AGAINST THE DRAFT:
ESSAYS ON CONSCIENTIOUS OBJECTION FROM THE RADICAL REFORMATION TO THE SECOND WORLD WAR

The composer Sir Michael Tippett unveiling the Conscientious Objector Stone in Tavistock Square, London, on International Conscientious Objectors' Day, 15 May 1994. (Reprinted by kind permission of the Peace Pledge Union)

PETER BROCK

Against the Draft

Essays on Conscientious Objection from the Radical Reformation to the Second World War

UNIVERSITY OF TORONTO PRESS
Toronto Buffalo London

Toronto Buffalo London
Printed in Canada

ISBN-13 978-0-8020-9073-7
ISBN-10 0-8020-9073-7

Printed on acid-free paper

Library and Archives Canada Cataloguing in Publication

Brock, Peter, 1920–
Against the draft : essays on conscientious objection from the Radical Reformation to the Second World War / Peter Brock.

Includes bibliographical references and index.
ISBN-13: 978-0-8020-9073-7
ISBN-10: 0-8020-9073-7

1. Conscientious objection – History. I. Title.

UB341.B76 2006 355.2'24'09 C2005-906170-7

University of Toronto Press acknowledges the financial assistance to its publishing program of the Canada Council for the Arts and the Ontario Arts Council.

University of Toronto Press acknowledges the financial support for its publishing activities of the Government of Canada through the Book Publishing Industry Development Program (BPIDP).

Contents

Illustrations

Foreword

'No ideology owes more to one academic than pacifism owes to Peter Brock. That the scope and richness of its historical tradition can now be recognized is largely the result of Brock's sympathetic and dedicated scholarship, which was begun, moreover, when pacifism was an unfashionable subject ...'[1] These were my words at a conference in Toronto in May 1991 to celebrate his distinguished career and to mark the publication of a second wave of what a representative of University of Toronto Press then told me were affectionately known in the trade as 'Brockbusters,' the major volumes that transformed our knowledge of the history of the principled rejection of all war.[2] Nearly a decade and a half later, they are truer than ever because Professor Brock, now in his mid-eighties, has used the intervening period to mine more seams of pacifist history and to unearth more nuggets in the form of both articles and books. His present volume, a third-generation Brockbuster, brings together twenty-five essays, written over the last three decades, that bear upon confrontations between governments which demand military service and subjects or citizens who refuse to supply it.

Of course, *Against the Draft* does not purport to examine all kinds of conscientious objection, a status that has often been invoked on non-pacifist grounds. Voluntarists, rejecting compulsion itself, have at times claimed it. Socialists and other progressives have sometimes done the same out of disapproval of the right-wing regime requiring their military service. And even those at the other end of the political spectrum, such as British pro-Nazis refusing to fight Hitler, have occasionally asserted the right of conscientious objection. Nonetheless, though dealing only with pacifism, this collection demonstrates the chronological span, scholarly precision, and cultural range of Brock's work. Being both a historian by profession and a pacifist by commitment, he has built up an expertise that runs the length of what he calls the 'unbroken line' of conscientious objection from 1525, when Conrad Grebel founded the Swiss Brethren, to the Second World War, when he himself went to prison in the same cause. Although a master of the broad canvas, as illustrated in this book by 'Experiences of Conscientious Objectors in the Soviet Union to 1945,' Brock has also, and perhaps more distinctively, been a skilled miniaturist. 'Six Weeks at Hawkspur Green' is a good example: at first glance a micro-study of limited significance, it turns out brilliantly to capture the best qualities – its largely humanitarian inspiration, its thoughtfulness, and its anxiety to serve the community – of British pacifism in the late 1930s and early 1940s. In addition, Brock's remarkable linguistic ability has enabled him to examine the primary sources and secondary literature of many countries (though here he apologizes for not knowing Japanese), which makes his work so impressively wide-ranging and at least implicitly comparative.

Moreover, the collected-essays format is admirably suited to his favoured approach to his subject. While he has a sharp eye for the wood (shown, for example, here in his shrewd comment that the appearance of pacifism, a by-product of imported Christianity, in late nineteenth-century Japan was a consequence of that country's decision to modernize), he has a particular love for the trees in all their variety. Discrete essays free him to explore the particular and identify the exceptional. Thus, although pacifists have generally been marginal or alienated members of society, as his own previous work has shown, the first essay in this book indicates that this was not true of the Brethren Church in Poland in the second half of the sixteenth century, which attracted members of the landowning elite. (Eventually, as this essay further reveals, they were to avail themselves of Socinus's 'ingenious logical distinctions' in an effort to minimize the conflict between their leading position in society and their pacifism.)

Above all, these essays reveal the diversity both of conscientious objection and of governmental responses to it. Brock's warts-and-all accounts of the positions taken by objectors contain a number of surprises, for me at least, among them that the Japanese pacifist leader Uchimura Kanzō once travelled all night on a crowded train to *dissuade* one of his followers who had resolved to refuse conscription during the Russo-Japanese War of 1904–5 from becoming a conscientious objector, and that some Soviet Mennonites not only welcomed Hitler's invading army as liberators in the Second World War but abandoned their non-resistance and volunteered to fight for it. I was also moved by a number of his accounts, particularly that of the three hundred or so Jehovah's Witnesses, 'simple men' but 'truly heroic,' who went to their deaths in Nazi Germany and Austria.

For their part, the authorities have sometimes handled objectors in unexpected ways. I assumed that 'The Confinement of Conscientious Objectors as Psychiatric Patients in First-World-War Germany' would be a tale of unrelieved official cruelty, whereas in fact it demonstrates that, given because 'religious conscience did not provide any excuse for refusing military orders' in that country, to refer objectors for psychiatric assessment was a humane attempt to avoid imposing a harsh military punishment. I was especially interested by the initial attempts of revolutionary regimes to accommodate religious pacifists. The Bolsheviks for a time felt some bond with those who had also been persecuted under Tsarism, and in any case expected that 'as the communist ethic transformed society, religion would wither away so that eventually no genuine COs would be left in the expanding socialist fatherland,' though their legal provision for exempting religious objectors did not stop some of their local military commanders shooting them instead. Similarly, some early French revolutionaries believed that the Quakers embodied some of their own values. Of their refusal to spill the blood of their enemies, a Girondin, Jacques-Pierre Brissot de Warville, wrote in 1790: 'This error of their humanity is so charming, that it is almost as good as truth.' This may be what non-pacifist readers will think about many of the conscientious objectors described in this learned and readable book.

Martin Ceadel
Professor of Politics, University of Oxford
and Fellow of New College, Oxford

NOTES

1 Harvey L. Dyck, ed., *The Pacifist Impulse in Historical Perspective* (Toronto: University of Toronto Press, 1996), 17.

2 The first consisted of *Pacifism in the United States: From the Colonial Era to the First World War* (Princeton: Princeton University Press, 1968), *Twentieth-Century Pacifism* (New York: Van Nostrand Reinhold, 1970), and *Pacifism in*

Europe to 1914 (Princeton: Princeton University Press, 1972). The second consisted of *The Quarker Peace Testimony 1660 to 1914* (York, UK: Sessions Book Trust, 1990), *Freedom from Violence: Sectarian Nonresistance from the Middle Ages to the Great War* (Toronto: University of Toronto Press, 1991), and *Freedom from War: Nonsectarian Pacifism 1814–1914* (Toronto: University of Toronto Press, 1991).

Acknowledgments

I wish to thank the following journals for permission to reprint – in revised form – articles of mine that appeared originally in their pages: *Adventist Heritage; East European Quarterly; Journal of Prisoners on Prisons; Journal of the Friends' Historical Society; Mennonite Quarterly Review; Ontario History; Peace & Change; Slavonic and East European Review; Tolstoy Studies Journal; War & Society; Xerography Debt.*

Further thanks for permission to reprint various items, or for information supplied, to: Robert Elmore (UK); William Hetherington (UK); Lawrence Klippenstein (Canada); Kvekerforlaget (Stavanger); A.L. Litvin (Kazan); Cedric Mc-Carthy (UK); and Hugh Mowat (UK).

I would also like to thank Christine Chattin for word-processing my manuscript, a task I am alas incapable of doing myself.

Finally, I am much indebted to Len Husband, humanities editor, and Frances Mundy, managing editor, at University of Toronto Press, for their support of my project, and to Ken Lewis for his careful copy-editing of my manuscript. Gillian Watts compiled the index.

AGAINST THE DRAFT

Introduction

The essays collected in this volume were written over a period of around three decades. They represent a by-product of my long-term research on the history of pacifism *sensu stricto* from antiquity to the end of the twentieth century, which I began at the outset of the 1950s. I would refer readers to the books I have published on this subject for a consecutive account of the cluster of ideas that have inspired conscientious objectors to military service (COs).[1] Plenty of books and articles on the subject by other authors, not all of them easily accessible, will be found in the endnotes of the present volume.

I have limited the time-range here to a period of 420 years – from 1525, that is, the start of the Radical Reformation, to the end of the Second World War in 1945. Before 1525 the phenomenon of conscientious objection to military service was, we may say, a submerged one. There were almost always a number of ways to evade being drafted. Besides, compulsion was not very often used to raise armies or militias: this was particularly true of India, where a long tradition of nonviolence stretched back more than two millennia without producing any conscientious objectors. True, there appear to have been cases of conscientious objection to military service among the early Christians before Emperor Constantine's reign. But no continuity in this respect exists thereafter through more than a thousand years. It seemed, therefore, most sensible to start this volume with the Radical Reformation of the sixteenth century and the unbroken line that begins at that time.

My reason for not including anything on the period after 1945 is a different one. For one thing, my contribution to the history of post-1945 conscientious objection has not been in the form of articles. Serious research here is still in an early stage. I can refer readers, however, to the thorough account by Jean A. Mansavage of 'legal conscientious objection' in the United States during the Vietnam War[2] and the volume of essays, edited by Charles C. Moskos and John Whiteclay Chambers II, on the 'new conscientious objection.'[3] These two works do not exhaust the list. And, at the time of writing, the Israeli army's 'refuseniks' are constantly in the news: the combatant soldier as conscientious objector, a new phenomenon, at any rate on such a wide scale.

The three opening essays in my book deal first with the incidence of conscientious objection among the antitrinitarian Polish Brethren of the sixteenth and early seventeenth centuries and then with the Dutch Mennonites, who later called themselves *Doopsgezinden*. These essays illustrate little-known aspects of the Anabaptist-Mennonite pattern of military exemption that started in 1525 and continued with variations into the twentieth century.

The Quaker peace testimony crystallized in England in the course of the 1650s. Most Quakers at first were not opposed to bearing arms: many fought for the Good Old Cause in the English Civil War. But after the Restoration conscientious objection fairly soon became a fixed tenet of the sect: those who broke this rule were disowned. In Britain, and on the other side of the Atlantic Ocean, Quaker 'sufferings' on account of refusal to perform compulsory militia service were carefully recorded by the Quaker Society of Friends. Essay 4 deals with the experiences of Quakers who were pressed into the Royal Navy: a part of Quaker history and also of English naval history since the overwhelming majority of those impressed were non-Quakers. The practice of naval impressment ceased at the end of the Napoleonic Wars in 1815: the impressment of Quakers had ceased long before that date.

In the eighteenth century Quakerism spread to France, though numbers remained very small there. Essay 5 deals with the response of this tiny religious community to the demands of the revolutionary and Napoleonic regimes. The installation in 1792 of the *levée-en-masse*, foreshadowing the universal military service system adopted during the next century throughout continental Europe, presented a difficult problem for sectarian pacifists. The essay includes discussion of the revolutionary authorities' attitude to conscientious objection; it also surveys the Jacobin regime's surprisingly positive reaction to the nonresistance (*Wehrlosigkeit*) of the Anabaptist-Mennonite communities newly incorporated into the French republic.

Essays 6 and 7 look respectively at the experiences of sectarian objectors in Upper Canada (today Ontario) and of — mainly Quaker – COs in the Channel Islands of Guernsey and Jersey. The militia ballot in Britain that selected men for service in that body had come to an end in 1831, but it persisted in Guernsey and Jersey as well as in Upper Canada. In the mother country after 1815, the efforts of pacifists were focused on other issues than conscription, which was reimposed only in 1916 after the outbreak of the First World War.

The situation was rather different in the United States because of the fiercely fought Civil War, which rent the country from 1861 to 1865. In the antebellum decades the militia had become a largely moribund institution. But with the outbreak of war, on each side the draft was imposed with increasing severity as the fortunes of war fluctuated. To the end it remained possible for draftees to hire a substitute. But for a denomination like the Quakers, who usually disowned members who chose this way out of service and some of whose members claimed unconditional exemption from bearing arms, a period of renewed suffering ensued on this score. A Vermont Quaker, named Cyrus Pringle, left a moving testimony to his loyalty to his Society's traditional testimony 'against all wars and fightings,'[4] while the fate of Civil War COs in general and the conscription legislation of the Unionist and Confederate governments are the subject of a well-researched monograph by E.N. Wright.[5] Most COs were indeed drawn from one of the major American peace sects – Quakers, Mennonites, and Brethren. But there were others, like the Brethren in Christ, for instance, who were nearly related to the Mennonites.[6] I have chosen for essay 8 the reaction to war and the draft of a recently created denomination, the Seventh-day Adventists, who were confined to the North because of their strong antislavery sympathies. This reaction may be followed best in the pages of the sect's organ, the *Review and Herald*: the sect's main concern was to convince the Unionist administration that its draftees, if they asked for exemption from bearing arms, should be entitled to this along with such established peace sects as the Quakers.[7]

During the second half of the nineteenth century, all states on the European continent introduced universal military service in place of the more flexible draft system inherited from the *ancien régime*. Only the Mennonites, at any rate those who still adhered to the sect's traditional principle of *Wehrlosigkeit*, managed to negotiate agreements with their governments that partially recognized their pacifist beliefs. In 1868 Prussia, and in 1874 Russia, replaced the existing draft system by universal military service. Prussia allowed Mennonites to perform their military service in a noncombatant capacity: they wore army uniforms but did not have to drill with weapons. In Russia, after a considerable number of Mennonites had decided on emigration to North America, the Tsarist government allowed those who remained to do their compulsory service in civilian forestry camps financed by the church.

Pacifist sectarians on the European continent found it difficult to survive in this situation: many escaped to the New World to avoid the burden of conscription on their young men. Quakers disappeared from the continent – except in Norway, where a small Society of Friends, centred in Stavanger, had been established at the end of the Napoleonic Wars by returning prisoners of war. These men, sailors for the most part, had been converted to Quakerism during their internment at Chatham near London. Neighbouring Quakers had visited them regularly in their prison ship in that port, and the men took their new-found faith back with them when they returned home. Essay 9 describes how subsequently Quaker COs fared when confronted with the Norwegian state's requirement that all its able-bodied young men be trained in arms. The situation changed in 1902 when religious COs were granted *de facto* exemption from the draft.

In another part of the continent, in Hungary, a fundamentalist peasant sect, the Nazarenes, from its inception in the 1840s continued to resist conscription. Its draftees endured long periods of imprisonment. Before the First World War their position became a little easier, but they still suffered severely. Even though they had made clear their willingness to perform noncombatant army service, the government failed to approve an exemption clause for conscripts belonging to the sect, who were drawn not only from Magyars but also from the country's ethnic minorities. In essay 10, 'Nazarenes Confront Conscription in Dualist Hungary,' I have given an overview of the fate of Nazarene COs to the outbreak of war in 1914.

Essays 11 and 12 centre on Tolstoy. The trial and imprisonment as a CO of Tolstoy's young Slovak disciple Albert Škarvan became a *cause célèbre*, located in dualist Hungary but unconnected with the Nazarene objectors whose witness was a collective one. In the Russian Empire, apart from the privileged Mennonites, a number of sectarian objectors, deprived of any legal protection, continued to suffer imprisonment on account of their resistance to the draft. Some of these young men were followers of Tolstoy, the former soldier and author of *War and Peace*, who had been preaching a doctrine of nonviolence since the end of the 1870s. But the Master was not only in touch with his own incarcerated disciples: he also corresponded – and sometimes visited in jail – COs from other religious traditions as well as a few who were unaffiliated Christians. In my essay on this subject, I have found the volumes of correspondence in Tolstoy's *Collected Works* (*Polnoe sobranie sochinenii*) a very valuable source.

Essay 13 deals with the emergence of conscientious objection in Japan around the end of the nineteenth century. Japanese pacifism of this period, though largely Christian, has certain characteristics that distinguish it from its Western counterpart. I illustrate these differences in the case of Uchimura Kanzō, one of the most creative figures in the history of modern Japanese Christianity.

Southwards from Japan across the ocean, during the years immediately prior to the Frist World War, the two British dominions of Australia and New Zealand became the scene of a curious episode in the history of conscientious objection. The 'boy conscription,' imposed in both countries at this time, is the subject of essay 14, which focuses on the experiences of teenage boys and their parents who, on grounds of conscience, actively resisted the measure.

The outbreak of the First World War in 1914 had marked a watershed in the history of conscientious objection, as in almost everything else. The majority of COs during that conflict were located in Britain or the United States, though they were to be found in other countries, too. Solid studies of conscientious objection in both Britain and the United States have been published.[8] My four essays, relating directly or indirectly to this period, treat topics that are not well covered in the literature. Essay 15 begins by discussing the samizdat journalism practised by COs in British prisons during the First World War. There was one such journal in almost every jail that housed a substantial enough number of objectors to act as contributors and readers. Unfortunately, only a few issues of these papers are still extant: they were produced in only one or two copies and circulated clandestinely. The essay concludes with an account of the only prison samizdat journal produced in Britain during the Second World War. I failed to discover a single original issue of Wormwood Scrubs Prison's *Flowery* (as the paper was called). But luckily, a pamphlet containing selected articles was published in 1945. The next essay (16) reviews the situation of those British First World War COs who were ready to serve in the Non-Combatant Corps (NCC). The establishment of a corps of this kind within the army was an innovation on the part of the government, which produced a second edition of the NCC in the Second World War. The NCC satisfied some COs, but it produced a number of problems that are discussed in the essay.

Two of the best-known COs in First-World-War Britain, the Quaker Stephen Hobhouse and the socialist Fenner Brockway, were responsible for compiling *English Prisons To-day,* which appeared in print in 1922 and proved a landmark in the development of the British prison system, propelling it in the direction of much-needed reform. The report's two editors found the inspiration for undertaking this arduous work in their recent experiences as jailed COs. In my essay on the two men (no. 17), I have highlighted the fact that they were pioneering the work of the New School of Convict Criminologists in North America today.

Two essays (18 and 19) deal with the fate of COs on the European continent during the First World War: usually a much harsher one than in the Anglo-American world. In Germany, for instance, COs were often confined in mental hospitals as psychiatric patients: a debate arose among German psychiatrists whether this was justified, at least in some cases. We know much less about COs in the wartime Russian Empire, except in the case of the Mennonites, who either continued to serve in the forestry camps or were assigned to civilian ambulance units attached to the Russian armies. Wartime non-Mennonite COs probably numbered around a thousand, though no exact figures exist. No legal exemption for these COs existed before the Revolution of 1917 brought relief.

During the interwar years there was no conscription either in the United States or in Britain and the other countries of the Commonwealth. It continued, however, in many states in continental Europe. Essays 20 and 21 deal with the flourishing pacifist movement that sprang up after the fall of the Russian monarchy in 1917 and the experiences of the COs who emerged from it. Virtually all these men were Christian sectarians: until his death in 1936, Tolstoy's close associate, Vladimir Chertkov, devoted his organizational skills to defending the rights of COs. With Lenin's approval, an extremely liberal CO decree was enacted on 4 January 1919. But long before Chertkov's death, the initially generous treatment of COs had been transformed into an oppressive system that eventually eliminated legal toleration for Soviet COs altogether. Essay 21 concludes with a look at the situation for the few remaining COs during the Second World War. I have also pointed out that a definitive history of conscientious objection in the Soviet Union before the Stalinist clampdown cannot be written until important Russian archival collections, now closed, become accessible to scholars. Of the conscriptionist countries of continental Europe outside the Soviet Union, I have chosen Poland for my essay 22. A complication here is that most COs in interwar Poland came from its Belarusian minority. My essay attempts to explain this phenomenon.

The literature on conscientious objection during the Second World War is large and growing.[9] Private archival depositories, like the Swarthmore College Peace Collection, as well as the government archives of countries where considerable numbers of COs were located, contain much as yet unexploited materials. Again, the essays included in this volume deal with little-known aspects of the subject. The six-weeks training camp at Hawkspur Green, the hitherto unrecorded 'pacifist episode during the Battle of Britain' described in essay 23, was remarkable for the intellectual calibre of the young COs who participated. Among the campers was the prominent Canadian philosopher George Grant, whose letters home provide insight into the camp life. Youthful rebellion against war, vanished fellowship, and lost innocence were the three most significant aspects in the Hawkspur experience in the memories of those who participated. The *dramatis personae* of the next essay (no. 24) were former members of the Non-Combatant Corps who volunteered as medical orderlies to accompany the British paratroopers first in 1944 in the Normandy D-Day assault and then in further campaigns against the Germans. Their commanding officer subsequently described his COs as 'excellent in battle.' My essay seeks an explanation for what might sound like an oxymoron: conscientious objection to combatant service and excellence in battle. Towards the end of the article, I make some comparisons between the experiences of these men and those of American noncombatant soldiers during the Second World War and the Vietnam War.

The last essay in the volume (no. 25) focuses on Nazi Germany, where the largest contingent of COs was provided by the Jehovah's Witnesses (JWs). Theirs was a truly heroic stand for peace and against a totalitarian state. Several hundred German Witnesses suffered the death penalty – usually by guillotining – for refusing induction into the armed forces after receiving their call-up notice. Female Witnesses, who had been incarcerated in concentration camps, consistently rejected work on the production of munitions, despite the fact that they were savagely punished for their disobedience of orders. Due primarily to the intensive archival research of a German historian of the post-45 generation, the nonviolent resistance of the Witnesses has become clear: once 'forgotten victims,' their role in the German resistance movement is now broadly recognized.[10] But this is a recent development. The treatment meted out to the Witness COs of Nazi Germany is unique in the history of conscientious objection. Hopefully, my essay, along with James Penton's recently published book (see essay 25, note 44), will make this tragic chapter better known among those interested in peace history who do not read German.

Six decades have elapsed since the conclusion of the Second World War and the dropping of atomic bombs on Hiroshima and Nagasaki. The Cold War has come and gone, though the nuclear threat remains to menace all living kind with the possibility of ultimate disaster – except perhaps for such tough little creatures as the cockroach. Methods of warfare have changed radically with the technological advances of the computer age, as we have seen recently in President Bush's lamentable attack on Iraq. Over the previous decades, some hitherto staunchly conscriptionist countries have abandoned the draft for the volunteer system, although many states still retain conscription.[11] For the time being, at any rate, there are still COs – enjoying varying degrees of tolerance according to the legislation in force in a given state. Objectors continue to draw their inspiration from a variety of sources: religious, humanist, and political. But in the 'new conscientious objection' there appears to be an increase in the incidence of selective objection,[12] even though we find selective COs staking their claims to exemption from military service in the First World War, and even before that time. A positive development during recent decades has been the increasing interest in conscientious objection shown by the United Nations Commission on Human Rights, which has passed a series of resolutions on the subject.[13] Decisions of the European Court of Human Rights have also marked a significant step forward, serving as a precedent 'for future appeals that conscientious objector status ... is protected under the European Human Rights Convention.'[14]

In conclusion, there is still much work to be done in the history of conscientious objection, especially for the period following 1945. But I will have to leave it to others to pursue this – to me – fascinating and, I believe, important topic.

NOTES

1 For example, *Pacifism in the United States: From the Colonial Era to the First World War* (Princeton NJ, 1968); *Pacifism in Europe to 1914* (Princeton NJ, 1970); *The Quaker Peace Testimony 1660 to 1914* (York UK, 1990); *Freedom from Violence: Sectarian Pacifism from the Middle Ages to the Great War* (Toronto,

1991); *Freedom from War: Nonsectarian Pacifism 1814–1914* (Toronto, 1991); and (with Nigel Young) *Pacifism in the Twentieth Century* (Syracuse NY, 1999).

2 Jean Anne Mansavage, '"A Sincere and Meaningful Belief": Legal Conscientious Objection during the Vietnam War' (Ph.D. diss., Texas A & M University, 2000), scheduled for publication shortly.

3 Charles C. Moskos and John Whiteclay Chambers II, eds, *The New Conscientious Objection: From Sacred to Secular Resistance* (New York and Oxford, 1993).

4 *The Civil War Diary of Cyrus Pringle* (Wallingford PA, 1962).

5 Edward Needles Wright, *Conscientious Objectors in the Civil War* (Philadelphia, 1931; reprint, New York, 1961). Wright's main focus is on the Quakers, though he does deal with most of the other peace sects which produced COs. We may note that a considerable number of Quakers served as combatants in the Union forces: disownment followed for this offence against the Society's discipline less frequently than one might have expected from the past practice of that body. See, for example, Jacquelyn S. Nelson, *Indiana Quakers Confront the Civil War* (Indianapolis, 1991), 101,261.

6 For the response of this small North American sect, known during its eighteenth-century beginnings as River Brethren, to the drafts imposed during the twentieth century, see the thoroughly researched and perceptive study by M.J. Heisey, *Peace and Persistence: Tracing the Brethren in Christ Peace Witness through Three Generations* (Kent OH and London, 2003).

7 A similar claim to exemption from Unionist conscription was drawn up in 1862 by fifteen above-draft-age 'Non-Resistant Abolitionists' (disciples of William Lloyd Garrison and ex-members of the defunct New England Non-Resistance Society). Eschewing any sympathy with the rebellious South, the signatories claimed, like the Seventh-day Adventists were to do, the same right to military exemption as that granted to Quakers. For the text of their 'Perpetual Protest,' see the *Bond of Peace* (Philadelphia), August 1869, 63, 64. The only signatory of note was Stephen Symonds Foster (1809–81), who had indeed been briefly imprisoned as a militia objector during his student days at Dartmouth College, from which he had graduated in 1838. But, by the eve of the Civil War his pacifism, like Garrison's, had become a purely personal faith. A colleague around this time called Foster, ironically, a 'non-resistant insurrectionist.' See the entries on Foster by Craig Phelan in Harold Josephson, ed., *Biographical Dictionary of Modern Peace Lenders* (Westport CT and London UK, 1985), 296, 297, and by Sandra Opdycke in the *American National Biography* (New York and Oxford UK, 1999), vol. 8, 307, 308; also W.H. van der Linden, *The International Peace Movement 1815–1874* (Amsterdam, 1987), 529–33, 535, 541, 543.

8 There are three surveys of conscientious objection in First-World-War Britain: John W. Graham, *Conscription and Conscience: A History, 1916–1919* (London, 1922; reprint, New York, 1969); David Boulton, *Objection Overruled* (London, 1967); and John Rae, *Conscience and Politics: The British Government and the Conscientious Objection to Military Service, 1916–1919* (Oxford, 1970). For conscientious objection in the United States during the First World War, see Norman Thomas, *Is Conscience a Crime?* (New York, 1927); and H.C. Peterson and Gilbert C. Fite, *Opponents of War, 1917–1918* (Madison WI, 1957), 121–38, 259–64, 274, 275, 323–5, 343, 344.

9 For Britain, see Denis Hayes, *Challenge of Conscience: The Story of the Conscientious Objectors of 1939–1949* (London, 1949), particularly valuable because of Hayes's role as publications editor to the Central Board for Conscientious Objectors; and Rachel Barker, *Conscience, Government and War: Conscientious Objection in Great Britain, 1939–45* (London, 1982). For the United States, see Mulford Q. Sibley and Philip E. Jacob, *Conscription of Conscience: The American State and the Conscientious Objector, 1940–1947* (Ithaca NY, 1952). And for Canada, see Thomas P. Socknat, *Witness against War: Pacifism in Canada, 1900–1945* (Toronto, 1987), 225–58, 341–8. There are also studies of conscientious objection during the Second World War in countries like Australia, New Zealand, Germany, and Denmark, where there were comparatively few COs.

10 See especially Detlef Garbe, *Zwischen Widerstand und Martyrium: Die Zeugen Jehovahs im 'Dritten Reich'* (4th edn, Munich, 1999).

11 For a comprehensive survey of the problem, see Bart Horeman and Marc Stolwijk, eds, *Refusing to Bear Arms: A World Survey of Conscription and Conscientious Objection to Military Service* (London, 1998).

12 Conscientious objection to military service is not easy to define exactly (especially today). Take the case of the Japanese-American (Nisei) draft resisters in the Second World War. When those among them of draft age, whom the authorities considered to be loyal, were inducted into the U.S. armed forces, several hundreds refused to go, arguing that they (and their families) had been wrongfully imprisoned; for they had in fact been deprived of their rights as Americans born. Most of them would have been ready to become combatant soldiers in different circumstances. In 1944 they were sentenced to terms of three to five years in prison. Some of these men served their sentences in McNeil Island Penitentiary in Washington State, where they mixed with COs of the conventional variety, including one Nisei, Gordon Hirabayashi, who was a Quaker. See Eric L. Muller, *Free to Die for Their Country: The Story of the Japanese American Draft Resisters in World War II* (Chicago and London, 2001), 167–70. The board set up by Pres-

ident Truman that amnestied them in 1947 considered these men to be 'closely analogous to conscientious objectors, and yet not within the fair interpretation of that phrase' (p. 181). That is certainly well put! Recent attempts at outlining the history of, and defining, conscientious objection to bearing arms are to be found in the following encyclopedia articles: Nigel Young, 'Conscientious Objection,' in Ervin Laszlo and Fong You Yoo, eds, *World Encyclopedia of Peace* (Oxford UK and New York), vol. 1, 187–92; L. William Yolton, 'Conscientious Objection,' in Roger S. Powers and William B. Vogele, eds, *Protest, Power, and Change: An Encyclopedia of Nonviolent Action from ACT-UP to Women's Suffrage* (New York and London, 1997), 124–8; Michael W. Hovey and Gordon C. Zahn, 'Conscientious Objection, Ethics of,' in Lester Kurtz, ed., *Encyclopedia of Violence, Peace, Conflict* (San Diego and London, 1999), vol. 1, 441–8; and Jesus Casquette, 'Draft, Resistance and Evasion of,' in ibid., 567–76.

13 Horeman and Stolwijk, eds, *Refusing*, 17.

14 Moskos and Chambers, eds, *New Conscientious Objection*, 192. But, writing in 1993, they added a rather ominous warning: 'The future is not bright for legal protection of conscientious objection in the non-Western world ... [E]ven in those states that implement the United Nations' proposals [for recognition of conscientious objection], legal problems of statute law and administrative process will persist throughout the evolution of the right of conscientious objection, problems enlarged by the growing secularization of conscience.'

1 Conscientious Objection among the Polish Antitrinitarians

In 1525 the idea of nonresistance (*Wehrlosigkeit*) emerged as a component of Reformation thought with the formation of the radical religious group known as the Swiss Brethren. Its founder was a young Zürich patrician and scholar, Conrad Grebel, who, along with the other Brethren, had accepted baptism of adult believers as the leading article of their creed. Although by no means all the early Anabaptists were pacifists, eventually nonparticipation in war became a central tenet of the whole sect. From Switzerland, Anabaptism spread to Germany and to the Netherlands, where the Frisian Menno Simons reorganized the movement, by this time in disarray after experiencing various internal upheavals as well as severe persecution from the authorities throughout Central Europe, both Protestant and Catholic. Before Menno's death in 1561 Anabaptists almost everywhere had become transformed into Mennonites – except for the sect's communitarian wing, the staunchly nonresistant Hutterites of Moravia.

From the outset there had been Anabaptists who refused to bear arms on the grounds of its being incompatible with their religious beliefs.[1] Later, Mennonites often gained from the authorities a blanket exemption for members of the sect, which protected them in case of conscription for the militia or the town watch.

Anabaptist beliefs eventually spread as far as Poland, which, along with its associated state Lithuania, enjoyed a greater measure of religious freedom than did most other European countries by the middle of the sixteenth century. As a result Poland-Lithuania soon began to give asylum to a number of radical religious refugees persecuted elsewhere by Protestants and Catholics alike, while extreme doctrines like Antitrinitarianism and Anabaptism, introduced into the country by these newcomers, now began to find native adherents, chiefly among the educated classes.

In 1565 a schism had occurred in the Reformed Church of Poland-Lithuania, with an Antitrinitarian minority splitting off from the main body in order to found a separate denomination of its own. Thus the Polish Brethren – or Minor – Church came into being.[2] At the beginning many of the Brethren adopted Anabaptist tenets, including the idea of nonresistance, which had reached them through previous contacts with the Hutterites in neighbouring Moravia. By no means all Polish Antitrinitarians, however, accepted pacifism as part of their Christian faith. The doctrine found its most ardent supporters among the Brethren in the Kingdom of Poland, whereas in the Kingdom's south-eastern borderlands and in the associated Grand Duchy of Lithuania the overwhelming majority of the Brethren Church membership continued to regard the sword, whether used to maintain internal order or to defend the country from external enemies, as a legitimate function of a Christian polity.

Yet, for all its religious toleration, the country was dominated politically and economically by the Polish – or Polonized – aristocracy and landed gentry, which excluded other classes from any voice in government. The 'golden liberty' (*złota wolność*) of the ruling élite included freedom for heretics persecuted almost everywhere else in Europe; yet the power of this élite rested on social oppression of the country folk and political discrimination against the townspeople. While the political culture of sixteenth-century Poland proved favourable to the development of the religious radicalism of the Polish Brethren Church, however unpopular such views may have been among both Protestants and Catholics, the country's social and economic conditions led the nobility to assume an increasingly important role in the affairs of the Brethren Church. We must hold this fact in mind while examining the military question within the Antitrinitarian community during the first four decades of the Church's existence, which will be the principal task of this essay. It is, moreover, the increasing dominance of the landowning class within the Brethren Church that differentiates its conscientious-objector problem from the way that issue presented itself in earlier or later religious pacifist groups, for in none of these latter did the landed nobility play any comparable role as a class.

Controversy over social issues had marked the years following the establishment of the Brethren Church in 1565. Leading ministers of the Church, especially in the Polish Kingdom, were meanwhile diligently spreading the gospel of nonresistance among the faithful. They told the nobles to sell their family estates, won by their ancestors as a reward 'for shedding blood,' and distribute the money thus gained among the poor.[3] It is not known exactly how many Brethren belonging to the landowning class were willing to obey this injunction but some there were who made this sacrifice enthusiastically: they gave up wealth and status to live as they believed a Christian should – humble and defenceless, trusting in their Saviour to uphold them during their sojourn in this transient world.[4] But, with the passing of time, the fervent convictions of the pioneers of the Brethren faith often gave way in the next generation to an adherence to the Church, certainly genuine but less willing to make a material sacrifice of the dimensions frequently undertaken by their fathers. A similar spiritual evolution took place at this time among the town congregations, too, though burgher members of course were subject to pressures somewhat different from those experienced by Brethren of gentry background.

What, we should now inquire, was the nature of military obligation in Poland in this period? Within what perimeters could confrontation take place between the Polish state and those members of the Brethren Church who espoused nonresistance and believed war to be forbidden to the true follower of Christ?

In 'feudal' Poland the enserfed peasantry, who for the most part remained loyal to their old religion, were not liable normally to bear arms. Military obligation, therefore, rested almost exclusively on the nobility and the burghers, the country's Antitrinitarians remaining subject in this respect to the same compulsions as were its citizens who still held to a belief in the Trinity.

In the sixteenth century attendance at musters of the general levy (*pospolite ruszenie*) continued to be obligatory for members of the landowning class as it had been in previous centuries. Even if by now this force had ceased to be an efficient instrument for defending the country, the general levy nevertheless was still called out both in wartime and at periodic intervals when the country was at peace. 'Failure to attend ... was punished by confiscation of lands.' By this date cases frequently occurred of gentry ignoring the summons to arms; of course, their absence was not the result of any conscientious objection to fighting. Opportunity to opt out by some form of monetary contribution seems as a rule to have been possible, though it was not formally sanctioned by the letter of the law. In Polish towns the male citizenry continued to be liable to assist in defence in case of attack. But an emergency of this kind occurred only rarely in this period; anyhow monetary commutation of service could take the place of actual physical participation.[5]

Within the Brethren Church the existence of conscientious objection to military service first became a matter of controversy in 1572 in the course of a polemical debate between two leading Antitrinitarian intellectuals, the Greek refugee from religious persecution, Jacobus Palaeologus, and the Pole Gregorius Paulus (to give them the names they used in their Latin works),[6] Palaeologus supporting the case for a just war and Paulus pleading for nonresistance. In the interregnum that had ensued on the death of the last Jagiellonian ruler, Zygmunt August, on 7 July, a state of emergency was at once declared and the country put on a war footing, which lasted until the election of a new ruler (Henry of Valois) in April of the following year. During this crisis Polish-Lithuanian landowners became liable once again for service in the general levy, to which body was entrusted in particular the defence of the eastern borderlands against attack from Muscovite, Cossack and Tatar foe. It was a time of troubles not only for the state as a whole, but for the – at any rate formally – antimilitarist Brethren Church as well.

For several years now the Church's radical ministers had been telling the Brethren that it was wrong either to carry a weapon in self-defence or to act as a magistrate (contemporaries then called this function the Office of the Sword) or to serve as a soldier, even when required to do so by the law of the land.[7] Thus it came about, writes Palaeologus, that 'under the influence of sermons ... delivered with oratorical passion, many nobles, some of them belonging to the kingdom's most illustrious families, refused to bear arms, lest they act contrary to the gospel and the teaching of Jesus Christ. But for refusing to take up arms there was an ancient penalty provided by law and that the most severe.'[8]

Although the question of conscientious objection had emerged into the open only as a result of the crisis of 1572, it is clear from the context of Palaeologus's antipacifist tract *De bello sententia,* written in August 1572 in support of the opponents of antimilitarism within the Church, that even before 1572 at least some Brethren, both nobles as well as commoners, had already rejected military service (as indeed according to the strict ethic then preached by most of their Church leaders they were required to do when drafted). In this tract, composed barely a month after the death of the last Jagiellonian king, Palaeologus enters into some detail concerning the ways and means by which pacifist

Brethren had been evading those military duties that involved the shedding of blood without directly confronting the state and at the same time preserving (so they hoped) their consciences more or less intact. It appears rather unlikely that practices of this kind could have come to the notice of the immigrant Antitrinitarian if they had been in use only for a matter of weeks, though it is true, of course, that the political situation at mid-summer 1572 now made the problem of urgent importance for the whole Brethren Church.

Palaeologus mentions three quasi-military alternatives that were, he tells us, generally acceptable to pacifist Brethren in order to avoid a clash with the authorities:

1. *Performance of watching duties.* In particular, an obligation of this kind formed part of the civic responsibility of the burghers, in Poland as in the rest of Europe. *Licere christiano homini excubias agere:* thus the anti-pacifist Palaeologus summarized the view of those Brethren pacifists ready to watch and guard against an enemy, if called upon to do so in an emergency. In such cases, though, as professed noncombatants we may presume they would have been unwilling actually to use any weapons they might have been required to carry while on guard duty (performed most likely on the town walls or in the streets of their city). But Palaeologus states, too, that in performance of such duties guards were likely to be ordered to sound an alarm if the enemy approached, so that thereby the latter might be uncovered the more easily. In the ensuing encounter blood would inevitably be shed; and in Palaeologus's view, even though Brethren had refrained from any direct part in it, this connivance at bloodshed altogether nullified their attempted stance of nonviolence. 'If,' he wrote, 'it is indeed wrong to kill an enemy striving to assault a city, it will be equally wrong to point out where he is hiding.'

2. *Payment of war taxes.* There were evidently Brethren ready to pay money to the government for the prosecution of war if required to do so, especially when that brought exemption from personal service as an indirect result. Again, Palaeologus seized on such conduct as an example of the pacifists' inconsistency, if not of their blatant hypocrisy. 'If it is wrong to bear arms,' he claimed, 'it will equally be wrong to pay tribute to the Commonwealth,' for the state in such circumstances would simply use the money it received to enlist more soldiers.

3. *Hiring of substitutes.* This practice, universal throughout Europe under the *ancien régime*, whereby a man liable for military duties paid

another to take his place in the ranks, appeared to Palaeologus to deserve censure even more than the first two alternatives. In his view (not indeed without justification), the hiring of a man to do what the hirer himself regarded as evil amounted to condoning wrongdoing on the part of others.[9] Nevertheless, some Brethren appear to have resorted to this practice as a way out of their dilemma as conscientious objectors to war.

One might think that the accommodating spirit shown by those ready thus to compromise with the state could be taken as proof at least of the pacifists' patriotism and of their civic loyalty. Palaeologus nevertheless continued to brand the pacifist Brethren as 'traitors' and 'deserters.' The main thrust of his writing lay of course in his positive plea on behalf of the Christian warrior; by defending this position he could hope to allay any fears the government might entertain as to the Brethren's continued loyalty to the state. To fight in defence of fatherland and faith indeed seemed to the Greek to be the clear duty of a follower of Jesus. Thus, he inevitably viewed an objector to military service as a bad Christian, who had failed to carry out what was clearly his religious obligation; for this reason such conduct brought disgrace to the whole Christian church, which, Palaeologus believed, had from the beginning approved of war for a just cause.[10]

Palaeologus's attack on pacifism evoked an immediate response from one of the Brethren Church's most prominent theologians: Gregorius Paulus. Paulus, along with other radical members of the Church who were now centred in Raków (in southern Poland), felt provoked on account of the bitterness with which a fellow Antitrinitarian had attacked the pacifist position. They were also shocked because this man had chosen a moment of acute political crisis for his onslaught. Charges of treason and desertion might well bring down reprisals on the heretic denomination, many of whose leaders espoused the pacifist cause; there were limits even in Poland to the liberty enjoyed by religious dissenters. Within a few months Paulus had completed his reply (*Responsio*), which he composed in the name of the Racovians as well as his own.[11] Its subtitle, *Bellum et iudicia forensia interdicta esse a Christo piis* (War and Lawsuits Are Forbidden by Christ to the Faithful), gives the gist of Paulus's argument; but we should note that he concentrates almost exclusively on the Office of the Sword, which he naturally considered to be incompatible with the Christian ethic. The military question emerges only incidentally in some brief comments on it made by the author.

In all this Paulus was perhaps wise. In the first place his caution with respect to that problem stemmed, as Kot suggests, from the fact of its being at the time a very sensitive issue: on a matter like that, 'it was no longer possible [for Paulus] to express himself ... with entire freedom.'[12] Secondly, it must have seemed to him of prime importance to place the problem of war within the wider framework of Christian nonresistance.

Palaeologus, writes Paulus, had presented in his tract 'an imaginary Christ [fictus Christus].' If Palaeologus's reproaches were indeed justified, then, declared Paulus angrily, the blame must fall on the real Jesus, who had first urged such conduct – on 'you, O Christ ... For were you not yourself a deserter and an unfeeling traitor to your people? You would neither take up arms for your country yourself or assist it nor command your followers to do so, either.'[13] Paulus concluded his tract by stigmatizing Palaeologus's championship of the sword when exercised by members of the church fellowship as a betrayal of Christ and his gospel and a reversion to paganism.

If Palaeologus's tone was invariably aggressive, Paulus – despite his belief in nonviolence – matched and indeed almost surpassed it. With this encounter of Pole with Greek, which took place in 1572–3, there now began within the Brethren Church a prolonged controversy over the sword, in which the military question constituted, however, only one of several related problems debated between the pacifist and nonpacifist Brethren. The problem of nonresistance also became the subject of prolonged discussion at successive Church synods. Whether in conference or in print, the two parties throughout remained far apart on this issue.

The most cogent exposition of nonresistance to emerge from the Polish Anabaptist camp was the work of the Lublin congregation's learned minister, Marcin Czechowic. It was published in the mid-1570s as Dialogue XII in a volume its author entitled simply *Christian Colloquies*.[14] To buttress his arguments in favour of conscientious objection to military service and to prevent his readers from thinking that nonresistance was a newfangled doctrine, as opponents of the pacifist Brethren had declared it to be, Czechowic added a Latin appendix in which he gathered supporting testimony taken from the writings of the early church fathers as well as from later theologians down to Erasmus.[15] What he sought to show by these extracts was, he wrote, that true 'Christians endure adversity patiently and do not have recourse, for injuries inflicted, either to arms or to the courts or to private revenge, because to take up arms or to proceed against anyone by war or by law does not belong to the evangelical purity of the Christian religion.'[16] In confirmation of the fact that the early Christians had refused military service, Czechowic quoted at length from Tertullian, whose hostility to soldiering provided both a precedent and a respectable pedigree for the stand of the Brethren Church's conscientious objectors.[17]

The controversial works of Palaeologus and Paulus on war and the magistracy had continued all this time to circulate in manuscript, mainly within Brethren Church circles. But in 1580 Szymon Budny, the leading minister among the socially conservative Lithuanian Brethren, published the whole of this polemical exchange in a weighty tome, to which he gave the title *Defensio verae sententiae de magistratu politico in ecclesiis christianis retinendo* (A Defence of the True Judgment That Public Office Should Be Retained in Christian Churches). Naturally the radicals of the Racovian party could not allow the taunts and jibes directed against them by Palaeologus to go unanswered now that Budny had made them public. Paulus, whom the Racovians approached first for a reply, begged to be excused; the task, he told them, would prove too much in view of his poor health. They next asked an Italian exile residing in Cracow named Faustus Socinus (Fausto Sozzini) to take on the job. Socinus, then aged forty-one and later to become famous as the founder of the Unitarian movement, was already highly respected for his theological learning as well as for his piety. His *Reply to Palaeologus* appeared in print (anonymously) in 1581.[18] In this work Socinus reviews in minute detail the whole problem of the Christian's relationship to the state. Answering Palaeologus point by point, and with a plethora of biblical references, Socinus succeeded in producing an effective defence of the Racovians' position even at the expense perhaps of wearying the reader. While he agreed that the Office of the Sword was needed in this world to restrain wrongdoers, he sought to show Christ's followers were forbidden by their Master to participate in its work. Above all, they must take the ethic of the Sermon on the Mount as their model for conduct while on earth.[19] Judged by that standard, war clearly became a sin if engaged in by the faithful.[20]

In the section of his book devoted to war, Socinus discusses briefly the question of conscientious objection. He deals in turn with the three practices Palaeologus claimed were pursued by pacifist Brethren in order to avoid direct confrontation with the authorities on the military question: (1) watching, (2) paying war taxes, and (3) hiring substitutes.

Whether such practices still continued in force, or whether Socinus raised them only in order to refute the assertions made by Palaeologus on this issue, we do not know for certain. But less than a decade had elapsed since Palaeologus wrote, and we may assume that the situation with regard to these practices remained generally unaltered.

(1) Like his opponent, Socinus, too, doubts if a genuine Christian would be justified in accepting a post in the watch or functioning as a military guard since, acting in such capacity, he would, Socinus agreed, find it next to impossible to avoid wounding or killing an enemy soldier. Socinus, we may note, did not assert that Palaeologus had been misinformed when stating that members of the Brethren Church had accepted duties of this kind on being summoned to bear arms either 'in the country's defence [pro patriae defensione]' or some other purpose like watching on a city's walls. While Socinus felt a man might just possibly succeed in maintaining a nonviolent stance in a position of this kind, he went out of his way nevertheless to show the extreme difficulty of reconciling watching and guard duty with the standards of behaviour he believed Christ had set up for his followers.[21]

(2) Payment of war taxes, on the other hand, seemed to Socinus entirely permissible. The tribute Jews paid to the Romans in New Testament times had gone largely to support the alien army and defend the alien Empire. When Christ approved rendering Caesar his due, he did not by this 'command or in any way sanction military service on the part of his own followers.' The latter were required to pay taxes to their rulers 'regardless of whether they made good or bad use of them.' And that principle, moreover, had been reinforced in St Paul's teaching (Romans 13:6, 7). In brief, Socinus believed that payment of a tax, even when it was known it would be used for warlike purposes, in no way undermined a Christian's loyalty to nonviolence or compromised his stand against military service.[22]

(3) Concerning the hiring of a substitute (*de aliquo pecunia conducendo, quo pro te militet*), Socinus takes up a more critical stance. He admits this practice furnished for the conscientious objector a convenient legal way out of his dilemma. Nevertheless, he could not approve of the direct hiring of a man to fight in one's place. He saw nothing wrong, though, if a draftee were excused personal service after having contributed to a tax imposed by the authorities to raise troops, even when in effect it meant that, with the money paid, 'another man could be hired who would fight for you, that is, ... would do what you refuse to do yourself.' The objector, in Socinus's opinion, would in this

case be paying a legitimate tribute and would no more be responsible for the death or damage ensuing as the final result of the transaction than he would be in the case of payment of a more general tax to the government.[23]

On the military question we find Socinus making one concession that may appear surprising in view of his condemnation of watching and guard duty whenever there was danger the watchman or guard might swerve from a strict adherence to nonviolence. For Socinus did not think it wrong for a Brother to take part in a military campaign when ordered to do so by the magistrate, provided some greater evil threatened were he not to participate. The drafted person might even appear armed at the muster – if he refrained from using his weapon either to kill or wound another human being. Yet, Socinus agreed, he should not thus proceed lightly and without taking certain steps beforehand in order to make clear his unwillingness, whatever the circumstances, actually to kill a fellow human being. 'It can happen,' wrote Socinus, 'that a Christian, at the commandment of the magistrate, may take up arms – first, however, having publicly declared, ... in such manner as to leave the magistrate in no doubt,' his determination not to use his weapons for homicide. For it was not in itself the bearing of arms that appeared wrong to Socinus, but their use for lethal purposes.[24]

Kot has pointed out correctly that in Socinus's work 'there breathes a spirit different from that felt in the arguments of Gregorius Paulus.'[25] Socinus indeed appears to have urged so far-reaching a concession with regard to military service as we have seen his treatise contained, not so much in an effort to curtail the Racovians' radical antimilitarism as to make its pacifism more palatable to the Brethren nobility. For many of them were already beginning to find this irksome, even in the Polish congregations where radicalism had been strongest. The laxity of Socinus's judgment on this point contrasts with the rigorism of his attitude to watching and guarding: an occupation in which burghers of course were mainly involved. So far as we know, none of the Racovians challenged Socinus here. At any rate the radical antimilitarists seem to have given his judgment at least their tacit consent.

During the early 1580s the military question remained a lively issue within the Brethren Church. It was debated, for instance, at a synod held early in March 1582 at Lubecz (near Nowogródek). The representatives from the Kingdom of Poland included prominent radicals like Czechowic, while among the 'Lithuanians' Budny took the lead in countering the arguments of the former in favour of nonresistance.

From Budny's account of the synod sessions (inserted in his book *On Sword-Bearing Rulership* published in 1583),[26] we learn that, in the past at any rate, the ministers of some congregations in the Kingdom of Poland had excluded from the sacrament those members who held office or served in the armed forces.[27] (As Budny pointed out with disapproval, if the powerful magnates of the Church's Lithuanian branch, who gave it protection in the Grand Duchy, had at that date belonged instead to the Polish branch, they would likely have been required to resign their social position and military authority if they had wished to remain in good standing in their congregations.) But the situation had now changed. For already some Antitrinitarian gentry in Poland were serving as soldiers and taking part in administration of the state, and there was no longer any question of such behaviour leading to disciplinary proceedings being instituted against them in the Church. Eventually Socinus was to replace Czechowic and the other Anabaptist Brethren leaders in the direction of the Church in the Polish Kingdom. And the Italian, we have seen, was from the very beginning anxious to smooth the path of those Brethren gentry who, in view of their fervent loyalty to the 'gentry republic [rzeczpospolita szlachecka]' of Poland, were finding conscientious objection to military service an increasingly difficult position to uphold (even though it remained the official position of their Church).

While Socinus, it is true, never ceased to assert that war, and homicide in general, were contrary to the Christian religion,[28] he continued to believe that this need not lead to a head-on collision with the state when a member of the Brethren nobility was called upon for military service. In February 1595, for instance, we find Socinus's father-in-law, Krzysztof Morsztyn, facing this problem when Poland's king, Zygmunt III, became involved in a war with Sweden, whose crown he claimed. The general levy was now called out for action on the north-eastern frontiers of the Commonwealth. Since Morsztyn, in addition to being an influential member of the Brethren Church, also held extensive landed property, he too became liable to serve under arms. To his father-in-law in his present dilemma Socinus gave the following advice: 'Concerning enlistment in the general levy, I would think that if there is no way to avoid it – either you must go or lose your property, it not being possible to give money so that another be hired to take your place – then you will not be breaking Christ's commandments if you arm yourself and set out on campaign, provided only that you refrain from killing or maiming anyone.' Socinus felt that a response of this kind was preferable to that of the man who adamantly refused to go on campaign. Even so, he was, in conclusion, forced to admit that he still remained uncertain as to what someone in Morsztyn's position ought to do in order to remain loyal both to his Saviour and to his fatherland.[29]

Twelve days later, writing to another prominent Antitrinitarian nobleman, Eliasz Arciszewski, Socinus repeated his warning against killing a man in war, while again expressing his approval if one of the faithful, when required to do so in defence of his country, should arm himself and set forth on campaign, provided of course that the draftee had previously done his utmost to obtain exemption from the authorities, perhaps by some kind of monetary contribution. For only in the unlikely circumstances of his being unsuccessful in this endeavour should he risk censure from the – naïve – purists among their coreligionists for choosing to obey the summons to arms when refusal to do so would bring shame not only on himself but on his whole family. In these circumstances, thought Socinus, it was a matter of choosing the lesser evil.[30]

Around the turn of the century the Brethren nobility, especially its younger generation, became even more insistent than before in demanding a revision of the Church's social and political ethic and a relaxation of the rigorism with respect to these issues, which had prevailed (at any rate in theory) hitherto in the congregations located in the Kingdom of Poland.[31] The climax came in the years 1601 and 1602. Then, in a series of closed sessions at the Church's centre at Raków, Socinus had delivered a course of lectures dealing with the pressing problems currently being debated within the Church.[32] *Inter alia* he presented the Brethren assembled there with an extensive revision of their Church's sociopolitical rigorism. And what their revered leader said now concerning sociopolitical ethics soon came to enjoy special authority throughout the Brethren Church.

In the course of his discussion of war during the 1601 sessions,[33] Socinus had indeed urged the unchristian character of all fighting, albeit in general terms, and he had continued to insist that a conscripted gentleman, who was a member of the Church, should try first to buy himself out of service. But in line with the views he had been expressing for over a decade, he went far towards approving active participation in military service on the part of the Antitrinitarian gentry when called out by the authorities in defence of their country.[34] (Voluntary enlistment in the army was of course an entirely different affair; something not to be condoned in one of the faithful.)

Despite the subtle qualifications Socinus was careful to make, his words had the effect of sweeping away any remaining reservations entertained by the Antitrinitarian gentry concerning the propriety of their taking part in war at the behest of the magistrate. His concessions in this respect appeared to give *carte blanche* to the kind of military activity in which they in fact had for long been engaged, if perhaps a little shamefacedly. Thereafter, there can have been few, if any, Brethren from the gentry, or indeed Brethren from any other class, who refused to bear arms when the state called upon them to do so. In 1601–2 Socinus had been speaking to a small and select group of Church leaders; his lectures – in the form of notes taken at the time by his friend and disciple Valentinus Smalcius – were to appear in print only in the twentieth century. But their content soon became known throughout the Church in a variety of ways. The publication in 1618 of an extensive section of Socinus's letters, including those we have cited from above, revealed to rank-and-file Brethren not privy to the deliberations of the Church leadership, *inter alia*, the far-reaching modifications carried out by Socinus in his latter years with regard to such topics as the magistracy, war, and self-defence. Even earlier, Christoff Ostorodt, a German-born Antitrinitarian minister, had incorporated much of the new Socinian doctrine in a book described by Kot as 'an official publication of the Church.'[35] Written primarily for the Church's small German-speaking membership, it appeared at Raków in 1604, the year of Socinus's death.[36]

Socinus's permissive attitude with respect to military obligation was reflected most clearly, however, in the discussions that took place during the open Church synods held at Raków in 1604 and 1605, at a time when the eastern borderlands of the Commonwealth were menaced by destructive Tatar raids. At the latter synod a resolution was passed – though, we should note, by no means unanimously – that forcible resistance to this kind of enemy was permissible, provided the Christian took every precaution not to kill or maim.[37] Despite the caution expressed here, Stanisław Szczotka was right in stressing the importance of this resolution: 'for the Polish [Brethren] it opened the way to armed resistance and, indirectly, to [full] military service. As a result we find more and more Brethren in the ranks of the army.'[38] Thus the year 1605 marked a turning point in the evolution of the Brethren Church's stand on the military question.

True, the Socinian reservations with regard to war remained to the end officially those of the Brethren Church as a whole. They were upheld by some of the clergy; and rigorists, as well as moderate Socinian pacifists, continued to exist within the brotherhood down to the time when the Polish Antitrinitarians were driven into exile in 1658–61, an act that reflected the mounting intolerance of the ruling Catholic majority. But long before this date the antimilitarists had dwindled to an insignificant minority.[39] Whereas in the course of the seventeenth century the Polish Brethren Church became increasingly radical in its theology, in their civic activities the Antitrinitarian gentry, who now formed the most influential element within the Church, blended more and more with their fellow nobles of Catholic or Calvinist persuasion. During the Russo-Polish War of 1632–4 Brethren cavaliers were conspicuous for their gallant behaviour on the battlefield, where they gained favourable notice from the Catholic king, Władysław IV. There were even some among them who now became professional soldiers, though the pastorate continued to regard this as unbecoming, if not actually sinful, in a member of the Brethren Church.

It may seem at first sight curious that for the four decades covered in this article I have not been able to cite the name of a single Polish Brother who actually refused to bear arms[40] nor any specific instance when a Brother evaded military service by some other means (with the exception perhaps of the ambiguous case of Faustus Socinus's father-in-law referred to above). But the reasons for the anonymity should be obvious, for whether it was a case of a Brother from the Polish gentry or of a burgher member of one of the Church's urban congregations, we have seen that ways existed of avoiding a direct clash on this issue. Means of evading service were always available in practice: by payment of commutation money perhaps, or by noncombatant duties of some kind, or even by hiring a substitute. True, the latter alternatives were at first frowned on by the Church, but they seem to have been resorted to, at any rate in an emergency. Since Brethren pacifists avoided a direct confrontation with the state over their conscientious rejection of military service, and in the absence of extensive Brethren Church archives surviving the Church's eventual suppression, we have to seek our evidence concerning Brethren conscientious objectors from literary sources, from the printed record, where the question is discussed only in general terms. If the worst came to the worst, of course, a gentleman conscientious objector could stand to lose his landed property – and his good name to boot. But only cases of the nonconscientious – non-Brethren – being thus punished are known to have occurred. The concessions Socinus recommended with regard to this problem in his Raków lectures of 1601–2 finally removed all possibility of a member of the Brethren Church being afflicted in this way.

The learned Italian's finely woven arguments and his ingenious logical distinctions passed, however, for the most part over the heads of rank-and-file Brethren from the gentry and of their non-noble coreligionists. Henceforward, participation in battle in defence of fatherland or native city appeared for almost all Polish Antitrinitarians to be not only a citizen's duty, but a Christian's obligation as well.[41]

NOTES

1 Jakob Gross and Ulrich Teck, members of the Anabaptist congregation at Waldshut, twenty-five miles north of Zürich in present-day Baden, refused in mid-1525 to bear arms in defence of their town. Gross, however, expressed his willingness to perform noncombatant duties.

2 The standard work on the social and political ideology of the Polish Brethren Church is by Stanisław Kot. Originally published in Polish in 1932, it was revised by the author and issued, in an English translation by Earl Morse Wilbur, under the title *Socinianism in Poland: The Social and Political Ideas of the Polish Antitrinitarians in the Sixteenth and Seventeenth Centuries* (Boston, 1957), hereafter *Socinianism in Poland*. All subsequent writers on the subject (including myself) remain deeply indebted to Kot's book. For the overall history of Polish Antitrinitarianism, see especially Wilbur, *A History of Unitarianism: Socinianism and Its Antecedents* (Cambridge MA, 1945), chaps. 19–39.

3 Stanisław Zachorowski, ed., 'Najstarsze synody arjan polskich z rękopisu kołoszwarskiego,' *Reformacja w Polsce*, vol. 1 (1921), 233. Such advice was given, for instance, at the synod held in 1568 at Pielesznica in the Cracow region by radical ministers like Marcin Czechowic, Piotr of Goniądz, and Grzegorz Paweł of Brzeziny (Gregorius Paulus). Their opinion, however, was contested by others present, and a heated discussion ensued over this issue.

4 Such a one, for instance, was Jan Niemojewski, owner of broad acres in the province of Kujawy, who for the sake of his conscience abandoned his ancestral property and all the pomp of nobility and donned 'a mean grey garment, without sword, without wallet, without attendant.' See Kot, *Socinianism in Poland*, 27–9.

5 Zdzisław Kaczmarczyk and Bogusław Leśnodorski, *Historia państwa i prawa Polski*, 2nd edn, vol. 2 (Warsaw, 1966), 136, 137; Tadeusz Korzon, *Dzieje*

wojen i wojskowości w Polsce, 2nd edn (Lwów-Warsaw-Cracow, 1923), vol. 1, 330, 331, vol. 2, 65. I would like to thank Prof. Zdzisław Pietrzyk of the Jagiellonian Library (Cracow) for his advice on bibliography at this point.

6 See especially Kot, *Socinianism in Poland*, chap. 5. Also Stanisław Estreicher, 'Pacyfizm w Polsce XVI stulecia' (hereafter Estreicher, 'Pacyfizm'), *Ruch prawniczy, ekonomiczny i socjologiczny*, vol. 11 (1931), 1, 8–11; Stanisław Szczotka, 'Synody arjan polskich od założenia Rakowa do wygnania z kraju (1569–1662)' (hereafter Szczotka, 'Synody'), *Reformacja w Polsce*, vol. 7/8 (1935–6), 26, 27; George H. Williams, *The Radical Reformation* (London, 1862), 734–6; and Domenico Caccamo, *Eretici italiani in Moravia, Polonia, Transilvania (1558–1611): Studi e documenti* (Florence, 1979), 153–7, 160. Sum mary biographies of, and guides to the literature on, the two protagonists can be found in the *Polski słownik biograficzny* (Wrocław and Cracow), vol. 9 (1960–1), 82–4 (Karol Górski on Paulus), and vol. 25 (1980), 67–72 (Lech Szczucki on Palaeologus).

7 Szymon Budny, *O urzędzie miecza używającem (1583)*, ed. S. Kot (Warsaw, 1932; hereafter Budny, *O urzędzie*), 20. Literally, 'the Office using the Sword'; Budny also uses the terms *urząd mieczowy* and *urząd z mieczem*.

8 Quoted in Kot, *Socinianism in Poland*, 52, from Palaeologus's preface (p. 2) to his *Defensio verae sententiae de magistratu politico in ecclesiis christianis reti nendo ...* (Łosk, 1580); hereafter *Defensio*. The preface was written in 1579. I have slightly revised the translation of this passage, which was made by Wilbur from Kot's Polish text. The penalty mentioned by Palaeologus was confiscation of estates; the Greek, though, makes no mention of such a penalty ever having been imposed on a member of the Brethren Church.

9 Palaeologus, 'De bello sententia,' in *Defensio*, 30, 31. We may note that the legitimacy of all three alternatives also became a matter of controversy among the two major pacifist sects of modern times, the Mennonites and the Quakers.

10 *Defensio*, 32, 44–9, 51 ('De bello sententia').

11 It was published in 1580 in *Defensio*, 56–81, along with Palaeologus's 'De bello sententia' and the latter's lengthy counterblast to Paulus, *Ad scriptum Fratrum Racoviensium de bello et iudiciis forensibus, Iacobi Palaeologi Responsio.* For an abbreviated translation of Paulus's tract, see my 'Gregorius Paulus against the Sword: A Polish Anabaptist on Nonresistance,' *Mennonite Quarterly Review* (hereafter *MQR*), vol. 65, no. 4 (October 1991), 427–36.

12 Kot, *Socinianism in Poland*, 59.

13 From my translation in the *MQR* cited above, 436. There is only one specific reference to war in Palaeologus's 'Reply' to Paulus: *Defensio*, 325, 326.

14 Marcin Czechowic, *Rozmowy chrystyjańskie* (Cracow, 1575), hereafter

Czechowic, *Rozmowy*. See the scholarly reprint edited by Lech Szczucki et al. (Warsaw-Łódź, 1979). Colloquy XII is to be found in this edition on pages 243–76. My translation of the sections of Colloquy XII dealing with war has been reprinted several times: in the *MQR*, vol. 52, no. 4 (October 1978), 287–93 ('A Polish Anabaptist against War: The Question of Conscientious Objection in Marcin Czechowic's *Christian Dialogues* of 1575'); also in my *Studies in Peace History* (York UK, 1991), 14–19. See essay 2 below.

15 Appendix ad Christianum lectorem continens testimonia patrum de vita et moribus Christianorum primitivae Ecclesiae.' Reprinted in Czechowic, *Rozmowy*, 1979 edn, 302–30.

16 Ibid., 303.

17 Ibid., 308, 309.

18 *Ad Iac. Palaeologi librum, cui titulus est, Defensio verae sententiae de magistratu politico, &c. pro Racoviensibus Responsio* (Cracow, 1581); hereafter Socinus, *Responsio*. See Kot, *Socinianism in Poland*, chap. 7; Ludwik Chmaj, *Faust Socyn (1539–1604)* (Warsaw, 1963), hereafter Chmaj, *Faust Socyn*), chap. 5; also Estreicher, 'Pacyfizm,' 11–13. Socinus's work was reprinted at Raków in 1627 and again (in 1668) in his *Opera omnia*, vol. II, 1–114, as part of the *Bibliotheca Fratrum Polonorum* (Amsterdam).

19 Socinus, *Responsio*, 46ff.

20 For Socinus's view of war in 1581, see Giovanni Pioli, *Fausto Socino: vita-opere-fortuna: Contributo alla storia del liberalismo religioso moderno* (Modena, 1952), 403–8. Pioli's study is the most detailed, hitherto, of Socinus's theological and socio-ethical ideas. But, though extremely thorough, he seems to me to devote excessive space to merely summarizing.

21 Socinus, *Responsio*, 257, 258. Like St Paul, Socinus regarded 'the powers that be' as 'God's ministers.' And, he stated, 'when we say that it is not lawful for a Christian to wage war or fight, we are speaking of a private person and not of the king, prince or magistrate.' For officers of state, waging war might well have been an entirely legitimate activity; they would only be acting as they believed was fitting for them. 'Not all those things which the Christian is forbidden to do are wrong in themselves and to be condemned,' he declared. But we must remember, of course, that Socinus, though he later modified his opinion on this point, at that time shared the Racovians' view that a faithful Christian could not himself become a ruler.

22 Ibid., 242–4, 251–3.

23 Ibid., 258.

24 Ibid., 264–7.

25 Kot, *Socinianism in Poland*, 91. In his letter to Márton Berzevicsy, dated 12 March 1583, Socinus stressed it was a misconception to regard his

treatise as an attack on government as such. His objective, he wrote, had been to define 'the obligation of individual Christians who did not participate in office [agitur ... de Christianorum hominum privatorum officio].' By doing this, he believed he was strengthening, rather than diminishing, the prestige of government in general (*Fausti Socini Senensis ad amicos epistolae* [Raków, 1618; hereafter *Epistolae*], 686).

26 Budny's *O urzędzie miecza używającem* was directed primarily against Colloquy XII of Czechowic's *Rozmowy chrystyjańskie* (1575), which had evidently made a considerable impression within the Brethren Church, for otherwise the anti-pacifist wing of the Church would scarcely have considered it necessary to publish a detailed rebuttal of its arguments. But unlike Czechowic's work, Budny's treatise included very little directly on the military question, its main argument revolving around the more general problems of office-holding and the existing social system.

27 Budny, *O urzędzie*, 30. The evidence as to this disciplinary measure is conflicting: we do not indeed know to what extent – or where – it was enforced.

28 He did this, for example, in a Latin work he completed at Lucławice in July 1599. It was published at Raków the following year in a Polish translation (*Okazanie* ...) and later in Latin in several slightly differing versions. I have consulted only one of the latter: *Quod Regni Poloniae et Magni Ducatus Lithuaniae homines, vulgo Evangelici dicti, qui solidae pietatis sunt studiosi, omnino deberent se illorum coetui adjungere, quo in iisdem locis falso atque immerito Arriani atque Ebionitae vocantur* (Raków, 1611). On pages 23–7 (*Okazanie*, 17–20), we find the author comparing his view of the sword, including war, with that of the Protestant mainstream. In contrast to the Old Testament times, 'under the New Testament,' declares Socinus (p. 25), 'God gave no earthly territory to his people'; from then on, they were to use only spiritual weapons against their enemies.

29 Letter to Morsztyn, dated 3 February 1595, *Epistolae*, 498. Socinus's approval here of hiring a substitute to take one's place in the general levy marks a retreat from his position in 1581, unless, of course, he regarded money paid in such circumstances as a tax formally unconnected with the hiring of a replacement.

30 Letter to Arciszewski, dated 15 February 1595, ibid., 407–9.

31 Kot, *Socinianism in Poland*, 112, 116. At a synod held at Lublin in 1593, resolutions (*konkluzyie*) had been passed *inter alia* allowing Brethren to participate in the punishment of murderers and adulterers – so long as the death penalty were not inflicted. In addition, a ruler converted to Antitrinitarianism might remain in office administering justice – so long as he did this in

accordance with the counsels of the Church (*z dokładem zborowym*). See Lech Szczucki and Janusz Tazbir, 'Księga wizytacji zborów podgórskich: Z rękopisu Biblioteki Nemzeti Muzeum w Budapeszcie,' *Archiwum Historii Filozofii i Myśli Społecznej*, vol. 3 (1958), 153, 154. Such resolutions, while opposed to the earlier rigorism, appear to me to be clearly Socinian in spirit, and probably in inspiration too. Tazbir, however, considers that they marked 'a victory of Budny's views' and that they approved 'the waging of wars' on the part of rulers who joined the Brethren Church. See his article 'Pacifism in the Ideology of the Polish Brethren,' *Polish Western Afffairs*, 15, no. 2 (1974), 211.

32 *Epitome colloquii Racoviae habiti anno 1601*, ed. Lech Szczucki and Janusz Tazbir (Warsaw, 1966; hereafter *Epitome*). For Socinus's lectures at Raków, see Kot, *Socinianism in Poland*, chap. 9, and Chamj, *Faust Socyn*, chap. 16. The compiler of the *Epitome* was Valentinus Smalcius (Schmaltz), an Antitrinitarian immigrant from Germany who stood very close to Socinus in his views. We may see this, in respect to sociopolitical ideology, in the section of his *Refutatio Thesium D. Wolfgangi Frantzii, theologiae doctoris et professoris publici in Academia Witebergensi* (Rakow, 1614) entitled 'De rebus civilibus' (387–96). Though approving a Christian magistracy – 'provided nothing be done contrary to the laws of Christ, and in particular against the royal law of love' – Smalcius states unambiguously his view of the 'unlawfulness' of all war if undertaken by the faithful: 'licere bella gerere, nec nos videmus, nec Frantzius ostendit' (387, 393–5). For Smalcius it was wrong for a Christian to destroy human life, whatever the reason.

33 *Epitome*, 83–5 ('De bello'). For a translation, see George H. Williams, ed., *The Polish Brethren: Documentation of the History and Thought of Unitarianism in the Polish-Lithuanian Commonwealth and in the Diaspora, 1601–1685*, Harvard Theological Studies, no. 30 (Missoula [MT], 1980), pt 1 (hereafter Williams, *Polish Brethren*), 125, 126.

34 It is clear from the *Epitome* that Socinus had the Brethren nobility in mind while he was speaking on war and military service, and it was the problems a refusal to bear arms would generate for members of this class that chiefly concerned him.

35 Kot, *Socinianism in Poland*, 123.

36 *Unterrichtung von den vornehmsten Hauptpuncten der christlichen Religion ...* Ostorodt's views on war are given on pages 177–95. 'Whether a Christian may take part in war is,' he wrote, 'a difficult question.' Indeed, because honest disagreement on this issue had existed among 'God-fearing and learned men' since the apostolic age, we had to act here as our own consciences told us to do. For his part, Ostorodt condemned all war, even

though he admitted that the majority of believers had not done so. He stressed, therefore, his desire not to exclude from fellowship those churchmen who, relying 'almost entirely on the Old Testament for their arguments,' dissented from the pacifist position. See also Williams, *Polish Brethren*, 155–62, 167. Ostorodt, like Socinus, believed that a Christian magistracy could function without having to shed blood either in punishing evildoers or in defence of the state.

37 At this synod, '... de publicis hostibus Tataris, quo Podoliam et vicina loca vastant, actum est, utrum eis se opponere et resistere licet. Ubi (quamvis a paucis) conclusum, resistere quidem licere, quatenus quis salva conscientia defendere possit, ita, ne aliquem eorum occidat, vel ita laedat, ut membrum eius mutilet. Id enim fieri praeter Christiani hominus debitum, potius inde migrandum et alibi domicilium quaerendum.' See Kazimierz Dobrowolski, ed., 'Nieznana kronika arjańska 1539–1605,' *Reformacja w Polsce*, vol. 4 (1926), 172. See also Szczotka, 'Synody,' 56, 57. The recommendation cited here, to flee the areas threatened by the Tatars rather than to attempt armed resistance, shows that old ideas died hard in the Brethren Church.

38 Ibid., 57. It is significant that, while not sanctioning bloodshed, the Brethren's famous Racovian Catechism, which was published in Polish in 1605 (and then in Latin in 1609), did not deal explicitly with the problem of war.

39 Towards the middle of the seventeenth century, the Church's German-speaking congregation in Danzig became a stronghold of sociopolitical rigorism, in part due to its proximity to the Mennonite communities of the Vistula delta. Rigorism indeed was now defended in print chiefly by German-speaking members of the Church like the Danzig occulist Daniel Zwicker and, especially, the immigrant Austrian baron Johann Ludwig von Wolzogen, who had joined the Brethren Church after finding refuge in Poland from persecution in his native land. In the course of his controversy around the middle of the seventeenth century with the Socinian minister Jonasz Szlichtyng *de magistratu, bello, et privata defensione*, Wolzogen expressed his conviction that a true Christian was bound to refuse to perform military service. 'What laws,' asked the baron, 'what compulsion can force a man who is a Christian to fight ... if his conscience tells him he should not do so?' He went on to cite with approval what he believed had been the practice of the early church in excluding soldiers from holy communion 'because ... shedding human blood is contrary to the Christian discipline'; that, in his view, was indeed 'a devout and Christian custom' (from Wolzogen's *Opera omnia exegetica, didactica, et polemica* [*Bibliotheca Fratrum Polonorum*, vol. 6], [Amsterdam, 1668], vol. 2, pt 2, 76, 78). In this same period, the Socinian minister Joachim Stegmann the younger, who translated many of Wolzo-

gen's works from German into Latin, was writing in support of pacifism, too, though he was less extreme in his views on nonresistance than his friend had been. (He appears, moreover, to have modified his antiwar position at a later date.) See Chmaj, *Samuel Przypkowski na tle prądów religyjnych XVII wieku* (Cracow, 1927), 50, 51, 80, 81, 157–71. In his treatise on the sword (extant only in brief excerpts included in the reply of his opponent Samuel Przypkowski), entitled 'Apologia prolixior: Tractatus de jure christiani magistratus,' Stegmann had declared forthrightly: 'No case can be cited of a Christian at the time of the Apostles ever having become a soldier' (from Przypkowski, *Cogitationes Sacrae ...* [Amsterdam, 1692], 760). Thus we find that even at this late date when most of the Polish Brethren had come to sanction war, Stegmann – as well as Wolzogen (and Zwicker) – still supported warmly the stand of the conscientious objector. But, of course, their advocacy was purely theoretical, for the question of military conscription had long ceased to be one that bothered the conscience of any of the Brethren in practice. Zwicker, now an exile in Amsterdam, summed up his view of the military question when he wrote: 'If ever there was anything the church [of the early centuries] unanimously agreed, it was this: that Christians must not fight and conduct wars, nor exercise civil authority and kill other men' (quoted in Peter G. Bietenholz, *Daniel Zwicker, 1612–1678: Peace, Tolerance and God the One and Only* [Florence, 1997], 152).

40 Cf. Tazbir (see note 31), 210: 'We do not know of a single case of an Arian [i.e., Polish Brethren] landed estate having been confiscated because its owner failed to turn up for a levy in mass or refused to take part in a war expedition.'

41 For a survey of the military question among the Polish Antitrinitarians from Faustus Socinus's first pronouncement on the matter to the final suppression of the Brethren Church, see my article 'Socinian Pacifism from 1581 to 1661,' *A Journal from the Radical Reformation*, vol. 4, no. 2 (Winter 1995), 33–48. The last statement by the Brethren Church reflecting Socinian pacifism came in 1680 in an editorial note by the exile Benedykt Wiszowaty, which was inserted in the edition of the Racovian Catechism (*Catechesis ecclesiarum polonicarum*) appearing in Amsterdam in that year. (For a translation, see Williams, *Polish Brethren*, pt 2, 714–17.) Thus ended what Williams has aptly called 'the second controversy over the sword' (p. 709) in the Brethren Church. Selected documents from this controversy appear in Polish translation in Zbigniew Ogonowski, ed., *Myśl ariańska w Polsce XVII wieku: Antologia tekstów* (Wrocław, 1991), 161–249.

2 A Polish Antitrinitarian in Defence of Conscientious Objection to Military Service (1575)

Marcin Czechowic[1] published his *Christian Colloquies* in Cracow in 1575 in the midst of the debate over the sword between various members of the Polish Brethren Church's intellectual élite. Czechowic was at the time the minister of the important Antitrinitarian congregation at Lublin. He wrote his bulky volume in Polish. 'A representative piece of pedagogical literature designed for the instruction of the young rather than ... a polemic with peers,'[2] the book was also intended for the use of adult Church members unacquainted with Latin. Indeed its learned author, endowed with a cooler disposition than the other leading protagonist of nonresistance, Gregorius Paulus, and master of a vigorous Polish prose style, was well qualified to defend the Racovian doctrine, including nonresistance. Though quite as convinced as Paulus of the rightness of this viewpoint, Czechowic was less impetuous in imputing evil motives to those who held different opinions and was better able to present opposing arguments – if only in order finally to refute them. Each dialogue took the form of a conversation between 'Teacher' and 'Pupil,' with the twelfth dialogue, 'On the Christian Life,' being devoted to the subject of nonresistance. Here Teacher expounds the views of Czechowic himself and of the radical party within the Polish Brethren Church, while Pupil presents those of the Church's antipacifists, among whom the most eloquent spokesman hitherto had been the visiting Greek Antitrinitarian scholar, Jacobus Palaeologus.

We may note that, unlike Paulus, who had avoided discussing directly the question of military service (presumably on account of the tense military situation prevailing in Poland while he was writing), Czechowic devotes a fairly lengthy section of the twelfth dialogue to this topic. At any rate, for our times, it is perhaps the most interesting part of the colloquy and I have therefore translated almost all of it into English and printed it below.[3] Here Czechowic unequivocally forbids the brethren to undertake such service even were it possible to do so without actually carrying arms. By implication, however, he allowed the payment of commutation money in exchange for exemption.

In 1583, eight years after the launching of Czechowic's *Christian Colloquies*, the leading anti-nonresistant Antitrinitarian, Szymon Budny, returned to the fray and published in Polish a lengthy rebuttal of Czechowic's exposition of nonresistance. It appeared under the title *On Sword-Bearing Rulership*. In this work, Budny concentrates mainly on the problem of the magistracy, which he defends as a Christian institution. In respect to military service, a topic to which however he devotes little space, Budny could detect no essential contradiction between the soldier's calling and the Christian life. True followers of Christ, in his view, should become conscientious conscripts and not conscientious objectors.

Discussion of nonresistance died down after the appearance of Budny's book, and the controversy over the sword that Palaeologus had launched with such vigour eleven years before seemed to have exhausted itself inconclusively. Budny himself was expelled from the Brethren Church in 1584 (for propagating non-adorantism, not antipacifism). This had removed the nonresistants' most effective opponent from the scene. Their cause, however, no longer prospered as it had in the past. The reasons for this are not too difficult to surmise. In the first place they, too, had lost several of their leaders. Paulus, for instance, already seriously ill, died at the beginning of the 1590s. Though Czechowic survived till 1613 and Niemojewski, his chief supporter in the Lublin congregation where he was pastor, till 1598, they no longer carried the same weight in the counsels of the Church as they had formerly done – which fact leads to a second, and deeper, cause of the decline of pacifism and social radicalism in the Brethren Church. As old age and death slowly took their toll of the generation of converts, younger men stepped into their shoes. For them, we have seen, the pacifist primitivism of the previous generation did not possess the same compelling power. They did not share the emotional attachment to nonresistance for which their fathers had sacrificed so much. Henceforward nonresistance became at most an intellectual tenet of their church to which they gave lip service but not love. It was only to be expected that, as members of the nobility began to exercise increasing influence within the Church, these nobles now found the restrictions placed by the nonresistant ethic on their political and social activities increasingly irksome. A Jan Niemojewski felt happy to exchange rank, wealth, and sword for the peace he gained through living as a humble and defenceless Christian. Those who came after him felt differently. The man who eased the transition from nonresistance and sociopolitical radicalism to sociopolitical conformity and the acceptance of war and self-defence was the Italian exile Faustus Socinus (see essay 1).

Marcin Czechowic on Conscientious Objection to Military Service

Pupil: [...][4] When the magistracy orders me either to take part in its warfare or to kill someone, as the Jewish kings, etc., also used to do, am I not to do this (for I am told I should listen to and obey the magistracy and I see that the Jews did this at the command of their kings, not only the good kings but the evil ones, too)?

Teacher: You must be obedient and subject to the magistracy and render to it what it commands – but only so far as the word of God allows and no further. You must always remember the vindication and answer of the apostles which they, too, made to such a magistracy that commanded them to obey it and not the Lord's commandment and their kind. They told their judges and superiors: Consider whether it be right in the sight of God to harken unto you rather than unto God (Acts 4:19). The same kind of thing is to be found in the Old Testament as well, where there are many instances when true glorifiers [of God] were unwilling to obey the magistracy or carry out its decrees if it commanded them to do what was contrary to God. Yes, indeed, they preferred to face hardships, great and strange, as well as danger to health rather than yield to the magistracy in respect to something that was against the will of God, who is himself the supreme magistrate, as we read in the third chapter of Daniel about the three young men[5] and in the sixth about Daniel himself. Against him all the counsellors made a decree that if he should dare (according to his usual custom) to ask a petition of God – or indeed of any man – for thirty days save of his king, Darius, he should be cast into the den of lions. Daniel did not then say he must obey this sacrilegious decree, [the outcome] of evil counsel, even though once already he had been delivered into captivity, nor that he should practice deceit by secretly praying to God behind closed doors. O no! Instead, in order to show clearly he loved and obeyed God and not any official decree, he opened the windows of his house and prayed publicly to God, even though he knew that according to that decree he should be cast among the lions.

Likewise we may read concerning Saul's servants (1 Sam. 22) that when the king, their vengeful lord, ordered them to kill Ahimelech,[6] the chief victim, along with the others, they were unwilling to carry out this deed that was wholly contrary to God. Hence you may observe how in the Old Testament there were glorifiers of God who were unwilling to obey the magistracy when its commands were contrary to God's. However, in the Old Testament many things were allowed which the New Covenant has forbidden the faithful to do. And whoever today would like to justify wars must also justify and practise circumcision and polygamy and divorce as well as many other things which do not square with the Gospel of Christ.

Now as for war, not only is it impossible to show from the Old Testament that the faithful should practise it, but we may very soon discover in the prophets that under the New Covenant Christ's servants are neither to fight nor to train for war on all the Lord's holy mountain – that is, from within the assembly of the faithful [...] Indeed in the last resort, if need be, and if you wish to trust more in the writings of men than in God's word, you can show here from the old as well as the new doctors – and even from the papist clergymen themselves (who are called priests) – that Christians, that is, spiritual Christians, may not fight.[7] Not merely may they not fight or condemn anyone to death, they may not even be present in a court of justice of this kind either. Yet some there are now who, against their own decrees and that ancient practice, dare to allow them to fight, forgetting about their own bishop, Martin.[8] He was ordered to go to war and, having not yet become a Christian before he left (as the Lombard's history testifies),[9] he then said simply. 'I have [now] become a Christian and I cannot fight.' Indeed it is certain that, even if the magistracy orders it, no true reborn Christian may fight. For it would be better to lose all, in the last resort even life itself, than to deviate in anything from the teachings of Christ and the apostles. Paul indeed writing to Titus (Titus 3:1, 2; also 2 Tim. 2:24), while he commands the faithful servants of Christ to obey the magistracy, at the same time, however, wishes them to be meek and gentle and to refrain from strife. The faithful, to be sure, can manage to achieve this if they always keep in mind that teaching of Christ's: Fear not those who kill the body but cannot do anything more, but rather fear him who, having destroyed the body, is also able to deliver the soul to hell (Matt. 10:28). And in order that you should not think this doctrine on war, Christian patience, the [magistrate's] office, and the other matters we have mentioned in this conversation, is a new doctrine and not the customary one for the faithful, I am putting these things in a separate section.[10] So in this way you will know there is no novelty here.

Pupil: I shall be glad to get this from you and to read it later. But now if I were to set out for war at the royal command, yet should kill no one while the others were killing, and moreover if I carried no weapon, would I be doing wrong?

[11]*Teacher*: Certainly you would be doing wrong, for there you would be yoked together with other unbelievers against the apostle's command (2 Cor. 6:14). Besides you would be venturing where we are commanded to abstain from all appearance of evil (1 Thess. 5:22), and if you had fellowship with the unfruitful works of darkness (Eph. 5:11) you would be tempting God and at the same time provoking not only the magistracy but also the rest of the knighthood thirsting for the enemy's blood. And in addition, if anything happened to you there, you would suffer deservedly as a busybody in other men's matters (1 Pet. 4:15); from it you would have neither a satisfied conscience nor recompense from God since you would have been acting against his word, whereas if you wished to practise deceit in the matter, then you would have at once to part from Christ because he abhors words of dissimulation. Moreover, your action would clash with that of Daniel the prophet and of those three young men [Shadrach, Meshach, and Abed-nego] who preferred, I say, to be slaughtered rather than retreat one step from their duty. I don't want to say anything further – find out for yourself whether you are acting according to the true faith.

[12]*Pupil*: Why did not John the Baptist condemn war and forbid the soldiers to fight, instead merely instructing them how they should behave while in service? Why, in addition, did Peter neither condemn soldiering nor forbid Cornelius the centurion to be a soldier any longer?

Teacher: Since you have cited two cases different both in respect to the office concerned and to the time, wishing with them both to prove one and the same thing, I must likewise divide my answer into two parts. In wishing to justify war and soldiering by means of John's answer, your argument in my opinion is both redundant and at the same time unconsidered. It is redundant because neither I nor any of the faithful believe there should not be wars and soldiers in this world. Indeed we know from our Lord Jesus Christ himself that, if ever, then in these final times there must be wars throughout the whole world. But nevertheless we may not deduce from this that, therefore, the little sheep of Christ's congregation should also take part in war. Your argument, on the other hand, is unconsidered because his own disciples were not enquiring then about war nor were the people of Israel, who did not need to do so for they knew well that without God's special counsel and commandment it was never right to fight. For whosoever should do this before receiving God's commandment would draw down on himself a substantial portion of God's wrath. This happened to Jehoshaphat when, against God's will, he went to the aid of Ahab in his war and had to flee ignominiously,[13] while the virtuous and godly Josiah, too, was killed.[14] It was not, therefore, Christ's disciples or his special apostles (who later were to become the builders of God's house) who questioned and took counsel with John about fighting, for at that time they had not yet come together. Moreover, the Lord Jesus had not yet been baptized, nor had he yet gathered disciples and made some of them his apostles. It was not right or proper for such people to enquire in such a matter. For if it was not right for David, who sought God's glory, to build the material house of God from wood and stone for no other reason except that he had shed much blood in battle – and even though he had never set out for war without seeking counsel of the Lord – then it would not have been right for soldiers enamoured of shedding the blood of strangers and the innocent (it was they who were enquiring about soldiering) to prepare the building of the spiritual home of God. This was the task of simple and sincere fishermen. In the same way, now, men of blood can neither build this house of God nor become [members of] it themselves so long as they have not repented and ceased to shed blood.

And who questioned John? Soldiers, of course. And these soldiers were not Jews, or else they would have been otherwise admonished and this would not have been recommended to them. Rather they were Romans maintaining a perpetual guard over the Jews, whom they had already conquered, in order that these should not at any time by some revolt or conspiracy break loose from their obedience and subjection. And now John replies wisely and circumspectly to such soldiers, who were asking – perhaps sincerely or perhaps wishing to trap him by guile – what they should do. Thus, although I have no idea whether they followed his counsel and conducted themselves afterwards according to it, his answer put an end to their questioning and they had to depart in silence. Indeed, if anyone today were interrogated by soldiers of this world, I don't know if they could answer better or more wisely, although if it were either the present or future disciples of Christ who were putting such questions we could – indeed we should – answer in a more satisfactory manner.

When you cite Peter and Cornelius you do so improperly and without justification, for neither did Cornelius ask nor did Peter answer any question on this subject. The latter, instead, spoke only of Christ in whom he believed, taking his spirit from the God that leads into all truth and teaches all those things taught by Christ, who told his own not to fight but to suffer – about which already enough has been said. And [Cornelius] was only baptized then so that, having died to the world and been reborn to God and having also renounced the self, he should take up his cross and follow after Christ – and no longer pursue the centurion's profession or command regiments.

Pupil: Would it ever be right, even with God's permission, for the magistracy to kill someone when it is so serious a matter to shed the blood of any?

[15]*Teacher*: Why would it not be right? For it is God's decision and his universal commandment that the wicked should be punished and the blood be shed of him who also sheds the blood of another (Gen. 9:6). It is right, I say, to do so for him into whose hand God himself gives the sword, as he entrusted it to that king of Babylon [for use] against the Israelites and strengthened his arm against them as well as against other nations (Ezek. 30:24).[16] Yes indeed, if any into whose hands God has given the sword should keep it back from blood, as God accused the Moabites of doing (Jer. 48:10), then shall he be cursed. The rulers of this world, then, must willy-nilly punish the wicked and shed their blood, but not the disciples of Christ, who must be willing rather that their own blood be poured out for righteousness' sake than that they should shed the blood of any.

Pupil: How will they be able to wage war and defend their states and subjects, if I and you and many others who have sincerely joined Christ will neither fight nor take part in war?

[17]*Teacher*: O we don't have to worry at all about that. For if the Lord will desire to punish someone by the sword of war, he has only to hiss and, be it from the uttermost parts of the earth, great numbers of robust and courageous soldiers will assemble, like the fly and the bee (Isa. 7:18, 19). And as for what you say about the defence of their state and of the towns and common people, in the first place the truth is that for this purpose all that is needed is a great host which can easily be

got together if only there is money. And secondly, it is no less true that every kingdom is defended by the same means by which it came into being at the beginning and was acquired [...] Lo! Were not Judah and Israel powerful kingdoms? Were not the Babylonian kingdom and many others – it would be wearisome for me to number and name them – were they not powerful as well? Behold, now there is not the faintest trace left of them, although they possessed men and wealth, courage and knowledge in abundance [...] However, to us faithful nothing of all this need be a cause of anxiety, for God has numbered the hairs of our heads. We need only to take care that we stand manfully at his summons. Then (as we have said time and again) having renounced the self we must take up his cross and follow after Christ the Lord in the exigencies of life, through him praising and calling upon God the Father in spirit and in truth. And he will himself defend those states where his faithful live, as he would have defended Sodom and preserved it from downfall if only there had been ten righteous men in that place.

NOTES

1 See Lech Szczucki, *Marcin Czechowic (1532-1613)* (Warsaw, 1964); also Peter Brock, 'Marcin Czechowic in Defense of Nonresistance, 1975,' *Conrad Grebel Review*, vol. 9, no. 3 (Fall 1991), 251–7.
2 George Hunston Williams, *The Radical Reformation* (London, 1962), 747.
3 Marcin Czechowic, *Rozmowy chrystyjańskie*, ed. Alina Linda et al. (Warsaw-Łódź, 1979), 272–6.
4 Marginal note: 'Whether the faithful may at the commandment of the magistracy kill someone or serve in war.'
5 Shadrach, Meshach, and Abed-nego.
6 A reference to the priest who was slain by Saul for allegedly conspiring against him on behalf of David.
7 In Polish the adjective *duchowny*, 'spiritual,' is also used as a noun with the meaning 'priest.' It is difficult to transmit Czechowic's play on words here.
8 A reference to St Martin of Tours in the fourth century.
9 This refers to Paul the Deacon's *Historia gentis Langobardorum*, composed in the eighth century and several times reprinted during the Renaissance and after.
10 Reference to the Latin appendix 'de vita et moribus Christianorum primitivae Ecclesiae,' printed in Czechowic, *Rozmowy*, 302–30.

11 Marginal note: 'Whether the faithful may go to war along with the rest, but without weapons and killing no one when the others kill.'

12 Marginal note: 'That John did not forbid the soldiers to fight and Peter did not forbid Cornelius to continue as a centurion.'

13 See 1 Kings 22:33.

14 See 2 Kings 23:29, 30.

15 Marginal note: 'God allows the magistracy alone to punish the wicked and shed blood.'

16 In fact, this particular verse refers to the king of Babylon's defeat of Pharaoh and not of the Israelites.

17 Marginal note: 'Kings can perfectly well wage war without Christ's disciples.'

3 Conscientious Objection among the *Doopsgezinden*

Anabaptism spread to the Netherlands in the early 1530s. At first its adherents belonged to the chiliastic, millenarian branch of the movement; even if peaceable in their outward stance, they were far from being nonresistants in the sense the Swiss Brethren, who authored the Schleitheim Confession of 1527, understood that term. Eventually the Frisian ex-Catholic priest Menno Simons succeeded briefly in uniting Dutch Anabaptists into a congregation of Christians striving for perfection and modelling itself on the primitive church. Henceforward Anabaptists, not only in the Netherlands but in Germany and elsewhere too, became known as Mennonites, though their designation as Anabaptists lingered on in the Netherlands, where the term *Doopsgezinden* (the Baptized) finally gained precedence over Mennonites.

Though Menno was not always consistent in his teaching on the subject, Dutch Anabaptists under his guidance adopted nonresistance as a central tenet of their belief. Henceforward Christians, in order to live on this earth 'without spot or wrinkle [zonder vlek of rimpel],' were obligated to reject military service if drafted.[1]

Menno died in 1561. The unity he achieved was unfortunately short-lived. Indeed the fissiparous trend began even before his death when, in 1557, the so-called 'Waterlanders,' centred in the 'waterland' area of north Holland, broke away because they felt the brotherhood was acting too severely in imposing the ban on those who had offended against the congregational discipline. 'Frisians' and 'Flemings' resulted from subsequent schisms until by the end of the century there were at least twenty Mennonite subsects. True, the majority of these were extremely small; still, some half a dozen had sizeable memberships.

The Dutch war for independence against Spain began in 1572. It was to continue intermittently until 1648; in the course of the struggle, the southern provinces (today's Belgium) were lost[2] and only the northern United Provinces, under the leadership of the House of Orange, achieved independence that was finally recognized internationally. (*De facto* independence had come in 1609.) Now for the first time the question of conscientious objection became a prime concern of the brotherhood.[3] The problem was not entirely new, as can be seen from a resolution taken at the conference held by the Waterlanders in 1568. Concerning those members who had taken part in military exercises when summoned to attend drills, it was decided: 'If a brother has taken part in this, he shall desist from it, confess to sorrow for the offence and ask the forgiveness of God and the church before he may be recognized as in peace with the church.'[4] Some form of disciplinary action against such an offender, combined with the ultimate sanction of disfellowshipping by the imposition of the ban, continued to be in force in all branches of the Dutch Mennonite brotherhood for a long time to come.

In the summer of 1572, at the outset of the war, the brotherhood had approached William of Orange with a free-will offering of over a thousand guilders, which was indeed a considerable sum of money. The prince, hard-pressed for funds to carry on the struggle against Spain, readily accepted the Mennonites' gift, giving them a receipt stating that the money would be used 'for the advancement of the common cause.' There can be no doubt that the latter knew what the prince meant by this. At the same time they presumed – correctly – that he would exert his influence to free draftees belonging to the brotherhood from the obligation to bear arms. Under the *ancien régime* an understanding of this kind was often reached between Mennonites and ruler: what the latter did with the money received was his business and not the brotherhood's.

'During the early years of the war, the period of the famous sieges of Alkmaar, Haarlem and Leiden, we know almost nothing about the stance of the *Doopsgezinden*,' writes van der Zijpp.[5] William of Orange and his successor, Maurice of Nassau, were men of a generally tolerant disposition, who now relaxed most of the restrictions hitherto existing on the Mennonites' exercise of their religion. They used their influence with the various authorities in the provinces of the northern Netherlands, united in name but largely decentralized in practice, to free drafted Mennonites from having to bear arms. (Hiring a substitute, always a possible option, was frowned on – though sometimes practised – by the brotherhood, many of whose members anyhow did not have the means to do this on their own.) In any case there was no sense in risking a confrontation on this issue between the *Doopsgezinden* and the state.

A landmark event came in 1575 when the province of North Holland, as a result of pressure from William of Orange, exempted members of the brotherhood from the obligation incumbent on all able-bodied male citizens of having to watch with weapons. This, incidentally, appears to be the first piece of legislation providing for conscientious objection to military service. In exchange for not performing their stint of duty armed, Mennonites were to come carrying 'a sharp spade and a basket' so as, in an emergency, to help dig ditches and build ramparts.[6] Whether such duties were ever actually enforced we do not know. We hear of no protest, though, from any of the brotherhood's branches concerning the character of such alternative service; they were presumably happy to have at last gained official recognition of their antiwar position and not too concerned with what might be demanded of them if hostilities reached the northern part of their country.

They knew, too, that the Calvinist clergy as well as some influential Dutch patriots opposed the prince's toleration of the Mennonites' scruples concerning arms-bearing. But a *modus vivendi* was usually worked out as well between the brotherhood and the other provincial or town authorities. Often exemption was granted on payment of a special tax (which, of course, was assigned to cover military expenses); sometimes, as in the case for instance of Middelburg, the amount varied according to the number of Mennonites who were liable for service. The brotherhood might try to bargain over the sum imposed, not always with success.[7] In the course of time the otherworldly sectaries, citizens of the kingdom of God alone, began to entertain patriotic sentiments towards the land where they could freely profess their nonresistant faith. The fact that some of the *Doopsgezinden,* who at the outset had almost all belonged to the poorer sections of the community, began to accumulate wealth through various commercial and industrial enterprises and acquire thereby a middle-class ethos, made it easier for most sections of the brotherhood to square the concessions to the state, described above, with their consciences.

The pattern of military exemption, worked out in the last three decades of the sixteenth century, continued into the next century when, from 1609, the United Provinces had gained *de facto* independence. In this 'golden age' of the Netherlands, Mennonites participated in the cultural upsurge that marked those years, producing a number of distinguished poets and painters as well as scientists and scholars. This intellectual and financial élite existed alongside primitivist congregations in town and countryside, which continued to nurture the ethos of an earlier generation. The existence of the United Provinces was not again seriously threatened until Louis XIV's armies invaded the country in 1672. Before that date occasional clashes over the military question were soon smoothed over, and then tension relaxed. During the Anglo-Dutch War of 1665–7 two developments occurred in the pattern of conscientious objection: they represented an amplification of earlier options for the brotherhood's draftees. First, the town council of Kampen, previously content with the payment of a tax, now demanded from its Mennonites the performance of noncombatant duties in case of attack by the enemy. (The principle of alternative service was, of course, implicit in North Holland's regulation of 1575.) The council assigned Mennonite draftees to the town's auxiliary fire service; their job was to man the fire engines and extinguish any conflagration arising from enemy action. Secondly, in 1665 the Frisian branch took the initiative by raising a large sum of money from their coreligionists and presenting it to the government. The church knew the authorities would use the 'gift' to outfit battleships needed for a successful prosecution of the naval war. Nominally this was a 'freewill' offering. But within a year the Frisians received their reward: the exemption of their draft-age men from military duties. (Again, this action reflected the stance of the *Doopsgezinden* in 1572.)

In the crisis years of 1672–3 the attitude of all branches of the brotherhood again displayed a mixture of loyalty to their country and attachment to their nonresistant legacy. In some places their draftees manned the fire engines and put out the fire-bombs hurled over city walls by the invaders. In Amsterdam, which had a large Mennonite community, they dug trenches and ramparts in order to stem the French advance northwards. A popular song of the time praised their conduct during the siege of Aardenburg in 1572 when they brought supplies to their fellow citizens defending the city walls: 'butter, bread, cheese, wine and beer, and all necessary victuals, brandy, and tobacco.' In addition, the brotherhood once more raised large sums of money, which they handed over to the government for use as they saw fit. They also responded positively to requests from the authorities to donate for the troops warm clothing and shoes as well as bedding and wigs. The government, in its turn, recognized that the Mennonites were 'good patriots [goede vaderlanders],' who rendered service to their country not with weapons but in ways that did not conflict with their consciences.[8]

Still, van der Zijpp is undoubtedly correct in calling the brotherhood's stance in 1672–3 a 'fossilized' version of the Mennonites' principle of defencelessness (*Wehrlosigkeit*), which they had inherited from the past. Were there any who dissented from this stance? The answer is yes. They were to be found among the small rigorist subsects, and particularly among the so-called *harde Vriezen*, who considered those forms of alternative service most closely connected with war to be incompatible with their peace principles. In February 1672 draftees from this group had rejected the order to dig trenches. To do that, they explained, was tantamount to waging war in person. Some families belonging to this group emigrated to Polish Prussia (Pomerania), where this kind of thing was not required from Mennonites. Eventually, though, even there noncombatant military service became law; but this happened only in 1868.

The war against France continued, on and off, until the Utrecht peace settlement of 1713–14. Mennonite draftees by this date usually served as auxiliary firemen, that is, if their church had not arranged to make a monetary contribution to the authorities. The official position of all branches of the brotherhood supported the stance of the conscientious objector (CO) throughout most of the eighteenth century. To give just one example, in a much read exposition of the Mennonite faith, Jacobus Rijsdijk (1690–1744), a respected pastor of the now united Waterlander-Flemish branches, condemned unconditionally any active participation in war. 'A Christian's weapons and warfare are ... spiritual ... so that war conflicts with the ethic [zedenleer], which ... teaches us never to shed human blood but to love our fellow man and treat him as we would wish him to treat us.'[9] Yet at the same time, as the eighteenth century advanced (a period incidentally of *Doopsgezinden* decline), two conflicting views emerged clearly on such matters as self-defence and military service. The 'strict Mennonites [fijne Mennisten]' clung to the traditional view that it was wrong for a true Christian to bear arms for whatever purpose, whereas the 'coarse Mennonites [groove Mennisten]' accepted bearing arms as a civic duty that was entirely compatible with their religious faith. Divisions on this issue sometimes split congregations, though in many congregations traditionalists and revisionists existed uneasily side by side with the ban not being exercised against those who bore arms. The revisionists were usually drawn from the theologically liberal sections of the brotherhood, who were often active in the radical 'Patriot' movement that emerged in the 1780s in opposition to the House of Orange; among the *groove Mennisten* there were pastors as well as laity. Among congregations made up exclusively of *fijne Mennisten*, those who bore arms continued to be disfellowshipped if they persisted in the practice. Such congregations continued, too, to furnish their draftees with a certificate of membership if this was required in order to gain exemption from military duties at the hands of the authorities.

Statistical material is not available to determine the relative strengths at any given time of the traditionalists and the revisionists. But the abandonment in 1799 of their church's military exemption by the brotherhood, less than four years after the radical Patriots had taken over the government of the country (behind the bayonets of the French revolutionary army), would seem to indicate that the revisionists had gained the ascendancy. The Batavian Republic that now replaced rule by the House of Orange on 4 May 1799 decreed that all the Republic's able-bodied male citizens, without exception, must serve in 'the armed civil guard,' for it was the duty of everyone to help defend 'the freedom and independence' of the country.

Some congregations attempted a protest, but opposition was soon dropped. As van der Zijpp comments: 'This shows indeed that indignation over the wrong done was not so very great; protest was made more from force of tradition than from the dictates of conscience. The religious conscience of the *Doopsgezinden* of that day no longer felt military service as a sin, as something in conflict with the commandments and spirit of the Gospel. With a few exceptions it was the spirit of the times that had won them over.'[10] With the vanishing of the Dutch Mennonites' legal exemption from bearing arms there disappeared, too, their conscientious objection to military service as a collectively held testimony against war. Van der Zijpp writes of the period following 1799: 'I have uncovered [in the archives] no cases of conscientious objection, though there are some instances when men hid or got out of service in some other way.'[11] The easiest method of escaping the draft was to hire a substitute, which, in the Netherlands as in most other countries, remained for conscientious and non-conscientious alike a legal way out. Doubtless there were still rigorist *Doopsgezinden* who availed themselves of this alternative, the best available in the circumstances. But such action would not leave any trace in the record. No one seems to have considered going to jail. Later in the new century, emigration to the United States was occasionally resorted to by rigorists in order to avoid the draft. But, as van der Zijpp remarks, by this date the principle of nonresistance had long ago lost all vitality within the Dutch Mennonite brotherhood.[12] It gained adherents again only after the Great War. But the Arbeidsgroep van Doopsgezinden tegen den Krijgsdienst (The Working Group of *Doopsgezinden* against Military Service) remained a small fellowship of dedicated pacifists within a church that included among its most respected leaders statesmen and magistrates and colonial administrators as well as army and navy officers.

This church, however, produced, as we have seen, during a period of just over two centuries and a quarter a considerable number of COs. We know a few of their names; one such was the well-known painter Salomon van Ruisdael. But most Mennonite COs were obscure men; none of them have left a record of their conscript experiences, which lacked the dramatic character present, for instance, in the case of Quakers pressed into the Royal Navy (discussed in the next essay). Most of what we know about Dutch Mennonite COs derives from the archival research of the *Doopsgezinden* pastor N. van der Zijpp. But his account of what is indeed a very complex subject is brief and leaves many questions unanswered. Further research into state and congregational archives is needed. But so far no scholar has undertaken this task, even though the topic clearly deserves further investigation.

NOTES

1 For the background of *Doopsgezinden* pacifism, see Peter Brock, *Pacifism in Europe to 1914* (Princeton NJ, 1972), 162–212 (chap. 5: 'The Dutch Mennonites'), and *Freedom from Violence: Sectarian Nonresistance from the Middle Ages to the Great War* (Toronto, 1991), 97–110 (chap. 9: 'The Rise and Fall of Nonresistance among the Dutch Mennonites').

2 In this area Mennonitism, along with other forms of Protestantism, was eventually suppressed. In towns like Bruges and Ghent, Mennonites drafted into the civic guard had avoided having to bear arms by hiring substitutes to take their place – that is, until the Spanish authorities put an end to the sect's existence in the southern Netherlands.

3 My account of conscientious objection among the Mennonite *Doopsgezinden* is based mainly on N. van der Zijpp, *De vroegere Doopsgezinden en de Krijgs-*

dienst (Wolvega, 1930); reprinted posthumously in *Uit het werk van Prof. Dr. N. van der Zijpp* (Amsterdam, n.d.), 5–39. My references below are to the 1930 pamphlet.

4 Quoted in John Horsch, *The Principle of Nonresistance as Held by the Mennonite Church: A Historical Survey* (Scottdale PA, 1927), 26.

5 Van der Zijpp, *Vroegere Doopsgezinden*, 18.

6 Ibid., 20.

7 Ibid., 18–20.

8 Ibid., 21, 22, 24, 26.

9 Quoted in Sjouke Voolstra, ed., *Vreemdelingen en bijwoners: Vredesgetuigenissen uit het Nederlandse Doperdom* (Amsterdam, 1979), 40, 41.

10 Van der Zijpp, *Vroegere Doospgezinden*, 27.

11 Ibid., 27, 28. We may note that Napoleon's brother, Louis, after he was made King of Holland in 1806, restored the Mennonites' military exemption as a gesture of goodwill towards the brotherhood. But the privilege was again withdrawn when in 1810 the northern Netherlands was incorporated directly into the French Empire. As a result, young *Doopsgezinden* were forced into the *grande armée*, many of them to perish on the battlefield. There were, however, some who succeeded in evading call-up.

12 Ibid., 28.

4 Experiences of Quakers Pressed into the Royal Navy

Readers of Herman Melville's *Billy Budd,* and those acquainted with Benjamin Britten's hauntingly beautiful opera based on Melville's story, will be familiar with the invidious form of conscription for England's Royal Navy practised until the end of the Napoleonic Wars ushered in for Britain many decades of peace. Until that date, especially when the country was at war (which it often was), 'press-gangs' roamed the ports and fishing villages that dotted the coasts of England and seized able-bodied young men for the Royal Navy, which was always short of seamen.[1] The practice amounted in fact to a legal form of kidnapping; naturally it was widely unpopular, particularly with the folk who lived on the seacoast.[2]

Melville's tale centres around Billy's 'arbitrary enlistment into the *Indomitable* ... on her way to join the Mediterranean fleet.' The year was 1797: Britain was in the midst of its prolonged conflict with the new revolutionary France. The 'Handsome Sailor' himself was not displeased at his new situation but there were on board other 'impressed ones,' taken by the 'gang' along with him, who chafed at the naval servitude that had been imposed on them and longed to be free to return to their homes and familiar occupations. Quakers were among those who had suffered at the hands of the press-gang; even though their clashes with the gang seem to have ceased long before the end of the eighteenth century, they made an impact on the Society of Friends. 'Sufferings' from naval impressment form an interesting chapter in the history of the Quaker peace testimony, not least because several of those who were 'impressed' have left a record of their experiences as reluctant tars.

Unlike today, during its first century the Society of Friends on both sides of the Atlantic had drawn many of its members from the seafaring community. In England they and their families lived on or near the coast; the menfolk sought employment, where possible, in vessels owned by coreligionists. In that case there would not – or at any rate should not – be guns: by the end of the 1650s, after a preliminary decade when the sword was not rejected, the Quaker discipline required Friends to reject the use of weapons to kill their fellow humans, and those who persisted in doing so were 'disowned.' At the close of 1660, in a 'Declaration from the Harmless and Innocent People called Quakers,' which they presented to King Charles II,[3] they had stated as their 'testimony to the whole world':

> All bloody principles and practices we ... do utterly deny ... with all outward wars and strife, and fightings with outward weapons ... The Spirit of Christ ... will never move us to fight and war against any man with outward weapons, neither for the Kingdom of Christ, nor for the kingdoms of this world ... So we, whom the Lord hath called into the obedience of his Truth, have denied all wars and fightings, and cannot again any more learn it ... our swords are broken into plowshares, and spears into pruninghooks; as prophesied of in Micah 4.

Of course, not all those Friends on whom the press-gang succeeded in getting its clutches were sailors, because members of coastal Quaker meetings were engaged in a number of other occupations: there were among them artisans and shopkeepers and fishermen as well as a few husbandmen. But whoever they were, they faced the same fate as the other pressed men once on board the man-of-war. Moreover, their consciences, backed by the threat of ultimate expulsion from their Society, told them they must refuse to cooperate in any warlike activity whatever the punishment might be for such disobedience.

The earliest record we have of how a Quaker reacted to this situation dates from 1661–2. Thomas Lurting had become a Quaker – and a pacifist – while serving as a boatswain's mate on a naval frigate. The English Commonwealth was then at war and so in these circumstances he was lucky to escape with his life after he had told the captain he was no longer prepared to fight. When he came home, he sought employment only in the merchant service. But his troubles were not at an end. In 1661, with a naval war threatening again with the Dutch Republic, 'early one morning, going from my [shore] quarters towards the ship I belonged unto, I met four press-masters.' There was no escaping them.

'They took hold of me, two under my arms and two under my hams, and lifted me upon their shoulders, and carried me about three hundred yards with my face upwards.' Eventually they released him (for reasons Lurting does not make altogether clear). But next year he was again to be confronted by naval impressment – this time on two occasions. Both incidents took place in the port of Harwich. His vessel had sailed there 'laden with corn.' As Lurting relates:

> No sooner we came to an anchor, but a press-gang came on board us; and the first man they laid their hands on was me, saying, 'You must go with us.' 'I hope not so,' said I. Then they swore that I was a lusty man, and should go. Then they laid hands on me and lifted me into their boat, and carried me on board the ship Mary, one Jeremiah Smith commander, who was a very loose and wicked man. So when I came to the ship side, they bad me go in, the which I had not freedom to do. Then they tied a rope about my waist, and with a tackle hoisted me, making a noise, as if I had been some monster, and lowered me down upon the main-hatches, where I sat about half an hour, that all might have their full view of me.

Aboard the man-of-war Lurting, for the time being, was left free to stroll around the ship. Night coming on, he curled up 'between two guns ... and slept very well.' For the next five days he refused to eat. He drank water from time to time but 'I was sensible if I had eat of their victuals, they would have kept me.' 'The seamen,' he goes on, 'were very kind to me, and many came in great tenderness, and proffered me of their victuals. I accepted of their love, but not of the victuals.' He had decided evidently to practise a passive resistance that foreshadows the technique devised by Gandhi centuries later. On the sixth day of his sojourn on the ship, the captain summoned Lurting to an interview. On the latter's failing to take off his hat, the former immediately recognized him as a Quaker. 'I know the Quakers very well,' said Captain Smith. It seems he knew that Quakers not only were unwilling to doff their hats on meeting social superiors but would not handle a weapon, either, and he now offered Lurting a noncombatant position. 'Thou shalt stand by me, and I will tell thee what I will have done, and thou shalt call the men to do it; or else thou shalt stand by the fore-braces, and I will call to thee to do so and so; and this is not killing of men, to hale a rope.'

But Lurting would not cooperate. The captain tried again. 'Thou shalt be with the coopers [who repaired casks], to hand beer for them, there is great occasion for it.' 'Well then [the captain, despite his Quaker's continuing refusals, was persistent], I will place you as the doctor's assistant. When a man comes down, that hath lost a leg or an arm, to hold the man, while the doctor cuts it off; this is not killing men, but saving men's lives.' Once more Lurting's response was negative: 'it's all an assistance,' he answered tersely. Finally the captain, after threatening to have him jailed, released the recalcitrant Quaker and returned presumably to his tippling, undoubtedly a more pleasant occupation.

After several days on shore Lurting returned to his ship, which remained at Harwich. The following day, 'being very hard at work, heaving out corn into a lighter, stripped in my shirt and drawers, ... a man-of-war's boat clapped us on board, and the coxswain jumped in; and swore, "Here's a lusty rogue come up," said he.' Lurting told the latter that he had no need to use force since he was ready to come along quietly: the use of force, however, would be resisted passively. The coxswain, as he told the captain of his vessel, immediately recognized Lurting as a Quaker, just as Captain Smith had done a few days before. The new captain, however, was not so accommodating as Smith had been. 'Thou art no Quaker,' he told Lurting, 'for here thou bringest corn, and of it is made bread, and by the strength of that bread, we kill the Dutch; and therefore no Quaker ... Art not thou as accessory to their death as we?' To this, sensing perhaps that the captain was not altogether serious and was merely trying to catch him out, Lurting replied with a delightful disregard of grammar: 'I am a man that have, and can feed my enemies; and well may I you, who pretend to be my friends.' Take him away, shouted the captain, 'he [really] is a Quaker.' A few days later Lurting was transferred to another warship. Its captain, at first very hostile ('swearing and cursing against the Quakers, like a madman'), must soon have realized that he was not likely to make a fighter again out of this now peaceable Christian. He gave orders that he be put on shore and there set free. 'And this,' Lurting writes, 'was the man that [had] said, "hanging was too good" for me' only six hours before.[4]

Lurting's narrative makes two things clear. In the first place, at least in the Royal Navy, there were around 1660 already many who identified Quakerism with a conscientious objection to arms-bearing on the seas as well as on land. Secondly, some naval commanders at any rate were aware, too, that they could do little with Quakers pressed into service: it was better to set them free, perhaps after having let off steam by abusing the whole sect of Quakers, and in this way not to risk demoralization of other members of the crew.

In 1665, four years after Lurting's last encounters with the agents of naval impressment and at the outset of another Anglo-Dutch naval war, a simple Yorkshire fisherman named Richard Seller was pressed on Scarborough pier while pursuing his occupation of fisherman. After he had eventually been released, he dictated an account of his 'sufferings' to a friend who, since Seller was almost certainly himself illiterate, wrote down 'the very words that proceeded from him, who sat before me weeping.'[5] Though in some respects Seller's experiences paralleled those of Lurting, the Yorkshireman was in for a number of much harder knocks before, as we shall see, his lot on board was eventually lightened:

> Refusing to go on board the ketch [Seller begins his story], they beat me very sore on the sand, and I refusing to go on board, they hoisted me in with a tackle on board of the ketch that pressed for the ship called the *Royal Prince*, and they bunched with their feet [so] that I fell into a tub, and was so maimed that they were forced to swaddle me up with clothes ... and they hauled me in at a gun-port on board ... the *Royal Prince*. And then the ship soon sailed for the battle area.

Fortunately, hearing of his plight, friends (presumably Quakers) had been able to supply Seller with a stock of food before the *Royal Prince* set sail. The food lasted him for several days.[6] Refusing to work while on board, he did not, therefore, have to fast, as Lurting had done, because he, too, had been unwilling to accept 'the King's victuals.' Asked by the captain for an explanation of his behaviour, Seller answered, 'my warfare was spiritual, therefore I durst not fight with carnal weapons.' This reply infuriated the captain, who began to beat him. On one of the crew, who came from the same neighbourhood as Seller, interceding on his behalf (he knew him, he said, 'to be an honest man and a good man'), the captain yelled, 'He is a Quaker, I will beat his brains out.' During the next few days, attempts were made to force 'the Quakerly dog' to go to work. But continued beatings and hanging by the wrists failed to persuade Seller to change his mind.[7]

The arrival of the admiral of the fleet, Sir Edward Spragge, who now took over the *Royal Prince* as his flagship, changed the situation – but not in Seller's favour, for Spragge had at once reproved members of the crew who, impressed by the Quaker's courage, had relaxed the severity of their beatings. The admiral ordered Seller to be locked up below deck in irons 'for refusing to fight.' Seller explains that the shackles placed around his ankles, which eventually made him temporarily lame, were attached to the 'bilboes,' i.e., an iron bar along which the shackles would slide so as to accommodate more than one prisoner if need be. The admiral had given further instructions for Seller's treatment: 'I charge you,' he said, 'all and every man, that none of you give or sell him any ... meat, drink, or water, for if you do, you shall have the same punishment as he hath.' Seller, sick and emaciated, survived owing to the kindness of some of the crew, especially the ship carpenter's mate. 'When I was set out to ease myself (which was but once in twenty four hours), I could neither stand nor go. So the officers that let me out, called some of my countrymen [i.e., fellow Yorkshiremen] to carry me into the ship's head to ease myself, and bring me back again to the irons.' The carpenter's mate during this walk surreptitiously supplied the prisoner daily with food; once he even managed to 'put about a pint of brandy' in Seller's pocket without anybody seeing![8]

Slowly, though, everyone aboard was getting used to this strange fellow: even Sir Edward Spragge showed him kindness now. Within a few weeks the English fleet was engaged in battle with 'the Hollanders' off Lowestoft: an action that ended in an English victory. Seller was present throughout the running battle with the Dutch. 'My employ,' he tells us, 'was to carry down the wounded men, and look out for fire-ships.' On one occasion, the lieutenant who had for so long harrassed him, seeing Seller smeared all over with blood and surmising he might have been wounded, asked: 'How came I to be so bloody?' 'I told him, It was with carrying down wounded men. So he took me in his arms and kissed me, and that was the same lieutenant that persecuted me with irons at the first.' Later, when the fleet had returned to Chatham, Sir Edward[9] congratulated Seller on his conduct during the recent fighting:

> Then, said he, Thou shalt have thy liberty to go on shore. I asked him, If I might go on shore to recruit, or go to my own being? He said, I should choose whether I would. I told him, I had rather go to my own being. He said, I should do so. Then I told him, There was one thing that I requested of him yet, that he would be pleased to give me a certificate under his hand, to certify that I am not run away. He said, Thou shalt have one to keep thee clear at home, and also in thy fishing; for he knew I was a fisherman.

But no sooner had the ex-sailor reached London on his way back to Yorkshire than 'two press-crews' approached him. 'This is Sir Edward's Quaker,' they said, 'you are welcome to shore. Will you please go to the tavern with us.' And Seller concludes his narrative as follows:

> I told them, I would not go, nor drink any thing. Then they wished me well home. Also they [had] proffered me my pay, before I came off on board, and said, I [had] deserved it as well as any man on board. But I refused, and told them, I had of my own, that I hoped would serve me home. And the lieutenant was troubled because I would take nothing; he would have given me twenty shillings, but I would not take it.[10]

Seller's readiness to perform noncombatant duties in lieu of handling a weapon strikes the reader, for it contrasts with Lurting's position. The latter had categorically refused to assist the ship's doctor in tending the wounded, if the occasion for this had arisen, since he considered to do so would have been tantamount to support of war. Doubtless he was ready to extend aid to any human being in need of it: it was the idea of an exchange, perceived as implicit in the proposal, that he had rejected. On the other hand, the guileless fisherman, who, moreover, had had to cope with an actual conflict situation and not a theoretical battle scenario, displayed no hesitation in caring for the wounded combatants and fire-ship watching. He also accepted gratefully the reward for his noncombatant service in the form of Sir Edward's certificate, which would, he knew, protect him against any further attempts to press him. Clearly Besse, in compiling his bulky record of Quaker sufferings for Truth, saw nothing in Seller's conduct that conflicted with this collective 'testimony of a good conscience.' Yet the divergence between these two testimonies, both in practice acceptable expressions of the Quaker conscience, have continued to reoccur in the history of conscientious objection generally: the gap between the two views never fully bridged.

Seller had indeed been exceptionally fortunate in being able to produce from his pocket a certificate from no less a person than Admiral Sir Edward Spragge. For the rest of the century and beyond, the Society was much concerned to rescue any of its members who had been seized for the navy. 'At times,' writes Hirst, 'in the hunt for seamen the gaols were invaded and Friends lying imprisoned for [nonpayment of] tithes were carried away.'[11] In 1671, on the eve of a new war, a Friend wrote to George Fox's wife, Margaret Fell: 'Here is a great pressing seamen.'[12] Even Scottish Quakers, a small community compared to their English, Welsh, or Irish brethren, were not spared the onus of naval impressment, notwithstanding the fact that, until the Act of union of 1707, Scotland remained an independent kingdom united with England only by the person of the monarch. In 1672, after the war forecast by Margaret Fell's correspondent had broken out, the Quaker meeting in Aberdeen recorded,

> That the magistrates of the town have put Alexander Somerville, mariner, our Friend, in prison, ... that they have ... denied to liberate him unless he give bond as the rest of the seamen have done and this having not only an appearance but plainly implying an engagement [to] answer them and list himself for the war. Friends thought fit to advise him not to give any engagement either by word or writ lest otherwise it might mar his peace and reflect on truth.[13]

In 1695 we hear of a Quaker of Danish origin, Gerard Sefferenson, who was torn from 'his wife and child' by a press-gang and 'kept on board by force.' He appealed to the Society's executive organ, the Meeting for Sufferings, to help obtain his release.[14] Indeed, for a couple of decades now, the Meeting for Sufferings had spent much time over 'the often sufferings of Friends by being impressed into the King's ships of war.' The Meeting decided to ask Daniel Lobdy, a member of the meeting at the coastal town of Deal, to try to obtain such men's release. 'Any expenses he incurred were reimbursed by the Monthly or Quarterly Meetings concerned, and [Hirst adds] he proved very serviceable in his mission.'[15]

One of those who suffered impressment during this period was a nineteen-year-old lad named Thomas Chalkley (1675–1741). The incident took place in 1694: seven years later, Chalkley left England for Pennsylvania, where he became one of colonial Quakerism's best-known travelling ministers. He was to tell the story later in his *Journal* (i.e., autobiography). The press-gang had seized him near his home in Southwark across the river from the city of London. On board he was kept in the ship's hold along with other pressed men, whose coarse language appalled the youth brought up in a strict Quaker family atmosphere. When, the morning after, in the presence of the ship's officers the lieutenant urged him to consent to serve in the King's navy,

> I answered that I was willing to serve him in my business, and according to my conscience; but as for war and fighting, Christ had forbid it in His excellent Sermon on the Mount; and for that reason I could not bear arms, nor be instrumental to destroy or kill men. Then the lieutenant looked on me ... and said, 'Gentlemen, what shall we do with this fellow? He swears he will not fight.' The Commander of the vessel made answer, 'No, no, he will neither swear nor fight.' Upon which they turned me on shore.[16]

Margaret Hirst, who alone of historians of Quakerism has examined at least some of the British Society of Friends' extensive meeting records to try and measure the impact on it of naval impressment over a period of at least a century, points to the experience of Quakers who, in 1701, had been freed from fifteen to twenty years' captivity in Algiers, as 'the hardest case perhaps' of all. Friends had raised the money to ransom them from the corsairs. But on reaching England, naturally 'very desirous to see Friends' faces,' they had been confronted with the possibility of being pressed into a warship before they had even set foot on land. The Meeting for Sufferings immediately contacted the Admiralty: these men, said the meeting, had been 'redeemed at the particular charge of Friends and not at the Government charge.' Friends' intervention was successful, except that several months later one of the returned Quaker captives was to fall a victim to the press-gang as he was about to set out for Pennsylvania, 'and was not released until a deputation from the Meeting for Sufferings had laid the case personally before the Lords of the Admiralty.'[17]

Quakers living along the extended coastline of the North American continent, at any rate if they stayed at home, did not have to fear the operations of the press-gang. These were confined to Great Britain. However, American Friends who gained their livelihood from the sea ran a related risk if the ship on which they were serving as mariners made the transatlantic passage. The vessel could be stopped on the high seas by an English man-of-war and one or more of its tars removed onto the battleship. The nearer the vessel approached the shores of England the greater, of course, the risk. We are lucky in possessing an autobiographical account by one young Quaker who went through this experience. John Smith's artless narrative was apparently composed not long after the events it described, but it was published only after the author's death.[18]

In January 1704 Smith, at the age of twenty-three, had been drafted into the Massachusetts militia. He came from a Quaker home and shared his parents' faith. It was indeed a period of intense Indian warfare with a very real threat of conflict also with the French in Québec, so it is not surprising that the young man found himself in jail. The year following his release from prison, Smith, who evidently fancied life on the sea, joined the crew of a ship bound for London that was owned by a well-to-do New England Quaker. All went well until the ship reached Plymouth (England) in mid-April 1705. There the vessel was stopped by a man-of-war, and Smith along with another young Quaker sailor, Thomas Anthony, was removed.[19]

The two were now no longer merchant mariners but ordinary seamen of the Royal Navy subject to its officers' commands. A troublesome situation indeed for a Quaker CO! And the situation soon worsened when the vessel cruised southwards in search of the enemy. Smith writes:

> The lieutenant ... swore divers times that he would run us through with his sword ... The day after we sailed, the ship we were in took a French prize ... When they were going to engage, they placed us to a gun, and commanded us to fight, but we told them we could not, for Christ and his apostles spake to the contrary; but they not regarding what we said, hauled us about the deck to make us work, but we signified we could not on any such account.

The lieutenant seems to have directed his anger chiefly against Smith, though Anthony took the same position as Smith. After a severe caning failed to make the Quaker work, the lieutenant ordered the boatswain 'to take him to the geers [i.e., rigging], and bring the cat and nine tails, at which time [Smith writes] I was freely given up to suffer what they might be permitted to inflict on me; and being at the geers on my knees, it arose in my mind to pray for my persecutors.' The captain, who from the beginning appeared to Smith to have been 'more moderate' than his lieutenant, eventually after the ship had returned to Plymouth let his two Quakers go. He had tried to break them in, but, he told them as they left, 'we were not men for his purpose.'[20]

There is evidence to show that Smith and Anthony's was not an isolated case. In the course of research for his study of Quakerism on the island of Nantucket, where most Friends had been engaged in one way or another with the whaling industry, Robert Leach succeeded in unearthing nineteen certificates of membership issued during the

Seven Years' War of 1755–63 by local meetings to Friends 'bound on a whale voyage.' Hopefully, such certificates would shield their recipients from impressment into the Royal Navy, if the whaler were boarded somewhere on its voyage. At least, it would serve as evidence that the men were genuine in their refusal to fight, since knowledge of the Quaker objection to war was fairly general by this date.[21] But it is only occasionally that we get a glimpse of the fate of such people. Again, Chalkley's *Journal* illustrates the frequency with which naval impressment of this kind continued to be practised even after the Treaty of Utrecht in 1713 ushered in a long period of peace. For instance, in 1735, which he tells us was a time 'of very great pressing for seamen' (open war came four years later), a merchant ship owned by Chalkley, in which he was transporting a cargo from Philadelphia, was boarded by the press-gang as it approached the English coast. He succeeded in hiding some of the men whom the gang sought (Quaker mariners possibly among them).[22]

As the second half of the eighteenth century advanced, the danger of naval impressment receded for Quakers. The Meeting for Sufferings now became increasingly concerned with another issue: Quaker shipowners who yielded to the temptation of arming their vessels against pirates and enemy privateers.[23] In the earlier period, however, Friends in England spent much time and energy in rescuing their coreligionists from the clutches of the press-gang. Pressed Quakers, for the most part, did not succumb to the various pressures placed on them, maintaining an often solitary witness to the peace principles of their Society.

NOTES

1 See David Hannay, 'Impressment,' *The Encyclopaedia Britannica*, 11th edition (Cambridge, 1911), vol. 14, 346, 347. A press-gang 'consisted of a captain, one or more lieutenants, and a band of trustworthy men.' Each gang had received a commission to carry out *inter alia* its work of pressing 'able bodied persons' for the fleet (ibid., vol. 22, 229). See also Michael Lewis, *The Navy of Britain: A Historical Portrait* (London, 1948), 310–12, 317, 318, 322–7; Constance Braithwaite, *Conscientious Objection to Various Compulsions under British Law* (York UK, 1995), 103, 104; R.J. Hill, ed., *The Oxford Illustrated History of the Royal Navy* (Oxford, 1995), 133–9 (from essay by Daniel A. Baugh, 'The Eighteenth-Century Navy as a National Institution, 1690–1815').

2 The well-known Victorian novelist Elizabeth Gaskell has depicted an

impressment on the Yorkshire coast in her novel *Sylvia's Lovers* (1863). The event took place in an area thickly settled by Quakers.

3 Reprinted in Licia Kuenning, ed., *Historical Writings of Quakers against War* (Glenside PA, 2002), 181–8.

4 Thomas Lurting, *The Fighting Sailor Turn'd Peaceable Christian* (1710); reprinted in Kuenning, ed., *Historical Writings*, 15–20. See also Margaret E. Hirst, *The Quakers in Peace and War: An Account of Their Peace Principles and Practice* (London, 1923), 52–4, 84, 85.

5 Seller's narrative is reproduced in Joseph Besse, *A Collection of the Sufferings of the People Called Quakers, for the Testimony of a Good Conscience* (London, 1753), vol. 2, 112–20. The narrative has been reprinted many times. It is to be found in my *Records of Conscience: Three Autobiographical Narratives by Conscientious Objectors 1665–1865* (York, 1993), 5–29. References below are to this edition. See also Hirst, *Quakers*, 80–5.

6 *Records of Conscience*, 6, 10.

7 Ibid., 6–9.

8 Ibid., 9–11.

9 In fact, it was only after these naval encounters that Spragge was knighted, although Seller gives him the title throughout his narrative; and I have followed him here.

10 *Records of Conscience*, 25–8. It would seem that, at the time of his pressing, Seller was still unmarried.

11 Hirst, *Quakers*, 78.

12 Ellis Hookes to Margaret Fell, March 1671, quoted in ibid.

13 Quoted in Peter Brock, *Pacifism in Europe to 1914* (Princeton NJ, 1972), 286.

14 Hirst, *Quakers*, 78, quoting from the minutes of Meeting for Sufferings for 1695.

15 Ibid.

16 Ibid., 178, quoting from Thomas Chalkley's *Journal*.

17 Ibid., 78. Quakers were great travellers, despite the risks travelling involved in those days, and they were among those seized by Algerian or Moroccan pirates. Some never returned; others did so only after many years' captivity. 'Collections for the redemption of these unhappy people,' writes Hirst, 'are a common item in the Quaker records of the time' (ibid., 79).

18 *A Narrative of Some Sufferings, for His Christian Peaceable Testimony, by John Smith, Late of Chester County, Deceased ...* (Philadelphia, 1800), reprinted in my *Records of Conscience*, cited in note 5 above. References below are to this edition.'

19 A ... merchant seaman was liable to be impressed almost in sight of [a]

home port, should a man of war happen to be short of hands' (Antony Preston, *History of the Royal Navy* [Greenwich CT, 1983], 75).

20 Smith, *Narrative*, 39–45. It is worth noting that when Smith and Anthony eventually got to London, they stayed with Thomas Lurting, who, we know, had been pressed around four decades earlier.

21 Peter Brock, *Pacifism in the United States: From the Colonial Era to the First World War* (Princeton NJ, 1968), 33, 34.

22 Hirst, *Quakers*, 178, 179.

23 See ibid., 226–33.

5 Conscientious Objectors in Revolutionary and Napoleonic France

The French Revolution, with the *levée-en-masse*, introduced the idea of universal military service as an instrument of the modern nation-state. For the first time in history thousands of young men were now drafted into the French army to fight a series of wars against neighbouring states intent on restoring the *ancien régime*. Casualties rose on an unprecedented scale. Alongside the fervent patriotism of wide sections of the populace there existed, especially in the countryside, extensive incidence of desertion from the Revolutionary armies and other forms of – usually passive – resistance to conscription. Recent studies of these *réfractaires*, however, make little, if any, mention of conscientious objection to military service.[1] This silence is puzzling since, as the endnotes to this essay show, there already exists a modest literature, in French as well as in English, on the subject of conscientious objection in France during the Revolutionary period; and, moreover, leading figures among both Girondins and Jacobins were directly involved in the problem. The two groups from which at this date objectors derived, both of them small, were the Quakers and the Mennonites (then known in France as Anabaptists). The present essay reviews the attitude of successive Revolutionary governments to religious conscientious objection and the efforts of the two sects to gain exemption from military service for their young conscripts as well as a more considerate attitude on the part of local authorities, and it concludes by reviewing briefly the fate of French conscientious objectors (COs) in the Napoleonic era.

French Quakers were confined to Languedoc, centring in and around the village of Congénies. But shortly before the Revolution an American Quaker whaler from Nantucket, William Rotch, had settled with family and assistants in Dunkirk in order to carry on, with the support of the French authorities, a business that had been largely ruined during the War of Independence. Rotch set up a meeting for worship in that town with English as the usual language of ministry. In 1785, the year in which the Rotch group arrived in France, a young Protestant nobleman and ex-officer, Jean de Marcillac Le Cointe,[2] whose reading about Quakerism had led to his conversion to that faith and abandonment of an army career as inconsistent with the views of the Society of Friends on war, made contact with the Congénies group. He soon became their spokesman. The origins of the Congénies Quakers are unclear; an offshoot of the *inspirés* around the mid-1730s, at the beginning they had had no direct contact with Friends elsewhere. Their worship and beliefs, however, largely coincided with those held by the latter. As a result of Marcillac's efforts, formal affiliation to the Society of Friends in London was completed by 1789.

Before that date Quakers in France had not been much troubled by the military question. In the 1780s approximately one hundred Quaker families were then resident in the Congénies area; according to a contemporary English Quaker report,[3] 'they mostly follow mechanic employments, some husbandry.' 'They do not bear arms but hire substitutes when drawn for the militia'; even though this practice contradicted the discipline of both British and American Friends, the latter refrained, at this date at any rate, from censuring their French coreligionists, thus showing more understanding for the difficulties of continental Friends than was usual. Elsewhere, hiring a substitute or even paying a fine in lieu of bearing arms, if persisted in, normally led to the disownment of the delinquent member of the Society. As for the Quakers in Dunkirk, Rotch before settling there had applied for, and been granted by a government anxious to accommodate this kind of immigrant, not merely 'full and free enjoyment of our religion' but also 'entire exemption from military requisitions of every kind.'[4]

The situation changed, of course, as the revolution gained momentum and the danger of foreign intervention against it mounted, with increasing pressure to mobilize the country's manpower in expectation of war. Marcillac, now an M.D. practising in Paris and specializing in the cure of gout, with his accustomed energy and the assistance of William Rotch and his son Benjamin, set about obtaining guarantees from the new government that their young men would not be forced into the armed forces: since the establishment of a National Guard in mid-1790, a veiled threat of military compulsion at some future date had threatened. They sought the same kind of exemption, at the least, as the *ancien régime* had given their Society. Quakers were fortunate in enjoying in this period widespread respect among France's advanced thinkers. Voltaire, among others, had adhered to the notion of 'the good Quaker' and praised Quaker Pennsylvania as the kind of quasi-Utopian commonwealth to which humankind should aspire.[5] '"Quaker and Pennsylvania" had become bywords in France, representing ... a more or less vaguely conceived ideal.'[6] This view, however remote from reality, was shared by many of the leading Girondin intellectuals and politicians prominent in the National Assembly of 1789–91.

Marcillac, therefore, set about winning, in particular, the support of the Girondins for his project. He was already acquainted with Jacques-Pierre Brissot de Warville, a leading member of the group, while Brissot himself had often been in close contact with the Quakers since his first visit to London in 1779. He collaborated with them in connection with his activities as an abolitionist. Indeed, the Société des Amis de Noirs, in which Brissot held a key position, drew its inspiration in part from Quaker efforts to end slavery.[7] During his visit to the United States in 1788, Brissot had gone out of his way to talk to members of the Society of Friends; among others, he met that active and ardent Quaker pacifist – 'the good' – Warner Mifflin, and he also conversed with President Washington himself on the subject of Quaker beliefs and their role in the Revolutionary War (about whose 'pacific neutrality' Brissot incidentally was rather critical).[8] Though a deist with strong anticlerical views, Brissot regarded Quakerism very sympathetically.[9] Moreover, in theory at least, he almost accepted their pacifism. At any rate he believed that universal peace would arrive if humanity as a whole followed 'these wise men' in resolving 'never to take [up] arms or contribute to the expences of any war.' Though himself 'convinced of the sacred and divine principle which authorises resistance to oppression,' he believed as strongly in the Quakers' right to refuse military service. While he knew about their objection to paying fines in lieu of serving with weapons and their willingness to suffer repeated distraint of property rather than comply with this alternative, he did not see this as an obstacle to granting them exemption in France. 'It would be very easy,' he wrote, 'to reconcile the wants of the state, and the duty of the citizen, with the religious principles of the Quakers. You might subject them only to pacific taxes, and require them to pay a larger proportion of them.'[10]

In a postscript to his *New Travels* added in 1790, Brissot argues cogently that, in reality, the spirit now leading French revolutionaries to approve an armed defence of liberty was virtually identical with the spirit that had animated the Society of Friends in refusing to bear arms for whatever cause. He wrote:

> If the old government had an interest in inviting Quakers to France, this interest is doubled since the Revolution. The spirit of that Society agrees with the spirit of French liberty in the following particulars:
>
> That Society has made great establishments without effusion of blood; the National Assembly has renounced the idea of conquest, which is almost universally the cause of war. The Society practises universal tolerance; the Assembly ordains it. The Society observes simplicity of worship; the Assembly leads to it. The Society practises good morals, which are the strongest supports of a free government; the political regeneration of France, which the Assembly is about to consummate, conducts necessarily to a regeneration of morals.
>
> If the French are armed from North to South, it is for liberty, it is for the terror of despotism, it is to obey the commands of God; for God has willed that man should be free, since he has endowed him with reason; he has willed that he should use all efforts to defend himself from that tyranny which defaces the only image of Deity in man, his virtues and his talents.
>
> But notwithstanding this ardour in the French to arm themselves in so holy a cause; they do not less respect the religious opinions of the Quakers, which forbid them to spill the blood of their enemies. This error of their humanity is so charming, that it is almost as good as a truth. We are all striving for the same object, universal fraternity; the Quakers by gentleness, we by resistance. Their means are those of a society, ours those of a powerful nation.[11]

The Quakers' decision, taken in the second half of 1790, to petition the legislature *inter alia* for military exemption for members of the Society in case of conscription seems to have originated with Marcillac. But Brissot was consulted at every step in the procedure. Marcillac already knew, of course, that Brissot took an extremely favourable view of the Quakers' noncombatancy. Thus, writing to a prominent London Quaker, the publisher James Phillips,[12] Marcillac in his letter, dated 9 January 1791,[13] spoke of conversations he had held with Brissot 'and some other good patriots,' all of them Girondin members of the National Assembly 'well disposed' towards the Quakers. They included Jean-Paul Rabaut Saint-Etienne, who came from a Protestant background, and the *abbé* Henri Grégoire, who had become the constitutional bishop of Blois, and was later to write about Quakers – as well as Mennonites – in his pioneering history of religious sectarianism.[14] These French well-wishers advised Marcillac 'that the success [of his petition] would much depend on the zeal and the address with which the President [of the Assembly] should present it.' Therefore, they urged, the Quakers should defer presentation of the petition for 'a couple of weeks when it was said Mirabeau would be chosen President: and as he [too] is well disposed towards us and a great friend of Rabaut, Grégoire, Warville etc., he will have pleasure in seconding the application with that energy and eloquence which has hitherto enabled him to combat all his rivals with success.' 'It is to be hoped,' thus Marcillac concludes his account, 'that in this day of returning liberty to France we shall be treated with even more consideration [than before 1789], if the Lord is pleased to favour us in the undertaking.'

Furnished with authorization from the Congénies Quakers to act as 'Député extraordinaire des Amis de France à l'Assemblée Nationale' and accompanied by the Rotches, father and son, Marcillac appeared on 10 February 1791 before the National Assembly, where Mirabeau had now embarked on his fifteen-day stint as president of that body.[15] The night before, some minor alterations had been made in the text of the petition Marcillac had composed. This was done at the request of the Rotches, who, however, on account of their ignorance of the French language had difficulty in getting all the changes made that they would have liked: 'the time was so short,' wrote William Rotch, 'that we were obliged to let it pass with much fewer amendments than we wished.'

On the day itself the Assembly chamber was packed. Deputies attended in large numbers and every place was taken in the galleries for the public, so that many 'spectators' had to be turned away. However, it seems to have been mainly 'the novelty of the object' that attracted so many people rather than interest in the Quaker religion. On entering the Assembly chamber, the three Quakers, according to an old custom of the Society of Friends, had kept their hats on.[16] They had also refused to wear national cockades, though pressed to do so; and they persisted in their refusal even after being told that it was 'required by law, to prevent distinction,' and that their safety might be endangered through mob violence generated by their failure to conform on this point. Nonetheless, despite such nonconformity, which was probably attributed to the harmless peculiarities of their sect, the Quakers were given a good reception by the Assembly; at one point of the proceedings, an unidentified deputy had whispered to Benjamin Rotch, 'I rejoice to see something of your principles brought before this Assembly.' Brissot, who had been asked by the Quaker delegation to give a last look at their text just before entering the Assembly chamber, stood all the time at Marcillac's 'elbow' as he read the Petition to the gathered Assemblymen, so as 'to correct him [William Rotch reports] in his emphasis, which [Brissot] frequently did, unperceived, I believe except by us.' After the reading was concluded, the president of the Assembly, Mirabeau, read his answer, upon which he politely invited the three Quakers to stay for the rest of the sitting.[17]

The main thrust of the Quakers' Petition[18] was directed towards gaining military exemption for their members. But it also included a request for exemption from taking civic oaths and for permission to use the simple forms of registering births, marriages, and deaths that were customary in their Society.[19] Appeal was made to freedom of conscience and to the principle of religious toleration which recent French legislation had exhibited, thereby setting an example to the nations. 'We hope that sooner or later they will follow it.' Among the Friends' dearest principles, the petitioners stated, was that of nonviolence, for the sake of which they had endured severe persecution. This principle prevented them from taking up arms and killing their fellow men 'for any reason whatsoever': a principle which, they believed, 'was in accordance with the holy scriptures,' for Christ had told his followers not to render evil for evil but to do good even to enemies. Britain and the United States had both freed Quakers from bearing arms 'without regarding them on that account as useless members of society.' Therefore Frenchmen, show generosity, the petitioners urged. 'You have sworn never to imbrue your hands with blood for the sake of conquest. This resolve brings you, and indeed the whole world, closer to universal peace. Thus you surely cannot view with hostility those who, by their example, hasten its arrival. In Pennsylvania [Quakers] have already shown that huge structures may be erected and maintained without military preparations and without shedding human blood.'[20] The petitioners concluded by reviewing the various material advantages which they believed would accrue to France – 'a country indeed dear to us' – if the Assembly encouraged their Society by granting it what had been requested.[21]

In his response, Mirabeau expressed his admiration for the Quakers' principles considered 'as a philanthropic system'; and he asked their delegates to have full confidence in legislators representing a France now in the process of regeneration and anxious for the maintenance of international peace and the rights of man. Nevertheless, with respect to their pacifism he told the delegates he entertained serious reservations. Though 'doubtless in theory a beautiful principle' doing credit to their humanity, in practice he thought it did not look so fine:

> Don't you think the defence of yourselves and your neighbours to be a religious duty also? Otherwise you would surely be overwhelmed by tyrants! Since we have gained liberty for you as well as for ourselves, why would you refuse to preserve it?
>
> If your brethren in Pennsylvania had been settled nearer its savage inhabitants, would they have allowed their wives, children, and old people to be slaughtered rather than resist? And aren't stupid tyrants and ferocious conquerors equally savages? ...
>
> Whenever I meet a Quaker I intend to say to him: My brother, if you possess the right to be free, you have also an obligation to prevent anyone from making you a slave. Loving your neighbour, you must not allow a tyrant to destroy him: to do so would be the same as to kill him yourself. Do you desire peace? Well, then, it is surely weakness that calls forth war. A general readiness to resist would procure universal peace.[22]

The Quaker delegates' labours were not concluded when the sitting ended and they had returned to their hotel. They quickly realized that they must seize the opportunity resulting from the good impression that they appeared to have made at the Assembly and do some further lobbying among influential members of that body. Among those they visited only Talleyrand proved entirely unreceptive. 'After endeavouring to impress him with the foundation of our Petition,' writes William Rotch, 'he made no reply, but let us pass silently away.' On the other hand, General de Lafayette, despite his military rank, promised his support for the Quakers in the course of a dinner party to which he had invited them. Among those visited it was the Girondin Rabaut who showed most understanding for Quaker nonviolence. He regarded this tenet, he told the three Friends, as 'pure Christianity.' Without committing himself personally to their position, he summarized it as follows: 'If an assassin comes to take my life, and I conscientiously refrain from taking his to save it, I may trust to some interposition for my deliverance. If however, no interposition appearing, I still refrain from precipitating a soul unprepared into Eternity, and he is suffered to effect his purpose on me, I may hope to find mercy for myself.' Marcillac and the two Rotches also organized a series of soirées at the hotel where the latter were staying. These gatherings were attended chiefly by Girondins: there Quaker doctrines were expounded and 'religious subjects' discussed until late into the night.[23]

The Assembly had in fact taken no decision whether or not to grant the Quaker petitioners' requests, merely ordering that the Quaker Petition and Mirabeau's reply should be printed at the Assembly's expense while at the same time transmitting the Petition to the Comité de Constitution for examination.[24] No further action in the matter is recorded; the Quakers' requests remained unanswered.[25]

Thus the outcome of Quaker efforts had proved ambiguous. No assurance of military exemption of any kind had been gained, although the current legislators had indeed displayed – in general terms – their goodwill towards the Quakers and towards their peaceable principles, too. A note of dissatisfaction, combined with restrained optimism concerning the present situation, emerged in a letter Marcillac sent to Phillips in London at the beginning of May. 'Although,' he wrote, 'I believe the spirit of general toleration has so far prevailed as not to oblige us at present to bear arms, nor to take an oath, nevertheless it is their intention not to consider us as active citizens in Languedoc and Dunkirk, and I protest always against that, whilst I consider it the duty of every citizen to contribute to the maintenance of his country with his pecuniary means and intellectual faculties.'[26]

In 1792 compulsion was employed in connection with the National Guard, which had been established two years earlier, but 'passive' citizens were excluded from this draft. The position of the Quakers with regard to military requirements remained as unclear after the presentation of their Petition as it had been before. After the outbreak of war with Austria on 20 April 1792 and the subsequent declaration on 11 July that the Fatherland was in danger, the situation began steadily to worsen. Marcillac wrote despondingly to London Friends about 'divers trials, which in our weak state we have found painful and grievous, the civic oath, the obligation imposed by the National Assembly to mount guard personally and to arm.' French Friends, including himself, had not felt able in good conscience to comply with 'these trying requisitions.' 'I [have had],' he wrote, 'several times opportunity of testifying in public that our refusal to bear arms was not in disobedience to the laws of the [state], but in obedience to the heavenly principles of our Master and Saviour Jesus Christ.'[27] An even more pessimistic report came next month from the pen of a Congénies Quaker writing to a London Quaker:

> This nation is in a desperate condition ... The authorities seize upon, indiscriminately, from the body of citizens a large number of men between the ages of 16 and 50. And we, too, shall not be exempt from the ballot. Judge, dear friend, in what a sad state we find ourselves and what a trial we are having to undergo. While one law ordains that all citizens without exception must mount guard within the confines of their district, another requires everyone, the young as well as the old, to wear the cockade; and anyone in our area who doesn't do this may expect to be roughly handled.[28]

In practice the Congénies Quakers seem to have reached a compromise with the local authorities in respect of the now compulsory National Guard. If called upon to do their spell of duty, they served – but not with a lethal weapon. By mutual agreement they went armed merely with a wooden truncheon.[29]

Meanwhile Brissot and the other Girondins, who continued to be extremely influential in the Legislative Assembly and for a time in its successor, the National Convention, too, had become enthusiastic supporters of war against the enemies of the Revolution, which they regarded as a crusade for liberty. In the course of 1793, however, Brissot and most of his Girondin colleagues fell victim to the Terror, organized by the Jacobins to eliminate not only adherents of the *ancien régime* or centrists of various kinds but their political rivals on the left as well.

By this date indeed the Dunkirk Quakers, after experiencing difficulties as a result of their refusal to illuminate their windows in celebration of French victories, had left the country for good. The Rotches sailed for England shortly before France declared war against the latter on 1 February 1793. In addition, in this tense atmosphere a promising scheme, devised by Marcillac with the support of English Quakers, to establish at Chambord a school for the training of poor children in trades and crafts, had collapsed – in large part because of Quaker insistence that any pupils, who were also Friends, should be guaranteed *inter alia* exemption from military service.[30] And in 1795 Marcillac himself left for the United States; when he returned to France in 1798, he had ceased to be a Quaker. Henceforward, the peasant boys of Congénies, and the simple Quaker villagers their parents, were left to face alone, as best they could, the *levée-en-masse* and the military demands of successive revolutionary administrations and finally of the Napoleonic Empire. For most of this period France was at war with Britain, while America was far away: thus Quakers abroad could be of little use in helping French Quakers respond to the military question.

The 'legend' of the Good Quaker, we have seen, was common to many French intellectuals at that time, and especially to those on the political left. Revolutionary politicians, including of course the Jacobins, knew about the Quaker Petition of February 1791 asking for exemption from military service[31] and were thus already acquainted with this aspect of the Quaker faith. However, it was not the Quakers but the Mennonites who, in 1793, became briefly the objects of the Jacobins' interest. These Mennonites, therefore, when receiving from the latter a measure of toleration for their noncombatancy, may in fact have been benefiting from the vogue which the peaceable Quakers enjoyed among French revolutionaries generally.[32]

The Mennonites settled in France under the *ancien régime* were an offshoot of the anabaptist Swiss Brethren, who had emerged in Zürich around 1525. Calling themselves 'defenceless Christians' and, like their Swiss predecessors, proponents of the principle of *Wehrlosigkeit* (nonresistance), these sectaries refused steadfastly to bear arms, though, unlike the Quakers, they were prepared either to pay commutation money in exchange for military exemption or, if it came to the worst, to undertake noncombatant duties in militia or army. In fact, before 1789 in Alsace, where most of them lived, their military obligations had been light, as they were too in that period in the two small enclaves formed by the principality of Salm and the county of Montbéliard.[33]

With the outbreak of revolution the situation altered for Mennonites in France, as we have seen it did too for the French Quakers. At first, however, the government assured Mennonites that in case of a military draft – for example, for the National Guard – their religiously motivated objection to bearing arms would be respected, as it had been in the past, in exchange for a monetary payment. But once war had broken out, and young Frenchmen began to be conscripted – and killed – then attitudes towards the Mennonites began to change, at any rate at the local level. There tolerance – or indifference – sometimes gave way to open or veiled hostility. In the district of St-Hippolyte, for example, the authorities described the Mennonites' objection to bearing arms as a 'dangerous' principle. If followed by others (which they appeared to think quite likely), it would leave this frontier area open to attack by the enemy. They accused the Mennonites of 'ill will and hatred of the Revolution.' 'When the Fatherland is in danger, all citizens who are not public functionaries ought to render service in person.'[34] The fact that the Mennonites, who still spoke only German, also rejected civic oaths as unchristian, wore beards then widely regarded as a remnant of barbarism, and followed a different form of worship from that of their fellow citizens, all added to the suspicion with which the average Frenchmen regarded them, at any rate in times of war when such peculiarities emphasized the sectarians' otherness.[35]

In the summer of 1793 the Committee of Public Safety took under consideration the Mennonites' claim for military exemption. The Committee's deliberations had been prompted by pressure exerted on the National Convention from concerned subordinate bodies like the Council General of Doubs; it was not asked to hand down some authoritative ruling in the matter. In addition, the Mennonites had appointed a delegation, which sought from the highest authority in the land a confirmation of their military exemption now being contested at a lower level. The initiative in sending a delegation to Paris seems to have originated with Mennonite congregations in the freshly annexed territories of Montbéliard and Salm.

Mennonites in the (former) principality of Salm had recently been encouraged by the warmth of feeling displayed towards them by a three-man delegation sent in March 1793 to inspect the newly acquired area. 'Good and brave men' was how one of the three inspectors, Goupilleau de Montaigu, described these rural sectaries; indeed, he had become convinced there were 'no better people on the face of the earth' than they were. And he compared them favourably to the Quakers, whom he also greatly admired. Back in Paris, Goupilleau promoted the Mennonites' cause with the Committee of Public Safety, and his efforts on their behalf appear in some way to have been coordinated with the lobbying of the Mennonite delegation which had arrived in the capital at the beginning of August.[36] The Petition, which the latter brought with them and presented – in a French translation – to the Convention on 8 August, asked that Mennonite conscripts be allowed to pay a sum of money in place of serving in person. It cited in support the fact that Mennonites had already been allowed to do this in the American Republic: a good precedent considering the prestige enjoyed by the latter in revolutionary France.

The matter was referred for a decision to the Committee of Public Safety. And on 19 August 1793 this body issued what was indeed not formally a decree, but simply a recommendation, in effect brief guidelines directed to local authorities, concerning the proper procedure to be adopted in dealing with drafted Mennonites. Among those signing, or confirming, this document we find the names of such prominent Jacobins as Robespierre, Carnot, Couthon, Hérault de Séchelles, and St Just. 'We have observed the simple hearts of these people,' states their *arrêté*, 'and believing a good government ought to employ all kinds of virtue for the public good we ask you to treat the Anabaptists with a mildness that matches their character, to prevent them from being harrassed in any way, and finally to allow them to serve in such branches of the armed forces as they may agree to, like the pioneers or the teamsters, or even to allow them to pay money in lieu of serving personally.'[37]

Historians have expressed surprise at finding 'totalitarian democrats' like Robespierre and proponents of conscription like Carnot approving a document such as this, which clearly 'created a privilege' for one particular group of citizens, thus undermining the principle of equality to which the Jacobins adhered with such tenacity.[38] 'Conscientious objection,' writes a military historian, 'was tolerated ... probably because it was marginal, rather than out of a libertarian concern' on the part of the men who signed.[39] True, but it is clear the latter were impelled to bend in favour of the Mennonites and make an exception in their case to the Jacobins' cherished egalitarianism not primarily on account of the marginality of the Mennonites but because these people seemed now to incarnate other principles to which the Jacobins were also devoted. They exemplified an idyll of rustic virtue and an Eden of lost simplicity; and contemplation of this delightful prospect won the heart of even a Robespierre or a St Just.

For the time being, then, the Mennonites' fears were laid to rest. Their young men would not be required to fight; henceforward they could serve their country in some more-or-less acceptable fashion. (Payment of commutation money was indeed the way of escape that they preferred.) Nevertheless matters did not go altogether smoothly, despite this official act of grace on the part of the central Revolutionary government. The authorities on the spot, civilian as well as military, showed a tendency to ignore the monetary alternative to noncombatant army service offered by the Committee of Public Safety; efforts were sometimes made either to push the Mennonite draftees into the pioneer corps or enrol them as teamsters alongside the troops, even when this was against their wishes.[40] We learn, too, of denunciations lodged against the Mennonites by private individuals; it was alleged, for example, that they were not truly nonviolent since some were known to have fired shots at thieves stealing fruit from their orchards. Voices were raised demanding that, on account of their attitude to military service, they should be deprived of active citizenship.[41] However, it was not until after the fall of Robespierre in July 1794 and the installation in power of the Directory in August 1795 that the central government withdrew explicitly any possibility for Mennonite conscripts to escape army service by means of a monetary payment: henceforward, it was now decreed, 'they will be assigned to sapper or pioneer battalions – service which can in no way offend their religious opinions.'[42]

The Jacobins' grant of exemption of August 1793 represents the apex of the French Mennonites' struggle to be free of the yoke of conscription. Half a century later its printed text, the pages now yellow with age, still remained a treasured possession of elderly Mennonites of the Salm congregation,[43] even though the younger generation of French Mennonites had by now abandoned the traditional nonresistance and were ready to bear arms alongside other conscripts. But in fact, as Séguy writes, after 1798 'the privilege conceded by the Convention has disappeared ... Jacobin egalitarian logic has swept it away, thus undoing with one stroke of the pen the timid act framed by the sentimentality rather than the legal judgment of the men of the Convention [la sentimentalité peu juridique des conventionnels].'[44]

Under Directory, Consulate, and Empire, the fate of both Quaker and Mennonite pacifism became increasingly precarious as the government's manpower requirements rose. The Mennonites indeed had some claim to special treatment within the ranks of the army; the Quakers, though, had none. While the army usually assigned the Mennonite boys to a formally noncombatant branch, even though that might entail handling military equipment,[45] Quaker conscripts were not so fortunate. Nevertheless, they appear to have been successful in avoiding, somehow or other, the use of their weapons to kill. Friends in France could report to their brethren in London in 1815 after the war was over: 'Not one of our members has to blush for having done violence to any.'[46] Such determination, they felt, did not merit the censure which their conscripts might otherwise have deserved. The Welsh Quaker Evan Rees, a committed pacifist who became active in the London Peace Society from its foundation in 1816, had visited French

Quakers at Congénies early in 1815. Writing home, he reported: 'Those who profess with us here, have a testimony against war, but when compelled to march, serve in the army. Several of their young men have been taken by the conscription, few of them are returned. One of them lost both his legs in Prussia, and is supposed to have died as a consequence; a second was killed in Spain; the parents of a third are still mourning, uncertain of the fate of their eldest son, swept away to the bloody plains of Moscow, where, in all possibility, he has fallen a victim to (another's) ambition.' While regretting French Quakers' failure to maintain a consistent witness against military service, he nevertheless stressed the extremely difficult situation which the tiny Society, made up of humble folk and 'subject to many trials to which we are strangers,' had had to face during the Napoleonic era.[47]

The French Revolution evoked from France's new rulers a much wider measure of consideration for COs than was again to occur in that country until in 1962 General Charles de Gaulle succeeded in overriding an unfriendly parliament and legalizing conscientious objection, this time on a broader base than the Revolutionary legislators had contemplated around 170 years earlier. In the 1960s, we may note, numbers at first did not greatly exceed those in the Revolutionary period.[48]

We have already seen the difference between the treatment of Mennonites in 1793 and the response made to the Quaker request for military exemption two and a half years before. The reason for this lay not in any difference in outlook between Girondins and Jacobins, for their attitude on this question was roughly the same, but in the more uncompromising stance towards military requirements taken up by the Quakers. In theory, at any rate, they stood for unconditional exemption of their conscripted members. Despite their belief in war as an effective instrument for defending a free republic and for extending liberty to the rest of humankind, what had prompted both Girondins and Jacobins to look benevolently at the noncombatancy of the two peace sects in their midst was a feeling that these sectaries reflected, as it were, the reverse side of their own libertarian belligerency; that these people were already practising brotherhood, the idea of *fraternité* which was still only an aspiration for the revolutionaries themselves; and, moreover, that they had realized in advance the goal, common to all progressive men and women, of an ultimately peaceful world. The revolutionaries (in their own opinion, at any rate) were pacifists at heart; they had been compelled to fight as a result of the otherwise ineradicable warlikeness of the foes of freedom. Quakers in France, and even more the Mennonites in that country, were indeed fortunate in appearing as the heroes of one of the 'legends' of the French Enlightenment. But, before long, legend gave place to harsh reality; young Mennonites and Quakers now found themselves on the battlefields where the Napoleonic armies fought with the rest of Europe. Only one essential characteristic differentiated them from other Frenchmen in uniform: they would not kill.

NOTES

1 Michel Auvray, *Objecteurs, insoumis, déserteus: Histoire des réfractaires en France* (Paris, 1983); Alan Forrest, *Conscripts and Deserters: The Army and French Society during the Revolution and Empire* (New York and Oxford, 1989). Auvray covers the period between 1789 and 1815 on pages 65–94. On page 5 Forrest writes: 'The *objecteur,* the man of conscience, emerged in the nineteenth century ... In the period that concerns us, those rejecting military obligation would seem to have acted from more prosaic motives ... In the hundreds of depositions made to tribunals and the numerous interrogations that accompanied the trials of deserters and *insoumis* there is nothing to suggest a resistance rooted in a principled opposition to war.' That last sentence is, I am sure, true; one has to look elsewhere for evidence of such principled war resistance. Subsequently Forrest, without mentioning the Quakers, does devote six lines (on page 54) to the 'conscientious objection to war' of 'certain religious groups' like the Alsace Mennonites. He refers, too, to the authorities of Colmar district assigning the latter early in 1796 to work as army teamsters in lieu of bearing arms.

2 Henry van Etten, *Chronique de la vie Quaker française 1745–1945: Deux siècles de vie religieuse* (2nd edn, Paris, 1947) 45, 46. See also his article 'Les Quakers et la Révolution française,' *Revue internationale d'histoire politique et constitutionelle,* N.S. vol. 6 (1956), 285.

3 Library of the Religious Society of Friends (London), MS vol. 314 (France MSS), no. 78: 'Note describing the usages of Friends in the south of France, n.d.' Though it is undated, a reference to Marcillac as a former 'captain of horse [who] being convinced of the unlawfulness of arms quitted the Service' indicates that the note was composed in the second half of the 1780s and reflects the pre-Revolutionary situation. The number of persons then belonging to the Congénies Quaker group is estimated here as between 250 and 280.

4 Quoted in Margaret E. Hirst, *The Quakers in Peace and War: An Account of Their Peace Principles and Practice* (London, 1923), 466.
5 See especially the excellent monograph by Edith Philips, *The Good Quaker in French Legend* (Philadelphia, 1932). Chapter 5 (133–65) is entitled 'Quaker Ideas and the French Revolution.'
6 Ibid., 133.
7 See Lenore Loft, 'Quakers, Brissot and Eighteenth-Century Abolitionists,' *Journal of the Friends' Historical Society*, vol. 55 (1989), 277–89.
8 J.-P. Brissot de Warville, *New Travels in the United States of America Performed in 1788* (London, 1792; reprinted as Brissot de Warville, *On America*, vol. 1 [New York, 1970]), 189–93, 414–16.
9 Cf. Philips, *Good Quaker*, 200: 'Quakerism seemed to the Deists to be the form which popular religion ought to take. They recognized that the masses needed more than an intellectual concept of God, and here, in Quakerism, was a "natural" religion ready made.' In his discussion of Quaker nonviolence, Brissot remarks: 'Reason is the only weapon they use' (*New Travels*, 418).
10 Brissot, *New Travels*, 417. I am not sure, however, if Brissot's proposal here would have satisfied the stricter Quakers, who objected in principle to any requirements exacted in exchange for exemption from any act they regarded as in itself wrong. Thus, the suggested 'larger proportion' of an otherwise innocuous tax would seem to be unacceptable according to such – perhaps excessively sensitive – consciences.
11 Ibid., 418–20.
12 James Phillips was also a personal friend of Brissot and one of the founders of the Society for the Abolition of the Slave Trade in 1787. Writing to Brissot at the end of 1790, he had pointed out to the latter that the new government was being unfair to the French Quakers in making active citizenship dependent on readiness to bear arms. See James C. Dybikowski, 'Edmond Philip Bridel's Translations of Quaker Writings for French Quakers,' *Quaker History*, vol. 77 (1988), 111, 116. Bridel had been a schoolmate of Brissot's but later moved to London, where he became a teacher and writer of elementary-school textbooks. See ibid., 110.
13 I have cited from the contemporary translation in Friends Library (London), MS vol. 314 (France MSS), no. 58. Van Etten, *Chronique*, has printed the French original on pages 69–72.
14 *Histoire des sectes religieuses* (Paris). This work went through three editions: 2 vols, 1810; 2 vols, 1814; and 6 vols, 1828–45. Grégoire died in 1831.
15 Several of the friendly deputies consulted earlier had suggested to Marcillac that he should present Mirabeau beforehand with an outline of Quaker

beliefs in French. It is not clear if this was actually done, though Marcillac, in his letter to Phillips, had expressed his intention of doing so and of sending Mirabeau as well several of William Penn's writings recently translated into French. See Dybikowski, 'E.P. Bridel,' 116–19.

16 Van Etten, *Chronique*, 78.

17 William Rotch, *Memorandum Written by William Rotch in the Eightieth Year of His Age* (Boston and New York, 1916), 52–6.

18 Its full French text, together with that of Mirabeau's response, has been printed at least four times: *Procès-verbal de l'Assemblée Nationale, imprimé par son ordre: Douzième livraison* (Paris), vol. 46, no. 558, 12–20 ('Du Jeudi 10 Février 1791, au soir'); *Pétition respectueuse des amis de la Société chrétienne, appelés Quakers, prononcée à l'Assemblée Nationale le Jeudi 10 Février 1791* (À Paris, chez Baudouin, Imprimeur de l'Assemblée Nationale ...), 7 pp.; Van Etten, *Chronique*, 72–8; and Jeanne-Henriette Louis, 'William Rotch, Quaker américain et les Anabaptistes-Mennonites de Salm, avocats de la liberté intérieure pendant la Révolution française,' *Revue de littérature comparée*, vol. 63 (1989), 588–92. The Library of the Society of Friends (London), hereafter cited as LSF, possesses copies of early printings in pamphlet form of English translations of the two documents; see Box 33 and Box 179. Rotch, *Memorandum*, also includes translations of the two documents; see pages 70–81. (The name of the translator is not given.) It is interesting to note also that the petition, at any rate as printed, omits the aristocratic 'de' from Marcillac's signature. See also Louis, 'La pétition presentée par Jean de Marcillac, et William et Benjamin Rotch, à l'Assemblée Nationale le 10 Février 1791,' in Elise Marienstras, ed., *L'Amérique et la France: Deux révolutions* (Paris, 1990), 205–10.

19 *Pétition respectueuse*, 3, 4. I have checked my translation with several of the previous ones.

20 Ibid., 2, 3.

21 Ibid., 4, 5.

22 Ibid., 5–7.

23 Rotch, *Memorandum*, 56–9; Van Etten, *Chronique*, 79, 80.

24 'L'Assemblée a ordonné l'impression de l'Adresse et de la réponse, et renvoyé au Comité de Constitution l'examen de la Pétition.' This concluding sentence of the account published in the Assembly's *Procès-verbal* (see note 18 above), 20, was not included in the printed pamphlet, whose text has formed the basis of subsequent reprints. Thus the Assembly's recommendation that the matter be considered by the Comité de Constitution has escaped the attention of later researchers.

25 A search was most kindly made on my behalf in the Archives de France

(Paris) to discover if in fact the Comité de Constitution took any action on the Quakers' Petition. Unfortunately nothing was discovered. (See letter from Yves Beauvalot for the Directeur Général, dated 28 February 1994.) The relevant documentation may have been lost. But it seems more likely, since the National Assembly was dissolved at the end of September 1791, that the Comité had not yet got round to considering the Petition.

26 Letter dated 1 May 1791 (English translation), LSF, MS vol. 314 (France MSS), no. 61.

27 Letter dated 16 July 1792 to Robert Grubb and Mary Dudley, ibid., no. 70 (extracts in Van Etten, *Chronique*, 80, 81).

28 Louis-Antoine Majolier to John Eliot, letter dated 18 August 1792, ibid., no. 72. In the letter cited above (in note 27), Marcillac reports his arrest in Paris for not wearing 'the national cockade'; he felt himself lucky in obtaining a speedy release.

29 Edmond Jaulmes, *Les Quakers français: Étude historique* (Nîmes, 1898), 41.

30 Brock, *The Quaker Peace Testimony 1660 to 1914* (York UK, 1990), 226.

31 See, for example, the document dated 3 August 1793, cited by Charles Mathiot, *Recherches historiques sur les Anabaptistes de l'ancienne principauté de Montbéliard, d'Alsace et du territoire de Belfort* (1922). I have used the edition of 1969, with Roger Boigeol as co-author, published at Flavion (Belgium); see p. 141.

32 This is suggested as a possibility by Louis, 'William Rotch,' 588. If such were indeed the case, it was certainly paradoxical, as she points out, that the Quaker Petition had proved fruitless, whereas the more obscure Mennonites were now to gain their objective, at any rate partially – 'thanks to the analogy established between them and the Quakers.'

33 In Montbéliard, indeed, no militia service seems to have been demanded from anyone; see Mathiot, *Recherches*, 137, n. 196.

34 Document dated 16 November 1792 requiring the enrolment in the National Guard of a local Mennonite farmer Peter Eicher; reprinted from the Archives du Doubs by Mathiot, *Recherches*, 138–40. Unexpectedly, on appeal this decision was overturned next year by the Council General of Doubs, which based its position in part on the favourable hearing granted the Quakers' similar stance by the National Assembly in February 1791. The Council General also took into consideration 'the quiet, secluded, and tranquil life of the Anabaptists [i.e., Mennonites], their special aptitude for agricultural work as well as for fruit-growing, their promptness in paying taxes, and the impossibility of their ever becoming disturbers of the peace.' See ibid., 140, 141.

35 Jean Séguy, *Les assemblées anabaptistes-Mennonites de France* (Paris and The

Hague, 1977), chap. 5, especially its documentary appendices. See also his brief account, *Les Mennonites dans la Révolution française* (Montbéliard, 1989).

36 Séguy, *Les assemblées*, 359–61.

37 Ibid., 361, 392, 393. Though from its first printing the date of the *arrêté* is given as 18 August, the correct date is almost certainly one day later. See Mathiot, *Recherches*, 142 n. 201; Séguy, *Les assemblées*, 414, n. 71.

38 Séguy, 362; Brock, *Freedom from Violence: Sectarian Nonresistance from the Middle Ages to the Great War* (Toronto, 1991), 145.

39 Michel L. Martin in Charles C. Moskos and John Whiteclay Chambers II, eds, *The New Conscientious Objection: From Sacred to Secular Resistance* (New York and Oxford, 1993), 82.

40 Séguy, *Les assemblées*, 394–7.

41 Mathiot, *Recherches*, 144, 146, 147, 150.

42 Letter from the Ministry of War, dated 28 December 1798; cited in full in Séguy, *Les assemblées*, 398. See also ibid., 363.

43 Alfred Michiels, *Les Anabaptistes des Vosges* (Paris, 1860), 17. Claude Jérôme, 'Les Anabaptistes-Mennonites de Salm aux XVIIIe et XIXe siècles,' *L'Essor*, vol. 46, no. 91 (April 1976), 18, col. 2, gives a reproduction of the original leaflet containing the text of the *arrêté*.

44 Séguy, *Les assemblées*, 363.

45 In fact, Mennonites usually did not raise strong objections to this – provided only that they were not required actually to bear arms and participate in killing. Michiels, *Anabaptistes*, 18, 19, relates how on one occasion a Mennonite in the baggage train of Napoleon's army campaigning against the Prussians saved his life during a skirmish by calling out in German: 'Don't shoot at me, for my religion forbids me to defend myself.' The 'enemy' immediately recognized that he was a Mennonite and did not fire; the lad was then taken prisoner peaceably. Three months later, the Prussians, familiar with Mennonite noncombatancy from the settlements of that industrious sect in the Vistula basin, let him go.

46 Cited in Hirst, *Quakers*, 470.

47 *Memoirs of Evan Rees: Consisting Chiefly of Extracts from His Letters* (London, 1853), 30, 31.

48 Martin, in Moskos and Chambers, eds, *The New Conscientious Objection*, 84 n. 39: 'there were fewer than one hundred COs between 1945 and 1955, their number reached more than two hundred in the early 1960s.'

6 The Peace Sects of Upper Canada and the Military Question

The province of Upper Canada, when it came into existence in 1791, was still largely wilderness. It bordered on the south with the new American republic, which presented a potential threat to its continued existence under the British crown. A native population was spread thinly over the land; it did not represent, though, a serious obstacle in the way of settlement by persons of European origin. In these circumstances the British government at home as well as the administrators it sent out to govern this remote frontier province regarded the promotion of European settlement as one of their priorities. Skilled craftsmen and especially farmers with experience would be needed in large numbers to clear the virgin forest and bring under cultivation those areas of the province below the Canadian Shield where the soil was suited to agricultural use.

Colonel Simcoe, the province's first lieutenant-governor, looking around for suitable settlers, soon decided that among the best people in this respect were the 'plain folk' farming land in Pennsylvania, New York, and New Jersey; Quakers (Society of Friends), Mennonites, and Tunkers, in particular.[1] They were frugal and hard-working, honest and law-abiding (in all matters that did not go against their conscience), skilled farmers who had worked the land for centuries. Moreover, during the recent Revolutionary War they had, with few exceptions, preserved their traditional loyalty to the British crown. While they had begun slowly to adjust themselves to the new political situation in their country, many of them would likely welcome an opportunity to move to British territory, especially if – as was the case in Upper Canada – they could obtain cheap and plentiful arable land. Their families tended to be large, and movement westward was already in full swing in the case of plain as well as other farming folk in the American east. There was in fact only one rather ticklish question to negotiate. All three sects mentioned above objected on religious grounds to bearing arms; they had for long held a testimony against participation in warfare, disfellowshipping members who failed to abide by this rule.[2] Thus, on 20 August 1792 we find Simcoe telling Henry Dundas in Whitehall: 'I have not hesitated to promise to the Quakers and other sects, the similar exemption from Militia duties which they have met with under the British government.'[3] Simcoe's promise found confirmation next year in the first of a succession of militia acts passed into law by the provincial assembly.

According to this act, all able-bodied males between the ages of sixteen and fifty were obliged to enrol in the militia and either to muster on the annual training day or find a substitute who could do so. Small fines resulted from a failure to enrol or to muster. But section 22 exempted from actually serving in the militia 'the persons called Quakers, Mennonites, and Tunkers, who from certain scruples of conscience, decline bearing arms.' To obtain this privilege, each draftee was obliged to produce 'a certificate of his being a Quaker, Mennonite or Tunker, signed by any three or more of the people who are or shall be by them authorized to grant certificates for this or any other purpose of which a pastor, minister or preacher shall be one.' But 'instead of such service,' 'composition money' had to be paid annually to the authorities amounting to one pound in peace time and five pounds 'in time of actual invasion or insurrection.' Failure to do this brought a penalty: 'distress and sale of the ... offender's goods and chattels, returning so much of the said distress as shall exceed' the amount of the fine 'after deducting the expenses of levying the same.' The right of appeal was given to those who felt themselves 'oppressed' by the manner in which a distraint was carried out.[4]

These provisions, modelled on English legislation, remained basically in force during the War of 1812 and governed the military obligation of members of the peace sects during the period of American invasion. In 1808, though, the legislators, having apparently realized that Quakers did not possess pastors, ministers, or preachers, in the sense at any rate that the other two peace sects did, added 'the clerk of the meeting' to the church officers authorized to issue certificates of membership to applicants for exemption.[5] And next year the Assembly made it legal, 'in case of actual invasion or emergency,' 'to impress such Horses, Carriages and Oxen' as the service might require, with monetary compensation to the owner for the period of their use by the military.[6]

The lieutenant-governor and legislators undoubtedly hoped that the exemptions they had granted the three peace sects would satisfy them. In this they were mistaken, however, and especially in regard to the Quakers. Perhaps Lord Dorchester, more familiar in Whitehall with the local Quaker lobby there than was a military man such as Simcoe, had an inkling of this when he wrote laconically to the latter: 'Quakers are a useful People and of good Example in a young Country; Exemptions may be carried too far.'[7] Quakers, in fact, were at this period absolutists with respect to all forms of military service; they believed it wrong to accept any alternative to bearing arms, such as paying commutation money in exchange for exemption or voluntarily permitting use of their property for military purposes or – still worse – accepting payment for such use. After some hesitation they even forbade members to accept government grants of land to United Empire Loyalists since, as Canada Half Yearly Meeting declared in August 1810, acceptance infringed the Society's peace testimony, the awards being made 'for actual service in war or for aiding or assisting therein.' And they disowned members who disobeyed the rules of the Society on any of these points. Some of the earliest Quaker settlers in Upper Canada had indeed been Empire Loyalists who, during the American Revolution, had taken up arms for their king despite the peace testimony of their Society that strictly forbade this. If such persons wished to continue in membership, as many of them did, they were obliged to express regret for such action in front of the meeting.

In these circumstances, Quaker militia draftees wanting to remain Friends in good standing could neither present a certificate to the authorities so as to establish their bona fide membership of the Quakers' Society, as the legislation required, nor pay the annual commutation money which would have freed them from the obligation of attending annual musters or joining the militia if it was called out for active service in case of invasion or other emergency. Naturally Quaker meetings frowned even more severely on such alternatives as paying for a substitute at musters. The uncompromising stance of the Society of Friends on this question was to lead on occasion to confrontation in Upper Canada with the state, as it had done elsewhere where Quakers were settled. The situation, as we shall see, would become more acute in time of war and threat of invasion.

For Mennonites and Tunkers such considerations as impeded the

Quakers from enjoying the privileges granted them by law did not operate. They regarded fulfilment of the same demands as the Quakers' religion found unacceptable to be a legitimate way to carry out Christ's injunction to render unto Caesar the things that are Caesar's. They did not see them as incompatible with their cherished doctrine of nonresistance, of defencelessness (*Wehrlosigkeit*). Their young men would not now have to bear arms personally. They knew, of course, that any money they paid in commutation of militia service would in all likelihood be used for military purposes, but that was Caesar's responsibility, not theirs. They reasoned along the same lines when they acted as teamsters for the army or loaned their horses or carts to transport military supplies or sold the products of their farms to feed soldiers. They had always acted in this way since the beginnings of their sect in the sixteenth century. But there were two matters on which they felt they had legitimate grounds for complaint. First came the fact that the money required in commutation of militia service represented a 'very substantial sum' (the historian John Moir's description), which pioneer farmers, especially those with the large families usual with Mennonite settlers, often found exceedingly burdensome. But, despite prolonged – and often intensive – lobbying and the presentation of countless petitions to the legislature, it was not until 1837 that the annual sum demanded was reduced by half to ten shillings.[8]

Their second grievance received much more rapid attention from the government, largely because the existing arrangement was more obviously unfair to Mennonites and Tunkers than was the overly large commutation fee. That fee in the end was usually produced by the draftee's church if he or his family could not afford to pay. But the situation was different in the case of males old enough to be drafted into the militia but still too young to receive the adult baptism which formally bestowed membership in the Mennonite and Tunker churches. These young fellows were usually in every sense part of their church community, having been reared in the traditional faith which they shared with their nearest kin and their neighbours, and they would enter into full communion with the church once the moment for their baptism arrived around the age of twenty-one. Yet, without practising deceit (which of course they were not prepared to do), their church officers could not supply them with the certificate of membership required by law. For Mennonites and Tunkers the kind of confrontation with the law that those uncompromising libertarians, the Quakers, seemed sometimes almost to enjoy was highly distasteful; it was alien to their tradition of rendering Caesar his due. Since they, too, frowned on the idea of furnishing a substitute militiaman, an option always open to the nonconscientious, without a change in the law the only alternative open was distraint on family property. If this last did not suffice, the boy would be committed 'to the common gaol of the district' until the fine was paid.

This defect in legislation was removed in 1810 when the as yet unbaptized members of these brotherhoods were included in a blanket exemption. This concession came, though, only after intensive lobbying by leaders of the two sects, in which the Tunker John Winger played the major role. In a petition they drew up for presentation to the Legislative Assembly they stated:

> Whereas many of Our Sons now under age and incapable of judging in matters of conscience, are not as yet actually considered as Church members, and cannot of course secure the necessary certificates, we therefore humbly pray the same indulgence may be extended to them that is granted to ourselves, their parents, that is that they may be exempted from serving in the Militia by paying the commutation money until they arrive at the age of twenty-one, or until they be admitted as Church Members.[9]

Though perhaps it had been slow to act, the Legislative Assembly now showed a commendable understanding of the two sects' position and a broadness of view that did credit to the members of the House. The legislation they passed drew attention to the fact that draft-age sons of Mennonites and Tunkers who were 'minors' could not take advantage of the militia exemption granted the peace sects because they could not 'obtain the certificate required' until they were twenty-one, 'according to the rules and regulations' of the two sects. Henceforward all that would be needed from the draftee would be a certificate giving his name and confirming that his father was a Mennonite or a Tunker and that he had been 'brought up and educated in the principles' of his family's sect.[10]

Now that this anomaly had been eliminated, relations between sect and state were not disturbed by the military question, at any rate so far as the Mennonites and Tunkers were concerned. How, though, did the Quakers, recalcitrant on principle, fare with respect to this same question that had been answered to the satisfaction of their nonresistant brethren? Surviving Canadian Quaker archives, which became increasingly abundant as the nineteenth century advanced, are for the period dealt with here fairly sparse (Canada Half Yearly Meeting, established in 1810, had as yet only three constituent Monthly Meetings). Nevertheless, they are abundant in comparison with those left by contemporary Canadian Mennonites or the much smaller Tunker sect; and the records of Canada Half Yearly Meeting and of Yonge Street Preparative and Monthly Meetings, along with those of Adolphustown Monthly Meeting, situated in the Bay of Quinte area, and of Pelham Preparative and Monthly Meeting in the southwest, provide sufficient materials to show the pattern of Quaker war resistance before and during the War of 1812–14.[11]

Yonge Street Quakers, whose farms were situated along that major military transportation route leading northwards until it petered out in the bush, were especially vulnerable to military demands during the invasion crisis. As John McIntyre has noted: 'The Quaker settlers of Yonge Street lived within twenty-five miles of the colonial capital on a road built by the government to help protect the capital in case of war.' Moreover, despite their loyalty to the British crown, like a high proportion of the provincial population at that date they were recent immigrants from the United States, and this could easily bring them under suspicion with the authorities, especially as they continued to maintain close ties with their brethren to the south. The difficulties experienced by Yonge Street Quakers in respect of both requisitioning of their farm produce by the military and of recruitment into the militia appear to have been greater than those of Quakers further removed from the scene of action. One of their number, a farmer named Clayton Jones, later recorded his family's experiences during this time of trial:

> Father was exempt by age, but brothers William and John were both drafted in the Militia. William, neither willing to fight nor to go to jail took refuge, with some others, in the woods. There was often parties in search of him, but never caught him. The officers took Thomas prisoner, and took him before Colonel Graham, who sent him to jail, where he lay about 6 weeks, and by father interceding for him with Col. Graham, he at length gave an order for his release, and I think was not troubled any more ... While Thomas lay in jail, a young man, a Friend, Joseph Roberts died there, rather than violate his conscience.[12]

Of course, not all Quaker draftees were as staunch pacifists as Joseph Roberts proved to be. Some, like Clayton's brother William, since they were unwilling either to fight or go to jail, became what we would call today draft-dodgers – or, more politely, draft-evaders.

Quaker response to military obligation during the war years was shaped by the experience of the previous two decades, and this in turn by the way the Quaker peace testimony had developed on both sides of the Atlantic over nearly one and a half centuries. Basically there was nothing new here. From the Meeting minutes we learn details of the burdensome distraints levied on Quaker draftees and their families for refusing either to present certificates of membership or pay the exemption fees. In 1810, for instance, Pelham Monthly Meeting recorded of members at Black Creek: 'Taken by distress by a warrant under the hand and seal of John Warren, Justice of the Peace, ... from the following [six] Friends property to the amount' of $80. From another entry around the same time we learn that 'Distraints on the property of Friends of Pelham for Militia Fines' consisted of such items as sacks of wheat, sheep, and a heifer.[13] But most of the archival materials dealing with military obligation concern cases of Quaker delinquency. The offence was brought to the notice of the Meeting; attempts were then made to persuade the offender to acknowledge that his conduct had been wrong; and, if he remained unrepentant, he was eventually disowned.

The most flagrant infraction of the Quaker discipline was of course attendance in person or by substitute at a muster of the militia. In time of peace there was usually only one training day in the course of the year; for most of our period this occasion took place on 4 June.[14] Few Quaker draftees seem to have been guilty of this offence, even though normally militia duty was extremely light, whereas the penalty for nonattendance, at least for the form which Quaker noncompliance took, was quite severe. It might even involve imprisonment if the objector was a poor man with insufficient property on which a distraint could be made. Those who transgressed on this issue were often in rebellion against their Society's discipline in other matters, too. Take the case of a young member of Adolphustown Monthly Meeting in 1801. The meeting minutes report first 'that Allen Clark had Deviated from plainness[,] been concerned in makeing [*sic*] a horse race and attended training,' and then, after the Meeting had taken the matter 'under care' (the phrase always used in such cases), it reported regretfully a couple of months later that 'Allen Clark [was] not disposed to reform his ways.' One must presume that he was eventually disowned! In 1807 this was the fate of Robert Hubb junior from the same Meeting for 'attempting a training, and mariing [*sic*] out of the order used among us,' that is, for marrying outside the Society of Friends.[15] In Pelham Monthly Meeting, for instance, whereas in 1805 William Doan had been cleared of the charge of paying a military fine, in 1811 'Ezekiel Dennis having had a right of membership amongst Friends, but not taking heed of the dictates of truth in his own breast hath gone out so far as to comply with Military requisitions attending training and also appears out of plainness.' Disownment followed.[16] Cases of a similar character can be found, too, among Yonge Street Friends.

The issue of certificates to draftees, envisaged in the legislation for Quaker as well as for the other two peace sects, was rejected by the Quakers as incompatible with a consistent witness against war. On at least one occasion, however, responsible Friends broke this rule, presumably hoping thereby to save draftees from incurring the penalties that resulted from the Society's uncompromising stand. On 18 February 1808 Yonge Street Monthly Meeting reported disapprovingly: 'Many Friends have so far complied with the requisitions of Military men, as to grant them Certificates, Certifying our Right of Membership; and signed by three members, whereby our Sufferings become Lessened.'[17]

The outbreak of war with the United States in mid-1812 brought increased requisitioning on the part of the military, which weighed heavily on Yonge Street Quakers in particular. Serving as teamster for the army – hauling cannon or military stores, for instance – led to disciplinary action against the offender by his Meeting, ending inevitably in disownment if due contrition were not shown.[18]

In contrast to the active war resistance of the Quakers, Mennonites during the war years followed a policy of 'passive war service' (as the historian Frank Epp has aptly called it). Their settlements along the Grand River had come into the front line when in October 1813 an American army chased the British forces as far as the River Thames. Mennonite exemption from bearing arms was guaranteed by law; they encountered no difficulties on this score even in this time of crisis. Doubtless Mennonite farmers would have preferred to be left altogether in peace, but when the British military imposed on them various requisitions and auxiliary services (for example, as teamsters), they performed their duties efficiently and cheerfully. We know that to do so was not frowned on by their church authorities. Their cheerfulness was perhaps increased when they discovered they could put in claims, sometimes quite substantial ones, for losses sustained 'when employed in military transport.'[19]

The Quakers, though they would have disowned one of their own members who made claims of this kind (unless he were persuaded to express a proper degree of regret), did not openly criticize the Mennonites or Tunkers for doing this. After all, Quaker pacifists and Mennonite nonresistants were allies vis-à-vis the military establishment. However, one criticism, a severe one, the Mennonite stance on this issue did receive from a private soldier in the British Army! But Irish-born George Ferguson (1786–1851) was an unusual trooper: already virtually a pacifist himself, after demobilization he became a pioneer of Canadian Methodism. In the autobiography he wrote in retirement, he has this to say of the nonresistant teamsters he met with during his army career in the autumn of 1812:

> I have found some so conscientious and pious that they would not take up arms to defend their property and their families, but take four dollars a day to carry arms, ammunition, men and provisions to assist those whom they supposed were murdering their fellow-men! What consistency! If a man is scrupulous about fighting, from principle, let him carry out that principle in every particular, and Amen to it, but such conduct as that above alluded to is contemptible.[20]

The Treaty of Ghent, signed on 24 December 1814, brought the war with the United States to an end; next year the war in Europe ceased, too, ushering in a long period of peace. The military question lost much of its urgency for the Canadian peace sects, even though compulsory militia service continued into the early 1840s, in contrast to Britain, where the last militia draft took place in 1831. Mennonites and Tunkers, if drafted for service in the militia, just paid their fines and were then left in peace on their farms. The situation for propertyless young Quakers, since their Society, as we have seen, refused any compromise, remained more difficult. As late as 1839 a visiting English Friend wrote home that two young Quakers 'had been thrown into jail at Hamilton, and detained there for sixteen days in consequence of their being unable, on conscientious grounds, to serve in the militia.'[21] But, as in the home country as well as in the neighbouring American republic, the militia system was by now in a state of decrepitude. Canada would not face military conscription until the next century.

During the period examined here, the question of military obligation had not soured relations between peace sect and secular state, even in the war crisis of 1812–15. Tension at times there had been. But eventually some sort of accommodation was always reached. Even if the Quakers never attained the grant they wished for of unconditional exemption from military service, they were used, after all, over a long period of time, to enduring 'militia sufferings,' which anyhow were not particularly severe. The government, on its side, did not lose its respect for the Friends' positive citizenship in other aspects of life and was normally prepared to overlook their 'peculiar' stance on the military question. The Mennonites and Tunkers adopted, as we have seen, a much less aggressive attitude, and consequently there existed in their case fewer possibilities of confrontation between military obligation and sectarian conscience. All three peace sects had played a modest, but valuable, role in pioneering the new and undeveloped country. The government realized that they constituted a valuable asset, while the sectarians for their part valued this recognition as a guarantee of free development. The resulting *modus vivendi* between the two sides was not perfect, but it proved a workable compromise.

NOTES

1 Gerald M. Craig, *Upper Canada: The Formative Years 1784–1841* (Toronto, 1963), 44–6. Craig refers to Dunkards (today known as Brethren, none of whom emigrated to Canada at this period) as one of the three Canadian peace sects, instead of to Tunkers (today known as Brethren in Christ). Both sects practised adult baptism by immersion, that is by dipping (*Tunken* in their German dialect means 'to dip'). See also Frank H. Epp, *Mennonites in Canada 1786–1920: The History of a Separate People* (Toronto, 1974), chap. 4 ('The Nonresistors and the Militia'); E. Morris Sider, 'Nonresistance in the Early Brethren in Christ Church in Ontario,' *Mennonite Quarterly Review* (hereafter *MQR*), vol. 31, no. 4 (October 1957), 278–80; Richard MacMaster, 'Friends in the Niagara Peninsula 1786–1802,' in Albert Schrauwers, ed., *Faith, Friends and Fragmentation: Essays on Nineteenth Century Quakerism in Canada* (Toronto: Canadian Friends Historical Association, 1995), 1, 9, 10.

2 See my *Freedom from Violence: Sectarian Nonresistance from the Middle Ages to the Great War* (Toronto, 1991) and *The Quaker Peace Testimony 1660 to 1914* (York UK, 1990).

3 E.A. Cruikshank, ed., *The Correspondence of Lieut. Governor John Graves Simcoe ...*, vol. 1: *1789–1793* (Toronto: Ontario Historical Society, 1923), 198, 199. This multi-volume collection is often referred to as the *Simcoe Papers*. For an overview of British Quakers as conscientious objectors to bearing arms dur-

ing the period to the end of the Napoleonic wars, see Constance Braithwaite, *Conscientious Objection to Various Compulsions under British Law* (York, 1995), 111–19. In Britain compulsory recruitment to the militia was carried out since 1757 by ballot. This provision was not included in Canadian legislation on the subject.

4 33 George III, chap. 1, sect. 22 (1793). Next year an act raised the age of liability for service in the militia to sixty but kept it at fifty for members of the three peace sects, except 'in time of war or other emergency,' when they would also be liable for service until the age of sixty (with exemption as before by paying commutation money).

5 48 George III, chap. 1, sect. 27 (1808). At the same time liability for paying peacetime commutation money was again raised to the age of sixty.

6 49 George III, chap. 2 (1809).

7 *Simcoe Papers*, vol. 2, *1793–1794*, 3, letter dated 4 August 1793. The government in Upper Canada, like the home government, continued, however, to regard Quakers positively despite their peculiar ideas on war. In 1806, for instance, we find Lieutenant-Governor Francis Gore telling Friends: 'I have no doubts of your proving peaceful and good subjects to His Majesty as well as industrious and respectable members of society' (quoted in Arthur Garratt Dorland, *The Quakers in Canada, a History* [Toronto, 1968], 94).

8 John S. Moir, ed., *Church and State in Canada 1627–1867: Basic Documents* (Toronto, 1967), 152, 153. See also L.F. Burkholder, *A Brief History of the Mennonites in Ontario* (Toronto, 1935), 349–51; William Janzen, *Limits on Liberty: The Experience of Mennonite, Hutterite, and Doukhobor Communities in Canada* (Toronto, 1990), 163, 164; Epp, *Mennonites in Canada*, 101–6; Brock, *Freedom from Violence*, 225–7.

9 *The Journals of the Legislative Assembly of Upper Canada*, vol. 2 in Alexander Fraser, ed., *Eighth Report of the Bureau of Archives for the Province of Ontario 1911* (Toronto, 1912), 301, 302; also J. Boyd Cressman, 'History of the First Mennonite Church of Kitchener, Ontario,' *MQR*, vol. 13, no. 3 (July 1939), 168, and Sider, 'Nonresistance,' 280, 281.

10 50 George III, chap. 11 (1810).

11 I would like to thank Dr Neil Semple for examining on my behalf the microfilms of these records deposited in the Archives of Ontario (AO), as part of the Religious Society of Friends Papers (Ms. 303). Dorland made use of some of these materials in his *Quakers in Canada*, 315, 317, 318. See also Elma Starr, ed., 'Quakers Opposed War Preparations in Upper Canada: Extracts from the Minute Book of Yonge Street Preparative and Monthly Meeting 1804–1818,' *Canadian Friend*, vol. 69, no. 1 (February/March 1973), 10, 11.

12 Quoted in Albert Schrauwers, *Awaiting the Millennium: The Children of Peace and the Village of Hope, 1812–1889* (Toronto, 1993), 44, 45. See also W. John McIntyre, *Children of Peace* (Montreal and Kingston, 1994), 36, 37, 189. The schismatic Children of Peace, who departed from Yonge Street Monthly Meeting in 1812 under the leadership of David Willson, fairly soon shed their pacifism, but that happened only after the war was over. See Schrauwers, *Awaiting the Millennium*, 46–8.

13 AO, Ms. 303, D-1-10, reel 50, Pelham Monthly Meeting, File 8, Militia Fines. See also Dorland, *Quakers in Canada*, 317, and Starr, ed., 'Quakers,' 10, for data on militia distraints imposed on Yonge Street Quakers between 1810 and 1817.

14 A.B. Sherk, 'Early Militia Matters in Upper Canada, 1808–1842,' Ontario Historical Society, *Papers and Records*, vol. 13 (1915), 67–70.

15 AO, Ms. 303, B-2-1, Adolphustown Monthly Meeting, 1798–1813, reel 14.

16 Ibid., C-3-45, Pelham Monthly Meeting, 1806–1830, reel 41. Birthright membership was the custom among Quakers in contrast to the other two peace sects, which granted membership to the children of members only on adult baptism.

17 Ibid., B-2-83, Yonge Street Monthly Meeting, 1806–1818, reel 27, p. 35.

18 See, for example, ibid., B-2-76, Yonge Street Preparative Meeting, 1804–1818, reel 267, pp. 27, 31, 32; C-3-45, Pelham Monthly Meeting, 1806–1830, reel 41, n.p. (1 Sept. 1813); B-1-9, Canada Half Yearly Meeting, 1810–1830, reel 13, p. 34. All entries date from 1813–15, years of war emergency. Disownment resulted even when the team and equipment belonged to the offender.

19 Epp, *Mennonites in Canada*, 104, 105; Harold S. Bender, 'New Source Material for the History of the Mennonites in Ontario,' *MQR*, vol. 3, no. 1 (January 1929), 42–6. Henry Wanner, for instance, claimed £128 for the loss of 'one waggon one horse and harnis five bags' (p. 45).

20 'Journal of George Ferguson,' United Church of Canada Archives (Toronto), 25; also 39, 40. See Arthur E. Kewley, 'The Swaddler Preacher: The Rev. George Ferguson – Loyal to King and Conscience,' in Canadian Methodist Historical Society, *Papers*, vol. 10 (1995), ed. N. Semple, 7–17, for an account of Ferguson's experiences while in the British Army. I thank Dr Semple for bringing this essay to my attention.

21 The Quaker visitor was Joseph John Gurney, the brother of Elizabeth Fry. I have republished his account in my anthology, *Liberty and Conscience: A Documentary History of the Experiences of Conscientious Objectors in America through the Civil War* (New York, 2002), 74–6.

7 Militia Objectors in the Channel Islands

The Channel Islands constitute the last territories of the Duchy of Normandy still attached to the British crown. Divided administratively into the bailiwicks of Jersey and Guernsey (which includes the smaller islands of Alderney and Sark), they look politically to Britain, while geographically they belong to the European continent and, until the later nineteenth century, the mother tongue of the majority of the population was French. As a result of the frequent wars with France and intermittent war scares, the British government fortified the islands against possible invasion: the last time a defensive tower was erected was as late as the 1850s. At the Reformation the Church of England had taken over in the islands ecclesiastically, with the Anglican parish forming the unit of local government. Towards the end of the eighteenth century, however, the arrival of Methodist missionaries from England presented a serious challenge to the Anglican establishment; eventually nonconformity became the predominant faith of the islanders. In due course, tiny Quaker meetings in Guernsey and Jersey introduced the idea of pacifism into a society that at this time was often militarily on the alert and fearful of foreign invasion. But, because of the small numbers involved, Quaker pacifism did not present a serious problem for the authorities.

In England, the situation for Quakers vis-à-vis the military question was rather different since the Society of Friends formed a very much larger community than it did in the Channel Islands. Since the early 1660s, when a refusal to bear arms became a fixed tenet of the Society of Friends, along with the obligation not to accept any alternative such as the payment of a fine in lieu thereof, the militia ballot became a source of Quaker 'sufferings.'[1] Propertied Friends, who were drafted, suffered distraints on their goods, while the propertyless were often jailed for a short spell. During the French Revolutionary and Napoleonic wars, the law was tightened, and law enforcement stiffened. As the militia act of 1802 (42 Geo. III c. 90) put it:

> If no goods or chattels belonging to such Quaker [i.e., one balloted to serve in the militia] can be found, sufficient to levy such distress [and buy a substitute] ... then it shall be lawful for [two] Deputy Lieutenants [of the county] to commit such Quaker to the common gaol, there to remain without bail or mainprize, for the space of three months, or until he shall have paid such sum of money as such Deputy Lieutenants shall have agreed to pay to such substitutes as aforesaid.

After 1815 imprisonment of Quakers became extremely rare, even though a militia ballot continued until 1831 to be enforced in England from time to time. Thereafter, the militia draft was suspended indefinitely, and military conscription in Britain was not again imposed until 1916. However, discussion of the militia question went on sporadically in Quaker meetings and in the Quaker press (the first Quaker papers commenced in 1843), especially when in the 1840s and 1850s the government contemplated reactivating the militia ballot. In 1846, for instance, letters appeared in the *British Friend* for and (more) against the idea of forming 'anti-militia clubs,' members of which – Quakers together with non-Quakers – would pool their resources to buy a substitute for any member balloted for service.[2] Friends were indeed interested in countering proposals to reimpose militia conscription; they followed parliamentary debates carefully, petitioning the government in the matter when they thought this appropriate. In the end the government, even during the Crimean War, decided to retain the principle of voluntary enlistment for the armed forces. In 1852 a militia act was passed (15 & 16 Vic. c. 50), which eliminated the possibility of imprisoning Quakers should the militia draft be reimposed. According to section 33 of this act, the two deputy lieutenants of the county were stripped of their power 'to commit a Quaker to the common gaol if no goods or chattels belonging to such Quaker can be found sufficient to levy a distress to defray the expense of providing and hiring a substitute for such Quaker.'

Let us now turn back to the Channel Islands. There militia conscription continued after 1831, and a handful of Quaker – or near-Quaker – militia objectors found themselves, if only briefly, in 'the common gaol.' In Jersey, Guernsey, Alderney, and Sark alike the local militias, regulated by the laws passed by the *Etats* (States) of the two bailiwicks, drew for their rank and file on draftees. This situation remained unchanged until after the outbreak of the First World War.

Quakerism took root first in Guernsey. It was brought there in the second half of the 1770s by an itinerant Quaker minister from France, Claude Gay, whose wife had owned property in the island. Gay preached there in French and distributed a leaflet in French expounding Quaker views. And he succeeded in converting two teenage boys, Nicholas Naftel and his older brother, Thomas André, whose family ran a watch and clock business in the town of St Peter's Port. Several other Guernsey people followed the example of the Naftel brothers and became Friends. They began to meet regularly for worship, and eventually, membership slowly growing, they were able to build a meeting house.[3] Numbers, however, always remained small.

Almost at once the Naftel brothers were confronted with a demand from the local militia to do a stint of service. Nicholas records in his *Memoirs* that his older brother's 'religious opinions soon made him bear his testimony against wars and fightings, he being of age to serve in the militia, there being a strict law to that effect. Expecting to be sent to prison for non-compliance at one time he put his night-cap in his pocket as he started for the Court, but the law proceedings were stopped in an extraordinary manner.'[4] Instead of jail, Thomas André received a fine for each of the two occasions he had refused the summons to muster with the militia. The 'Crime Book' of the Court, which on 24 April 1779 consisted of the bailiff, William Le Marchant, and ten jurats, records that, on a charge being brought by the militia captain, Michael Robinson, Naftel was fined three 'livres tournois' for the first offence and six for the second offence.[5] The court based its verdict on Guernsey's militia ordinance of 19 January 1756. This stated that 'chaque personne, obligée à porter les armes, se trouvera au lieu et à l'heure appointée' for the militia muster. The fine for nonattendance was to be increased with each failure to muster.[6] Thomas André presumably paid his fine – or else someone else did so on his behalf – even though it was in this period contrary to the Quaker discipline to do this. Anyhow, according to Guernsey's pioneer historian, Edith Carey, 'it does not appear that any further proceedings were taken against him.'[7]

Nicholas Naftel was equally fortunate in his experiences with the militia as his brother had been. He had, however, been slower in taking a resolute stance in conformity with his newly found faith. He writes in his *Memoirs* that, even after his acceptance of Quaker principles, he continued to muster with the militia when called upon to do so:

> I wore a red coat and had to serve my turn at the watch house or tower every six weeks or two months. But I no longer enjoyed the life, for my brother's influence became stronger, and I felt myself in duty bound to leave the Militia, but I did not give it up readily, and suffered much in mind. But very reluctantly I omitted to keep my watch, and when the Captain of my Company asked me 'Why?' I told him, 'for conscience sake.' He replied 'Then I must have you to Court,' but, although the law is very severe in these Islands I was never prosecuted then or since.[8]

The Naftel brothers' militia experiences took place in peacetime. With the reopening of war with France in 1793 the situation changed, and with Napoleon's accession to power the threat of an invasion of the islands became more real. The authorities now viewed the small Quaker community's anti-militia stance less benignly than they had done twenty years earlier. When a Friend named Thomas Gallienne was drafted for militia service and refused to muster, he was incarcerated in Castle Cornet. 'While there he was wheeled in a cart up and down the Castle ... yard with a gun strapped in front of him before a company of soldiers, and then taken to prison.'[9]

At this time no Quaker meeting existed yet in Jersey, though from the beginning of the century there were one or two individual Friends on the island. A formal meeting, attended by a handful of members, was set up only in 1831; it was attached, as in the case of Guernsey's Quaker meeting, to the nearest mainland quarterly meeting (i.e., Sussex, Surrey, and Hampshire). The earliest Jersey militia objector I have been able to discover was apparently not himself a member of the Society of Friends, though he worshipped with Friends and had adopted the peculiar dress still worn by Quakers at this time as well as their pacifism. This man was John Asplet, a plasterer by trade and highly respected by his fellow citizens as 'a man of strong and earnest convictions.' He clashed with the authorities in 1827 and 1828 on account of his refusal to drill when drafted for militia service:

> He was dragged before the Court; he was fined heavily; the Sheriffs seized and sold his possessions; he was imprisoned with ruffians and felons; and finally he was banished from the Island.[10] He bore all this

> with as much modesty as resignation and courage. He did not parade his wrongs or exhibit himself as a hero or martyr ... not one word of anger did he ever utter against those who had so cruelly and so wantonly persecuted him.[11]

A few years after Asplet's run-in with the Jersey militia, the famous Elizabeth Fry visited the island in 1833, accompanied by her husband and one of her daughters. Of course, she paid a visit to the local prison and commented on what she saw within its walls. But she also went on a Sunday morning to a Quaker meeting. She found there 'a little band of persons, in very humble life, who professed the principles of Friends, one or two only ... being members of the Society.' The meeting was held 'in the cottage of Jean Renaud, an old patriarch residing on the sea shore,' near St Hélier. 'There was,' she went on, 'a quaint old fashioned effect about the low large room in which they assembled ... The appearance of the congregation was in keeping with the apartment, seated on planks, supported by temporary props.' The language of ministry at the meeting was the Jersey French patois, and when the visitors spoke, their ministry had to be translated as most of those present could not understand English.[12]

These humble and obscure folk hardly presented a threat to the military security of the island, even if a state of alert continued there for at least another half century. In 1872 a small Quaker meeting house was built in St Hélier, but in 1886 only five members are recorded for Jersey.[13] Nevertheless, even though militia conscription in England had ceased long ago, in 1886 once more two young Jerseymen, neither of them Quakers, were jailed for refusing, on grounds of conscience, to drill when drafted for militia service. In England a concerned Friend, Richard Binns, writing to the two Quaker papers to inform their readership of this sorry happening, began his letter with the words: 'Incredible as it may appear, yet there has been this year a case of persecution for conscience' sake' in this British dependency. He went on to describe what had happened:

> Two sons of Edward Voisin [Albert and Ernest], of Jersey, for refusing on religious grounds to serve in the Militia, were sent to prison, and confined for four days during last winter's frost in separate granite cells lighted by a grating, without heat of any kind, a plank to lie on, no straw, only four blankets, and these taken away in the day-time, when their own warm clothing was replaced by prison garb. Their exercise, half an hour's

> parade with criminals on Sunday round the grave of a murderer. Should they refuse to serve next year they expect a month's hard labour.[14]

British Quakers were shocked: they perhaps felt a little guilty because, if the militia draft were reintroduced in Britain, they would no longer under any circumstances be sent to jail. The militia act of 1852 had specifically freed them from this penalty, whereas non-Quakers, however conscientious as in the case of the Voisin brothers, would not be exempted even on the mainland. (It seems indeed that since the mid-1870s, in Jersey too, where militia conscription continued, members of the Society of Friends were among the categories of persons exempted from service, along with ministers of religion, schoolteachers, etc.; see below.) Were they right to accept this kind of privileged position? asked British Quakers. In 1916 the Society of Friends was decisively to reject any special consideration for its members in the conscription legislation then passed by parliament.

The Voisin case had caused quite a stir among Quakers in Britain, and in August of the same year, the Society's executive body, the Meeting for Sufferings, appointed a committee of three to look into the matter and report back to them.[15] This committee's report, submitted on 3 September, constitutes our main source for the case.[16]

Edward Voisin, the boys' father, a respected citizen of the island, though he had served in the Royal Jersey Militia Artillery for many years, from the beginning had been uneasy as to whether, as a Christian, he could bear arms with intent to kill. In 1874 a 'perusal of [the Quaker, Jonathan] Dymond's Essays was the means of confirming' his growing belief that to do this was wrong. He had, therefore, written a letter to the officer in command of his militia regiment, in which he stated:

> For a space of about thirteen years ... I have endeavoured faithfully to obey the orders of my superiors in rank ... I tried in vain to drive the thought away ... that I was wrong in ... countenancing a system involving destruction of human life ... Of late I have very seriously considered the question, and weighed arguments on both sides; moreover, I have carefully searched the Scriptures, and, from the teachings of that book, which contains the will of God, I find that we are urged to guard against the very *feelings* from which arise the quarrels of nations and of individuals. Consequently, ... my doubts have grown to a deep conviction that ... no man, under any pretence whatever, has the right to take the life of another, and

> that I ought not to do that which my conscience so strongly condemns. I must, therefore, beg of you not to consider me any longer as forming a part of the Battery under your command.

From that time on, Voisin resolutely maintained his anti-militia stance, refusing, according to the committee's report, 'not only to serve or provide any kind of substitute, but even to consent to payment on his behalf of the fines imposed by the authorities.' Early in the next decade, he was hauled up in court for failing to register his underage sons for militia service. But on each occasion the authorities hesitated to imprison this intrepid antimilitarist, despite his failure to pay any of the fines imposed on him in court. Meanwhile, Voisin was active as secretary of the Jersey Anti-Compulsory Militia League in campaigning against the militia draft.[17]

Two members of the Meeting for Sufferings' committee visited Jersey and reported back as follows:

> Edward Voisin is a solicitor of good position, residing in the country ... so that his sons [aged respectively twenty and seventeen] had been accustomed to a comfortable, though by no means luxurious, mode of living; yet they have neither flinched from this suffering, nor any desire to dwell on it or make much of it. We have been very favourably impressed with their demeanour. Their father has carefully abstained from in any way urging upon them his own views of what is right, yet they appear thoroughly to share his convictions.

The two Quaker visitors also reported that, especially among the island's working class, the militia draft was widely unpopular. On the other hand, 'there are many who uphold it, or at least readily acquiesce in it.' Among opponents of the draft were both political objectors and those who objected on religious grounds. 'Several of these declared their readiness to go to prison rather than serve, but only one of them, the President of the [Anti-Compulsory Militia] League, submitted to imprisonment, rather than pay the fine, and his courage failed him before he had been in prison two hours, so that he paid the fine and was released next morning.'[18]

In the end, the Voisin brothers did not have to serve another, and longer, term in jail, as they had expected they would have to do. This happy outcome resulted from British Friends' energetic – and ultimately successful – lobbying of the home secretary on their behalf. The home secretary, in turn, ordered the lieutenant-governor of Jersey to exercise his prerogative of granting exemptions from militia service to persons not otherwise legally entitled to this. The Quaker Meeting for Sufferings, we may note, had been extremely tactful in approaching the home secretary. Its Memorial had stated:

> Edward Voisin and his sons are not members of our Society, but their views on this subject are identical with our own, and we submit that it will be entirely in accordance with the spirit of the law, thus to extend the exemption which it already contains [i.e., with respect to Quakers]. Nor could such an exemption be considered as furnishing any precedent for cases in which religious objections may be alleged, but in which there is no such proof as has been supplied by Edward Voisin and his sons that the objections are based on genuine conviction.

Friends pointed out that they made this suggestion on their own, without the knowledge of the Voisins themselves. The latter, while they would certainly welcome relief from their present unenviable situation, did 'not seek for themselves any peculiar privilege or favour.' Friends concluded as follows:

> Our action in presenting this Memorial is solely prompted by the sympathy and admiration which we feel for those who, sharing our convictions, have nobly sustained a protest against what we believe to be the unchristian character of the military system, but who are unprotected by the provisions which the legislature of Jersey, at the instance of the authorities at home, has enacted in favour of our members.[19]

By 1889 Edward Voisin, together with his whole family, had joined the Society of Friends.[20] Obviously his views on other issues than the military question coincided with those of the Quakers. And the Society of Friends' warm support for his sons during their clash with the military must have strengthened his ties with the local meeting.

A decade earlier, a rather similar case in Guernsey had drawn the attention of Friends on the mainland. The draftee in question was the eighteen-year-old Henry Cumber, junior, son of a local Quaker but himself not yet a member of the Society. It was also Richard Binns (at that time living in Derby) who, because of his contacts with Quakers in the Channel Islands, now alerted readers of the *Friend* to the full implications of the case for Quakers. 'Surely,' he wrote, 'we ought to use our influence as far as possible to extend any advantage we possess to others, and not to rest satisfied because we have made things comfortable for ourselves.' We must, he urged his coreligionists, 'make a determined effort to extend the exemption with which we are favoured to all who conscientiously object to military service.'[21]

The Cumber case opened on 22 February 1875 when the draftee appeared before the Police Court, the bailiff, Sir P. Stafford Carey, presiding with four jurats also present. The island's French-language official gazette reported the trial in some detail:

> *M. Henri Cumber*, fils, est cité devant la Cour, sur la poursuite de M. le major Pirie, pour se voir condamner à payer une amende d'une livre un sou tournois pour n'être pas présenté a l'Arsenal après y avoir été dûment convoqué comme milicien. Le prévenu prétend que, comme membre de la Société religieuse des amis, des raisons de conscience le forcent à ne pas servir dans la milice.
>
> *La père* du prévenu observe qu'en Angleterre la raison émise par son fils serait admise. Son père et son grand père sont membres de la même religion, religion qui n'admet pas l'usage des armes. Le témoin cite, à l'appui de sa thèse [i.e., as to his son's sincerity], le cas de M. Thomas Quertier, qui a préferé subir l'emprisonnement plutôt que de remplir ses dévoirs de milicien, quoiqu' à cette époque il ne fut même pas membre de ce secte religieux.
>
> *M. le procureur*, d'accord du reste avec M. le baillif, a observé que tout natif de Guernesey était obligé de remplir les devoirs de la milice, que, du reste, par son âge, le prévenu ne faisait pas partie encore de la société des amis, et que de titre ne pouvait donner droit à l'exemption des devoir de la milice.
>
> En conséquence, la Cour a condamné M. Henri Cumber à amende demandée.[22]

Thus Guernsey, we see, at this date did not recognize the Society of Friends as a body whose members were entitled to exemption from militia service. Anyhow, the teenager, Henry Cumber, was not yet formally a member of the Society of Friends, a point the prosecution – and the authorities in general – appeared to stress. Since the boy followed Quaker practice in rejecting payment of a fine in such circumstances, he was jailed. True, his imprisonment lasted only twenty-four hours. But he was threatened with further summonses when the amount of the fine could be doubled and trebled with the likelihood of his term of imprisonment for refusing to pay being correspondingly increased. In a Memorial to the home secretary, British Quakers asked the minister why, 'if the abolition of imprisonment in our case be just and expedient in England, ... it should not be equally just and expedient in the Island of Guernsey or in any other portion of the Queen's dominions.'[23] British Friends' intervention on Cumber's behalf seems to have been effective, for the young man encountered no further difficulties on account of his conscientious objection vis-à-vis the militia.

In fact, henceforward the island authorities, at least informally, exempted young Quakers from the obligation of serving in the militia. There must indeed have been very few of them liable for service. At a meeting of the Royal Court in May 1913, held to discuss a new militia ordinance, the question was raised as to what categories were exempted from militia service. It was presumed that Quakers would not be required to bear arms. As Jurat Leale put it, 'this very small community had had the privilege of not serving in the Militia for many years.' But should they be totally exempt or should they possibly have to perform some kind of noncombatant service in lieu of arms-drill? Jurat Leale was in favour of exempting them unconditionally. 'From information he had received it was very difficult to become a Quaker, unless his parents were Quakers before him.' After further debate, the Court finally decided unanimously to grant Quakers unconditional exemption from service in the militia.[24]

This essay has dealt with a minute group of pacifists over a time span of approximately 135 years. Yet the story is not without significance for the history of conscientious objection. First of all, we can see here how a handful of young men, subjects of the British crown, continued to confront the draft after compulsory militia service had ended on the English mainland: this indeed is a story that has been largely forgotten. Next, we may watch how fear of invasion ensured that the militia draft remained in force in the islands and estimate the impact such a situation made on their tiny pacifist communities. Lastly, the story illustrates the Quakers' deeply held conviction that it was not right for them to enjoy a privileged position vis-à-vis the draft, even though the Society of Friends expressed gratitude to the government for its toleration of a minority, and often unpopular, stance. The story is, of course, incomplete. But, told in outline, it provides nevertheless sufficient detail to make the above points clear.

NOTES

1 See Margaret E. Hirst, *The Quakers in Peace and War: An Account of Their Peace Principles and Practice* (London, 1923), 73–6, 197–200, 205–7, 213–15, 244–7; Constance Braithwaite, *Conscientious Objection to Various Compulsions under British Law* (York UK, 1995), 106–19; also Peter Brock, *The Quaker Peace Testimony 1660 to 1914* (York, 1990), chap. 4, and J.R. Western, *The English Militia in the Eighteenth Century: The Story of a Political Issue, 1660–1802* (London and Toronto, 1965), 251, 285.

2 *British Friend* (Glasgow), vol. 4, no. 1 (January 1846), 22; no. 2 (February 1846), 51, 52. See Brock, *Pacifism in Europe to 1914* (Princeton NJ, 1972), 334.

3 See John Ormerod Greenwood, *Quaker Encounters*, vol. 2: *Vines on the Mountains* (York, 1997), 61–4.

4 Quoted in Edith Carey, *The Beginnings of Quakerism in Guernsey* (12-page reprint from the *Transactions of the Guernsey Society of Natural Science for 1918*), 5. Carey's article is based largely on Nicholas Naftel's *Memoirs*, which she states was published in the United States in 1888. I have not been able to locate a copy of this book in any library on either side of the Atlantic.

5 'Livre en Crime (Crime Book),' vol. 15, Office of the Greffe, Guernsey, fol. 115 (entry for 24 April 1779).

6 'Jugements, Ordonnances et Ordres du Conseil: Novembre 1745 à Avril 1957,' Office of the Greffe, fol. 109, rev.

7 Carey, *Beginnings*, 5.

8 Ibid., 6.

9 Ibid., 8. Carey gives an approximate date of 1799–1800 for this incident. During the second half of the 1790s, even more alarming to the authorities than Quaker militia recalcitrance had been the refusal of the islands' Methodists, a much larger community, to perform militia drills on Sundays; they claimed that this was contrary to their religious principles. These men were truly conscientious objectors but not to military service *per se*, since they were prepared to drill on weekdays. We may compare them to the later Seventh-day Adventists, who, when drafted into the army, objected to drilling on their Saturday Sabbath. Members of this denomination, however, have usually maintained a noncombatant stance as 'conscientious cooperators' on the other days of the week (see essay 8 below). Channel Islands Methodists suffered repeated terms of imprisonment, ranging from several days to several weeks, until the intervention at the end of the century of influential Evangelicals in England led the government to order the island administrations to allow Methodist militiamen to perform their militia drill

exclusively on weekdays. See Matthieu Lelièvre, *Histoire du Méthodisme dans les Iles de la Manche* (Paris and London, 1885), chap. 5 ('Les exercises militaire du dimanche 1794–1799,' pp. 349–80).

10 Act of the *Etats* of Jersey, 18 October 1798: 'Chaque habitant capable de porter armes, doit son service personnel à la défense de son pays ... La sûreté de l'Île dépend essentiellement des forces de la milice, de sa bonne discipline et uniformité de service.' According to the act, anyone who persisted in refusing militia service would be expelled from the island and not allowed to return until he pledged his willingness to perform such service. See Lelièvre, *Histoire*, 367, 368. Asplet's exile was probably fairly brief: sources available to me give no details.

11 Quoted from the *Jersey Magazine* (January and March 1837) in Anthea Hall, 'History of the Quakers in Jersey,' *Société Jersiaise: 128th Annual Bulletin for 2003*, vol. 28, pt. 3, 383. Since Asplet was a committed freemason and membership of a freemasons' lodge was in that period not permitted by the Quaker discipline, one must presume he was not formally a member of the Society. Lists of Friends in Jersey at this time do not exist.

12 Katharine Fry and Rachel Elizabeth Cresswell, eds, *Memoirs of the Life of Elizabeth Fry, with Extracts from Her Journal and Letters* (2nd rev. edn, London, 1848; reprinted 1974, Montclair NJ), vol. 2, 121.

13 See *List of Members of the Society of Friends, Belonging to the Quarterly Meeting of Sussex, Surrey, Hants, &c.* (London, 1886). The names of attenders are not listed here: there were probably more attenders than formal members in the Jersey meeting.

14 Richard Binns (Reigate), letter to the editor entitled 'Military Persecution under British Law,' published both in the *Friend*, N.S., vol. 26, no. 307 (May 1886), 115, and the *British Friend*, vol. 44, no. 5 (May 1886), 107.

15 *Extracts from the Minutes and Proceedings of the Yearly of Friends Held in London ... 1887*, 90, 91.

16 Ibid., 92–6.

17 Hall, 'History,' 384.

18 The committee's report (page 96) states that 'several applications for exemption on the ground of conscientious objection' were recently made to the lieutenant-governor of Jersey, who had 'the power to grant exemptions from active service in the Militia, in special cases, other than those expressly provided for by the law.'

19 *Extracts ... 1887*, 91, 92. The sources available to me do not indicate to what religious denomination, if any, Edward Voisin belonged at the time of his boys' refusal of militia service. He may already have been attending Quaker meeting.

20 *List of Members ...* (1889), 18.

21 Binns, letter to the editor, *The Friend*, N.S., vol. 16, no. 190 (August 1876), 208. See also the brief article by 'D.O.' entitled 'Imprisonment for Refusing Military Training,' ibid., N.S., vol. 15, no. 174 (April 1875), 103.

22 *La Gazette Officielle de Guernesey*, vol. 88, no. 17 (27 February 1875). See also 'Livre en Crime (Crime Book),' N.S. vol. 42, fol. 38 (entry for 22 February 1875). The 'crime' was committed on 15 February. We may note the reference here to Thomas Quertier's earlier imprisonment as a militia objector before he joined the Society of Friends. (How many other such cases lie buried in the islands' archives and island press of the nineteenth century?) Quertier is listed as one of three Guernsey Quakers in *List of Members ...* (1874), 14.

23 *Extracts ... 1875*, 60–2; *Extracts ... 1876*, 59.

24 *Guernsey Advertiser* (24 May 1913), newspaper cutting in the Library of the Society of Friends, London, vol. QQ/69. In 1913 the Quaker meeting in Guernsey had thirteen members plus a few attenders, whereas the meeting in Jersey, the larger island, had only eleven members in that year.

8 When Seventh-day Adventists First Faced the Draft: Civil-War America

The church of the Seventh-day Adventists traced its origins back to the millenarium movement, led by William Miller (1782–1849), that had swept the northern United States during the early 1840s. When in 1844 the promised millennium failed to materialize, Miller was discredited. But his movement survived, though it remained a small denomination for some time: when the Civil War commenced, it numbered only some 3,500 members, with 125 congregations situated exclusively in the northern states. Prime responsibility for introducing the observance of Saturday as the Sabbath day of worship lay with a remarkable couple, Ellen and James White. From the mid-1850s the organ of the Seventh-day Adventists, the *Advent Review and Sabbath Herald*, began from time to time to print articles expressing a pacifist point of view. But it was only after the outbreak of the Civil War that, with the backing of at least Ellen White, the Adventists adopted pacifism as the official position of the church though with several leading members dissenting vigorously.[1]

Strongly antislavery and pro-Unionist, Seventh-day Adventists, when drafted for military service, could at first – such was then the law – pay a commutation fee of $300 in lieu of serving, despite the fact that the denomination was not as yet recognized officially as a peace sect, a status given from the outset of the war to Quakers, Mennonites and Amish, and Dunkers (later known as the Church of the Brethren). This recognition, however, Adventists gained potentially under the act of 24 February 1864; hopefully when Adventist draftees produced a certificate from their congregation stating that their church forbade participation in war, exemption would now be granted. As a result of the threat of conscription, 'many of our brethren,' James White, then editor of the *Review and Herald*, had written a little earlier, 'were greatly excited, and trembled at the prospect of a draft.'[2]

Discussion had begun in August 1862 in the *Review and Herald* with a leading article entitled 'The Nation,' written by White himself.[3] The article drew attention to the seeming contradiction between the Adventists' strongly antislavery position and the fact that until then they had stood aside from the war. But 'the requirements of war' conflicted with both the fourth commandment ('Remember the Sabbath day, to keep it holy') and the sixth ('Thou shalt not kill'). Nevertheless, White went on, if a brother were drafted, 'the government assumes the responsibility of the violation of the law of God, and it would be madness to resist.' Refusal to obey might end in the resister being shot by the military: this 'goes too far, we think, in taking the responsibility of suicide.'

Two points are worth pointing out in connection with White's arguments. In the first place, he gives prominence to the sabbatarian objection to military service that became of primary importance to the sect in the wars of the twentieth century. Once in the army, it was feared, the Seventh-day Adventist would not be allowed to observe Saturday as his day of rest and prayer. (Were he permitted to do so, and were this to become the only grounds of his objection, the reasons for refusing to serve would naturally disappear.) Secondly, White implied that the disproportionately heavy cost of a refusal to fight, together with his belief that any guilt involved in breaking God's laws rested on the shoulders of the government, made it inexpedient to resist the draft. In addition, the strength of the government's case in the midst of a struggle against 'the most hellish rebellion since that of Satan and his angels' was a factor to be taken into consideration in reaching a decision on how to act.

From August until the end of October, week after week, the controversy over White's article filled many columns of the *Review and Herald*, and a large amount of further correspondence remained unpublished. Leading brethren wrote in their opinions. The immediacy of the issue facing brethren of draft age gave an added urgency to the discussion which White's advocacy of compromise had generated. His views aroused the opposition, in particular, of a group of pacifist militants: 'those who have been most highly tinctured with the fanaticism growing out of extreme non-resistance,' wrote White, 'are generally the most clamorous against our article.' He had never given any encouragement to voluntary enlistment, he explained to his readers: Seventh-day Adventists 'would make poor soldiers, unless they first lost the spirit of truth.' His article was aimed primarily at checking the extreme antidraft position which had been growing among them.[4]

The general impression created by White's conclusions seems to have been one of confusion, and even of dismay among some brethren.[5] Brother White's views carried weight but, of course, did not have final authority among them. Besides, it was not quite clear from his article precisely what course he did advise drafted Adventists to take, although those who interpreted him as recommending submission even to the point of bearing arms would appear to have been correct. Tempers at times began to get frayed, so that we find one writer, R.F. Cottrell, commencing his contribution on 'Non-resistance' with the words: 'There is no necessity for brethren to go to war with each other on *peace principles*.' For him, 'the only question was whether it was [our] duty to decline serving in the army at all hazards, even of life itself. It is by no means certain that a man's life would be taken because he declined fighting for conscience sake.' If death were the only alternative to submission, however, he thought that he, too, would opt with Brother White for the latter, at least until God should grant further guidance.[6] For Brother Henry E. Carver, on the other hand, such conduct smacked of apostasy: 'untenable and dangerous ground,' he called it. Despite his abomination of the Southern slaveholders' rebellion, he had 'for years had a deeply-settled conviction (whether wrong or not) that under no circumstances was it justifiable in a follower of the Lamb to use carnal weapons to take the lives of his fellowmen.' If an act was wrong, should it not be shunned at all cost, even that of martyrdom? Surely the individual was not entitled to transfer to the government responsibility before God for his own actions?[7] J.M. Waggoner, a leading minister in Burlington (Michigan), was another brother who, though respectful towards White's views (while confessing himself rather startled by them at first), nevertheless supported the pacifist position. He opposed the idea of paying commutation money in lieu of personal service, preferring to 'trust in God for the consequences' of a refusal to fight. Exemption on such terms was 'not only doubtful in principle, but inefficient as a practical measure of relief. Not over one in one hundred, if as many, could avail themselves of its provisions, while the poor, the great mass of our brethren, whose consciences are as tender and as valuable as those of the rich, stand precisely where they would stand without it.' Thus it would create a rift in the brotherhood between the well-to-do minority and the rest.

Many contributors, however, expressed in varying degrees their approval of participation in the struggle that was being waged in their earthly homeland. There was the enthusiastic pro-war position of Joseph Clarke, who, pleading with the editor that Seventh-day Adventists should be allowed to become combatants, contributed two articles with the titles 'The War! The War!' and 'The Sword *vs.* Fanaticism.' He wanted 'to see treason receive its just deserts.' 'I have had my fancy full of Gideons and Jephthahs, and fighting Davids, and loyal Barzillais,' he writes; 'I have thought of brave Joshua, and the mighty men of war that arose to deliver the Israel of God, from time to time.' He had dreamed, his mind full of heroes of Old Testament times, of the day 'when a regiment of Sabbath-keepers would strike this rebellion a staggering blow.' He had only scorn for those many brethren who were 'whining lest they might be drafted.' Were not 'the military powers of earthly governments' instituted by God for our protection? Was not the time to refuse their summons when they were acting unrighteously, and not in the present crusade against Confederate wickedness?[8]

Several prominent ministers supported a pro-war position, though in more restrained terms than the excitable Clarke, who had evidently been deeply stirred by seeming parallels between the apocalyptic happenings related in scripture and the events of his own day. J.N. Loughborough, who had joined the Adventist movement back in the forties and was now among the most respected leaders of its sabbatarian wing, implied that even in an unjust cause the guilt lay with the state and not with the conscript, quoting as his authority John the Baptist's admonition to the Roman soldiers, instruments of an alien domination, to be content with their wages.[9]

Towards the end of the discussion, after he had published selected opinions both pro and con from the correspondence and articles which flowed in to him, James White restated his views on the attitude his church should adopt towards the coming draft. This was, in fact, not merely a restatement but a slight modification of the position taken in his 'Nation' article, although it was still not without considerable ambiguity. He reproved what he designated extreme points of view on either side: both those who wished to give unqualified support to the war effort and the brethren who called for unconditional nonresistance. 'We cannot see how God can be glorified by his loyal people taking up arms' was, however, his final summing up. If the whole nation had followed God's will, some other path than war would have been found to resolve the country's problems. Seventh-day Adventists he called upon to wage a war whose weapons were not carnal:

> We did say in case of a military draft, it would be madness to resist. And certainly, no true disciple of non-resistance would resist a military draft ... We have advised no man to go to war. We have struck at that fanaticism which grows out of extreme non-resistance, and have labored to lead our people to seek the Lord and trust in him for deliverance. How this can and will come, we have no light at present.[10]

And so the debate petered out in this way rather inconclusively. Behind the editorial desk of James White, however, we may detect the figure of his wife, the charismatic Ellen White. She had not participated in the discussions in the *Review and Herald*, perhaps because it would not have appeared seemly to the Brethren for a woman to do so. More important was the fact of Ellen White's prophetic role in the sect: a prophetess does not confide her utterances to the columns of a newspaper even when it is edited by her husband. Several months before the attack on Fort Sumter, Ellen White had had a vision of the coming bloody conflict between the states.[11] The war, when it came, she viewed as a judgment of God on wickedness on both sides; yet her intense hatred of slavery, offspring of the abolitionist connections of her circle in earlier days, aroused in her warm sympathy for the struggle being waged by the North. She was, then, no neutral. But, at the same time, she saw the end of kingdoms of this world at hand. 'Prophecy shows us that the great day of God is right upon us,' she wrote in 1863. God's people, her people, must – in spite of their hatred of the satanic iniquity of slavery – hold themselves apart from the armed struggle and wait quietly and peacefully for the second coming. After the indecisive debate in the *Review and Herald* that we have dealt with above, and before conscription actually touched any of the brethren directly, Ellen White, it seems, reached certainty on the stand that the brotherhood should collectively take in reply to the army's call whenever it should come. 'I was shown,' she wrote, 'that God's people, who are His peculiar treasure, cannot engage in this perplexing war, for it is opposed to every principle of their faith.' In the armed forces it would be impossible for them to follow the voice of conscience if, as would inevitably happen, the commands of the officers directed them otherwise. 'There would be a continual violation of conscience.' However, she went on to criticize those who had acted impetuously in proclaiming their willingness to suffer prison and death rather than submit to the draft. Instead, 'those who feel that in the fear of God they cannot conscientiously engage in this war, will be very quiet, and when interrogated will simply state what they are obliged to say in order to answer the inquirer.' They must make quite clear, too, their abhorrence of the rebellion.[12]

Thus the Seventh-day Adventists, even those who at first appeared to hesitate or rejected outright the pacifist viewpoint, closed their ranks. Through a human agency God had spoken, dissipating their doubts. True, there was little likelihood of universal peace ever being established among the nations of this world; but in the short space before the establishment of a new dispensation on earth, God's children, it was now clear, must refrain from shedding human blood and desecrating the Sabbath. To court martyrdom was wrong. To avoid martyrdom, on the other hand, action was needed; the government must be informed of the reasons for their refusal to bear arms, and advantage taken of the legal provision for exemption provided by successive federal conscription acts.

Although membership in a peace church was not a requirement of the act of March 1863, the act of February 1864 demanded such membership from applicants as a prerequisite for exemption as conscientious objectors. However, opting out of service still remained possible even after February for all those prepared to pay, although only enrolment as a conscientious objector brought the privilege either of having the commutation money devoted to humanitarian purposes or of choosing, as an alternative, the army medical service or work with freedmen. Content that, simply by paying, their scruples concerning the taking of human life and work on their Sabbath were not infringed, Seventh-day Adventists did not at first – even after February 1864 – insist on their recognition as a noncombatant denomination within the meaning of the act. Poorer members were helped out with the necessary money by the church as a whole, while some evidently accepted induction into the army, when drafted, hoping nevertheless to be able to take advantage of the recent act and be assigned noncombatant duties.[13] But on 4 July Congress passed an amending act which, although it did not alter in any way the provisions made in February for conscientious objectors, did abolish the general privilege of escaping military service through commutation.

The brotherhood, fearful that a mere letter of support from one of their congregations would not be sufficient, now became alarmed that their men, since they did not belong to a recognized nonresistant denomination, would be drafted into combatant service in the army, where they would find themselves forced to break both the fourth and the sixth commandments. As one of them wrote: 'Not having had a long existence as a distinct people, and our organization having but recently been perfected, our sentiments are not yet extensively known.' So it came about that on 2 August the three members of their general conference executive committee drew up a 'Statement of Principles' for presentation to the government of Michigan, in which state the church's headquarters at Battle Creek was located. There is no trace in the document, the first public statement of the group's noncombatancy, of any of the doubts or hesitations or divergencies in view that had revealed themselves only two years earlier in the debates in the *Review and Herald*. One of the three authors was, indeed, none other than J.N. Loughborough, who in those discussions had championed the case for full participation in the present contest. But now, according to the 'Statement,' the church was 'unanimous in their views' that war is contrary to Christian teachings; in fact, 'they have ever been conscientiously opposed to bearing arms.' For the performance of military duties, the 'Statement' went on, would prevent them from an exact observance of the fourth and the sixth commandments; neither would their Saturdays be free from labour nor their hands from the stain of blood. 'Our practice,' the authors continued, 'has uniformly been consistent with these principles. Hence our people have not felt free to enlist into the service. In none of our denominational publications have we advocated or encouraged the practice of bearing arms.'

Similar statements were presented soon afterwards to the governors of the other states where Seventh-day Adventists were to be found in any numbers: Wisconsin, Illinois, and Pennsylvania. The object of these approaches to the state authorities was to gain confirmation at the highest level locally – that is, in their home states where their views and practices ought to have been best known – that they were, in truth, a people whose principles forbade them to fight, who were therefore entitled to the exemption granted formally to several similar denominations in the act of the previous February. All but the governor of Illinois, who does not appear to have given an answer, replied that they believed that members of the church were, indeed, covered by the recent legislation. And even from Illinois a certain Colonel Thomas J. Turner could be quoted as having said that, in his view, the Seventh-day Adventists were 'as truly noncombatants as the Society of Friends.'

And so, armed with the 'Statement of Principles' of 2 August and the supporting letter of the governor of Michigan, which had been printed as a pamphlet under the title of *The Draft* together with several other documents, a leading minister, John N. Andrews, was sent from Battle Creek to Washington around the end of August to plead his church's claims to noncombatant status. In the capital Andrews had a friendly talk with the provost marshal general, Brigadier-General James B. Fry, who assured him that the act intended exemption to apply not merely to Quakers or members of the older peace sects but to all denominations whose members were precluded from bearing arms, and that he would issue orders to that effect. Andrews was further advised that, in addition to producing confirmation of membership in good standing and, preferably, too, of consistency of conduct from neighbours, conscripted Adventists should present a copy of *The Draft* to the district marshal 'as showing the position of our people.'[14]

Andrews had succeeded in his mission. Henceforward, until conscription ended, there was no major conflict between Seventh-day Adventists and the military authorities. But attempts to create a fund from which to pay the fines of poorer members (while this alternative was open) soon broke down – perhaps because the sect at that time did not possess enough well-to-do members to make this a practicable plan. Anyhow, we find most of their draftees entering the army and opting there for hospital or freedman work, according to the provisions of the February act. Trouble occasionally resulted, however, from unsympathetic officers attempting to make the men perform duties which went against their conscience. At the end of the war, at their third annual session in May 1865, the church once again confirmed its noncombatant stand. 'While we ... cheerfully render to Caesar the things which the Scriptures show to be his,' the conference stated, 'we are compelled to decline all participation in acts of war and bloodshed as being inconsistent with the duties enjoined upon us by our divine Master toward our enemies and toward all mankind.'

The noncombatancy which the Seventh-day Adventists had achieved, not without much soul-searching and spiritual travail, was a doctrine of multiple roots. In the first place, these Adventists shared with the other pacifist groups the belief that participation in war, the shedding of human blood for whatever cause, was contrary to the Christian faith. Loving one's enemies and killing them in battle seemed to them a contradiction impossible to resolve. The gospels forbade the use of any weapon but the sword of the spirit. Resist not evil, turn the other cheek – these were Christ's clear command. 'Could this scripture be obeyed on the battlefield?' asked a writer in the *Review and*

Herald.[15] Even here, however, the Adventists put much greater emphasis on the Old Testament commandment, 'Thou shalt not kill,' than most of the other peace sects of that day did. Moreover, in general, their discussions of the war issue and the draft were heavily interlaced not only with biblical citations but with fantastic interpretations of them based on prophecy. Secondly, refusal to bear arms stemmed in the case of these Adventists from a deeply ingrained otherworldiness, a desire for nonconformity to this world even more intensely felt than that which underlay, for instance, the pacifism of the Mennonites. What, indeed, had God's people to do with the fighting of this world that was about to be destroyed and replaced by another where they would come into their own? And, thirdly, we get the sabbatarian objection, an element that had basically nothing in common with pacifism. Unwillingness to risk the desecration of their Sabbath as a result of military orders was not, of course, their sole reason for refusing army service: Seventh-day Adventist conscientious objectors insisted on their status as nonresistants even after induction into the army. Still, especially among some of their leaders, the question of Sabbath keeping had figured prominently in their thought.

NOTES

1 For Seventh-day Adventists in the Civil War, see Roger Guion Davis, 'Conscientious Cooperators: The Seventh-day Adventists and Military Service, 1860–1945' (Ph.D. diss., George Washington University, 1970), chaps. 3 and 4; R.D. Graybill (who is critical of some of Davis's conclusions), 'This Perplexing War: Why Adventists Avoided Military Service in the Civil War,' *Insight* (Washington DC), 10 October 1978, 4–8; Peter Brock, *Freedom from Violence: Sectarian Nonresistance from the Middle Ages to the Great War* (Toronto, 1991), chap. 21; and George R. Knight, 'Adventism and Military Service: Individual Conscience in Ethical Tension,' in Theron F. Schlabach and Thomas T. Hughes, eds, *Proclaim Peace: Christian Pacifism from Unexpected Quarters* (Urbana and Chicago, 1997), 157–66, 169, 170.

2 *Advent Review and Sabbath Herald*, vol. 20, no. 20 (14 October 1862), 159.

3 Ibid., no. 11 (12 August 1862), 84. See also J.N. Loughborough, *Rise and Progress of the Seventh-day Adventists* (Battle Creek MI, 1892), 243, 244.

4 *Advent Review and Sabbath Herald*, vol. 20, no. 15 (9 September 1862), 118; no. 16 (16 September 1862), 124.

5 See, for example, ibid., no. 17 (23 September 1862), 136, for comments on

White's article sent in by readers. One puzzled Adventist, A.G. Carter, from Rubicon (Wisconsin), writes: 'I acknowledge that I am a right-out-and-out coward when I am required to go into the carnal war, and if the same law that was to be binding on us that was on the Jews, I would surely show my heels. See Deut. XX, 8. "And the officers shall speak further unto the people and say, What man is there that is fearful and faint-hearted, let him go and return unto his house, lest his brethren's heart faint as well as his heart." But let me have a place in that war whose weapons are not carnal, and I will stick as close as a brother.'

6 Ibid., no. 20 (14 October 1862), 158.

7 Ibid., no. 21 (21 October 1862), 166, 167.

8 Ibid., no. 17 (23 September 1862), 132–5.

9 Ibid., no. 18 (30 September 1862), 140.

10 Ibid., no. 11 (12 August 1862), 167.

11 Arthur Whitefield Spalding, *Origin and History of Seventh-day Adventists*, vol. 1 (Washington DC, 1961), 315, 316.

12 Mrs. E.G. White, *Testimonies for the Church*, 3rd edn, vol. 1 (Mountain View CA, n.d.), 356–8, 360–2.

13 See, for example, *Review and Herald*, vol. 24, no. 6 (5 July 1864), for reference to a brother who had been drafted and was then with the Unionist army in Virginia.

14 See Francis McLellan Wilcox, *Seventh-day Adventists in Time of War* (Washington DC, 1936), 58–62, 83, 84; also Spalding, *Origin and History*, vol. 1, 323, 324, 407; and Davis, 'Conscientious Cooperators,' 84–91. The Adventists published in pamphlet form two editions of their policy statement on the draft. They were printed in Battle Creek (Michigan) at the Steam Press of the Seventh-day Adventist Publishing Association.

15 Cited in Wilcox, *Seventh-day Adventists*, 38 (from an article in the *Review and Herald*, 7 March 1865, by George W. Amadon, one of the framers of the Statement of Principles of 2 August 1864).

9 Quaker Conscientious Objectors in Norway, 1814–1902

Norwegian Quakerism dates back to the latter years of the Napoleonic Wars and has persisted, with various ups and downs, to the present day – unlike the other Quaker societies on the European continent in France, Germany, and Denmark that all died out in the course of the nineteenth century. The chief reason for this collapse lay in the oppressive burden of universal military service that became increasingly oppressive during the age of *Realpolitik*. It is, therefore, worth examining how the small group of Friends managed to survive in conscriptionist Norway.

Its birthplace was not Norway itself but a prisoner-of-war ship in the English port of Chatham. Among the sailors from the Scandinavian countries fighting alongside Napoleon, who were interned on that ship, were some twenty Norwegians whom visiting Friends from a nearby Quaker Meeting had succeeded in converting to their faith. When these men returned home in 1814, they continued to worship together either in the seaport of Stavanger on the west coast of Norway or in Christiania (now Oslo), the capital. Though the Meeting in the capital died out, the one in Stavanger survived, despite initial birth-pains, and eventually expanded to other areas in the rural west of the country.

Before leaving England, Friends there had given each returnee a certificate, stating that its holder had indeed become a Quaker and that Quakers held a 'testimony' against war which precluded them 'for conscience sake' from bearing arms.[1] Back home, these Quaker converts faced fierce hostility from the state church. 'To be a Norwegian without being a Lutheran was impossible according to Norwegian law ... Until 1845 there was no legal means of canceling one's membership in the state church.'[2] Moreover, Norway's new constitution, which had been promulgated on the occasion of the country's being forcibly coupled henceforward in a union with Sweden instead of Denmark, specifically laid down that military service in defence of the country was one of the obligations of Norwegian citizenship. In 1818 the government was ready to exempt Quakers from this duty. They would be subject to certain restrictions, including exercise of the suffrage, but would not be required to bear arms. But the parliament (*Storting*) rejected this proposal, which the majority of members considered too liberal! Attempts to proselytize could be punished with banishment, and it was not until the passing of the Dissenter Law in 1845 that the organization of denominations outside the Evangelical Lutheran Church ceased to be illegal. Henceforward it became possible to leave the state church without joining another denomination, 'thus ending the requirement of mandatory church attendance.' But the struggle for religious freedom in Norway was by no means over: as Peder Eidberg correctly remarks, long after 1845 free church members (including the Quakers) remained 'second class citizens.'[3]

In these circumstances it is no wonder that Norwegian Quakerism at the beginning grew very slowly, if it grew at all. There were still only ten members of Stavanger Meeting in 1825, and that figure had dropped to nine a decade later.[4] Quakers, like other religious nonconformists, were subject to constant harrassment by church and state alike. Emigration to the New World proved one way out. There were a number of Quakers, for example, among those who sailed for the United States in 1825 on the *Restaurationen*. The search for religious freedom, along with a desire to exchange the dismal poverty of many Norwegian farmers, fishermen, and rural craftsmen, prompted a steady stream of emigration throughout the rest of the century and on into the next. Only the outbreak of the Great War brought this demographic movement to an end.

The survival of the Quaker community at Stavanger was due, in large part, to the talented leadership of Endre Dahl (1816–65) and Asbjørn Kloster (1826–76). Both men were firmly committed to their Society's peace testimony. They both knew English well, and their contacts with British Friends, whom they kept informed of conditions in Norway, brought rich dividends in the steady interest and support of the latter in their plight. British Friends were prepared to petition their government to intervene on behalf of the Norwegian Quakers and to memorialize the *Storting* 'on behalf of our brethren in religious profession within the Kingdom of Norway who are subject to persecution on account of their religious principles.'[5]

At first Norwegian Quakers do not seem to have clashed with the authorities over the draft, which consisted of an annual spell of military training for a period of five years.[6] There were indeed so few Quakers, and those few presumably in most cases not liable to be called up for the annual training. That alone can easily explain the situation. When one of the Kristiansand Quakers, Tønnes Johnson, a returnee from the prison ship in Chatham, applied to become a burgher of his town, he asked to be excused from the obligation, incumbent on others who achieved this status, of bearing arms if called upon to do so. The answer to his application was affirmative, but with the proviso that he must find a substitute if drafted.[7] In 1828 a sailor named Peder Osmundsen Gilje, presumably a Quaker though that is not absolutely certain, had refused on grounds of conscience to take the required oath or to muster when drafted for a stint of military service. In the upshot, he was only lightly punished for his failure to conform to the law.[8] There may have been a few more Quaker COs during this early period, but record of them seems to have been lost. In fact, it is not until 1845 that we hear of a CO who was indubitably a Quaker. This was Andreas Bryne from Stavanger, evidently a prosperous citizen since he was a burgher of that town and thus more likely to be drafted than most other Norwegian Quakers in town and country who did not enjoy burgher status. Called up for service, Bryne appeared at the muster in his civilian clothes and unarmed, except for his walking stick. For this misbehaviour, he was at once fined and then spent three days in the Stavanger town jail for refusing to pay the fine or find a substitute to take his place on the muster ground.[9]

The Dissenter Law of 1845 had explicitly stated that no one could be exempted from the draft on grounds of conscience (*ingen troesbekjendelse kan fritages fra værneplikten*): that would be to sanction a special privilege for one group in the community, a view that reflected the parliamentarian majority's egalitarian impulse. Of course, the Quakers continued to clash with the authorities over a number of issues besides the military draft: the official oath, for instance, and taxes for state schools or for the upkeep of the established church. These taxes proved extremely oppressive for Quakers and other dissenters. Indeed, throughout the century any of these issues could land a Quaker in jail! And, as Ernst Lapin points out with respect to the draft, for long 'there were no clear legal guidelines regarding how to treat conscientious objectors so that Friends' refusal to perform military service was considered to be simply insubordination. There continued to be quite a lot of difference in the ways various branches of the armed forces tackled the problem.'[10]

Such differences in approach emerged in the CO *cause célèbre* in 1848, the year of revolutions on the European continent. In that year a twenty-one-year-old up-country farm labourer (*søvant*) named Søren Olsen (1827–79) was called up for service in the Norwegian navy. He reported for service in Stavanger on 7 June but at once made clear he would not take part in any activity connected with killing. He was not to return home until near the end of that year. Back in his village in Rennesøy, he then sat down and wrote an account of his captivity. His memoir, which he entitled *A Testimony against War and Fighting*,[11] 'a small handwritten book of 59 pages,' first appeared in print only in 1998 – almost 120 years after its author's death. The manuscript had been gathering dust in the Stavanger municipal archives for many decades after its deposit there by the local Society of Friends. We now have access to a document which, whatever its constructional and other defects, reveals the mindset of a CO of that era, along with other documents that show the response of the Norwegian authorities to this unusual able-bodied rating (*matros*) as well as the reaction of the press to his startling actions.

The situation in Norway at this time was volatile. Though the country remained at peace, neighbouring Denmark was engaged in an armed struggle with Prussia over the two provinces of Schleswig and Holstein that continued off and on until mid-1850. It is little wonder that some Norwegian authorities took a dim view of COs. In March of that year, Endre Dahl had written to Asbjørn Kloster to tell him of the continued difficulties one of their members, Andreas Bryne, was having with the draft: he 'has several times been distrained on for refusing to bear arms. He appeared before the justice, a few days ago, when he was treated by the courtier very severely, and assailed with many scornful expressions.' Dahl agreed that, on the whole, 'the magistrates are favourably inclined towards us,' but 'there are individuals, who have great pleasure in stripping us, and in exercising the law.'[12] Bryne received scornful words; Olsen's fate was much harder. In fact, he was to suffer more severely than any other Norwegian CO in that century. Apart from the impact of the current international situation, the severity of his treatment was due in all likelihood to the fact that, a few years earlier, then sixteen-year-old Olsen, dreaming of a career on the sea, had taken an oath to serve king and country as a naval rating when occasion for this arose: here was an able-bodied seaman in the making. Therefore, writes Aarek, 'when he became a CO he was not only refusing military service; he also broke the oath he had taken earlier.'[13]

In addition, in 1848 Olsen had not yet joined the Society of Friends, though he now shared their beliefs and attended their worship. His connection with the Quakers, in fact, went back to his childhood.[14] One of his uncles belonged to the Society, while Asbjørn Kloster was a friend of his family. Before sailing from Stavanger – by easy stages – to the naval depot at Fredriksvern, the captain had allowed Olsen to go on shore. Thus given the opportunity to visit Friends there, Olsen had asked them for a letter of support that he could use in the trials that he knew lay ahead. Quakers in Stavanger had indeed no difficulty in supplying the conscript sailor with a 'certificate,' signed by Elias Tastad, confirming that Olsen's refusal to bear arms was the result of religious conviction. The young man's claim to be a Quaker in all but name was quite genuine. 'He is a man of good character, honest and well-intentioned. In recent years he has been convinced [of the Truth] by the light of Christ's spirit in his soul.'[15] Like his coreligionists he was a good citizen, ready to obey the law of his country when this did not conflict with his conscience. Olsen, we may note, seems to have been afflicted by a sense of his own unworthiness: a feeling that may have inhibited him from applying for membership in the Society.

Arrived in Fredriksvern, the young man managed to send a letter to his friends, the Stavanger Quakers, reporting on the course of his life since he had left them. He wrote:

> In a tender and living love, I think of you, Friends, and always remember you. We arrived at Horten on the 14th inst.; and when I, for conscience sake, refused to work in any thing appertaining to war, I was put in prison after being subjected to many examinations, and expected to have been beaten. On the 18th, I was removed to this place, and have been again examined, and am expecting some further punishment. I will therefore be patient, though I often feel something that is evil passing through my mind, and am scarcely able to be as watchful as I ought. I have nothing to glory in but weakness and infirmities: the Lord is my confidence and my comfort in tribulation.[16]

At Fredriksvern Olsen's interrogators were indeed formidable. The farm labourer, with little or no book learning,[17] had now to face the counsel for the prosecution (called in Norwegian the *aktor*). Exactly why did he refuse service? the latter had asked him.

> I answered that it was because of my conscience that I refused to serve. I did not feel free to assault a fellow human being; and if I were to do this against my conviction, I believed I would experience a continuing uneasiness in my conscience ... I told him I believed it was right to obey the king and the government so long as they behaved in consonance with God's law. But in case of a conflict between the two, I believed it was right to obey God rather than men. The counsel then asked me whether in peacetime I could not bear arms [om jeg kunde gaae med til orlogs i fredstider] just as an exercise. To that I at once answered, 'No' because I felt exercising in this way to be more or less the same as the thing itself.[18]

Throughout the hearings, Olsen always made his religious affiliation clear: he shared Quaker principles but was not an actual member of the Society of Friends. His captors seem to have respected him for his sincerity; and they treated him as if he was a Quaker. Nevertheless, the naval courtmartial (*Sømilitaire Ret*) at Fredriksvern did not feel competent to hand down a lighter sentence than the one laid down by the law as proper in such cases. While recommending 'mercy,' the sentence was that Olsen should receive twenty-seven lashes of the cat-o'-nine-tails on three successive days: a penalty that, without exaggeration, Olsen described as likely to permanently cripple a man if he was fortunate enough to survive![19] Still, the sentence had to be approved by the Supreme Court, and meanwhile Stavanger Friends had been busy in enlisting the help of British Quakers in getting Olsen's harsh sentence reduced or perhaps gaining an amnesty for him as a prisoner of conscience. Waiting for the final outcome in his prison cell ('a very uncomfortable room' was how one observer described it) was a trying ordeal. 'I often feel,' Olsen admitted in a letter to his Stavanger friends, 'that impatience is ready to break in upon me; but the Lord be praised, who, up to this time, has preserved me, and I do find it an excellent thing, when the distress of my heart is made to burst forth before the Lord.'[20]

Matters indeed moved slowly: it was no wonder that the young man grew impatient. Meanwhile, a second case of Quaker conscientious objection in Norway had come to light. We know little of this CO, who was a recent convert to Quakerism, beyond his name, Torbjørn Thorsen Hæggem, and the fact that, after being jailed for fifteen days in his home province of Hjelmeland, he was freed.[21]

Olsen's conscript troubles were finally ended when, on 19 November, he was released from prison and soon on his way home. The Norwegian-Swedish bureaucracy, like other bureaucracies, worked slowly. In mid-August British Quakers had drawn up a petition on behalf of Olsen and Hæggem, which was presented to the Swedish ambassador in London by two weighty Friends, Samuel Gurney (brother of the famous prison reformer Elizabeth Fry) and George Stacey, clerk of London Yearly Meeting. The two men 'were kindly received,'[22] and their intervention had its effect. Two months later Olsen's sentence was commuted, on the King of Sweden's recommendation and with the earlier sanction of the Supreme Court (*Høyesterett*), from one of flogging to ten days' solitary confinement on bread and water.[23] Olsen's friends reported, even 'after twenty weeks' imprisonment, the last ten days on water and bread [, he] looked happy and healthy.'[24] Back at home, Olsen received a letter from the naval authorities at Fredriksvern telling him he owed them money for board and lodging while under arrest in their lock-up. In reply, Olsen informed them in forthright fashion that he had neither the means to pay nor any intention of doing so if ever he acquired the means. He heard no more after that.[25]

For half a decade after 1848 there do not seem to have been any COs in Norway. But drafting of Quakers of military age begins again in 1854. From mid-century on, Norwegian Friends were to be visited by a series of vigorous and articulate British and American Quaker ministers, all of the evangelical persuasion. These men and women went from one rural meeting to another preaching and gathering in converts from the churchless seekers who abounded along the fjords and in the remote mountain valleys from Stavanger northwards and westwards. The testimony 'against war and fighting' figured prominently in the message they conveyed, usually perforce through interpreters from the Norwegian Quaker community. Among the most active in this work (to mention just a few names) were James Backhouse, Joseph Buckley, and Sarah Ann and Robert Doeg from Britain, and Lindley Murray Hoag, Sybil and Eli Jones, and Alice and John F. Hanson from the United States.[26] The last named was of Norwegian origin and knew his parents' language well. During the 1850s and 1860s these activities generated something like a religious awakening. Membership in Norway's Society of Friends rose from 41 in 1845, reaching a peak of 166 in 1865. But by 1881 the number had fallen to 149. Endre Dahl was forced to admit that was not very 'encouraging.'[27] A major cause of this rather depressing situation was the continuous emigration across the Atlantic draining off a large number of potential members.

Even the intrepid Søren Olsen left Norway for Marshall County, Iowa, in 1854, together with most of his family. There he finally joined the Society, where he became a pillar of the only Norwegian-speaking Quaker meeting in the United States in LeGrand, Iowa. Several other jailed COs followed his example. They were still liable to the draft in their native land; they probably felt they had already borne sufficient witness to Truth as they saw it and there was no need to suffer further. And they probably wished, too, to rear their sons in a society free from the burden of military conscription (even during the Civil War years there was provision for the exemption of religious COs). But some decided to stay and face the consequences. We know the names of twenty Quaker COs between 1854 and 1874, together with the length of their sentence(s) and where they were incarcerated. Then there was a twenty-two-year gap with no record of any Quaker COs drafted: a rather mysterious hiatus. The list of draftees begins again in 1896.[28] While occasionally a CO might receive only a fine, several were jailed more than once.[29] Two were released without further ado by sympathetic officers who were assigned to deal with their cases, but this was exceptional treatment. Even when officers were friendly, they mostly felt they were not authorized to relax the law, which prescribed a prison sentence for this type of offence. Sentences ranged from five days to six months, thirty to forty days being usual. They were almost always served either in the castle at Bergen, which had been converted into a prison, or in the town jails in Stavanger or Kristiansand.

Is it possible, even though none of these men left a memoir such as Søren Olsen composed, to penetrate beyond the impersonality of a list and discover what their CO experience meant to them and to the religious fellowship to which they belonged? Several sources are indeed available that can shed light here, though inevitably much remains in shadow. Chief of these are the observations of visiting Quaker ministers like Joseph Buckley and James Backhouse and finally John F. Hanson.

Backhouse, an amateur botanist of distinction, had himself as a young man been a CO; he was balloted for the militia in 1831, which was the last time military conscription took place in Great Britain until it was reimposed in 1916. Backhouse had refused either to muster in his own person or to hire a substitute, which was then open to the non-conscientious as to the conscientious draftee. The authorities thereupon hired a substitute on his behalf and charged him six pounds, seven shillings, and six pence to cover the cost and, upon Backhouse's failing to pay – on grounds of conscience – levied a distress on his property; 'a spring clock was taken' from his home. Though Backhouse told the authorities he believed there were – hopefully many – Christians in the armed forces, it was clear how he thought a Quaker at any rate should react if called upon to bear arms.[30]

In 1860, during his last visit to Norway, he noted in his 'Journal' as he travelled up-country: 'we were greeted by one of our young friends, who had lately been a prisoner of the Lord at Bergen, where he was incarcerated for three weeks for maintaining his allegiance to the Prince of Peace, by refusing military service.'[31] Backhouse continued his journey along rough tracks where only ponies could make it through the thick snow on the passes to and from the Quaker-inhabited valley of Røldal (it was June!). At one point, he relates, the Quaker party was joined by some soldiers returning home on leave:

> The men of peace, and these men of war, travelled very quietly together; and some of the former used the opportunity of calling the attention of the latter to the nonconformity of their profession to the peaceable principles of the Gospel of Christ, the Prince of Peace. It was a subject they had thought very little about. They had considered active obedience to the Government a matter of necessity, though it was against their inclination. The precepts of the King of Kings overriding the commands of earthly 'powers that be' did not seem to have entered their minds; but might, with the information they received, at least explain to them the grounds of the refusal of two other Røldal neighbours to bear arms and their imprisonment for so doing.[32]

Let us turn now to the memoirs of Joseph Buckley, who visited Norway in 1856 and again a decade later in 1866. Like Backhouse, this sedate Quaker businessman from the English Midlands was impressed by the magnificent mountain scenery amidst which the overwhelming majority of Norway's Quakers lived. 'The situation is one of surpassing beauty,' he remarks on one occasion. Of Søvde he writes: 'The views were extensive and exquisitely beautiful.'[33] He was equally impressed by the poverty of most members and attenders at rural Quaker meetings: these crofters and fishermen lived extremely simply – and also happily, it would seem – even though they lacked most of the civilized amenities which the citizens of Buckley's home town of Manchester enjoyed. When in 1856 he planned a visit to an isolated

Quaker community up-country, he had to travel first by boat along the fjord. Disembarking, 'we ... walked some distance over a wild, stony sort of moorland to Stagland, to the residence of Søren Stakland, where we were heartily welcomed by the family. They live in a snug farmhouse ... with an air of cheerfulness about the whole.' Stakland's son, Elias, who had spent thirty days in Bergen castle the previous year, had recently been drafted again. 'He was taken to Bergen, where he was delivered as a prisoner.' However, this time he was more fortunate. After waiting several hours, 'a man, high in authority, came to inform him that he might return to his home on condition that he would promise to surrender himself a State prisoner when requested.' With typical Quaker scrupulosity the young man, when he gave his promise, added the proviso, 'life and health permitting.'[34]

It is from Buckley's memoirs that we learn about non-Quakers in the Røldal valley who objected to bearing arms. One of them was Jon Øen, a seeker, whose incarceration in Bergen castle in 1857 coincided with Elias Stakland's. 'But they were not allowed any intercourse with each other, except a few minutes before J.O. entered his cell.' When the latter returned home, Endre Dahl had reported that 'he looked pale, and was not in good health, but was enjoying that peace which the world can neither give nor take away.'[35] Whether the pacifism of these groups of seekers in Røldal and elsewhere was spontaneously generated or not is difficult to discover. But some influence of Quakers living in the same area is likely.

In 1856 Sarah Ann Doeg, who, like Buckley, was visiting Røldal with her husband, Robert, made the following entry in her diary about their return journey:

> Off again next morning very early, as we stood waiting for the boat, my mind was drawn in sympathy and love to a youth who had come with us, in obedience to the powers that be, summoned to prepare for service as a soldier. One of our company asked him if he would be a man's soldier, or a soldier of Jesus Christ? He turned away and wept. I endeavoured to encourage him to be faithful to his God and not to fear man. (This young man afterwards cheerfully endured imprisonment in Bergen castle for not serving.)[36]

The entry is tantalizing, since Sarah Ann Doeg does not name the young man who wept and then decided to become a CO. I do not think it can be Jan Øen unless his incarceration in Bergen castle next year was his second experience of prison. While clearly the young man was not a Quaker, for a Norwegian Quaker would never have consented to be drafted, he very likely came from a home background that was familiar with Friends' peace testimony, that is, from one of the groups of seekers in the Røldal valley.

When Buckley returned to Norway in 1866, he took up his previous concern for the Society's COs, although his main focus of course was on visitation and missionizing. At the outset, in mid-June, he attended Yearly Meeting in Stavanger, which he noted was well attended. Later he was to declare that he felt very much at home 'among this simple, earnest people.' At the Yearly Meeting he learnt of two young Quakers currently in jail 'for refusing to bear arms': one for six months in Kristiansand and the other for thirty-five days in Bergen castle. On 12 July, in the course of his travelling ministry and accompanied by Endre Dahl, who acted as his interpreter, Buckley finally reached Bergen. The record of his visit begins:

> It rains heavily. Bergen is said to have 200 rainy days in a year. We have been to the castle, where we were courteously permitted to visit the prisoner, Jon Rinden, jun., of Botn, in Røldal, who refused to take up arms. He has been ordered to this place to give his reasons for not complying with a request to learn the art of war. He attended the order, came to Bergen and appeared before the officials, who heard his reasons, and then committed him to prison, deferring further judgment until Government Commissioners had been communicated with. The cell in which he is confined is on the first floor. It is small, and the window is boarded up; about one foot being left for light and ventilation. The furniture consists of a bed, a table, a chair, and a stove.[37] There was also a can of water, and a small bread basket. I think a New Testament was on the table. The young man, who is twenty-five years of age, is comely of person, with calm animation resting in his countenance. He spoke cheerfully and seemed resigned, whilst he felt his situation.

On the vessel taking Buckley and Dahl back to Stavanger, it chanced that one of the twelve government commissioners, whose task it was to take the final decision how to treat a CO, was their fellow passenger. Dahl had a lengthy conversation with him. The commissioner

> stated that the law is laid down very strictly against such persons; thirty days' close imprisonment, with bread and water for the first refusal, and

every refusal to increase in number of days. He said that they were so impressed with the sincerity of Friends, and that they conscientiously object to serve, that they deal as leniently as possible in their cases, shortening the time of confinement as far as they think prudent.

This was in fact the procedure adopted in the case of Jon Rinden, who was released from prison after fifteen days. For eleven of those days, he had been forced 'to be present on the training ground where soldiers are exercised in the art of warfare': presumably with the aim of intimidating the refractory conscript so as to make him willing to handle a weapon, though no violence was used for this purpose. Before his departure from Norway, Buckley saw the young man again: 'he looks cheerful and well,' he reported.[38]

The threat of exile had always existed as an ultimate sanction against Norway's dissenters. But it was not used against Quaker COs – until the end of the 1860s. In April 1870 London Meeting for Sufferings received a letter from Endre Dahl on behalf of Norwegian Friends. 'Two young men,' he wrote, 'have been suffering (the one two months,' the other five and a quarter months') imprisonment and solitary confinement during last year in Christiansand for refusing military service and were set at liberty on condition of promising to leave the country, or else they would, according to the military laws, be liable to imprisonment so long as they should continue to refuse military service.'[39] Martin Nag has been able to identify the two men as Søren Thorsen Skjørestad and Peder Andreas Tou from Strand. Tou at any rate emigrated to America in 1870.[40]

The comment of the leading historian of conscientious objection in Norway is well taken: even the harshest punishment imposed on a Norwegian CO during the nineteenth century was, he writes, 'not much by later standards.' Sentences, we have seen, were usually short, at most six months.[41] True, objectors might be drafted and punished more than once for what was virtually the same offence, but this was fairly rare. Many COs were placed in solitary confinement, for most if not all of their sentence, and this was often accompanied by a bread-and-water diet. True, too, that was unpleasant. But peasant lads were used at home to a spartan life. At first conscientious objectors had been drawn almost exclusively either from the Quaker community or from isolated individuals who shared Quaker principles.[42]

From the last part of the 1880s there began, however, to appear objectors not connected with the Quakers. Most of them belonged to other small dissenter groups ... but there [were] also a couple of cases where the motivation was not specifically religious. Thus the number of objectors rose, particularly after 1895, but it was still very small: in the 1890s there were 7–8 objectors a year on the average, and we know about only 44 objectors during the last fifteen years of the 19th century.[43]

One of the main concerns of the newly emergent peace movement soon became the legalization of conscientious objection, whether on religious or nonreligious grounds. Peace societies had been established in major urban centres in the mid-1890s, with a central office in Christiania. Articles on the subject of conscientious objection now began to appear in the Norwegian Peace Society's paper, as well as in the press generally, and the matter was raised in the Norwegian parliament, and the Swedish parliament as well. Tønnes Sandstøl, who, along with another Christian pacifist Nikolai Julius Sørensen, led the Norwegian peace movement in this period, was an attender at Quaker meetings in Stavanger, where he taught school. Though he never formally joined the Society of Friends, he was a Quaker in all but name. As in England, Quakers in Norway participated in the work of the Peace Society out of proportion to their numerical strength in the country.[44]

Once again a handful of young Quakers were being jailed for refusing to bear arms when drafted for a spell of service. One of them was Søren Stakland, son of the five-times jailed Elias Stakland, who had resisted the impulse to emigrate. Stakland junior spent 120 days 'behind bars' between 1896 and 1898: his case got publicity in the press. Though his time in prison must indubitably have been an ordeal, Søren Stakland knew he was no longer virtually alone in his resistance to the military machine, as his father and the other Quaker COs had been a quarter of a century or so earlier. That perception may have been an important factor in stemming emigration and in the re-emergence of conscientious objection among Norwegian Quakers noted above. Indeed, imprisoning a Quaker for following his conscience did not go down very well in *fin-de-siècle* Norway.

Stavanger Friends kept London Yearly Meeting informed on all such matters. On 6 July 1899, for instance, the Continental Committee of its executive body, the Meeting for Sufferings, recorded in its minutes:

> By a letter from P. Fugellie [a Norwegian Friend] we learn that, to go to learn military exercises in Norway, one young Friend is now in prison for 50 days, this being the fourth time he has thus suffered;[45] that another, who has several times been thus imprisoned, has been summoned again;

> another is in prison, and three others are being tried by the courts for refusing military service. Walter Morice [a member of the Continental Committee] is encouraged to send some notice of these circumstances to some of the [British] periodicals.

And next year we find the following minute entered on 5 July 1900:

> During [this year's] Yearly Meeting much interest was felt and expressed on behalf of young men imprisoned in Norway for refusing to bear arms. A committee was appointed to send letters of encouragement to them, and also to endeavour to interest the King of Norway and Sweden on their behalf. One of these young men is a Friend who has already been in prison several times on this occasion.[46]

Clearly British Friends' concern extended not only to their coreligionists in Norway but to all 'who, whether connected with our Society or not, are now suffering for conscience' sake on account of their refusal of compulsory military service.'[47] They were aware that, 'as the younger people often emigrate to avoid military service, the number of Friends [in Norway] is steadily decreasing.'[48] They also knew that they were dealing here with an issue that now transcended the restricted boundaries of their denominational life; it was a question of religious freedom. And their view was shared by Quakers in Norway.

Successive military laws passed by the *Storting* in 1854, 1866, 1876, and 1885 had contained no provision for conscientious objection. In the 1890s the Norwegian peace movement called ever more insistently for a change in the law that would allow civilian work for COs in place of military service. In 1898 a crisis situation emerged for Friends when the clerk of Norway Yearly Meeting, Thorstein Bryne, informed the authorities that his Society would no longer supply the names of members liable for the draft as by law it was obligated to do. After a fine was twice imposed for failure to report names of potential Quaker conscripts, Friends decided to relinquish their status as a legally recognized religious denomination since, as they stated, 'this duty Friends considered contrary to their testimony against the military system.' And it was not until the 1930s that the Society regained official recognition. As a Quaker CO from Flekkefjord, Oluf Nilsen Tjersland, declared: 'I cannot understand what advantage the state can have from putting us in prison because we cannot for conscience' sake perform military service.' Their imprisonment, he went on, cost the state money, whereas, if COs were permitted to work at a civilian job, they would be able at no cost to the state to contribute to society's well-being.[49]

Two bills drafted around this time by Sørensen proposing the exemption of genuine COs, who would henceforward be allowed to perform civilian work, were defeated in the *Storting*. But on 6 August 1900 the Department of Defence, evidently realizing that jailing such men added nothing to the military strength of the country, issued a circular (no. 29) recommending that the army employ conscripts who objected to handling weapons solely on noncombatant duties. Among such duties it listed work in the kitchens or workshops, or as medical orderlies or in the transport section. But, of course, though this might satisfy some consciences, Quakers certainly rejected a compromise of this kind. As London Friends explained to the Norwegian Home Department:

> The transfer of conscripts permitted by the regulations in Circular No. 29 is not a real relief from military service, inasmuch as the conscripts set to work as cooks, handworkers, and in transport or hospital work would still be doing what are essential parts of the military system ... The Society of Friends in Stavanger ... inform us that ... they see little difference between a man being employed to transport army stores, including ammunition, or otherwise serving the soldiers with food, horses, &c., and the actual use of the horses or ammunition against an enemy. They also point out that men employed in the services named as non-combatant will be in military clothing, under military command, and thus will form an integral part of the system of warfare, in which they feel themselves forbidden to take part by the spirit and teaching of the New Testament.[50]

A further matter bothered Quakers, in Norway as well as abroad. Circular 29, since it granted noncombatant status only to members of a religious denomination which forbade its members to participate in war, appeared in practice to restrict CO exemption to Quakers. Apart from nonreligious objectors, who, we have seen, were growing in numbers, none of the small non-Quaker denominations which supplied the majority of objectors at this time required members to refuse to bear arms. Although most members might take this position, pacifism was not a fixed tenet of the sect. As London Friends explained: 'We think that no other religious sect in Norway expressly forbids its members to be soldiers. But there are not a few individuals, both in other sects and in the Lutheran Church, who have as strong and real conviction of the unlawfulness of all war as our Society has, who ... in some cases have suffered the shame and loss caused by imprisonment on account of their faithfulness to that conviction,' while many more, as had happened with Friends, sought relief by emigrating to a land free of the burden of conscription.[51] Among these near-pacifist denominations were the indigenous Assembly of God (*Kristi Menighed*) and the Free Friends (*Frie Venner*), located in the far north, as well as imported sects like the Seventh-day Adventists, the Pentecostals, and the Salvation Army.

At the outset of the new century, the campaign to legalize conscientious objection in Norway was stepped up. Partial success came when, on 18 February 1902, the army issued a circular exempting all religious objectors from the draft (*Kommanderende Generals Cirkulære nr. 1*), an ordinance that had the force of law though not formally a legislative act. True, the struggle continued for a further two decades until nonreligious objectors were covered by the same blanket exemption as religious COs. But henceforward Quakers and COs from other religious denominations remained untroubled by the military question. They just stayed home instead of being lodged in a jail or finding refuge on an emigrant ship. Since no plan to set up a scheme of alternative civilian service was envisaged in the circular,[52] an old problem facing Quaker COs did not arise, namely whether they should accept an alternative in lieu of bearing arms or stand out for unconditional exemption.[53]

In May 1900 London Yearly Meeting had sent a Memorial to King Oscar II: it was polite but firm, and it included non-Quakers among the list of imprisoned COs appended to the Memorial. This document stressed, too, that the issue involved 'the great principle of religious tolerance in Norway.' London Friends asked the king 'respectfully' to help to set these men free; 'although they cannot serve their country in the army, they will yet make good and faithful citizens, whose example will tend to the highest welfare of the nation.' It was not right to treat them 'as criminals' for following what Quakers believed was 'the teaching of our Lord Jesus Christ.'[54] Though two weighty Friends, John Bellows and Edmund Wright Brooks, took the Memorial to Sweden to deliver to the king, they were not successful in presenting it to him themselves. 'The king declined to grant a personal interview on the ground that [the two] Friends were not his subjects.' So the Memorial had to be 'handed to an officer on the King's yacht.' However, Brooks assured London Friends, there was 'every reason to believe that it was placed in the King's hands.'[55] The two Quaker emissaries also succeeded in getting a sympathetic deputy (Jakob Byström) to insert the Memorial in the printed proceedings of the Second Chamber of the Swedish parliament early in 1901.[56]

It was understandable that King Oscar had felt he could not intervene as London Friends wished he would do; after all, Sweden was a constitutional monarchy. Eventually, in September, John Morland, clerk of London Yearly Meeting, received a brief note from the chargé d'affaires at the Swedish-Norwegian legation informing him that the king had received the Quakers' Memorial 'in favour of certain Norwegian subjects.' However, 'neither the King nor His Norwegian Government feel able to intervene in the present case, as sentence has been passed according to the law.'[57]

So it was left, in the end, for the army authorities in Norway to find a practical solution to a problem that was more a matter of religious freedom than a military question. It is doubtful, though, if they would have felt obliged to seek a solution if Quakers at home and abroad and the Norwegian peace movement, largely inspired by Quaker ideals of peace, had not exerted continuous pressure in this direction.[58] For more than half a century, young Quakers, backed by the older members of the Society of Friends, had consistently chosen either to face the possibility of repeated imprisonment or to emigrate to a distant land. It was the behaviour of this tiny group of religious dissenters that in Norway provided a role model during the 1890s and early 1900s for the campaign to legalize conscientious objection in the case of all who genuinely took that stand.

NOTES

1 Quoted in my monograph *The Quaker Peace Testimony 1660 to 1914* (York UK, 1990), 237. Chapter 21 of that book, entitled 'Norwegian Quakers, Conscription, and Emigration,' surveys the development of the pacifist movement in Norway and the situation of both religious and secular COs in that country to 1914.

2 Peder A. Eidberg, 'Norwegian Free Churches and Religious Liberty,' *Journal of State and Church*, vol. 37, no. 4 (Autumn 1995), 871.

3 Ibid., 871–3, 876–8.

4 John Ormerod Greenwood, *Quaker Encounters*, vol. 2: *Vines on the Mountains* (York, 1977), 181.

5 Ibid., 182.
6 Andreas Seierstad, *Kyrkjelegt Reformarbeid i Norig i nittande hundreaaret*, vol. 1 (Bergen, 1923), 242. See Ørnulf Nåvik, *Vernepliktens Historie 950–1996*, 2nd edn. (Oslo, 1997), 104, 120, 122, 123, for information about conscription legislation in Norway during the nineteenth century.
7 Anne Emilie Jansen, *Det norske kvekersamfunns historie i förste halvdel av det 19. hundreåret* (Stavanger, 1967), 51.
8 Seierstad, *Kyrkjelegt Reformarbeid*, 240, 241.
9 Ernst Lapin, *Vennenes Samfunn Kvekerne 1846–1848* (Stavanger, 1999), 158.
10 Ibid., 155.
11 Søren Olsen, *Et lidet Viidnesbyrd mod Krig og Fægtning*, ed. Hans Eirik Aarek (Stavanger, 1998). Olsen's memoir is printed on pages 31–53. Aarek, together with lengthy introductory and concluding sections, has also printed a number of official and private documents relating to Olsen's case, and the texts of contemporary press articles which deal with the case. Especially valuable is his overview of conscientious objection in Norway from 1814 to the 1980s ('Oversikt over militærnektingens historie i Norge,' 17–22). The English translation of the memoir's title given by Aarek is excellent, but it omits the second word of the Norwegian original: the archaic adjective *lidet*, that is, 'suffering.' In his insertion of this word, Olsen is obviously in tune with Quaker usage from the seventeenth century on.
12 George Richardson, *The Rise and Progress of the Society of Friends in Norway* (London, 1849), 115.
13 Aarek in Olsen, *Et lidet Viidnesbyrd*, 18.
14 Ibid., 55–63.
15 Ibid., 56.
16 Richardson, *Rise*, 120. The letter, given in English translation, is dated 28 June 1848.
17 Citation about Olsen from a letter from a Norwegian Quaker: 'He ... has had scarcely any school learning (but what he has acquired since he grew up)' (ibid.).
18 Olsen, *Et lidet Viidnesbyrd*, 42.
19 Ibid., 46: 'det er næsten livsstraf,' he told his parents.
20 Richardson, *Rise*, 120, 121. Letter dated 2 July 1848.
21 Aarek in Olsen, *Et lidet Viidnesbyrd*, 58, 95, 107, 116. Aarek notes that there were several more (probably Quaker) COs at this time from Rogaland who were jailed in Kristiansand, but their names are not known.
22 Minutes of the Continental Committee of the Meeting for Sufferings of the Yearly Meeting of the Society of Friends, London (MS. in the Library of the

Religious Society of Friends), exercise book 1, 5 September 1848, fols. 60, 62. Aarek, in Olsen, *Et lidet Viidnesbyrd*, 87, gives brief biographical data concerning the four Friends who drew up the petition in their capacity of members of the Continental Committee.

23 Aarek, ibid., 79, 107.

24 Richardson, *Rise*, 121.

25 Aarek, in Olsen, *Et lidet Viidnesbyrd*, 53.

26 Greenwood, *Quaker Encounters*, vol. II, 184–95.

27 *Extracts from the Minutes and Proceedings of the Yearly Meeting of Friends held in London ... 1861*, 42, 43; *1865*, 45; *1866*, 30; *1881*, 53.

28 The basic list was compiled by the visiting American Quaker minister John Frederick Hanson. It was printed first anonymously in Norwegian in *Vennen*, vol. 1, no. 4 (April 1901), 51, and then reprinted over three-quarters of a century later in Hanson's *Skitser fra Vennernes Samfunds Historie fram Vennen 1900–1902* (Ås, 1978), 11; it also appeared in his *Light and Shade in the Land of the Midnight Sun* (Oskaloosa IA, 1903), 84–7. Lapin, *Vennenes Samfunn*, 156, table 48, includes all the names assembled by Hanson and adds two more (Iver Olsen Sætre [1865] and Carl Røiseland [1866]). In *Vennen*, vol. 1, no. 4 (April 1901), 57, Hanson attributes the gap in Quaker CO cases between 1874 and 1896 to the emigration to America of young Friends before they became liable to the draft. He writes: 'They did not see any point in sitting in prison in their homeland.' I am not completely satisfied by this explanation since the situation for Norwegian COs during these two decades did not differ essentially from the one prevailing during the two previous decades. Certainly emigration may have radically reduced the number of COs but scarcely accounts for their total absence during the latter period.

29 Between 1855 and 1859 Elias Stakland received five prison sentences, and Gudmund I. Erland five between 1861 and 1866 (with a fine for 1865).

30 See Sarah Backhouse, *Memoir of James Backhouse by His Sister* (York and London, 1870), 43–5.

31 Ibid., 207, 208 (15 June 1860). The young Friend was probably Elias S. Stakland.

32 Ibid., 208, 209. It is difficult to identify the Røldal COs referred to here. For details about two Quaker COs from this area, John Olsen Botn/Øyna and John Johnsen Botn/Rinden, see Martin Nag, *Et lysende sted: Røldal-kvekerne, myte og virkelighet* (Stavanger, 1994), 45.

33 *Memoirs of Joseph Buckley: Edited by His Daughter* (Glasgow and London, 1874), 503, 250.

34 Ibid., 254, 255. See also 276, 277. Elias Strakland was subsequently jailed four times for draft refusal, each time in Bergen castle.

35 Ibid., 282, 283; Greenwood, *Quaker Encounters*, vol. 2, 192, 193.

36 Hanson, *Light and Shade*, 159.

37 Lodging for Quaker COs in Bergen castle had certainly improved over the previous decade. When Mathias M. Husebø and Elias Stakland did time there in 1854 and 1855 respectively (thirty days each), they were not allowed any books in their cell nor pen, ink, and paper (letter from Stavanger Friends, dated 18 December 1856; Aarek in *Et lidet Viidnesbyrd*, 100).

38 Buckley, *Memoirs*, 494, 500, 514–16, 532, 533. John Rinden, junior, appears in Norwegian sources as John Johnsen Botn. We may also note that there appears to have been more flexibility in deciding on the actual length of sentence in CO cases than the government commissioner in question allowed for.

39 *Extracts ... 1870*, 35.

40 Nag, *Det indre lys: Strand-kvekerne – deres nærmiljø i Ryfilke og i Amerika* (Ås, 1983), 183–5.

41 Nils Ivar Agøy, 'The Norwegian Peace Movement and the Question of Conscientious Objection to Military Service, 1855–1922,' in Katsuya Kodama and Unto Vesa, eds, *Towards a Comparative Analysis of Peace Movements* (Aldershot UK, 1990), 91. According to Agøy, 'in the military jurisdiction covering south-west Norway, where most of the Norwegian Quakers lived and where most of the 19th century objectors came from, the objectors received much harsher treatment than elsewhere; while the two Eastern Norwegian jurisdictions handed out the lightest sentences.'

42 Like Knud Knudsen and his family, farming folk in the Røldal valley, who eventually emigrated to the United States.

43 Agøy, 'Norwegian Peace Movement,' 90.

44 For surveys of the movement to legalize conscientious objection, see Agøy, 'Regulating Conscientious Objection in Norway from the 1890s to 1922,' *Peace & Change*, vol. 15, no. 1 (January 1990), 6–20, and my *Quaker Peace Testimony*, 248–56, 362–4. For a detailed archive-based study of conscientious objection in Norway from the mid-1880s on, see Agøy, *'Kampen mot Vernetvangen': Militærnekterspørsmålet i Norge 1885–1922* (Oslo, 1987), *passim*; Quakers, however, figure only incidentally in Agøy's work.

45 Though the minute does not mention his name, I am almost sure that this man was Søren Stakland, who would now have added another 50 days to his previous 120, making a total of 170 days – just short of the six months' sentence which Carl Røiseland served in 1866.

46 Minutes, Continental Committee ... Society of Friends, London, exercise

book 5, fols. 35, 61, 62. London Yearly Meeting's 'Address to those in Norway who are in prison, or otherwise suffering, for refusing military service' was printed in *Extracts ... 1900*, 72, 73.

47 *Extracts ... 1900*, 56. See also *Extracts ... 1898*, 104.

48 *Extracts ... 1898*, 104. The report continued as follows: 'Two young men, one a member and the other an attender, have during the past two years refused to render military service or practise drill; the former has been imprisoned on both occasions, and this faithful testimony, with some other cases of those not connected with our Society, attracted much attention. Much sympathy with the objection to war has thus been called forth, finding expression in the newspapers and otherwise.' Agøy, '*Kampen*,' 58, cites from a document, issued by the Kristiania Peace Society in 1896, arguing that the continued imprisonment of their young men would extinguish Norwegian Quakerism as a result of emigration: a deplorable loss of valuable citizens.

49 In a letter to *Fred* (Peace), no. 10 (1900), 77, quoted in Agøy, '*Kampen*,' 51, 52.

50 *Extracts ... 1901*, 162.

51 Ibid., 163.

52 However, in their letter to the acting consul-general for Sweden and Norway, dated 18 December 1900, London Friends clearly approved of the idea of the Norwegian state requiring COs to undergo alternative civilian service. 'We have learned,' they write, 'through the Norwegian Press that a proposal has been made for allowing conscripts with these scruples to be engaged in improving and planting with trees some uncultivated parts of the country ... Such work would, we believe, be accepted as a real relief by the conscripts who cannot give military service.' The provision of 'some useful work for the State, entirely free from the military system' would 'thus avoid the lamentable fact that honourable citizens are put into prison, like evil-doers, alone from faithfulness to their convictions of conscience' (*Extracts ... 1901*, 162, 163). Such a scheme clearly resembles the Russian Empire's forestry camps for its Mennonite COs. In World War One, we may note, the British Society of Friends produced a number of CO absolutists, who were unwilling to accept any condition of exemption.

53 In a few exceptional instances, religious COs failed to gain exemption and were imprisoned. But normally in these cases they now received a speedy pardon and were freed from further punishment. See Agøy, '*Kampen*,' 200–9.

54 *Extracts* ... 1900, 73–5. The Memorial singled out Søren Stakland (see above) for special mention: 'The only son of his widowed mother, [he] has been brought away from their farm on four separate occasions in the years 1896

to 1899' and lodged in jail, leaving his poor mother to cope alone on the family farm.

55 *Extracts ... 1901*, 121, 157, 158.

56 Minutes, Continental Committee ... Society of Friends, London, exercise book 5, fol. 74.

57 Letter dated 7 September 1900; *Extracts ... 1901*, 159.

58 Agøy, '*Kampen*,' 127–9 (3:III, 'Initiativer fra Kwekerne').

10 Nazarenes Confront Conscription in Dualist Hungary

The Nazarenes[1] originated as an offshoot of the Swiss *Neutäufer*, or Evangelical Baptists,[2] a denomination which had come into existence in the early 1830s in part as a result of Mennonite influence. Its founder, Samuel Heinrich Frölich,[3] taught nonresistance and rejection of oaths as well as adult baptism, and his followers, when conscripted, consistently refused combatant service in the army. Among Frölich's converts in 1839–40 were three Hungarian locksmiths who had come to Zürich in connection with their craft. Their names were Lajos Hencsey, János Denkel, and János Kropacsek. These men returned immediately to Hungary and began to spread their new religion among the peasantry and artisans of their native land. Hencsey, who had taken the lead at first, died in 1844, but his two companions continued his work, though progress was very slow throughout the 1840s. Around mid-century the Nazarenes, who were also known as Believers in Christ or Disciples of Christ, began to organize more systematically despite the severe repression of the sect by the 'Bach régime,' which ruled the Habsburg Empire after the defeat of the revolutionary movements of 1848. This period was one of testing for the new sect; nevertheless, the Nazarene faith survived somehow until the coming of the constitutional era in the Empire eased the situation to some extent. In 1867 the dualist system was inaugurated, and Hungary became an equal partner of the Austrian lands of the Empire with its own parliament and government.

Since Nazarenes in Hungary formed an almost exclusively peasant sect, many members were illiterate, especially in the early days. They were concentrated mainly in the south-west districts of the country in the Great Hungarian Plain, or *Alföld*.[4] One of the sect's strengths lay in its ability to recruit members from all the nationalities that inhabited this ethnically mixed area. Although Magyars predominated among them, Serbs, Rumanians, and Germans also joined in considerable numbers. Though more converts came from the Protestant and Orthodox churches than from the Catholic, the clergy of all these denominations were alike opposed to the sect's spread. Since the Hungarian government refused to recognize it as a 'received' religion, the hostility of church and state seriously impeded its growth, so that it is perhaps surprising that it continued slowly to expand. For this the missionary zeal of its members was largely responsible. By the beginning of the twentieth century the Nazarenes of Hungary numbered between 13,000 and 15,000.[5]

In their religious faith the Nazarenes were 'very close to the Mennonites.'[6] The similarities attracted the attention of Dutch Mennonite scholars towards the end of the last century. First J.G. de Hoop Scheffer and then Samuel Cramer and C.B. Hylkema published articles on the sect.[7] The Nazarenes' steady refusal of military service, which was based on a simple adherence to the Sermon on the Mount ('resist not evil'), also aroused the interest of the British Quakers. In the mid-1890s Tolstoy became concerned with their fate, and Dr Dušan Makovický, his Slovak disciple and later personal physician (see essay 12 below), compiled a short account of their beliefs and practice that still remains one of the best sources for the study of the sect.[8] Though the Nazarenes lived quiet and inoffensive lives and earned respect even of opponents for their honesty and high moral standards, which often contrasted favourably with the uncouth manners and rough ways prevailing among their neighbours, they clashed dramatically with the state in connection with their nonresistant stance. It was mainly this conflict that led outsiders, both at home and abroad, to examine the beliefs and activities of the sect. The Nazarenes themselves published no literature except items like hymn books (in several languages) that they needed for their religious services.

The sources for my survey of Nazarene nonresistance up to the outbreak of the First World War are fragmentary – and not always reliable. Even though the materials I have used include works in several languages, they still leave large gaps in the story. There is sometimes tantalizing uncertainty even in respect to basic facts and important developments.

The first case of conscientious objection that I have been able to discover dates around 1857. Then we learn of three young Nazarene recruits from the Bácska area who, on their induction into the army, refused to take the military oath and persisted in their refusal despite beatings and imprisonment. 'One was shot because he did not give in and the other two died as a result of their flogging.' There were evidently other cases at this time of resistance to military service and of the imprisonment and even execution of Nazarene objectors.[9]

In the Austro-Prussian War of 1866 we hear of more executions of Hungarian Nazarene objectors and of prison sentences of ten to fifteen years being meted out not infrequently to those objectors who were fortunate enough to escape the death penalty.[10] The Nazarenes were now winning adherents even among the *Grenzer*, the soldier population of the frontier districts administered from Vienna until 1881, when they were handed back to Hungary. Though converts remained few in number, the authorities were naturally alarmed at the possibility that the loyalty of these special troops might be undermined. For instance, in September 1869 a twenty-year-old *Grenzjüngling*, Michael Irre, from the Bánát area, when called up to perform the military service which was the hereditary obligation of his family, announced to the commanding officer's surprise that he would not don the uniform or take the military oath since to fight was contrary to Christian love. Repeated attempts were then made forcibly to dress him in army uniform and place a rifle in his hands, but without success. 'I would prefer to be shot than to take up arms,' Irre told them. 'If from the start we do not put a stop to this aberration,' reported Captain Kastner in panic to his superiors, 'we must expect that Nazarenism, which in this kind of behaviour should be regarded as a threat to the state, will very quickly be accepted generally.' After solitary confinement on bread and water had failed to break Irre's resistance, he was sentenced to five years in a military prison.[11]

Meanwhile Hungary had concluded the Compromise (*Ausgleich*) with Austria in 1867, and the establishment of dualism brought self-rule for the Hungarians on a constitutional basis. The imperial army, however, remained a joint undertaking directly under the command of the emperor-king. In August 1869 the Imperial War Office issued an order which would allow Nazarene recruits, if they persisted in refusing to bear arms, to transfer to the army medical corps, where they could work as hospital orderlies for the rest of their military service without having to bear arms. This sensible concession was modelled on a similar exemption given to members of the small Mennonite community of Galicia in the previous year, when the introduction of universal military service did away with the wider military exemption they had enjoyed under the old regime. However, in 1875 the War Office reversed its decision in favour of the Nazarenes and ordered them once again to perform service with weapons along with the rest. The ostensible reason given for this was that young men of military age were said to be joining the sect in order to escape armed service. This seems unlikely considering the puritan discipline that the Nazarenes imposed on their members. Along with the other legal liabilities from which the sect suffered, such discipline would not make membership in the church attractive for shirkers.[12] Yet the fact that the Nazarenes did make converts even among serving soldiers undoubtedly made the army authorities suspicious. They seem to have been genuinely afraid of the effect concessions to the Nazarenes would have on military discipline. In October 1870 the commander of the Buda garrison had reported: 'There are many cases of soldiers on the reserve who on joining the Nazarene religion have wanted to opt out of their obligation of armed service and have been unwilling to serve with the colours.'[13]

The liberals who held power in Hungary uninterruptedly until 1905 – whatever their shortcomings in respect to social policy and the politically unprivileged – showed considerable tolerance in religious matters. The founding fathers of dualist Hungary, Ferenc Deák and József Eötvös, seem to have been anxious to legalize the position of the sect, and one of their followers, Dániel Iranyi, strove for many years, in vain, to obtain official recognition for the Nazarenes, though it is very doubtful that any of these politicians was prepared to go so far as to advocate the right of conscientious objection. In 1872 two British Quakers travelling in the ministry in Central Europe visited Budapest and intervened with Deák and some of his parliamentary colleagues on behalf of the Nazarenes. One of the visitors reported home: 'We found a unanimous testimony – upon the whole (except their exclusive views) favourable to the Nazarenes ... They are decidedly on the increase. ... Their reverence for Holy Scripture is striking. They bear a faithful testimony against Oaths and War.'[14]

When fighting broke out in 1878 as a result of Austria-Hungary's occupation of the Turkish territories of Bosnia and Herzegovina, which the Treaty of Berlin had placed under Habsburg administration, Hungarian soldiers were involved. Once again there are stories of Nazarene conscripts being executed for resisting military duties.[15] But thereafter, since Austria-Hungary was not to be caught up in war again until

1914, there are no more reports of Nazarenes having to pay with their lives for their loyalty to nonresistance. They continued, however, to suffer severely on this score from long and repeated terms of imprisonment. The sect repeatedly petitioned both the Hungarian Ministry of Religion and Education in Budapest and the imperial authorities in Vienna for relief – but in vain.

In one of their confessions of faith, dated 1875, the Nazarenes stated their readiness to obey the powers that be in everything that was not contrary to their consciences. They willingly accepted military service insofar as it did not entail killing their fellow men. In support of their stand, they quoted from the Sermon on the Mount: 'Ye have heard that it hath been said, "Thou shalt love thy neighbour, and hate thy enemy. But I say unto you, Love your enemies, ..." '(Matthew 5:43, 44). 'We are quite prepared,' they went on, 'to take up weapons for the purpose of cleaning them but we won't exercise with them. For if we were ever required to use them, since we cannot kill men we would have to hand them back and our king would then be grieved with us.' They concluded by asserting that they would gladly serve as medical orderlies or such like and even carry a small weapon (*die kleinere Handwaffe*).[16] The sect was indeed far from the stand of the 'absolutist' objectors of Great Britain and the United States during the two World Wars. There is considerable evidence of the conciliatory stand taken up by many Nazarenes in respect to all military demands except swearing the oath and the bearing of arms. But the allegations made by opponents of the sect – that in some places the Nazarenes would accept new members only after they had done their military service and that many fled the country to escape service – do not appear to be justified.[17]

From the 1890s the authorities began to take a slightly more lenient attitude towards Nazarene objectors, though treatment remained severe. Laws passed by the Hungarian parliament in 1894 and 1895 had at last extended semi-recognition to the sect, but this did not touch the subject of military service. Nazarene leaders composed a new series of petitions which they presented to the authorities in Budapest and Vienna. Explaining why the recent laws did not satisfy their consciences, they asked for exemption from actually carrying arms while in service as well as from the obligation to take the military oath and attend the prayers which were obligatory for the troops. Might they not be allowed, they asked, to substitute for the oath a simple affirmation and to serve in a unit like the medical corps where they would not be required to bear arms? The answer of Baron Gyula Wlassics, then minister of religion and education, to one of these petitions ran as follows: 'The concessions and requests relating to military service cannot, however, be seriously considered until the aforesaid denomination gains legal recognition as a public religious body.'[18] Thus the bureaucracy seems to have drawn a vicious circle around the Nazarenes.

It is true that the military authorities by this time had indeed become more lenient, yet their leniency was narrowly circumscribed.[19] It consisted merely in increased willingness to assign Nazarene conscripts to noncombatant service in the medical corps, but often only after they had passed through a long ordeal. On the basis of his personal investigations and a survey of the Hungarian press over a ten-year period, Makovický describes the process as follows:

> Frequently they test the Nazarene recruits by using force to try to make them handle weapons. They attempt in various ways to make them serve like other soldiers, but the Nazarenes almost always prefer to let them tie the rifle onto their neck or their arms ... and torture them in other ways rather than give in. Some are then sent to the military asylum at Nagyszombat [Trnava], others are hauled before the tribunal and sentenced to shorter or longer terms of imprisonment. Some of these men are transferred to the medical corps after completion of their sentences but others are sent back for another trial and then incarcerated in penal barracks or fortress prisons and dungeons ... There they spend long years (sometimes as much as ten) and more than one has died there before the expiration of his term.[20]

The same author goes on to give details, including names and dates, of a number of 'characteristic' cases (though it is not easy to judge if they are so or not). A few examples may be cited here from Makovický's account. We learn, for instance, that when in 1892 Joća Radovanov, a Serbian Nazarene from the Bácska area, was sentenced to two years' imprisonment for refusing to handle a rifle, his brother had already served eight years in military jails for a similar offence. Yet their mother encouraged her younger son, too, to take a stand against military service. Another young Serb from the Bácska area, Sava Nićetin, seems to have spent the whole decade and more in prison; at any rate, in 1895 when Makovický was writing he was already in the fifth year of a series of sentences totalling fifteen years. At one point they had placed him in a cell where he could scarcely move and had attached a rifle to his body. But he would not touch it even though this would have ended his torture. Jur Dovala was a former thief who, while serving in the army, had been sent to jail for stealing. There he was converted by a Nazarene prisoner, a baker by trade. On completion of his sentence, Dovala was returned to the ranks, where, to the astonishment of all, he then refused to bear arms, bringing upon himself repeated terms of hard labour. It was in fact seven and a half years before he was finally released. Dovala's is by no means the only case of an ordinary prisoner's conversion to the Nazarene faith.[21] Outside jail, too, Nazarene objectors sometimes succeeded in winning over fellow conscripts as well as soldiers on the reserve. These men, as Makovický shows, were sure to incur harsh penalties when they in turn refused to bear arms.[22]

The sources at my disposal do not indicate clearly either the proportion of Nazarene objectors who were now being assigned to the medical corps or at exactly what stage in their army career this transfer took place. Makovický notes that in 1892 in one military hospital in Pest more than half of the forty orderlies were Nazarenes.[23] But no overall statistics appear to exist. In fact, in the absence of clear-cut regulations on the subject, the treatment of Nazarene objectors differed from one regiment to another. Apparently one commanding officer might be lenient and another might be severe (just as the tribunals and boards dealing with British and American conscientious objectors during the two World Wars were to differ considerably in their decisions). Undoubtedly Nazarenes who were born into the sect fared better than did those who were not (in the same way, we may remark, that the applications of members of established peace churches like the Mennonites or Quakers were not infrequently to be given more consideration by the bodies set up to deal with wartime objectors than those coming from men who were not so connected). In the worst situation of all were the soldiers – whether in military prisons or in the ranks – who were converted to the Nazarene faith. All observers are agreed on the state of alarm produced in the military when they contemplated the effect such conversions might have on army discipline. Thus they were set on imposing on such people penalties of sufficient harshness to deter all but the most courageous spirits.

In the light of presently accessible sources, the situation at the outset of the past century does not seem to have changed appreciably from that of a decade earlier. In 1903 Samuel Cramer reported, on the basis of information derived from members of the Evangelical Baptist Church, which had remained in fairly close touch with the Hungarian

Nazarenes, that there were still men in prison who had been there up to twelve years. One of his informants wrote: 'I know that in one year the number imprisoned [in Szeged alone] amounted to as many as 52. But the figure alters from year to year.'[24] Writing around the same time, Vladimir Bonch-Bruevich, a Russian Marxist expert on sectarianism, painted a somewhat similar picture of continuing incarceration of Nazarene objectors.[25] Yet during the decade preceding the outbreak of the First World War, the number of objectors assigned to noncombatant service seems to have slowly increased, while the number of prison sentences declined. The fact that by this time the sect had begun to lose something of its missionary dynamism, and thus constituted less of a threat to army discipline, may have made the authorities more tolerant. After all, the number of those joining the Nazarenes had proved relatively small and the danger of subversion was shown to be unreal. However, the sources to which I have had access throw little, if any, light on this period and preclude any definite statement.[26]

No *Martyrs' Mirror* exists for the Hungarian Nazarenes. Since they left no records and wrote no history, the task of compiling such a volume would be virtually impossible. Yet their 'sufferings' on account of loyalty to nonresistance, which have continued – with intervals – until today in both Hungary and the neighbouring states, equal, and even surpass, those endured elsewhere by other peace sects (except perhaps for the Jehovah's Witnesses).

We may now ask why Nazarene conscripts in Hungary never acquired at least the regular exemption allowing service in a noncombatant branch of the army that Prussia-Germany and Habsburg Austria had granted to their Mennonite subjects after the introduction of universal military service. The reason for this lies, I think, in certain differences between the Mennonites and Nazarenes. The Mennonites in Central and Eastern Europe were no longer an expansive community; they lived apart from the surrounding world, divided from it in the case of Russia and Austrian Galicia by an ethnic barrier and in the case of Prussia by a sectarian wall. As contacts between sect and society inevitably grew, it was the Mennonites who tended to become acculturated to the surrounding society, while few, if any, outsiders now became Mennonites. But it was (and perhaps still remains) quite different with the Nazarenes.

For another thing they were a new sect, whereas Mennonite peculiarities had been hallowed, as it were, by more than three centuries of existence. The Nazarenes in the Hungarian *Alföld* were ploughing virgin soil. Their converts there were torn from the bosom of the established churches or from the clutches of the military establishment. They appeared, and to some extent actually were, a threat to church, state, and army. It was the sect's potential for expansion, and not its nonresistant principles, that was the primary cause of the cruel treatment meted out for so long to its conscientious objectors. For the Nazarenes proved as willing as many Mennonites then were to accept army service if only they could be exempted from actually bearing arms. Yet this exemption was granted the latter and steadily withheld from the former, despite their repeated pleas. There existed, indeed, an additional complication in the case of the Hungarian Nazarenes. Their activities centred in an area of social and ethnic tension, and their members were drawn mostly from poverty-stricken peasants and from the national minorities – two categories that often overlapped. And in dualist Hungary this in itself was sufficient to make the sect suspect in the eyes of a government, liberal in name but increasingly chauvinist in its aspirations to establish Magyar hegemony over the non-Magyar inhabitants of the state. Moreover, this government represented almost exclusively the numerically small upper strata of society, with the landowning nobility in particular playing a major role in administration. Thus a sect like the Nazarenes, which acted as a channel for rural protest against an oppressive agrarian system, became doubly suspect in the eyes of the authorities always on the watch for signs of peasant discontent, whether Magyar or non-Magyar, and unrest among the non-Magyar nationalities. However pacifist their principles might be, the Nazarenes represented an implicit threat to the existing order. They were fond of answering the question 'What would happen if your refusal to fight were to spread?' by saying, 'If everyone were like us, then there would be no need for police or soldiers.'[27] But an expansion of the sect, however peaceable, was just what the authorities feared. They seemed really frightened that it would evolve from a group of evangelical nonresistants into a Münster-like movement which would gather into its fold all those nurturing grievances of a social or national character. This had to be prevented at any cost. Therefore, so long as the Nazarenes maintained their missionary drive, the lot of their conscientious objectors must be made hard. Concessions granted to non-missionizing Mennonites appeared as inopportune in respect to an expansive denomination like the Nazarenes.[28] Whereas the question of military service had not been acute in the age of Mennonite expansion, the Nazarenes came into existence and grew in the age of universal conscription. This fact was chiefly responsible for the sad plight of the Nazarene nonresistants in dualist Hungary.

After 1914, despite the willingness of most Nazarene conscripts to perform noncombatant army service, they continued to suffer severe penalties on account of their refusal to act as combatants. Their fate in the two World Wars is not altogether clear: while some Nazarenes served as noncombatants, more were imprisoned, and a few may even have been executed.[29] Trianon Hungary was not permitted to have conscription. But in interwar Yugoslavia and Rumania, Nazarenes, the majority of whom were ethnic Hungarians, were repeatedly jailed for resisting military service. As a middle-aged Yugoslav Nazarene remarked: 'I was imprisoned by the Magyars and I shall be in prison again here. All this has passed over my head.' Accounts of harassment, and even torture, of imprisoned Nazarene draftees appeared from time to time in the Yugoslav opposition press; and the situation in Rumania was not much better.[30] For many decades after the Second World War, the treatment of Nazarene conscientious objectors was even more savage than during the interwar period! In Tito's Yugoslavia, where most Nazarenes were now located, 'Nazarene recruits spent up to 12 years in prison, depending on the year they were recruited.' After the disintegration of communist Yugoslavia, the situation improved somewhat since assignment to noncombatant army service now became possible. However, recruits who demanded alternative service of a civilian character still faced imprisonment. By this time, though, there were few Nazarenes left in Serbia and Montenegro, that is, rump Yugoslavia. They had 'fled en masse' to escape the comprehensive religious discrimination to which they had been subjected over the years.[31]

NOTES

1 See the *Mennonite Encyclopedia* (hereafter *ME*), vol. 3, 815. See also my *Pacifism in Europe to 1914* (Princeton NJ, 1972), 495–8, 540, 541, and 'Some Materials on Nazarene Conscientious Objectors in Nineteenth-Century Hungary,' *Mennonite Quarterly Review*, vol. 57, no. 1 (January 1983), 64–72.

2 See *ME*, vol. 1, 138, 139. In the United States they are known as the Apostolic Christian Church.

3 See ibid., vol. 2, 414, 415.

4 There were some Nazarenes in the Austrian half of the Empire as well as in Serbia. Croatia, then an associate state of Hungary, and Bosnia, which from

1878 on was administered by Austria-Hungary, also contained a few members of the sect.

5 Samuel Cramer, 'Nazarener, ungarische,' *Realencyklopädie für protestantische Theologie und Kirche*, ed. J.J. Herzog and D. Albert Hauck, vol. 13 (3rd edn, 1903), 672.

6 *ME*, vol. 3, 815: 'The Nazarene doctrine is simple. The Bible is their only and absolute norm of religious knowledge. The reading of the Scriptures is considered an unquestioned duty; fulfilling its commands is the way of salvation. The principle command is to bear the cross for Christ's sake, and to practice self-denial and love. Absolute nonresistance, patient bearing of all insults, rejection of military service and the oath, and abstention from cursing, are among their principles. They baptize by immersion after the age of 18 years.' In addition, their church government also parallels that of the Mennonite denominations.

7 De Hoop Scheffer and Hylkema published their pieces in *Doopsgezinde Bijdragen* (Leiden) for 1891 and 1904 respectively. But these are rather paraphrases of the work of others than original articles.

8 *Nazarénové v Uhrách* (Prague, 1896). Makovický, as a Slovak, knew Hungarian well. 'He obtained reports and statements about the Nazarene movement either personally, or by correspondence with various persons, or from newspapers, etc. In his papers [now deposited in the Literary Archive of the National Museum in Prague] are preserved a large number of original and authentic documents. Makovický visited remote areas in order to observe the life of the Nazarenes, participated in their assemblies, talked with them, and noted down their beliefs in minute detail, sometimes to the point of pedantry. In particular he obtained many reports from local people, especially clergy, with whom he corresponded for this purpose. They provided him with information about the movement in different parts of the country' (from Stěpán Kolafa, 'Nástin života a díla Dušana Makovického,' *Slovanské štúdie*, vol. 4: *Z ohlasov L.N. Tolstého na Slovensku* [Bratislava, 1960], 170). See also the same author's article, 'Archiv Dušana Makovického,' *Slovenská literatura*, 6, no. 3 (1959), 358.

9 Pál Biró, 'A Nazarénusok Bácskában,' *Vasárnapi Ujság*, 31 July 1870. See also Lajos Zsigmond Szeberényi, *Nazarénismus* (Nagy-Becskerek, 1888), 76. Biró writes of this incident: 'I well remember it happened in 1857 ...' But could his memory perhaps have led him slightly astray and at least the execution have taken place during the Italian war of 1859, when severer measures against war resisters might be expected than in peacetime?

10 György Schwalm in *Evangelikus Egyházi Szemle* (hereafter *EES*), vol. 2, no. 2 (February 1905), 23. Schwalm was a Lutheran minister, who knew the Naz-

arene communities well and had collected a great deal of material on them. He is generally reliable, though of course not altogether sympathetic. In late 1904 and early 1905 he contributed to a long review article on De Hoop Scheffer's and Cramer's writings on the Nazarenes (cited above), which was spread over a number of issues and contained some additional information drawn from his own researches. He gave it in Hungarian the same title as De Hoop Scheffer's article: 'A tizenhatodik századnak ujrakeresztelöi jelenben uj életre ébredve Magyarországon' ('De Doopsgezinden der zestiende eeuw, nu in Hongarije herboren').

11 Szeberényi, 'Die Secte der Nazarener in Ungarn,' *Jahrbücher für protestantische Theologie* (1890), 502–4; Schwalm, *EES*, vol. 2, no. 1 (January 1905), 9, and no. 2 (February 1905), 20, 21. The documents given in Szeberényi's work, which was translated by Schwalm from the Hungarian original (cited above), were in fact inserted by the translator. Below I refer to this translation as Szeberényi-Schwalm.

12 Heinrich von Himmel, 'Von den Nazarenen,' *Pester Lloyd* (Budapest), 4 June 1897. Himmel was a retired colonel who wrote with sympathy of the Nazarenes' plight in respect to military service. He pointed out that, apart from their religious scruples against handling weapons, they were quite ready to fulfil their army service in a noncombatant capacity, whether as orderlies in military hospitals or as clerks in the army administration.

13 Antal Szöllösi, 'A Nazarénusokról,' *Magyar Protestans Egyházi és Iskolai Figyelmezö*, vol. 2, no. 10/11 (October/November 1871), 484. Such men may not have been eligible for the conditional exemption granted temporarily to the Nazarenes in 1869. This would explain the severe treatment still being recommended for 'Nazarene soldiers' in an order issued by the commander-in-chief of the home forces (*honvéd*) in the spring of 1874. But possibly my source – Antal Ujlaki, *Bibliás emberek (Nazarénusokról)* (Szeged, 1897), 86–8 – has given the wrong date here.

14 *J. Bevan Braithwaite: A Friend of the Nineteenth Century. By His Children* (London, 1909), 205, 206. Letter dated 22 September 1872.

15 For example: Cramer, 674; [Gustav Szeberényi], 'A magyarországi Nazarénusok,' *Békéscsabai Evangélikusok Lapja*, vol. 8, no. 4 (May 1941), 57.

16 Szeberényi-Schwalm, 506; Makovický, *Nazarénové*, 19. I have printed in English translation the section in this document on compulsory military service in my 'Some Materials,' 67. It was drawn up for presentation to the Ministry of Religion and Education. I was fortunate in finding a copy of the rare sixteen-page pamphlet, reproducing its text, in the municipal library of Hódmezövásárhely, where it had been printed in 1876: *A Kristusban hivö gyülekezetek vallás és egyház szertartasi szabályai*. We should note, however,

that there were Nazarene objectors – probably a minority but this is not clear – who refused to carry a weapon under any circumstances. Makovický, on the same page in which he gives this 'confession' in translation, writes as follows: 'They are ready to become medical orderlies, batmen or army cooks; some however are unwilling, even as medical orderlies, to wear side-arms and thus, since going out into the streets without arms is forbidden, they remain inside barracks throughout their whole term of service, i.e. for three years.' It seems, though, that in this case they were not otherwise punished for failing to carry a weapon.

17 See Makovický, *Nazarénové*, 11. Some Nazarenes did emigrate to the United States, where they joined the Apostolic Christian Church, but usually their departure from Hungary was not connected with their objection to military service.

18 *Debreceni Protestáns Lap*, 12 February 1898, 91; 'A Nazarénusok,' *Erdélyi Protestáns Lap* (Kolozsvár), 9 February 1899, 50.

19 Makovický, *Nazarénové*, 18–24 (section entitled 'Odpor proti vojenčině'), gives a fairly detailed account of Nazarene conscientious objection during the first half of the 1890s. For no other period is so much information available on this subject – though even so it is not in fact very much!

20 Ibid., 19, 20.

21 Apart from Makovický's work, on which this paragraph is based, an example of such a conversion can be found in István Tömörkény, *Munkák és napok a Tisza paratján: Cikkek, riportok, tanulmányok 1884–1916* (Budapest, 1963), 33. Tömörkény's article on the Nazarenes was originally published in 1895; it is based on personal observation of the sect. See also the case of the locksmith Karoly Ethei, a leading member of the Nazarene congregation at Hódmezövásárhely, a centre of Nazarene activities in south Hungary, who had spent twelve years in prison for robbery with violence before becoming a Nazarene. I have printed his brief defence of conscientious objection to military service, which he made during his official interrogation in December 1863, in my 'Some Materials,' 64, 65.

22 Makovický, *Nazarénové*, 21–3.

23 Ibid., 23.

24 Cramer, ed., 'Nazarener-Briefe,' *Mennonitische Blätter* (Danzig), vol. 50, no. 7 (July 1903), 56. See also Schwalm in *EES*, vol. 11, no. 3 (March 1905), 38, 39; *Peace and Goodwill* (Wisbech), vol. 5, no. 5 (1899), 67. This last paper, edited by English Quaker and peace advocate Priscilla Peckover, published reports from time to time on the peace witness of the Nazarenes in Hungary and Serbia.

25 Vladimir Bonch-Bruevich, 'Nazareny v Vengrii i Serbii,' in *Iz mira sektantov:*

Sbornik statei (Moscow, 1922), 296–8. While the section on conscientious objection in Hungary (pages 288–98) is based to a considerable extent on Makovický, it does contain fresh materials especially for the decade following the appearance of the latter's work. Materials in Hungarian and Czech were translated for Bonch-Bruevich by the Slovak Tolstoyan, Dr Albert Škarvan, who had himself refused further service in the Austro-Hungarian army in 1895 (see essay 12 below).

26 The Nazarenes faced a very difficult situation in the First World War. While many of their young men served in noncombatant branches of the army, sometimes receiving military decorations for this service, others suffered imprisonment and even perhaps death for their opposition to bearing arms. See John W. Graham, *Conscription and Conscience: A History 1916–1919* (London, 1922), 356, 357; Sándor Palotay and Jenö Szigeti, 'A Nazarénusok' (Budapest, mimeo., 1969), 5.

27 Szeberényi-Schwalm, 505, 506.

28 Whether in Russia, Prussia, or Austrian Galicia, Mennonite conscientious objectors in eastern Europe, even after the imposition of universal military service, were by law guaranteed at least some form of noncombatant alternative service.

29 Jenö Szigeti and László Kardos, *Boldog emberek közössége: A magyároszagi nazarénusok* (Budapest, 1988), 272, 274, 288–93.

30 See *'Nazarenes' in Yugoslavia* (Syracuse NY, 1928) and *Report of the Conference of the Yugoslavian and Roumanian Delegates in Brussels ... with Regard to the Nazarenes in Their Respective Countries* (Syracuse NY, 1928).

31 See Bojan Aleksov, 'The Dynamics of Extinction: The Religious Community in Yugoslavia after 1945' (M.A. thesis, Central European University [Budapest], 1999), chap. 2. I must thank the author for giving me a copy of his thesis.

11 Tolstoy and the Imprisonment of Conscientious Objectors in Imperial Russia

In 1896, with his mind much occupied with the Dukhobor soldiers and their provocative burning of military weapons during the previous summer, Tolstoy set about writing a play which he called *And the Light Shineth in Darkness (I svet vo t'me svetit)*.[1] He continued intermittently into the following year, and even beyond, but he never completed the work. After finishing four acts, he abandoned it. Of the fifth act, he got barely a page onto paper.

The hero of the drama is a young Russian prince, Boris (Boria) Aleksandrovich Cheremshanov, who, because of his belief in Tolstoyan-style nonresistance, refused induction into the army when called up as a conscript. 'Let them beat the life out of you in a [penal] battalion, anything's better than serving these deluders,' he tells the soldiers detailed to guard him after his arrest. His family are, of course, disgusted at his behaviour. He had owed his conversion to a progressive landowner, Nikolai Ivanovich Sarintsev (a.k.a. Lev Nikolaevich Tolstoy), whose allegiance to the Tolstoyan gospel, unlike the more resolute Boria's, had been hitherto largely a matter of theory. At the outset of act 5, Boris is incarcerated in the barracks of a penal battalion of the Russian army. To break his will the commanding officer sends Boris to the punishment cells. 'We'll flog him,' he says. But Boris does not yield. In the eyes of the world, the young man is a ruined man – and a fool as well: as a university graduate, he would not have had to serve for very long.

The play, which Tolstoy himself valued highly and Bernard Shaw praised to the skies,[2] is indeed no masterpiece, even though it contains some powerful scenes. But it does express in dramatic form Tolstoy's sanguine belief that the young men who in Russia, and abroad, were refusing to perform military service on grounds of conscience when summoned to do this by the state represented 'a light shining in darkness' that would slowly transform the world and establish peace among humankind.

True, few if any Russian conscientious objectors to military service (COs) were princes. They were mostly villagers or craftsmen, religious dissenters belonging to rural sects that espoused pacifism at least in theory, like the Dukhobors, Molokans,[3] and Malevantsy. There were, of course, among the COs disciples of the Master, too; and Tolstoyans were sometimes of middle class or gentry origin. Since the imposition in Russia of conscription in 1874, only Mennonites, centred in south Russia (today Ukraine), were exempt from military service. Their draftees were assigned to forestry camps run by the church under the general supervision of the government. Other COs (and these were the people Tolstoy was really concerned about) faced a variety of punitive measures. The pacifist section of the Dukhobors solved the problem by emigrating as a group to Canada at the end of the century.[4]

In a long essay entitled 'The Law of Violence and the Law of Love,' which he wrote in 1908 shortly before his death, Tolstoy recalled the names of thirty-two imprisoned COs with whom he had been in personal contact.[5] At least sixteen more names of jailed COs occur in his *Collected Works*, though this does not necessarily mean he was in contact with them all. Several of these men visited him at Iasnaia Poliana; and with some of them he corresponded, often over a prolonged period of time, at first during their imprisonment and then after their release from jail. His CO correspondents, while they were usually peasants and largely self-educated, counted among the most articulate of their kind: rural philosophers whose homely wisdom obviously appealed to Tolstoy. We possess no reliable statistics from the number of COs imprisoned during the four decades between 1874 and 1914. Excluding Dukhobor soldiers who had refused to handle a gun during the last half-decade of the century, a rough estimate might be 150.[6] Thus Tolstoy was probably acquainted in some fashion with around a third of the CO cases that occurred in the Russian Empire during his lifetime.[7]

Contemplating the stand taken by COs both in Russia and abroad in such conscriptionist countries as Austria-Hungary, Bulgaria, or the Netherlands, Tolstoy saw these people as standard-bearers pointing the way to a warless world. He contrasted their behaviour with that of the churches and the secular states these bodies everywhere supported. 'It is obvious,' Tolstoy wrote in 1906, 'that mankind has made little progress during the nineteen centuries since Christ if it is still possible to persecute men on account of their lofty spiritual aspirations and noble actions.'[8] Though none he knew of had yet paid with their lives for their beliefs, Tolstoy always felt uneasy at being himself spared suffering of any kind, especially as he realized that many Russian COs modelled their lives on his interpretation of the Christian gospel. As he told a jailed CO in 1910: 'Whenever I receive letters from friends in your situation, my feelings are mixed. I experience joy and compassion but at the same time I feel envious of you. I am ashamed at being left in freedom to enjoy all life's comforts. And I never fail to experience such feelings when I read the letters you people send me.'[9]

In the eyes of the Russian authorities, 'conscientious objection was a dual crime: it was a violation of civic duty as well as military duty.'[10] They feared, too, that the virus might spread; and this may have been the reason why some military tribunals preferred to sentence COs to incarceration in a civilian prison rather than to confinement in a penal battalion,[11] though the practice was not applied consistently.[12] The spread of pacifist sectarianism among the various Cossack hosts, with their special military obligations, as well as into an area like the Turkestan military district (*okrug*),[13] added to the alarm of the military, even though this probably did not represent a real threat to military security.

The first CO with whose case Tolstoy became actively involved was the twenty-one-year-old Aleksei Zaliubovskii, who refused to handle a weapon when called up for military service in 1885.[14] His decision had been prompted by reading some of Tolstoy's writings. Zaliubovskii himself came from a military family (his brother was an artillery officer) with no connections with any pacifist sect: Tolstoy, therefore, felt especially concerned since he had been largely responsible for the young man's resistance to the military machine and for the pain which this was causing the latter's family. He now exerted himself on Zaliubovskii's behalf, attempting to influence public opinion in his favour and putting pressure on the bureaucracy to ameliorate his impending fate – but without success. Zaliubovskii was sentenced to two years in a penal battalion and served out his full sentence, though he was thereafter left in peace by the army.[15]

In Tolstoy's relations with imprisoned COs over the next quarter-century, two features stand out. In the first place come his untiring efforts to bring each case as it became known to him before the general public and, above all, urge civilian bureaucracy and army command alike to give these men fair treatment and avoid punishing them repeatedly for what was essentially the same offence. In line with his belief that suffering in a good cause, suffering that was voluntarily undertaken, was the Christian way of combating evil, Tolstoy felt that the COs' witness of suffering possessed positive value. Therefore, we do not find him urging the government to allow not merely Mennonites, but all genuine COs, to undertake alternative civilian service – or possibly some kind of noncombatant work within the framework of the army. Some COs with whom he was acquainted, like N.S. Akulov, were ready to accept alternative civilian service, though Akulov was not successful in obtaining it.[16] While refusing to plead for a change in the law in favour of COs, Tolstoy at the same time believed that it was his duty to ameliorate their lot in so far as that was possible without compromising on principle. We find him, for instance, appealing in October 1896 to Lieutenant-Colonel Koz'min, commanding officer of the penal company (*rota*) stationed at Irkutsk, on behalf of two Ukrainian COs serving time there. Tolstoy first pointed to the deplorable example of another CO, Evdokhim Drozhzhin, whose death in the penal battalion at Voronezh two years earlier as a result of ill treatment ('he was tortured by cold, hunger and solitary confinement' while suffering from consumption contracted during his confinement)[17] had made quite a stir even outside Tolstoyan circles. And he continued:

> Judging by the position you occupy I presume your views on life and the obligations incumbent on man are completely different from mine. I cannot hide from you that I regard the duty you have undertaken as incompatible with Christianity, and I would be happy if you – and all others in your situation – could break free from participation in such activities. Still, knowing my own many sins, present and past, and all my weaknesses and transgressions, not only should I not tell you what you should do, instead, I should regard you as my brother in Christ, showing you respect and love.[18]

It is not clear that such an approach was the one most likely to evoke an answering chord in the letter's recipient. But Tolstoy's primary intention was certainly not to persuade the colonel he should give up his job; rather, he wished to show there were persons of influence in society concerned with these men's fate.

Even in old age, Tolstoy was willing to travel considerable distances to visit imprisoned COs and talk to those in charge of the captives.

And he always went out of his way to gather information about COs he knew were already in the hands of the military but not yet sentenced. Early in February 1898, for instance, we find him writing to a lawyer friend employed in a military tribunal in Vilna (Vilnius). He asks him for further details concerning a CO about whom his friend had learnt in the course of his duties. Tolstoy at once had wanted to know the man's name and present location.[19] He followed up these enquiries with suggestions as to how this man and his companions could be helped, first in their long and painful journey on foot across Siberia and then in the distant province of Iakutsk, where they had been sentenced to spend up to eighteen years of administrative exile. If their friends sent money, Tolstoy adds, they must be careful to prevent the authorities there from getting hold of it.[20]

The second recurring feature in Tolstoy's relationship with imprisoned COs was his concern for their personal welfare and spiritual equilibrium in often trying circumstances. He tried to cheer them when they felt depressed or discouraged. To one man he wrote: 'Those few minutes of weakness which you experienced only prove that your normal condition is not one of weakness but of spiritual strength.'[21] To another, who was overwhelmed with despair when the prison authorities deprived him of reading matter in his cell, he wrote: 'I can very well understand how hard it must be for a young man like you to endure rigorous imprisonment.' Still, since his conscience was clear, he should realize he was in fact much better off than many outside jail, who were affected with all sorts of worries and temptations: 'A time will come when you will look back with satisfaction on the time you spent in prison.' Tolstoy went on to suggest that the man should arrange his life according to a daily program combining physical labour, prayer, and meditation, and – if possible – mixing with others in the prison.[22] A sense of isolation, in particular, could make things hard. To be incarcerated in a jail where there were no other COs, as happened in 1907 to Ivan Deriabin, a railway worker from Ufa province who had to serve his four-year term in Tomsk, could intimidate a more intrepid spirit than this anxious youth. Deriabin wrote to Tolstoy for 'advice and support' in his ordeal. The latter in his reply told him of others who, although their sentences were even longer than his, were filled with 'tranquillity and gentleness.' 'If you were to read their [prison] letters and hear what those who visited them have to say about them, you would be deeply moved.'[23]

Tolstoy showed a remarkable understanding, worthy of the great novelist, of those potential COs who, unable for one or another reason to resist the pressure, agreed after all to serve in the armed forces. A case in point was that of Leopold Sulerzhitskii, a talented young actor and theatrical director, who belonged to the Tolstoy family circle. Arrested in 1896 on account of his failure to comply with the draft, 'Suler' (as he was known to his friends) suffered a deep depression as a result of the distress his action was causing his family, and he agreed eventually to serve in the navy. While Tolstoy's leading disciple, Vladimir Chertkov, was disapproving, the Master himself told 'Suler' that he was doing the right thing. His was indeed 'a terrible dilemma,' but he had interpreted the law of love they both acknowledged as meaning that he should avoid inflicting pain on aged parents. That circumstance certainly did not make military service right. But this particular draftee Tolstoy thought was correct in the decision he had made. In fact, after his discharge from the navy, 'Suler' continued to take part in the Tolstoyan movement; he was to be one of those most active in helping in the emigration of the Dukhobors to Canada at the end of the century.[24]

The only CO with whom Tolstoy seems finally to have lost patience was the Ukrainian Baptist, Evtikhii Goncharenko, who, after being released from a penal battalion, had showered Tolstoy with complaints about what he considered inadequate financial assistance for himself and family. Tolstoy, we must add, also found Goncharenko's narrow religiosity difficult to stomach. The man was tough and obviously sincere but seemingly an inveterate grumbler.

Tolstoy, unlike some of his disciples, was clearly not a doctrinaire. This comes out in his response thirteen years later to a draftee who had written to ask his advice as to whether he should refuse to serve. Even though the young man had come to the conclusion that all war was evil and, for a Christian at any rate, the CO position was the correct one, he could not make up his mind how he should proceed after receiving his call-up notice. (Unlike in Sulerzhitskii's case, there do not appear to have been any family complications to make a clear-cut decision difficult.) Tolstoy began his reply: 'Concerning your question only you can give the answer. [If your conscience tells you that it is wrong] to take the military oath and learn how to kill other human beings, [then you must resist induction into the army].' However, Tolstoy went on:

> One may possibly feel one does not possess sufficient strength to face all the consequences of such a refusal. That, though, is not to cast in doubt

> what course of action is the correct one. I certainly sympathize with you in this trial. But one piece of counsel I do have. If you finally decide that you do not have the strength to resist induction, do not pretend that, by failing to resist, you have done what was right.[25]

Induction of conscripts into the armed forces followed the complicated procedures set out in the universal military service law of 1874, which remained virtually unchanged until the outbreak of war in 1914. 'Military obligation boards ... were established [by this law] in every provincial capital and in every district. A structure of deferments and exemptions was established in accord with the social, occupational and educational needs of the state ... Following the granting of all possible exemptions and deferments, a lottery was established to determine who from among the remaining group of those aged 21 would be inducted into the military.' Men with higher educational qualifications were required to serve for a shorter term than those who possessed at most a primary education. From a pool of 700,000 to 900,000 men, between 200,000 were drafted into service annually, the call-up taking place in October.[26]

Tolstoy became intimately acquainted with the intricacies of the draft, in part through his prolonged contacts with non-Mennonite COs who became caught up in its working. In the powerful exposition of his faith he completed in 1893, *The Kingdom of God Is within You* (*Tsarstvo bozhie vnutri vas*), he paints a sombre picture of the treatment meted out to any draftee who objected on grounds of conscience to enrolment. 'No attention is paid to his arguments ... it is supposed he is a sectary and therefore does not understand Christianity in the right sense.' An Orthodox priest is then called for to convince him he is wrong. When this proves without avail, the military board, now suspecting the man may be a revolutionary, hands him over to the police for further questioning. But the young man declares repeatedly that 'he ... is opposed to any use of force.' Thus the gendarmes find no basis for criminal charges and, having 'put him into uniform,' hand him over under guard to the regiment to which he has been assigned. There he refuses to handle a weapon, explaining that his disobedience of orders results from his belief that 'as a Christian he cannot voluntarily prepare himself to commit murder.' The senior officers, at least, are usually not unsympathetic to this strange fellow. But they are at a loss to know what to do with him while they await instructions from St Petersburg. 'To save appearance, though, they shut the young man up in prison.' Sometimes, on orders from the capital, the CO is sent to a lunatic asylum for psychiatric examination. 'The doctors examine him ... and, naturally finding in him no symptoms of mental disease, send him back to the army' – and back to square one! (One solution, of course, was to sentence the man to a term in a civilian prison. If they decided to keep him in the army, as most often they did, that usually meant more delays.) Tolstoy goes on:

> Again they write to Petersburg, and thence comes the decree to transfer the young man to some division of the army stationed on the frontier, in some place where the army is under martial law ... They transfer him to a division stationed on the Zacaspian border, and in company with convicts send him to a [commanding] officer who is notorious for his harshness and severity. All this time ... the young man is roughly treated, kept in cold, hunger, and filth, and life is made burdensome to him generally. But all these sufferings do not compel him to change his resolution. On the Zacaspian border, where he is again requested to go on guard fully armed, he again declines to obey ... All this takes place in the presence of the other soldiers. To let such a refusal pass unpunished is impossible, and the young man is put on ... trial for breach of discipline ... and ... sentenced to two years [in a penal battalion].[27]

Sometimes the delinquent soldier is released before the expiry of his sentence only to be sent into administrative exile in Siberia not infrequently for as much as eighteen years. 'In all cases,' Tolstoy concluded, 'the government has adopted the same timorous, undecided, and secretive course of action.'[28]

Little had changed at the time of Tolstoy's death seventeen years later. The year 1905 seemed to many in Russia to presage a new era. The October Manifesto led to the release of a number of imprisoned COs, though this proved only a temporary lull. Early that year, Tolstoy had received a letter from two young sailors, Timofei Tregubov and Mikhail Zakharov, who were incarcerated in the fortress prison at Kronstadt. Zakharov was a villager, while Tregubov had worked as a locksmith in a provincial town. Previously in the reserve, the two men had been recalled to the colours at the outbreak of war and assigned to serve on the battleship *Borodino*. When their ship sailed for the Far East, they had declared their unwillingness – on grounds of conscience – to go too, unless they would be allowed to serve in a noncombatant capacity as ambulance men. They were then taken off the ship and put in jail to await trial. There they managed to smuggle out a letter to Tolstoy, asking him to intercede with the authorities because these had deprived them of their Bibles, their only consolation in an unhappy situation. A court martial subsequently sentenced both men to three years in a penal battalion. Since the court's decision mentioned 'reading certain religio-philosophical works' as one of the factors leading the two men to take their present 'erroneous, indeed fanatical' stance, it seems probable it was Tolstoy who had, if indirectly, made them COs – along with previous contact with one or another of the groups which had adopted his message.[29]

Three years later, in August 1908, Tolstoy was overjoyed to receive a similar letter, this time from an anonymous group of thirty-two soldiers and sailors. Congratulating him on his eightieth birthday, the men told him that they were all now convinced of the incompatibility of service in the armed forces with Christianity. In reply, Tolstoy wrote: 'Violence is upheld only by armies.' If those who served in the military understood that learning to kill fellow human beings was contrary to the Gospel law of love, then they would refuse any longer to serve.[30] Whether the men took Tolstoy's advice is not known.

Undoubtedly Tolstoy's view of the CO question is stamped with his hostility to the political and religious establishment of imperial Russia. Moreover, each CO case was *sui generis*. Indeed one might expect this, considering the variety of social, ethnic,[31] and religious backgrounds from which such people were drawn throughout the period. Apart from Dukhobors in the Caucasus (until their emigration at the end of the century), most imprisoned COs came from small pacifist sects like the Dobroliubovtsy, Malevantsy, Molokan Skakuny, Netovtsy, or Sabbatarians, most of whose adherents were villagers. South Russia, that is, Ukraine, was often a centre for such groups. There were also Free Christians, as most Tolstoyans called themselves, who might be peasants, artisans, or merchants or, like the Master himself, were from the landowning class. Occasionally a peasant lad, reared in the Orthodox Church, unexpectedly – a Tolstoyan without knowing it – took a CO stand when he was drafted. But there were not very many such cases. Likewise, Evangelical Christians, Baptists and Seventh-day Adventists, though they were to predominate among non-Mennonite COs from 1914 on, had produced few COs before the outbreak of war. Thus Tolstoy's CO friends represented a motley group. Still, despite the individual character of each CO's witness, sources like Tolstoy's letters, not intended for publication, or the exile Tolstoyan journal, *The Free Word*

(*Svobodnoe slovo*, 1901–5),[32] in general confirm his account, from which I have cited above.

Tolstoy, we have seen, felt guilty at not being placed behind bars when the government incarcerated young men, often for many years, because they had acted as he told them a Christian should do. He knew, indeed, what went on in penal battalions and other 'correctional institutions' (*ispravitel'niia arestantskiia otdeleniia*) as well as among those exiled to distant regions of Siberia (the scene of some of the most poignant chapters in his novel *Resurrection*), even if personal experience was limited to visits to COs in civilian jails or military fortresses situated not too far from home.

He strove, too, to publicize the often deplorable conditions found in such places: that would be a service not only to COs but to their unhappy criminal inmates. With Tolstoy's warm support, the Chertkovs had published in exile a volume on the Dukhobor soldiers who, after the sect's burning of weapons, had been sentenced to a term in a penal battalion.[33] Even more revealing of conditions in these battalions was the memoir by a young peasant, which the Chertkovs were to edit and publish in 1905 just before they returned to Russia. In the early 1890s Nikolai Iziumchenko had converted to Tolstoyism while fulfilling his conscript service, and he then spent two years in the penal battalion at Voronezh for refusing to continue as a combatant soldier. His account, which runs to sixty-four printed pages,[34] reveals a picture, on the one hand, of brutality and humiliation inflicted on the hapless prisoners and, on the other, of humanity on the part of both guards and officers. On one occasion, for instance, the latter together with their families joined the prisoners in a ball held to celebrate the battalion's twenty-fifth anniversary, the officers' wives dancing mazurkas with the prisoners.[35] Iziumchenko concludes his account with truly Tolstoyan optimism: 'Soon after I left the battalion twenty-four men were sent there all at once for the very [same] offence [as mine].'[36]

Seventeen years later Tolstoy, less than two months before his death, received a visit at Iasnaia Poliana from a young peasant CO, Andrei Kudrin, who had recently been released from a penal battalion where he had spent the previous three years and nine months. In April 1906 while Kudrin was awaiting trial, Tolstoy described him as 'one of those fighters for Christian truth, who serve God by serving humankind and thus help to bring in the kingdom of God on earth.'[37] The two men remained in touch from then on. Tolstoy praised Kudrin's serenity throughout his long imprisonment, and he rejoiced that the number of such people was increasing. Kudrin was evidently a talkative fellow, so that Tolstoy now seized the opportunity to get him to tell his life story, including the years he had spent in the hands of the military.[38] Kudrin's words were carefully noted down by Tolstoy's secretary, Valentin Bulgakov.[39] Tolstoy was delighted with the result, finding Kudrin's account of his experiences as a CO simple, sincere, and accurate. The latter did not hide his occasional bouts of depression when he came near to throwing in the sponge. He certainly had had some difficult moments. In the army detention barracks, for instance, he was put for three days in the 'hole' (*'temnii kartser'*) on reduced diet for behaviour the colonel of the regiment, to which he had been assigned, considered to be insolent. (Kudrin had the habit of addressing the officers as 'brother.') But his guards surreptitiously passed to him part of their own rations through the bars of his cell.[40]

What must certainly have pleased Tolstoy most as he leafed through his secretary's manuscript were Kudrin's concluding remarks describing the way in which in the penal battalion he was saved from despair and from abandoning his resolve never to handle a weapon or become a soldier. During his final months in confinement, he had become friendly with another CO, Peter Kolachev, a village schoolteacher who occupied the cell next to his in the penal battalion barracks. Kolachev had introduced him to the writings of the radical Tolstoy, which circulated clandestinely among the prisoners. It was such reading matter and his companion's encouragement that gave Kudrin new courage to persist until the time for his release arrived.[41]

Tolstoy's belief that the light generated by his fictional Prince Boris and the prince's real counterparts, whom the Russian state consigned to prison or penal battalion, would eventually dissipate the gathering war clouds darkening the world's horizons proved only too soon unfounded. Nevertheless, Tolstoy's hopes, however utopian, constitute an essential element of his *Weltanschauung* as this evolved from the late 1870s on. And the relationship which he established over the next three decades with successive generations of draft resisters forms an important part of his biography, though one that has often been lost sight of in the plethora of detail making up this extraordinary life. The new regimes introduced by the February and October revolutions of 1917 were to recognize the COs then released from jail as victims of tsarist oppression, alongside the political prisoners who had suffered during the imperial era. Tolstoy surely would have agreed with this.

NOTES

1 Tolstoy had already contemplated such a play in 1893. The drama has appeared twice in English translation: first by Louise and Aylmer Maude in *Plays by Leo Tolstoy* (London, 1923) (hereafter Maude, *Plays*), and then by Marvin Kantor with Tanya Tulchinsky in *Tolstoy's Plays*, vol. 3 (Evanston IL, 1998). The Russian text can be found in Tolstoy's *Polnoe sobranie sochinenii* (Moscow-Leningrad) (hereafter *PSS*), vol. 31 (1954), 113–84, followed by a detailed history of its composition and printing (*Istoriia pisaniia i pechataniia*) on pages 291–300.

2 See Aylmer Maude's preface to *Plays*, xi–xiii.

3 See Nicholas B. Breyfogle, 'Swords into Plowshares: Opposition to Military Service among Religious Sectarians, 1770s to 1874,' in Eric Lohr and Marshall Poe, eds, *The Military and Society in Russia, 1450–1917* (Leiden, 2002), 441–67, for early dilemmas of Molokans and Dukhobors vis-à-vis military service.

4 Universal military service was not introduced until 1887 into the Caucasus *guberniia* where the Dukhobors then lived. At first their conscripts had not protested against bearing arms: resistance came only a little later under the direction of Peter Verigin. For the traditional scholarly view of these events, including the famous 'burning of weapons' in 1895, see George Woodcock and Ivan Avakumovic, *The Doukhobors* (Toronto and Ottawa, 1997), chap. 4. Recently Breyfogle has added a new dimension to the subject, especially in his 'Rethinking the Origins of the Doukhobor Arms-Burning: 1886–1893,' in Andrew Donskov et al., eds, *The Doukhobor Centenary in Canada: A Multidisciplinary Perspective on Their Unity and Diversity* (Ottawa, 2000), 55–82.

5 'Zakon nasiliia i zakon liubvi,' *PSS*, vol. 37 (Moscow, 1956), 187; in the translation by Mary Koutouzow Tolstoy, *The Law of Love and the Law of Violence* (New York / Chicago / San Francisco, 1970), 59.

6 The main source here is the thirty-seven-page typescript report 'Kratkie svedeniia ob otkazavshikhsia ot voinnoi sluzhby v Rossii po religioznym ubezhdeniiam' (January 1912) in the Pavel Miliukov Papers in the State Archive of the Russian Federation, Moscow (GARF), fond 579, op. 1, d. 2568 (cited below as Mil. MS). I must thank Lynne Viola and Denis Kozlov for their help in obtaining from Russia a photocopy of the document. This document gives a list of 117 cases, out of which 103 cases fall between 1880 and 1910. There is no indication of who compiled the list or why it was undertaken. But for the role of the historian and Kadet Party leader, Miliukov, as a liberal internationalist and peace advocate, see Thomas Riha, *A Russian European: Paul Miliukov in Russian Politics* (Notre Dame IN, 1969),

207–8, and D.A. Sdvizhkov, 'Idei nenasiliia v obrazovannykh sloiakh Germanii i Rossii nakanune Pervoi mirovoi voiny,' in T. Pavlova, ed., *Nenasilie kak mirovozzrenie i obraz zhizni (istoricheskii rakurs)* (Moscow, 2000), 138, 139. Materials on COs who were convicted by Russian military tribunals must lie buried in military archives surviving from the imperial era, but a research project in that quarter does not seem feasible within the foreseeable future, given the dimensions of the task and the scattered character of the evidence. At least two COs composed autobiographical accounts that have not so far surfaced, but they may still be extant; see unpaginated notice in *Svobodnoe slovo* (Christchurch, England), no. 2 (January-February 1902).

7 Miliukov's list is certainly incomplete, especially with respect to the nineteenth century. For instance, CO cases which do not appear there were known to Tolstoy.

8 *PSS*, vol. 36 (1936), 279.

9 Ibid., vol. 82 (1956), 153, 154. Ernest Simmons quotes from a letter Tolstoy wrote to Iakov Chaga, a peasant Tolstoyan jailed in 1903 for refusing induction into the army: 'I am ashamed of myself that at a time when you sit with so-called criminals in a foul prison, I live in sumptuous fashion with criminals not so-called [...] The most powerful feeling that I experience towards such as you is love as well as gratitude for all those millions of people who will be benefited by your act.' See Ernest J. Simmons, *Leo Tolstoy* (Boston, 1946), 632; the letter was printed in *PSS*, vol. 75 (1956), 19, 20.

10 Joshua A. Sanborn, *Drafting the Russian Nation: Military Conscription, Total War, and Mass Politics, 1905–1925* (Dekalb IL, 2003), 185.

11 In 1907 Sergei Prozretskii, a well-to-do citizen of Riga, when inducted not only refused to handle a weapon, but also refused stubbornly to wear an army uniform. See Mil. MS, fol. 25. (Most COs did not object to uniform: indeed, wearing uniform was unavoidable for all who had to serve in a penal battalion.) Prozretskii was then sentenced to five years in a civilian prison. Possibly his uncompromising stance may have led his court martial to take this decision. I doubt, though, if that had been Prozretskii's aim: five years in a pre-revolutionary convict prison was not necessarily preferable to two to three years in a penal battalion.

12 Tolstoy's *Collected Works* contain a number of references to a CO persuading one or more fellow soldiers to adopt his position. A prime example of such pacifist impregnation is that of Petr Ol'khovik and Kirill Sereda in 1896.

13 *Svobodnoe slovo*, no. 8 (November-December 1903), cols. 9, 10; Mil. MS, fol. 12.

14 The earliest mention of a specific Russian CO in Tolstoy's *Collected Works* (*PSS*), dating to 22 July 1881 ('Dnevnik'), refers to Ivan Siutaev, a son of the

Tolstoy-style village philosopher Vasilii Siutaev (1820–92). In 1877 Ivan had refused to serve in the army and was jailed for a number of years, including time in the notorious Schlüsselburg fortress as well as in a lunatic asylum. See *PSS*, vol. 49 (1952), 54; 63 (1934), 365, 366; 85 (1935), 118, 120, 121. In his 'V chem moia vera?' completed on 22 January 1884, Tolstoy writes that, in contrast to the contemporary churches' virtually unanimous rejection of the pacifism of the early church (and of Christ himself), 'only recently there was one [Russian] peasant who, on the basis of the Gospels, refused military service.' This was, of course, Ivan Siutaev (*PSS*, vol. 23 [1957], 367, 558).

15 *PSS*, vol. 63 (1934), 301–6; also Simmons, *Leo Tolstoy*, 387, 388, and my *Freedom from War: Nonsectarian Pacifism 1814–1914* (Toronto, 1991), 212.

16 In a few rare cases, COs were allowed noncombatant service in the army: for example, Fedor Burov, a reserve soldier from Poltava *guberniia*, in 1904, or the Sabbatarian Iatsenko, also a soldier CO, in 1908. See Mil. MS, fols. 13, 30. Perhaps the fact that these two men had been part of the army before declaring their unwillingness to handle a weapon may have made it easier for the military to grant this concession. On the other hand, it could have resulted primarily from the liberal attitude of the local command under which the men served. Available sources remain silent on this point.

17 Drozhzhin's was only the most notorious case of a CO dying before the expiry of his sentence either from a disease contracted during confinement or from ill treatment or (as in Drozhzhin's case) of a combination of both these factors. Tuberculosis and typhus were the most frequent killers: they did not distinguish between COs and criminals, who both fell victims. Not only Tolstoy's *Collected Works* but also the Miliukov report contain other cases covering over two decades. See Mil. MS, fols. 18, 19, 23, 31. Alexsandr Varnavskii, for example, served his sentence in the civilian jail at Kherson: 'Here he was several times beaten severely with the butt of a rifle so that he was left unconscious. His cell was icy cold; its floor, on which he had to sleep in the absence of a bed, was cemented and with water everywhere.' He died in 1911 from tuberculosis with over two years of a five-year sentence still to go. Tolstoy took a great interest in his fate and corresponded with him on various subjects over a number of years. And well he might, since Varnavskii's was an interesting case: while a guard in a penal battalion, he had had a row with one of its noncommissioned officers, seemingly in connection with his own conversion around that time to Christian pacifism. See Mil. MS, fol. 23.

18 *PSS*, 69 (1954), 184–6; also printed in *Pis'ma Petra Vasil'evicha Ol'khovika* (Christchurch and Croydon, 1897), 25–7, and in my *Freedom from War*, 212–14. For Drozhzhin, see also Mil. MS, fols. 3–5.

19 PSS, vol. 71 (1954), 278, 279.

20 Ibid., 289, 290.

21 Ibid., vol. 75 (1956), 47.

22 Ibid., vol. 77 (1956), 205, 206. In this case, the books confiscated were probably nonfiction writings by Tolstoy. Prison authorities sometimes considered these to be unsuitable reading for inmates in their charge.

23 Ibid., vol. 80 (1955), 35, 36. Tolstoy was thinking in particular of Anton Ikonnikov, a railway machinist from Riazan province, with whom he corresponded on various topics from 1906 until his death. Ikonnikov, a former social democrat turned Tolstoyan, spent nearly seven years in confinement between 1901 and 1911. One might almost say he was Tolstoy's favourite CO. He was particularly effective in 'missionizing' on behalf of pacifism among his fellow soldiers in camp or military correctional institution (see Mil. MS, fol. 16). In the course of his prison odyssey, Ikonnikov was in 1909 incarcerated in a Warsaw army command prison, where convicts were kept shackled day and night, along with three other soldier COs. Later, one of them, Fedor Bannov, after serving three years of a four-year sentence of Siberian *katorga* in Nerchinsk, attempted to escape from jail, was caught, and then sentenced to an additional four years' penal servitude plus twenty days in solitary confinement (see Tolstoy, *PSS*, vol. 80 [1955], 96; Mil. MS, fol. 22). For two successful draft-evaders (better located than was Bannov for this operation), see *Svobodnoe slovo*, 4 (April 1903), col. 14; Mil. MS, fol. 10. Because of his rash venture, which occurred after Tolstoy's death, Bannov received the severest punishment of all the CO cases I have encountered in the pre-war period. Before the First World War the maximum penalty imposed on a non-escapee CO was six years' penal servitude (*katorga*) with an addition possible of up to eighteen years' administrative exile, usually in Iakutsk.

24 *Freedom from War*, 214, 215.

25 *PSS*, vol. 79 (1955), 81, 82. Tolstoy's correspondent was Boris Nikolaevich Denshchikov. The editors of *PSS* were unable to discover any further details about him or his subsequent fate. In order to help Denshchikov reach a decision, Tolstoy sent him copies of two letters written to himself by COs in jail. 'One,' he explained, 'will show you the hardships [trudnost'] involved in refusing service and the other how easy it can be.' The second letter, as one might guess, was from Ikonnikov.

26 Henry H. Hirshbiel, 'Conscription in Russia,' in Joseph L. Wieczynski, ed., *The Modern Encyclopedia of Russian and Soviet History* (Gulf Breeze FL), vol. 8 (1978), 7; N.N. Golovin, *The Russian Army in World War I* (New Haven CT 1969), 1–29.

27 I have used Constance Garnett's translation, *The Kingdom of God Is within You* (Lincoln NE and London, 1984), 225–9.

28 Ibid., 228, 229.

29 *PSS*, vol. 55 (1937), 119, 493. See also Mil. MS, fols. 17, 18.

30 *PSS*, vol. 78 (1956), 214, 215. The Miliukov report for 1909 (Mil. MS, fol. 33) gives details about a CO named Nikolai Ivanov, whose conversion from revolutionary socialism to Christian pacifism resulted from his encounter with Tolstoy's writings on nonviolence while a deserter from the navy. Ivanov decided to give himself up to the police believing that was what he should do as a Tolstoyan, and was sentenced to two years in a naval disciplinary detachment but released before his term was up for saving its commander from drowning. But the navy command, rather meanly, returned him to the regular navy. When he refused, 'on account of his religious convictions,' to carry out his duties there, like Tregubov and Zakharov before him he was thrown into the Kronstadt jail, whence he escaped and was once more on the run. 'Until now no further news of him [Do sikh por ne naiden],' the report concludes. Ivanov's name does not appear in the *Collected Works*; so it is doubtful if Tolstoy was ever aware of this colourful disciple of his. Reservist and soldier COs, we may note, become increasingly visible in the Miliukov report from the Russo-Japanese War onwards.

31 The overwhelming majority of imprisoned COs were Slavs, Ukrainians and Belarusans among them, probably not possessing any well-defined ethnic identity separate from that of Great Russians. But Tolstoy was in touch with a Latvian (Karl Siksne), a Moldavian, that is, a Rumanian (Ivan Kurtysh), and a Jew who had converted to Tolstoyism (Chaim Dymshits).

32 See, for example, *Svobodnoe slovo*, no. 4 (April 1903), cols. 11–13; no. 8 (November-December 1903), col. 10; no. 9 (January-February 1904), cols. 7–9; no. 11 (May-June 1904), col. 8; no. 13 (September-November 1904), cols. 6–19.

33 Vladimir and Aleksandra Chertkov, eds, *Dukhobortsy v distsiplinarnom batal'one* (Christchurch, 1902). The Chertkovs promised a complementary volume on Dukhobors in prisons ('Dukhobortsy v tiurmakh'), but this was never published, presumably for lack of funds. See V. Chertkov, ed., *Christian Martyrdom in Russia: Persecution of the Spirit-Wrestlers (or Doukhobortsi) in the Caucasus* (London, 1897), 50–6, 72, 104–8, for examples of the savage treatment of Dukhobor draftees in the penal battalions to which they had been sent after 1895. Tolstoy (and Chertkov) more than once sent letters of protest to the commanding officers responsible for these barbarities. Such protests seem sometimes to have had an effect. See, for example, Pavel

Biriukov, ed., *Dukhobortsy: Sbornik statei, vospominanii, pisem i drugikh dokumentov* (Moscow, 1908), 86–90.

34 *V distsiplinarnom batal'one: Zapiski N.T. Iziumchenko* (Christchurch, 1905); Peter Brock and John L.H. Keep, eds, *Life in a Penal Battalion of the Imperial Russian Army: The Tolstoyan N.T. Iziumchenko's Story* (York, 2001). The translation is by John Keep.

35 Ibid., 61–3.

36 Ibid., 63. Iziumchenko, though, was lucky in not being flogged during his two years in the Voronezh penal battalion. As the acerbic Drozhzhin, his companion in captivity, had remarked: 'Well, brother, evidently it's not your destiny to get yourself beaten' (57). But the kind of rough treatment that sons of the village, like Drozhzhin or Iziumchenko, could take in their stride, was to induce a severe mental breakdown in the young Kharkov merchant Pavel Bezverkhii. After being sentenced in 1906 to a term in a penal battalion, 'he was ... punished continuously with exceptional cruelty.' Tolstoy was largely instrumental in gaining his release in the following year after his sanity had come under question. See Mil. MS, fol. 21.

37 *PSS*, vol. 76 (1956), 154. See also ibid., vol. 77 (1956), 44.

38 A.I. Kudrin, *Chto Andrei Ivanovich Kudrin razskazal' Tolstomu* (Berlin, [1911?]) (hereafter, *Chto Kudrin raszkazal'*); *Récit d'André Ivanovitch Koudrine sur son refus du service militaire (rapporté d'après ses propres paroles)* (Geneva, 1912). (Kudrin's *razskaz* has also been published in Russia in the journal *Istinnaia svoboda* no. 3 [1920], 9–19, but I have not seen this item.) In his preface the translator, Petr Nikolaev, apologizes for his inability to reproduce the racy colloquialisms present in Kudrin's oral narrative. Kudrin had been reared among the Molokans of Samara, but, at the age of eighteen, finding the sect's faith too narrow for his taste, he broke away. Under the influence of the pacifist Dobroliubov's teachings, he decided to refuse military service when in 1905 he was drafted. Later, the writings of Tolstoy confirmed him in his stand. See also Mil. MS, fols. 20, 21.

39 Next year Bulgakov was himself drafted in March but in the following month was exempted 'permanently' on grounds of health (Mil. MS, fol. 36).

40 *Chto Kurdin razskazal,'* 32–4.

41 Ibid., 45, 46.

12 The Škarvan Case: The Trial and Imprisonment of a Slovak Tolstoyan

Early in February 1895 Tolstoy received a letter from his devoted Slovak disciple, Dušan Makovický, informing him that a young Slovak army doctor of peasant origin, Albert Škarvan (1869–1926), shortly before completing his conscript service in the Austro-Hungarian army had, on grounds of conscience, refused further service and was now under arrest. Through Makovický, Tolstoy was already acquainted with Škarvan's name; he knew the young man had come under the spell of Tolstoyan ideas. But this influence had not been strong enough to prevent him from joining the army (though as a noncombatant, it is true) when, on completing his medical studies at the University of Innsbruck towards the end of 1894, he had received his call-up notice.

Replying to Makovický, Tolstoy admitted to being excited by the news of Škarvan's resolute action. 'When I learn about deeds of this kind,' he wrote, 'I always feel a strong admixture of apprehension, exultation, compassion, and joy.' He was fearful lest such action should stem from a love of notoriety or egotism. But if it reflected the divine truth, then indeed it was a matter for rejoicing even if 'the man were to get burnt' in the process. 'I hope, I am sure, that our dear Škarvan has acted as he has acted because he cannot act in any other way.' In that case God would be manifesting himself through him, and then any hardships he had to suffer would be easy to endure. 'Please,' Tolstoy concluded, 'write and tell me everything you know [about Škarvan]. Can we help him in some way? And give him my love.'[1]

Meanwhile, in northern Hungary (present-day Slovakia) the Škarvan case pursued its course. When Škarvan took his momentous step, his regiment was stationed in the town of Košice (Kaschau). His initial defiance of the military had occurred on 7 February, and he remained in confinement of one or another sort until his final release from prison on 25 October. The army authorities had not at first known quite what to make of the case or what to do with this strange young man. The case, indeed, was unprecedented since in Austria-Hungary, apart from Mennonites, only the peasant sect of Nazarenes objected on principle to military service (see essay 10 above). They were sentenced to repeated terms of lengthy imprisonment. This fate now hung over Škarvan's head: a kindly army major warned him that, as an educated man used to the comforts of life, he would never be able to endure such treatment, and the major ended by a personal appeal to his prisoner:

> I don't wish [he said] to enter into a philosophical discussion with you because that does not form part of my function. I just want to tell you this. Have you properly considered what you are doing and what will be the consequences of your action? You know, don't you, that if you persist in your present intention, they'll throw you into jail and no one can be sure if they won't keep you there for many years? And what will you have achieved? Absolutely nothing. You're a serious man, you've read and thought a lot. But I must say this: you would be acting more sensibly, even though you are unwilling to renounce your idea, if you would first complete the short term of service still remaining and then devote yourself to the investigation and promotion of your ideas. There are, you know, in our country too, people who support the idea of disarmament and peace. So, if this question indeed interests you and you have the talent, you can devote yourself to its study. In the course of time you may even become a member of parliament and then you can try to achieve something for peace! But if you continue as you are doing now, you will waste away in jail and no one will take any notice of you. Don't think you're the first to act as you are doing now! For a long time there have been in our monarchy sectarians – the so called Nazarenes – and they, like you, refuse to be soldiers ... Every Nazarene male sits out in prison his 6–8 years, indeed sometimes it is 10–12 years. Most of them die during this time. And if they do survive such prolonged punishment and finally serve out their sentences, they emerge from prison broken old men. But of course these are uneducated people, religious fanatics and mystics; an educated man like you would never endure such treatment.[2]

After a few weeks the military authorities decided to send Škarvan under escort to Vienna. There he was placed in the psychiatric ward of one of that city's leading hospitals. After keeping him under examination for nine weeks, the doctors decided unanimously that Škarvan, however odd his views might appear to many people, was undoubtedly sane. Thus the hopes entertained by the military of consigning him to a lunatic asylum for good were frustrated. He was then taken back to Kaschau and soon put on trial there.

On the way to the Imperial capital, the Vienna express had stopped at a station near where Makovický had a country medical practice. The tolerant military escort allowed the latter to travel for several stops with Škarvan. Among various mementos brought back from a recent visit to Russia, Makovický was able to show a photo of Tolstoy to Škarvan, who felt immensely encouraged by this glimpse of 'grandpa, as we used to call him among ourselves,' he adds in his memoirs.[3] In the psychiatric ward a little later, Škarvan experienced another reinvigorating contact with Tolstoy when a Ruthenian acquaintance of his, named Shevchuk, then living in Vienna and an almost daily visitor at the hospital, brought him a copy of the freshly appeared story *Master and Man*. Reading it, Škarvan's spirits revived. 'The labourer Nikita put me to shame by his sacrificial life and his beautiful death. As I read the story, I felt ashamed of my meanness of spirit. A good book is often a help in life.'[4]

It had been in the Vienna psychiatric ward that Škarvan met the great love of his life. It was to be a fairly brief encounter that would end sadly in mutual recrimination. After it was over, Škarvan told his story in a long letter he wrote to Tolstoy, who was fascinated by it. He found it, he told Škarvan, 'very moving.' He saw it as 'a drama' – a tragedy – involving two persons with quite different characters. The letter was never published, but it has been preserved in the manuscript collection of the Tolstoy Museum in Moscow.[5] The beloved one was an Austrian countess, a widow of Polish origin, Adela Mazzuchelli.[6] 'She possesses,' Škarvan told the Master, 'the most exuberant nature of any woman I have ever known. Indeed I loved her ever so dearly. She was the only person I could tell everything to, everything I felt and everything I did.'

Adela had arrived in the psychiatric ward during the fifth week of the Slovak's sojourn there: she was visiting another patient, a cavalry officer named Carina, to whom she had become emotionally attached. She soon switched her affections to Škarvan – to her previous lover's dismay. Škarvan confessed to Tolstoy that he had often felt awkward in the presence of upper-class women. But there was never the slightest constraint in his relationship with Adela: he always felt at ease with this 'proud aristocrat.'

Adela continued to be Carina's visitor. But every day Adela and Albert took a stroll together in the hospital garden; they usually had supper together, too, in Albert's room, which he tidied up especially for her. While Adela brought dainty morsels she had bought in the town in order to supplement the hospital fare, 'I would lay the table,' he told Tolstoy, 'wash the dishes, make the tea, etc.' Often she brought her three children with her for the day; and to them Škarvan would tell stories. (He was a wonderful storyteller.) They all, adults and children, played games together in the garden; it was springtime and the blossoms were out. Adela spent more and more of her time at the hospital; in fact, as she confessed, she now felt bored at home. She had never met anyone like Albert before; she felt that his *Weltanschauung* (she did not use that word though) was utterly different from anything she had known about before and that his act of defiance could not be assessed by the rules of life she had been taught.

She listened to him like a bright yet innocent child as he explained the reasons that had led him to his 'act' and expounded the Tolstoyan gospel that had at least brought him inner peace after he had despaired of the world and its ways. She showered him with questions and would listen to his reply with intense emotion, her nose convulsed and her lips twitching. She would interrupt him when she did not understand something or failed to follow his argument, sometimes asking for time to think over what he was telling her, especially when this appeared particularly challenging. 'She filled me with admiration,' writes Škarvan. But naturally she worried and perplexed Carina. Relations between the two men were rapidly to cool.

At first Škarvan attempted to keep the affair on a platonic level. Not long before he was scheduled to leave the hospital, Škarvan received from the countess the first of three letters written in German, which he included almost in full in his report to Tolstoy. She told her 'dear friend' of her delight in his company. 'I would gladly talk to you without interruption for hours on end.' And she dared not think what would happen to her when he left the hospital. She did not wish, though, to place any obstacles in the way of his becoming reconciled with his former fiancée, who had broken off her engagement to Škarvan after his act of defiance. What she offered him was her sincere friendship. She once again intended to become Carina's wife; her feelings for Albert he had made her realize were indeed of a different – and more elevated – kind than those she entertained towards her other – and most faithful – admirer.

Albert answered her letter without delay: it was now the day before he was due to leave Vienna for good. He loved her, he told her, because he loved God and she was striving to love God, too. Not unexpectedly, she interpreted this letter as a reciprocation of her own love for Albert rather than merely a recognition of the love they both now felt for God. Her second letter, therefore, reflected a sense of triumph. 'You are mine!' she began. 'You love me as I love you.' (The doctor was no longer *Sie* but *Du*.) 'No one is nearer to me than you are.' True, she loved him as a creature of God, but she loved him, too, as a man. She begged him not to leave her; she needed his help if she was not to fall back into her old lifestyle. 'At first I could not comprehend why you had chosen to go to prison; now I understand why.'

Škarvan's reaction was mixed. He obviously wished to keep free of emotional entanglements; at the same time, as he told Tolstoy, he knew she had come to 'worship' him. He could not fail, either, to notice the mounting passion expressed in her letters. On the eve of his departure, therefore, he felt awkward. With Carina hovering in the background, he hesitated to fulfil her desire for a passionate farewell, even though he saw how unhappy his unwillingness to do so made her: she looked to him as if she were ready to commit suicide. He became frightened and, suddenly, he kissed her on the lips, telling her to be at the railway station early next morning.

Of course she was there, along with a friend of Škarvan's from the city who had come on his own account. Though she looked pale after a sleepless night, Albert thought her enchanting – no longer the haughty high-society lady but 'a simple country lass.' Now for the first time he, too, used the familiar second person singular in place of the formal second person plural which, despite their increasing intimacy, he had hitherto always employed in addressing her. The kindly military escort allowed her to travel with Škarvan as far as Marchegg several stations down the line; he even left them by themselves in the carriage reserved for the prisoner and his guard. Albert felt blissfully happy as he talked to Adela about God and His love for humankind. Škarvan described to Tolstoy how deeply he had been moved after she had alighted from the train, by the sight of her standing on the platform at Marchegg as if immobilized by shock, clutching her gloves and her hat, which the strong wind had blown off so that her abundant tresses streamed in all directions.

Back again in the barracks at Košice, Škarvan finally went on trial before a military court, which on 4 July sentenced him to lose his medical diploma (the MD gave the right to practise medicine) and at the same time to serve four months in a military prison, including a month in solitary confinement and two days each month on a bread-and-water punishment diet. This may sound like harsh treatment. But compared to what the courts meted out to the unhappy Nazarenes (happy Nazarenes, Tolstoy might have been inclined to say, since they were enabled to suffer intensely for their beliefs), Škarvan's fate was comparatively mild. He had been an officer in the joint Austro-Hungarian army; and in the Habsburg monarchy that counted for something, even in a military prison.

Škarvan indeed had felt in fine fettle as he returned from Vienna to face the music. In his memoirs he recalls the scene: 'It was then spring ... warm, sunny, joyful spring. There were flowers in bloom [in the barracks garden], and the air was scented, and the birds were warbling all around ... What joy it was to be alive!' His conscript colleagues, their term of service completed, had all gone home by now. But a new batch of young conscript doctors had taken their place. These now greeted Škarvan warmly: no doubt they were curious to see this peculiar fellow about whom the senior officers must have told them. The young men laughed together as if without a care in the world. 'No one,' Škarvan concluded, 'looking at our jolly gathering would have imagined that, on the threshold of prison, one could enjoy oneself in such an almost childlike way. And indeed I have wondered myself that it could be so.'[7]

Even after entering jail, Škarvan kept in good spirits, despite his grim surroundings and the spartan lifestyle to which he was now subjected. The chapters of his memoirs in which he describes life in an Austro-Hungarian military prison, especially his two weeks 'in solitary,' constitute a valuable contribution to prison literature.

Though housed separately from the other prisoners, who were all private soldiers, Škarvan had many opportunities to talk to them and to observe the much harsher treatment to which they were subjected:

> What from the beginning struck me in prison [he wrote] was that convicts are not at all, as we tend to think of them (I don't know why), evil people; they are not sinister persons. The more I came directly in contact with convicts, the more I became convinced that, as happens outside in conditions of freedom, here too we can indeed find both good men and bad men. Though I looked intensely, I could perceive no brand mark burnt into a prisoner's soul, no trace there of any inborn brutality, and no spe-

> cially perverse disposition or range of feelings. True, in prisons men pick up certain unpleasant characteristics not usually found in people outside. But these are traits acquired in the course of incarceration.[8]

Škarvan describes the constant shouting of the guards, their coarse and brutal language, and the humiliating body searches and friskings which they inflicted on the ordinary prisoners as well as the insanitary cells into which the latter were locked for the long evenings and the unhealthy conditions in which most of them had to work during the day. The meals provided by the jail authorities were wretched. Škarvan, as an officer, was permitted, however, to purchase extra food outside the prison. He experienced a feeling of guilt at the privileges he enjoyed, even though he was at the same time a convicted prisoner. Indeed, the sight of the shaven head of the ordinary prisoner and the grotesque prison uniform he was required to wear, 'which branded him as a convict in the eyes of everyone,' distressed Škarvan. He felt, as a follower of Tolstoy, that he should be suffering as his fellow inmates were suffering; yet he dreaded the thought of ever being reduced to their level.

Surrounded by dirt and afflicted by fleas, bedbugs, and body lice, these men were always filthy – except for the very occasional bath. But this, Škarvan tells us, 'was not ... a bath in the usual meaning of the word, for all the prisoners bathed in the same water. Thus, one man simply exchanged his own filth for the filth of another! ... I am certain, apart from pigs, no animals would have entered liquid of this character. Yet the convicts were glad to go into the water for the dirt that adhered to their bodies tormented them.' They treated the occasion as a time to have some fun and, naked, indulged in horseplay as if they were still schoolboys.[9] For a few minutes they were able to forget the miseries of existence. Škarvan explained to his readers that the reason why he had decided now 'to write about what [he had seen] and ... experienced in these places of torture existing in our purportedly "enlightened" age' was because 'the public knows little about life in our military prisons.'[10]

Towards the end of his sentence, Škarvan, as a result of a minor infraction of prison regulations, had been placed for fourteen days in solitary confinement, the 'hole' dreaded so much by the ordinary convicts that they 'would prefer to be chained up than spend even a day' in a solitary punishment cell. 'In solitary,' Škarvan writes, 'what above all hits one at the outset is the cramped space and the stifling and stale atmosphere. I felt exactly as if I were in a mouldy animal-hutch.' Soon he became engaged in battle with hundreds of bedbugs that infested his new residence: 'a loathsome and bold foe' that prevented him from sleeping until his 'merciless attack on the enemy' had been successful. 'But at last, on the third night, when all that remained of the enemy were the corpses strewing the battlefield, I was once more able to sleep. However, from the squashed bugs there now arose within my cell a worse stench than existed anywhere else in the prison.' Somehow or other, Škarvan got through his fourteen days: the bedbugs disposed of, 'a feeling of gentle calmness [had] settled on me, which ousted the burden of the present, so that my spirit remained at rest. I once again felt happy.' He slept soundly at night and awoke refreshed, ready to face whatever the new day would bring him.[11]

For the spring and most of the summer of 1895, Škarvan's name does not appear in Tolstoy's correspondence, but Slovak and other visitors may have brought news of him to Iasnaia Poliana during this period. Or it may have been that Tolstoy, with his mind filled with pressing matters nearer at home, including several Russian conscientious objectors in jail or awaiting trial, may have let the Škarvan case escape temporarily from his memory, though he was certainly aware that the young man remained locked up. But early in September we find him asking Makovický: 'How is dear Škarvan getting on? Do you or his other friends – or his mother – see him? And is he in good spirits?' He has to think of his soul, Tolstoy went on, if he is to survive his ordeal. 'And that is going to be difficult to do both because he is young and strong and because he is a physician so that all his youthful energy is now directed towards the body. Anyhow please keep me informed about everything you know about him. I know already what the papers write about him' – most of it slander! But that should not disturb Škarvan.

Tolstoy wanted to hear exactly how the young man spent his time in jail. 'Does he read? Does he work?' The Russian asked Makovický to pass on to Škarvan one piece of advice: he should so organize his prison day as to divide his time, so far as possible, equally between intellectual and physical pursuits. For instance, let him learn a foreign language; let him practise a manual craft. Finally, Tolstoy again asked Makovický to tell him in what way he could help Škarvan. 'We his friends are a small group but we do indeed truly love him.'[12]

It was not only in Russia but also in his own Hungary that Škarvan's 'deed' had found him friends. In the Hungarian capital, Budapest, a circle of active Tolstoyans had emerged under the leadership of Eugen Heinrich Schmitt, who had begun to propagate the Tolstoyan gospel on the pages of his journal published in German, *Die Religion des Geistes* (The Religion of the Spirit).[13] On hearing of Škarvan's trial and imprisonment, Schmitt had set to and composed an outspoken 'Manifesto' protesting against the government's action. In August he sent Tolstoy a draft informing him that he intended to publish the manifesto in his paper. Tolstoy agreed that 'the idea of the Manifesto' was excellent but, he added, 'I have not been so taken with the form' that Schmitt had given it. A document of that kind should be 'easily understood by persons without a literary education.' Tolstoy advised his Hungarian disciple to write 'simply and clearly' so as to achieve the effect he desired.[14]

Meanwhile, inside his prison, Škarvan's romance continued to develop. Adela had at once followed him to Košice, and there by a combination of feminine charm and aristocratic bearing she succeeded in persuading the prison authorities to allow her to see Albert twice a day, though they required that a guard be present at every meeting. She and Albert continued their dialogue on the spiritual life and the ideal society. But from time to time – Carina apparently forgotten – Adela would raise the question of their life together after Albert came out of jail. 'I'll leave Vienna and come with my children and be with you wherever you may happen to be.' She did not intend now to marry again, she told him, nor did she wish to interfere in any way with his occupations. But he would come every evening to her house for supper. As in the hospital, he would slice the bread ('no one else can do that like you') and play with the children and tell them stories. 'And so the time will pass ...' Škarvan confessed to Tolstoy that he found her 'chatter' delightful: those meetings undoubtedly helped him through a difficult period.

Within the prison walls, with the jail guard sitting discreetly beside them, their relationship reached a climax. Finally Albert became fully conscious that Adela was not merely a 'beloved sister' as he had pretended till then, but a woman whom he loved. 'As she chattered away ... I could not refrain from stroking her curls ... Only a tiny push was needed for the thin partition which lay between us to fall, and then I would [know] for sure that I was passionately, madly, in love with the woman who was Adela.' ('What a mixture of animal and divinity humans are.')

The partition fell when Adela said goodbye to him as he was led away to spend two weeks in solitary confinement in the punishment cells for that minor infringement of the prison rules. Earlier he had kissed her – but 'as a sister'; now, for the first time, the countess took the initiative. 'And what a kiss that was!' he told Tolstoy.

> With that kiss everything seemed changed. Adela, lifting the veil which covered her face, had pressed her lips to mine. And, in our speechless contact, I had experienced a feeling of rapture. Throughout my body I felt the sweet poison of passion, of physical desire for a woman. I felt it surge through my body; I felt it in every limb, to the tips of my fingers. I had never before felt desire take hold of me so overwhelmingly; hitherto she had not exerted as strong an attraction on me as now. It was as if in that kiss she received confirmation of her longing that I should belong to her and to her alone. It was as if she were telling me: you can occupy yourself in any way you wish but you must belong to me. Apart from me no one will – or can – love you. She left the room but the passion she had aroused in me remained ... My cheeks were on fire. I felt her slender waist and her soft hair as if they were still beside me. The violet perfume she always used scented the room. To sleep with her seemed to me now both innocent and natural – and so desirable!

While he remained in confinement, Škarvan just let matters drift. Underneath, he obviously felt uneasy at some of the implications of their changed relationship. Still, it was wonderful to have her there to brighten the dreary scene he was daily forced to witness behind the prison walls.

In the spirit of the Master, he considered it would be wrong to conceal any of his imperfections, including his lapses from sexual purity, from the woman who loved him. It was during Adela's last visit at Košice that he gave her a letter in which he made, as it were, full confession of his sins. 'Since we had become so close to each other I wanted her to know all of me. For this purpose ... I had in my letter to tell her everything. I wrote there ... frankly and openly of the physical desire I felt for her and about my whole sexual life from the very beginning.' She responded that very same day to her 'dearest Belo.' She was in no way surprised, she wrote, at what he now told her; after all, none of us are perfect and, therefore, must not demand too much of each other. 'Surely a kiss bestowed out of true love is not unclean'; rather, it proves the purity of such love. Come what might, they should face the future with confidence: 'the most important thing is that we understand each other, that in spirit we are one. Everything else is unimportant.' She asked him to respond to her letter promptly.

Albert felt at first reassured by the letter; he did not doubt Adela's sincerity for a moment. But soon misgivings began to arise. For instance, might not marriage with the woman he loved conflict with his love of God? He wondered, too, if any woman would have the power to retain his love. Even after the arrival of children, might he not yearn to become again a pilgrim in search of God? Or suppose his wife were to die in childbirth, a not infrequent occurrence at that time, surely he would feel like a murderer? 'I know,' he told Tolstoy, 'there were far better and more important things to do in life than procreate offspring when I really didn't want children.' Thus, while marriage attracted him, at the same time it scared him. Reading Škarvan's contorted prose with its misty aspirations towards the godhead, one cannot doubt that the romance between Adela and Albert was doomed from the outset. In Škarvan's relationship to Adela there may also have been a touch of class: a consciousness on Albert's part that the elegant young Viennese lady and the boy from the village were not likely to make a success of life on the long haul. He probably suspected that his main attraction for Adela lay in his novelty, which would wear off sooner or later. Their parting soon came, a bitter one, and it was for good. Adela had felt rejected by her dearest Belo, and she could not forgive him for this.

Meanwhile, Tolstoy continued to feel concern for the jailed Slovak. Learning from Makovický towards the end of September of the exalted 'spiritual state' which Škarvan had maintained throughout his imprisonment, he expressed his joy at this news and at the expectation of Škarvan's imminent release from jail. Makovický had asked the Russian if perhaps he could help Škarvan financially when he came out. And to this request Tolstoy responded a little ambiguously. 'I don't myself have money available' at the moment, he wrote. 'I could certainly collect some but I think it better not to have to do so.'[15]

For all Tolstoy's willingness to help, his potentialities as a fundraiser were not inexhaustible. A few months earlier, the Dukhobor crisis had reached its climax with their solemn burning of weapons on 28–9 June, and the efforts of Russian Tolstoyans were now centred on campaigning on the Dukhobors' behalf. That involved heavy expenditure.

In fact, Škarvan did not require much financial assistance after leaving prison on 25 October. He lived at home. His needs were simple and easily satisfied. True, he could no longer earn a living as a doctor since the annulment of his diploma took away the legal right to do this. (He did indeed occupy his time by giving medical aid to the peasants in the surrounding countryside, where there was an insufficiency of trained doctors. But he did this mostly without charging since his patients lacked the means to pay.) Škarvan's major worry concerned his old mother.[16] But the kindly Makovický was already helping her financially while Škarvan was in jail, and he continued to send her money after the latter's release.

Replying to the letter Škarvan had written to him shortly before his release from jail, Tolstoy told him his letter had caused him much heartfelt joy. Indeed, from the way Škarvan wrote he had at once recognized in his young friend 'a brother in spirit,' 'a new found travelling companion along the way.' He admired his steadfastness in his ordeal and his courageous spirit and his energy in pursuing the good. Tolstoy's fears that Škarvan might give way in prison had been, he now saw, without foundation. He felt they shared the same outlook on life, and he urged Škarvan to continue to follow his conscience whatever the consequences.

Tolstoy ended his letter with three requests. First, he asked Škarvan his opinion of Schmitt and his journal. What do people in general think of him and how far does his influence extend? 'Putting aside his often angry tone and hurried style and the bombast and verbosity of much of his writing, I see in him a sincere and very talented man and, most important of all, a person who is not a materialist but a believer in spiritual values and, therefore, one who is akin to us.' Not only Tolstoy but many others were to have their doubts about this somewhat enigmatic Hungarian (of German background). It shows the confidence Tolstoy already felt in Škarvan that he should make these enquiries; of course, he knew, too, that the latter, living not so very far away from Budapest, would be in a position to give him a reliable answer.

Next Tolstoy asked Škarvan if he would be able to translate some of his current writings into German, especially such items as could not then appear in Russia. He must already have been aware of Škarvan's linguistic ability: a master of at least three foreign languages, the latter was eventually to translate *inter alia* Tolstoy's *Resurrection* into his Slovak mother tongue.

The most intriguing item came in the last paragraph of Tolstoy's letter. There he urged Škarvan to tell him all he could about his family, his friends, and his present way of life. 'It all touches me very closely because indeed you are very dear to me.' In particular – 'if it won't be disagreeable to do so' – please do tell me all about 'your Viennese lady-friend [venska dama].'[17]

Tolstoy was always pleased to receive Škarvan's letters; he seems to have enjoyed giving his young friend advice not only about his love life but also, of course, about the condition of his soul as well as his lifestyle. Early in 1896, Tolstoy had sought news of him from Makovický: 'What's happened to Škarvan? Where is he and what is he doing? How is his spiritual state? Please tell me everything about him.' Then he added: 'I find his Memoirs very valuable: people will read them with much profit.'[18] In fact, Škarvan, early in December 1895, had sent part of his memoirs to Tolstoy, who, after he had read with much satisfaction the sections sent, passed them on to his friend and disciple, Vladimir Chertkov, for eventual publication. Further instalments followed. Škarvan presumably composed his work in Russian. But since he had not yet acquired the fluency in that language that he later achieved – he was also a novice writer – Chertkov probably had to do a considerable amount of editing. At any rate, it was not until 1898 that the memoirs appeared at Chertkov's exile Russian-language press in England.

As Tolstoy had explained to Škarvan: 'Your Memoirs have especially touched me since, at this very moment, our young friend the painter, [Leopold] Sulerzhitskii, is incarcerated in the psychiatric ward of Moscow's military hospital for refusing army service.' He, too, had written an account of his time under arrest, and Tolstoy promised to send Škarvan a copy. Though Tolstoy did not allude to this, Sulerzhitskii, we know, was soon to yield to family pressure and give up his resistance to entering the armed forces, Tolstoy showing remarkable understanding of the young man's dilemma and telling him he must do what his conscience told him was right. Undoubtedly with Sulerzhitskii's case in mind, Tolstoy a little hesitantly now assured Škarvan that if, as seemed likely, he was called up for service again, he would retain his undiminished 'respect and love' were he to opt to obey the call to rejoin the army.[19]

Škarvan, however, was made of sterner stuff than Sulerzhitskii was. (Or perhaps external circumstances made it easier for him to maintain his resistant stance?) In June 1896, shortly before he was due to report again for another spell of military duty, Škarvan had received an invitation from Chertkov to visit Russia and money to cover the expenses of the journey. The Austrian authorities, glad probably to be rid of this difficult subject, allowed him to leave the country despite his conscript situation. Next month, Tolstoy and his wife welcomed Škarvan to the hospitality of Iasnaia Poliana, where he spent part of his time until, in February 1897, the Russian authorities expelled him as an undesirable alien.[20] (He had been active, along with Russian Tolstoyans, in campaigning on behalf of the Dukhobors.) From Russia he moved on to England, beginning an unhappy exile, filled increasingly with longing for his Slovak homeland. Exile came to an end only in 1910 when the Habsburg authorities granted him an amnesty, at the same time returning his medical diploma so that he could now set up a country practice within view of his beloved Mount Kriván. The remainder of his life was spent in happy obscurity. He died on 29 March 1926 at Liptovský Hradok.

The year 1910 was also that of Tolstoy's death. The two men, though they continued to correspond (Škarvan confiding some of his constant marital troubles[21] to 'grandpa'), were gradually to drift apart. The Slovak acknowledged his debt to the Russian seer, who had led him out of spiritual darkness up into the light. But, while remaining an adherent of nonviolence, he had eventually succeeded in shaping a *Weltanschauung* of his own. The precise shape of Škarvan's later philosophy of life can only emerge after more scholarly study of his extensive correspondence and diaries located in Slovak and Czech archives. As for Tolstoy, Škarvan had played at one point in time a special role in his bodyguard of war resisters. Others were to take that place without, however, ousting the Slovak from Tolstoy's affections or obliterating him from his memory.

NOTES

1 Tolstoy to Makovický, 10 February 1895, in Tolstoy's *Polnoe sobranie sochinenii* (Moscow-Leningrad) (hereafter *PSS*), vol. 68 (1954), 29. For Makovický, see Tomáš Winkler, *Tragické hľadanie života: Dušan Makovický – Život a dielo v dokumentoch* (Martin, 1991).

2 Quoted in my *Freedom from War: Nonsectarian Pacifism 1814–1914* (Toronto, 1991), 237.

3 Albert Škarvan, *Zápisky vojenského lekára*, ed. Rudolf Chmel (Bratislava, 1991), 66, 67. The Slovak version of Škarvan's memoirs first appeared in book form in 1920. I have translated and edited the parts dealing with his prison experiences: *Life in an Austro-Hungarian Military Prison: The Slovak Tolstoyan Dr. Albert Škarvan's Story* (Syracuse NY, 2002).

4 Škarvan, *Zápisky*, 74, 75.
5 Škarvan to Tolstoy, 11 October 1895, MS., Tolstoy Museum (Moscow) Archives. I would like to thank the Tolstoy Museum for making these letters accessible to me and Dr Olga Velikanova (Toronto) for providing me with a typescript of the portions of Škarvan's letter (written in Russian with many Slovakisms) that were relevant to my theme. Without such aid, I would never have succeeded by myself in deciphering Škarvan's handwriting! My thanks here, too, to Professor Donna Orwin.
6 For further details, see my article 'Adela and Albert: A Tolstoyan Love Story,' *Canadian Slavonic Papers*, vol. 45, no. 3/4 (November–December 2003), 395–408. I have incorporated parts of this article in the present essay.
7 Škarvan, *Zápisky*, 93.
8 Škarvan, *Life*, 15.
9 Ibid., 26, 31, 32.
10 Ibid., 23, 24.
11 Ibid., 40–58.
12 Tolstoy to Makovický, 11 September 1895, *PSS*, vol. 68, 175, 176.
13 For Schmitt, see my 'Tolstoyism and the Hungarian Peasant,' *Slavonic and East European Review*, vol. 58, no. 3 (July 1980), 345–69.
14 Tolstoy to E.H. Schmitt, mid-September 1895, *PSS*, vol. 68, 177–80.
15 Tolstoy to Makovický, 29 September 1895, *PSS*, vol. 68, 187, 188.
16 Škarvan was very close to his mother, a widow who kept a shop in a small town in the Slovak highlands. While his father had been Czech by origin, his mother was of Slovak peasant stock. It was she who had brought Albert up to be a conscious Slovak patriot, and his strong cultural nationalism owed a lot to her.
17 Tolstoy to Škarvan, 14 November 1895, *PSS*, vol. 68, 254–66.
18 Tolstoy to Makovický, 22 February 1896, *PSS*, vol. 69 (1954), 45, 46.
19 Tolstoy to Škarvan, 16 December 1895, *PSS*, vol. 68, 277, 278. For Sulerzhitskii, see my *Freedom from War*, 214, 215, 377.
20 Winkler, *Tragické hľadanie*, 82–5. Škarvan seems to have feared that Austria-Hungary might ask for his extradition as a draft dodger.
21 Škarvan married three times. His first two marriages – to an Italian and Hungarian respectively – were disastrous. But he found domestic happiness in middle age when he married Margita Sokolová, who survived him. Like Tolstoy, Škarvan obviously encountered difficulties in squaring his aspiration for Christian asceticism with his strong sexual drive. The twenty-four-year-old Russian Marxist, Vladimir Bonch-Bruevich, not yet an Old Bolshevik, met the exiled Škarvan in 1896 at the community established by Vladimir Chertkov at Purleigh in England. 'Several times,' Bonch-

Bruevich writes, 'I felt like opening his head to discover what he was thinking about. I could not rid myself of the idea that, behind the mask of Tolstoyan humility and search for Christian truth, he thought – only about women.' One day 'a tall, finely proportioned, golden-haired young English girl arrived at the community. Škarvan gazed at her with his intent and far from Platonic glance as if he was penetrating her through and through' (quoted in Winkler, ibid., 86).

13 The Emergence of Conscientious Objection in Japan

Paradoxically, the emergence in Japan of conscientious objection to military service reflected that country's westernization: it represented one small link in the modernizing of Japan that took place during the later nineteenth and early twentieth century. British India, with its long tradition of *ahimsa* (nonviolence), experienced the impact of pacifist ideas, which originated in Europe and North America, more deeply than Japan was to do; however, because universal military service was never introduced in India, conscientious objection never became an issue there. India, indeed, produced Gandhi, but Japan produced the first conscientious objectors (COs) in the oriental (and African) world.[1]

In Japan conscription for the armed forces had been introduced in 1873,[2] the same year in which Christianity was legalized, and five years after the Meiji Restoration of 1868, which launched the process of modernization. True, only in the next century was Japan to start out on its career of overseas expansion. But in many ways pacifism from the outset remained alien to its people's outlook. Despite all the reforms that were to transform Japanese society, the culture of Japan was to retain a strong traditional element. The army and its officers were generally regarded with the same high esteem that the old samurai warrior class had been in the past. Armed forces and national pride were closely associated: outside ideologies like pacifism – indeed like Christianity itself – were looked at askance by a large section of the population.

Pacifist ideas began to circulate in Japan from the 1880s. In August 1889 William Jones, a British Quaker travelling on behalf of the London Peace Society, visited Tokyo. He had been invited by some Quaker missionaries then working in Japan. In a public lecture he gave in the Japanese capital, Jones described war's horrors and cruelties while pointing to the brotherly love which Jesus had taught as the only way to create a peaceful world. The twenty-year-old poet, recently converted to Christianity, Kitamura Tōkoku,[3] who knew English well, was deeply impressed by Jones's address. It was indeed Kitamura who now 'introduced pacifism into Japan.'[4] He and several other young enthusiasts established the first peace society in Japan: Kitamura became editor of its journal, established in 1892. Kitamura, though himself a Christian who worked closely with the Anglo-American Quaker missionaries, viewed pacifism as a belief inherent in all religions. 'Jesus Christ, Buddha, or Confucius,' he exclaimed, 'which one didn't prohibit men from fighting and destroying one another?'[5] Kitamura's suicide in 1894 illustrates the tension set up in the minds of Japan's early pacifists: the first to espouse the ideal of world peace in a society steeped in a centuries-old military tradition.

After Kitamura the pioneer, the next important figure in the history of Japanese pacifism was Uchimura Kanzō (1861–1930).[6] Uchimura became a pacifist only after he had reached the age of forty. But much earlier in his career he had become a Christian and had distinguished himself as a political nonconformist as well. The Russo-Japanese War of 1904–5 provided the first test for his newly found pacifism, which he based on his reading of the New Testament. In the summer of 1903, in answer to the bellicose pronouncement of ten University of Tokyo professors calling on the government to declare war on Russia immediately, Uchimura had declared: 'I not only oppose war with Russia; I absolutely oppose all wars.'

Reared in a samurai family, Uchimura, however, retained an intense patriotism throughout his life, while at the same time he unhesitatingly opposed Japanese militarism and expansionism as contrary to the Christian ethic. He strove to free Japanese Christianity from the tutelage of missionary religion. But it was only slowly that he gained adherents to his *Weltanschauung*; and it was not until after the First World War that he founded the Mukyōkai movement, 'Churchless Christianity' or 'Non-Churchism,' organized loosely on a congregational basis. The special Japanese quality of Uchimura's religious viewpoint permitted him to present pacifism in a form acceptable to many of his fellow countrymen, even though they had been repelled by the Westernism of the more missionary-bound churches. Thus, after 1945, his ideas exercised posthumously a powerful influence on the postwar peace movement.

During the war with Russia, Uchimura had deplored the fact that, on both sides, the Christian churches were among the most enthusiastic supporters of war. He urged Christians to adopt 'nonresistance' both as a personal and as a state ethic; and he cited the pacifist Church Father, Tertullian, in support of this view. 'War may be right and just by some other principle [than the Christian one], but not according to the Gospel of Jesus Christ,' who taught that '"the meek shall possess the earth."'[7] With respect to the question of conscientious objection, however, Uchimura took up a somewhat ambiguous position. While he himself was above draft age, some of his followers faced the question of how to respond if they were drafted for military service, a question that naturally became particularly acute in wartime. In an article he wrote in October 1904 entitled 'A Pacifist's Death in War,' Uchimura advised Christian conscripts against refusing to serve, even though he believed that nonresistance still remained in principle obligatory for them as for other Christians. For if pacifist draftees refused induction into the army, they would be regarded as cowards, and this would give pacifism a bad name generally. In addition, the only practical outcome of their refusal would be the conscription in their place of other young men. In contrast, the pacifist who became a soldier, if he died on service (as he well might), would provide a splendid example of self-sacrifice and thereby enhance the reputation of the pacifist cause. In some curious passages of this article, which he printed in italics (that is, in their equivalent in the original Japanese) as if to emphasize the importance he attributed to the ideas he was expressing, Uchimura wrote:

> If there is any such thing as 'the beauty of war,' it is not the death of a ruffian who likes war and knows not the value of life but the death of a pacifist who appreciates the nobility of life and the joy of peace ... It sounds like a contradiction to say that pacifists make the best soldiers, but it is ... a fact ... As pacifism finally becomes the accepted philosophy, those who deserve the glory will not be those who like us proclaim our pacifism with our pens but those pacifists who shed their life's blood on the battlefield and become the sacrifices to war.[8]

Howes points out that Uchimura's focus here – and elsewhere – is exclusively on the sacrificial dedication of the conscript's life in battle, and that he seems to lose sight of the fact that the latter might also have to take life before dying a hero's death (unless, of course, he somehow avoided actually killing anyone).[9]

Even more puzzling for the student of Western pacifism than his theoretical stance at this moment was Uchimura's reaction to the news that one of his young followers, a schoolteacher, had actually received a draft notice from the army authorities and then had decided to refuse induction in protest against the waging of war:

> As soon as he heard of the plan, Uchimura travelled all night on a crowded train to confer with the young man, urging him not to take such drastic action because of the problems it would pose for his family. He might not begrudge the consequent loss of his own life, but his family would have to live with the antagonism their neighbours felt for his intransigence ... This incident [marks] the beginning of Uchimura's attitude that the pacifist should not shirk his duty to serve in the military ... The responsibility for the taking of human life rested with the men who allowed their governments to start wars, not with the hapless draftees.[10]

We do, however, know of one Japanese Christian who became a conscientious objector during the Russo-Japanese War. This was Yabe Kiyoshi.[11] Yabe's pacifism was derived chiefly from his independent study of the Bible. After he had become a Christian at the age of eighteen, the Old Testament commandment – 'Thou shalt not kill' (whose pacifist interpretation he probably owed to the teaching of the Seventh-day Adventists) – combined with the doctrine of nonresistance that he discovered in the Sermon on the Mount to impress upon him the need to oppose fighting, if he were to be true to his religion and his conscience. On the eve of war with Russia, he courageously demonstrated publicly in favour of peace. 'War is a sin which disobeys God's will,' he called out to passers-by, many of whom, we are told, either answered with abuse or threw stones at him.

In 1905 Yabe, then not quite twenty-one and a student at Doshisha University in Kyoto, had received his call-up papers. William Hoover describes what ensued for him as follows: 'Yabe was ordered to enter military service with the Sendai regiment. He courageously told the regimental commander that he would not enter the army. He announced that as a citizen he was not a person to evade the draft but, as a servant of God, he could in no way kill an enemy soldier. He said that he preferred his own death rather than take the life of another ... Yabe was arrested, tried, and found guilty. After serving two months in prison for draft evasion, Yabe again received an induction notice. Expecting to die, he ... left home after a funeral-like send off by family and friends.' Evidently he succeeded in convincing the commander of the regiment to which he had been assigned that it was on grounds of conscience that he could on no account bear arms, for he was permitted to do his conscript service in the army medical corps. 'Yabe's actions made him Japan's first conscientious objector.'[12]

The decade from 1906 to 1915 Yabe spent studying in the United States. During this period he joined the United Brethren in Christ Church, which had been founded by Philip Otterbein in 1800. Though this church never adopted a pacifist position, it had contained from its early days a minority that was nonresistant. After completing his BD degree at the University of Chicago Divinity School, Yabe returned to Japan as a United Brethren missionary, remaining a staunch pacifist until his death in 1935. While as missionary and minister he refrained from proselytizing for pacifism, he succeeded by his example and influence in quietly spreading this faith among those with whom he came in contact. For instance, both Kagawa Toyhiko,[13] the most famous Japanese pacifist of the post-1914 era, and Tabata Shinobu, the leading spokesman for a pacifist interpretation of the Constitution of 1947, owed something of their dedication to peace to Yabe's influence.

Yabe's stand as a conscientious objector was taken independently of Uchimura, whose pacifism, we have seen, stopped short of personal war resistance. Yabe does not appear, either, to have been acquainted with Tolstoy's writings, which constituted an important factor in the emergent pacifism of a number of young Japanese intellectuals around this time.[14]

I have only been able to uncover two cases in Japan of conscientious objection to the draft during the period before the First World War – and one of these, we have seen, was abortive! Undoubtedly there must have been other cases that were not recorded, especially since many of the country's first socialists were also pacifists and Tolstoy's writings on nonviolence circulated in Japan at that date, even though on a very limited scale. Of course, many pacifists were above draft age and, therefore, not liable to conscription; still, some of them were at least potential draftees, who presumably had to grapple with the question whether to bear arms or not if required to do so.

Pacifism remained for many decades a rather tender plant in Japan.[15] But after 1945 and the country's military defeat, with the menace of the nuclear bomb overshadowing the world, the peace movement, including pacifists and nonpacifists, became an important factor in Japanese public life. Yet, because a draft has not been imposed since the end of the war, the question of conscientious objection has only been of peripheral importance there during the post-war era. However, even though COs in Japan have been few in number, especially if compared with the situation in North America or many European countries, they have shown that conscientious objection could take root in an Oriental culture while differing with regard to some points from the Western model.

NOTES

1 For the background of early Japanese pacifism, see my *Freedom from War: Nonsectarian Pacifism 1814–1914* (Toronto, 1991), 278–88, 404–7. (I have drawn parts of the present essay from the chapter in *Freedom from War* entitled 'The Dawn of Christian Pacifism in Japan.') Since, regretably, I do not know Japanese, I have found immensely valuable the volume edited by Nobuya Bamba and John F. Howes, *Pacifism in Japan: The Christian and Socialist Tradition* (Vancouver, 1978).

2 Janet Hunter, ed., *Concise Dictionary of Modern Japanese History* (Berkeley / Los Angeles / London, 1984), 27, 28: 'Initially, the system ... permitted exemption and service by proxy ... The system was reformed [between 1879 and 1889]; the abolition of exemption and service by proxy established the obligation of all [able-bodied] men to military service.'

3 See the entry on Kitamura by Bamba in Harold Josephson, ed., *Biographical Dictionary of Modern Peace Leaders* (hereafter *BDMPL*) (Westport CT and London, 1985), 512–14.

4 Bamba in *Pacifism in Japan*, 15.

5 Quoted in ibid., 58.

6 See the entry on Uchimura by Howes in *BDMPL*, 970–3.

7 *The Complete Works of Kanzō Uchimura*, ed. Taijiro Yamamoto and Yoichi Muto, vol. 7 (Tokyo, 1973), 131, 132.

8 Quoted by Howes in *Pacifism in Japan*, 116.

9 Ibid., 116–19. Uchimura, writes Howes, 'seems to have accepted the Samurai assumption that to enter combat is to accept one's own death.' Uchimura's response to Japan's naval victory over Russia at the outset of the war was one of intense nationalism; he later admitted that his attitude showed inconsistency in one who had proclaimed himself an absolute pacifist. At the time, however, to quote Howes again, 'no amount of opposition to his government's action could overcome this expression of joy that his nation was trouncing one of the world's greatest powers.' Tolstoy, on the other side, had followed Russian reverses with concern and even regret.

Still, he never faltered in his allegiance to nonviolence, even though emotionally – like Uchimura – he was not free from patriotic feelings at this time of national crisis.

10 Ibid., 119.

11 See the entry on Yabe by William D. Hoover in *BDMPL*, 1039, 1040.

12 There is some uncertainty about Yabe's denominational affiliation at the time of his becoming a CO in 1905. I think Bamba's statement that he was then a Seventh-day Adventist is most likely correct. But Japanese Christians have not been as concerned about denominational distinctions as the Western missionaries. As Howes remarks: 'For the Japanese, the big break was the conversion, and they looked at denominational affiliation as of very subordinate significance to their new life in Christ. The missionaries, eager for converts, were not as casual, and so converts were sometimes listed as members of denominations in which they had little interest and little knowledge of doctrinal differences.' See my *Freedom from War*, 406 n. 21.

13 Yuzo Ota in *Pacifism in Japan*, 172. Yuzo Ota considers that Kagawa, though already an antimilitarist, was not yet fully committed to pacifism *sensu stricto*. He later became Japan's internationally best known Christian pacifist, though some of his actions in the 1930s and 1940s are certainly open to criticism from a pacifist point of view.

14 Kagawa read some of Tolstoy's writings on nonviolence while still in high school. As a result, the boy refused to participate in the military drill that was compulsory in his school and received corporal punishment for his disobedience.

15 See Cyril H. Powles, 'Pacifism in Japan, 1918–1945,' in Peter Brock and Thomas P. Socknat, eds, *Challenge to Mars: Essays on Pacifism from 1918 to 1945* (Toronto, 1999), 433, 435, 436, for conscientious objection in that country during the Second World War, with Jehovah's Witnesses now playing the main role here. Powles's essay is based mainly on sources in Japanese.

14 'Boy Conscription' in Australia and New Zealand: The Experiences of the Conscientious Resisters

Britain fought the Boer War on the voluntary system. But during the early years of the twentieth century, the movement to introduce compulsory military service, which prevailed throughout the European continent, gained in strength. It was led by Lord Roberts and the National Service League, of which the Boer War hero became president. The League gained wide support among Conservatives. But most liberals and left-wingers and the whole peace movement opposed its program: its realization, they believed, would lead to the militarization of youth and bring war a step nearer. Some British private schools included military training in the curriculum, but a cadet corps was not established in any state-funded school.

During the years immediately preceding the First World War, the British dominions of Australia and New Zealand, whose citizens prided themselves on their open society and pioneer democracy, outdid Britain's conscriptionists by establishing compulsory military training for teenagers. The legislation laid down penalties, including fines and imprisonment, for parents and their boys who resisted. Most of the resistance to 'boy conscription,' however, was not on grounds of conscience. This essay examines the experiences of Australian and New Zealand youngsters whose refusal to obey the state when it ordered them to drill did indeed stem from conscience.

Australia

The menace of the 'yellow peril,' especially after Japan had defeated Russia in 1905, became a powerful propaganda weapon in the hands of Australian advocates of conscription. The Defence Act of 1911 imposed military training on all males of European origin resident in the country for more than six months, if they were between the ages of twelve and twenty-six. Cadet corps were to be set up to accommodate the conscripted youths. The main burden was placed upon the Junior and Senior Cadets, aged 12–14 and 14–18 respectively. These lads were required to put in 120 days' training a year, which averaged out at roughly two hours a week. The training requirements for the various age groups differed slightly, while the top age groups, for the time being, were not called up for service.

The Act contained no provision for conscientious objection, even on grounds of religion (as in the case of the Quakers). 'Punishments for evasion were harsh.' Boys evading training could incur fines between £5 and £100, followed by imprisonment and/or military detention, when they would be forced to drill. 'Failure to enlist or to attend a medical examination, or advising or aiding a conscript to refuse to perform any of his military duties incurred a penalty of six months' imprisonment with hard labour.' Thus, parents or guardians who conscientiously objected to their boys undergoing military training could be prosecuted in the courts along with the recalcitrant youths. In 1913 an amendment to the Defence Act now 'made it an offence to miss a single compulsory drill.'[1]

The scene was set for a confrontation between the authorities and the anti-conscriptionist forces. Opposition to boy conscription was drawn from two main sources. In the first place, there were the socialist antimilitarists, who were inflexibly opposed to the pro-conscription position of the Australian Labour Party. These people were connected with the anarcho-syndicalist Industrial Workers of the World (IWW or 'Wobblies,' as they were commonly known), an organization with strong support among the miners of New South Wales. One of their leaders, Harry Holland, who edited the Sydney *International Socialist*, put his case against boy conscription as follows:

> I strongly object to the whole business, inasmuch as it amounts to teaching boys to do murder for a class purpose, and I am perfectly satisfied that it is only a matter of time when conscripts will be called upon to shoot down working men in time of industrial conflict ... If the Defence Act were not a murder scheme, and if the working classes really had a country to fight for, surely we might expect men, and not schoolboys to do the work of defending it.[2]

Holland was obviously not a nonresistant or Quaker-style pacifist. But clearly he conscientiously objected to conscription in his country as at present constituted.

Secondly, Australia's religious pacifists, spearheaded by the Quaker Society of Friends, despite their small numbers, provided needed enthusiasm and organizational ability for the opposition movement. Early in 1912 two Quakers, John F. Hills and John P. Fletcher, a visiting Friend from England, had established the Australian Freedom League, specifically aimed at abolishing boy conscription as quickly as possible; it soon began to issue a journal entitled *Freedom*, which campaigned vigorously and drew support from the burgeoning Australian peace movement. It also published a series of pamphlets and leaflets which were distributed widely, and it publicized CO cases that came to its notice. While the main impetus behind the League's activities derived from the Quakers, membership was open to all who agreed with its goals whether from religious or secular motives. Membership of the Australian General Meeting of Friends, established in 1902 but still part of London Yearly Meeting, was small: on the eve of the First World War it numbered only 664,[3] apart, that is, from attenders at Quaker meeting who had not so far joined the Society. Australian Friends, though, could draw on support from their British coreligionists, 'both in finance and personnel.'[4] In addition to Fletcher, mentioned above, Harriette and W.H.F. Alexander, Alfred Brown, Mary and Herbert Corder, Alexander Rowntree, and Herbert Thorp, prominent members of London Yearly Meeting, arrived in Australasia, where their presence added strength to the resistance movement. Perusal of the printed *Extracts from the Minutes and Proceedings of Friends Held in London* for the Years 1911–1914, as well as files of the *Australian Friend* and the London *Friend* for these years, shows the alarm and deep concern felt by English Friends for the situation in Australia and New Zealand: their own time of troubles was to arrive in 1916 when conscription was reimposed in Britain. But, as W.N. Oats points out, 'they came ... out to Australia and New Zealand in 1911–1912 ... not to direct an anti-conscription conspiracy or to encourage law-breakers on the streets, but to give support to an already dedicated core of Australian [and New Zealand] Quakers.'[5] And these local Quakers, we know, formed just one component, though a very important one, in a wider campaign against conscription.[6]

For the experiences of the conscientious resisters to boy conscription in Australia, I have drawn chiefly on the monograph by the Australian historian John Barrett.[7] In his chapter 5, entitled 'Fines and Fortresses,' he provides 'case histories' of conscientious objectors to boy conscription, parents and boys. Barrett's approach is scholarly. He is not pleading for a cause as some anti-conscriptionist writers on the subject have done. The value of the data he presents about the COs is, I think, augmented by his general thesis: that anti-conscriptionist writers have exaggerated the strength of the opposition movement. 'Even the boys forced to do the training,' he writes, 'mostly liked it, or did not mind too much – although it was sometimes a nuisance.' Those rebelling were few in number. He pays tribute, though, to those among them who were genuine COs: 'all honour to those who [rebelled] for good reasons, for they were principled and brave.' He even goes so far as to call these boys 'martyrs,' who sometimes endured 'agony' in standing by what they believed was right. (If an anti-conscriptionist had written this, Barrett would probably have called it an exaggeration, perhaps not incorrectly.) 'For some lads,' he concludes, 'there were fortresses and cells by the sea, but for more trainees there were drillhalls and training grounds that were almost a club.'[8] I should mention, too, that, in addition to official and other archives hitherto not utilized, Barrett had access to the papers of one of the best-known boy COs (Tom Roberts, see below), which were in possession of his daughter.[9] So far as I know, no other conscientious resisters in either dominion have left personal papers that can illuminate aspects of their struggle.

Let us now look more closely at the experiences of these youths and the parents who supported them. We may divide them into four classes: (1) socialist antimilitarists of various kinds; (2) libertarian objectors to conscription *per se*; (3) non-Quaker religious COs; and (4) Quakers.

(1) Harry Holland, the socialist journalist and union organizer (see above), and Alfred Giles, a socialist butcher from Broken Hill in New South Wales, were apparently the first parents to be convicted – in April 1912 – for not registering teenage sons liable for service; the court imposed fines, not to pay which meant, of course, a jail sentence. 'Harry Holland took himself and his family to New Zealand without either paying the fine or going to jail.' In New Zealand after the war was over, Holland became one of the leaders of the parliamentary Labour Party until his death in 1933. But before his departure from Australia, his son, Roy Holland, spent a short time in jail. Roy's father, whom Barrett describes as 'a difficult man,' had declared in rather

patriarchal style: 'Roy has no choice whatever in the matter, and while he is under 21 years of age I shall firmly refuse to allow him to take any part whatever in the abominable military crimes.' The boy evidently had no intention of rebelling against his father.

The Giles family fared less well. Alfred Giles, the father, having refused to pay his fine, a stiff £100, was sent to jail for three months, although a successful appeal to the Supreme Court brought his release after a short time. Then came the ordeal of his son, Frank, who in the following September was given a two-week prison sentence after refusing to pay the fine imposed by the court. The boy was able to present a glowing testimonial from his employer, but this did not help. Frank spent his first week in jail 'on bread and water and the other days on very little better.' His parents, visiting the boy in the middle of his sentence, were shocked to see him dressed in prison uniform. Alfred Giles described the visit as follows:

> We had to go into a little room and sit on a form facing an iron barred window, and then the boy was brought in and placed about six feet from the window outside and a warder stood between us, his father and mother. We were warned not to tell the boy anything that was going on, only speak on family matters. The boy said he was that weak after the first 7 days he could hardly lift his hands to his face, from starvation. At the gaol the authorities tried everything to get the boy to give in, and let them send and ask me to pay the fine, but he would not. The prison doctor even went so far as to tell the boy that he would have to do the full time on bread and water the next time he was sent up there. They told him he would be looked on as a criminal and all sorts of harsh things, but the boy had too much courage to give in.[10]

On his release, Frank was fêted by the Amalgamated Miners' Association in his home town of Broken Hill; they presented him with a gold medal. But soon after returning home, Frank received another notice requiring him to attend drill and, on his ignoring this order, 'late in January 1913 a warrant for his arrest was issued.' Frank, along with his brother, who might expect to be drafted too, now went into hiding.[11] He clearly did not fancy another spell of prison clothes, bread-and-water, iron bars, and hostile warders nor evidently did his brother like the idea of suffering a similar fate. And their parents sympathized with the boys' dilemma and helped to shield them from discovery by the authorities.

Harry Flintoff, a nineteen-year-old cabinetmaker's apprentice in Richmond, Victoria, early on got caught up in the anti-conscriptionist movement, becoming secretary of the Australian Freedom League in his home town. He was also active as a left-wing socialist. Thus inevitably, when drafted, he became a conscientious resister. His first spell in military detention, now the standard penalty for uncooperative boy conscripts, came in December 1913 when he received fourteen days. He subsequently received further sentences: twenty days in March 1914 and, within three weeks of his release, a further twenty-one days in April of that year. Flintoff's forced location was at Fort Queenscliff on an offshore island by the sea. Treatment there was worse than was usual in a civilian jail 'Harry,' Barrett relates of his first spell of detention, 'was dragged around the parade ground by two soldiers – he being the only one of about 50 detainees to refuse to drill.' The boy was tough, but his widowed mother's distress worried him, and this began to wear his high spirits down. To quote further from Barrett:

> What his friends called his normal self-possession was lost after seven days in a cell at Fort Queenscliff. It was a solidly built wooden cell, 9ft × 9ft × 8ft high, with an iron door, and dimly lit by two tiny windows (though with good ventilators). It contained only a bed, from which the bedding was removed at 6.30 am to be returned twelve hours later. Harry was in solitary confinement except when another trouble-maker happened to be put with him for a time, and some days he was on reduced rations. Flintoff left his mark on the cell: 63 years afterwards, in March 1977, H.E. FLINTOFF could still be seen punched (with a table fork?) into the wooden walls. The cell also left its mark on Flintoff. To [a friend] he wrote, 'For God sake do something or this will drive me mad and will not drive me to drill,' adding pathetically in the margin, 'Can someone call to see me.'

But he survived solitary as he had survived the previous manhandling on the drill ground. Eventually, though, his hitherto resilient spirit broke. During his third detention, knowledge of a letter of his having been deliberately held up seems to have acted as a catalyst for his collapse. When noncombatant duties during training were offered him, an informal arrangement not provided for in the Defence Act, he agreed to this compromise. As he wrote to a friend, 'I would not have given in only I was weak and sick, and my bodie [*sic*] would not stand any more ... but if they get cockey I will again refuse.' And he signed the letter 'Your heartbroken Friend, Harry.' In mid-sentence Flintoff decided he had had enough; he succeeded in escaping unperceived from Queenscliff Fort and, like Frank Giles, hid until boy conscription had ended.[12]

There are several not easily resolvable questions about Flintoff's case. In the first place, the fact that the boy had a little earlier aspired to become a non-commissioned army officer was brought up against him at his third trial. The prosecutor then claimed that his present stance was hypocritical, that his desire to 'pose as a martyr and a hero' was the result solely of outside prompting. But, as Barrett points out, 'it was a painful pose to maintain.' There is indeed no reason to believe that Flintoff's transformation into an antimilitarist activist and draft resister was not sincere. Secondly, there is some difference of opinion concerning his motives for resisting the draft. His widow told Barrett in 1977 that her husband's stance had been due to Christian belief and not socialism: he later became a Methodist home missionary. On the other hand, his elder brother belonged to the Victorian Socialist Party and likely influenced the boy's political development, and the latter's participation at this time in left-wing activities is well documented. Barrett suggests that contacts with Quakers in the Australian Freedom League and with religious COs around this time may have led Flintoff to return, while he was still incarcerated in Queenscliff Fort, to the Christianity in which he had been reared.[13] If Barrett is correct, then we can perceive Flintoff moving at this point from a selective – socialist – objection to war to a Christian pacifist objection to all war.

Vivian and his younger brother Victor Yeo were also working-class COs: their father, a self-educated man, was a miner who had emigrated from England to work in the coalfields at Broken Hill. Though he had once served in the British army, he was now an out-and-out pacifist 'on humanitarian and economic grounds' as well as a socialist. 'If he had to take the oath again or be shot, they might shoot him,' he told his friends. And he brought up his sons to hate war. Vivian went to jail for a couple of weeks after refusing to drill and then went into hiding. Victor was made of sterner stuff. 'A sort of Benjamin to his parents,' though only fourteen, he adopted their anti-warism with enthusiasm. On successive occasions, late in 1912 and again in 1913, he refused orders to drill as a drafted cadet, and, each time refusing to pay his fine or allow anyone else to do this, he was sentenced by the magistrate. On the first occasion he was sent to prison for two months. Released after serving only twelve days through the good offices of the member of parliament for Broken Hill, who happened also to be the minister for external affairs, Victor was picked up some six months later and sentenced this time to two months' detention, which he served, however, in the jail at Broken Hill instead of in a fortress as had been the court's original intention. His jail task was to knit socks: that was no hardship. But, Barrett writes, 'Victor was frequently restricted to a diet of bread and water, and was confined to his cell for all but two hours in every 24.' After release he had remarked jokingly 'that he knew now how little a pound of bread was'; for a hungry fourteen-year-old a cob, that is, the small loaf of bread served in prison meals, was certainly an unsatisfactory diet! After an abortive attempt to prosecute him once again, Victor was left alone since the authorities wished to avoid the bad publicity their treatment of young Yeo had already brought in its wake.[14]

(2) Joshua Ratcliff was neither a socialist nor a Christian but a rationalist. He objected to any son of his being drafted, not on pacifist grounds, but because he considered this infringed the rights of a free citizen. By profession a merchant, his firm specialized in imported teas; he remained a respectable member of society for all his individualistic views, which led him, on this issue, to clash with the law and boldly confront the authorities. He joined the Australian Freedom League and took an active part in its work alongside Quakers and other anti-conscriptionists. Hauled into court in July 1913 for not allowing his drafted teenage son to drill, Ratcliff was fined £5. The boy would presumably have refused to comply if forced into the cadet corps. But his stamina was not put to the test since Ratcliff senior, though a born Australian, with his business interests hitherto all in the state of Victoria, decided to move to England together with his wife and two sons, both of whom he feared would be liable to boy conscription if he stayed. Unhappily, he did not foresee that in 1916 Great Britain would re-introduce conscription, whereas ironically Australia was to remain conscription-free for almost the whole of the First World War![15]

The Size brothers, William aged seventeen and John aged nineteen, were farm boys. They helped their mother to run the small family farm at Oakland, South Australia. When drafted into the Senior Cadet Corps, they had at first drilled but then stopped, claiming that the state had no right to demand military service from its citizens. Mrs Size was apparently a convinced libertarian with, according to Barrett, 'strong feelings about British freedom.' Some Quakers, who interviewed the boys after their clash with the law, wrote: 'They are big, well-grown lads, shy at first among strangers, typical Colonial youths, accustomed to rough life, and enjoying a spirit of independence, but one would gather good lads to their mother. The father is rather a poor tool ...' In September 1913 the two brothers were sentenced to twenty days in military detention and despatched to Fort Largs.[16] If endurance is a proof of sincerity, then the Sizes' ordeal in the fort provided such proof. The account they gave of their conscript troubles is worth quoting at length: the conditions they describe are confirmed by evidence provided by cadets at other locations. The brothers declared:

> We slept [on the night of our arrival at the fort] in tents with the rest. An officer called us all next morning and gave us five minutes to fall in. At the 'Fall-in' all fell into rank except us. We stood about half a dozen yards away. We [felt] it wrong to submit to the drill. The officer again ordered us into the ranks. On our second refusal he sent the cook for a file of men and we were marched into the cell. There we found four others ... [Later,] in the fort square they told us to fall in. We refused. They then took hold of us, pushed us into the ranks, and as we refused to Right Turn they turned us. The order 'Quick March' being given, we were pushed and hustled along. The other lads were marched off out of sight and hearing. Then the Master Gunner said (among other things): 'Put the grips on them!' 'Get them by the scruff of the neck!' 'Drag them around!' 'Put your knee into them and break their backs!' He bent his own knee as he spoke. This display of threats having failed, we were marched off ... and then put in the cell ... We were put upon bread and water. We had just the slice of bread and a cup of water three times a day. The water was nasty. These rations were kept on several days and made us very weak. We did not get anything better till Sunday came. After that when the officers found that starving us made no impression on us they gave us better food except when other lads were sent to share the cell; then it was bread and water again, once for three days on end. The cell was about 12 feet by 9 feet, we should judge. One night seven others were put into it besides ourselves. There was a plank bed for two only; so seven slept, or tried to, without any bed, six on the cement floor and one on a sort of stool. We were each provided with one blanket only. The bedding was not put in the cell till our last week there. We were at the Fort from September 23rd till October 13th, 1913.[17]

Release came in due course. The brothers, however, continued to disregard notices to attend drill, so that four months later, in February 1914, they found themselves in court again. The magistrate, as might be expected, sentenced them once more to a spell in detention. But now the brothers were divided, John being sent again to Fort Largs while William was lodged in Fort Glanville on this occasion. Their treatment differed, too. At Fort Largs, John spent ten days of his time in solitary with its accompanying dietary restrictions, whereas in Fort Glanville, William, the younger brother, enjoyed a comparatively easy time. Barrett suggests that perhaps in this way the military authorities hoped to persuade at least one of the boys to conform and commence to drill. 'The Sizes endured it all unmoved.' The conclusion of their story came after the outbreak of war in August 1914 and the subsequent winding down of boy conscription. Both brothers, believing Prussian militarism incarnated the spirit of compulsion, then volunteered for overseas service. 'What they did not like was compulsion.'[18]

(3) It is rather surprising that so few religious COs surfaced in the course of boy conscription. But, apart from small peace sects like the Seventh-day Adventists (who have always been ready to accept noncombatant service in the army) and the Christadelphians, only the Quakers rejected military service in principle. Barrett mentions 'the eccentric A.L. Henzell' from South Australia, who, as a Christian pacifist, refused to allow his offspring to drill. Another father, who opposed boy conscription 'on Christian principles' was the Rev. Alfred Madsen, a Methodist clergyman of the evangelical persuasion from Melbourne. Active in his local branch of the Australian Freedom League, Madsen was no eccentric but a respected minister of his church. In September 1912 he was fined £2 for failing to register his son William, aged fourteen, when he became liable for the draft. Madsen paid the fine, but the army was nonplussed as to how to proceed. Some officers wished to have Madsen fined at fortnightly intervals until he finally consented to register his son. Others were doubtful if such a procedure was legal. Finally, the army decided to issue a regulation permitting an area officer to register any boy whose parents had not done this on his behalf. The regulation appeared in June 1913. Madsen, incidentally, dropped his opposition to conscription in the course of the First World War; he then urged his coreligionists to vote 'yes' in the conscription referendum of 1916–17.[19]

The most clear-cut cases of non-Quaker Christian pacifist conscientious resisters were provided by the two Krygger boys, Edgar Roy from Ballarat and Walter from Northcote, both aged around seventeen when conscripted. Edgar Roy's case came up first. In court Edgar Roy was defended by a lawyer from the Australian Freedom League, who pleaded that the boy's religious freedom, guaranteed by Section 116 of the Constitution, was being infringed. According to the latter's statement, he believed that evil should not be opposed by military force: he was, though, willing 'to fight the devil, not with armies and navies, but with the word of God.' Since Christ had taught his followers to turn the other cheek, military training was 'as much a sin in the sight of God as gambling, racing, or any other sin.' The court turned down the lawyer's plea for exemption, chiefly on the grounds that a cadet could be employed in some capacity that did not require him to bear arms. Therefore, the boy 'was ordered 64 hours in custody, the time he was short of drills.' The latter then appealed to the High Court, which handed down a negative judgment based on an extremely narrow definition of religious freedom. But the significance of the High Court's ruling lay in the fact that it successfully blocked any further attempts to argue that compulsion to undergo military training in the case of someone who objected to this on religious grounds was an infringement of that person's rights.

Next year Walter Krygger attempted just that, but naturally without success. Walter worked in a shoe shop; off duty he acted as secretary of the local branch of the Australian Freedom League. When in December 1913 he was taken to court for ignoring the order to join the Senior Cadet Corps, he stated he was 'a Christian,' who strove to 'follow the teachings of the Bible.' There is no evidence he belonged to any particular denomination, but his mother, a devout Christian, was clearly a strong influence on Walter's religious development. When on 15 December the magistrate sentenced him to twenty-eight days' detention at Fort Queenscliff, his mother called out from her seat in the courthouse, 'There's no encouragement for boys to be Christians.'

Walter was a delicate and sensitive lad in contrast to some of his fellow COs, who found it easier to stick it out than he was to do. The crude language and obstreperous behaviour of most of the recalcitrant cadets, who shared his incarceration in Fort Queenscliff, shocked him profoundly. And the guards' conduct was not much better. 'It seems,' he told his mother, 'as if I am in amongst a lot of devils.' In the letter he wrote her at 4:30 a.m. on the morning after his arrival at the fort, he continued in the same strain: 'I miss you but Mother Dear pray for me. God help me fight the good fight of faith. Pray earnestly for me. I am almost crying as if in fact I am and I can't help it ... I have been praying almost all night. I pray for each of you by name.' He believed, he told her, that he was not alone, for God was indeed with him. He had also discovered that another CO, no other than the intrepid Harry Flintoff, was his companion in the fort, and that was a great comfort. (And Barrett suggests that Krygger's ardent Christian faith may have been a factor in Flintoff's return to Christianity, although there is no concrete evidence for this.) Flintoff, for his part, in the trying days ahead for the two boys did his best to keep up the more timorous Krygger's spirits. He wrote to the latter's mother, 'But Mrs. Krygger, will you kindly write couraging [*sic*] letters to Walter not sad. Don't tell him you are broken hearted as you are making him lose his courage.' Walter's refusal to drill was met by a rough response from the corporal in charge of operations, an obvious bully who had been a champion boxer before he joined the army. The frail Walter was manhandled more than once either by this corporal or by other soldiers he had called in to assist him. Exactly what happened is now difficult to discover; at any rate, there is reason to think Walter somewhat exaggerated the degree of ill treatment he received. Three representatives of the Australian Freedom League, who visited Fort Queenscliff at this time, reported: 'Krygger resents ... a little rough handling ... as a piece of injustice which seeks to violate his conscience, and it is that subjective element which makes all the difference.' As so often, Barrett provides us with a balanced judgment of a complex situation when he writes: 'It was a miserable and frightening time for someone as susceptible as Krygger.'

For all his susceptibility, Walter got through his twenty-eight days in military detention without yielding to the various pressures on him to conform. The officers at the Fort failed to make the boy either drill or handle a weapon. Four months later, in May 1914, Krygger received a second spell of detention: this time twenty instead of twenty-eight days. Once more he underwent some rough treatment, which he appears to have handled more successfully than during his earlier sentence. Again to quote Barrett: 'Krygger was learning to rough it a little! Nevertheless, it remains obvious that the tender Walter Krygger suffered severely for his Christian conscience.' After his May spell in the fortress by the sea, the army left Walter alone.[20]

(4) Australian Quakers, so far as I can discover, produced only seven conscientious resisters to boy conscription: four of them were teenagers, two were fathers, and one was a grandfather. The small number of Quaker COs, despite the Society's long established peace testimony, can be explained by the fact that the General Meeting of Australian Friends was a small community, especially if we compare it to London

Yearly Meeting or Yearly Meetings in the United States. Each of these cases, however, aroused considerable interest when reported in the press. Imprisoning Quakers for following their conscience in obedience to a well-known tenet of their faith made a bad impression in early twentieth-century Australia. Many persons who felt that socialists and anarcho-syndicalists and unaffiliated religious resisters deserved most, if not all, of what they got were disturbed when they read about members of the generally respected – and respectable – Society of Friends receiving the same treatment as these maverick members of society. Not all shared this view, of course. But enough people did so to make *causes célèbres* out of several prosecutions involving Quakers.

Let us begin with the senior Quaker conscientious resister, Francis Hopkins. His failure under the Defence Act to register his grandson, for whom he acted as guardian, led to his being summoned to court on 20 December 1912. The magistrate was kind: he could have imposed a fine of as much as £100. Instead, he levied a mere £3 with a pound or two more for costs. This leniency was presumably due to the respect generally felt for Hopkins as a Quaker and a model citizen. However, soon afterwards the old gentleman died, according to his obituary, largely as a result of 'the worry and trial of this case.'[21] Margaret Hirst mentions another Friend, Christopher Flinn from Melbourne, who was fined and distrained upon for failure to register his son, aged fourteen.'[22] In the case of the Ingles, both father and son were imprisoned. William had emigrated from England in 1911 and was now living at Hectorsville in South Australia. From there he had written a letter to the editor of the Australian Freedom League's paper, in which he stated:

> I feel there is some underhand work in trying to get young children [medically] passed at the age of eleven and then pass them on to the senior cadets. If that is not the object why examine the boys only? ... I appeal to all parents to stand firm against the Act, which does not give freedom to conscience, and demand, as British subjects, we shall have no taint of conscription in the Empire.[23]

Friend William Ingle was soon to have to carry out his advice to others with respect to his own fourteen-year-old son, Herbert. Refusing to register the boy and making clear he would not, under any circumstances, permit his son to drill, in April 1913 he was summoned to the court in Adelaide, where the following bizarre dialogue occurred between the magistrate and Ingle senior:

> INGLE: My defence is that I am here as a Christian, as a follower of Christ, and to obey the Defence Act my conscience and my religion will be violated.
>
> MAGISTRATE: To put it shortly, you object to this Act?
>
> INGLE: How can my child love and serve his fellow-men if ...
>
> MAGISTRATE (interrupting): We don't want that. That is a matter for the churches.
>
> INGLE: I was told there was a conscience clause, but my child would be compelled to take an oath to serve the King. If a child agrees to join the military and in a battle an officer said to him, 'carry that box of ammunition to the men fighting,' is he compelled to obey the officer?
>
> MAGISTRATE: Don't you understand discipline? The officer must be obeyed.
>
> INGLE: Yes, well, there is no difference between carrying the ammunition and shooting a man.[24]

The magistrate then proceeded to fine Ingle £1.10.0 (incidentally a very lenient penalty) with the option of going to prison for fourteen days in lieu of payment. Ingle chose the jail term.

The area officer by that date was empowered to register a boy conscript if his parents had failed to do so. This now happened with Herbert Ingle, who, as we might expect, failed to turn up for the statutory drilling. Sentenced to fourteen days' detention, he served his sentence at Fort Largs. Proving uncooperative at the fort, he received the kind of treatment there with which we are already familiar: solitary confinement, a restricted diet, and seemingly a beating, too. On the boy's release, Ingle senior decided to take his family back to England: like Joshua Ratcliff, he mistakenly believed he could live in the land of his birth without fear of conscription.[25]

The Quaker, Sidney Crosland, was a bank clerk in Newcastle, New South Wales. Aged eighteen, he was called up as a cadet in April 1913. Failing to attend any drills, he was then summoned to court, where the magistrate gave him a fifty-six-day sentence, later reduced to three weeks. He served his time in the Victoria Barracks in Sydney. 'He was offered non-combatant clerical work,' writes Hirst, 'but refused it, and though after his release he still abstained from drill, he was not again prosecuted.' Crosland clearly made a good impression on those he came into contact with. In court the magistrate who sentenced him had told the military prosecutor: 'It seems to me that to you the most important thing in the world is the military test, while to the defendant religious principles are highest.' In barracks, though Crosland continued unyielding, no ill treatment was reported during his stay there: a contrast to the experiences of most other conscientious resisters in similar circumstances. And, a nice footnote to Crosland's story, his bank gave him back his job after he had served his sentence in detention. But, to give Barrett once again the last word: 'What were his sufferings, nonetheless, and those of his family?'[26]

In October 1913 another young Quaker became entangled in the net of boy conscription. This was Douglas Allen from Melbourne. Refusing to drill, he was sentenced to twenty days' detention to be served in a fortress. The magistrate at his trial made it clear that the Defence Act included no provision for conscientious objection: in this, of course, he was quite correct. His view was confirmed by no less an authority than the prime minister and minister for defence when, in the following March, a delegation of Australian Friends, carrying a protest letter form the Meeting for Sufferings of London Yearly Meeting, attempted to persuade the government to exempt genuine conscientious objectors from the current conscription. In reply, they were told that, although leniency would be practised as far as possible, no exemptions were possible. 'The law cannot be altered.'[27]

The last Quaker boy conscript to make his appearance was Thomas Roberts from Brighton in the state of Victoria. His case was to gain more publicity than any other. His parents, Susanna and Fred Roberts, were devoted members of their local Friends' meeting. Humble folk – Fred was a plumber and active trade unionist – they brought their son up strictly but lovingly. Tom was taught the meaning of the Society's peace testimony and needed no pressuring on the part of his parents to refuse to drill or cooperate when he was conscripted into the cadet corps. In his case the law took several years to catch up on him. Not surprisingly, his parents had not registered him for service, but they were never prosecuted. Like Tolstoy in Russia a little earlier, they were anxious to shoulder the punishment themselves. After all, the boy was only following out what they had taught him was right, was the correct Christian conduct. Fred wrote in this strain to various army authorities, including the Minister of Defence, while Susanna pleaded, as the likelihood of Tom's being sentenced to military detention grew stronger, that her son was recovering from a serious illness so that he was in no condition to face the 'rough and brutal' régime prevailing in army detention centres. Susanna, however, really had not needed to worry. For Tom, like some of the conscientious resisters discussed above, was quite tough. Poor though his health was at this stage in his growth, the sixteen-year-old experienced no difficulty in pulling through his three weeks at Fort Queenscliff. He received this sentence in June 1914 – after the court had given him the chance to put in the sixty-four hours of drill that the army calculated he had failed to attend!

The London *Friend* reported on Tom's incarceration in its issue of 31 July: 'On the third day, for continued refusal to drill, he was court-martialled, and sentenced to seven days' solitary confinement. This was in a cell ten feet by ten feet, and unlighted except by a grating. He had a wooden stretcher with mattress and blankets, which were only allowed him at night. He had two half-hours' exercise daily, was placed on half-diet, and was not permitted to read or write.' The specific order the boy was punished for refusing was to do signalling: some might have regarded this as a noncombatant occupation, but not Tom (or his parents). Allowed a letter home, young Roberts told his parents he was being very careful not to act in any way he thought they would disapprove of. And, Barrett adds, childlike 'he closed the letter with 25 clear and unashamed kisses.' Meanwhile Tom's parents were creating a rumpus in the outside world, accusing the authorities – correctly – of treating their Quaker boy like a hardened criminal. 'June 1914 became something of a Tom Roberts month in press and parliament,' writes Barrett. Though responses differed, almost all agreed, including those who were in favour of compulsory military training, that solitary confinement in military detention centres of the kind that Tom Roberts was forced to endure was indeed wrong. The government, though it tried to play down the affair, was eventually forced to give parliament a promise that in the future it would not impose solitary confinement on boy conscripts – and Tom himself was not again required to drill. 'Anti-conscriptionists remained sceptical, but it is probable that Tom Roberts was the last compulsory trainee to undergo this punishment.'[28]

The number of unambiguously conscientious resisters to boy conscription in Australia was very small: the names of some twenty are known, whether teenagers or parents. Although a few more names may eventually surface (there must surely have been several Seventh-day Adventists objecting to handling a weapon as well as working on their Saturday Sabbath), that would be unlikely to greatly raise the figure. Yet by mid-1914 there had been over 13,500 prosecutions under the Defence Act, with the number of boys incarcerated in fortress or military barracks exceeding 5,000.[29] Bobbie Oliver raises a pertinent question when she asks 'how many of these boys failed to attend drill on conscientious grounds, and how many for other reasons, such as duties at home or at work, or sheer dislike of the process.'[30] Barrett does not hesitate to describe almost all those boys who refused to drill and were then sentenced to military detention as 'out-and-out shirkers,' 'the delinquent mob,' though he concedes that, apart from the handful of genuine COs, for whom we have seen he expressed his respect and even admiration, there were some who resisted from mixed motives. In fact, he goes on, conditions in the various detention centres were quite good, even if very occasionally a conscientious resister might suffer some ill treatment. And he concludes, 'Most of those who faced fines and fortresses under the Defence Act did not suffer very much, and some (probably most) could only have benefited from them.'[31] The experiences of a young fellow like Walter Krygger would indeed seem to indicate that the moral calibre of his fellow inmates was not very high.

But this does not tell the whole story. Quaker publicists, like Hills and Fletcher, and anti-conscriptionists like the Rev. Leyton Richards, a Congregational minister visiting from England, and Miss Rebecca Swann, representing the Australian Freedom League in Sydney, diverged radically from Barrett's subsequent assessment. They noted the obvious bias of magistrates against these boys, whom they usually treated harshly as if they were criminals. The mostly inarticulate youths indeed were rarely given a fair trial. Instead, the normal procedure was to sentence them in batches with no adult accompanying them to give support. The boys, for the most part, were entirely unfamiliar with court procedure and seldom stammered out even a few words in their own defence, though Miss Swann claimed that they had often intended to do this. Richards (and others too) believed that a majority of the incarcerated boys were sincere in their opposition to drilling, despite their usually being unable to formulate their conscientious objection in precise terms. Criminalization by the courts and the army could only exert a negative influence on their development. Richards wrote:

> Australia is making rebels in scores and hundreds. Most of the lads who appear before the Court are decent, respectable lads, who have felt out,

> rather than thought out, their objection to militarism ... [Their treatment] is a violation of inherited liberties ... [but] they are suffering to keep Australia free. ... It needs no little courage for a youth in his teens to face the array of policemen, soldiers, officers, lawyers, clerks and officials, who throng the court and who for the most part seem to regard the prosecution of the boys as a comedy. It needs *more* courage to face life in a military *fortress*. There the boys are beyond the jurisdiction of the civil courts – they must drill for 6 hours a day or face a military punishment.[32]

The reader must judge whether Richards's or Barrett's account carries most conviction. The truth, of course, may lie somewhere between the two views.

New Zealand

Boy conscription in New Zealand, while differing in detail, contains many parallels with boy conscription in that country's northern – and much larger – neighbour. The same may be said of the anti-conscriptionist movements in the two countries. The basis in New Zealand for this measure lay in the Defence Amendment Act, finally passed into law in November 1910. 'The first step in putting the new scheme into operation was the compulsory registration of all boys between the ages of 14 and 20. Registration commenced on 3 April 1911 ... and continued until 17 July.'[33]

Unlike Australia, New Zealand made provision in its Defence Act for conscientious objection. The trouble was that exemption was very badly formulated. In the first place, it could be claimed only from combatant duties. This would satisfy Seventh-day Adventists, for instance, but not Quakers or Christadelphians, who objected to noncombatant service in the armed forces. Secondly, 'the law suggested that the potential objector must first register, be enrolled, take the oath of allegiance, be ordered to parade, and only then be in a position to state his religious objections to bearing arms ... For the individual who objected to military service, it was necessary to belong to the military before he could object.' Few COs found this acceptable. Moreover, the exact procedure whereby a draftee could establish his claim to exemption as a religious objector was unclear. Since the law did not entitle a Magistrates Court to make this decision, could the army command decide on the conscript's fate? In the third place, the legislation and the Army Department Memorandum of April 1911, which sought to lay down rules for the practical implementation of the law in this respect, made a curious distinction between religious objectors and conscientious objectors. Only the former were entitled to claim exemption; the latter – presumably humanitarian and political COs of various kinds – were excluded from consideration. The shifting governments that held power during this period refused to intervene.[34]

As in Australia, the anti-conscriptionist forces were drawn from various elements. However, the religious component was weaker in New Zealand. The Society of Friends, the country's most conspicuous pacifist sect at this time, numbered only 143 members[35] plus a few attenders. There is no record of any New Zealand Quaker being involved in boy conscription, although Quakers were active here, too, in the campaign against that measure.[36] Socialist antimilitarists, on the other hand, played a more central role in this campaign than they did in Australia. Almost all the teenage conscientious resisters came from the socialist camp. The centre of resistance was in Christchurch on the South Island. In this city the Anti-Militarist League, established in June 1910, had its headquarters, and the city's branch of the New Zealand Socialist Party was one of the party's most active sections in the ensuing anti-conscriptionist campaign. Above all, Christchurch was the birthplace in February 1912 of the Passive Resisters Union (PRU). Membership of the union was restricted to boys liable for the current draft. Branches were soon set up in other cities of the two islands. The boys called themselves the 'We won'ts' and carried out numerous public protests against the Defence Act. The PRU also published a lively paper with the eloquent title of the *Repeal*. In young Reg Williams, the union's joint secretary, along with James K. Worral, the group had a brilliant publicist and talented organizer. Under Williams's guidance, it worked closely with militant labour, especially the coalminers, and with bourgeois bodies like the New Zealand Freedom League, which a Quaker, Egerton Gill, had set up early in 1912, in Auckland in the North Island. The government claimed that only 'an infinitesimal number' of people were opposed to the Act, and that resistance was confined mainly to Christchurch.[37] But the evidence proves the contrary.

In December 1912 an amended Defence Act was passed that marked a slight improvement in the status of the teenage resisters. In the first place, as in Australia, military detention replaced imprisonment, with its accompanying social stigma, for those boys who refused to pay the fine imposed for failure to drill. James Allen, the minister of defence, declared that military detention did not possess an 'essentially' penal character: the objective was to persuade the delinquent teenager to perform his national service. Unpaid fines could be recovered by deduction from wages instead of incarcerating the boy, provided, that is, that he was now prepared to drill. Secondly, the amended act specifically exempted members of pacifist denominations from drilling (along with a vague requirement for the performance of equivalent alternative service). Though this concession lifted the burden off the shoulders of Quakers and a few others, it did not cover religious objectors who belonged to churches not requiring their members to be COs if drafted. And, of course, exemption even now did not extend to so-called 'conscientious objectors' who did not plead religious belief as their motive (see above). Allen indeed realized the shortcomings of the new legislation as regards religious objectors and was anxious 'to so widen the clause as to make the religious objection of the individual as apart from the denomination ... ground for exemption from military training.' But the solicitor-general told him this was not possible: the wording of the Act must be observed in the form in which parliament had passed it.[38]

Though Allen gave up entirely on the nonreligious conscientious resisters – 'regular young anarchists' encouraged by their 'fathers and mothers ... to break the law' – he continued to worry over the problem of the religious objectors. Perhaps a scheme of alternative service along the lines suggested in the recent legislation might be the solution? So he began to ask various bodies, official and non-official, for advice as to how such a program should be framed; among them was the Society of Friends. Naturally Friends responded with a decided negative.[39] A little earlier, they had told the government that they were even contemplating emigration *en masse* (something Mennonites in Russia had done some four decades earlier) if boy conscription continued. In their reply to Allen, they very politely told the minister of defence:

> After careful deliberation, they see no other way of consistently upholding their [peace] testimony than by declining to undertake any duty that will bring them under military control or the operation of the Defence Act. Nor can they define any duties that, whilst meeting the consciences of some, may violate those of others.[40]

The point made here was spelled out by two Quaker visitors from England in private correspondence. One noted that the goal was to abolish conscription altogether and not to make it work better; therefore 'we cannot do anything that will help to make conscription popular by removing any anti-militarist difficulties.' And the other declared that Friends had no business to find ways to make the Defence Act work more efficiently when 'the Christchurch lads are winning ... by their refusal to undertake *any* duties on Ripa Island.'[41]

And that brings us back to the struggle waged by the conscientious resisters themselves when confronted with orders to drill. The course of events was more or less the same as in Australia: at first a prison sentence was imposed for failure to pay the fine for failure to drill, and later, military detention for nonpayment replaced this. The first boy to be jailed was William Cornish from Wellington in the North Island, who was sentenced in July 1911 to three weeks in prison. He was followed shortly afterwards by Harry Cooke, whose father was secretary of the Christchurch branch of the Socialist Party. His sentence was the same as Cornish's. On their release both boys were fêted by the anti-conscriptionists at receptions in their honour, while the antimilitarist *Maoriland Worker* began publication of a 'Roll of Honour,' on which they listed the names of boys who had been prosecuted for not drilling under the Act. 'The Government,' Weitzel writes, 'chose selectively, striking largely at young leaders of the antimilitarist movement.' Since 'jailing of "political prisoners" was unprecedented in New Zealand,' the revelation 'that the incarcerated youths shared the same quarters as convicted criminals ... [outraged] much of the public and the Government was embarrassed.'[42] For a while it ceased prosecutions, but, early in 1912, it commenced them again, seeing no alternative so long as the Defence Act was in force. To the accompaniment of mounting indignation on the part of the anti-conscriptionists, joined by increasing numbers hitherto neutral, Lyttleton jail in Christchurch, as well as prisons in other cities, began to accommodate increasing numbers of resisters. James Worral, the PRU's joint secretary, and Alex, Harry Cooke's brother, were among the first to be lodged there as well as Harry Cooke himself, whose first sentence had been served in Timaru prison. When it was Reg Williams's turn to enter Lyttleton Gaol, he had asked himself as, at Reception, he and the other teenage COs were put into prison uniform: 'Was it Russia or New Zealand?' The jail, according to Williams, was 'a school of brutality, debauchery, and immorality.'[43]

Conditions may have been a little better at the various barracks to which resisters, now all sentenced to military detention, were sent from mid-1913 on.[44] At Otago Heads, for example, supervision appears to have been lax since two resisters, incarcerated there, succeeded in escaping. (However, after they had been recaptured, twenty-eight days were added to their sentence!) On the other hand, pressure to drill was more intense since the whole purpose of military detention was to make the reluctant boys handle weapons under the threat of punishment if they refused. This comes out particularly clearly in the case of the military barracks on Ripa Island. 'Ripa Island,' Weitzel writes, 'smacked strongly of a maximum security facility and, symbolically at least, reflected the determination of the Government that military punishment should be a real punishment.' Most of the conscientious resisters sent there were socialists; they included Reg Williams and James Worral of the Christchurch PRU as well as some young miners from the West Coast. But the internees included a Baptist Sunday-school teacher named James Nuttall. After arriving on Ripa Island, the boys took up a consistently non-cooperative stance. Ordered 'to clean guns and practice semaphore, they refused, were put in close confinement, and began a hunger strike, for which they were sentenced to an additional seven days.'

The military authorities, rather surprisingly, did not prevent the boys from writing quite openly to friends outside: they did not have to smuggle their letters out. The anti-conscriptionists were furious when they learnt of the way COs were being treated on Ripa Island, but they received little satisfaction from the minister of defence, who was unsympathetic to those whom he called pejoratively 'conscientious objectors.' The most he would concede was that any internee unwilling to work on a military job would be given non-military employment inside the barracks. This, of course, was quite unacceptable to the boys concerned, who had already gone on a work strike. And, writes Weitzel, 'since breaches of the regulations while under military detention were punishabale by more military detention, the boys in effect were serving indeterminate sentences.' And, indeed, one boy was incarcerated for over three months. Yet, as Nuttall, the Baptist in the group, pointed out to a friend outside, the situation had its positive side; the longer they stayed in detention, the more money they would be costing the government. 'They have the most determined renegades here,' the teenager went on, 'we are all old fighters for the cause, and if we break down, the cause of anti-militarism will have suffered a great set back.'[45]

There is even more ambiguity about the number of New Zealand boys who, at some stage, resisted the order to drill than there is in the case of Australia. In 1912, of the 1,923 convictions obtained by the New Zealand police '120 lads chose a prison sentence in lieu of the fine.' But it is not clear whether all those who were jailed were *conscientious* resisters. The prosecutions continued throughout 1913 and most of 1914. 'In the year ending 30 April 1914 ... 234 objectors [were] sentenced to military detention,' and incarceration of recalcitrants continued until the outbreak of war eventually put an end to boy conscription. The measure was indeed becoming increasingly unpopular, but, as Weitzel points out, it is not possible to say whether, if war had not come, the government would eventually have been driven to modify or abolish boy conscription altogether.[46]

In neither Australia nor New Zealand were the numbers of teenage conscientious resisters, and the parents and guardians who were penalized for failing to register them for service, very large, though, we have seen, the exact figures of those who objected to drilling at least in some measure owing to conscience, are difficult to ascertain. While the penalties imposed on the boys were sometimes severe, and might also involve cat-and-mouse treatment, they were fairly mild in comparison with the handling COs sometimes experienced elsewhere and in other periods. But there are three aspects of boy conscription in Australasia that are truly deplorable, never mind the fact that most boy conscripts, as Barrett argues persuasively, enjoyed the experience and profited willy-nilly from their time on the muster ground. Firstly there is the lack, in Australia of any formal provision for conscientious objection and in New Zealand of totally inadequate provision for COs. In the second place, the handling of children from twelve years old and up according to the Defence legislation of the two countries was surely unique in its harshness. Although the schools of many countries, including Britain and the United States, have, we know, included military training in their curricula, to the best of my knowledge nowhere were boys imprisoned for refusing to drill. Thirdly, there is no doubt that, in the fortresses and prison barracks of the two countries where many of the boy resisters were incarcerated, brutality was employed deliberately in order to frighten the boys, taken from their families and locked up there by themselves, into ultimate compliance.

Some of them, to their credit, did indeed refuse compliance and suffered the consequences. The Australian historian Bobbie Oliver has sought to discover the source of this lamentable falling away from the democratic ethos that inspired the political tradition of her country.

(Her conclusions, echoing the anti-compulsionists' slogan, 'Child compulsion: our country's shame,' could validly be applied to New Zealand, too.) She points as a major cause to 'the concurrent existence of two contradictory features of ... society: a much-praised and well publicized spirit of equality, freedom and independence and ... a strongly authoritarian, repressive strand.' It was the spirit of freedom that in this case provided the inspiration for the anti-conscriptionists and the conscientious resisters to boy conscription, while authoritarianism was the driving force behind those who approved and administered the measure.[47]

NOTES

1 Bobbie Oliver, *Peacemongers: Conscientious Objectors to Military Service in Australia, 1911–1945* (South Fremantle, 1997), 16, 17.

2 *The Argus*, 2 April 1912, quoted in Thomas W. Tanner, *Compulsory Citizen Soldiers* (Waterloo, New South Wales, 1980), 196.

3 Margaret E. Hirst, *The Quakers in Peace and War: An Account of Their Peace Principles and Practice* (London, 1923), 488.

4 William N. Oats, 'The Campaign against Conscription in Australia – 1911 to 1914,' *Journal of the Friends' Historical Society*, vol. 55, no. 7 (1989), 217.

5 Ibid., 207.

6 For the role in Australia of these Quaker visitors from the UK, see Peter Brock, *The Quaker Peace Testimony 1660 to 1914* (York UK, 1990), 279–82, 370, 373.

7 John Barrett, *Falling In: Australians and 'Boy Conscription,' 1911–1915* (Sydney, 1979). An alternative source is the much earlier study by John Percy Fletcher and John Francis Hills, *Conscription under Camouflage: An Account of Compulsory Military Training in Australasia down to the Outbreak of the Great War* (Glenelg, 1919). But I have not used it here, preferring Barrett for the reasons I give in the text.

8 Barrett, *Falling In*, 3, 199, 207, 288. Barrett concedes (pp. 191, 192) that his case histories are those of 'notable resisters.' 'These cases – from Harry Holland to Tom Roberts – received most publicity at the time ... they were the most notorious cases.' There were, he adds, a few other cases that he does not discuss. My reading confirms his belief that there were, however, not many more such cases.

9 Ibid., 301, 302.

10 Barrett (ibid., 177) comments: 'Even after allowing for some exaggeration in

that account, it is clear that Frank Giles had a hard fortnight.' Indeed, a generous estimate but, from what I have read about prisons in the English-speaking world of that time, I can see no sign of exaggeration in Alfred Giles's account.

11 Ibid., 170, 171, 175–7; Tanner, *Compulsory Citizen Soldiers*, 196, 197.

12 Barrett, *Falling In*, 183–6.

13 Ibid., 183, 184, 186, 187. Curiously, the Australian Quaker anti-conscriptionist J.F. Hills considered – privately – that Flintoff had, as Barrett puts it, 'let the side down' by escaping from detention (p. 188).

14 Ibid., 177, 178. Barrett mentions briefly one further case that may fall into my category (1): that of William Henry Bennett, a labourer on the railways, who was prosecuted on two occasions for refusing to permit his son to drill. Bennett junior was a sixteen-year-old and worked as a shop assistant. The father was fined a small sum, which his wife paid, while the son seems to have escaped scot-free.

15 Ibid., 172, 173.

16 Ibid., 187, 188, 200.

17 Tanner, *Compulsory Citizen Soldiers*, 214, quoting from the *Argus*. See also p. 215. The soldiers in charge of the detention fortresses by the sea were artillerymen: plenty of guns around, therefore, for the interned boys to polish!

18 Barrett, *Falling In*, 187, 188.

19 Ibid., 173, 174.

20 Ibid., 178–84. Barrett (p. 178) states that the two Kryggers may possibly have been cousins not brothers: the sources do not make this clear. I should mention here that Barrett (p. 100) cites one more case of a non-Quaker religious CO. In 1914 Roy A. Seaman was sent to Fort Queenscliff for twenty days. As a Christian, he had told the magistrate, he could not train as a soldier. The former responded sharply: 'This is not a matter of conscience, [the training] is only physical education.'

21 Ibid., 176; Oats, 'Campaign,' 212.

22 Hirst, *Quakers*, 491.

23 Oliver, *Peacemongers*, 23, 24, quoting from *Freedom*.

24 Quoted in Oats, 'Campaign,' 212, 213.

25 Ibid., 213; Barrett, *Falling In*, 175.

26 Barrett, *Falling In*, 175, 176; Hirst, *Quakers*, 491.

27 Hirst, *Quakers*, 491.

28 Ibid., 491, 491; Barrett, *Falling In*, 105–7, 188–90; Oats, 'Campaign,' 213. In adult life, Tom Roberts became a carpenter and builder. Like his parents, he remained a committed pacifist and Labour supporter. His daughter Thelma's wish, after the outbreak of the Second World War, to join the

Women's Auxiliary Australian Air Force caused him pain, and he forbade her to join up. Thelma reported that this was 'the only argument [she] had with him'! See Barrett, *Falling In*, 188.

29 Oats, 'Campaign,' 216, 217. See also Oliver, *Peacemongers*, 23, who presents slightly different figures from Oats's. For Seventh-day Adventists, see Barrett, *Falling In*, 100–2.

30 Oliver, *Peacemongers*, 24.

31 Barrett, *Falling In*, 192–9.

32 Oliver, *Peacemongers*, 25, 26.

33 R.L. Weitzel, 'Pacifists and Anti-militarists in New Zealand, 1909–1914,' *New Zealand Journal of History*, vol. 7, no. 2 (October 1973), 129.

34 Ibid., 136, 137.

35 Hirst, *Quakers*, 488.

36 For the role of Quaker visitors from the UK in the New Zealand anti-conscriptionist movement, see Brock, *Quaker Peace Testimony*, 285, 286.

37 Weitzel, 'Pacifists,' 137.

38 Ibid., 138, 139.

39 Ibid., 146.

40 Hirst, *Quakers*, 490.

41 Weitzel, 'Pacifists,' 146, quoting from letters from John Fletcher and W.H.F. Alexander. The emphasis is mine – P.B. For Ripa Island, see below in the text.

42 Ibid., 132, 133, 136.

43 Reg Williams, 'The Truth about Lyttleton Gaol,' *The Repeal* (Christchurch), May 1913, 10, 16.

44 In addition to Ripa Island in Lyttleton Harbour, Weitzel ('Pacifists,' 138) mentions three prison barracks, taken over by the Defence Department to house boys punished for refusing to drill: Point Halswell (Wellington), Otago Heads (Dunedin), and North Head (Auckland).

45 Ibid., 144, 145. Reg Williams, we may note, became a CO again during the First World War after conscription had been reintroduced in 1916. (This time, though, it was not boy conscription.) See David Grant, *Out in the Cold: Pacifists and Conscientious Objectors in New Zealand during World War II* (Auckland, 1986), 17. It is also worth noting that some Labour leaders like Robert Semple, who had supported the pre-war campaign against boy conscription and continued to be anti-compulsionist throughout the First World War, adopted an extremely unsympathetic attitude to COs when they were in power during the Second World War, branding a large number of them as 'defaulters' and interning them in semi-penal cantonments. In February 1941, Semple in his capacity as minister of national service, had

told religious leaders pleading for a more positive treatment of COs than the government appeared willing to adopt: 'By 1943 every young man at present of military age will be out of this country [i.e., on overseas service] or in camp. If we are too liberal [to COs] and too sympathetic with the fellow who wants to dodge we will have trouble' (quoted in J.E. Cookson, 'Illiberal New Zealand: The Formation of Government Policy on Conscientious Objection, 1940–1,' *New Zealand Journal of History*, vol. 17, no. 2 [October 1983], 123). See also Grant, *Out in the Cold*, 118, 119. The authoritarian democracy of Second-World-War New Zealand was not only hostile to COs, it also jailed pacifist activists above draft age, such as the Methodist minister Ormond Burton (1893–1974), a First World War veteran, regimental historian, and New Zealand patriot, who had become a pacifist after that conflict was over. During the Second World War he also clashed with the pro-war majority in his own church.

46 Weitzel, 'Pacifists,' 141, 147. It appears that, among the conscientious boy resisters of pre-war New Zealand there were no Maoris. This contrasts with the situation after the introduction of general conscription in 1916 when there were over one hundred Maori defaulters: the government treated them with the same harshness it inflicted on white conscientious objectors. These defaulters were largely inspired by the principled nonviolent resistance to the aggressive policies of the Pakeha, that is, white New Zealanders, which was led by Te Whiti at Parihaka until his death in 1907. See Dick Scott, *Ask That Mountain: The Story of Parihaka* (Auckland, 1981 edn); and Paul Baker, *King and Country Call: New Zealanders, Conscription and the Great War* (Auckland, 1988), 213, 214, 217–21. The section of the Maoris that followed Te Whiti – years before Gandhi launched his *satyagraha* movement – had broken with their people's warrior tradition: to some extent at any rate, the leader had seemingly been influenced by the pacifist element in the Christianity brought to New Zealand by the missionaries.

47 Oliver, *Peacemongers*, 9.

15 Prison Samizdat of British Conscientious Objectors in Two World Wars

Prison samizdat has been described, I think correctly, as 'the real prison press' in contrast to the prison press sponsored by, or at least approved by, the jail administration. This samizdat constitutes an underground activity carried on by prisoners 'without the sanction of prison officials,' and often in conditions of 'considerable adversity.'[1] The discovery of a samizdat journal is likely to lead to the punishment of those responsible for its production and distribution, and the destruction of all copies that the authorities have been able to discover. The unfettered expression of opinion in its pages represents a challenge to the prison establishment that cannot easily be tolerated.

The successful pursuit of prison samizdat journalism requires secrecy above all – the concealment of successive issues of the journal so as to prevent confiscation by the jail authorities. To guarantee this secrecy there is need for the presence within the prison population of a closed and reasonably compact group – political prisoners perhaps, or religious or working-class dissidents – among whom the samizdat journal can circulate without the likelihood of a reader, purposely or through negligence, bringing it to the attention of the authorities. Free circulation of the journal among prisoners would almost certainly expose it sooner or later – indeed, probably sooner rather than later – to this danger and thus put an end to the journal's existence. Editor, contributors, and readers of such samizdat are inevitably drawn from one prisoner group, and the contents of the journal will be oriented towards the interests and concerns of this group. The existence in a given prison of a group of this kind presumably explains why samizdat makes an appearance there, since it provides a potential readership for the journal.

First World War

The most extensive English-language prison samizdat network before mid-twentieth century emerged in First-World-War Britain among conscientious objectors (COs), incarcerated on account of their resistance to the military conscription introduced there in January 1916. This chapter in the history of 'jailhouse journalism' is not, I think, widely known and it may, therefore, be of interest if I outline the story.

During the First World War the community of British COs numbered some sixteen thousand men. It embraced religious pacifists, including active Quaker absolutists who refused all offers of alternative service, as well as humanitarian and socialist war resisters. Very few COs were given unconditional exemption, though this was a possible option. Those who failed to gain the exemption they wished for from the tribunals, which were set up by the government as part of the administration of conscription and granted alternative service to COs either in the army's Non-Combatant Corps or in a civilian occupation, were invariably sent to prison. Some of these men served repeated sentences virtually for the same offence. The COs possessed a vigorous organization in the No-Conscription Fellowship. Among the Fellowship's leaders were devout Christian pacifists, like the Quaker Edward Grubb, exempt from call-up because of his age, and socialist pacifists, like Clifford Allen and Fenner Brockway, who both spent prolonged periods in jail for their refusal of military service.[2] Eventually the government released those imprisoned objectors who were ready to accept work in semi-penal conditions under what was known as the Home Office Scheme. Those men who rejected the Scheme remained in jail even after the war ended in November 1918. Only in April 1919 did the release of these imprisoned objectors begin in earnest; it was completed in the following November. By that date a whole year had elapsed since the conclusion of an armistice between the belligerent powers.[3]

The regimen in British prisons at that date still retained much of the harshness of the penitentiary system introduced by penal reformers in Britain and North America a century or so earlier.[4] A new wave of prison reform originating around the turn of the century had, by 1914, done away with some of the worst horrors of the previous system: the treadwheel and crank, the convicts' cropped hair, the lock-step movement of prisoners, and some of the more barbarous punishments. But the silence rule, dietary punishment, and the penalty of solitary confinement, as well as the hated broad-arrow prison uniform, remained. And so, of course, did Britain's antique jails constructed in the previous century. COs did not suffer worse treatment in prison than common criminals, but they did endure the same, though some amelioration took place near the end of the war. This, then, was the environment in which the CO samizdat took root and flourished for several years. It ended with the release of the COs.

CO samizdat appeared in at least eight prisons in which COs were confined. Methods of production were similar because the conditions of production did not vary much from jail to jail. No writing materials were then allowed in British prisons, apart that is from a slate with chalk and pen, ink, and form letter issued specifically for the periodic letter home and collected afterwards by one of the warders. Thus these journals had usually to be 'written with such fragments of pencil as were obtainable, and in most cases toilet paper was the only paper to be had.' They usually appeared 'in the form of illustrated magazines.' Contents included verse and prose. Humour, a commodity in short supply in jails, occupied a prominent place in both these styles of writing. There were also articles on socialism and pacifism, literature and philosophy, as well as short stories and pencilled sketches.[5]

An anonymous author, writing in 1919, who surveyed this ephemeral press without claiming to have seen all the journals he discussed, let alone all issues of a given journal, calls the *Joyland Journal*, produced by COs in Mountjoy Prison, Dublin, 'undoubtedly ... the most artistic publication' from among the COs' nine known samizdat organs. He describes 'its sketches, cartoons, headlines, and cover designs,' creations of Arthur Wragg, as 'first-class work.' (Wragg's antiwar drawings and illustrations became popular in the 1930s in pacifist circles.) 'The *Joyland Journal* was bound in cloth, so that in its journey from cell to cell it might be properly preserved.'[6] Here, as in the case of the other journals, only one copy was made; this copy then circulated among the prison's CO population. Eventually it would, hopefully, be smuggled out of the prison, probably by the so-called 'foot post,' by which means letters and pencils were brought by COs into and out of jails.

John Graham, a Quaker prison chaplain who became the first historian of conscientious objection in First-World-War Britain, tells us that in the course of his duties as chaplain he came into possession of just one issue of a samizdat journal. 'The edges of its leaves,' he writes, are tattered, in spite of its cover of sacking decorated with an inscription.'[7]

Because of his wartime prison chaplainship and the trust jailed COs placed in him, Graham became well acquainted with the working of their samizdat. We learn from him that its surreptitious circulation from cell to cell 'became much more easy under the later [government] regulations, when conversation was allowed [for COs] in the exercise yard, and men could walk two or three together.' Sometimes a journal might somehow be passed from one cell window to another. For the brown toilet paper, Graham goes on, 'prison pen and ink were appropriated as opportunity arose. Leads for writing were imported. Pencils and the precious manuscripts were concealed inside waistbands and the hems of waistcoats. An innocent-looking ball of wax used in the daily work might be discovered to have a movable top, revealing a bottle of ink underneath.'[8]

Returning now to our survey of CO samizdat, the *Literary Outlet* was the product of one W. Dixon's initiative while he was incarcerated in Birmingham and Hull prisons. 'It was neatly produced, with artistic coverings, and a number of illustrations were scattered through it.' It featured a special series of articles on socialism. Another one-man effort was the *Court Martial*, produced in Winchester Prison by a prominent member of the No-Conscription Fellowship, W.J. Chamberlain. But it ceased publication after only four issues due to Chamberlain's breakdown under the strain of prison. It was an exclusively humorous magazine, its editor claiming his paper to be 'the organ of the Absolutely Its.' The pages 'were neatly written in imitation print, with a get-up similar to that of a smart modern newspaper.' Of a size little bigger than a bus ticket, it was perhaps conceived more as a joke than a serious contribution to the prison press. The *Lincoln Leader* was largely a newsheeet, but it included cartoons after the artist, Arthur Wragg, was transferred from Mountjoy Prison in Dublin. The CO samizdat journal produced in Dorchester Prison was unique in that it was written entirely in Esperanto. Entitled *Instigilo* (Stimulus), 'it was well bound in cloth' with excellent illustrations. In fact 'the entire makeup was exceptionally attractive' and up to the standard of the 'best monthly magazines,' according to one testimony. I wonder, though, how many of the COs then in Dorchester Prison were able to read Esperanto?

The fortnightly *Canterbury Clinker* was edited by Alfred Barratt Brown, an absolutist Quaker CO who, after the war, became prominent in the adult education movement and was eventually appointed principal of Ruskin College, Oxford, a centre for extramural students at that university. Brown composed most of the verses published in the columns of the journal, often parodies of familiar pieces adapted to the conditions of prison life. 'The *Canterbury Clinker*,' writes the anonymous author quoted above (who may have been Barratt Brown himself), 'was apparently written on the fly-leaves of the editor's books, and since it was done with pen and ink, one concludes that the publication day coincided with his letter-writing day.'[9]

About the three remaining CO samizdat journals, the *Winchester Whisperer*, *Old Lags Hansard* in Wandsworth Prison, and the *Walton Leader* in Liverpool, we know rather more than about the other six from the reminiscences of men who participated in their publication and/or circulation.

Let us begin with Winchester Prison's samizdat journal, to which its editors gave the title the *Whisperer*. That title was derived from the fact that, as a result of the silence rule then in force in British jails, prisoners wishing to communicate with each other resorted to whispering when they perceived a 'screw' was not looking their way. Young Harold Bing, serving a lengthy sentence in that jail, reported the following in an interview he gave many years later to the Imperial War Museum Sound Archives, London:

> The only writing facility in a cell was a slate and the slate pencil and therefore if you filled your slate you had to rub it all out again. There was no writing material except periodically when you were allowed to have the notepaper in your cell and a pen and ink to write your monthly or fortnightly letter. But here again a little ingenuity was used and some prisoners managed to make little ink wells by taking a block of cobblers wax – which was used for waxing the thread for making mailbags and so on – making a hole in it, sinking a thimble into the wax and then covering it up with another piece of wax. So that what appeared to be a block of wax was in fact a block of wax with a lid and when you lifted the lid there was a thimble sunk into the wax. And that thimble you filled with ink when you had your fortnightly or monthly ink for writing your letter. With inkpots of that kind there was produced in Winchester Prison a periodical called the *Winchester Whisperer*. It was written on the small brown sheets of toilet paper with which we were supplied – different people writing little essays or poems or humorous remarks, sometimes little cartoons or sketches. And all these bits of paper were passed surreptitiously from hand to hand and reached the editor who bound them together with a bit of mailbag canvas, used for repairing, for a cover, and this issue of the *Winchester Whisperer* was then passed round secretly hidden under people's waistcoats or up their sleeves. And as it happened, despite many

> searches, no copy of the *Winchester Whisperer* was ever captured by the warders, though I think some of them suspected its existence. And all the copies were finally smuggled out and placed in some depository in London, in some library. I used as a pen a needle, writing with the hollow end – dipping the hollow end into the ink. This meant of course one had to be always dipping the needle into the ink for almost every word. But it did produce thin writing so that you could get a good deal on one small sheet of toilet paper.[10]

The *Whisperer* was produced in a size easy to conceal from the vigilant eyes of a prison warder: approximately five inches square, it 'was bound with mailbag hessian with the title embroidered on the front.' Though the writing was small, young eyes could read it without difficulty. The *Whisperer*'s editor-in-chief was a talented poet and translator, Alan McDougall, who spent over two years in prison as a libertarian CO until finally, through a prolonged hunger strike, he forced the authorities to release him, by then just 'a walking number in misfitting broad-arrows and shuffling shoes.' In his memoirs the same friend, who thus described McDougall during their shared sojourn in Winchester Prison, wrote of his paper: 'The *Winchester Whisperer* was, with the exception of Alan McDougall's contributions, great tripe. It was also good fun.' His own verse contributions to the paper he modestly categorized as 'poor stuff all of it.' He also noted that McDougall allowed him to publish an 'unbowdlerized' poem using four-letter words – to the dismay 'of that considerable section of Winchester pacifists who were Christians.'[11]

For information about the samizdat journal of the 'conchies' in Wandsworth Prison, where many COs were then incarcerated, I am indebted to a fragment from the hitherto unpublished memoirs of Harold Blake, which has been reproduced by Felicity Goodall in her book on conscientious objectors in the two world wars. Beginning with the paper's editor, whose name unfortunately is not supplied, Blake writes:

> He was, in build and feature, almost the double of Mr. Lloyd George. This man undertook the publishing of a newssheet which he designated the *Old Lags Hansard*. This periodical was written by hand in block characters on sheets of toilet paper, and sewn together with thread; and on account of the labour involved, only one copy of each issue was published. However, it went the rounds passing from hand to hand, and finally when it

> had fulfilled its intended purpose, it was contrived that it should fall into the hands of Mr. Walker, the Chief Warder. The vastly amusing part about the whole business was that the last page always contained the announcement, 'Look out for the next number, to be published on ... [date]' and in spite of all the efforts of the authorities to trace its origin, we were not disappointed. Once indeed it was a day late, as they made the declared date a search day; but the editor presented his apologies in his editorial to the effect that he was a day late in publishing 'owing to an official raid on our offices.'[12]

The final CO samizdat journal we have to consider is the *Walton Leader.* Since its editor was Fenner Brockway, who served his major sentence as a CO in this Liverpool jail, we are well informed about how this paper functioned, for Brockway included a detailed account of this episode of his variegated political life in both versions of his autobiography that appeared in print during the latter part of his career.[13]

After doing time in Pentonville and Wandsworth and at Wormwood Scrubs, all located in London, Brockway entered Liverpool's Walton Prison in a defiant mood. 'I had gone through my period of initiation,' he tells us, 'and no longer had the spiritual exultation of a novice ... I would pit my wits against those of the authorities and defeat them whenever I could.' He considered he had already learnt a lot from his prison experience.[14]

There were at that time around sixty COs in Walton Prison located in the basement of one of the cellblocks. This concentration of the group made circulation of a samizdat journal easier than if the COs had been scattered in cells throughout the prison. Brockway soon decided it should be his first prison 'task' to produce such a paper. The No-Conscription Fellowship had already begun to smuggle leads into prisons concealed in a packet 'beneath the arch of the foot' of a CO entering jail. The leads were useful for passing written messages. 'The supreme disability which we had to overcome,' writes Brockway, 'was the rule forbidding communication between prisoners.' Under these conditions 'to speak was not always easy.' In addition, possession of such leads greatly facilitated the production of an underground journal.[15] Soon the project got under way. This is how Brockway tells the story:

> With a pencil in my hand I immediately began to plan a prison newspaper. The *Walton Leader* was produced twice a week and was quite a creditable journal. It consisted of about forty toilet paper pages, and included

> news items, cartoons, serious articles, humorous stories and correspondence. Our cartoonist was Arthur Wragg, whose work is now often to be seen in the press; the news items were sent in by prisoners who had received letters and visits or who had newly come in, whilst articles, stories and letters were contributed in abundance ... We were rapidly becoming experts in breaking the prison rules, and some of the warders, who became increasingly friendly, made this easier by winking their eyes at offences so long as their chiefs did not get to know.[16]
>
> One item in the *Walton Leader* might have brought us charges under the Official Secrets Act. An incoming objector brought us a detailed account of the slaughter at Passchendaele written by a deserter who was in the guard room at the same time. The story moved us all deeply. Should we complain of our safe conditions whilst others were facing almost inevitable death? One of our boys even withdrew and joined the army because he could not accept the comparison. It was ironical that whilst the Press outside was not allowed to publish the story a prison paper was able to do so.[17]
>
> A copy of the *Walton Leader* was discovered and I was tried by the Visiting Magistrates. They had no doubt that I produced it and I did not deny it, but they had no evidence. In a normal Court I could not have been found guilty, but they sentenced me to six days on bread and water in the punishment cells. I was taken to a dark basement cell where the furniture consisted of a stool, a chamber pot and a Bible. The second day I became weak and lay on the floor, using the Bible as a pillow, but I found that by the third day I had become adjusted. At night I was permitted to lie on a bed board, which was at least warmer than the stone floor.[18]

The *Walton Leader* was a more ambitious effort than any other CO prison samizdat of that period. Indeed, over a hundred issues were produced. In its commentary on political events, whether at home or abroad, the journal naturally reflected its editor's socialism. But Brockway, while greeting with enthusiasm the fall of the Romanov dynasty in February 1917, was extremely critical of the Provisional Government's continued prosecution of the war.

The paper, until its discovery by the authorities, bore clearly the imprint of its editor's personality. 'I used to spend hours in the production of the prison paper,' Brockway tells us in his autobiography, 'rewriting in small, neat capital letters every contribution, leaving only the cartoons in the original form.'[19]

The reader's subscription, one piece of toilet paper for each issue,[20] was collected by the cleaner on the landing where the COs were located (a young Welsh CO nicknamed 'Raj') when prisoners were at work. 'And,' writes Brockway, 'each evening I found my supply made up plentifully.' But, he goes on:

> ... with the distribution side of the paper I was dissatisfied; to pass a copy from prisoner to prisoner took a week and news and articles became stale. The solution of this difficulty came to me suddenly. We all used the lavatory and in privacy: why not make it the reading room for the paper? I hid it there and tapped out a telephone pipe 'Call to all Cells' announcing that it would be there every Tuesday and Thursday morning. I ought to have anticipated the result. On Tuesday and Thursday morning there were queues; if a prisoner were unlucky enough to get the wrong cubicle, he was back again before long. The prison authorities were puzzled. Why Tuesdays and Thursdays? The Medical Officer was ordered to report on the diet on Mondays and Wednesdays ... but, alas, before his report was prepared the *Walton Leader* was discovered by an unusually inquisitive or officious warder.[21]

Thus one of the most interesting ventures in prison samizdat came to a sudden end.

During the First World War, COs in Britain, from mid-1916 to mid-1919, had produced at least nine samizdat journals. There may well have been more such papers, now lost, for toilet paper is fragile and the network readership was volatile. There were indeed a number of other prisons in which COs were incarcerated in varying numbers. What, then, of Wormwood Scrubs, Reading, Exeter, Bristol, Norwich, Cardiff, Strangeways (Manchester), Armley (Leeds), Durham, and a number of other jails? And what of the Scottish prisons? But if samizdat was produced by COs in any of these institutions, it has seemingly vanished without a trace. A key factor in producing these journals appears to have been the presence in a given prison of at least one individual with journalistic talent, ready first to take the initiative and then to oversee the journal's production and distribution. Without such a person, presumably a samizdat journal would not emerge, even if other favourable factors such as a sizeable group of COs within the given institution might be present.

One last point is worth noting: the elitist character of this CO samizdat. It did not circulate among the general prison population, but only among a small group with special concerns of its own, to which the contributors addressed themselves in what they wrote for these journals. I have explained the reasons for this restricted circulation and appeal. I believe they were valid ones; at the same time the elitism of this samizdat should not be slurred over. So far as I know, CO samizdat did not circulate either among the Irish nationalists incarcerated in British jails during the First World War, even though Fenner Brockway at any rate was in contact with them. But, then, of course, they possessed a tightly organized communications network of their own.

Second World War

Flowery dell – a prison cell in the traditional rhyming slang of English thieves. Therefore British conscientious objectors (COs) imprisoned in London's Wormwood Scrubs Prison in the Second World War gave their underground paper the title *The Flowery.* Seventeen, or possibly eighteen, issues appeared between August 1942 and March 1944, and the paper had a succession of six different editors.[22] *The Flowery* had been the brainchild primarily of Herbert F. Moore, who edited its first five issues in the course of eight months spent at the Scrubs. Moore was not only an accomplished journalist but a charismatic character. A fellow CO, Bob Hockley, who occupied the cell next door to Moore's, relates in his prison memoir that Moore's presence there 'transformed' his life in prison.[23] When one editor was released from jail at the expiry of his sentence, he handed the editorship over to his successor. By the spring of 1944, however, few COs remained at Wormwood Scrubs; so the paper folded up. Writing at the end of the year, *The Flowery*'s last editor, Howard Hutchins, explained that, leaving prison the previous June, 'I could find nobody to undertake the editorship, so the publication stopped ... my issues were the last. I did two numbers, the first was taken out [of Wormwood Scrubs] by one named Armstrong ... a reliable chap ... The second of my efforts was in circulation when I went sick in hospital. When I returned, owing to some scare I found that the whole outfit ... had been so efficiently hidden that some demolition was [needed] to recover everything: copy, ink, etc.'[24] Another of the paper's later editors has described the somewhat 'scary' atmosphere facing both the paper's contributors and its readers towards the end. He writes:

> When Leslie Tarlton approached me with the suggestion that I should take over the editorship of *The Flowery* on his release, discipline was at a

low ebb in the prison and I had no qualms about taking over the job. Almost immediately, however, there began a general tightening-up of the regulations and my term of office was spent in an atmosphere of 'turning-over' [i.e., frisking], 'scrubbing-out' [i.e., of prisoner's cell], inspections, etc., which kept me on tenterhooks all the time.

Not that the risk of being caught with the magazine was very great, nor probably would the consequences have been very serious, but I did not like the idea of losing an edition over which a great deal of trouble had been taken, or precious 'copy,' which was not too prolific. However, all difficulties were successfully overcome, and I got the editions passed out with a third in circulation, and handed my successor some 'copy' to give him a start.

We had one or two narrow squeaks, of course. At one period there was a P.O. (Principal Officer) on duty with a mania for 'turning-over,' this practice being to lock up a group of eleven cells before the occupants went down in the morning. One never knew which group would be chosen as he jumped about all over the Hall. However, one chap asked me for the current issue of *The Flowery* to read one evening when he thought he would be fairly safe. Next morning of course his group of cells was chosen for a search before he had time to dispose of the magazine. Fortunately the 'screws' were far from zealous in their duties and *The Flowery* survived this occasion between the chap's foot and sock.

I was fortunate in not being subjected to a proper search during this time, but I went about in some trepidation for, in addition to a wad of 'copy,' I usually had in my 'flowery dell' a stock of paper from the shop clerk's books, a bottle each of black, red and violet inks, a couple of pens, a rubber and other items. These I hid in the best place I knew – the ventilator – but I believe even this expedient was not unknown to the officials.

Needless to say, the foregoing state of affairs made my colleagues anxious not to hang on to a copy of *The Flowery* for long, and consequently I found that I had it in my possession nearly all the time. This got a bit too unhealthy, so I used to hide the material in the workshop when I did not require it for editorial purposes.

Once I stuffed a wad of matter in a sack of hessian waste. Imagine my dismay on returning from another part of the shop to find that in my absence a 'screw' and a couple of C.O.s had taken away the sack to an inaccessible part of the building for further disposal.

To my relief however, a colleague nearby calmly fished the packet from his shirt and modestly explained that when he saw the lay of the land he had whisked it out of the sack. In this incident he displayed all-round

> astuteness: first, in knowing that something was in the sack when I thought no one had seen me secrete it; secondly, in realising that it was *The Flowery*; and thirdly, in whipping it out under the very nose of the 'screw' and while the prisoners were actually in the act of taking the sack away, for he had no means of knowing beforehand what they intended to do.
>
> There was a wide diversity of temperament revealed in the attitude of the C.O.s to *The Flowery*. On the one hand, there were the fellows who were too timid to accept the paper at all for fear of being caught with it (mostly chaps with short sentences), or too timid to scribble down a few words on a piece of toilet paper for insertion in the mag. On the other hand, an artist whom I commissioned to design a cover would almost make my hair stand on end by handing me a bottle of red ink or some material when we were surrounded by hordes of prisoners and officers, at the same time making loud comments on the whole business!
>
> The majority of the C.O.s, on the whole, thoroughly entered into the spirit of the thing, and I personally consider that the effort – and the risk of being 'cased' –was well worth while, if only for the fact that it put a bit of a kick into prison life, gave something to occupy one's time and thoughts during a long sentence and helped to pass the time more quickly.[25]

Fenner Brockway, a veteran of CO prison samizdat in the First World War, wrote the preface to the pamphlet containing extracts from the paper, which appeared in June 1945. In it he told readers how much he regretted that the Central Board for Conscientious Objectors (CBCO), of which he was chairman, had been unable 'to reproduce *The Flowery* in full in its original form.' The paper, he goes on, 'was written in hand on sheets of ruled prison paper bound together with the stout waxed thread supplied to the prisoners for their task of making mailbags for the General Post Office (GPO). Careful folding of the sheets, a few stitches with the stout needle, and the process of binding, such a problem for most publishers during wartime, was complete.' At Wormwood Scrubs and other British jails of that time, prisoners, we know, were permitted use of pen, ink, and paper only for the purpose of writing the monthly letter out. Otherwise, a smallish slate, together with chalk and a rag for erasing what had been written, was all that was available.

A striking feature of each issue of *The Flowery* was its cover. The Scrubs community of COs contained some extremely talented artists whose fingers were probably better adapted to this task than to sewing mailbags for the GPO. One cover, for instance, depicted a heavily barred cell window, another the prison's neo-Gothic turrets and grim cellblocks. 'Sometimes the artist showed a neat sense of humour as, for instance, in the first issue of 1943 – when the New Year was illustrated by the figure of a little child bearing a bag marked "43" and knocking at a locked prison door marked "Reception." Beneath was the caption "Starting a stretch."' One cover artist devised a tasteful colour design in shaded pink and pale blue as the result of somehow – somewhere – purloining a bottle of red ink. Readers were so pleased with the outcome of the artist's 'theft' that the editor used the scheme for three successive issues.

Only one copy of each issue was produced. Let me quote Brockway again on the process of production and methods of distribution; he obviously obtained his information direct from those who had participated in one capacity or another in the enterprise: 'Every issue,' he writes, 'of course involved risks to all associated with it – not only the editor and contributors, but the readers. The writers and artists would usually prepare their contributions seated in the one quarter of their cells outside the view of the inquisitive eye at the spy-hole in the door. The binder would fold and sew the sheets in a similar way or inside the protection of the mailbag on which he was working. The reader would hide the precious journal inside his shirt or sock until he was ready to pass it in a flash to another prisoner as they met in corridor or queue. Discovery meant almost certainly a day or two on bread and water and solitary confinement.'

Considering the high risk of discovery, it is surprising that only one issue, that of February 1943, was uncovered by a prison officer – through no fault of the man who was carrying it, since he had taken 'all reasonable precautions' to preserve secrecy. The officer, however, did not report the delinquent as he was supposed to do according to the prison rules. He just destroyed the paper on the spot. Brockway supposed he did this out of kindness, adding wryly: 'though perhaps without due appreciation of literary and artistic merit.'

At first the risk of discovery had been comparatively small, at any rate in comparison with the situation which developed later. In a review of the *Flowery* booklet in *Peace News*, the famous composer Michael Tippett, who served a short sentence in Wormwood Scrubs as a CO in 1943, wrote:

> The Scrubs was a natural place for such a project. There was a floating criminal population of nearly 800 first offenders, with a certain number of penal servitude men en route to one of the penal camps, which meant that the percentage of warders to prisoners was low ... Part of the 800 were the group of conchies, numbering at one time nearly 150, which had a workshop to themselves ('Mail Bags Two'). So the opportunities for communication were liberal.[26]

Besides illustrations, each issue of *The Flowery* contained a variety of contributions in both verse and prose: serious articles alongside humorous pieces. There may not have been any masterpieces, but *The Flowery*'s literary standard was remarkably high considering the circumstances in which it was produced.[27] The Food Relief campaigner Roy Walker, for instance, who spent virtually the whole of two sentences at Wormwood Scrubs in solitary confinement because he had consistently refused all prison labour, still managed to contribute several clever poems to *The Flowery.*

Herbert Moore, introducing the paper – anonymously, of course – in its first issue of August 1942, had set the tone. 'The editor,' he wrote, 'wishes to apologise right away for everything except for one thing. He apologises for the writing, the spelling and the syntax. He apologises for the paper, the nib and the ink ... He apologises for all the contributors who have "started the ball rolling" but he thanks them most gratefully for risking it. What he does not apologise for is the spirit in which it was conceived, and which was one of cooperation with all those "inside" with him, ... who are standing against war. This effort has helped him. May it also help his readers.' Moore then gave readers some advice. They should be prepared 'to accept full responsibility' if a prison officer should discover he had the paper. 'It is to be retained one night or dinner-time only, and passed on to a known C.O. It is only to be read in the cell, with the door shut, and should not be taken if there is a possibility of a special release': a necessary precaution since at this time the authorities were releasing COs without prior notice if their application to an Appellate Tribunal had been successful. Readers were also asked not to fold the paper: It was a fragile artefact that could easily disintegrate when treated roughly. 'If,' Moore concluded, 'a certain P.O. [Principal Officer] with a reputation for seeing even the ridge of a cigarette paper under a convict's jacket, should be about, we can only say that *Flowery* should be hastily swallowed in two large gulps. Nor should that prove difficult to those who have actually eaten, shall we say, a fish dinner. After all, it may be bad, but it doesn't smell!' And the stockfish, served as a frequent main course for midday dinner at the wartime Scrubs, was truly malodorous.

Humour seems to have predominated over serious content. As a versifier declared in the issue of December 1942: 'If this booklet brings to birth / Naught of value save its mirth, / We could no apter subject find, / Knowing well how sorrow might consume the mind; / For of joy one smile surmounts a span, / For to laugh is proper to the man.' Indeed, the serious contributions seem to have been rather slight. An exception was the article Sidney Greaves wrote for *The Flowery* during the evening prior to his discharge from the Scrubs. It described the work at the Hungerford Club, to which he was returning.[28] The Club, situated under an arch of Hungerford Bridge in central London, cared for down-and-outs whose verminous and filthy condition made them unwelcome in the capital's air-raid shelters. It was run by the Anglican Pacifist Fellowship and staffed by a dedicated group of COs and their friends, who earned praise even from the wartime coalition government's Ministry of Health.

The Flowery's humour often poked fun at the 'screws' (as the prison officers were known in jail slang) and, above them, the Principal Officers, 'encased in ribboned uniform for show.' One of the most successful contributions (authored by H.R. Moir) consisted of a series of 'Nature Notes: Birds in Scrubland,' accompanied by illustrations depicting the various birds: the Lesser Wryneck or *Wormwoodia Scrubicus*, whose 'mournful tones pervade the scrubs at all hours'; the Scrubby Bullfinch (*Stevii Prisonicus*), whose 'gentle call ... is known to all .. "Git-abucket, Git-abucket"'; and two 'pretty (Jail) birds ... [nicknamed] on account of their head plumage ... "Goldilocks."' The latter, the Notes report, 'appear to be in full song throughout Scrubland at about 8:30 in the morning. Their appealing cry, "Kumm-on-Lad, Anser-y' naym," pierces the densest November fog ... The two species ... share song peculiarity and beak structures. The plumage, too, is uniform.' But not only the prison staff, including the Anglican chaplain ('*Ecclesiasticus Carolae Tudorii* ... the only bird of "pray" ever to figure in heraldry') and 'rarer ornithological visitors to these climes,' like the visiting Justices of the Peace with 'their cry, "Any gumplaints?"' became figures of fun for the magazine's contributors, the naïve CO was also game for them. An example of this is the 'Conversation Piece' composed for *The Flowery*'s first number, presenting a dialogue between an 'old lag' and the innocent CO in the neighbouring cell, who is extremely bewildered by his neighbour's slang.

I have based this essay almost exclusively on the 1945 pamphlet referred to above. In fact, the pamphlet had been quite a long time in gestation – before appearing in mid-1945. The idea of publishing extracts from the paper seems to have originated with Herbert Moore, *The Flowery*'s first editor and *spiritus movens*, after his release from the Scrubs early in 1943. He approached the CBCO, where Denis Hayes was press officer, with a proposal for a booklet. The CBCO's Quaker secretary, Stephen Thorne, was rather lukewarm. He considered 'that on the whole it is worth publishing though I think some of it rather slight.'[29] Hayes warned Moore that members of the CBCO doubted if the moment was appropriate for such a venture. They knew there were COs at the Scrubs, who believed publication of such a booklet was inadvisable. 'The Board could not rule out the possibility of a special search in Scrubs following the issue of the pamphlet ... If publication were to take place in defiance of the C.O.s at present in Scrubs, the Board would lay itself open to serious attack.' He hoped that publication would be possible later – 'either when the present magazine was discontinued or at the end of the war.' Even though the CBCO hoped they would not do so, the Board, of course, would not try to obstruct Moore and his friends if they decided to go ahead with publication on their own. The CBCO did ask Moore, though, 'to give the Board an opportunity to notify the C.O.s in prison that you were to proceed with publication.' Hayes expressed his regret at having to turn down Moore's proposal. 'I am afraid the whole matter will be rather a disappointment to you, but I think you will agree that the longer the magazine is able to continue the greater the tradition which it can fairly be said that you and the first contributors commenced to build up.'[30]

Thus Moore's proposal was put into cold storage, though not abandoned altogether. The CBCO eventually went ahead with publication after production of the paper at the Scrubs had definitely ceased and the war was drawing to a close. Hayes now sent Brockway a copy of the proposed booklet, asking for his comments on the materials it would contain: 'I have already done a good deal of pruning,' he stated. Brockway's negative response is surprising in view of the enthusiastic welcome he gave to *The Flowery* in the preface he wrote to the booklet, printed a couple of months later. What, however, he now wrote was this:

> I am frankly a bit disappointed ... It has made me feel the difference between the C.O.s in prison during the last war and this war more than anything I have read. Our surreptitious prison papers were full of discussion on social and political problems and on what we could do when we got out to help the struggle against war and for a society and world of cooperation. But the 'Flowery' is terribly subjective and introvert and soul-saving. The humour is good – but so was ours. The nature notes are grand, but for gawd's sake leave out the apology for the semi-hunger strike and for its conclusion. This is really introversion to the point of imbecility.

He would, he went on, gladly write a preface. 'But it will be about the technique and contents of the illegal papers of the last war and not about the "Flowery." In view of this over-ruthless criticism I think this note had better be seen by yourself and a few privileged persons only!'[31]

Brockway must have had second thoughts. At any rate, his preface contained very little about the First World War and was full of factual information about the production of *The Flowery* as well as nice things about its contributors. Brockway indeed made a valid point when he compared the strongly socio-political stance of most prison COs during the First World War, at any rate the vocal ones, with the more 'subjective and soul-saving' bias of the Second World War's British prisoners of conscience. One need not, of course, share Brockway's preference for the former.

Except for the confiscated issue, it would seem that all remaining issues of *The Flowery* had been successfully smuggled out of the Scrubs, despite the fact that only one copy of each issue existed inside prison. At the end of the war, the lawyer Denis Hayes, who had worked for the Central Board for Conscientious Objectors throughout the war years, was in possession of copies of nearly all the original issues, while the penultimate *Flowery* editor, Howard Whitten, possessed two issues that Hayes did not have. These originals provided the source for the 1945 pamphlet. But, alas, they appear to be no longer extant, though of course some – or all – may eventually surface again.[32] It seems probable that, after the appearance of the pamphlet *Flowery,* Hayes returned the issues of the paper in his possession to their respective editors, who had in fact merely loaned them to him while the question of publication was still unresolved. This may prove a key to eventual recovery of the vanished original issues, that is, if in fact they still exist!

During the First World War almost every British prison had had its CO underground press. But, in the next global conflict, so far as I am aware, among British prisons only Wormwood Scrubs produced a CO samizdat – a result perhaps of the smaller proportion of COs who then spent time in jail. It is sad, therefore, that the original issues of this unique journal may have vanished for ever.[33]

NOTES

1 Paul Wright in *Journal of Prisoners on Prisons*, vol. 10, no. 1/2 (1999), 130, 131; reprinted from *Prison Legal News*, vol. 10, no. 4 (April 1999).

2 After the war the two men were eventually raised to the British peerage for political services, in 1932 and 1964 respectively; Lord Allen of Hurtwood died in 1939 and Lord Brockway in 1988. While remaining active in the promotion of peace, by this time both had rejected unconditional pacifism.

3 See Constance Braithwaite, *Conscientious Objection to Various Compulsions under British Law* (York UK, 1955), 128–69, for an informative survey of conscientious objection to military service in First-World-War Britain. To 31 July 1919, '5,739 objectors were sentenced by court martial. 1,548 objectors were sentenced more than once and of these 893 were sentenced more than twice ... At least 843 objectors were in prison for twenty months or more; some were in prison for more than three years' (ibid., 153).

4 The classic account here, so far as Britain is concerned, is Michael Ignatieff, *A Just Measure of Pain: The Penitentiary in the Industrial Revolution, 1750–1850* (New York, 1980).

5 The *C.O. Clink Chronicle* (London, [1919]), 1. This sixteen-page pamphlet, published by the National Labour Press, contains extracts from the CO samizdat, mainly verse. While sometimes quite clever or entertaining, the extracts are never of a strikingly high literary calibre. But, of course, that was not the objective of the writers, who aimed simply at keeping up the spirits of their fellow 'conchies' in trying circumstances.

6 Ibid., 2. I have only been able to trace a single original issue of one of these journals. (Though it is very likely that more may be extant, toilet paper does not provide the most durable material for purposes of publication!)

7 John W. Graham, *Conscription and Conscience: A History 1916–1919* (London, 1922), 280, 282. The item owned by Graham was no. 6 of the *Winchester Whisperer*, Christmas 1918. It is now in the collections of the Library of the Religious Society of Friends, London.

8 Ibid., 279, 280. Graham refers here to a weekly samizdat journal edited by

an absolutist CO named Albert Taylor, arrested while a 'prospective parliamentary Labour candidate for Rossendale.' But I have been unable to identify this paper. See also David Boulton, *Objection Overruled* (London, 1967), 228.

9 *C.O. Clink Chronicle*, 1, 2; Boulton, *Objection Overruled*, 228, 229.

10 Quoted in Felicity Goodall, *A Question of Conscience: Conscientious Objection in the Two World Wars* (Stroud UK, 1997), 35–7. Bing later became active in the War Resisters' International, especially during the interwar years. What a pity, though, he was not more specific here as to the depository where he says all copies of the CO samizdat smuggled out of the various prisons were to be found!

11 George Baker, *The Soul of a Skunk: The Autobiography of a Conscientious Objector* (London, 1930), 199, 200, 253, 254. While McDougall printed classical Greek in his jail samizdat, the imprisoned Quaker pacifist Stephen Hobhouse found solace in reading the Greek New Testament in his cell. I had considered this proof of the superior classical culture of an important section of the CO community in First-World-War Britain over that of a later generation, not to speak of North Americans generally – until I read this: Within recent years George Edwards of Louisville, Kentucky, a retired seminary New Testament professor, 'taught Greek to some prisoners at La Grange Prison who had requested the instruction so that they could read the New Testament in its original language. Ray [Cullen, one of the inmates] took the course and did so well that he began teaching Greek to still other prisoners' (from *Fellowship* [Nyack NY], vol. 66, no. 11–12 [November-December, 2000], 25).

12 Goodall, *A Question of Conscience*, 37.

13 Fenner Brockway, *Inside the Left: Thirty Years of Platform, Prison and Parliament* (London, 1942; reprinted 1947); and his second autobiography, *Towards Tomorrow* (London, 1977).

14 Brockway, *Inside the Left*, 95.

15 Ibid., 95, 96.

16 Ibid., 98–101.

17 Boulton, *Objection Overruled*, 230, describes this as a 'scoop.' 'At a time when such reports were prohibited in the national newspapers, a tiny prison journal told in graphic terms of the wave upon wave of "cannon fodder" sent "over the top" by the generals, suffering decimation for the sake of a few feet of land – or a cow-shed.'

18 Brockway, *Towards Tomorrow*, 51, 52.

19 Brockway, *Inside the Left*, 99.

20 Described by Brockway as 'a primitive but very useful form of payment'

(from his introduction to *The Flowery, 1942–4: The Scrubs 'Conchie' Review* [London, 1945], 4). This pamphlet, published by the Central Board for Conscientious Objectors, contains excerpts from the samizdat journal produced by COs incarcerated in Wormwood Scrubs Prison during the Second World War.

21 Brockway, *Inside the Left*, 99, 100.

22 In a brief report entitled 'A Secret Paper Ran 1½ Years at the Scrubs,' published in the *News Chronicle* (press cutting in the Archives of the Central Board for Conscientious Objectors, Library of the Religious Society of Friends, London, MSS 914, Series 8, Box 2 ['The Flowery']), Louise Morgan claimed to have been shown seventeen issues of the paper immediately prior to writing her article. Together with the issue destroyed by a prison officer, that would make eighteen issues in all. Others have stated that the total was seventeen. Morgan describes the issues she perused as 'grimy and tattered from being secretly passed from man to man and hidden inside shirt or sock.' *The Flowery*'s successive editors were Herbert Moore, Leslie Tarlton, Ernest Daniell, Arthur Chamberlain, Howard Whitten, and Howard Hutchins.

23 Robert Hockley, *Beyond the Next Hill: My Story*, ed. Hilary Clark (Wolverhampton: The Model Printers, 1998), 58–94.

24 Howard Hutchins to Denis Hayes, 17 December 1944, Friends Library (London), MSS 914, Series B, Box 2. For safe keeping, copy, ink, etc. must have been so well concealed, probably in landing walls or cell flooring or walls, that 'demolition' was needed to retrieve them!

25 Ernest Daniell, '"The Flowery" Comes to Town,' Central Board for Conscientious Objectors, *Bulletin*, no. 63 (May 1945), 123, 124.

26 *Peace News*, 29 June 1945.

27 According to Louise Morgan, the paper's editors and artists included 'a bank cashier, local government officer, printing operative and barber.'

28 Printed in Denis Hayes, *Challenge of Conscience: The Story of the Conscientious Objectors of 1939–1949* (London, 1949), 226–8. Greaves was an unconditionalist CO with a six-months sentence, who had moved rapidly from Anglicanism to Quakerism. After the war he became a medical doctor. See 10850/2 (2 reels: Greaves), Sound Archive, Imperial War Museum (London).

29 Stephen Thorne to Fenner Brockway, 1 April 1943, Friends Library (London), MSS 914, Series 8, Box 2.

30 Denis Hayes to Herbert Moore, 7 June 1943, ibid.

31 Hayes to Brockway, 9 March 1945 and Brockway's reply to Hayes, n.d., ibid., Cf. the suggestion of *The Flowery*'s last editor, Howard Hutchins, in

his letter to Hayes dated 17 December 1944: 'I am wondering if it would be advisable to limit the articles to those concerned with prison life.' 'Informative or controversial articles' could be 'read anywhere.' This advice, though it sounds sensible, was not followed. On the other hand, the inclusion of a wider selection of articles than Hutchins proposed, gave readers a more accurate idea of the character of the paper.

32 See letter, dated 28 August 2003, from Tabitha Driver, Library of the Religious Society of Friends, London, where the CBCO archives are now located. The London *Friend* (9 July 2004, p. 3) published my letter asking readers to 'help me to locate present possessors of the original issues.' So far at any rate, there has been no response.

33 American COs in the Second World War produced at least one CO prison samizdat. Its sponsors, Lowell Naeve and Jim Peck, at Danbury Prison gave it the not very original title *The Clink*. 'The men quickly learned that the pages of *Life* magazine [which was permitted in the prison], once hand-washed, yielded enough ink to print their own cartoons, poetry, drawings and articles' (Scott H. Bennett, *Radical Pacifism: The War Resisters League and Gandhian Nonviolence in America, 1915–1963* [Syracuse NY, 2003], 116, 117). For a survey of the American prison press, almost exclusively journals sanctioned by the prison authorities and not samizdat, see James McGraith Morris, *Jailhouse Journalism: The Fourth Estate behind Bars* (Jefferson NC, 1998). It spans the period from 1800 to the 1990s.

16 Weaponless in the British Armed Forces: The Non-Combatant Corps in the First World War

The Non-Combatant Corps (NCC), established by the British government in the two world wars of the last century, was a striking phenomenon in the history of conscientious objection. Under the British conscription legislation of 1916 and 1939, service in the NCC was one among several forms of exemption that a conscientious objector (CO) might receive; and such service was open to any objector, religious or secular, who was considered to be sincere.

Governments in other lands sometimes also made provision for COs, who were ready to serve in their country's army or navy, to do so without bearing arms. But noncombatant service was carried out in every case within a different framework than the one in which the NCC worked. For instance, when universal military service was introduced in Prussia in 1868, only Mennonites were exempted from combatant duties. Their conscripts were allowed, instead, to perform their service in certain branches of the army regarded by the government as of a noncombatant character.[1] This privilege was continued for the Prussian Mennonites after 1870 when a united German Empire came into being. Later, the Soviet government in the 1920s allowed Mennonite conscripts to serve without arms in the Red Army.[2] Though we find COs eventually serving as noncombatant soldiers in some countries on the European continent as well as in wartime Australia, New Zealand, and Canada, they did so on an individual basis. And with respect to 'legal conscientious objection' during the twentieth century in the United States, while certainly noncombatant service in the armed forces has been one of several alternatives offered to American COs, no special corps was set up to accommodate COs who accepted noncombatant duties. Such men usually did their national service in the Medical Corps, and the situation remained unchanged until the abolition of conscription at the end of the Vietnam War.[3]

On the other side of the Cold War's so called 'Iron Curtain,' the Communist rulers of the German Democratic Republic (DDR) in 1964, after the building of the Berlin Wall in 1961 and the introduction of conscription for the Nationale Volksarmee (NVA) in 1962, created a noncombatant branch of their army known as the *Baueinheiten* (construction units), to which recognized COs – 'convinced pacifists' – were assigned. This noncombatant corps, unique in the Soviet bloc, continued until the fall of communism in 1990, by which date, despite continued disinformation and despite discrimination practised against them by the authorities, members of these units were acting as foci for the expanding peace movement in the DDR. Apart from the officers and NCOs, who were combatant soldiers, the *Bausoldaten* were drawn exclusively from COs, many of them members of the Evangelical-Lutheran Church. The Church, which formed the major religious denomination in the DDR and included a few absolute pacifists in the leadership and many more among its young adherents, steadfastly supported its noncombatant conscripts alongside those members – the overwhelming majority – who chose combatant service: at one point, to the annoyance of the Party, it even implied that the position of the former was the one nearest to that of the gospels. During the quarter-century of the *Baueinheiten*'s existence, a complex pattern of give and take, friction and détente, developed on this issue between church and state. Over the twenty-six years of their existence, approximately ten thousand COs, including some whose objections were based on humanist rather than strictly religious motives, served in the construction units.[4] Those COs, on the other hand, who were unwilling to become *Bausoldaten*, like the JWs, were either jailed or became draft exiles. These men (*Totalverweigerer*) objected, in particular, to the kind of work the army usually required its COs to perform, such as building military airfields, servicing army bases, or enlarging the army's communications network. Unfortunately, the State Security Service shortly before the fall of communism succeeded in destroying much of the official documentation concerning COs in the DDR.

Because of their special characteristics alluded to at the beginning of this essay it should, now, be worthwhile to take a look at how the NCC functioned during the First World War. (For a glimpse at its Second World War edition, see essay 24 below.)

During the First World War the original intention of the British government seems to have been to limit exemption for COs to noncombatant army service.[5] But in the end the Military Service Act of January 1916 (5 & 6 Geo 5, c. 104), which with only minor changes defined the treatment of conscientious objection for the rest of the war, provided for three categories of CO exemption – unconditional exemption or exemption conditional on the applicant undertaking either alternative civilian service or noncombatant duties in the armed forces. On 10 March, Army Order 112 (1916) set up a Non-Combatant Corps, which was placed under the direction of the Adjutant-General's Department. Shortly afterwards, an Army Council Instruction (551 [1916]) defined what kind of training NCC men would have to undergo as follows: 'Companies of the NCC will be trained in squad drill without arms and in the various forms of tools used in field engineering. The privates will be equipped as infantry except that they will not be armed or trained with arms of any description.' NCC men, however, were debarred from serving in the firing line: 'a restriction,' as John Rae points out, that 'excluded such tasks as erecting barbed wire and burying the dead [but] denied to conscientious objectors the opportunity to share the dangers and deprivations of the trenches.' Rae lists the kind of labour on which the men were actually employed: building of roads, erection of huts in army camps, loading and unloading of ships and railway waggons, and the burning of excreta ('an unpleasant task euphemistically defined as "sanitary work"'). And he adds, these were the kind of jobs 'usually undertaken by pioneer or labour battalions, or even by defaulters.'[6]

In contrast to their fellows incarcerated in Britain's jails, the NCC men of the First World War did not usually leave a record of their comparatively tame wartime experiences. We lack here the view from inside. One young Yorkshireman, Horace Eaton, though, kept a diary during his time in the NCC; and after the war was over, he composed a memoir based on it. He had originally wanted, when called up, to join the Royal Army Medical Corps (RAMC) or the Friends Ambulance Unit and had even taken a St John's Ambulance course before induction. But his tribunal, held in March 1916, assigned him to the NCC. For several weeks he wondered what he should do: 'Should I refuse all service to the country in which I had been brought up and thus be sent to prison – or should I undertake non-combatant duties?' He chose to report for duty with the NCC: 'the right way,' he concluded, 'was to undertake any service I could conscientiously perform – which would not take the life or assist to take the life of another.' Soon, however, it looked as if Eaton was running into trouble. His NCC unit was employed first in building an aerodrome, which could only just possibly be defined as a noncombatant occupation, and then in working with the Royal Engineers on often more dubious projects. He writes:

> We had various duties to perform – sometimes assisting to build the stables and other times cleaning out various places in the town for soldiers' billets. One day a part of our company were sent to the railway station to unload a railway van for another company of soldiers. They moved almost everything except some rifles and ammunition and these they refused to handle. Regular soldiers had to be called upon to finish the work. We expected trouble – but heard nothing further, so probably the captain had smoothed over the affair.[7]

Eaton, as he knew, was luckier than some of his mates were to be. True, 'many objectors whose objection was confined to the actual taking of life were able to work conscientiously in the Non-Combatant Corps.'[8] This was particularly true of the Plymouth Brethren – in both world wars. But even the Seventh-day Adventists, whose sect called upon its members to choose noncombatant service when drafted, clashed from time to time with the army. I think Rae is correct when he writes: 'Disputes over the nature and conditions of work were sporadic and confined to a few.'[9] No unanimity existed among NCC men as to where to draw the line between acceptable tasks and those which they felt to be – at any rate indirectly – lethal and, therefore, unacceptable. The only point all were agreed on was that they would not handle a weapon for the purpose of killing another human being. 'Whereas nearly all noncombatants would refuse to handle ammunition, some would also refuse to stand guard over it, and some again would refuse to construct roads or railways that might be used to convey military supplies.' The army understandably 'found it difficult to select tasks that were at once useful to the prosecution of the war and inoffensive to scruples of the men.'[10] Sometimes the problem does not seem to have bothered the military authorities too much unless a fuss resulted in the press because of some abuse on their part.

Let us now look at some of the areas of conflict that emerged. In his memoir Eaton relates:

> A large number of an NCC at Newhaven ... refused to load munitions and were court martialled. Thirty-eight were sentenced to six months' impris-

> onment with hard labour ... Just about this time [end 1916 / early 1917] a part of our company were put upon certain work and they soon discovered it was to be a rifle range – so they refused to proceed further. The usual warnings were given about the penalties for disobedience, so part of No. 4 company were allotted the task – they too refused, but the officers got over the difficulty by ordering the members who were Plymouth Brethren to do it, and they complied as it appears to be a part of their belief to do as ordered – and those who give the order are responsible to God.[11]

The Seventh-day Adventists proved among the most cooperative NCC men. But their conscientious objection to working on their Saturday Sabbath proved a headache for the military since the Military Service Act did not provide any guidance as to how to deal with this issue. The problem was left to the local commander to cope with on his own. Most often, the men were sent to prison: a procedure that Rae rightly describes as both lacking 'flexibility' and showing 'little imagination.'[12]

Abuses were likely to occur when units of the NCC left England for work behind the lines in France – and even more likely to occur if such units were sent further overseas. For instance, in December 1917 'for refusing to handle military supplies' seventeen NCC men, stationed in France, were sentenced to more than eighty days' Field Punishment No. 1, a peculiarly painful ordeal that recalcitrant British soldiers were subjected to at that date. In response to protests, the undersecretary of state for war claimed, 'men in the Non-Combatant Corps can be called upon to carry out any duties other than those of a combatant nature.' There were also cases in 1917 and 1918 of COs in the RAMC being jailed for resisting transfer to combatant units after being sent overseas.[13]

In November 1917 fourteen Seventh-day Adventists, former students at a Missionary Training College run by their sect, had been sentenced to six months' hard labour by a Field General Court Martial for refusing to work on their Sabbath ('from sunset on Friday to sunset on Saturday'). This happened after they had been serving in France with the NCC for eighteen months. Hitherto they had met with no difficulties from the military authorities on account of their sabbatarian principles. The reason for the change in the army's attitude is not clear. After a month in a military prison, situated 'in the base where they were located,' they managed to smuggle out an account of the manhandling they – and other, non-conscientious prisoners – were forced to endure there. The No-Conscription Fellowship published this account several months later in its journal. It is worth quoting at length from this report, which was signed by twelve of the incarcerated Adventists:

Prison Experiences

On the 23rd November, 1917, we entered the prison, and were taken in charge by one of the warders (a sergeant), whose duty it was to take our personal property from us, and to array us in prison garments. During these preliminaries we are subjected to much abuse and bullying from the sergeant in question, and from several of his fellow N.C.O.'s. In the most offensive and blasphemous language we were told that this particular prison was the worst place in France, that they were able to break men's hearts there, and further, that we should be glad to work seven days a week after a few days with them. We were then interviewed by the Governor, who told us that we should be compelled to work Saturdays, as they were authorised to employ physical means in order to secure their object. On leaving the Governor we were set to work on the parade ground with some other prisoners who were working there. This was at three o'clock on Friday afternoon, one hour before our observance of the Sabbath Day commenced. We had plainly stated that we could not consistently continue work beyond four o'clock. By that time five or six sergeants, each armed with stick and revolver, had collected near the working party. As soon as we ceased work, with one accord these men rushed at us and knocked us down in turn with their fists. As each man rose from the ground this treatment was repeated. We still refused to work, and the attack was renewed with sticks. In several instances we were kicked brutally whilst on the ground. Two of the sergeants became so infuriated that they now drew their revolvers, but were prevented from levelling them by the intervention of several of their fellow N.C.O.'s. In no case was the slightest resistance offered by us. We were then rushed to the punishment cells, the sticks being freely used on the way, and several sergeants ran in amongst us deliberately tripping us, thus bringing us heavily to the ground on the square. On reaching the cells we were placed in irons – called 'figures of eight' on account of their shape – which are made in various sizes to grip the wrists securely one above the other behind the back. In some cases the irons were too small, and caused the most excruciating pain on being screwed up. In this helpless condition we were again punched severely about the face and body, after which we were isolated, each man in a small cell about 7 feet by 4½ feet, having a concrete floor and iron walls. The extreme cold was very trying in this condition.

Up to this point we had been dealt with collectively, but now our experiences were more or less individual. It must be remembered that we were all treated with varying degrees of brutality, although only a few exceptional instances are mentioned here. One of our number was selected by a sergeant as the ringleader. We can attribute this to nothing but the fact that he was the tallest amongst us, for we all ceased work at the stroke of the clock, and the choice of a ringleader seemed a kind of afterthought, nothing being mentioned about it until our entry to the cells. Here is the account which the young man chosen as ringleader gives of his experience in the Punishment cell:

Personal Statement by ———

In the cell passage the sergeants agreed that I was the ringleader, probably because I was the tallest. The smallest pair of 'figure eights' was brought and screwed down upon my wrists. So small was the pair that to get them on my flesh was ripped and cut in several places. The circulation was practically cut off, leaving my hands dead. I was then pushed into a cell, and pinned against the wall by one sergeant, whilst the others in a most passionate rage struck me continually about the head and in the stomach. Then one burly N.C.O. lifted me up bodily, and with his knee threw me backwards to the other side. The contact with the iron wall caused the irons to cut more, and sent acute pain to all my nerves. This kind of treatment continued until I dropped to the floor. I was picked up, but collapsed again, whereupon I was kicked several times in the middle of the back. Finally I became unconscious. I had made no opposition by force, or even uttered a word which could have given the slightest offence.

The next morning a staff sergeant and a sergeant visited me, and again violently knocked me about until I fell to the ground winded by a sharp punch. I felt pains and bruises everywhere; my eyes were blackened, and one was completely closed; my jaw seemed locked on one side, and my nerves were out of control. Towards 9 a.m., a corporal opened the cell door and ordered me to work. To my reply 'I cannot,' he seized me and threw me against the wall. He repeated the order, and receiving the same reply, drew his revolver, placing the barrel to my forehead, threatening to shoot me if I again objected. He reminded me that 'Dead men tell no tales.' He meant that his word (stating that his action was necessary in self-defence) would not be disputed. Seeing that I remained quite calm, and did not reply, he put up the revolver and left me with a curse.

About 10 a.m. I was taken out of my cell, and two cement blocks weighing about 35 lbs. each were roped round my neck, one hanging upon my chest, the other upon my back. With my wrists still in irons behind my back I was made to pace the passage at a quick march. At last, from exhaustion, I sank beneath the strain, and remained in a fit about an hour. When I came to, I was placed in the cell again till the afternoon, when the Governor visited me and gave permission for me to have my blankets. At 4 p.m., I was given six ounces of bread – the first food for twenty-four hours. At 3.40, my companions were sent back to their sections, but I was too ill to go, and remained the night and next day in the cell without further medical attention until 12 a.m. The food given for this day was two rations (6 ozs.) of bread. The next morning I was taken before the doctor, and a sergeant in a misleading way stated what had happened. In a casual way the doctor examined me, and gave me 'Light Duty,' stating that I had palpitation of the heart, and that the occurrence was unfortunate. With this I was promptly dismissed to my section.

Treatment of Other Prisoners

Apart from our own experiences we heard and saw many cases similar to a few we here mention ... As to the general conditions under which the prisoners live much could be written that would never be believed, and much could not be described in words. We were huddled fourteen men in each tent. Owing to shocking sanitary conditions, and the fact that it is impossible to wash in the two minutes allowed in the wash-house twice daily, the vilest diseases are prevalent. We were sleeping next to men suffering from venereal disease. In the sections where the men sleep there is provided one open bucket for the use of about sixty men, and latrine paper is almost impossible to obtain; the stench from these buckets is vile ...

Many men are covered with bad sores – the result of being unable to wash themselves properly. In wet weather the men's blankets are often wet through on account of the bad condition of the tents.

The ill-treatment which we received, and which is common throughout the prison, appeared to be administered, in the first instance, apart from the Governor's authority. He could not, however, have been totally ignorant of subsequent abuses. A chaplain from a neighbouring camp was passing the prison one day, and hearing shrieks from the cells he entered the prison and asked to see us (he knew we were in the prison). He was

> not permitted to see us, nor was he allowed inside the prison again, in spite of the fact that he held a service there once a week. Not once were we visited by the prison chaplain, nor were we allowed to have Bibles – our own were demanded from us on entering the prison.
>
> We certainly think that the authorities at home cannot be cognisant of the terrible conditions existing in our military prisons in the Field. The men absolutely hate their own country, so embittered does the life make them. It is common to hear men say that they will never fight again for their country. So emaciated and reduced were we by our stay of one month in prison that it was difficult for us at first to recognise several of our comrades.
>
> We should emphasise the fact that throughout our whole experience we remained quite passive. No resistance of any kind was offered at any time.
>
> We have seen the treatment of prisoners from other prisons whilst the men were out in working parties, and know the conditions in each case to be much the same. Indeed, it is the subject of much scandal and bad feeling among the British troops in the bases where the prisons are located.[14]

True, conditions in the trenches were far worse than in the worst military prison at the base: this must not be overlooked. Still, it does not excuse the British army authorities for gratuitously inflicting conditions of this kind on those it had in its charge.[15]

NCC men had been among the last COs to be released from their wartime obligations: the process came to an end in January 1920. Unlike other COs, those who served in the NCC were not disenfranchised for five years under the Representation of the People Act of 1918, nor were they excluded from government employment as in other cases COs were for several years.[16] On the other hand, the gratuity presented to soldiers still in the army in 1919 was denied to members of the NCC. To his credit Major-General Sir Wyndham Childs, director of personal services at the War Office, 'who had all along argued that the non-combatants were soldiers, protested against the unfair and illogical withholding of this gratuity, but he was overruled.'[17]

Around 3,300 COs served in the NCC during the First World War, with another 100 as noncombatants in the RAMC, out of a total number of around 16,100.[18] To the best of my knowledge, no figures are available concerning the religious affiliation of NCC men. Horace Eaton wrote of his mates: 'There are Primitives [i.e., Plymouth Brethren], Wesleyans, Congregationalists, Baptists, Roman Catholics, United Methodists, Seventh Day Adventists, International Bible Students [i.e., Jehovah's Witnesses], Jews, Church of England, Socialists and Atheists.'[19] Certainly a mixed bag! The absence of Quakers is striking. A few Quakers may have joined the RAMC, but I doubt if any Friends could have been found in the First World War edition of the NCC. When the Corps was established, prominent Quakers had joined with the No-Conscription Fellowship to frankly inform the government that 'the men for whom we speak can, under no circumstances, become part of this corps, which we observe will be under the control of the War Office, and in every sense part of the military machine.'[20] On the other side of the religious spectrum, the Christadelphians also forbade members to serve with the armed forces on pain of being disfellowshipped.

The creation of a separate noncombatant corps which, apart from its staff of officers and NCOs, was manned entirely by officially recognized COs of various sorts was, we know, an innovation of the British government. It appears to have been thought up in the heat of the moment, as it were, after the introduction of conscription at the beginning of 1916. The NCC had its positive aspects. One was that the conscription act included two other forms of CO exemption in addition to assignment to noncombatant service in the army. That was not intended to be a catch-all solution. Secondly, for certain pacifist religious sects, in particular, the NCC provided an acceptable way of combining loyalty to their country at war and adherence to biblical nonresistance of the 'Thou shalt not kill' variety. On the negative side stood firstly the reality, the way in which the authorities interpreted the sections of the Military Service Act which dealt with COs. In large numbers of cases, the Tribunals assigned to the NCC COs whose unwillingness to comply with this condition resulted in the imprisonment of men for following conscience, which was indeed contrary to the declared intentions of the government as well as the British tradition of freedom (a situation that was to be repeated in the Second World War on a diminished scale). In the second place, the failure of the authorities in most cases to permit COs, who had been assigned to noncombatant duties in the armed forces, to serve in the RAMC created a sense of frustration and unfulfilment among many COs, even though they were not ready to rebel and go to prison instead. (The British government's stance in the First World War contrasts with the more sensible policy of the U.S. administration in the Second World War and in the Vietnam War when noncombatant COs served with distinction as army medics.) Lastly, as this essay has shown, due to imprecise – and sometimes faulty – formulation of the duties of NCC men, clashes occurred from time to time between the latter and the army authorities. Though similar situations arose occasionally in the Second World War, the military authorities by that date proved more flexible in this respect as well as in respect of other issues involving COs in the armed forces.

NOTES

1 See John D. Thiesen, 'First Duty of the Citizen: Mennonite Identity and Military Exemption in Prussia, 1848–1877,' *Mennonite Quarterly Review*, vol. 72, no. 2 (April 1998), 169–86. The Royal Cabinet Order of 28 November 1868 allowed 'such members of old Mennonite families as did not voluntarily express their readiness to do military service under arms ... to fulfil the obligation to serve, by acting as attendants in military hospitals, or as clerks, &c., in the office of the district commander of the *Landswehr*, or as stewards, artizans, or drivers.' Such persons were 'exempt from training in the use of arms' (from translation of the Order in Robert Barclay [Jr], *The Inner Life of the Religious Societies of the Commonwealth: Considered Principally with Reference to the Influence of Church Organization on the Spread of Christianity*, 2nd edn [London, 1877], 616).

2 I have dealt briefly with this in essay 21 below.

3 See Mulford Q. Sibley and Philip E. Jacob, *Conscription of Conscience: The American Slate and the Conscientious Objector, 1940–1947* (Ithaca NY, 1952), 86–98, 104, 105; and Jean Anne Mansavage, '"A Sincere and Meaningful Belief": Legal Conscientious Objection during the Vietnam War' (Ph.D. diss., Texas A & M University, 2000), chap. 6 ('Serving God and Country: Noncombatant Conscientious Objectors').

4 In Germany, writes Robert Goeckel, 'the burden of World War II ... had led many, especially Christian youth, to reject military values.' And it was the resolve, during the first two years of conscription in the DDR, of some 1,500 young men to face imprisonment rather than become combatant soldiers that led the communist regime to change its mind and set up army construction units (*Baueinheiten*) to accommodate these refractory citizens. Though little has been published hitherto in English, the literature on the *Baueinheiten* in German, including non-government documentary materials, is quite extensive. (But some of it is not available in an easily accessible

form.) For an overview of their twenty-six year history (1964–1990) by an ex-*Bausoldat*, who has written extensively on the history of the construction units, see Bernd Eisenfeld, 'Wehrdienstverweigerung als Opposition,' 241, 242, 244–56, in Klaus-Dietmar Henke et al., eds, *Widerstand und Opposition in der DDR* (Cologne, 1999). See also Uwe Koch (formerly an absolutist CO in the DDR), 'Die Baueinheiten der Nationalen Volksarmee der DDR – Einrichtung, Entwicklung und Bedeutung,' 1835–79, in Materialen der Enquete-Kommission, *Aufarbeitung von Geschichte und Folgen der SED-Diktatur in Deutschland*, published by the German Parliament (*Bundestag*), vol. 2/3 (Baden-Baden, 1995); Heinz Janning, ed.; *Kriegs-/Ersatzdienst-Verweigerung in Ost und West* (Essen, 1990), 232–341; Horst Dähn, 'DDR – Protestantismus und Kriegsdienstverweigerung: Interpretation eines bisher nicht veröffentlichten Dokuments vom 12 März 1962,' *Berliner Dialog-Hefte: Die Zeitschrift für den christlichen–marxistischen Dialog*, vol. 3, no. 2 (1992), 15–22; Stephan Eschler (also a former *Bausoldat*), 'Staatsdienst im Zeichen des Goldenen Spatens: Wehrdienstverweigerung in der DDR und die Positionen der Evangelischen Kirchen zur Wehrdienstfrage' (pp. 94–206), and Peter Schicketanz, 'Die kirchenpolitische Situation und die Entstehung der Baueinheiten 1961–1964' (pp. 194–204), in Detlef Bald and Andreas Prüfert, eds, *Vom Krieg zur Militärreform* (Baden-Baden, 1997); and, particularly valuable for background, Robert F. Goeckel, *The Lutheran Church and the East German State: Political Conflict and Change under Ulbricht and Honecker* (Ithaca and London, 1990), esp. 66, 143, 143, 186, 187, 189, 190, 237, 238, 261, 264, 267, 269. One of the army's political officers told some *Bausoldaten* engaged in constructing a new military airfield: 'Being yourselves weaponless, you should feel quite at ease with your consciences in building our weapons. Then, when all your tasks are finished we will express our thanks to you' (quoted in Eisenfeld, 'Wehrdienstverweigerung,' 254). Members of Britain's Non-Combatant Corps in the two world wars, weaponless soldiers like the *Bausoldaten*, might have expected similar encouragement from the British army, and indeed they sometimes got it. But, as was to be the case with many of the *Bausoldaten*, some NCC men, we know, became increasingly unhappy at the nature of their work assignments and found themselves in jail for refusing work they regarded as objectionable. In the Second World War, at any rate, they were fortunate to find release from a burdensome routine by transferring to bomb disposal squads or medical paratrooper units: work that was both dangerous and humanitarian. See essay 24 below. In one respect the situation of the *Bausoldaten* was more fortunate than that of members of Britain's Non-Combatant Corps. In both world wars many NCC men felt keenly – and correctly – that a 'stigma' attached to the letters NCC on their forage caps, whereas in the DDR to choose to become a CO a *Bausoldat*, with the spade as an 'emblem' on the shoulders of his uniform, came to be 'a symbol of civil courage' with the populace at large. On the other hand, in the NCC one was not subjected to political indoctrination or required to vow to do all in one's power to increase the Fatherland's 'readiness for defence.' No wonder that over the years the *Bausoldaten* were to continue to press the government to institute a civilian alternative for the increasing number of COs who wished to carry out their national service in that way rather than in the army.

5 John Rae, *Conscience and Politics: The British Government and the Conscientious Objector to Military Service 1916–1919* (London, 1970), 25.

6 Ibid., 191, 192.

7 Quoted in Felicity Goodall, *A Question of Conscience: Conscientious Objection in the Two World Wars* (Stroud UK, 1997), xi, 6, 15–17.

8 Constance Braithwaite, *Conscientious Objection to Various Compulsions under British Law* (York UK, 1995), 161.

9 Rae, *Conscience*, 193.

10 Ibid., 87.

11 Quoted in Goodall, *A Question*, 17. In his *Annals of an Active Life* (2 vols, London, n.d.), vol. 1, 250, General Sir Nevil Macready assigned responsibility for the Newhaven incident to 'some Socialists' in the ranks of the NCC. He was obviously wrong. While there is some discrepancy in dating between Horace Eaton and the general, I think they are both referring to the same episode. General Macready, as the British army's adjutant-general, was at one stage responsible for giving the government advice as to the treatment of COs in the forthcoming conscription legislation. In his *Annals*, he confessed to having 'no sympathy with the state of mind' of a CO, whether 'religious or otherwise.' He made an exception, however, in the case of the Quakers, whom he admired. 'Their [pacifist] creed was old-established, consistent, and unaffected by the war.' As late as the mid-1920s, he thought all Quakers, after being called up, had been drafted into the Friends Ambulance Unit, organized by his Quaker friend in the Board of Trade, Sir George Newman. If he had ever discovered Corder Catchpool and other young Quaker absolutists, who mostly ended up in Wormwood Scrubs, that surely would have given him a shock! Or perhaps not.

12 Rae, *Conscience*, 193.

13 Braithwaite, *Conscientious Objection*, 157.

14 *The Tribunal*, no. 102 (4 April 1918), 1, 4. See also John W. Graham, *Conscription and Conscience: A History* (London, 1922), 152, 153; and David Boulton, *Objection Overruled* (London, 1967), 158–62.

15 See the *Tribunal*, no. 129 (17 October 1918), 3, for a report from five members of the NCC in France who, the previous January, had refused an order to tidy up the loose shells that had been spilled during 'a collision between a heavy ammunition train and another engine which was shunting some trucks.' Seven of the NCC men, detailed for this task, had refused to comply. They were subsequently court-martialled and sentenced to six months' imprisonment with hard labour. The first fourteen days they spent in a military prison before being transferred to a civilian jail. In the former, they suffered from the NCOs the same kind of bullying and brutal manhandling as the Adventists had experienced (see above). Failing to break their wills, the warders put them on a charge as a result of which the prison governor gave them penalties that included '14 days solitary confinement in irons (figures of eight) and punishment diet (bread and water)' as well as Field Punishment Nos. 1 and 2. The report concluded by asking readers to imagine what it was like: 'to stand in a small iron cell all day, with one's hands behind one for over 10 hours daily, and with nothing to do at all and nothing to look at.' Such punishment, if prolonged, usually ended in the man becoming insane. 'In addition to this we were shaved every morning with blunt razors.' Again, we should not forget that this 'terrible punishment' was what the British army meted out to delinquent soldiers and by no means solely to disobedient NCC men.

16 Rae, *Conscience*, 235–7.

17 Ibid., 194.

18 Graham, *Conscription*, 349; Braithwaite, *Conscientious Objection*, 141. Rae, *Conscience*, 71, 194, considers the correct figure to be about 2,900 since 'about 400 should be subtracted for the officers and NCOs who were not conscientious objectors.' They 'were selected from regular infantry personnel unfit for general service but fit for service abroad on lines of communication' (Army Council Instruction, No. 551 [1916]). According to this instruction, one officer and thirteen NCOs were assigned to ninety-four NCC privates, that is, COs. Of course, the above figures for membership in the NCC do not include men whom the Tribunals only too eagerly assigned 'non-combatant service in the Army,' knowing well that they were unwilling to accept this condition. See Graham, *Conscription*, 213; Boulton, *Objection Overruled*, 132; Rae, *Conscience*, 127, 128, 131.

19 Quoted in Goodall, *A Question*, 17, 18.

20 Letter to H.H. Asquith, dated 14 March 1916, in Boulton, *Objection Overruled*, 131, 132.

17 Hobhouse and Brockway: Conscientious Objectors as Pioneer Convict Criminologists

In the late twentieth century a New School of Convict Criminologists emerged in North America. Its roots went back earlier in the work of ex-convict academics like John Irwin, who published his path-breaking study, *The Felon*, in 1970. The two key characteristics of the research carried out by this school are the 'centrality of ... ethnographic methods' and the fact that the authors are all either themselves ex-prisoners or 'fellow travellers,' criminologists writing 'from a convict perspective,' so that the view from 'inside' always forms a significant component in penological theory.[1]

This essay deals with two convict criminologists whose work was done in Britain during the first quarter of last century. The motive of both men for undertaking the task of investigating the state of contemporary English prisons derived from their recent experience of being jailed as conscientious objectors (COs) during the First World War. So far as I am aware, the prison research of Stephen Hobhouse (1881–1961) and Fenner Brockway (1888–1988)[2] did not exert any direct influence on the later North American school of convict criminologists. In fact, I doubt if even their names were known to the latter, at least at the beginning. That, though, it seems to me, is a good reason for now reviewing the story of Hobhouse and Brockway's pioneer efforts, which had resulted in 1922 in a bulky volume of over 700 pages entitled *English Prisons To-day*.[3]

The initiative for the project lay with the Fabian partnership of Beatrice and Sidney Webb. Famous as pioneers of the Labour Party and as social historians (later even notorious as authors of *Soviet Communism: A New Civilization?* [1935]), the Webbs, as the war came to an end, were concluding work on their history *English Prisons under Local Govern-*

ment. They gave there a thoroughly researched account of English prisons from the sixteenth century down to the last quarter of the nineteenth century: the centralizing Prison Act of 1877, with the power it gave to the Board of Prison Commissioners in the Home Office, was a landmark in the history of prison administration. Eventually they brought the story to the end of the century. But they decided that others must cover the twentieth century, incorporating the insights gained by two classes of prisoners of conscience, often persons of education and literary talent – first the pre-war suffragettes and then the wartime COs. The COs were particularly important for this purpose, not only because the overwhelming majority of English prisoners were male but also because COs in jail had almost invariably been treated as common criminals.

The Webbs, in 1918, entrusted the job of supervising the undertaking to a specially appointed Prison System Enquiry Committee (PSEC). The committee was at first affiliated to the Labour Research Department; that body was, in turn, an affiliate of the Labour Party. But the PSEC soon broke away in protest and became an independent organization when the Labour Research Department, in order to raise additional funds, had agreed to 'sell information' (Bernard Shaw's phrase) to the Soviet Trade Delegation.[4]

The members of the PSEC were an impressive lot. In addition to the Webbs, the committee included Bernard Shaw, who throughout took an active part in its deliberations and in drafting its report,[5] the extremely capable Margery Fry, then secretary of the Howard League for Penal Reform, the Quaker MP T. Edmund Harvey, and the playwright Laurence Housman. The chairman of the committee was Sir Sydney Olivier, a socialist and former governor of Jamaica. The committee members were intelligent and diligent reformers, who were anxious to see fundamental changes in what they felt had become an antiquated and harsh method of dealing with crime, a system, moreover, that was increasingly shown to be ineffective. But who was to do the actual work of collecting, collating, and editing the materials that would ultimately appear as the committee's report?

The man chosen for this task was Stephen Hobhouse, whose account of his time in jail as a CO had recently appeared in a leading English journal.[6] Hobhouse, with his usual modesty, states that, in addition to being Beatrice Webb's nephew, the main reason why, in late 1918, he received this appointment (formally his position was that of secretary to the PSEC)

> was the fact that up to May 1919 the great majority of the C.O.s who had a long experience of prison were still, most unfairly, locked up; and this meant that I was almost the only available ex-prisoner with any literary competence for the job or any experience (such as I had gained through my seven years in a Whitehall office and my Chairmanship of the [Quaker] 'Emergency Committee' [for enemy aliens] in collecting evidence or conducting an enquiry.[7]

In fact, there was much more to Stephen Hobhouse than that! All who knew him at all intimately were impressed by his strength of character and transparent sincerity, his sound learning and wide cultural range, and, above all, his sensitivity to the suffering of all sentient beings. He was indeed a man who tried, however difficult that might be, to live up to his beliefs, in which endeavour he was supported by his devoted wife, Rosa née Waugh. Hobhouse having renounced his family fortune, the couple settled in Hoxton, a depressed area of London. He had been born with a silver spoon in his mouth: both his parents belonged to England's Liberal elite. Of humble origin, the Hobhouses in the eighteenth century had acquired wealth and political influence: the clan produced one peer of the realm and a series of members of parliament, some of whom reached cabinet rank. Stephen's 'fine old uncle Leonard' was the distinguished statesman and publicist, Lord Courtney of Penwith. (Courtney's wife, Kate, had visited Stephen in Exeter Prison and broken prison regulations by defiantly kissing her nephew 'heartily coming and going,' even though Rosa had told her she should not do so.)[8] Another uncle was the eminent international lawyer Alfred Cripps, later Lord Parmoor. The list could be extended. Hobhouse went to the prestigious English public school Eton College. While an undergraduate at Balliol College, Oxford, during the South African War, he had been a lively young patriot, drilling with the University Rifle Volunteers. He recalled later arguing on the war with his cousin, Emily Hobhouse, who was to win renown for her fearless denunciations of conditions in the 'concentration camps' in which the British forces herded Boer (Afrikaner) women and children.[9] Hobhouse went down from the university with an excellent classical degree. Subsequently, while in solitary confinement in Wormwood Scrubs Prison, he found reading the Greek New Testament – 'specially allowed' him – the greatest solace in those trying circumstances,[10] even though that work had not formed part of the classical curriculum at the university. In the early years of the new century, Hobhouse came across Tolstoy's *Confession*; and that began a spiritual migration from his family's Church of England to Quakerism combined with the Tolstoyan social gospel. In his autobiography he describes how, on a cold January morning, 'having to visit for some purpose or other the Oxford railway station, I bought casually a little green paper-covered book of sixty-four pages, published by the "Free Age Press."'[11] That started him on a life-long spiritual pilgrimage.

Beatrice Webb, though she disapproved of her nephew's stance as a CO,[12] had indeed judged his abilities correctly. In fact, she confessed to really quite liking her 'quixotic' nephew, despite 'his uncompromising virtue.' But she could not refrain from adding:

> Superficially he is not to my mind an attractive personality. His lugubrious manner and long doleful face, the absence of spontaneity and joy in everything he does, and a marked strain of self-conscious morality mars his very substantial gifts of character and intellect. Those who have actually worked with him report real self-effacement and a solidly wise judgement.[13]

Aunt Beatrice now installed Stephen in an office, assigned an assistant in the person of Arthur Creech-Jones, a fellow CO prisoner who later rose to cabinet rank in Attlee's Labour government, and left the two to get on with the job. Hobhouse soon mastered the existing literature on modern British prisons. As he explains, these materials were 'not large, the official not usually informative, and the non-official often untrustworthy.' However, soon thereafter he ran into difficulties. For the Board of Prison Commissioners and their chairman, Sir Evelyn Ruggles-Brice, presumably sensing that the image they would be given in the PSEC's report would be a largely negative one, proved very uncooperative. First of all, they barred access to any prisons. Then, it was only 'with difficulty by unofficial channels we secured the loan of a copy of the large volume of "standing orders" which regulated almost every detail of prison [life] and was supposed to be kept private for the staff only.' There were nearly 1,500 such standing orders relating to local prisons alone. In the Foreword to the PSEC's report, the editors were to complain of the Prison Commission being 'one of the most secluded of Government Departments.' Prison staff were ordered not to give the PSEC any information, though in fact around fifty staff members, 'governors, chaplains, doctors, and warders,' defied this order and either answered the committee's questionnaires or consented to a personal interview. These questionnaires, which Hobhouse tells us covered 'every conceivable feature and aspect of prison life,' became the basis for formulating the report. They were 'printed and widely circulated, especially to ex-prisoners, of whom nearly 300, mostly those who were C.O.s, gave us most valuable information.'

In addition, the committee had a remarkable piece of luck. The circumstances were quite dramatic. At the time it was necessary to keep the details from both the press and the prison commissioners, who were puzzled at certain disclosures in the committee's report. Many years later, however, Fenner Brockway could freely tell the story:

> We published a series of censored extracts from letters of convicts and we reproduced photographs taken in prison ... Certain prisons during the war [and immediately after] accommodated 'conchies' [released from jail] under the Home Office Scheme. They were allowed a good deal of freedom ... One of the 'conchies' at Dartmoor was put on the job of repairing the roof of the office. Instead of repairing the hole he enlarged it and let himself in. There he found a large manuscript volume containing copies of all the extracts from convicts' letters which had been censored by the Governors over a period of years. He climbed back on the roof with the volume, made a thorough job of repairing the hole, and when he had his next week-end leave (men on the Home Office Scheme had this privilege periodically), took his find home. These extracts reflected the reaction to imprisonment of hundreds of convicts more vividly than any other evidence.[14]

'There's nothing to beat a lagging for utterly debasing whatever was left in a man of what was good' (1905: *second year of first sentence*); 'This life reduces one to the level of a wild beast, and every bit of one's better self is literally torn out ... If you come to meet me in August, look out for something between a man and a beast, uncouth and uncivilized' (1907: *first sentence*); 'For God's sake and your own, and for the sake of us all, stretch out a hand and pluck me from this brand of hell (for it is hell)' (1910: *first year of second sentence*); 'The only thing that prison has done for me is to sow the seeds of revenge against a society that tolerates it' (1910: *second year of third sentence*); 'My bitterest enemy I would not send to prison. Never. This place makes curses and sots of men' (1911: *eleventh year of first sentence*); 'There is no uplifting influence, but everything tends to grind one down to the last indignity' (1912: *second year of second sentence*). And so on and so on ...[15]

Hobhouse confessed to being 'a slow worker.' After a couple of years working away at the report, he still seemed to be a long way from finishing the job. He was finding it hard to concentrate. 'I had never,' he writes, 'really recovered from the effect of fourteen months imprisonment set in the middle of my life in slum surroundings and other strains of the four war years.' In preparing the report on English prisons, 'I had to deal with so much that was sordid and sad and repressive, with the same unhappy experiences that had left my own soul wounded and scarred. In 1921 ... I began to feel the approach of a nervous breakdown.' The bustle and noise of the capital was getting on his nerves. Frequent headaches and pain in the stomach added to his distress. Fits of irritation, usually over unimportant matters, came and went; he was often depressed. His emotional life was disturbed: 'I lost ... the normal desires of a husband' – to the grief of his wife, who was now entering middle age and had hoped for a child.[16] Clearly, if there was to be a report, Stephen needed a responsible co-editor. Again it was Beatrice Webb who acted. The man she chose to help her nephew was Fenner Brockway. 'Stephen,' she told him, 'is in danger of being buried under the mountain of material he has piled up. I want you to rescue him from it.'

For Brockway, this offer came at just the right moment. After what he had experienced during almost two-and-a-half years in jail as a CO, 'I did not,' as he put it, 'feel that I should be free from prison until I had done what I could to expose and end the system.' His post as editor of the *Labour Leader* had been filled during his forced absence in jail, and he was scraping a living from various part-time jobs. Brockway did not come from a patrician background: his family were missionaries. But he was a brilliant journalist (as Mrs Webb recognized) and immensely energetic and, in his own way, as much an idealist as Hobhouse was. Brockway and his wife, Lilla, were then living in a cottage at Thorpe Bay in the county of Essex, and this location now became the PSEC's office. Here Brockway finished writing the committee's report on the basis of the chapters already drafted by Hobhouse, who, however, was relieved of the major editorial burden. Stephen was at hand, though, for consultation since the two families shared the cottage, which they christened Keir Cottage after the famous socialist leader, Keir Hardie. Brockway recalls that 'at Thorpe Bay Stephen was continually struggling against ill-health, his long war-time imprisonment had seriously undermined his frail physique. But with unfailing courage he stuck at our job, doing it with a conscientiousness which was a lesson to me.'[17]

The Hobhouse-Brockway collaboration was obviously a very harmonious one. Hobhouse paid the following tribute to his co-editor: 'I gradually handed over the work [to him], and I cannot speak too highly of the generous and skilful way in which he completed the tasks of compiling and editing the big volume of 735 pages which eventually appeared under our joint names.'[18]

At the last moment, however, an incident occurred that threatened to spoil the good working relationship between the two men. No less a personage than Bernard Shaw was the troublemaker, though certainly not a malicious one. Hobhouse found the episode 'at once amusing and painful.' 'Fenner,' according to his co-editor, 'was temporarily bewitched by the great name of "G.B.S."' He had invited Shaw to contribute a preface to the forthcoming volume, hoping in that way to increase its sales and give it the prestige that Shaw's name would bring. (Hobhouse, we may note, in order to increase sales, was ready to compromise his egalitarian *Weltanschauung* by including the academic acronym M.A. after his name.) To Hobhouse's 'horror,' Shaw included, among 'many wise and witty things about our present penal policy,' a proposal to 'extirpate utterly unmanageable criminals,' along with incurable invalids and morons, by sending them to the 'lethal chamber.' As Shaw told Brockway, 'there are people who have to be tenderly chloroformed out of existence.' When Brockway continued to insist on the inclusion of Shaw's introduction, which ran to thirty thousand words, Hobhouse threatened to withdraw his name as co-editor. That was something no one wanted. Shaw offered a compromise (surely with his tongue in his cheeks?): as an alternative to euthanasia, incurable criminals could be placed for life under the care of Quakers and other dedicated persons. The Webbs called a meeting of the committee at their London home, when a solution was found. Aunt Beatrice, her nephew thought, certainly considered him to be 'a sentimental fool.' But, knowing he was not going to change his mind on the matter, she was glad to obtain the famous man's imprimatur, as expressed by the presence of such a preface, for the Webbs' own *English Prisons under Local Government*, which was about to appear in print.[19]

Though Shaw wrote to Hobhouse telling him 'that he must now provide a preface himself,' in fact, *English Prisons To-day* contained only a short Foreword from the co-editors outlining their aims and research methods and providing acknowledgments to persons who had helped them in compiling the report. The penultimate paragraph of the Foreword brought the reader's attention to the Webbs' volume, 'published simultaneously with this work.' 'The two books should be read together for a right understanding of the growth of the prison system.'

In a short essay it is impossible to do justice to Hobhouse and Brockway's seminal work. A summary of its thirty-nine chapters[20] would not, I think, be helpful. Instead, I would like to focus on the major areas in the English prison system that their report singled out for criticism. Of course, Hobhouse and Brockway were *partis pris*, as indeed was the whole committee that sponsored their work. But what is important is the weight and validity of the evidence they amassed in support of their critique. The areas I have focused on are: (1) the silence rule, (2) prison uniforms, (3) prison buildings, (4) prison routine and labour, (5) prison staff and visiting justices, (6) punishments, (7) rehabilitation of prisoners, (8) medical treatment, and (9) sex life of prisoners.

1. In his personal prison memoir, Hobhouse pointed to 'the attempt to enforce complete silence and separation upon prisoners' as the harshest aspect of jail life, even though most prisoners, COs as well as 'crimos,' did their utmost to evade its enforcement at the risk of punishment if detected. In these circumstances, whenever possible 'talking without detection in a special kind of whisper, that will not carry more than a yard or two, becomes a fine art.' The only alternative to deception was 'mental as well as moral decay.'[21] The report castigated the prison commissioners for denying that the silence rule did not play an important role in the prison system. Reference to any prison's 'Punishment Book' would show how 'grossly misleading' such assertions were, even with regard to women's prisons. 'The first rule on the card which hangs in every prisoner's cell was, "Prisoners shall preserve silence."' The report quoted from interviews with ex-prisoners: all of them witnessed to the demoralizing effect of this rule. 'The silence system is a means of driving men mad,' said an ex-prisoner who had served a seven-year jail term. Experiments in permitting 'talking exercise' were criticized as insufficient: 'The privilege of talking is ... a human right[, which] should be denied no one,' a prisoner governor stated frankly, adding that the abolition of the silence rule, to be effective, must be carried out within the framework of an overhaul of the entire prison system. That was Hobhouse and Brockway's view, too.[22]

2. Most British COs, jailed during the First World War, as well as those who visited them in prison, found it hard to forget the prison uniform they were obliged to wear. Its humiliating effect probably exercised a still greater effect on common criminals. Though the prison commissioners denied the uniform was 'intended or designed as a

garb of shame,' Hobhouse and Brockway disagreed and cited not only ex-prisoners but warders, too, in support of their position. The dress was 'crudely cut, untidy, ill-fitting, and sprinkled with broad arrows ... On the jacket hangs an ugly yellow disc, bearing the prisoner's [cell] number.' For convicted males the colour of their uniform was a dismal drab. 'The cap, usually worn indoors and out, is made of a similar stuff.' An interviewee told the committee:

> After I put on the prison clothes, I had a difficulty to retain my self-respect. The ugliness of them, the dirty colour and the patches in the coat and trousers, the arrows denoting my criminality, the disc bearing the number of my cell – all had a degrading effect, making me less a man and more an outcast.

Often the clothing provided was insufficient in wintertime in the icy-cold cells. The report did not suggest prison uniforms should be abandoned and prisoners allowed to wear their own clothes. It confined itself to pointing out the defects of the existing prison dress.[23]

3. The report devoted a whole chapter to prison buildings.[24] Its conclusions were eminently sensible, and I shall quote them verbatim here as an illustration of the editors' restrained approach to a subject in which all concerned were indeed involved emotionally:

1. The architecture is depressing and inhuman.
2. There is a marked absence of colour and beauty both within and without the buildings. The grounds accessible to prisoners are generally bare and frequently without flowers or shrubs.
3. The cells are often dark, particularly in the basements and in the angles of the halls in the radial system. Many of the cells are sunless.
4. Frequently the cells are badly ventilated. Only two small window panes open at the most.
5. The heating and lighting arrangements for the cells are often inadequate.[25]

British prisons of this time were built either on the radial system (as in the case of Pentonville or Wandsworth prisons) or on the block system (as in the case of Wormwood Scrubs prison). They were all constructed in penitentiary style during the previous century when the avowed aim of imprisonment was to punish rather than rehabilitate. 'Few prisoners who approach them for the first time do so without a sense of hopelessness and terror' (Hobhouse and Brockway were undoubtedly expressing here their own feelings as well as that of other ex-prisoners whom they had interviewed). 'It is difficult to convey an impression of the hope-destroying, forbidding aspect of prison buildings.' They were repression incarnate in stone. Some of their interviewees, among them prison officials, had suggested that reform would come only if these hideous edifices were dynamited! 'And the suggestion is not extreme.'[26] Short of this radical solution, the editors were able to provide readers with some striking photos of prison interiors (which unfortunately cannot be reproduced here): the exterior of two wings of Wakefield prison illustrating the radial system; two views of the interior of the notorious prison 'on the moor' showing the way all British prison halls were built, including the wire-netting stretched across the first landing to prevent suicides; and one photo of an exercise yard at Wakefield.[27]

4. The editors devoted considerable space in several parts of their report to prison routine. Their findings could be summed up in one word – soulless. Indeed, no other word epitomized better, especially with regard to the deeply religious Hobhouse, the severity of the verdict passed in the report on the whole prison system. Beginning with Reception, 'the place of transition into the prison world,' the regime was one of 'rigid and monotonous uniformity.' Prisoners were subjected to an 'obtrusive and military discipline'; he/she lost his/her name and became 'A.3.21' or perhaps 'C.2.8.' 'Choice and personality' were systematically repressed. In addition to the universal silence, prisoners from the moment of waking to lights-out at night were deprived of privacy. The report gave a minute description of a prison cell, in which the prisoner spent long hours of solitude, as well as a detailed account of the daily routine, including the labour performed, the food served, and the sanitary conditions in the halls, which were extremely primitive.[28]

The editors found industrial training, an essential element in enabling the average prisoner to cope with life after release, 'unsatisfactory from almost every point of view.' The report continues:

> Prison industries ... are of the most elementary character and are performed in a crude, amateurish way. Only in a very few instances are they of any educational value to the prisoner, whilst they are a serious economic loss to the nation. The 'instructors' are rarely trained men, and efficient machinery and equipment are almost entirely lacking. The

workshops are frequently poor, and the prisoners work under conditions which give them little interest in their labour and no incentive to do well.

Ironically, the job of 'cleaner,' whose duties were often of a 'disagreeable' kind, was among the most sought after. Cleaners often managed to get extra food; they also had greater freedom of movement within the hall where they worked as well as the possibility of establishing a better relationship with the landing officer than the majority of prisoners who were assigned to a workshop. 'One of our ex-prisoner witnesses gives particulars of a case where a landing officer keeps the position of "cleaner" open for a certain habitual prisoner whenever he is discharged, knowing that he is certain to return within a short time.'[29] In the workshops prisoners normally received no wages for work accomplished. Though labour, 'except during the early stages of imprisonment,' was no longer regarded as penal and the treadwheel and crank had gone for good, according to the report 'the punitive element still characterises practically all prison work.' The editors cited a number of ex-prisoners to this effect. In particular, the latter pointed to mailbag making, the major occupation of prisoners, as a task rather than a craft. As one of the witnesses said of these 'eternal mail bags': 'All processes of mail bag work could be done better and more cheaply by machinery.'[30]

The punitive principle that still guided the prison commissioners spilled over into the areas of education and recreation. The report recommended that more money be spent on providing classes for prisoners, who were often illiterate or poorly educated, and improving the quality of instructors.[31] Prison libraries should be better stocked with books than they then were, and the possibilities of choice of reading matter extended. 'If prisoners have any appreciation of reading, the books provided by the library are their best prison friends ... Almost all prisoners who are not illiterate read books with avidity.'[32]

While letters and visits were regular occurrences in the life of prisoners, the report criticized the infrequency of letters permitted by the system. As a warder declared: 'The influence of relatives and friends from outside has a beneficial effect on a prisoner, and helps a man in those hours of solitude of which a prisoner has far too many.'[33] The editors were even more critical of the conditions under which visits took place: in a word, these were 'degrading.'[34] Such conditions illustrated once again the 'cruelty' of the English prison system of that time:

> Visits take place ordinarily under one of two arrangements, described in prison parlance as the 'meat-safe' and the 'cage' respectively. The former consists of two small compartments similar to telephone boxes, partitioned from each other by two screens of thick wire gauze about a foot apart. The visitors stand in one box, the prisoner with an officer behind him to 'censor' the conversation, in the other. The wire gauze so darkens everything seen through it that no clear impression can be obtained of the persons in the opposite box ... The second arrangement [brings to mind] the analogy of caged animals. A room is divided by two parallel rows of bars reaching from floor to ceiling, into two bare cages with a corridor between. The prisoner stands in one cage, the visitors in the other, and the officer sits in the corridor dividing them.

The wife of an ex-prisoner reported the shock she experienced at seeing her husband 'pressing forward through the bars, clasping them tightly, his face dirty and unshaved, his eyes distraught, his body clothed in a rough ill-fitting way. Just for a moment I felt that I was looking through the dim light at some fierce, uncouth animal at the Zoo. Then I forgot his looks. The only thing that mattered was that it was *he*.'[35] A Catholic priest testified to the fact that many prisoners, because of the humiliation they experienced during visits, dispensed with them altogether and relied instead solely on letters for communicating with the outside world. In exceptional circumstances, the governor could permit visits to take place in an open room. 'In this case the prisoner sits at one end of a table and the visitors at the other, with the officer midway'; the prisoner was required to keep his hands on the table in order that nothing could be passed from visitors to prisoner without the officer noticing.[36]

5. The report was critical both of the prison staff and of the visiting justices whose function it was to inspect the administration of the country's prisons. But it acknowledged that many of these officials strove to perform their duties conscientiously – within the framework of an 'essentially inhumane' prison system. It noted, too, that, in respect to convict prisons housing long-term offenders, the visiting justices were 'mostly of the land-owning class and out of touch with the conditions from which most convicts come.' And, from their side, convicts usually felt that it was 'of little use to expect redress [of their grievances] from the Visitors.'[37] The shortcomings of prison staff, in general, were due above all to the inadequacy of their training for work in a really

humane prison system. This was as true of the governors, 'selected primarily as disciplinarians,'[38] as of the rank-and-file prison officers, of the wardresses in women's prisons as of their male counterparts. 'It is quite obvious,' Hobhouse and Brockway conclude, 'that with a new system there must be a new prison staff and a new method of appointing it.'[39] A further criticism made by the editors related to the fact that most prisoners remained unaware of what their legal rights were as prisoners; theoretically such information was supposed to be available, but in fact there was overwhelming evidence it was not.

The report included a chapter on prison chaplains and volunteer prison visitors.[40] The editors' main complaint with respect to the latter was that there were not enough of them, especially in prisons for men. With respect to prison chaplains, the editors are obviously uncomfortable. They recognized that a minority were 'noble' people, hard-working, and 'wrestling with an almost impossible situation and doing their Master's work in shepherding their unhappy charges.'[41] But most of them were content to give the system their unconditional support. This was especially true of Church of England chaplains. They were appointed by the home secretary and, as prison officials, were directly responsible to the prison commissioners: there had by law to be an Anglican chaplain in every prison. As Hobhouse and Brockway knew from their own experience, the Sunday service could be a grim affair for the prisoners who attended, even if it usually provided an hour's relief from the monotonous daily routine. The evidence the editors received from ex-prisoners confirmed their own negative view. An ex-prisoner, who had done time in six jails, wrote:

> So long as the silence regulation is maintained, so long will the warders be required to sit on high chairs, so as to overlook the prisoners, and command them to 'kneel up, there!' when anyone adopts a too devotional attitude during prayers, lest he should be bowing his head to talk to his neighbour.

And another prisoner reported:

> It is a rule that during prayers a prisoner must sit with his back absolutely straight. It is an awful sight to see a warder step over from one form to another to a boy, who has broken down in tears, and get hold of his shirt collar and pull him straight.[42]

Almost all the warders interviewed agreed that the Anglican services were spiritually dead. Certainly the prisoners enjoyed the singing. But one warder considered that the latter, if given the choice, would have preferred extra time on exercise ('the monotonous exercise of the circular track') to attending the compulsory Sunday church service.

6. Hobhouse and Brockway saw the harshness of prison discipline and the multiplicity of petty regulations, 'which cannot possibly be kept,'[43] as the major cause of the frequent punishments to which prisoners were subjected. In fact, 'prisoners never feel immune from punishment.' The report lists a number of trivial 'offences' for which ex-prisoners reported receiving punishment, including 'tins unpolished,' 'leaving place [at work] to visit lavatory without permission,' 'singing,' 'talking,' 'whistling on exercise,' 'lending a book to fellow prisoner,' 'having pen concealed in cell,' 'giving another prisoner a piece of bread,' being 'caught with a needle and thread ... for the ... purpose of sewing on buttons when required.'[44] Dietary restrictions ('bread and water') and solitary confinement were the usual forms of punishment employed, with corporal punishment reserved for acts of violence directed either against a prison officer or another prisoner. The report, while not making any specific recommendations, pointed out, first, that 'punishment by lowering the diet is dangerous to health,' even when the prisoner is certified by the medical officer as fit to undergo such punishment, and secondly, that 'the infliction of corporal punishment has a demoralising effect upon the whole prison population and is degrading to the officer who performs the flogging.'[45] The reader was left to draw the proper conclusion.

8. The report devoted three chapters to the problem of the medical treatment of prisoners, including the mentally deficient.[46] After citing evidence that the health of prisoners on reception was below the national average, the report asks, 'how is it affected by imprisonment?' The answer given was that whereas, in the case of prisoners with short sentences, 'owing to the fact that so many of them are in a low condition of health on arrival,' an improvement in physique was usually noticeable, however, 'in the case of those who serve long sentences, ... they usually became seriously weakened.' Symptoms of this deterioration in health were nervous strain and marked 'loss of physical energy.'[47] Prisoners' reactions to the medical staff the editors found to be mixed. 'That much malingering occurs cannot be doubted.' Even so, complaints of inadequate treatment they considered to be often justified, and they considered prison hospitals to be particularly in need of

improvement – on the basis of non-exprisoner evidence.[48] They found 'very disturbing' the frequent use of 'forcible feeding' in the case of political prisoners, presumably either COs or Irish nationalists, who were on a hunger strike. It was often carried out with brutality and resulted in physical injury.

If political prisoners soon disappeared for the time being from British prisons, the mentally deficient were permanent fixtures there. In this period they numbered about four hundred in any given year.[49] Their treatment, as presented in the report, was truly horrifying: padded cells, reminiscent of eighteenth-century Bedlam, figured prominently. An ex-prisoner remarked: 'It amazed me to find such people in prison. The magistrates who sent them to prison appear to me to be guilty of crimes much greater than many of those they judge from day to day.' And a warder was even more scathing about the way the feeble-minded were treated: 'They only get worse caged up like animals for months,' he said. Another warder stated that, in his opinion, such people should be placed in the prison hospital.[50]

9. Hobhouse and Brockway confined their discussion of the sex life of prisoners to a brief appendix to the conclusions of their report.[51] If they were dealing with the subject today when we are much less inhibited, doubtless they would have dealt more extensively with the topic. Indeed, the questionnaire the PSEC circulated had not included any reference to sex. Despite this reticence, however, some of the answers they received, from non-prisoners as well as ex-prisoners, touched on the problem of sex in an institution, like a prison, 'involving the prolonged segregation of individuals of the same sex.' The report regarded the practice of homosexuality in British prisons as virtually impossible owing to 'the strict manner in which the system of separate confinement is usually carried out.' 'On the other hand,' the editors stated, 'it has again and again been asserted to us that auto-eroticism and the practice of masturbation arise in direct consequence of this segregation and of the intense monotony of the routine. Warders [as well as chaplains] appear to be almost unanimous in their testimony to the prevalence of this practice.' Some ex-prisoners, however, were convinced that the prison authorities 'secretly' placed 'sexual sedatives' in the prison meals. The editors thought that this was unlikely. But they were puzzled by the fact that many prisoners testified to a diminution of their sexual drive, especially during the early period of their imprisonment. The report suggested as an explanation of the seeming contradiction in the evidence presented between the desire for sexual outlet

and the loss of virility, that it was a matter of the stage which the prisoner had reached in his confinement.

'Freedom from sexual obsessions,' the report insisted, was impossible so long as the existing monotonous and generally repressive prison regime with its enforced silence and lengthy enclosure in a cell continued. As an ex-prisoner put it: 'What would be the effect of 19 hours behind a locked door on a youth between 16 and 21?' We may note that Hobhouse and Brockway shared the view, common in their day, that homosexuality and masturbation constituted 'perversions,' 'vices'; in the case of masturbation, they believed, the outcome was mental and moral deterioration and eventually insanity. Their final conclusion was that, since 'a completely normal life is from the nature of the case impossible in prison,' it was essential to create conditions which approximated to those existing outside prison walls and would thus empower inmates to avoid 'the formation of undesirable habits and mental tendencies.' The report failed to resolve the basic problem here. But later penologists and prison administrators have equally failed to come up with a satisfactory solution.

The editors included in their report, in addition to their thematic chapters which focus on local prisons for males, also chapters on various types of prisons: convict prisons housing those sentenced to no less than three years' penal servitude; Borstal institutions for juvenile delinquents under the age of twenty-one; and women's prisons. Much of what was written about local prisons applied also to these other types of prison. As the opening words of the chapter on 'Women Prisoners' stated:

> The variations in régime between men's and women's prisons are slightly in favour of the latter; but there is no radical difference. The same repressive system, the same idea of punishment with almost no thought of cure, runs through both systems. The wastefulness, the failure to individualise, the lack of serious training, and the cruelty which comes from looking upon people merely as bodies instead of as personalities are found in both. In both there are the small, nameless humiliations, the inevitable abuses, or a too-absolute power, and the infringement of rules to the prisoners' disadvantage.[52]

There were, of course, problems that related to women prisoners alone, the chief of which was the baby in prison. Convicted mothers were permitted to bring their babies with them during their incarceration, though usually a twelve-months' limit was imposed, and babies were born in prison, too. 'There is no doubt that much kindness is shown to these little children; they are well looked after, have good food, and are kept clean.' Their presence inside obviously had a positive effect on both the mother and the other prisoners. 'The crowing of a baby breaks the silence, a scrap of ribbon on its sleeve makes a touch of unwonted colour, and to many women the mere sight of a child is a relief.' Hobhouse and Brockway were obviously happy at last to have something really positive to say about prison administration. But they concluded by asking whether or not, in view of the impact 'unconscious memory' might have on later character, the children could perhaps be harmed – 'however remedial their influence upon others may be.'[53]

The report also had positive things to say about the way most convicted juvenile delinquents were being handled in Borstals. For those who remained in adult prisons, however, separation from adult prisoners was not effective: thus the chances of juveniles being 'contaminated' by criminals were high. An ex-prisoner was quoted as overhearing the following conversation carried on between a youth and an 'old lag' from one jail window to another:

> 'Say, kid, what're in for?'
> 'Pinchin' a bike.'
> 'When do you get out?'
> 'Tuesday week.'
> 'I shall be out two days later. You're just the kind of boy I want for a job. Meet me at such and such a place and time.'[54]

Whatever the editors' own views on these matters may have been, the report did not contain a plea for prison abolition nor did it advocate the abolition of capital punishment. But it did include a brief chapter on 'Executions.'[55] The thrust of the argument here was that the carrying out of the death penalty had 'a demoralizing effect upon the whole prison population.' It was 'degrading to every official concerned and certainly ought not to take place in a prison.'[56]

The message the editors wished to convey through the medium of their report was, first, that crime resulted largely from the defects of the existing society, which must take responsibility for this fact. Secondly, imprisonment in many instances, for example in the case of the feeble-minded or juveniles, was not the proper way to deal with the offender. Thirdly, when imprisonment appears to be the only way to deal with offenders, they must be segregated 'under conditions securing ... the minimum of suffering, but the maximum of wholesome happiness that is compatible with their isolation and their infirmity.'[57] But they stressed that, in order to achieve the goal, it was essential to revise current penological theory based essentially on the idea of retribution and deterrence.[58] The text of the report concluded with a 'note' by the chairman of the PSEC. Sir Sydney Olivier wrote there:

> In our prisons we put away men [and women] for our own convenience, and, for the sake of financial economy, control them by mechanical methods which not only deteriorate their own characters and dissipate their inheritance in humanity, but in the majority of cases ensure that if we release them we shall have to put them away again, and continue the process of their destruction till nothing but animal life can be said to remain to them.[59]

The publication of the report proved to be a landmark event in the history of penal reform in the British Isles. Brockway correctly assessed its importance when, with a touch of pride, he wrote: 'It became recognized as the standard work on the English Prison system.'[60] On the whole, reviews on both sides of the Atlantic were favourable. For instance, in England the influential *New Statesman* congratulated the two editors for presenting the facts 'lucidly, temperately and judicially'; they 'let the facts do their own pleading.'[61] And C.M. Lloyd in the prestigious literary journal edited by Sir John Squire, the *London Mercury,* wrote, 'the case that is made against our present penal system is a very strong one.'[62] True, the report covered only prisons in England and Wales, but conditions for the incarcerated in Scottish and Irish jails did not differ in any essential way from those in the area dealt with by Hobhouse and Brockway. Writers on the prison system in twentieth-century Britain have confirmed the significance of the PSEC's report. It was generally agreed that the 'massive description and policy analysis' presented by the editors[63] 'made an important contribution to the growing sense of disillusionment with imprisonment' as administered under Sir Evelyn Ruggles-Brice.[64] The report was felt to be an 'indictment' of the existing prison system, the innumerable shortcomings of which found, from then on, few apologists. In 1984 Garland Publishing chose the PSEC's report as the final volume in their thirty-title facsimile-reprint series on *Crime and Punishment in*

England 1850–1922, designed to document 'the dramatic changes in the extent and character of society's attitudes toward criminals during the period.'[65] That choice illustrated the historical role now assigned to Hobhouse and Brockway's work in the development of penological theory and the practice of imprisonment.

But, of course, the changes that ensued after 1922 were not due to the PSEC's report alone. Reform was on its way[66] and would eventually have come, though even more slowly than it did, without the report. Ruggles-Brice had retired while the report was in the press, and in 1922 one of the most active members of the PSEC, Alexander Paterson (1884–1947), became a member of the Prison Commission. He had helped draft the section in the report on Borstals. An old friend of Hobhouse's, he exercised a positive influence on his fellow commissioners in the direction of reform. 'He judged prison conditions by the same standard as he judged social conditions, by their effect on the human soul.' '"Men," he said, "come to prison as a punishment, not for punishment."'[67]

In later years Brockway expressed his dissatisfaction with the report, a feeling he claimed had been with him from the beginning; it was this dissatisfaction that prompted him seven years afterwards to write a book expounding (according to its title) *A New Way with Crime*. In the report, he later wrote critically, 'we had exposed the prison system but we had not made proposals for any comprehensive alternative.'[68] But Brockway seems now to have forgotten the aim he and Hobhouse (with the support of the committee) had consciously set themselves. They had written in their report:

> The object of the Enquiry has been the discovery of the facts, and not the preparation of proposals of reform. Before that can be done effectively the operation of the present system and its results must be carefully examined and precisely set forth, and it is to this preparatory task that we have devoted ourselves. All that this Report claims to be is a description (as accurate and complete as conditions have allowed) of the English Prison System as it is actually working to-day, accompanied by a study, based upon our evidence, of its physical, mental, and moral effects upon those who are subjected to it.

Only in the concluding chapter had the editors tried briefly to indicate 'the broad principles of any adequate scheme of reform.'[69]

The authors' programmatic statement, putting the emphasis on description, points ahead to the ethnographic key to the work of today's North American convict criminologists. In addition, Hobhouse and Brockway themselves, and most of the witnesses who provided them with evidence, were ex-prisoners. The carceral experience they all possessed supplied the other essential component in the writings of the New School of Convict Criminologists. The role of the two Englishmen as precursors of recent developments in criminology should not be forgotten: they deserve more than just a passing mention in the history of the prison.[70]

NOTES

1 Introduction to Jeffrey Ian Ross and Stephen C. Richards, eds, *Convict Criminology* (Belmont CA, 2003), 4–9.

2 For Brockway, besides his autobiographies listed below, see the entry by David Howell in the *Dictionary of National Biography: 1986–1990* (1996), 49, 50. The *DNB* does not contain an entry for Hobhouse, even though his books on the history of Christian mysticism (all written after 1922), added to his other activities, might have justified his inclusion.

3 Stephen Hobhouse and A. Fenner Brockway, eds, *English Prisons To-day: Being the Report of the Prison System Enquiry Committee* (London, 1922); hereafter *EPT*. A facsimile reprint appeared in 1984 (New York and London: Garland Publishing). Longman, Green and Company published the first edition.

4 Brockway, *Inside the Left: Thirty Years of Platform, Press, Prison and Parliament* (London, 1942), 122, 123.

5 Ibid., 123, 124: 'he read every line of what Stephen Hobhouse and I wrote and was active in suggestions ... The evidence of a prison chaplain who advocated sterner discipline made him angry; the proof came back annotated: "The scoundrel!"' Hobhouse on more than one occasion complained rather petulantly of lack of interest on the part of members of the PSEC. Shaw certainly could not be accused of this fault.

6 See Hobhouse, *An English Prison from Within* (July 1918). I have included extracts from Hobhouse's pamphlet in my *'These Strange Criminals': An Anthology of Prison Memoirs by Conscientious Objectors from the Great War to the Cold War* (Toronto, 2004), 15–27.

7 Hobhouse, *The Autobiography of Stephen Hobhouse: Reformer, Pacifist, Christian* (Boston, 1952), 175.

8 Sybil Oldfield, *Women against the Iron Fist: Alternatives to Militarism, 1900–1989* (Oxford, 1989), 39.

9 Hobhouse, *Autobiography,* 39.
10 Ibid., 165, 166.
11 Ibid., 59.
12 Ibid., 173: 'The Webbs had little or no sympathy with C.O.s and, while I was in the guardroom, I received a letter from my aunt urging me not to continue to be guilty of the sin of rebellion against a Government that was defending my liberties and my way of life.'
13 *The Diary of Beatrice Webb,* ed. Norman and Jeanne MacKenzie, vol. 3: 1905–1924, *'The Power to Alter Things'* (London, 1984), 230, 231, 286. Hobhouse has sometimes been referred to as a modern Quaker saint. But, as Tolstoy, echoing earlier theologians, once remarked, in this world there really are no saints because God has given even the best of us at least one sin.
14 Hobhouse, *Autobiography,* 176; Brockway, *Inside the Left,* 124–6. According to Hobhouse, three volumes were purloined in this way. Brockway comments on the contents of the letters: 'I was surprised by their literary power; it is evident these men had suffered so deeply that even their illiteracy became eloquent' (p. 125).
15 *EPT,* 523–6. Cf. the confirmatory 'Evidence of a Conscientious Objector on the Mental Effects of Imprisonment' (ibid., 645–50), printed by Hobhouse and Brockway as an appendix to their report. The young man, sentenced to four periods of imprisonment, spent a total of two and a half years in jail, with three months in solitary confinement. He attributed to his 'obstinacy and adaptability' the fact that, though 'not unscathed,' he survived his ordeal without lasting 'mental ill-effects.' Summing up, he declared the 'reformative influences of the English prison system' on the criminal to be 'nil.'
16 Hobhouse, *Autobiography,* 177, 186.
17 Brockway, *Inside the Left,* 120–2; and *Towards Tomorrow* (London, 1977), 61.
18 Hobhouse, *Autobiography,* 177. Brockway calculated that in its final form the report contained 'quarter of a million words' (*Inside the Left,* 122).
19 Hobhouse, *Autobiography,* 177, 178; Brockway, *Inside the Left,* 126–9, and *Towards Tomorrow,* 61.
20 The listing of chapters is idiosyncratic. First come chapters 1–23 (pp. 3–474) and then a second series of chapters 1–9 with a 'concluding chapter' (pp. 475–598). Pages 599–706 contain four appendices, of which the first ('Specimens of Evidence,' pp. 600–50) is the most valuable. The last appendix lists the principal printed sources used in compiling the report. Finally comes a useful analytical index (pp. 707–28). Pages 19–41 contain statistical tables on crime and imprisonment (with the emphasis on the twentieth century). The editors introduce the statistics with some comments on 'their signifi-

cance and limitations.' They were clearly aware of the defects inherent in criminal statistics of that period.

21 Hobhouse, *English Prison*, in my anthology, '*These Strange Criminals*,' 23, 27.

22 *EPT*, 355, 356, 562–70.

23 Ibid., 130–3.

24 Ibid., chap. 5 (86–92).

25 Ibid., 92. Twenty years later, during the Second World War, imprisoned COs found that little, if anything, had changed since Hobhouse and Brockway's day.

26 Ibid., 86, 90, 91.

27 The swivel-door latrine cubicles, with the top half open, are visible in the photo printed by Hobhouse and Brockway, although the editors do not call attention to this item. According to an ex-prison CO witness: 'The W.C.'s are unpleasantly public, with only half-height door over and under which anyone can see' (ibid., 637).

28 Ibid., 93–106, 126–48. With regard to prison sanitation, CO prisoners during the Second World War found the major deficiencies pointed out by Hobhouse and Brockway (p. 148) still present: 'Prisoners confined to their cells have great difficulty in visiting the W.C's'; 'lack of privacy in the W.C's'; and, above all, 'slops ... emptied and drinking water obtained simultaneously from one sink.'

29 Ibid., 109, 110.

30 Ibid., 113–15.

31 Ibid., 149–84.

32 Ibid., 178.

33 Ibid., 207.

34 Ibid., 213.

35 I suspect that this woman was the wife of a CO, though the report does not identify her as such.

36 Ibid., 210–12. Kate Courtney's visit to Stephen Hobhouse in Exeter prison was obviously an open-room visit. There were prisoners who preferred even the 'meat-safe' system to open-room visits, because in the former case it was easier to speak without being overheard by the guard, 'one officer frequently having to supervise several visits in neighbouring boxes.' Guards were known to stop the prisoner from referring to any jail happenings or visitors from discussing public events!

37 Ibid., 362, 406, 407.

38 Ibid., 384.

39 Ibid., 382.

40 Ibid., chap. 11 (185–205).

41 Ibid., 195.
42 Ibid., 190. During the Second World War warders in prison chapels still sat on high chairs overlooking the prisoners, even though the silence regulation had been relaxed.
43 Ibid., 245.
44 Ibid., 231–4.
45 Ibid., 245.
46 Ibid., chaps. 16–18 (251–91).
47 Ibid., 252, 253. The report devotes considerable space to the evidence of CO ex-prisoners describing the 'mental decay' they experienced during incarceration, though at the same time these men recorded certain beneficial effects of imprisonment – including solitary confinement! – like 'opportunity for reading or meditation' and various other 'spiritual benefits,' which the editors point out the common criminal was much less likely to be able to enjoy. See ibid., 488–500, 643–50. Compare 'Every day in prison brings its hour of desperation' with 'A certain amount of solitary confinement I found pleasant and restful.' Cf. also the letter written by the Quaker Malcolm Sparkes (later a prominent guild socialist) not long after his arrival in Wormwood Scrubs Prison in May 1917 to begin a sentence of twenty-three months' hard labour. 'It had taken [him] a good while,' he wrote, 'to get "tamed down" to prison.' But then he discovered that the Scrubs was 'a spiritual power house, in which a veritable Niagara of energy is being created and pent up, until it can be liberated for the service of God and humanity. The [Quaker] meetings for worhip are simply glorious.' 'It is a truly wonderful experience to be here' (quoted in Bert den Boggende, 'Reluctant Absolutists: Malcolm Sparkes' Conscientious Objections to World War I,' *Quaker Studies*, vol. 10, no. 1 [March 2005], 80).
48 Ibid., 256–83. An ex-prisoner reported, 'I cannot imagine any punishment much worse than being in a prison hospital' (p. 270).
49 Ibid., 285.
50 Ibid., 286, 287.
51 Ibid., 586–9.
52 Ibid., 336.
53 Ibid., 346, 347.
54 Ibid., 301.
55 Ibid., chap. 15 (246–9).
56 Ibid., 250. The insertion here of the clause, 'Leaving aside the question of the justifiability and expediency of capital punishment,' was, I think, intended as an indication that both Hobhouse and Brockway were opponents of the death penalty. Some members of the PSEC may not have been.

57 Ibid., 595.

58 For example, Sir Evelyn Ruggles-Brice, *The English Prison System* (London, 1921), viii, argued that, while reform of the prisoner was an inspiring and noble task, 'the primary and fundamental purpose of punishment, ... say what we will, must remain in its essence retributory and deterrent.'

59 *EPT*, 598.

60 Brockway, *Inside the Left, 125.*

61 *The Book Review Digest*, vol. 18: *Reviews of 1922 Books* (New York and London, 1923), 260.

62 *London Mercury*, vol. 6, no. 35 (September 1922).

63 Seán McConville, 'The Victorian Prison: England, 1865–1965,' in Norval Morris and David J. Rothman, eds, *The Oxford History of the Prison: The Practice of Punishment in Western Society* (New York and Oxford, 1995), 167.

64 Christopher Harding et al., *Imprisonment in England and Wales: A Concise History* (London, 1985), 261.

65 The editor of the series was Martin J. Wiener.

66 And new problems were to come, too, such as overcrowding of prisons and an increased level of violence, which was to some degree the result of the worldwide spread of drugs. Moreover, almost all the old penitentiary-style buildings remain in use today, slightly refurbished perhaps.

67 See the entry on Paterson by A. Maxwell in the *Dictionary of National Biography: 1941–1950* (1959), 658–61.

68 Brockway, *Inside the Left*, 129.

69 *EPT*, v.

70 In 1812, during the Napoleonic Wars, a local militia act (52 Geo. 3. c. 38) had ruled that Quakers, who refused to serve when balloted for the English militia, should not be 'confined among felons,' as had sometimes been happening. In twentieth-century wars, liberal provision of this kind was never practised with respect to COs. Ironically, if it had, Hobhouse and Brockway might never have produced their masterpiece!

18 The Confinement of Conscientious Objectors as Psychiatric Patients in First-World-War Germany

A vigorous pacifist movement sprang up in Germany after that country's defeat in November 1918 only to fall victim to Nazi repression when Hitler came to power in January 1933.[1] The Weimar pacifists drew their main inspiration from the war resistance of British conscientious objectors (COs), whose experiences received considerable publicity in post-war Germany, especially in the left-wing press. German pacifists in the Weimar Republic also knew of the existence of a few COs in wartime Germany, but little detailed information was then available. A pamphlet on the subject, covering the Habsburg Empire as well, was indeed published,[2] and articles occasionally appeared in journals and newspapers. However, no CO memoirs emerged, as was the case with respect to First-World-War Britain and the United States. Since 1945, attention has naturally focused on war resistance in Nazi Germany; scarcely any further progress has been made with reference to the earlier conflict.[3]

Who became a conscientious objector in Germany during the 1914–18 war? The few who took this position almost all based their objection to bearing arms on religious grounds. First we may mention the Mennonites, whose doctrine of nonresistance (*Wehrlosigkeit*) dated back to the early years of the Protestant Reformation. During the first half of the nineteenth century, Mennonite congregations, first in northwestern and then southern Germany, had mostly abandoned this doctrine, and their members now served in the armed forces when conscripted. But the more conservative *altmennonitische Gemeinden* in what was then called West Prussia (*Westpreussen*) continued to regard military service as opposed to their faith. We have seen earlier that when Prussia introduced universal military service their traditional

Wehrfreiheit, the legal privilege exempting them from military service, disappeared for good. However, the Royal Cabinet Order of 3 March 1868 permitted Mennonite conscripts, if they so wished, to serve in the army in a noncombatant capacity. After German unification, except in Bavaria and Württemberg, this concession was normally extended to the few pacifist conscripts emerging thereafter from Mennonite congregations in other parts of Germany. In the First World War most German Mennonites served as combatants, though in West Prussia about a third of their conscripts asked for noncombatant duties, which they had no trouble in obtaining.[4] For the German army no problem existed here. Around four hundred Mennonite soldiers died in battle: a considerable figure for a small religious group.

It was a denomination very different from the by now largely middle-class and highly respectable German Mennonites who took the most determined CO stand in First-World-War Germany. The Bible Students (*Ernste Bibelforscher*), known as Jehovah's Witnesses (JWs) after 1931, were drawn predominantly from factory workers, domestic servants, foresters, or peasants.[5] An offshoot of American millenarianism, the sect had spread to Germany at the end of the nineteenth century. By 1914, it numbered between three thousand and four thousand adherents there.[6]

Pastor Charles Russell (1852–1916), its founder, on the basis of abstruse biblical calculations, had predicted an imminent end of the world (an apocalypse that periodically had to be postponed). Then Christ would return to earth and, at the battle of Armageddon, the wicked would be destroyed by God's avenging angels. A righteous remnant among the living would remain unharmed to inherit the Kingdom of Heaven along with the resurrected righteous dead. Russell taught that all worldly governments were evil and that Bible Students should take no part in them. Though he opposed neither the death penalty for murder nor personal self-defence, he condemned participation in battle and advised his followers in conscriptionist countries, if drafted, to ask for service in the medical corps. In a widely circulated work, first published in 1904, which appeared soon after in German translation, Russell made it clear he supported conscientious objection. But in Russell's view a conscripted Bible Student, if refused noncombatant duties, could in the last resort train in weaponry without committing a sin. 'Even if compelled ... to fire our guns we need not feel compelled to shoot a fellow-creature.'[7]

Russell's tactful, and at the same time rather unrealistic, treatment of the issue probably explains why we do not hear of any Bible Student COs in Germany before 1914. Though the group was at that time still very small, it must have included some men liable to military service. But evidently the success or failure of their attempts to gain some form of noncombatant service has simply left no trace in the record. In peacetime, their leader's ambiguous proviso of resolving not to shoot-to-kill did not possess any immediate relevance. Once war had broken out, however, the problem soon took on a new aspect.

At first, though, most drafted Bible Students joined the army, hopeful of being assigned to the medical corps or some other noncombatant branch of the services. By 1915 around 350 of them were already in the forces. Although exact figures are not available, Detlef Garbe thinks, from the evidence at his disposal, that army commanders in most cases took a sympathetic view of their requests for noncombatancy; where this did not occur, the men evidently agreed to train as combatant soldiers, while presumably, as 'neutrals' opposed to human bloodshed, they resolved to avoid using their weapons to take life. But as one fierce military campaign followed another, compromise of the kind suggested by Russell increasingly appeared to the men concerned as a betrayal of the Bible Students' witness for peace.

Some conscripts now began to regard even work in the medical corps as unacceptable. Since no civilian alternative then existed for German COs, these men could only reject military service *in toto* and face court martial and prison. One of those who followed this path was Hero von Ahlften, later to become one of the leading members of the sect in interwar Germany. Von Ahlften took this stand after having served in the army for two years. But in 1917 he refused any longer to obey military orders, alleging that to do so would constitute 'collaboration in the work of the devil.' By this time the Bible Students' position with regard to the war had begun to worry both the churches (and especially the Protestants, from whose ranks members of the new sect were mainly recruited) and the military authorities. The latter became concerned that with the sect's growing membership and vigorous proselytizing, the mounting hostility of the Bible Students to the war effort would have an adverse effect on the troops as well as the civilian population with whom they came into contact.[8]

Garbe estimates the number of Bible Students refusing all service in the armed forces as around fifty, of whom twenty received five-year prison sentences. But, he adds, that is only an approximation; accurate statistics do not exist.[9]

Alongside the Bible Students, the Seventh-day Adventists figure most prominently among the COs of First-World-War Germany. Like the former, the Adventists, too, were millenarians, though their expectations of apocalypse were more remote. During the American Civil War, the founders, Ellen and James White, had taken a pacifist stand; Adventists, while ready to undertake noncombatant duties, refused to bear arms. They regarded themselves, they said, as 'conscientious cooperators.' The sect had spread to Germany in the late 1860s. Though growth was slow, by 1914 there were some twenty thousand Adventists in the German Empire. With respect to pre-war conscription, Adventist draftees do not seem to have encountered difficulties when they asked for assignment to the medical corps, though they occasionally met with trouble in connection with Sabbath observance. Refusal to work on Saturdays, the Adventists' Sabbath, could sometimes lead to a prison sentence.[10]

The sect's position changed radically with the outbreak of war in 1914. In August, the leadership, believing in the righteousness of their country's cause and under the strong impact of nationalism, declared the readiness of Adventists in the existing war emergency both to bear arms and perform army duties on the Sabbath. The overwhelming majority supported this decision, but about 2 per cent of the church's membership opposed it. The dissidents eventually broke away to form a separate 'Reform Movement' (*Reformationsbewegung*). However, even in the main Adventist body, the feeling continued to be widespread that their religion forbade them to kill, so that conscripted Adventists, as in the case of the Bible Students, often sought noncombatant status, which at first was frequently granted to them informally.[11] The 'Reformers,' on the other hand, rejected *Sanitätsdienst* along with combatant service. For their uncompromising stand, their COs received heavy prison sentences; for instance, two of their leaders, Adolph Czukta and Friedrich Wieck, who had both deserted after being drafted early on in the war, got five years each, and this severity was not unusual. A few Reformers, when called up, tried to escape service in the army by going into hiding. But they were usually discovered and were then court-martialled and jailed.[12]

Mennonite, Bible Student, and Seventh-day Adventist COs belonged to religious groups which, with different degrees of intensity, rejected participation in war as part of their Christian faith. Pacifists, at any rate of military age, did not emerge in any other denominations in First-World-War Germany. But we should mention the COs who lacked any sort of affiliation; their objection to fighting was a purely individual decision reached on their own. These men can be divided into the religious and the political and ethical. Our knowledge of the unaffiliated religious COs is drawn exclusively from case studies located in the publications of psychiatrists who examined them in the clinics to which the army had sent them for observation. Some of these men were obviously eccentrics, even when they succeeded in drawing a few followers around them. We read of several who refused to fight because an inner voice – perhaps God himself – had told them this was wrong. Their eccentricity, however, does not necessarily exclude the sincerity of their objections to war. (Can one indeed be sure how Joan of Arc, for instance, or George Fox would have fared under clinical observation?) At the same time there were some religious individualists rejecting participation in war who, we shall see, were indubitably sane and devoid of any trace of mental disturbance. The political and ethical individualists among the COs were mainly socialists or anarchists, with one or two whose antimilitarism derived from reading Tolstoy's moral treatises. In all, we only know of around half a dozen cases of this kind.[13] Of course, not all these men were absolute pacifists; several expressed willingness to fight in defence of a workers' state, their objection being to participation in an imperialist war. In comparison with the United Kingdom or the United States, where this type of objector figured quite prominently, for example, in the British No-Conscription Fellowship, political war resistance in Germany usually took other forms.

Whether political or religious, conscientious objection to military service in Germany lacked any kind of legal recognition. When, for instance, an army commander agreed to a conscript's request to be assigned to the *Sanitätsdienst* (actually the only army unit where exercising with weapons would not be required), this was a purely informal arrangement without any basis in law. It was done solely in order to avoid trouble; and it could be terminated at will – at least in theory, though no actual instances of this being done are known to have occurred.

The situation became more acute with the increase in numbers of absolutist objectors who rejected any form of alternative army service. For court martials had no alternative now except to sentence offenders of this kind to repeated terms of imprisonment, a course of action that for practical reasons the military authorities were usually reluctant to pursue. While the military code laid down specifically that religious conscience did not provide any excuse for refusing military orders,[14] the picture changed when mental disorder could be proved. And so in many cases, instead of immediately proceeding to sentence the delinquent, the military authorities decided first to ask for a *Gutachten* (expert opinion) in the matter from a psychiatrist. The CO was then transferred from military arrest to confinement in a psychiatric clinic until the doctors had completed the examination of the 'patient' and submitted their report to the army. As one of the psychiatrists most concerned in the problem noted: 'it was quite striking how the military authorities in the first instance always considered that a soldier, who in our Fatherland's hour of danger decides from allegedly religious or moral grounds to refuse to serve and persists in this decision after being informed of the severe punishment awaiting him, must be mentally ill.'[15]

The psychiatrists, for their part, could either declare the man in need of treatment and keep him shut up in the clinic for as long as necessary to effect a cure, on the same conditions as the other mental patients, or they could confirm his sanity. In the latter case, the CO would normally be returned to the army for trial and probable imprisonment. The psychiatrists might indeed recommend clemency if they thought the man's sincerity made this appropriate. But the court martial did not have to take their recommendation into account.

In general, 'the position of the psychiatrist around 1900 was not a particularly happy one,' especially as a result of his continued 'ignorance of the causes of mental illness' and his inability to treat it effectively.[16] Even in Germany, where perhaps most progress had been made, psychiatry still lacked the prestige enjoyed by other branches of the medical profession. On the other hand, psychiatric institutions had emerged in large numbers, which gave promise of future achievement. 'By 1911 ... Germany had almost 1,400 physicians specializing in psychiatry. This pool of research energy was unmatched anywhere else in the world.' The doctors practised their profession in the sixteen university psychiatric clinics as well as in a network of both public and private mental hospitals – or asylums (*Irrenanstalten*), as they were then called – spread across the country.[17] German psychiatrists, moreover, were not only trained rigorously in medical science; they had often received a classical education, and some had studied *inter alia* both ethics and the psychology of religion. For such persons, the conscientious objector may have provided a welcome relief from the more mundane cases handed over to them for observation by the wartime army.

I have been able to discover published reports by ten German psychiatrists who discuss, in greater or less detail, the COs they examined.[18] Further reports in hospital or military archives may, of course, have survived the ravages of time and the devastation Germany suffered during the Second World War. But I suspect they would not add substantially to the picture. We should note that almost all the CO case studies available date from late 1916 on; understandably so since, as we have seen, the incidence of CO absolutism expanded during these latter years.

Broadly speaking, the psychiatrists, in their attitude to the COs they were observing in their clinics, divide into two groups: (1) those regarding most of the COs as sane (however much they might differ as to what was thereafter to be done with them); and (2) those considering the COs, with a few exceptions perhaps, as suffering from some sort of mental disorder which had caused them to refuse military service. Terms used by the latter group include *psychisch-gestört, geisteskrank*, or simply *irre* (the reports, of course, usually went into some detail as to the symptoms of mental illness the men were said to display).

The outstanding figure in our first group of psychiatrists was undoubtedly *Generaloberartzt* Robert Gaupp, professor of psychiatry at the University of Tübingen and, since 1906, director of that university's psychiatric clinic. His findings were based on observation of thirteen COs; and Gaupp published these case studies in several medical journals.[19]

In some instances, Gaupp had felt obliged, in an *Obergutachten*, to overturn the negative opinion of a medical subordinate, who had declared patients 'insane' (*verrückt*) or 'paranoic' on the grounds that 'their thinking and their explanations' reflected some religious delusion (*Wahn*). This view, Gaupp stated decisively, was in the case of most of the COs under observation, incorrect.[20] Instead, their refusal to serve in the army (at any rate as combatants) resulted quite logically from their literal, and often uncritical, interpretation of the Sermon on the Mount and similar passages in the Bible. Unlike most other Christians, Gaupp explained, the COs believed that these injunctions, reflecting human brotherhood and the idea of nonviolence, applied not merely to individuals but to the community as a whole. They were prepared to suffer the consequences of following Christ's teaching uncompromisingly; for them, God's commands took precedence over human law. When Quakers and Mennonites, Gaupp went on to point out, took exactly the same position as these men did, no one accused them of being paranoid. 'Psychiatry,' Gaupp concluded, 'must, especially in times of great upheaval, avoid committing the dangerous mistake of branding unusual behaviour out of hand as pathological.'[21]

While judging several of the unaffiliated COs he had examined to be indeed paranoid, and therefore in need of further clinical treatment,[22] Gaupp at the same time stressed that it was easier for members of pacifist sects to refuse military service than for individuals to do so if they lacked the support of a religious community. Nevertheless, the latter could be as sincere – and sane – as the products of sectarian pacifism. As an instance of this, he dealt at some length with the case of a twenty-two-year-old gardener whom the army had sent to his clinic for observation. This man – 'intelligent, honest, hard working' – displayed no pathological symptoms, no evidence of mental illness. Moreover, he had no sectarian affiliation.[23]

Gaupp apparently had no hesitation in handing back to the army the COs he considered were not mentally ill, whether they were Bible Students, Adventists, or unaffiliated. He felt he really had no alternative. The same viewpoint was expressed as follows by another university specialist Wilhelm Schmidt, *Privatdozent* in psychiatry and neurology at the University of Göttingen and an admirer of Gaupp:

> I consider it quite wrong to label the 'fanatic' as mentally ill. It is indeed in the first instance an injustice done to the 'accused.' True, one would like to free such a person from the possibility of eventual punishment, the more so since we have to do here with men inspired by the highest ethical motives. But if we describe them in our report as mentally ill we shall be injuring them as human beings because we do not recognize they acted out of their convictions, and thus we shall hurt their feelings by treading them, as it were, in the dirt. I think that the punishment which they are likely to suffer can only raise their morale by giving them a sense of martyrdom. It will certainly harm them less than the self-doubt that an authoritative declaration they are mentally ill will most certainly induce in them.[24]

Schmidt went on to criticize many of his fellow psychiatrists for their materialist outlook, which had left them incapable of understanding the contribution some religious 'fanatics' had made to the spiritual advancement of humankind.[25]

Yet the subsequent fate of the CO patients he had handed back to the army as sane obviously did bother Gaupp. A fellow psychiatrist wrote: 'The question of how one is to proceed in such cases is no concern of the medical profession.'[26] But Gaupp clearly disagreed. And he did his best to persuade the military authorities to deal as lightly as possible with the COs he had discharged from his clinic; he seems to have been fairly successful in these endeavours. On his release from clinical confinement the young gardener, mentioned above, was, for instance, given a prison term which he did not in fact have to serve, since the time he had spent under observation in Gaupp's clinic was counted in his favour. The military court, instead, sent him back to Gaupp's clinic – not as an inmate this time but as a gardener! 'The promise,' wrote the professor, 'he then made to keep his religious viewpoint to himself and not to influence others, he has honestly kept.'[27]

A major factor prompting caution in assigning to some form of mental sickness a man's refusal to bear arms lay in the realization of many psychiatrists how little in fact science knew as yet about the nature of religion and its manifestations in history. As one of the psychiatrists most active in observing COs under clinical conditions wrote: 'Satisfactory methods of measuring religious experience do not exist. Therefore in every expert opinion an element of the subjective will always be present.'[28] There was also need for greater clarity in the use of terms such as 'religious delusion,' especially with respect to the phenomenon of conscientious objection.[29] In addition, systematization of the cases of conscientious objection emerging during the war, very important for its proper understanding, was in this expert's view only at a beginning.[30]

Aware of the shortcomings of their discipline with respect to the psychology of religion, unwilling to consign a sane person to a mental institution for an indefinite period, yet at the same time reluctant to hand him back to the army with the probability of his then having to endure lengthy incarceration in a military jail, some psychiatrists, when they came to compose their *Gutachten*, tried to fuse the two alternatives legally open to them and gain for sanity the freedom from imprisonment which the declared lunatic would enjoy within the confines of his mental institution.

Here, for instance, is such an attempt: 'The forensic opinion ... must be that B., when he committed his act of disobedience, was not unconscious of what he was doing or mentally disturbed [nicht in einem Zustand von Bewusstlosigkeit oder krankhafter Störung der Geistestätigkeit]. On the other hand, perhaps one can point to the man's unusually low level of education, along with a not particularly high level of intelligence, as factors leading one to consider him, in respect to any future legal punishment,[31] as possessing a diminished sense of responsibility.'[32]

Our second group of psychiatrists, those considering conscientious objection to military service to be almost always the outcome of mental disorder, did not possess a practitioner of the eminence of Gaupp – though perhaps Geheim Sanitätsrat professor Josef Peretti might have disagreed with this judgment. Peretti, as director of the mental hospital at Dusseldorf-Grafenberg and professor of psychiatry at the Academy of Applied Medicine in that city, found himself entrusted with overseeing the assessment of some twelve hundred soldiers who had been sent to his clinic at Grafenberg and to a neighboring hospital for nervous complaints. The men suffered from a wide variety of mental illnesses. A disciple of his famous contemporary Emil Kraepelin, then professor of psychiatry at the University of Munich, Peretti in his clinical methods closely followed the latter, who had elevated 'the two ... nonorganic ... psychoses – manic-depressive illness and schizophrenia – to the top of the pyramid where they remain in only slightly modified form to this day as the object of endeavor of serious psychiatry.'[33] Only two genuine CO cases seem to have come to Peretti's attention, both of them Bible Students. One of them, 'a 33-year old preacher' he described as a paranoic, who lacked any sense of responsibility. The other man, aged forty-four, had served as a conscript before the war. Peretti characterized him as a person 'of weak intellect.' His decision to refuse to serve any longer in the army Peretti attributed to a literal interpretation of selected passages from the Bible and, above all, to the influence exercised on him by a 'paranoid teacher.'[34]

Obviously, Peretti saw no essential distinction between these two men and the other patients placed under his care who suffered from a variety of war neuroses, including psychopaths and 'degenerates,'[35] epileptics, and those attempting to escape further service through self-inflicted wounds. We do not know what happened to his two Bible Students; as a result of his recommendation to the military, we may, however, presume that their confinement in the Grafenberg asylum continued until the end of the war.[36]

Another opponent of Gaupp's and Schmidt's view of conscientious objection, Adolf Hoppe, proved himself nevertheless rather more flexible in his attitude than Peretti. Hoppe ran a private psychiatric clinic at Rinteln; perhaps because of an interest in the psychology of religion, he became involved with *Kriegsdienstverweigerer* of various kinds, who had been placed for observation in the Military Section of the psychiatric clinic of the Cologne Academy.

As with Peretti, only two of Hoppe's patients from the army had refused military service on grounds of conscience. Case A at the age of twelve had heard 'heavenly voices' urging him to hate evil and follow the good. As an adult, he formed a small religious sect of his own, numbering around one hundred adherents – mostly women. When conscripted, he had refused to put on uniform or obey military orders; the war, he said, was the work of the devil. In the clinic, the man was quiet and well behaved, helpful towards his fellow patients, and extremely religious. Hoppe diagnosed him as suffering from *dementia praecox*. His mental illness – 'his hallucinations and delusions' – and not his religious convictions constitute, Hoppe believed, the main reason for his refusing military service. Case B, a man in his mid-thirties, was a Bible Student, who had long been a religious seeker before joining that sect. When drafted, he served at first in a noncombatant capacity. However, two years later, when ordered to the front, he had refused to obey and was sentenced to a year in jail. 'After his release he at once asked his commander, both in writing and orally, to be employed in the medical corps.' This officer then passed the matter over to the court, which in turn ordered the man to be sent to the psychiatric clinic in Cologne for examination. On the basis of 'life-style, character and behaviour,' Hoppe in his *Gutachten* characterized the man certainly as a psychopath, but not sufficiently ill to be certified as insane. B would therefore have been handed back to the army if the war had not ended soon after.[37]

Hoppe detected a false sentimentality in the generally favourable view of COs taken by some of his colleagues. In his opinion, when COs were not mentally ill, they were probably shirkers. The rise in the number of religious COs during the later years of the war he attributed to war weariness. He refused to take seriously their readiness to suffer; rather, they displayed, he thought, a striking readiness to escape from unpleasant obligations incumbent on the citizenry. True, they could not be called cowards or hypocrites. But most of them, he considered, to be 'ethically of inferior quality.'[38]

Arthur Hübner, an expert in criminal psychology, was another psychiatrist critical of sentimentality vis-à-vis COs. He warned, too, against showing uncritical sympathy towards the general run of 'world reformers [Weltverbesserer]'; such people could often be imposters. As chief physician at the University of Bonn's clinic for nervous illnesses, he had been called upon to deal with COs placed there for observation by the military. He evidently felt irritated at the way uneducated 'agricultural labourers, craftsmen and small shopkeepers' quoted uncritically endless biblical passages to prove that Christians were forbidden to fight.[39]

Among COs Hübner examined, he found only one whose intellectual capacity he could at least respect. This man, whose name he does not reveal,[40] was by profession a lawyer (*ein ehemaliger Rechtsanwalt*). A libertarian socialist prepared to fight in defence of a worker's state, he had disobeyed his call-up notice in order to engage in open antiwar propaganda. The military had arrested him several times and, in the belief he was probably insane, had finally sent him in 1916 to the Bonn clinic. 'With weak lungs,' writes Hübner, 'and a squint he looked undernourished and neglected. From a psychiatrist's viewpoint we may describe him as a complete degenerate.' The clinic soon released the man as a harmless crackpot, attributing his peculiar views on war – not quite correctly — to the influence of Tolstoy. And the military authorities thereafter wisely left him alone.

The wartime confinement in psychiatric clinics of COs of the more uncompromising type had resulted in the first instance from the German army's desire to discover whether, as it suspected, refusal to serve had indeed resulted from mental illness. This was the military authorities' natural response to what was to them a strange, and rather distasteful, phenomenon. But, of course, they possessed no means of keeping such men locked up for the duration of the war as a convenient way of handling the problem if the examining psychiatrists decided no good medical reasons in fact existed for doing so.

The psychiatrists took their task very seriously, whatever the decision they finally gave in a given case. Specialists like Robert Gaupp consistently presented an independent judgment, based on an interpretation of the medical data according to the best of their professional knowledge. When the CO appeared to them to be sane, they stated this clearly in the *Gutachten* which the military had asked them to provide. The man was then released from clinical custody. What happened to him next was, formally, the army's business alone. But in these circumstances some psychiatrists, impressed by the sincerity of their 'patients,' felt impelled to offer a recommendation for clemency, which to its credit the army seems often to have followed.

The obverse side of this situation lay in the fact that the COs' fate depended solely on the attitude of the examining psychiatrist. A superior might reverse the negative opinion of a junior physician, and in an

Obergutachten declare the man sane with the consequent decision to discharge him. But the patient had no right of appeal: all depended on the senior psychiatrist's judgment. Indeed, throughout, the confined COs remained silent partners in the process to which they were involuntarily submitted.

We have seen that examining psychiatrists tended to presuppose a psychotic state in a man who had refused to defend his country in its hour of need. It was indeed difficult for these highly educated professionals to enter into the mindset of simple, and often inarticulate, artisans and peasants.[41] Nor was it at all easy, as some psychiatrists admitted, to distinguish between eccentric behaviour and thought that were still within the bounds of sanity and a psychotic condition that might be harmless (and therefore not need further hospitalization) or could be dangerous, at least to the patient's well-being (and would, therefore, require continued clinical confinement). Even in the case of Gaupp, whose attitude on this question demands our respect,[42] it is not clear – on the available evidence – how far those few COs he described as mentally ill were in fact sick – or, at any rate, how far their objection to military service derived from an existing mental sickness and not from conscience, as in the case of the undoubtedly sane.

Since the absolutist objection to all forms of army service that most often led the military authorities to send COs to psychiatric clinics for examination was largely absent during the early years of the war, confinement of the allegedly psychotic COs in such institutions came fairly late and thus was brief. The end of the war soon brought release. Nevertheless, the situation was potentially dangerous; as in all instances that have occurred when the state has attempted to rid itself of persons whose political or social behaviour was unwelcome by confining them in institutions established for the care of the mentally ill, a precedent might be set. In such circumstances, infringement of human rights is perhaps less immediately obvious than in the case of confinement in a penal institution, but the removal of the dissident from society and the imposition of silence are usually even more effective.

NOTES

1 See Guido Grünewald, 'Kriegsdienstverweigerung in der Weimar Republik,' in A. Gestrich et al., eds, *Gewaltfreiheit: Pazifistische Konzepte im 19. und 20. Jahrhundert (Jahrbuch für historische Friedensforschung,* 5) (Münster, 1996), 80–102.

2 Martha Steinitz, Olga Misar, and Helene Stöcker, *Kriegsdienstverweigerer in Deutschland und Osterreich* (Berlin, 1923). See also Johann Ohrtmann, *Die Bewegung der Kriegsdienstgegner: Ein schlicter Bericht von schlichtem Heldentum* (Heide in Holstein, 1932), 8–11. No figures are available as to the total number of conscientious objectors in First-World-War Germany.

3 A partial exception is Detlef Garbe's impressive study *Zwischen Widerstand und Martyrium: Das Zeugen Jehovas im 'Dritten Reich,'* 4th edn (Munich, 1999), which in its background chapter contains three pages, minutely documented like the rest of the book, on the First World War (pp. 46–8). See also Grünewald, *Zur Geschichte der Kriegsdienstverweigerung ... 1650 bis 1945*, 2nd edn (Essen, 1982), 32–8, a popular account based largely on Steinitz et al. Garbe (p. 47, no. 17) is, to my knowledge, the only German writer who has referred to the existence of a 'relatively detailed' medical literature on COs in First-World-War Germany by contemporary psychiatrists; in passing, he cited three such articles. These articles provided me with a starting point for the present study. Subsequently I discovered that present-day Swiss psychiatry is acquainted, too, with at least some of this literature. After all, from the First World War onwards, the Swiss military authorities have frequently followed the German example of placing absolutist COs of an unusual type, especially Jehovah's Witnesses, in psychiatric clinics for observation; and, indeed, since that period, psychiatry in German-speaking Switzerland has had close links with German psychiatry. See J. Janner, 'Die forensisch-psychiatrische und sanitätsdienstliche Beurteilung von Dienstverweigerern,' *Schweizerische Medizinische Wochenschrift*, vol. 93 (1963), 819–26.

4 Christian Neff, 'Die Wehrlosigkeit der Mennoniten und der Weltkrieg,' *Die Eiche*, vol. 12 (1924), 182; Harold S. Bender in the *Mennonite Encyclopedia*, vol. 3 (1957), 680. The noncombatant exemption covered Alsatian Mennonites, who became German citizens after the Franco-Prussian war of 1870, and their young men took advantage of this privilege; see Jean Séguy, *Les assemblées anabaptistes-mennonites de France* (Paris and The Hague, 1977), 576. It is possible that conscripts from the *Neutäufer* (New Baptists), a sect closely related to the Mennonites which had fairly recently spread from Switzerland, may have been covered by this privilege, too. But I have come across no instances of this; not surprisingly, since there were very few New Baptists in Germany.

5 M. James Penton, *Apocalypse Delayed: The Story of Jehovah's Witnesses* (Toronto, 1985), 255.

6 Garbe, *Zwischen Widerstand*, 45. Exact figures are not available for this period. But we do know that in 1918 there were 3,868 *Verkündiger* ready to

proclaim the new faith, organized in nearly one hundred congregations (ibid., 58).

7 Charles Taze Russell, *The New Creation*: series VI in *Studies in the Scriptures* (Brooklyn NY, 1912), 594–5. 'So bleibe man in der Linie,' if the requested *Sanitätsdienst* is refused, 'aber erinnere sich dass dem Befehl, einen Nebenmenschen niederzuschiessen, Gehorsam nicht geschuldet wird' (quoted by Garbe, *Zwischen Widerstand*, 47, from Russell, *Die neue Schöpfung*, 551). Russell seems to have derived his antimilitarism from contacts with George Stetson, a member of the pacifist Advent Christian Church; see Penton, *Apocalypse*, 16, 17, 309, 313.

8 Garbe, *Zwischen Widerstand*, 47, 48.

9 Ibid., 47, n. 15, 58.

10 See my *Freedom from Violence: Sectarian Nonresistance from the Middle Ages to the Great War* (Toronto, 1991), 250–3.

11 Jacob Michael Patt, 'The History of the Advent Movement in Germany' (Ph.D. diss., Stanford University, 1958), 257–9, 262, 271, 272. 'After the church authorities gave their open support to the government,' writes Patt, 'Adventist enlisted men could not easily defend their opposition to Sabbath labor and regular military duties and they could no longer hope for the leniency previously given them.' Nevertheless, 'a few Adventist soldiers ... maintained their religious scruples and had to pay the harsh consequences.'

12 Ibid., 269, 270, 274. In the summer of 1917, the police in Pomerania uncovered an Adventist group which offered refuge to soldiers deserting because of religious objections to continued service in the army. See Benjamin Ziemann, 'Verweigerungsformen von Frontsoldaten in der deutschen Armee 1914–1918,' in A. Gestrich, ed., *Gewalt im Krieg: Ausubüng, Erfahrung und Verweigerung von Gewalt in Kriegen des 20. Jahrhunderts* (Münster, 1995), 11. A. Balbach, *The History of the Seventh Day Adventist Reform Movement* (Roanoke VA, 1999), 36, 37, mentions a report presented by Brother Otto Wipf at a conference in Yugoslavia in 1933, in which Wipf claimed that some Reformers were executed as COs during the First World War. First 'one out of every ten' inductees was shot; then, if the rest failed to yield and shoulder a weapon, 'every fifth man ... and every second one' was shot. Wipf concluded that only 'the day of judgment' would reveal the number of Reformer COs who were annihilated by the German military. Michael W. Casey (Pepperdine University), to whom I am grateful for bringing my attention to this source, understandably doubts the accuracy of Wipf's report. I am also grateful to Professor Casey for sending me xeroxes of three accounts of German Pentecostals allegedly executed as COs during the

First World War. See *The Bridegroom's Messenger* (Atlanta GA), no. 171 (1 June 1915), 3, and no. 218 (Nov./Dec. 1919), 1; and *Weekly Evangel* (St Louis MO), no. 95 (1 June 1915), 1. As in the case of Wipf's account, these reports supply few concrete details. But they date from the war itself, and the authors (F. Bartleman and Eric Booth-Clibborn), who were leading Pentecostals in the United States, were well informed concerning the Pentecostal community in wartime Germany. They were both fluent in German. All this makes their information likely to be generally correct. Most Pentecostals, whether in Germany or elsewhere, were still pacifists. The report in the *Weekly Evangel* states that some German Pentecostal conscripts, evidently unwilling to face prison or psychiatric ward or firing squad, went 'with the armies, not knowing how to do otherwise, but praying that God [would] save them from taking the life of any man.'

13 Ohrtmann, *Die Bewegung*, 10; Grünewald, *Zur Geschichte*, 33–8. Grünewald (p. 38) mentions the name of an anarchist objector from Hamburg, Hans Schreier, who died during his imprisonment in Spandau military jail, where a number of other COs were held. See also John W. Graham, *Conscription and Conscience: A History 1916–1919* (London, 1922), 258, 259.

14 'A person cannot escape punishment for doing something or failing to do something because this results from his conscience or from a tenet of his religion' (Art. 48 in A. Romer and Carl Rissom, eds, *Militär-strafgesetzbuch für das Deutsche Reich vom 20 Juni 1872 ...* [Berlin, 1912], 153). According to the editors (p. 323), refusal by members of a sect like the Seventh-day Adventists to bear arms (or work on their Sabbath) is thereby made subject to punishment by military law. Whether any kind of exemption should be granted must be left entirely to the discretion of the commanding officer. But in such cases it would be appropriate to call in the assistance of an army chaplain.

15 Robert Gaupp, 'Dienstverweigerung aus religiösen (und politischen) Gründen und ihre gerichtsärztliche Beurteilung,' *Medizinisches Correspondenz-Blatt des Württembergischen ärztlichen Landesvereins*, vol. 88 (1918), 168. Gaupp's opinion is confirmed by the only available case of this kind from the pre-war era; see M. Köppen, 'Über einen reinen Fall von überwertiger Idee und über seine forensische Beurteilung,' *Charité-Annalen*, vol. 29 (1905), 304–13. Köppen describes how in 1901, under the influence of Tolstoy and other antiwar writers the reservist Paul M., 'a simple shoemaker,' had refused further service. His regimental commander had then placed him in a hospital for psychiatric examination; however, the final result, in the form of a *Gutachten* by Köppen himself, only confirmed the man's sanity even if his concern for peace and world reform, in Köppen's opinion, might be called obsessive.

16 Erwin H. Ackerknecht, *A Short History of Psychiatry*, 2nd edn, translated from the German by Sula Wolff (New York and London, 1968), 82.

17 Edward Shorter, *A History of Psychiatry: From the Era of the Asylum to the Age of Prozac* (New York, 1997), 81. Cf. Dirk Blasius, *'Einfache Seelenstörung': Geschichte der deutschen Psychiatrie, 1800–1945* (Frankfurt am Main, 1994), 61–115 ('Psychiatrie im deutschen Kaiserreich').

18 One report was anonymous. For biographical data about some of the remaining authors, I am grateful to Professor Edward Shorter.

19 In his article (cited above, note 15) in the *Medizinisches Correspondenz Blatt*, vol. 88 (1918), 167–9 and 175–7, Gaupp discusses eleven CO cases. In two additional (and largely overlapping) articles, both entitled 'Die gerichtsärztliche Beurteilung der militärischen Dientsverweigerung aus religiösen Gründen,' he deals with two more cases: *Münchener Medizinische Wochenschrift: Organ für amtliche und praktische Ärzte*, vol. 64 (1917), 950, 951, and *Zeitschrift für die gesamte Neurologie und Psychiatrie: Originalien* (cited below as *ZNPO*), vol. 15 (1918), 92, 93.

20 Gaupp, *Correspondenz-Blatt*, 176.

21 Ibid., 177.

22 Ibid., 168, 169. It is difficult to know whether Gaupp was always correct here. The men in question were undoubtedly rather unusual characters: one, for instance, had refused to serve because an inner voice he believed was God's had told him war was the devil's work; another had refused because Jesus had brought him the same message; a student, reared in a family of socialists and antimilitarists, had displayed suicidal tendencies along with his consistent war resistance as well as a martyr-complex; a garment worker, whose father was a member of an intentional religious community, had combined personal asceticism with a stubborn refusal to wear military uniform; a refractory conscript had led the life of a tramp wandering, homeless, from one end of Germany to another. But whether their objection to military service resulted from any paranoid or psychotic characteristics they may have possessed is another matter. As Gaupp himself stated: religious behaviour can indeed be 'abnormal, that is, deviating from the normal, but it is not [necessarily] pathological in the sense of a symptom of an existing mental illness.'

23 Ibid., 175, 176.

24 Wilhelm Schmidt, *Forensisch-psychiatrische Erfahrungen im Kriege* (Berlin, 1918), 121. This book was Schmidt's *Habilitationsschrift*; it was based on 107 cases of military delinquency sent by the army between January 1915 and mid-1917 to the psychiatric clinic at the University of Freiburg, where Schmidt was then working. Only one of the cases, however, was that of a

CO: an Adventist but seemingly a member of the main branch and not of the Reformation Movement. The man had served as a non-commissioned officer in an artillery regiment for two years before coming to the conclusion that combatant service was forbidden by the Bible – as his denomination had previously taught.

25 Ibid. A rather similar response was made by some of the theologians and jurists attending Gaupp's first lecture on COs at the Tübingen Medical Society on 29 January 1917 in the course of the discussion that followed his lecture. His second lecture was given on 23 February 1918 in Stuttgart as a *Militärärztlicher Fortbildungsvortrag*.

26 'Kriegsärztlicher Abend der Zehlendorfer Lazarette am 24 Juli 1918 – Zwei Soldaten, die jeden Dienst verweigerten,' report in *Neurologisches Centralblatt*, vol. 37 (1918), 704. The CO assessed as completely sane was an Adventist; the other 'patient,' whose religious affiliation was not given, was said to suffer from hebephrenia, that is, 'psychosis in the young.'

27 Gaupp, *Correspondenz-Blatt*, 176.

28 S. Loeb, 'Dienstverweigerung aus religiösen Gründen und ihre gerichtsärztliche Beurteilung,' *Psychiatrisch-Neurologische Wochenschrift*, vol. 20 (1918), 204. Loeb worked as chief physician in the military reserve hospital at Ahrweiler. There he had been personally responsible for assessing the case of a thirty-three-year-old Seventh-day Adventist CO, who had served in the army as a combatant soldier before becoming convinced that this was incompatible with his religious faith. Loeb's *Gutachten*, while granting that the man might be regarded as a fanatic, dismissed the idea of his being mentally ill. However, Loeb at the same time pointed out that there was really 'no sharp dividing line' between a religious fanatic who was sane and one who was insane (*verrückt*). Details of this case are given in ibid., 191–4. For a similar case (this time of a Bible Student) and similar psychiatric conclusions, see W. Horstmann (Stralsund), 'Religiosität oder Wahn?' *ZNPO*, vol. 49 (1919), 218, 220–6, 230, 231. Horstmann's opinion reversed that of 'a well-known and experienced psychiatrist,' who had declared the man first to be a psychopath, then a paranoiac, but in any case not responsible for his actions – and therefore legally exempt from military service while undergoing treatment in an asylum.

29 Ibid., 199, 201.

30 Ibid., 200.

31 This opinion was given around the end of the war when changes in the law were to be expected.

32 O. Marienfeld, 'Über einen Fall von Kriegsdienstverweigerung aus religiösen Gründen,' *Psychiatrisch-Neurologische Wochenschrift*, vol. 25

(1923), 158 (from a report on the case of a Polish Bible Student from Poznania sent by the army for observation to the psychiatric clinic at Rostock-Gehlsheim in March 1918). See pages 156–8 for an account of this CO case, written apparently several years after the war was over.

33 Shorter, *History of Psychiatry*, 107, 108.

34 Josef Peretti, 'Erfahrungen über psycho-pathologische Zustände bei Kriegsteilnehmern,' *Schmidts Jahrbücher der in- und ausländischen gesamten Medizin*, vol. 84 (1917), esp. 259.

35 For the place of the concept of degeneration in nineteenth-and early twentieth-century psychiatry, see Ackerknecht, *Short History*, 54–9; Shorter, *History of Psychiatry*, 93, 94.

36 Peretti concluded his brief account of the Bible Student preacher's case with the words: 'Das Gutachten musste sich für Unzurechnungsfähigkeit ausprechen.'

37 Adolf Hoppe, 'Militärischer Ungehorsam aus religiöser Überzeugung,' *ZNPO*, vol. 45 (1919), 395–9.

38 Ibid., 400–11. Marienfeld, 'Über einen Fall,' 160, comments aptly on Hoppe's arguments: 'That a man is ready to face prison, or even the death penalty, for the sake of his idea does not seem to support the theory that this idea springs from war weariness. I consider it must have deeper roots.'

39 A.H. Hübner, *Über Wahrsager, Weltverbesserer, Nerven und Geisteskrankheiten im Kriege: Vortrag gehalten in der Anthropologischen Gesellschaft in Bonn* (Bonn, 1918), 3, 13–19. See also E. Meyer, 'Religiöse Wahnideen und Kriegsdienst,' *Deutsche Medizinische Wochenschrift*, vol. 44 (1918), 645, for a similarly negative view of the intellectual capacity of two (presumably) Bible Student COs kept for observation in a psychiatric clinic in Königsberg.

40 From Grünewald, *Zur Geschichte*, 33–6, we can identify him as Erwin Cuntze.

41 Across the Atlantic, members of a Board of Inquiry, which had been set up by the U.S. administration in June 1918 to investigate that country's CO situation, encountered the same difficulties with respect to Mennonite ploughboys who appeared before them. Almost echoing the words of some of the German psychiatrists vis-à-vis their sectarian COs, the army lawyer on the Board described the Mennonite CO as follows: 'He shuffles awkwardly into the room – he seems only half awake. His features are heavy, dull and almost bovine.' 'It is difficult to realize that we have among our citizenry a class of men who are so intellectually inferior and so unworthy to assume its burdens and responsibilities.' In the majority of cases examined 'their ignorance and stupidity' amazed him. See Walter Guest Kellogg, *The Conscientious Objector* (New York, 1919), 38–41. For the Board it was the

middle-class Quaker COs who were the good boys; Board members easily established rapport with them as I suppose psychiatrists in Germany might have done with the middle-class Mennonite COs who served as noncombatants in the German army, had they ever encountered any of them.

42 Gaupp's general attitude, however, was far from liberal, as Blasius, '*Einfache Seelenstörung*,' 120–3, 130, 140, has shown. In the interwar years he became a leading protagonist of German 'racial hygiene.' According to Blasius, his strongly nationalist psychiatry 'prepared the ground for National Socialist psychiatry' (p. 120).

19 Imperial Russia at War and the Conscientious Objector, August 1914 – February 1917

In the First World War, between the outbreak of hostilities in August 1914 and the fall of the monarchy in February 1917, the Russian Empire produced more conscientious objectors to military service (COs) than did any other country in Europe for the whole period of the war, except Great Britain. The basic cause of this phenomenon lay in the existence of a rich tradition of sectarianism within the Empire. True, not all these sects were pacifist. But some sects espoused nonviolence; in the case of others, a sizeable number of their adherents held that it was wrong for a Christian to bear arms. The conversion of the great novelist Leo Tolstoy to Christian pacifism in the late 1870s helped to spread the idea of nonviolence (nonresistance as Tolstoy called it) and gain recruits for the pacifist cause, even though the Tsarist autocracy hindered the spread of his socio-political writings and continued to jail his disciples when they refused to perform military service if drafted.[1]

The strength of the Russian army at the outset of the war was around 2,700,000 men; by the beginning of 1917, the figure had risen to around 6,900,000.[2] COs constituted indeed an infinitesimal fraction of the total number of men under arms during this period. From the point of view of the military, the main worry, especially when the war was going badly, was that COs might encourage malingering or outright desertion from the forces, that the line between conscientious objection to bearing arms and draft-dodging might blur. For COs, of course, there was no question of such mergence; virtually all of them based their stand on a religious principle.

A historian of conscientious objection during the early Soviet period has pointed out the 'extreme difficulty' presented by any attempt to analyse the relationship of Russian sects at that time to military service. For one thing, there were so many of them; their doctrines, too, had changed over time since their often obscure origins. Repression by the Tsarist autocracy sometimes caused them to conceal their true beliefs from the authorities and general public alike. Those sects that reflected folk piety rather than middle- or upper-class religiosity produced at most only an oral devotional literature.[3]

We may divide the sects producing COs into four categories. In the first place come the Mennonites, who enjoyed a privileged position with respect to military service. Spiritual descendants of the sixteenth-century Anabaptists, Mennonites adhered to nonresistance (*Wehrlosigkeit*): any member who agreed to bear arms was excluded from the congregation of believers. By the conscription act of 1874, Mennonite draftees were assigned to work in forestry camps (*Forsteidienst*) (see above). The forestry servicemen wore special uniforms and were under semi-military discipline. However, the Mennonite brotherhood financed the camps on the basis of a rate levied on church members according to their income; and it was in charge of the day-to-day running of the camps, while the work program was the responsibility of government-appointed forestry officials. During the Russo-Japanese War, Mennonite draftees were allowed to volunteer for ambulance work on the Far Eastern front. The men remained civilians but worked alongside the military under the umbrella of a non-military body, usually the Red Cross. This became a precedent in the Mennonite response to the First World War.

Beginning in August 1914, with government approval, Mennonite 'recruits could choose whether they served in forestry camps, or in ambulance units attached to army medical corps at the front, or sometimes in military hospitals.'[4] Men were allowed, if they wished, to transfer from a forestry camp to an army medical unit. Mennonites, after preliminary training, served both on Russia's western front and on the Caucasian front facing Turkey.[5] By this date, with the exception of a few isolated pockets of rigorism Mennonites had become enthusiastic supporters of the monarchy, anxious to serve the Emperor in war as in peacetime, provided their conscientious scruples concerning arms-bearing were respected. No other COs in the Empire enjoyed this status.

Secondly, many COs were drawn from a variety of indigenous sects. The Molokans, or Spiritual Christians, undoubtedly produced more COs than any other sect in this category. But, although they espoused nonviolence officially, most of their draftees, especially from among the more well-to-do sections of the sect, did not refuse to bear arms. Perhaps the most consistent pacifists among these indigenous sects were the Malevantsy, followers of the charismatic Kondratii Malevannyi, who had been influenced by Tolstoy's teachings. His disciples, on the Tolstoyan model, were vegetarians and refused to bear arms when drafted. They also abstained from alcoholic drinks and from smoking.[6] The sect, which remained small in numbers, was at first confined to Ukraine, though in the early twentieth century it began to spread slowly outside that area. The Judaizers and Sabbatarians, who celebrated Saturdays as their sabbath, were drawn, on the other hand, from the Great Russian population of the Empire.[7] Other small groups producing COs included the Dobroliubovtsy, Dukhobors, Jehovists, Netovtsy, New Israelites, as well as the Trezvenniki, who espoused not only teetotalism but nonresistance and vegetarianism as well.[8] A curiosity is provided by a small rural sect whose members called themselves Quakers. They carried their nonviolent ethic to the extreme of never killing body lice, at any rate purposefully! How they acquired their name is unclear: no connection has been established with the Anglo-American Quaker Society of Friends.

Thirdly, the Tolstoyans – sometimes known as Free Christians – if not yet very numerous, formed an important component of the Russian pacifist movement through the Master's powerful testimony from the late 1870s on behalf of nonviolence and through his unstinting support for COs, which ceased only with his death in 1910. Near the end of his life, Tolstoy defended conscientious objection in the following words: 'The motive for these refusals is always the same: ... the belief that a civil law exacting military service, that is to say the preparedness to kill by order from above, can only be in opposition to all religious and moral law which is always founded on love of one's neighbor.'[9] Unlike the Mennonites, Tolstoyans and some Russian sectarian pacifists were radical antimilitarists, who regarded the state with hostility and, when war came, opposed it vigorously.

Lastly come the Baptists and Evangelical Christians as well as the Seventh-day Adventists, sects that were originally imported from abroad by foreign-born missionaries. The Russian Baptist Union had been established in the 1880s, including from its inception a number of small evangelical groups centred in the south of the Empire. Some of these groups were known collectively as Stundists. In 1909, under the leadership of Ivan Prokhanov, a sizeable group of Baptists had split with the main body and formed an All-Russian Union of Evangelical

Christians, though the two denominations did not differ essentially on doctrine.[10]

Before the war neither sect espoused pacifism. When war broke out in 1914, Russian Baptist leaders gave unconditional support to the war effort. The Evangelical Christians did so too – but differences of opinion soon revealed themselves in that body. Though Prokhanov was pro-war, a minority took a pacifist stand; and there were pastors who urged their draft-age members to refuse to bear arms.[11] In fact, even before the war, Evangelical Christians had shown more tolerance towards pacifism in their midst than the Baptists had done.[12] The Seventh-day Adventists were an import from the United States via Germany. While American Adventists have maintained down to the present a position of noncombatancy established by church leaders during the Civil War, noncombatancy was largely abandoned on the European continent even before the outbreak of war in 1914. After war was declared, leaders of the church in both Germany and Russia had assured their respective governments of their support in the ensuing military struggle, even though that would mean Adventists on one side of the battle-line would be shooting at Adventists fighting on the other side.

In the Russian Empire before the war, Adventist COs seem to have been in good standing in their congregations, and after the outbreak of hostilities, the sect produced a larger number of COs during wartime than one might expect from its comparatively small numbers in Russia at that time. What indeed is difficult to explain is the large number of COs emerging from two denominations – Baptists and Evangelical Christians – which, we have seen, had taken an unambiguously non-pacifist stand before the war and had hastened in August 1914 to rally behind their country's war effort. The pacifist wave in these two denominations was, however, to gain momentum during the years following the Bolshevik revolution and subsided only with the repression of religion inaugurated by Stalin in the late 1920s.

In May 1917 a prominent Tolstoyan, Konstantin Shokhor-Trotskii, had received from the Department of Religious Affairs of the Ministry of Internal Affairs a list (*vedomost'*) giving a statistical breakdown of the religious affiliation of men who had been tried by military courts for refusing to perform military service 'on grounds of conscience.'[13] The list covered the period from the general mobilization in July/August 1914 to 1 April 1917. Fifteen sects are mentioned by name, with a total of 588 objectors plus an additional 249 whose religious affiliation was not known, making a total of 837 objectors. The list contains a further breakdown according to military districts (*voennye okruga*), of which thirty are listed. The list is undoubtedly incomplete, especially since at the time it was compiled a number of COs were awaiting trial and sentencing and, therefore, did not figure there.[14] However, the proportion of COs contributed by the various groups is not likely to have differed radically even if we were in possession of complete figures.

The Evangelical Christians head the list with 256 COs, followed by the Baptists with 114 and the Seventh-day Adventists with 70. Thus the non-indigenous category provided the overwhelming majority of COs whose religious affiliation appeared on the list. Of the sects of Slavic origin, Molokans contributed 28 objectors, Malevantsy 27, Tolstoyans (together with Free Christians) 26, Dukhobors and Sabbatarians 16 each, Dobroliubovtsy 13, with several others contributing less than 10. The fact that staunchly pacifist sects, like the Trezvenniki, do not figure on the list may be explained perhaps by their being submerged in the 'affiliation-unknown' category. Likewise, the comparatively small number on the list from the indigenous sects in comparison with those belonging to the three sects of foreign origin may be deceptive, since objectors from the mostly small and rural Slavic pacifist sects probably also lie hidden under the designation 'affiliation-unknown.'

The experiences of wartime COs appearing before army tribunals varied considerably not only from one military district to another but from one case to another in the same military district. Apparently there was no established norm.[15] For instance, in 1916 COs tried in the Moscow military district received sentences as comparatively mild as two years in a penal battalion and as severe as fifteen years' *katorga* (i.e., penal servitude), with the average sentence situated somewhere in between. As before the war, military tribunals sometimes deprived COs of their civil rights.[16] Overall, with the declaration of war, sentences had increased in severity: three years in a penal battalion to be followed by anything between four and twenty years' *katorga* was not unusual. (We have no overall statistics, though, concerning the length of sentences given COs during the war years.) By the beginning of 1917, we find COs being sentenced to penal servitude for life (*bessrochnaia katorga*).[17] But liberation was then close at hand.

Increased wartime penalties for conscientious objection were understandable. For one thing, refusal to fight for one's country might easily be interpreted as sympathy with the enemy as well as a failure to perform one's duty as a citizen. Moreover, 'the numbers [of COs] shot up and got steadily worse.'[18] That must have seemed alarming.

For a detailed memoir recounting a CO's experience of life in a penal battalion, we have to go back to the 1890s.[19] But, in a lengthy report submitted to the Provisional Government by two leading Tolstoyans,[20] we do get a few glimpses of the conscript troubles as well as the mind-set of non-Mennonite wartime COs. The available evidence, though, relates exclusively to the early stages of their army career.

While all COs were united in their refusal ever to shoot to kill, some objectors, in the absence of a civilian alternative, were anxious to perform noncombatant service – preferably ambulance work – within the framework of the army.[21] (This was what the law allowed Mennonite draftees to do.) In 1915 in Kazan, for instance, we find private Filipov pleading with his company commander to assign him to an ambulance unit, though he was willing to undertake 'any noncombatant duties ... which my conscience could accept so that I will be of use to the Fatherland ... Only I won't kill.' His request, however, was rejected, and a military court finally sentenced him to seven years in a civilian prison. From the Kazan court, one Pantelyushik received a similar penalty for taking the same stance, even though his superiors described him 'as gentle and unassuming, ... and punctilious in carrying out his duties as long as these did not entail handling a weapon.' For the same year, a CO named Golik told the Moscow military district court that, while he 'categorically' refused to carry a gun, he was quite ready to be a stretcher-bearer or army baker or camp cook or even to dig trenches. He did not object to taking a military oath (which most COs were not ready to do). He considered it was his duty 'to protect the Tsar and the Fatherland by every means not entailing having to kill.' He wished, moreover, to serve without pay: it was enough that he was doing his duty. All this to no avail; the court sentenced him to sixteen years' *katorga*. Next year we find private Sarikov, though 'ready to work joyfully in the barracks or camp kitchen,' being sentenced to fifteen years of the same for his refusal to become a combatant soldier. In only one of the nineteen cases discussed in the Tolstoyans' report was a CO's request to be assigned to noncombatant service in the army granted.[22]

We read of an eighteen-year-old CO, Nikolai Iakhovskii, belonging to the Malevantsy sect in Ukraine, being subjected in the autumn of 1915 to a fictive execution. After he had been told he had been sentenced to death, ten soldiers charged with bayonets fixed; they lunged at him and knocked him down so that he at once lost consciousness.

His fellow draftees afterwards said of him: 'Iakhovskii has undergone death once; next time he will have nothing to fear.'[23]

Several of the COs whom the Tolstoyans report as willing to accept noncombatant service in the army, at the same time expressed their readiness to face a firing squad rather than handle a weapon. But were there, we may ask, any executions of COs during the First World War as would happen during the ensuing Russian Civil War and then again in the Soviet Union around the outset of the Second World War? There were indeed rumours of such executions, but, to my knowledge, no reliable evidence exists that any took place in this period.

Sufficient evidence is not available to judge how frequently manhandling and torture were employed to induce submission on the part of a CO, nor do we know in how many cases such methods were successful.[24] There was no Tolstoy any longer to bring abuses of this kind to the attention of the public and exert moral influence on the government to stop them; anyhow it was wartime when any talk of war resistance was regarded as dangerous by most people. The Tolstoyans were themselves a suspect group.

Isolation must have been one of the most difficult circumstances encountered by non-Mennonite COs. (Of course, some of them could also rely on support from their coreligionists, whether they belonged to a sizeable denomination like the Molokans or a small one like the Malevantsy.) And Adventist COs often found it hard to explain their unwillingness to work on Saturdays in addition to carrying a gun on a weekday. Newly drafted men may have fared better than the reservists or serving soldiers, who only now declared their conscientious objection to fighting: the military were likely to regard such men as shirkers or cowards, even if some of them had joined a pacifist sect since their previous stint of army service. The many religious seekers among the COs, who lacked a sectarian label (they had mostly been reared in the Orthodox Church), must have provided a puzzle to the usually unsophisticated army command, who had to deal with them.[25] But there is no evidence to show that such men fared worse in camp or military court than COs with denominational affiliations. Perhaps the fact that they did not possess a group affiliation made them appear less of a menace than COs belonging to a body with expansive potential.

The ethnic composition of the wartime CO community is difficult to define with any exactitude, and an attempt at quantification is out of the question in view of the paucity of sources. Mennonites, despite steady acculturation to Russian society, retained their German-Dutch ancestral identity. In the case of the much smaller church of the Seventh-day Adventists, an 'ethnic and cultural gravitation towards Germany' made most of them reluctant to fight not only on religious grounds but also because of politically motivated objections.[26] The overwhelming majority of other COs, for whom the law provided no alternative in either civilian service or noncombatant army duties, were for sure ethnically Slavic. Can we discover any further breakdown?

The listing of 837 wartime COs, printed by the Soviet publicist Putintsev,[27] gives no indication of either the ethnic identity or the geographical provenance of these men. The breakdown here is by religious affiliation and army corps to which the men had been assigned. However, a list appended to the United Council of Religious Communities and Groups' report of 18 August 1919[28] does throw light on this problem. The list contains, after taking into account 3 errata, the names of 608 non-Mennonite COs arranged in alphabetical order. There is no indication of religious affiliation. But, apart from 11 cases where there is only a blank, the *guberniia* in which each man was drafted is given. Considering most COs were villagers or the products of small country towns, they would usually have been called up in the area of their birth. Obviously we may find here a key to ethnic identity, provided we realize its limited utility.

Since almost all these men must have been drafted between July/August 1914 and February 1917,[29] we have information here for this period concerning nearly 600 men, that is, around three-quarters of the non-Mennonite COs. The list shows 242 of the men were drafted in Ukraine, Kiev *guberniia* leading with 116 names, followed by Kharkov with 49, Poltava with 29, Chernihov with 14, Ekaterinoslav with 12, plus 23 from Ukrainian *gubernii* contributing less than 10 COs.[30] Thus around two-fifths of the total came from Ukraine. Moreover, no *guberniia* outside Ukraine produced more than 28 names, with the majority of the names being spread around a large number of ethnically Russian (and Belarusian) *gubernii*.[31]

Ukraine, we know, was the centre of the 'Russian' Baptist movement and its offshoot, the Evangelical Christians – the two denominations producing the largest number of wartime COs – as well as of a number of small pacifist sects like the Malevantsy; and it was also the home of the 'Russian' Mennonites. Of course, not all those drafted in Ukrainian *gubernii* were ethnically Ukrainian. (On the other hand, some COs from other *gubernii*, for example Kuban, were undoubtedly Ukrainians.) These facts may in part explain the large concentration of COs among the ethnically Ukrainian section of the Empire's population. There is, though, little evidence of separate ethnic *consciousness* among these men. The villagers among them presumably spoke a Ukrainian dialect, but their allegiance was to their religious brotherhood, which was trans-ethnic in character. It was religion, then, rather than 'ethnie,' or nationality, that defined their identity.

The February Revolution brought the release of all political prisoners, including COs.[32] Ironically, the victims of savage wartime sentences had had to serve at most two and a half years, whereas their peacetime predecessors had faced as long as six years' incarceration, followed often by long years in Siberia. With the benefit of hindsight, we can see that the threat to national security, which the authorities believed these *religiozniki* posed, was highly exaggerated. Most of the latter wished to help their country if given the opportunity to do so without compromising their belief in nonviolence, and even antimilitarist activists among the Tolstoyans confined themselves to peaceable methods of opposing the war. Though a sizeable proportion of COs were ethnically Ukrainian, such people nurtured no separatist aspirations. Indeed, Lenin and the Soviet leadership, though doctrinaire atheists, were wiser than the rulers of Imperial Russia when they introduced their extremely liberal CO decree of 4 January 1919. But this is another story.[33]

NOTES

1 See essay 10 above.

2 N.N. Golovin. *The Russian Army in World War I* (Archon Books reprint, 1969), 109; and his *Voenniia usiliia Rossii v mirovoi voine* (Paris, 1939), vol. 1, 181–4.

3 Konstantin Vladimirovich Stvolygin, 'Politika osvobozhdeniia grazhdan ot voinskoi povinnosti po religioznym ubezhdeniiam v Sovetskom gosudarstve (1918–1939 gg.)' (Candidate of Historical Sciences dissertation, University of Minsk, 1997), chap. 3, section 1. See also his *Alternativnaia sluzhba: istoriia i sovremennost'* (Minsk, 1991), 6–7.

4 Lawrence Klippenstein, 'Otkaz ot voennoi sluzhby po motivam sovesti v mennonitskikh obshchinakh tsarkoi Rossii,' in Tatiana A. Pavlova, ed., *Dolgii put' rossiiskogo patsifizma: Ideal mezhdunarodnogo i vnutrennego mira i religiozno-filosofskoi i obshchestvennopoliticheskoi mysli Rossii* (Moscow, 1997), 164–6.

5 For reminiscences of Mennonite draftees in forestry camps and in ambulance units alongside the troops, see Waldemar Guenther et al., eds, *'Our Guys': Alternate Service for Mennonites in Russia under the Romanows*, translated from the German by Peter H. Friesen (Winnipeg, n.d.). Most of the book deals with the First World War. The original German edition was entitled *'Onsi Tjedils'* (Yarrow BC, 1966). The motivation of the Mennonite ambulance units was very similar to that of the Friends Ambulance Unit (FAU) organized – unofficially – by a group of British Quakers. The FAU worked during the First World War on the Franco-German front: it included non-Quakers as well as members of the Society of Friends.

6 F.M. Putintsev, *Politicheskaia rol' i taktika sekt* (Moscow, 1935), 457.

7 Ibid., 465.

8 Ibid., 471.

9 Leo Tolstoy, *The Law of Love and the Law of Violence*, translated from the Russian by Mary Koutouzow Tolstoy (New York, 1970), 59.

10 Paul D. Steeves, 'Evangelical Christians in Russia,' in Joseph L. Wieczynski, ed., *The Modern Encyclopedia of Russian and Soviet History*, vol. 11 (Gulf Breeze FL, 1979), 12–15.

11 Wilhelm Kahle, *Evangelische Christen in Russland und der Sovetunion: Ivan Stepanovich Prochanov (1869–1935) und der Weg der Evangeliumschristen und Baptisten* (Wuppertal and Kassel, 1978), 391, 392.

12 Ibid., 386.

13 Printed in Putintsev, *Politicheskaia rol,'* 96, 97.

14 'Kratkaia zapiska o litsakh, otkazyvaushikhsia ot voennoi sluzhby po religioznym ubezhdeniiam pri tsarskom i vremennom pravitel'stvakh,' report by OSROG (United Council of Religious Communities and Groups), 18 August 1919, in the Russian State Military Archive, Moscow (RGVA), fond 11 [Vseroglavshtab], op. 8, d. 924, 1. 29 (1).

15 Joshua A. Sanborn, *Drafting the Russian Nation: Military Conscription, Total War, and Mass Politics, 1905–1925* (De Kalb IL, 2003), 185, 186.

16 Ibid. Sanborn had access to the court records of some military districts, but of course many such records are still inaccessible or are no longer extant.

17 Kratkaia zapiska, 1. 29 (1). Daniel Heinz, 'Adventisty sed'mogo dnia i otkaz ot uchastiia v voennikh deistviakh v Rossiiskoi Imperii,' in Pavlova, ed., *Dolgii put'* (p. 175) cites the case of an Adventist who, in March 1917, was sentenced to eighteen years in prison plus Siberian exile.

18 Sanborn, *Drafting the Russian Nation*, 185: 'In Kiev military district there were 5 objectors convicted of refusing to serve in 1914 and 44 in 1915. In Moscow military district, the numbers were 4 and 71 respectively, of whom

the vast majority (53) were peasants.' In May 1916 the minister of internal affairs reported that 'the rate of refusals ... was "gradually increasing."'

19 Peter Brock and John L.H. Keep, eds, *Life in a Penal Battalion of the Imperial Russian Army: The Tolstoyan N.T. Iziumchenko's Story* (York UK, 2001). The translation of the memoir is by John Keep.

20 'Dokladnaia zapiska ob otnoshenii k otkazyvaiushchimsia po religioznym pobuzhdeniiam ot voennoi sluzhby,' a privately printed collection of materials compiled by Vladimir Chertkov and Konstantin Shokhor-Trotskii, and presented to the Provisional Government, 15 April 1917; copy in the Russian State Historical Archive, St Petersburg, fond 821 (Department of Religious Affairs, Ministry of Internal Affairs), op. 133, d. 314, 1. 424–56. The information I am referring to here is contained in appendices II–IV.

21 Tolstoyans had discussed the question of noncombatant army service before the war without coming to any consensus. See Mark Popovskii, *Russkie muzhiki rasskazyvaiut: Posledovateli L.N. Tolstogo v Sovetskom Soiuze 1918–1977* (London, 1983), 48. My impression is that many Tolstoyans, possibly a majority, took an unconditional CO stand, though I have no firm evidence for this statement.

22 Dokladnaia zapiska, 1. 47 (7) – 48 (9).

23 Ibid., 1. 48 rev. (10) – 50 (13). See my article 'The Fictive Execution of a Russian Conscientious Objector in World War One,' *Peace and Reconciliation*, vol. 3, no. 4 (November/December 2002), 5–7. Cf. the similar treatment by the Confederate military of an eighteen-year-old Quaker draftee from Tennessee, Tilghman Vestal; see my anthology *Liberty and Conscience: A Documentary History of the Experiences of Conscientious Objectors in America through the Civil War* (New York, 2002), 159–66.

24 Cf. the case of the nineteen-year-old Ukrainian Baptist CO, Ivan Danil'chenko, drafted in September 1915. Refusing to carry a gun, the boy was repeatedly tortured: beaten unconscious with rifle butts, starved, forced to stand with a heavy sack filled with gravel on his back until, exhausted, he collapsed onto the ground, etc. After several months of this kind of treatment, he managed to smuggle out a letter to a sympathetic military attorney asking whether legally such 'humiliation' could be imposed on him without a court order. The Tolstoyans, who report this case (Dokladnaia zapiska, 1. 50 [13]), eventually lost sight of the man. Did he die as the result of his sufferings? Or had he agreed in the end to bear arms?

25 A good example of a CO whose position resulted directly from study of the Bible and 'the voice of conscience' is Arkadii Manulam. Born a Jew, Manulam joined the Orthodox Church when he became an adult. But a reading of the New Testament now convinced him that Christianity and war were

totally incompatible, and, when drafted in 1915, he decided to become a CO at whatever cost. It cost him a sentence of eight years' penal servitude from the Odessa military district court. See Dokladnaia zapiska, 1. 50 rev. (14), 51 (15). For another odd man out, see the case of the reservist Roman Korop, recalled to the colours early in 1916; ibid., 1. 52 (17), 52 rev. (18). Private Korop, 'after a long religious search,' could no longer, he said, conscientiously serve as a soldier. He wrote from his village to his commanding officer to tell him that he would remain at home until they removed him by force to face, he knew, certain punishment. He asked pardon for the trouble he was causing. 'But I can act in no other way.'

26 Heinz, 'Adventisty,' in Pavlova, ed., *Dolgii put,'* 175.

27 See note 6 above.

28 The list is entitled 'Spisok lits, otkazyvavshikhsia ot voennoi sluzhby po religioznym ubezhdeniiam pri tsarskom i vremennom pravitel'stvakh.'

29 Because (1) only a small number of COs emerged under the Provisional Government, and (2) comparison with the fairly comprehensive thirty-seven-page report on non-Mennonite COs in the Pavel Miliukov Papers, dated January 1912 ('Kratkaia svedeniia ...' State Archive of the Russian Federation, Moscow [GARF], fond 579, op. 1, d. 2568), shows an overlap of only thirteen names.

30 Taurida (8), Podolia (6), Kherson and Volynia (4), and Odessa (1).

31 Kratkaia zapiska, 1. 32 (1) – 48 (17).

32 In collaboration with the Tolstoyan leadership, the Provisional Government soon began work on an alternative civilian service law for COs. (One of its ministers, the Kadet, A.I. Shingarev, had in 1912 vainly tried to persuade the Third Duma to introduce such legislation.) Although the provincial authorities might sometimes try to re-draft a former CO or force pacifist sectarians living near the battle zone to dig trenches, the Provisional Government strove to prevent such occurrences. See Kratkaia zapiska, 1. 30 (2), 31 (3). The CO question under the Provisional Government needs further – archival – research.

33 See essay 20 below.

20 Vladimir Chertkov and the Tolstoyan Antimilitarist Movement in the Soviet Union

In October 1918, a year after the overthrow of Russia's Provisional Government, Vladimir Chertkov (1854–1936),[1] the former Tsarist army officer who became leader of the Tolstoyan movement after the death of the Master, established an organization to defend the rights of conscientious objectors (COs), and he gained for it the collaboration of the chief sects then supporting a pacifist position. At the same time as this United Council of Religious Communities and Groups (Ob'edinennyi sovet religioznykh obshchin i grupp – OSROG) came into existence, the chairman of the revolutionary Military Council (Revvoensovet), Lev Trotskii, had issued a decree, dated 22 October 1918, assigning COs specifically to army medical units after they had been certified as sincere by a board specially appointed for this task. Religious conviction as the basis for refusal to bear arms remained an essential condition for exemption.

Undoubtedly some pacifist sectarians would have found the decree quite acceptable; they sought only the freedom from actually bearing arms. Work as medical orderlies in military hospitals would have satisfied their consciences and left them with no grounds for complaint. But the Tolstoyans, in particular, objected strongly to the terms of the decree, and Chertkov, who still enjoyed good relations with the Soviet leadership, became their chief spokesman. OSROG, under Chertkov's direction, now petitioned the authorities for a more generously framed CO law. In response, the latter appointed a committee to do just this, inviting Chertkov to become one of its members. The other members included Vladimir D. Bonch-Bruevich, an old friend of the pacifist Dukhobors and the Bolsheviks' expert on sectarianism, and Emilian Iaroslavskii, who, despite his representing the military on the committee, was not unfavourably disposed towards COs. Most importantly, the president of the Council of People's Commissars (Sovnarkom), Vladimir Lenin, believed the existing provisions for COs to be inadequate; in his view, they would only cause more suffering to a group which had already endured enough hardship. Eventually these people, if treated properly, would, he thought, abandon their pacifism and rally to the defence of the workers' state.

The committee held six meetings. Chertkov pressed his views vigorously, pointing out that, while most COs would be satisfied with alternative civilian service, there were some – 'Christian anarchists' – who would not accept any alternative to doing something they believed was right. They were absolutists (like the absolutists, we may add, including many Quakers, who had taken a similar stance in First-World-War Britain). Chertkov also pointed out that the restriction of pacifism to members of religious denominations would exclude many genuine COs who remained unaffiliated. These men were 'free Christians,' independent spirits who refused to attach to their spiritual quest any organizational label.

Chertkov's rejection on behalf of his organization of noncombatant service in the army as a CO alternative – even if performed in a medical unit – met with strong disagreement from Iaroslavskii, who told the Tolstoyan leader that it was 'his primary obligation to make clear to those people, who call themselves disciples of Lev Nikolaevich Tolstoi, that to help the sick, the wounded, the mutilated and those who have lost blood [in combat] is not to participate in violence, is not an act of violence.' In fact, however, the CO decree, issued on 4 January 1919, by the Council of People's Commissars under Lenin's signature, contained no reference to noncombatant army service of any kind. Chertkov's viewpoint had prevailed – largely due to Lenin's intervention.

The decree contained three clauses and a brief note at the end expanding on OSROG's role in administering the decree:

1. Religious COs might substitute for military service such civilian activities as 'medical service, principally in hospitals for contagious diseases, or some other appropriate, socially useful work selected by the inductees themselves, on the basis of a decision of a people's court.' The length of service was to be the same as for conscripts in the armed forces.
2. The Moscow headquarters of OSROG was entrusted with the task of providing the People's Court with 'expert witness,' so that it could

reach a just decision in each case. 'The expert witness should include information that a definite religious conviction excludes participation in military service and that the particular person is acting sincerely and conscientiously.' (No mention was made of membership of a pacifist denomination, or indeed of any religious body, as being essential for gaining exemption as a CO.)

3. 'In exceptional cases' OSROG, if it were unanimous in its decision, might petition 'the presidium of the All-Russian Central Committee of Soviets for complete exemption from military service, without substitution of another civic duty, if it can be especially shown that such a substitution is impermissible not only on the basis of religious conviction in general but also on the basis of sectarian literature as well as the personal conduct of the person concerned.'[2]

The decree of 4 January 1919, when compared with CO legislation in other countries earlier and later, is remarkable for the generosity of its terms and the broad range of options it offered objectors. True, in Britain in both world wars, according to the letter of the law, if not always in practice, even nonreligious objectors could gain exemption if deemed acting from conscientious motives. Such objectors were not included, however, in Lenin's decree. Otherwise, the latter is not exceeded in its liberality by any similar legislation. Though Lenin and his colleagues undoubtedly acted from motives of expediency, surely expediency was also not entirely absent in the considerations prompting, for example, the British legislators in their wartime stance?

At first the authorities accepted all those whom OSROG recommended for exemption. But soon the former became dissatisfied with the way Chertkov and his United Council were interpreting the decree: the feeling grew that anti-Bolshevism, rather than conscience and religious sentiment, provided the motive behind many applications for exemption. It is difficult at this distance in time, and in the inaccessibility of concrete evidence, to judge whether these suspicions were justified. OSROG, on the other hand, considered that it had grounds for grievance in the no longer beleaguered government's treatment of COs, since the protracted civil war as well as any immediate threat of foreign intervention had virtually ended by the autumn of 1920.[3]

The final outcome of this struggle saw the ousting of Chertkov and OSROG from the key position in administering the government's CO policy. On 14 December 1920 Sovnarkom issued an 'amendment and supplement to the decree of 4 January 1919,'[4] by which OSROG's expertise was replaced by 'an expert commission' appointed by the government. 'The People's Court,' the document explained, 'summons for testimony experts who are informed and sympathetic representatives of the corresponding religious confession, primarily from among those who are living in the particular locality and are closely acquainted with the belief and manner of the followers of a particular confession, as well as other persons who possess appropriate information and experience.' Applicants were required now to appear personally before a People's Court; OSROG – or one of its affiliates – was no longer permitted to present the applicant's case in lieu of the man himself. While unconditional exemption might be granted exceptionally, objectors who did not belong to a religious sect, though not specifically excluded from exemption, were clearly in a more ambiguous position than under the original decree.

In fact, a couple of years later the Commissariat for Justice, for the purpose of enabling a reduction in the number of religious groups whose members were eligible for exemption as COs, was to limit exemption to a list of sects which had sponsored conscientious objection under the Tsars, their members suffering severe penalties for their loyalty to this tenet of their faith.[5] But the COs' champions within the party leadership like Bonch-Bruevich were for the time being still able to ward off attempts to seriously restrict – or even abolish – CO exemption.

The Tolstoyans formed, in fact, a rather nebulous group. They did not keep membership lists or hold regular religious services, nor did they insist on any creed to which all had to subscribe. But the sacredness of human life and strict vegetarianism remained fixed tenets of their faith from the genesis of the movement in the 1880s when Tolstoy began preaching his gospel of nonviolence. Few of them, if conscripted, would be ready to accept noncombatant service in the army; some insisted on unconditional exemption, preferring prison to compromise on this issue. At first growth was slow, with the majority of converts coming from the educated classes. By the early 1920s, however, peasants and artisans had come to predominate numerically,[6] even if it was still members of the urban intelligentsia who gave the group its spiritual direction.

At the end of the First World War, we may detect three different, though overlapping, types among the adherents of Tolstoyism. In the first place, there were those who lived in villages and cultivated the soil as peasants. Some of these people owned their own plots of land;

others gained a living as agricultural labourers. There may have been villages where all, or nearly all, the inhabitants thought of themselves as Tolstoyans, though with varying degrees of intensity. Next came the Tolstoyan communitarians, most of them of peasant or artisan background with a few members of the intelligentsia, who had chosen life on the soil as a vocation. These intentional income-pooling communities seem to have been surprisingly successful, especially in comparison with many similar ventures elsewhere, perhaps because most of their members were accustomed to work on the land. The Tolstoyan experiment in living[7] came to an abrupt end in the late 1930s when all their agricultural colonies were closed by the Soviet authorities. The Tolstoyans had pleaded in vain that, apart from the use of violence, they really shared the same ideals and goals as the Communists.[8] Lastly, in Moscow and other major cities, the Tolstoyan movement consisted largely of members of the intelligentsia. In the capital (as Moscow had become under the Soviets), Tolstoyan activities centred in the Society of True Freedom in Memory of L.N. Tolstoy, which was established in mid-1917 and continued to exist until the end of 1923. At its height, the Society numbered around two thousand members.

The Tolstoyan intelligentsia might differ as to the degree of educational qualifications each member possessed. But they shared a common urbanism. And it was the Moscow Tolstoyans, with Chertkov playing the leading role, who shaped the newly emergent antimilitarist movement and represented it in negotiations with the Soviet government, especially with respect to CO legislation. Though other pacifists participated in OSROG, that organization was staffed largely by Moscow Tolstoyans with the assistance of urban Tolstoyans in the provinces, who acted as intermediaries between Moscow headquarters and COs outside the immediate Moscow area.

The Moscow Tolstoyan leadership included both 'old Tolstoyans,' like Ivan Gorbunov-Posadov and I.M. Tregubov as well of course as Chertkov himself, and younger men in their late twenties and thirties, like M.V. Muratov, K.C. Shokhor-Trotskii, and the elder Chertkov's son, Vladimir Vladimirovich Chertkov, who was to succeed in preserving his father's papers throughout the whole dark Stalinist era. Chertkov's wife, Anna, too, gave devoted service to the cause until her death in 1927.[9] It is worth noting that, despite their staunch antimilitarism and pacifist activism (for as long as this was at all possible), none of these people suffered imprisonment – or a worse fate. Was this luck, or chance, or a result of the aureole continuing – even under Stalinism –

to surround the figure of Lev Tolstoy and reflected in some fashion on their own more humble persons?

OSROG, the main aim of which was to defend the interests of COs and promote 'freedom of conscience' in general as well as to link in a closer union the 'various free religious currents' supporting pacifism and nonviolence, had resulted from Tolstoyan initiative.[10] It started activities in October 1918 – with Chertkov as its president, assisted by Shokhor-Trotskii, who also displayed immense energy and resourcefulness in dealing with a complex and sensitive situation. The executive committee consisted of eleven members; besides the Tolstoyans, Baptists, Evangelical Christians, Mennonites, Seventh-day Adventists, and Teetotalers (*Trezvenniki*) sat on the committee, too. Smaller pacifist sects like the Dobroliubovtsy, Dukhobors, Jehovists (Ilin's followers), Malevantsy, New Israelites, Netovtsy (a branch of the Old Believers), Sabbatarians, and Skakuny (the staunchly pacifist section of the largish Molokan denomination, now only partially adhering to absolute pacifism) – sects whose members were mostly located in the countryside or provincial towns – were represented on the United Council by the Tolstoyans, who also acted as spokespeople for the numerous COs who remained unaffiliated to any religious group.[11]

Immediately the CO decree of 4 January 1919 appeared, OSROG printed thousands of copies in leaflet form and began to distribute them widely; it circulated them, in fact, in any part of the country to which it had access and especially in areas where pacifist sectarians were settled. The latter acted as local distributors; of course, they handed out leaflets, too, among their neighbours who were not pacifists and helped in this way to convert some of them to 'the gospel of non-resistance' and to lead their sons, when drafted, to choose the CO option instead of the army. Since war weariness was widespread throughout the country after years first of international conflict and then of civil strife, the message contained in the leaflets frequently met with a positive response both in town and countryside.

OSROG did not leave the work of propaganda to sectarian volunteers. It proceeded to set up a network of agents drawn from convinced supporters of the antimilitarist movement, who also gave legal advice to COs, informing them of their rights and of official procedures by which they could establish their claim for exemption or initiate an appeal if their application was turned down. The latter functions proved especially useful in the months that followed the promulgation of the decree when the exemption process differed widely from one

People's Court to another;[12] in fact, uniformity of procedure was never established. To facilitate the agents' work, OSROG provided them with a printed questionnaire (*osprosnii list*) for CO applicants to fill in; the information, thus gathered, would help the agents in preparing the dossiers in which they formulated their expertise and also aid the COs themselves to clarify the grounds on which they based their objection to bearing arms.

The United Council affiliates sought to provide the 'expertise' required by the decree in all CO cases; in the Moscow area, of course, the central office fulfilled this function. The provincial affiliates kept in close touch with Chertkov and his colleagues, reporting on their work and seeking the latter's advice in difficult or contested cases. Providing expertise often proved a delicate, time consuming, and mentally exhausting occupation in view of the hostility not infrequently shown by local authorities (in contrast to the at first generally positive attitude of the central government). By the end of 1920, OSROG had 117 agents – representatives (*upolnomochennye*) – working in the field. They were to be found scattered over thirty-four regions.[13]

For Chertkov and his colleagues these were exciting times. It must have seemed to them that a new dawn had indeed come, that the cause of nonviolence and human brotherhood would now be realized in the new Soviet state, just emerging from the horrors of civil war. In a report prepared later for war resisters abroad, they told the latter: 'the Moscow U.C. could hardly cope with all the applications for certificates of sincerity, and its secretary and other voluntary workers were working day and night, as every hour of delay meant an extra hour of imprisonment or even death for a CO. The applications for certificates came in bundles, sometimes all the young people of a village applying at one time. More than 30,000 cases of conscientious objection were registered at the U.C. office.'[14]

The United Council normally held meetings of its executive committee (*Prezidium*) twice weekly. Meetings took place in Chertkov's private apartment: an illustration of the key role played by the Tolstoyan leader in OSROG's work. Periodic gatherings of representatives from its provincial affiliates also took place there. These gatherings helped to acquaint the most active supporters of the antimilitarist movement with each other. Spread over a vast area, such people often suffered from a feeling of isolation; they had few means of getting to know each other personally.

Although at first OSROG and central Soviet authorities, on the whole, worked harmoniously, in part because of the friendly relations existing between Chertkov and Bonch-Bruevich, gradually tension arose and misunderstandings multiplied. The government became alarmed at the mass character of the CO movement; some officials felt that through the United Council's negligence, draftees were escaping service by declaring themselves COs – and getting away with it! In particular, exemptions given as a result of the council's expertise to such persons as former army officers, Orthodox priests, and members of the medical profession irritated many officials.

A further cause of alarm, on the part of the Soviet military in particular, lay in occasional attempts by pacifist sectarians living in the provinces (including Tolstoyans) to proselytize among the troops stationed in their vicinity. Desertion rates in this period were high: the possibility of escaping further service in the Red Army might seem attractive to privates and non-commissioned officers, who longed to get back to their families at home. Some of these men, often from the same background as the pacifist peasant sectarians, may have been genuinely attracted to the idea of nonviolence and could rightly be ranked as soldier-COs. But the army was probably correct in its assumption that this was not often the case and that most of these men had really little idea of evangelical nonviolence, despite their verbal adherence to it.

At a conference of sectarians held in Moscow during 6–10 June 1920 – a venture sponsored by OSROG with government support – the question of army desertion emerged several times, giving rise to some rather wild oratory. This may indeed have been why the People's Commissariat of Justice was a little later to describe OSROG – rather inelegantly – as 'a pretty formless anarchistic capitalist association of predominantly bourgeois-intelligentsia groups and persons.' Chertkov voiced the opinion of many delegates in urging 'mass refusals' of military service; this phenomenon, he said, should not alarm pacifists. 'We should rejoice at refusals of military service on whatever grounds; we must not try to dissuade men from doing this.' Another Tolstoyan (Pyrikov) echoed Chertkov's sentiments; he, too, welcomed all deserters from the Red Army. 'Under Tsarist rule,' he stated, 'there were one million deserters, under Kerenskii two million, while today just how many there are nobody knows. Deserters are men who are still weak [i.e., in their antiwar convictions] but they are becoming stronger' in this regard. One delegate demanded why all who refused to bear arms, for whatever reason, should not – pragmatically – be regarded as acting (even unconsciously) from religious conviction.

With regard to labour conscription, which figured alongside the military question as the chief item on the conference agenda, while many Tolstoyans opposed such a measure unconditionally as a form of slavery, delegates representing the major pacifist sects tended, as in the case of the military draft, to express a more moderate view than the Tolstoyans did. For instance, Vladimir Teppone stated: 'As a religious movement, we [Seventh-day Adventists] consider it permissible to obey a labour direction, provided it does not conflict with our conscience. If it does so, then we have no alternative but to refuse obedience.'[15]

The tone of some of the conference sessions as well as the fact that the Tolstoyan delegation was the largest one and easily the most outspoken in its antimilitarist stance, cannot have been welcome in some government circles. We must remember that by no means all influential members of the Soviet hierarchy shared Bonch-Bruevich's benevolent attitude to sectarians. The latter, though a convinced atheist, viewed these people in a different light from most of his fellow atheist militants, who sought to destroy all vestiges of religion as soon as possible.

Getel,' in her study of OSROG, has traced the stages by which the relationship between the pacifists and the Soviet government slowly deteriorated.[16] The government made repeated attempts at controlling the way OSROG used its expertise to win exemption for a wide range of COs – within the terms of the decree of 4 January 1919. OSROG, on the other hand, complained of the way officials, especially in the provinces, circumvented its requirements, thus depriving potential COs of the rights they enjoyed according to Soviet law. In April 1920, and again in January 1921, the authorities raided the offices of OSROG, carrying off its records (which then came into the hands of the secret police, known in that period as the Cheka) and starting an official investigation of the United Council's activities. In the meantime, the OSROG offices were sealed by the secret police, an action severely hampering the organization's work. From its side the Council took steps to counteract these hostile measures. Through Bonch-Bruevich's intermediacy, on 8 September 1920 Chertkov obtained an audience with Lenin, who appeared to be sympathetic. Lenin promised to look into cases of infringement of the CO decree if Chertkov would give him a detailed account of such occurrences; and Chertkov did this in a letter dated 10 November 1920. In the end the Soviet leader entrusted the matter to a specially appointed committee under the chairmanship of the eminent Marxist historian M.N. Pokrovskii. This committee, in turn, rejected Chertkov's allegations as unfounded.[17] And there the matter rested.

A severe blow was dealt OSROG at the end of 1920 when the amending decree of 14 December (see above) removed out of its hands the task, assigned it in the original decree of 4 January 1919, of supplying the expertise for every CO application – and thus virtually putting in its power the possibility of gaining exemption in all cases it regarded as genuine. (The authorities, we know, considered that the United Council often gave the benefit of the doubt to applicants whose sincerity was at best dubious.) 'OSROG continued to exist simply as a legal-aid organization.' The larger pacifist denominations now acted directly on behalf of COs from their midst (as the Mennonites already did) and no longer relied on OSROG to do this. With respect to COs, therefore, the role of the latter narrowed to that of representing applicants coming from a Tolstoyan milieu or those applicants who did not belong to any organized religious group. The small rural pacifist sects also seem to have continued to rely on OSROG for assistance in obtaining exemption for their COs. At any rate, in comparison with the two previous years, henceforward 'its work' was 'on a much smaller scale.'[18]

OSROG leaders, despite setbacks and wavering relations with government and party, went on spreading the pacifist message with unabated energy. The Soviet authorities raised no objections to their organizing another large-scale conference of their supporters. It was held in Moscow in March 1921. Ironically, this all-Russian Congress of Sectarian Agricultural and Production Associations coincided with the trial of Chertkov and six other Tolstoyan leaders; they were, however, soon released from custody and allowed to continue work with OSROG.[19] No penalties were imposed; the government's behaviour, though, contained an implicit warning to them to be careful how they acted in the future.

While delegates at the conference protested against the mounting persecution of religion in Soviet Russia, they remained generally favourable to a communist restructuring of society, a point that would be well regarded among the sectarians' official sympathizers. But the delegates unanimously condemned the recent change in CO legislation, predicting dire consequences from the ousting of OSROG from its role in the exemption process. For one thing, henceforward soldier-COs were not likely to gain exemption, however sincere might be their objections to continued bearing of arms. 'Prisons, concentration camps and other places of incarceration once again begin to be filled with martyrs for the faith who, on account of their religious convictions or the call of conscience, are unwilling to continue to participate in war.' It was asserted that several such people had recently been shot for persisting in their stand.[20]

Different opinions exist today as to how and when OSROG came to an end; such discrepancies may eventually be cleared up when the archives are more fully investigated. At present the most likely date for its closure appears to be 1923. For Chertkov himself, around a decade later, gave 1923 as the year when his organization ceased activities. However, he did add the proviso 'if he was not mistaken.' Thus, Klibanov may still be correct when he states that the end came in 1922. At any rate, the author who claims 1928 as the closing date is surely mistaken. Concerning the circumstances of OSROG's demise, there are also discrepancies. The American civil libertarian Roger Baldwin, who visited Russia in 1927, claims the organization voluntarily ceased activity ('tactfully dissolved' is how he puts it) when it realized it could no longer carry on its antimilitarist activity effectively as a result of harassment from the secret police and obstacles put in its way by the government.[21] Though an outsider, Baldwin gained his information on COs in the Soviet Union from the Moscow Tolstoyans not long after the events he described in his book. His version does indeed appear likely. On the other hand, a party publication issued in 1933 states that OSROG was dissolved by the authorities (in 1922) 'in connection with its proven counter-revolutionary activity.'[22] Again, only further investigation of the archives can confirm one or other account.

Even though prospects for the antimilitarist movement looked increasingly unpromising, Chertkov continued to be optimistic; in fact, when times became still more grim, he does not seem to have abandoned hope in ultimate success. When the prominent German pacifist and feminist Helen Stöcker visited Moscow in September 1923, Chertkov told her that he believed 'even more firmly than ever ... in a spiritual regeneration of vast circles of the Russian people, especially among the peasants.' This, he believed, would, sooner or later, 'put an end to all hatred, all killing of men.' For him, it was 'a joy, a happiness, to live in Russia.'[23]

Within six years Stalin had put an end to the Tolstoyan movement. Though Chertkov himself remained untouched until his death in 1936 (a representative of the government attended his funeral and even said some nice things about the departed), the sole surviving Tolstoyan organization, the Moscow Vegetarian Society, which was founded in 1909, had been closed in 1929. Its newsletter was banned (the censorship had already put a stop to the publication of pacifist literature of any kind), and further public activity on the part of the Tolstoyans was prohibited. Tolstoyans could no longer obtain visas to attend international peace congresses abroad; it was a risky business even to ask for a visa for such a purpose. Though the Soviet government claimed to be peace-loving and in favour of world disarmament, it forbade independent pacifist activity at home. Roger Baldwin was aptly to describe this as 'a state monopoly of pacifism and militarism.' Chertkov now asked war resisters in the West to exercise great caution in reporting on the antimilitarist movement in the Soviet Union and the position of COs there: precautions that became increasingly necessary as the international situation deteriorated during the 1930s. He warned them, too, not to attempt to send peace literature to antimilitarists inside the Soviet Union. Recipients might be penalized for this, since it was an offence either to mail such matter within the country or receive such items from abroad. The penalty could be severe: internal exile or imprisonment as well as probable loss of regular employment.

Subject to increasing official harassment and faced with the ongoing Soviet collectivization of the land, the Tolstoyan agricultural colonies survived for a few more years.[24] But before the decade was finished, they too were shut down. A number of the communitarians were sent to labour camps, where many of them died; many suffered less harsh forms of incarceration, often though for lengthy periods of time; and some were executed. (See essay 21.) A sad conclusion to a movement that had worked to create by peaceful example a nonviolent society based on communist principles!

Appendix

In his old age, the American civil libertarian Roger Baldwin recalled the contacts he had had with Vladimir Chertkov during his visit to the Soviet Union in the summer of 1927. I reprint below the relevant passages from Roger Baldwin, 'Recollections of a Life in Civil Liberties – II: Russia, Communism, and United Fronts, 1920–1940,' *Civil Liberties Review*, vol. 2, no. 4 (Fall 1975), 18. Most of the information about conscientious objectors in Baldwin's *Liberty under the Soviets* (1928), which was to result from this visit, came from Chertkov and his circle. In his

'Recollections,' however, Baldwin refers to Chertkov as Lebedev: a lapse of memory presumably as Chertkov senior died in 1936 and Chertkov junior in 1963, so that neither man could then have been endangered by the mention of his name. For Baldwin's life, see the entry by Norman Dorsen in the *American National Biography* (New York and Oxford, 1999), vol. 2, 61–3.

From Roger Baldwin's 'Recollections' (1975)

I sought out ... the Tolstoians, to whom I had introductions from [American] Quakers, pacifists and conscientious objectors ... Their saint, Tolstoi, was revered by all Russians and honored by the Bolsheviks with the usual museum and street and village names. I met the Nestor of the cult, octogenarian Lebedev, Tolstoi's former secretary and literary executor, a white-bearded old saint right out of a Bible picture. I also met his son, a clerk in the state bank, leader of the Moscow group.

They had, they said, considerable freedom to carry on pacifist activity, but their young men of military age were going to prison for refusal of service, and some of their people had been arrested for allegedly encouraging such refusal. It sounded like home during World War I. I attended a court trial of several of the boys in a crowded room before three judges. They got a better deal than most objectors in the United States did during the war – a public civil trial with the chance to state their views freely, and short sentences to prison.

The Tolstoians arranged a public meeting for me in an open hall with no apparent surveillance. Several hundred attended, and a lively question period followed my talk on civil liberties in the United States. I was astonished when two young men arose to ask questions, stating that they were prisoners of conscience out of jail just for the evening by permission of the warden so they could attend. No warden at home would conceivably have risked his job by taking such a chance.

The Tolstoians had their troubles with the GPU, like everybody else with a dissenting line. I heard old Mr. Lebedev repeatedly on the phone trying to get information about some arrested Tolstoians, and apparently rarely succeeding. But the Tolstoians were treated, on the whole, with consideration by the government. They did not belong to the historically hostile classes; they were workers, many of them small farmers, and they were willing to help the economy if they could keep their freedom to follow their principles. My experience with the Tolstoians left me with no different feeling about their relation to government than the relation of pacifists or conscientious objectors to government at home – except for their caution about attracting attention of the police to private group meetings. No other groups dissenting from government policy at any point were permitted to operate.

NOTES

1 See the entry on Chertkov by William B. Edgerton in Harold Josephson, ed., *Biographical Dictionary of Modern Peace Leaders* (Westport CT and London, 1985), 162, 163.
2 For the history of the decree and its text in English translation, see Paul D. Steeves, ed., *The Modern Encyclopedia of Religions in Russia and the Soviet Union* (Gulf Breeze FL), vol. 5 (1993), 223–5. The decree's Russian text is given in A.I. Klibanov, 'Sektantstvo i stroitelsvo vooruzhennykh sil sovetskoy respubliki (1918–1921 gg.),' in his *Religioznoe sektantstvo i sovremennost (Sotsiologicheskie i istoricheskie ocherki)* (Moscow, 1969), 195, 196. The insertion of the decree's rather convoluted third clause was due primarily to Lenin, who foresaw trouble from a small group of intransigent absolutists if unconditional exemption were not granted them. See Alexei Zverev and Bruno Coppieters, 'V.D. Bonch-Bruevich and the Doukhobors: On the Conscientious Objection Policies of the Bolsheviks,' *Canadian Ethnic Studies*, vol. 27, no. 3 (1995), 80.
3 See Klibanov, 'Sektantstvo,' 202, 203.
4 The text of this amendment, in English translation, is given in *Modern Encyclopedia*, vol. 5, 225, 226.
5 Zverev and Coppieters, 'V.D. Bonch-Bruevich,' 84.
6 Mark Popovskii, *Russkie muzhiki rasskazyvaiut: Posledovateli L.N. Tolstogo v Sovetskom Soiuze 1918–1977 -Dokumentalnyi rasskaz o krestianakh-tolstovtsakh po materialam vyvezennogo na Zapad krestianskogo arkhiva* (London, 1983), 66. Popovskii (in the late 1970s) was the first to reveal the existence of Tolstoyan survivors in the Soviet Union. In 1983, now an exile, he published an account of their earlier communitarian activities based on archives the Tolstoyans had carefully preserved from confiscation by the authorities.
7 Essential reading here is Edgerton, ed., *Memoirs of Peasant Tolstoyans in Soviet Russia* (Bloomington and Indianopolis 1993). For the Russian edition of these memoirs, see A.B. Roginskii, ed., *Vospominaniia krest'ian-tolstovtsev 1910–1930 - e gody* (Moscow, 1989).
8 Among the Tolstoyan leaders, I.M. Tregubov was perhaps the most ready in

expressing his admiration for the Communists' goals and in pointing to the pacifist sectarians as the latter's natural allies in building the new society, which the Soviet Union aimed to become. Speaking at the Seventh All-Russian Congress of Soviets in December 1919, he told the delegates, 'We will not reproach you, and you will not reproach us ... because we are each going toward Communism along different paths. Let each act according to his own conscience and reason' (quoted in Steeves, 'Tolstoyans in Russia and the USSR,' in *The Modern Encyclopedia of Russian and Soviet History*, vol. 39 [1985], 119). For a hardline Bolshevik critique of the 'mendacious' tactics employed by members of the sectarian 'left,' like Tregubov, particularly with reference to military service, see F.M. Putintsev, *Politicheskaia rol' i taktika sekt* (Moscow, 1935), 358–66. Putintsev, of course, was writing during the Stalinist era; a decade or so earlier, the Soviet authorities had not entirely rebuffed such overtures on the part of the Tolstoyans and other sectarians.

9 Klibanov, 'Materialy o religioznom sektantstve w rukopisnom sobranii V.G. Chertkova,' in his *Religioznoe sektantstvo*, 182. This essay provides valuable information concerning the Chertkov Papers in the Russian State Library (Moscow), including their still uncatalogued sections. In the 1920s the 'old Tolstoyans,' Pavel Biriukov and Valentin Bulgakov, lived much of the time abroad, so that neither was particularly active in OSROG or in the antimilitarist movement as a whole.

10 Zverev and Coppieters, 'V.D. Bonch-Bruevich,' 79.

11 Roginskii, ed., *Vospominaniia*, 465. The Trezvenniki, though a small group, had their headquarters in Moscow, unlike the other largely rural minor pacifist sects.

12 E.I. Getel,' 'Ob'edinennii sovet religioznykh obshchin i grupp kak odno iz proiavlenii russkogo patsifizma,' in T.A. Pavlova, ed., *Dolgii put' rossiiskogo patsifizma: Ideal mezhdunarodnogo i vnutrennego mira v religiozno – filosofskoi i obshchestvenno – politicheskoi mysli Rossii* (Moscow, 1997), 307.

13 Roginskii, *Vospominaniia*, 466. In regions where pacifist sectarians were numerous, OSROG appointed representatives in villages and small country towns. Otherwise they seem to have worked in the provincial capitals. Roginskii lists the thirty-four regions in the following order: Petrograd, Novgorod, Smolensk, Vitebsk, Tula, Orel, Vladimir, Nizhni Novgorod, Riazan, Viatka, Kazan, Tambov, Penza, Simbirsk, Saratov, Samara, Tsaritsyn, Astrakan, Uralsk, Orenburg, Ufa, Voronezh, Homel, Mogilev, Kiev, Kharkov, Poltava, Kremenchug, Sumy, Armavir, Piatigorsk, Omsk, Barnaul, and Irkutsk. Thus, not only were the European republics included but Siberia as far as Irkutsk. It is likely that the archives of all – or at least some – of these

regions listed by Roginskii may still contain even today materials relating to the COs of the interwar period – documents relating to their hearings, for instance, or reports of their trials if they were unsuccessful in gaining exemption. A formidable task indeed awaits future researchers!

14 From 'The Antimilitarist Movement in Russia,' printed in *WRI Bulletin No. IV* (March 1924) and reprinted in my *Studies in Peace History* (Toronto, 1991), 90. Although its exact dating is a little uncertain, the passage cited obviously refers to 1919–20 when OSROG's work was at its height. Statistics of CO applications vary from writer to writer (including myself, I regret to have to say) – ranging usually between 30,000 and 40,000 for the period between 1919 and 1921. But it is never quite clear if the given figure refers only to COs dealt with by the Moscow headquarters of OSROG or if it also includes CO applications handled directly by that body's provincial affiliates. More accurate statistics should emerge after further examination of the relevant archives.

15 Klibanov, 'Sektantstvo,' 198–202.

16 Getel,' 'Ob'edinnenii,' 308–12. (See also Roger N. Baldwin, *Liberty under the Soviets* [New York, 1928], 257.)

17 Getel,' 'Ob'edinnenii,' 312; Klibanov, 'Sektanstvo,' 202.

18 Getel,' 'Ob'edinnenii,' 312; 'The Antimilitarist Movement,' 91.

19 Getel,' 'Ob'edinnenii,' 313.

20 Ibid., 312.

21 Zverev and Coppieters, 'V.D. Bonch-Bruevich,' 89 n. 50; Getel,' 'Ob'edinnenii,' 314; Baldwin, *Liberty*, 257.

22 *Leninskii Sbornik* (Moscow, Kraus reprint, 1966), vol. 24 (1933), 188. Klibanov, of course, may have based his 1922 dating of closure on this source.

23 Brock, *Studies*, 86.

24 Getel' ('Ob'edinnenii,' 315, 317 n. 55) cites an extremely courageous instance of antimilitarist activism from as late as 1936. In that year a member of the Tolstoyan agricultural colony in Ukraine, 'the commune of Fraternal Labour [Bratskii trud],' sent letters to Stalin and the Comintern, enclosing the text of the commune's antiwar manifesto addressed to the War Resisters' International in connection with the latter's forthcoming antimilitarist congress. The manifesto called *inter alia* for the establishment worldwide of 'nonviolent communism.' Unfortunately we do not know what was the addressees' reaction, if any, to this bold initiative.

21 Experiences of Conscientious Objectors in the Soviet Union to 1945

During the First World War, as shown in a previous essay, draftees in the Russian Empire refusing to bear arms continued to receive prison sentences as had been the rule in peacetime – unless they were Mennonites, who were assigned either to forestry work (*Forsteidienst*) or to Red Cross ambulance units alongside the troops, or the occasional lucky non-Mennonite conscientious objector (CO) permitted by his commanding officer to perform some kind of noncombatant service. The revolution of March 1917 had brought release from prison. Tolstoyan leaders, headed by Vladimir Chertkov, the Master's closest associate, now began negotiations with the Provisional Government for the establishment of alternative civilian service for genuine COs. The takeover of power by the Bolsheviks in November 1917, however, nullified these efforts. Henceforward pacifists would have to deal with the new ruling elite.

At first the new government had relied on volunteers in the continuing war, first against the external enemy and then against the regime's internal foes. But an increasingly threatening military situation during the early months of 1918 led Lenin and his fellow Bolsheviks to reverse their stance and return to the conscriptionist policy of the former monarchy. Chertkov, meanwhile, had set up the United Council of Religious Communities and Groups (Ob'edinennyi sovet religioznykh obshchin i grupp – OSROG) to represent the interests of conscientious objectors, and OSROG now entered into lengthy negotiations with the government to insure that satisfactory conditions of exemption for COs were included in any new conscriptionist legislation. (See essay 20 above.) The final outcome of these negotiations did credit to Lenin's tolerance and generosity – or, at any rate, to his unwillingness to penalize religious sectarians, who had also been victims of the Tsarist tyranny, sharing the fate of socialist dissidents in prison and exile. He expected anyhow, we know, that, as the communist ethic transformed society, religion would wither away so that eventually no genuine COs would be left in the expanding socialist fatherland.

The decree of 4 January 1919 was extremely liberal. It provided not only alternative civilian work for conscientious objectors, but even unconditional exemption for COs whose consciences forbade them to undertake an alternative obligation for acting as they thought right.[1] At first the machinery of exemption was placed in the hands of OSROG, but subsequent amendments to the decree gradually whittled away that body's administrative functions. After Lenin's death in 1924, further restrictions were imposed, and in 1929, we have seen, the last surviving pacifist organization, the Tolstoyan Vegetarian Society in Moscow, was closed. Open pacifist activity was no longer permitted. During the Stalinist terror of the 1930s, conscientious objection to service in the Red Army virtually ended; at least it went underground. And by 1939, the Soviet government was able to claim that no CO applications had been received over the past two years. It, therefore, removed provision for conscientious objection from the statute book.

The pacifist community in the early Soviet Union consisted almost exclusively of sectarians of one kind or another: the law spoke of 'religious conviction,' that is, belief in a Supreme Being, as the essential basis of a claim for exemption from bearing arms.[2] We may divide Soviet pacifist sectarians into three groups. In the first place come the Mennonites, centred in Ukraine with branch settlements in other parts of the country. Of German origin, they still retained their German dialect and culture though, with the passing of the years, becoming increasingly acculturated to their Slavic environment. Their position as nonresistants had been seriously compromised during the stormy period at the end of the war when many of their young men took up arms, forming the so-called *Selbstschutz*, self-defence units, to protect their settlements against attacks by peasant bandits and Ukrainian partisans.[3] Secondly, Baptists[4] and Evangelical Christians, also of foreign origin (along with the Seventh-day Adventists),[5] contributed the largest number of post-war COs, though eventually most of their church leaders were pressured by the authorities into rejecting pacifism and the CO position. Thirdly come a number of indigenous Slavic sects which, at least in theory, espoused nonresistance: among the best known were the Dobroliubovtsy, Malevantsy, New Israelites, Sabbatarians, Skakuny (the Molokan subsect that remained staunchly pacifist), and the Teetotalers (*Trezvenniki*). Lastly, the Tolstoyans, often calling themselves Free Christians and espousing vegetarianism as well as communitarianism, remained an extremely influential component of the CO movement: they were respected by the government, in name at least, because of the Master's continuing reputation and so long as Chertkov lived (he died in 1936), though in reality subject to increasing persecution that included long sentences served in Siberian labour camps.[6]

In this essay I shall attempt to give readers, on the basis of the sources presently available to me, some idea of what the Soviet conscientious objector experienced after his decision to resist the draft in one or another form. The options offered the CO ranged, as we know, from unconditional exemption to informal permission to a drafted soldier to perform his service without being required to bear arms. Unfortunately, unless in the future hitherto unexplored archives reveal some unsuspected treasure, Soviet CO experience during the interwar years led to very few autobiographical accounts (if we exclude brief autobiographical passages encapsulated in personal correspondence). In fact, I know of only three narratives of this sort. One comes from a Tolstoyan peasant, Iakov Dragunovskii, a self-educated man who in addition wrote poems, essays, and diaries, none of them lacking in literary quality; it was composed in the 1920s.[7] The other two are Mennonite compilations published in Canada after 1945: one a volume on Mennonites in the Red Army[8] containing the reminiscences of a single individual, the other a book on Soviet alternative service, which is multi-authored and contains contributions from some twenty-four writers.[9] Unlike Dragunovskii, these Mennonite memoirists composed their accounts decades after the events and personal feelings they were describing. Undoubtedly they strove to be truthful, but, as we all know, memory can play strange tricks![10]

Under the Protection of Lenin's Decree: An Umbrella with Holes

Paradoxically, we shall begin the story by considering the fate of around one hundred religious COs who were shot by local Bolshevik authorities, civilian officials in collusion with military officers, for refusing to bear arms during the civil-war years 1919–20. The executions took place in the provinces, remote from the state capital, where both the central government and the COs' defence organization, OSROG, were located. The authorities who ordered the executions were either ignorant of Lenin's CO decree or ignored it purposefully, regarding those who refused to fight in the Red Army as enemies who deserved death for their resistance.

In most instances, families or friends of the men sentenced to death, or local OSROG agents, managed to convey news of the death sentences to the OSROG headquarters in Moscow. Though communications in existing circumstances could be slow, OSROG in turn hastened to intervene with the government to save the men's lives. 'The authorities at the Kremlin would telegraph to stop proceedings and to forward the men to Moscow. But it was impossible to get word of many cases in time; and in others, local military officers, knowing Moscow's attitude, held up telegrams of appeal until too late to stop the executions.'[11] Moreover, the central government seems to have been powerless to bring the perpetrators of such outrages to justice; the best it would do, when it could not stop proceedings, was to issue a severe reprimand. Most of the victims of this terrorism were peasants. Tolstoyans formed the largest group but there were also Baptists, Evangelical Christians, and members of other sects as well as a few independent spirits, whose faith had not led them to join any one religious group.[12]

Cases occurred of executions on a large scale, like the one that occurred in August 1920 when a group of thirty-four sectarians, Baptists and Molokans, from villages in the province of Voronezh faced the firing squad before a reprieve from Moscow could be enforced.[13] But usually COs were executed singly or in small groups of up to ten or so persons. Sometimes army deserters were executed alongside them, too.

Some of those who suffered the death penalty were absolutists unwilling to perform even civilian alternative service. This view, we know, was prevalent particularly among the Tolstoyans. But Lenin had provided for such people in his decree, which enabled them to receive unconditional exemption from military service. Others were less uncompromising and stood out – to the point of death – for a civilian alternative to serving in the army.

A letter from a Tolstoyan absolutist, written to his parents and smuggled out of jail on the eve of his execution, gives us insight into the state of mind of men about to suffer death for their beliefs. (Bulgakov was to entitle his account of the executions, 'How they suffered death for their faith.') Semen Dragunovskii, along with seven other village lads, all Tolstoyans, from the province of Smolensk, had been (in Semen's words) 'condemned ... by the Smolensk military court to be shot.' He asked his parents not to worry about him, even if a reprieve failed to come in time to halt his execution. 'I myself chose this path ... let them do what they want with me, ... I forgive them and I will suffer in the name of Christ. The body returns to the earth from which it came but the soul is God's and must return to him.[14] As I was writing these lines,' Semen continued, 'I remembered all of you ... I felt bitter and wept and could not go on writing for a long time. I felt sorry about leaving you all ... [But] death is not terrible for me.'[15] Semen's sufferings, however, did not end with the firing squad. Since the bullet had not killed him, 'he was shoved into the pit and covered with dirt while he was still half-alive. For a long time his groans could be heard coming from his dirt-covered grave.'[16] Semen Dragunovskii and his seven companions may have incurred the death sentence by their stubborn refusal to compromise. Semen, in his farewell letter to his parents, told them: 'At court we were given the choice of working in a hospital for contagious diseases or on the railroad; but we refused all of it, and they called us counterrevolutionaries and sentenced us to death.'[17]

In December 1920, exactly a year after Semen's execution, his cousin Iakov Dragunovskii, together with his three brothers, all of them Tolstoyans (Tolstoyism seems almost to have become the family faith), were serving jail terms as COs in the Demidov Prison (Smolensk province). William Edgerton has described Iakov as 'an honest, courageous, impassioned man, intolerant of compromise and hypocrisy.'[18] He was clearly also a man of sensitivity, unwilling to come to terms with the harshness and cruelty he was forced to observe in the Russia of his day. Now, as he sat in his prison cell beginning a letter to the COs' Moscow friends, Anna and Vladimir Chertkov, he broke off to tell them what he suddenly saw through the grated window of his cell. 'I looked out the window into the prison courtyard and saw a detachment of armed men. Part of the detachment went up to the second story of the prison with some ropes. We assumed that they were going to take some dangerous criminals to the courtroom. But imagine our horror when we saw them bring out fourteen men, tied together in pairs, who had been sentenced to be shot. ... I was filled with horror; ... and I felt a stabbing pain in my heart. O my God, my God! What is going on in this world, in broad daylight, and who is doing it? Men – reasonable creatures, created for life and joy ... There they have been taken out, all fourteen men – four for banditry and ten for refusing to go to war, condemned to death for refusing to kill people ... All those living men have walked off .. to the pits that have been prepared for them.'

At any rate the executed COs, so Iakov consoled himself, would be at peace knowing that they had 'sacrificed themselves in the cause of love.' The local People's Court had passed sentence of death on these men, despite 'expert' evidence produced from OSROG testifying to their sincerity as religious conscientious objectors. 'They were all condemned as deserters and shot,' even though one of the group had previously received a prison sentence from the People's Court, seeming thus to confirm in oblique fashion the court's belief in his sincerity.[19] Scenes such as the one Iakov Dragunovskii witnessed illustrate the varied – and often irregular – practice of provincial People's Courts and local Red Army commanders in dealing with the unfortunate COs who fell into their hands during this period. Though irregularities occurred after the period of civil war was over, the death penalty ceased to be handed out to recalcitrant objectors. (The treatment of deserters or those already in the army who claimed to have developed an objection to fighting is another matter.) The central authorities could not prevent all arbitrary local decisions, but the most flagrant breaches of Lenin's CO decree were not repeated.

Iakov Dragunovskii's own experiences as a CO, which he shared with his three brothers, further illustrate the uncertain behaviour vis-à-vis COs of local authorities at that time.[20] A First World War veteran discharged from the army on account of wounds received during combat, Iakov only became a Tolstoyan early in 1919 as a result of reading the works of the Master, which figured prominently in the thousand-book library this poorly educated farmer eventually succeeded in acquiring. Called up for service in the Red Army in the autumn of 1920, Iakov has left us an account of his conscript troubles which soon landed him in jail.

Though he does not specifically mention this, I think that as a fervid Tolstoyan, he would have been unwilling to accept a civilian alternative to service in the army, thus prejudicing his case in the minds of the local draft authorities who might possibly have been more understanding if Iakov had shown himself less intransigent. As it was, they submitted him and his fellow Tolstoyan COs to some pretty rough treatment, beating up most of them and threatening to shoot them all if they continued to passively resist induction into the forces. Sentenced to imprisonment, they finally ended up in 'the Smolensk forced-labour concentration camp' controlled by the Cheka, a penal institution that Iakov describes in lurid detail in his CO memoir. (Two of the group, unable to endure the 'horrors' of life in this penal camp, abandoned their CO stand and consented to become combatant soldiers, feeling further resistance to be in vain.) After nearly two years, despite intercession on their behalf by the Council of Soviets in the village where they had lived, OSROG succeeded in gaining the men's release, even though it was no longer officially in charge of the CO exemption process. Chertkov and two other members of OSROG's council now certified that the men were 'well known to it for their sincere, steadfast, and consistent effort to live according to the free-Christian philosophy of life, the most outstanding exponent of which was Leo Tolstoy. Moreover, the United Council vouches for the fact that [they] are free of any kind of counterrevolutionary tendencies ... and have acted exclusively from religious motives.'

Describing his interrogation by members of the regional 'politburo,' Iakov helps us to understand the kind of questions the authorities put to COs who appeared before them. The tribunal, of course, wanted to know how he, an army veteran, had become a believer in nonviolence, including vegetarianism. They tried to make him sign a statement in which he confessed to 'being guilty of agitation against the Soviet government.' Of course, Iakov absolutely refused to do so, though they threatened to get the Cheka to shoot him. 'Do you know, you muddle-headed devil, ... [the] Provincial Cheka won't stand on ceremony the way we've done.'

Significant, too, was the manner in which the tribunal tried to catch Iakov up in inconsistencies in his nonviolence. Yes, he told them, after reading Tolstoy he no longer ate meat. 'And now,' he went on, 'I know I can't eat meat, not just because of what Tolstoy said about it, but because my innermost feelings won't let me even consider the idea that it's possible to eat meat.' At once a tribunal member interposed (it was November): 'How is it that you won't eat meat but you still wear a fur coat?' Iakov did not try to excuse this. 'It really goes against my conscience to wear it,' he replied. But he was still a sinner and weak in many respects: 'I still haven't figured out how to get along without a fur coat in winter.' He had to admit that he had not yet been able to think the matter through to a satisfactory decision in line with his conscience that he knew must be right.

I have perhaps given undue attention to Iakov Dragunovskii's brief

CO memoir, but it is unique of its kind. Among non-Mennonite Soviet objectors of the interwar period, to the best of my knowledge, apart from Iakov no other objector has left a CO memoir, that is, not counting the statements outlining COs' reasons for their objecting to military service which have been preserved in the Chertkov Papers. A lacuna of this kind is understandable. Few, if any, of these men shared Iakov's literary talents; none of them were to emigrate overseas, where our Mennonite CO memoirists were able, decades later, in tranquil Canada, to distil their recollections of their service years in the Soviet Union. Besides, the overwhelming majority of Soviet COs, at any rate during the Lenin era, had obtained exemption on fairly easy terms. They remained on their farms (most of them were peasant lads), or obtained work in civilian hospitals, or entered some other occupation according to their choice and to what was then available (an option permitted, we know, by the decree of 4 January 1919). Though documents relating to their alternative civilian service undoubtedly exist, it is doubtful if any of them are of an autobiographical character.[21]

While Tolstoyans (like contemporary British Quakers, I should add) were often rather flamboyant in their rejection of every kind of compulsory alternative to doing what they believed, as Christians, was right, the overwhelming majority of COs welcomed the opportunity Lenin's decree offered them to perform a job unconnected with the military. They caused the authorities no trouble if handled properly. And, even taking into consideration the terrible fate of those COs shot during the years of civil war (contrary, we must again stress, to the express wishes of Lenin and the Kremlin), it is impossible to withhold tribute from those responsible during this early period for administering the law regarding COs: a law which the Tolstoyan elite and the United Council in Moscow helped to carry out, working very closely – though not, indeed, without periodic friction – with appropriate Soviet authorities.

Most COs, then, kept a low profile, trusting in the United Council to represent their interests if these were challenged. Take the case of Vladimir Martsinkovskii, for instance, originally a practising member of the Orthodox Church, who after the war drew close to the Evangelical Christians. He did not formally leave the Orthodox faith, but he did accept the pacifism of his new coreligionists. When summoned to an interview with the OGPU in December 1922, he explained that, though unwilling to join the army or use a weapon even in self-defence, at the same time he thought it wrong to carry on any kind of public antimilitarist agitation. That, in his view, would lead nowhere, unless accompanied by an inner conversion in the spirit of love, including love of enemies; in short, before becoming a CO a man must be born again, which could never happen as a result of political propaganda. He also assured his interrogator of his belief that the authorities must be obeyed in all things not against conscience. Partly because Martsinkovskii, already in his late thirties, possessed high educational qualifications (he held a professorship of ethics at the University of Samara) and partly because he had already received a certificate of exemption from a People's Court in September 1919, he was not again troubled over the military question before he left the Soviet Union next year for good.[22]

Before moving on to discuss the post-Lenin experiences of COs in Soviet prisons and labour camps when now more than ever, for many of them, in the telling phrase of the American poet Robert Lowell, 'experience is what you do not want to experience,'[23] I would like to turn briefly to the lot of COs in areas controlled during the civil war by White armies. The trouble is that the record here is very defective; communication with territories controlled by the Soviets, where we know the COs' friends possessed a stable base, was uncertain, but White forces, on the move for much of the time, scarcely had time or inclination to keep a record of these strange people, who refused to kill whether on orders from the Whites or the Reds.

In mid-1919, according to Toews, 'many young Mennonites were forcibly inducted into the White Army; others willingly cooperated with Denikin.'[24] The Mennonite *Selbstschutz* had only recently disbanded officially; pockets of combatancy remained unsuppressed during the months to come. Mennonites drafted by Denikin's soldiers were likely to receive short shrift if they pleaded religious scruples concerning the bearing of arms, though it is not excluded that some may have been consigned to medical or other noncombatant duties – if only to prevent trouble from their brethren among the fighting Mennonites in Denikin's army. What happened to non-Mennonite COs inducted into this force is unknown. Probably some were shot,[25] while others may have been assigned noncombatant duties just as Mennonite pacifists in the White ranks may have been, too. Iakov Dragunovskii tells us that his consistently pacifist brother, Vasilii, 'had refused ... when he was under Denikin to fight against his fellow Russians' (or indeed against anyone else); exactly under what circumstances Iakov unfortunately does not tell us.[26]

Perhaps the most interesting item throwing light on COs in White Army territories, written decades later, comes from the volume of Mennonite CO reminiscences edited by Hans Rempel, referred to above. Aaron H. Langemann, born in Omsk in 1900, was inducted, along with forty-one other young Mennonites into Admiral Kolchak's army in May 1919. Omsk then lay in an area controlled by the White leader's forces. The Mennonites at once made known their unwillingness, as members of a nonresistant sect, to bear arms or exercise in weaponry. Perhaps some of Kolchak's officers were already acquainted with the Mennonites and their customs. Anyhow, the men were assigned to medical duties (*Sanitätsdienst*), which began with a six-weeks' course in first-aid and other training needed if they were employed near the front line. 'The training was hard work,' Langemann recollects. Later he and another Mennonite, after passing an examination, were transferred to the medical unit's office, whereas the rest worked in the divisional stables, for which menial employment they received considerably less pay than the privileged office workers.

Now constantly on the retreat, before the end of the year Kolchak's forces had been decisively defeated by the Red Army. The admiral was shot by the Bolsheviks in 1920 in Irkutsk. Kolchak's Mennonites, as we may call them, now became soldiers of the Red Army, still I think preserving their informal noncombatant status, until – probably through appeal to Lenin's CO decree and the intercession in the Kremlin of OSROG, which had Mennonite representatives in its council – they were transferred to alternative civilian service, becoming *Ersatzdienstler* instead of *Front-Sanitäter*. Langemann gained employment in a flour-mill belonging to a relative until his demobilization in August 1921, just over two years since his induction into Kolchak's army.[27] Langemann's odyssey may not have been typical of Russian CO experience. But it reflects the complex character of that experience as a whole.

In Soviet Prisons and Forced Labour Camps: The Post-Lenin Experience

Sovietologists have disagreed concerning the course of Soviet penal policy during the first two decades of the new regime. Were the post-1945 forced labour camps described so graphically by Alexander Solzhenitsyn already implicit from the very beginning of Soviet rule? Or were they preceded by a 'progressive' penal policy, with rehabilitation of the offender rather than punishment or deterrence – or any exterior economic objective – predominant in the minds of those who framed that policy?

If the latter thesis is correct (and it seems to me to be the more convincing one), the year 1929 is the crucial date marking 'the transition from the [progressive] penal policy of NEP to the Stalinist policy,' a policy closely connected with the beginning of large-scale and rapid industrialization. Industrialization of this kind at once brought the need for a greatly expanded labour force.[28] Stalin's use of mass terror as an instrument of government constituted another factor in bringing to an end the progressive penal policy of the early years of Soviet rule.[29]

Soviet COs suffered incarceration both under 'progressive' auspices and in the early stages of the Gulag. We have seen that even during Lenin's lifetime and despite the decree of 4 January 1919, COs were jailed (and even shot). But this was against the wishes of the Kremlin. Such cases occurred in the provinces; the central government had proved powerless to put a stop to such outrages. But from 1924 on, with the increasingly restrictive CO legislation, objectors now found themselves in prison, not as the result of some flagrant abuse, but as a consequence of due legal process. Chertkov and his colleagues could not prevent this happening; they could only be supportive of their young friends in their ordeal. Some of these might earlier have received exemption, only now to be tried and jailed.

Sentences ranged from a month or two to three (and occasionally five) years, with 'cat-and-mouse treatment of COs' not uncommon. Sentences might also include a deprivation of civil rights for a given number of years as well as a fine to be levied on the offender's property.[30] In contrast, however, to this harsh practice at the centre, in villages and small provincial towns officials sometimes adopted a much more relaxed attitude. There men liable to prosecution according to the letter of the law, who would invariably have received a prison sentence if they had lived in a city, might be left alone. Their neighbours in village or small-town office realized very well that such people were sincere. Why, then, should they bother with them when they knew they would make bad soldiers?

'Conscientious objectors,' Roger Baldwin reports of the situation in the Moscow area, 'are sent to the civil prisons just like ordinary criminals and under the same regime. I was told by some of the men themselves that keepers usually see that they are unusually intelligent, and recognizing that they are not criminals, put them in higher prison grades and in better jobs.'[31] Civil prisons were mostly antique structures, inherited from the Imperial era; 'conditions ... were often primitive.'[32] Overcrowding, especially in provincial jails, and damp – and often dirty – jail cells, were among the more serious defects of the prison system at that time. Yet, the authorities, not without justification, looked on the system as 'reformatory' in intent; they liked to designate prison as 'a house of reform' (*ispravdom*), a point of view not always shared by the inmates! Still, in many prisons, schools had been established for those criminals who, in freedom, had received little or no education, and all prisoners received training, which hopefully would help them to find honest employment after leaving jail.

Jailed COs, though some reported spells in solitary confinement (presumably as a result of an infraction of prison regulations), experienced positive aspects of the prevailing Soviet progressive penal policy. For instance, COs, like other prisoners, sometimes gained early release for one or another reason. We hear of one CO (V.C. Mishnin) who received a three-month furlough – in the summer of 1925 – to return to the family farm, which was short of labour in harvest season, 'after which he has to return to prison and finish his term,' which would expire near the end of the year.[33] Dr Idzhevsky, a Tolstoyan medical man, was allowed to practise his profession inside prison ('and twice a week his friends can see him,' the WRI report adds).[34] Vegetarians among jailed COs (all Tolstoyans, we know, followed the Master in adopting a vegetarian diet) usually received consideration from the prison authorities, at least to the extent that friends outside could provide them with the food they required.

Towards the end of the 1920s, in line with the progressive penal policy still in place though approaching its demise, 'virtually all Moscow prisoners were employed in factories or on estates which had been expropriated from private owners, and they were instructed by staff teachers.'[35] CO prisoners, of course, benefited from this program; transfer to a farm colony must have been a pleasant change for those brought up in the country after the close confinement and fetid atmosphere of the ramshackle Soviet prisons of that day.

Open antimilitarist activity ceased in 1929. The law still acknowledged the claim of a limited number of pacifist sects to receive CO status. Recognized sects included Mennonites as well as some smaller groups. But for some years already Baptists, Evangelical Christians, Seventh-day Adventists, and Tolstoyans had faced the likelihood of imprisonment when they opted for conscientious objection; the law no longer regarded them as people whose pacifism was motivated by genuinely religious convictions.[36] At the same time an ominous change began with regard to the type of incarceration to which COs were subjected. In line with the all-Union shift from 'progressive' penal policy to the program of internal exile and forced labour camps with which Stalin replaced it, COs, by now greatly reduced in numbers and diminishing still further with each successive year, served their sentences in accord with this new style of dealing with offenders, especially political ones. We hear, for instance, of that intrepid Tolstoyan, Boris Peskov, who had refused to work in jail and as a total resister had gone on hunger strike too, being 'banished to the cold North where, with others, he is suffering great privation' (according to a report smuggled to war resisters abroad at the beginning of the 1930s).[37] Even earlier, staff members of the Moscow Vegetarian Society not long before its closure, including the office secretary and two women volunteer typists, had been exiled to Siberia for three years for assisting Tolstoyan COs in their efforts to gain exemption from military service.[38]

The fate of (non-Mennonite) COs in the 1930s and beyond remains unclear. How many of them were there, and how exactly did the authorities treat them? I do not think we shall ever obtain a satisfactory answer to these questions. Possibly the still inaccessible parts of the Chertkov Papers may supply partial answers. But Chertkov's group was no longer able, as it had done in the 1920s, to act as an umbrella organization, linking COs of various persuasions and providing them with legal aid as well as intervening, when necessary, with a by no means always unsympathetic Kremlin. True, Chertkov died in his bed, but that was probably because Stalin did not perceive him as a threat.

Before leaving the subject of Soviet prison COs, I would like to say a word or two about a form of incarceration that, in principle at any rate, is remedial (or protective) rather than either punitive or aiming at rehabilitation: confinement in a mental hospital (or lunatic asylum, to use the pejorative term formerly in general use). In Second-World-War America, more than once the authorities were to attempt to have recalcitrant COs certified as insane.[39] We need not be surprised, therefore, if attempts were made in the Soviet Union to put COs away in a mental institution; after all, it was to happen in the case of other Soviet dissidents and was certainly a convenient way of getting rid of potential troublemakers. I have, however, been able to discover at most two cases of such an abuse of the law. In this period, however, with Chertkov and other friends of the CO acting as watch-dogs, the authorities –

even in a country as vast as the Soviet Union – could not have concealed for long arbitrary action of this kind and held a CO in continued duress on the plea he was insane.

At some unspecified date an Evangelical Christian named Nikolai Vasil'evitch Asiev, my first case, who taught singing in a Moscow school, had claimed exemption as a CO. For reasons that are not entirely clear to me, the authorities sent him to a mental hospital for examination. After six months he was released and not troubled any further in connection with military service. At the same time the doctors declared that he was suffering from 'religious mania' since he had told them it was God who had forbidden him to bear arms and he remained, moreover, indifferent to the consequences of his refusal to become a soldier. As a result of having been declared mentally ill, Asiev was not permitted to return to his teaching post. At the end of the decade, in 1929, an imprisoned Tolstoyan CO found himself in the same predicament as Asiev earlier (the latter, though, had been hitherto a free man). 'The military authorities,' we are told, 'declared [him] insane. [He] is getting on better in the asylum than in prison. He is working in the kitchen garden and has been allowed to go home on leave.'[40] All in all, the Soviet authorities, military as well as civilian, do not seem to have taken 'the asylum' seriously as a way of dealing with their CO problem.

In the Red Army

Until 1917 readiness to accept noncombatant duties on an informal basis proved the only way for a CO, who was not a Mennonite, to escape prison or penal battalion. This way out continued to exist informally under the Soviets. But now it was an alternative that *faute de mieux* Mennonites also chose. Unfortunately we know virtually nothing about the non-Mennonite CO soldiers who served in the Red Army.[41] But several Mennonites have left accounts of their years as 'defenceless' conscript soldiers. There is, for instance, the memoir by Gerhard Penner, who served for the required two years from 1924 to 1926, first in the 134th Infantry Regiment and then in the 45th Artillery Regiment. In each regiment he served alongside Mennonite boys who had opted in the same way he had done for noncombatant army service. Penner's memoir runs to 113 printed pages; the other accounts are very much shorter. For what I have written below, I am largely indebted to his detailed, but at the same time lively, narrative.

When, at the end of his two years' conscript service, Penner finally came to say farewell to his fellow Mennonite noncombatants, he was overwhelmed by a sense of camaraderie[42] engendered by the long months of hardship and joy they had shared: a group separated from their fellow soldiers both by their *plattdeutsch* dialect, which they spoke among themselves, and by their common religious faith and their belief, however immature, in nonresistance (*Wehrlosigkeit*) as the principle which underlay the lifestyle of their folk at home. They remained, then, a people apart, even if outwardly they wore army uniform and were subject to military discipline like the rest of the regiment.

At the outset Penner and the others made clear that, as Mennonites, they would not train in weaponry or take part in military instruction of any kind and that, moreover, the law guaranteed them noncombatant status. Two years earlier, however, Penner, like other Mennonites of military age in his neighbourhood, had been forced to perform rifle drill, their protests dismissed peremptorily by the local commissar, who told them: 'These military exercises are quite harmless; they've nothing to do with killing anyone.' The only way they could escape going through the motions of drilling was by feigning sick. But this did not always work![43] Fortunately things went off better now. Penner and the others were able to produce certificates from a People's Court attesting that they were Mennonites and genuinely opposed to participation in war. The 'Comrade Commandant,' Penner relates, was a little taken aback by all this. 'Who on earth are the Mennonites?' he exclaimed. 'Never in my life have I ever heard of them.' He would have to consult his senior officers, he told the boys, before deciding how to proceed. The Mennonites agreed, meanwhile, to be present at military exercises; they were not ready, though, to participate in them actively. In a few days news came that the matter was settled satisfactorily.[44]

Red Army practice in the 1920s was to assign such CO conscripts to medical, commissariat and clerical work, and other auxiliary branches of the army which did not entail training in weaponry.[45] Penner, for instance, worked for much of his time in the pharmacy of a military hospital. Only once was he challenged by an order to perform work of a directly military nature.[46]

In retrospect, the negative aspects of army service retreated into the background in Penner's mind, as they must have done in the memories of the hundreds of other Mennonite draftees inducted into the Red Army during the 1920s. They could give thanks to the Lord that, unlike some of their fellows who at call-up had yielded to the pressures of commissars and politruks and agreed to become combatants, they had stood firm: 'a small Mennonite flock who continued to adhere to the principle of nonresistance (*Wehrlosigkeit*).'[47] The bedbugs in the interstices of the wooden barrack-room bunks often making sleep impossible, the lousy food usually sufficient but almost inedible when compared with what mother had prepared for them at home, the insults from unsympathetic officers who taunted them as 'damned Germans' and uncultured yokels, and the two hours every weekday devoted to political 'education' when the instructor poured scorn on all manifestations of religion and told them lie after lie about life in the capitalist countries of the West:[48] these unpleasant aspects of Red Army life yielded in time to more favourable impressions. For Penner, there were fond memories of leisure hours spent with his Mennonite comrades. They used to sing – not only hymns but German folksongs they had learnt at home. Indeed, they sang so well that the Russian officers soon began to invite them to give concerts for their benefit.

For a raw farm lad as Penner then was, the Red Army provided educational facilities his home environment had not given him as well as entry into a wider world than the village of his birth, beyond which he had not adventured hitherto. The story is an old one: the educational achievements of compulsory military service with conscriptionist armies widening the horizons of country lads and urban youths and giving them a schooling they would otherwise have lacked. (But although this is largely true, in no way does it remove the fact – that the main purpose of armies is to wage war, educational aspects being merely side issues, with the essential debate revolving really around the question of just-war *versus* pacifism.)

For the first time now Penner saw the inside of an Orthodox church and was present at one of their services (though, when he could get leave, he normally attended Sunday worship at a Baptist chapel). Above all, he and his Mennonite comrades would never forget the thrilling experience of visiting, often more than once, the ancient churches and monasteries of Kiev, while they were stationed near that city and could easily reach its sights during their time off. The history of Rus' opened out before them as it had never done earlier.

Among Penner's happiest recollections of his years in the Red Army were his memories of the dear old general in command of the 45th Artillery Regiment. 'Grandpa' was how the Mennonites liked to refer to him among themselves. 'Never did he attack or abuse us on account of our nonresistance. He recognized us Mennonites as able, hardworking, and honest lads,' who were ready to undertake any 'weaponless' service in the army. In fact, he took the Mennonites under his wing and protected them against the ill will towards them of some of his junior officers.[49]

On the whole, I think the Red Army's treatment of its Mennonite soldier COs, at any rate, does it credit – even outside the command of the 'dear old general' of the 45th Artillery Regiment. I am not so sure, though, of its record with respect to the non Mennonite COs, who have left such few traces in the record, though undoubtedly they were present in its ranks too. Penner, for instance, tells us of a Russian Baptist CO who, recently drafted, turned up in the barracks of the 45th Artillery Regiment in the autumn of 1925. By then the status of Baptist applicants for CO status was anomalous. The man was not ready to accept noncombatant army service. So a court martial was set up; the Mennonite COs in the regiment were ordered to attend (possibly an act of intimidation in case they thought of insubordination); and the court proceeded to interrogate the Baptist as to his beliefs. The trial concluded with a sentence of two years in an army penal battalion, after which the man would be liable to serve his two years as a draftee.[50] The Red Army, thus, could provide some COs with memories far different from those it left with Penner and his Mennonite comrades.

In Labour Battalions

A new era in the history of Soviet COs begins around 1927 with their consignment to work in one or another type of labour battalion. Such an arrangement differs radically from earlier alternatives to service in the army, which for the most part meant direction of recognized COs to undertake work of a civilian character on an individual basis.

The establishment of these labour battalions, in which others served as well as COs, connected up with the advancing Soviet industrialization, though they had preceded by a little inauguration of Stalin's Five Year Plan in 1928. From the early 1930s it seems that all sectarians whose claims to CO status gained recognition from the authorities were employed in this way if they could not be persuaded to enter the army. Herded together, the COs were now more amenable to political indoctrination. Thus this new method of dealing with them, in addition to its primary aim of furthering the country's economic development, possessed a political purpose, too.

The work program went through two stages, with 1929 as the dividing line. The only sources available to me for this period of an autobiographical character are exclusively Mennonite, but other COs certainly participated.[51]

In the first stage much of the work undertaken by COs resembled what Mennonite draftees had done in Tsarist times in the camps run by the *Forsteidienst*: work in the extensive forests located in the Ural Mountains and in Siberia existed alongside draining swamps and making rivers navigable and constructing railways. Some of the draftees, though, worked as clerks in the camp office or as attendants in the medical clinic attached to each camp or in the camp kitchen. Others were assigned to the stables or worked as cleaners within the camp compound. Campers were often sent home during the winter months since in the harsh climate of the Urals and Siberia work closed down with the onset of winter.

Much of this program was familiar to Mennonites at least. One difference for them, though, between present and past lay in the almost entire absence of visiting preachers (distance for one thing made this very difficult) and the daily presence of political indoctrination which, as in the Red Army, COs found extremely hard to bear. The object of the instructors in these courses was to undermine the men's religious beliefs; if their faith collapsed, this would be a victory for atheism and might lead on to acceptance of combatant service. However, although Sunday worship was forbidden, the Mennonite boys (perhaps the other COs too?) found a way to circumvent the design of the hated politruks: they just walked out into the woods during a Sunday afternoon and worshipped informally under the trees surrounded by the vast silence of the primitive forestland.

They toiled often deep into the night. Work norms were excessively high in projects like railway construction; and, moreover, everything was normally done by manual labour, for machines at that time were in extremely short supply. The Mennonite boys were, of course, accustomed in the summer season to work long hours on the family farm; indeed, they were not afraid of hard work. Still, in camp food was rarely as plentiful as the nature of their employment required: that did not make heavy labour easy. In addition, as one of them remarked, 'the constant pressure on them to shoulder a rifle did not help to make their service lighter.'[52]

All in all, the two years spent in labour camp seem to have passed quite quickly – and not too unpleasantly (especially since winters were often spent at home). Frank Rempel was right when he said of himself and his mates that they could not claim they were martyrs for Mennonite nonresistance like their sixteenth-century ancestors. In fact, in their own experience the preceding and succeeding years proved far worse, with the menace of starvation and deportation – and death. In camp they worked hard now, but life passed tranquilly. They had their troubles, it is true: political indoctrination, for instance, and the swarms of mosquitoes that made sleep almost impossible during the summer nights. But, Rempel explained: 'our relationship with the [camp] authorities was by and large excellent. We fulfilled our work-norms, and even overfulfilled them!'[53]

Just as Mennonite COs in Second-World-War America gained the reputation of being 'the good boys' of the government-sponsored Civilian Public Service, their predecessors in Soviet Russia could with equal justice be called the good boys of the labour battalions. This indeed was in line with the teachings of their church, which required the faithful to render unto Caesar his due as a divine commandment that it was a sin to disobey.[54]

These boys were often inarticulate; after all, many of them had received only a very rudimentary education. How, then, did they fare in explaining their beliefs to those who decided whether they were eligible for this kind of service? Peter Peters, for instance, freely admitted that, at his appearance before the People's Court at the outset of his CO career, the presiding magistrate seemed to know more about the Bible than he or any of the twenty-five or thirty other Mennonite draftees who had been called up at the same time. The judge, of course, made full use of the Old Testament and the Israelites' wars that God had approved. Fortunately for these farm boys, who tried not very successfully to fend off the judge's arguments by referring to Jesus' peaceable gospel, they could rely on their congregations for assistance in presenting their case in court.

Indeed, Peters and his companions had received coaching in the community before their court hearing. A handwritten exercise-book, with set questions and answers concerning military service based on past experience with CO hearings, circulated in the village. Prospective applicants for CO status copied out the questions and answers and then handed the book on to another applicant. 'We learnt the questions and answers by heart,' writes Peters, 'before we went ahead with the court hearing.' Peters and his fellow Mennonite draftees were lucky, too, in being able to have Aron Toews from the Chortitza colony as their 'expert' witness. The old preacher indeed enjoyed years of experience in this role. 'He had his own place at a desk on the left side of the courtroom. However,' Peters goes on, 'he didn't always have an easy job with us youngsters because many of us had great difficulty both in writing and expressing our thoughts.'[55]

We may note that COs from other sects, at this date at any rate, often lacked community backing: no coaching for them in the home village and no kindly Preacher Toews to make up for their educational deficiencies when they faced a hostile tribunal anxious to catch them out on the Scriptures or show up their inconsistencies as they presented their case for exemption. But whether ultimately the Mennonite situation described here was a healthier one than that of the beleaguered COs from other sects, about that I have indeed my doubts.

For all COs, whether Mennonites or from some other section of the sectarian pacifist community, the second stage in the development of labour battalions marked a turn for the worse. During the first two years, that is, 1927 and 1928, oversight had rested with the Ministry of the Interior, with the Ministry of Transport in charge of such activities as railway construction. From 1929 on, the Ministry of Industry took over in many sectors. Such activities as stone quarrying, or coal mining in the Far East, or the construction nearer home of the power station at Zaporozhe, or the manufacture of turpentine from the oleo-resin secreted in certain coniferous trees, now predominated among the tasks assigned to COs and others who served with them in the labour battalions, renamed 'tylovoye opoltshchenyiy (TOs)' or 'hinterland reserves.' With regard to the work of the TOs, the need of heavy industry figured ever more prominently.

While Mennonite COs who worked on the Dnieper power station project were only a few miles from home and could thus keep in close touch with families and church, the days when forestry workers received a furlough for the whole winter had gone forever. But there were more serious signs of worsening conditions. The control of the military over these 'soldiers of labour' tightened, while the pressures to become combatant soldiers increased. As Klippenstein aptly puts it, 'new recruits were now in effect not COs but "TOs."' Apart from conscientious objectors, the work force for the TOs was drawn largely from elements considered to be antisocial and therefore untrustworthy as soldiers: priests' sons and choristers,[56] for instance, and boys whose parents the authorities regarded as kulaks. All these people were required to serve for three years instead of the two years which was statutory for drafted soldiers. Hitherto COs likewise had served a two-year draft term. But now the authorities designated some COs as kulaks' sons and made them serve an extra year (and deprived them, too, of full pay for the job and of the right to vote, as happened with Mennonite as well as non-Mennonite TOs), whereas COs in the same battalion, judged to be from poor peasant families, were released as before at the end of two years.

It became increasingly clear, as collectivization of agriculture gathered momentum along with industrialization and the threat of war clouded the international atmosphere, that the patience of Stalin's administration with the dwindling number of COs was wearing out. True, the problem was a tiny one in comparison to others the government faced. But it occupied the attention of those officials directly connected with the TOs. As an army officer, assigned to work with the latter, told Hans Rempel: 'We are really not particularly concerned with the labour of you COs. We can easily get others who will do it. What we are concerned about is to try and free you from your religious mindset [Glaubenshaltung], and for that purpose every method and every means is justifiable.' As Rempel comments, only strong religious conviction could enable a man to stand firm in face of pressures of that sort.[57]

The year 1935 – possibly 1934 – would appear to have been the last in which the authorities were prepared to accept application for CO status. For instance, J. Neufeld began to serve as a TO in March 1934, along with ten other Mennonite draftees from the Molochna colony and two from the Old Colony in Chortitza. The latter were all released after two years' service. But Neufeld was kept until March 1937 – as a kulak's son. On leaving home his father had given him a pocket New Testament, and his mother bade him farewell with the words of Psalm 37, verse 5: 'Commit thy way unto the Lord; trust also in him; and he shall bring it to pass' (AV).[58] He treasured her words; they helped him, when he came back, to face the break-up of the Mennonite fellowship that, at the conclusion of his service, he found had taken a devastating toll in broken lives and dispossessed families since he had left home three years before.

Mennonites, as ethnic Germans and as kulaks, were beginning to be considered as unfit for army service, an unreliable element which might betray the Fatherland to its foes. This disqualification, though reflecting official hostility that generated much trouble for the sect, at least relieved these young men of some of the suffering resulting from a refusal to bear arms. Successive contingents of draftees during the second half of the 1930s were, however, obliged to attend the annual period of military training that was obligatory for all able-bodied men preceding and succeeding their conscript army years, or in the event they were lucky enough not to be drafted.[59]

But how much worse was the situation of ethnically Slavic sectarian COs whom the Fatherland sought for its armed services, often even when they derived from the more well-to-do peasantry! Unless by good chance they met with a sympathetic army commander or understanding territorial officer, willing in one instance to assign them to noncombatant duties if they were willing to perform these or on another occasion to turn a blind eye to their unwillingness on muster-day to exercise with the weapons they had been issued with, then their fate was sealed: either Gulag or weary years in some civilian jail. How many resisted, how many yielded to almost insupportable pressure, what was the combined total of those in the two categories? – these are questions to which we have no answer. The archives could contain clues, but, as with so many historical questions, we may have to put up finally with partial and unsatisfactory solutions.

The Second World War erupted on 1 September 1939 when German troops marched into Poland; the Soviet Union entered the international conflict when Nazi Germany invaded its territories on 22 June 1941. Professor Klibanov, the Soviet Union's most distinguished sociologist of religion and the man who in his day knew more about Russian sectarian pacifism than any other scholar, once declared with pride: 'During the years of the great Fatherland War the faithful of every sect and church ... fought courageously with the German fascist aggressors.'[60]

But were there really no COs left?

They must certainly have been few in numbers, especially if we think of the vast human resources of the Soviet Union. But there is evidence, if fragmented evidence, of their existence throughout the years from 1939 to 1945. Indeed, it would be surprising if the tens of thousands of young sectarians who had opted for conscientious objection during the interwar years, most of them still of military age during the Great Fatherland War, had unanimously, as it were, renounced their conviction that fighting was wrong and were now ready to shoulder a rifle and shoot to kill. Of course, for the Russian people the war against Hitler was, as perhaps never in their history with a war before, 'the good war' – to use a term recently become popular in North America. As happened in the case of pacifists in Britain and the United States and elsewhere, many pacifists in the Soviet Union must have felt quite sincerely that it was now their duty to defend their country with arms – and have put their nonviolence into cold storage until the Nazis were defeated. (In the national crisis, too, Stalin, from his side, lifted the anti-religious campaign insofar as to make substantial concessions to both the Orthodox Church and the leading sectarian groups.) Nevertheless, national consensus on the military question was not quite complete.

We learn, for instance, from the Tolstoyan peasant memoirs published in recent years of young men, raised in the Tolstoyan communities, who had during the years of war died at the hands of the firing squad for refusing induction into the Red Army.[61] Older Tolstoyans, too, though they had their dilemmas in such matters as home-guard duties, succeeded in preserving a pacifist stance. Of course, we must remember also, many of them spent long years in the Gulag archipelago, from where some of them never returned: however grim their fate, this removed the need to worry over being ordered to handle a lethal weapon.

Wilhelm Kahle – but only briefly – refers to two cases of wartime COs: one an Evangelical Christian named Iuri Koesche, who was executed in 1941 for his stand, and the other a Baptist named Gulyuk (no first name given), who perhaps survived.[62] As happened with German Mennonites in Hitler's army, who had still entertained scruples when required to bear arms even though their church abandoned nonresistance altogether in 1934, Soviet pacifists, when drafted, could have obtained relief for their conscience by various kinds of compromise, some of which we have discussed above. Then there was the Labour Army (*Trudarmiia*), the wartime successor of the TOs: this corps, which was not furnished with weapons, contained many men of military age who were for security reasons considered unreliable.[63]

Finally, we should take a look at the Mennonites of the wartime Soviet Union. After Stalin's suppression of their worship, dispersal, with few exceptions, of their settlements, and the arrest and imprisonment of their spiritual leaders, who often disappeared without trace, they could scarcely feel any particularly warm sentiments towards the worker's fatherland whose rulers had branded them as pariahs; even if they often continued to have friendly relations with their Slavic neighbours, who, after all, were victims of the same terror as they were themselves. We know, indeed, that many Slav peasants welcomed the invading Germans with bread and salt, the Nazis rejecting the possibilities this opened up because they viewed Slavs in general as *Untermenschen*. But they regarded Soviet Mennonites as *ausländer Deutsche*; they were anxious to settle them on German soil – or soil they regarded as German – and bestow on them all the privileges enjoyed by the German *Volk*.

Here, indeed, lay a great danger to the Russian Mennonites' moral integrity. After all, only half a decade before, their finest spirits had been urging the young men of the church to stand firm in their adherence to nonresistance in face of government pressure to relinquish this centuries-old tenet of their faith. Alone among the more important pacifist sects (if we exclude the Tolstoyans), Mennonites resisted the strong government pressure to issue an official statement rejecting, or at any rate severely restricting, the church's support for conscientious objection. Once the *Selbstschutz* crisis was over, combatant service once again ceased to be a Mennonite option; members in good standing had no choice but to refuse to bear arms – inside or outside army ranks – if they wished to keep their church membership.[64] And, we have seen, many youngsters – for all the defects of their education – continued to stand up to official browbeating, whether in noncombatant units of the army or in labour battalions. True, many Mennonite COs of the 1920s had left the country in the great exodus of that era. But the majority of families remained to face the Soviet inferno that soon followed.

When the German armies advanced into Soviet territory in mid-1941, only some four years after the last Mennonite COs had been released from service in a Soviet labour battalion, most young and able-bodied Mennonites in the occupied territories readily volunteered for combatant service in one or other unit of the German army. 'Men from various villages,' one of them relates, 'joined our unit and soon there were hundreds of them varying in age range from seventeen to forty years. The older men served as clerks, as cooks and in similar capacities ... The principle of non-resistance was forgotten and the men felt it their duty to assist in the struggle against the fearful oppression we had been subjected to for so long.'[65] This development harked back to the *Selbstschutz*; indeed, units bearing that name sprang up again informally under German patronage in Mennonite villages as protection against Soviet partisans or against brigands.[66] However, when the Germans resorted to conscription, a few Mennonites, recent Soviet COs, endeavoured when called up to obtain some kind of noncombatant employment in the German army: we have no means, though, of knowing whether any who tried for this were successful.

Mennonites – men, women, and children – who found refuge in Germany during the latter months of the war, as well as Mennonite servicemen who formed part of the retreating German forces, were liable to forced repatriation when the war was over. The Western allies handed over around two-thirds of these Mennonite displaced persons (DPs) to face almost certain retribution – exile and worse – on arrival back in the Soviet Union: one of several shameful acts perpetrated by the West in the immediate post-war period.

Mennonites in areas which escaped Nazi occupation fared differently from their brethren who passed for a time under German rule. In Siberian exile, at least some semblance of community life survived, even if underground, as it were, to re-emerge during the second half of the century in a renewal process that continued into the post-communist era. As ethnic Germans, Mennonites of draft age were not taken into the wartime army. If they escaped prison or forced labour camp, they were likely to be directed into the *Trudarmiia* – 'in any case far from the front lines.' In the post-war years, nurtured by some of the fellowship's spiritual leaders, the doctrine of nonresistance began slowly to revive. But this remained a personal matter dependent on 'the convictions of the individual.' The post-war Soviet Union made no provision for conscientious objection of any sort. Still, the authorities usually adopted a pragmatic attitude and directed the Mennonite youngsters informally to some employment during their term of service that did not offend their conscience.[67]

The antimilitarist movement in the interwar Soviet Union vanished almost as if it had never been: one among countless other victims of Stalin's terror. After the fall of communism, the fragile Russian peace movement, anxious to assert the rights of conscientious objectors, sought precedents and inspiration in the experiences of COs of an earlier period.[68] For nearly two decades, Soviet COs and their supporters had struggled to maintain the claims of conscience against the increasingly totalitarian state. They lost – but, hopefully, their struggle was not in vain.

NOTES

1 For the history of the decree and its text in English translation, see Paul D. Steeves, ed., *The Modern Encyclopedia of Religions in Russia and the Soviet Union* (Gulf Breeze FL), vol. 5 (1993), 223–5. The decree's Russian text is

given in A.I. Klibanov, *Religioznoe sektantstvo i sovremennost (Sotsiologicheskie i istoricheskie ocherki)* (Moscow, 1969), 195, 196. See essay 20.

2 For a time Chertkov found a way around this restriction and was able to gain exemption even for – the very few – ethical-humanist COs. See my 'Recognition of Non-religious Conscientious Objection in Lenin's Russia: Vladimir Chertkov's Solution,' *Reconciliation Quarterly* (Spring 1998), 19–22. Chertkov, however, does not appear to have sought exemption for selective conscientious objectors (if there were any).

3 See John B. Toews, 'The Origins and Activities of the Mennonite *Selbstschutz* in the Ukraine (1918–1919),' *Mennonite Quarterly Review* (hereafter *MQR*), vol. 46, no. 1 (January 1972), 5–40, and his 'The Russian Mennonites and the Military Question (1921–1927),' *MQR*, vol. 43, no. 2 (April 1969), 153–68; also Lawrence Klippenstein, 'Mennonite Pacifism and State Service in Russia: A Case Study in Church-State Relations: 1789–1936' (Ph.D. diss., University of Minnesota, 1984), and his essay 'Mennonites and Military Service in the Soviet Union to 1939,' in Peter Brock and Thomas P. Socknat, eds, *Challenge to Mars: Essays on Pacifism from 1918 to 1945* (Toronto, 1999), 3–20. My colleague Harvey L. Dyck has microfilmed a vast collection of documents – almost miraculously preserved – from hitherto lost Mennonite archives. Some of these documents concern COs in the Soviet Union, Mennonite and others. See H.L. Dyck et al., eds, *Mennonites in Southern Ukraine, 1789–1944: A Guide to Holdings and Microfilmed Documents from the State Archives of the Zaporozhe Region* (Toronto, 2001).

4 See Steeves, 'Russian Baptists and the Military Question, 1918–1929,' in Brock and Socknat, eds, *Challenge*, 21–40.

5 For an overall view of Adventist noncombatancy, see Daniel Heinz, 'Adventisty sed'mogo dnia i otkaz ot uchastiia v voennykh deiistviakh: Istoricheskaia perspektiva,' in Tatiana Pavlova et al., eds, *Nenasilie kak mirovozzrenie i obraz zhizni (istoricheskiy rakurs)* (Moscow, 2000), 116–27.

6 For an overview of conscientious objection in the interwar Soviet Union, see my privately printed booklet (in 50 copies), *Soviet Conscientious Objectors, 1917–1939: A Chapter in the History of Twentieth-Century Pacifism* (Toronto, 1999) – full of typos, alas! See also Bruno Coppieters, 'Die pazifistischen Sekten, die Bolschewiki und das Recht auf Wehrdienstverweigerung,' in Reiner Steinweg, ed., *Lehren aus Geschichte? Historische Friedensforschung* (Frankfurt am Main, 1990), 308–60; A.A. Kalinin, R.V. Muranov, E.A. Zakharova, *Al'ternativnaia grazhdanskaia sluzhba: Proshlie, nastoiashchee, budushchee ...* (Moscow, 2000), 8–17; and Konstantin Vladimirovich Stvolygin, 'Politika osvobozhdeniia grazhdan ot voinnskoy povinnosti po religioznym ubezhdenniiam v Sovetskom gosudarstve

(1918–1939 gg.' (Candidate of Historical Sciences dissertation, University of Minsk, 1997). Stvolygin's work is the most thorough and detailed treatment of the subject so far: it focuses on the Soviet government's treatment of COs and uses Russian state archives, in some cases no longer accessible, at least to foreign scholars. A useful addition to the literature based on archival sources, though covering only the period to 1925, is Joshua A. Sanborn, *Drafting the Russian Nation: Military Conscription, Total War, and Mars Politics, 1905–1925* (De Kalb IL, 2003), 190–9.

7 Iakov Dragunovskii, 'Memoirs about Arrest on 31 October 1920 for Refusal of Military Service,' printed in English translation in William Edgerton, ed., *Memoirs of Peasant Tolstoyans in the Soviet Russia* (Bloomington and Indianapolis, 1993), 199–209.

8 Gerhard Penner, *Mennoniten dienen in der Roten Armee* (Winnipeg, 1975).

9 Hans Rempel, ed., *Waffen der Wehrlosen: Ersatzdienst der Mennoniten der UdSSR* (Winnipeg, 1980). Some of the contributions to the volume record CO experiences in the Red Army and not in civilian *Ersatzdienst*.

10 As Klippenstein and others here have indicated, Mennonite archives in North America as well as Mennonite papers there in private hands contain some autobiographical materials throwing light on the CO experience in the interwar Soviet Union. But I doubt if they have anything of particular significance to contribute.

11 Roger N. Baldwin, *Liberty under the Soviets* (New York, 1928), 256. Undoubtedly Baldwin received this information from Tolstoyan friends during his visit to the Soviet Union in 1927. It corresponds to what we know from other sources.

12 See Valentin Bulgakov, 'Kak umiraiut' za veru,' *Sovremenniia Zapiski* (Paris), vol. 29 (1929), 189–223, for details about thirteen individual cases of execution. The article also appeared in pamphlet form in Czech and German. Bulgakov was one of Tolstoy's secretaries; he obtained information for his account from documents in possession of his Moscow Tolstoyan colleagues and relied, too, on his own and his colleagues' memory of these recent tragic events. As virtually all such cases coming to the central government's attention were channelled to it through OSROG, that body, therefore, possessed a reasonably accurate picture of what transpired.

13 Ibid., 214, 215.

14 Semen was echoing here the words of Ecclesiastes 12:7: 'then shall the dust return to the earth as it was; and the spirit shall return unto God, who gave it' (AV).

15 Edgerton, ed., *Memoirs*, xxi, xxii. Semen Dragunovskii's letter, dated 21 December 1919, remained hidden for over sixty years, along with other

manuscript material produced by post-1918 Tolstoyans, until in the 1980s publication of such documents became possible, first abroad and then in Russia itself.

16 Ibid., xxii. These gruesome details come from oral tradition in the Dragunovskii family. I do not see any reason to doubt their general accuracy.

17 Ibid. The most widely publicized case among the COs executed during this period was that of Vasilii Egorovich Tarakin, an unaffiliated Christian pacifist from the province of Vladimir, who was shot – formally 'as a deserter' – on 2 July 1919. See Bulgakov, 'Kak umiraiut'," 197–201. Of course, pacifists throughout the world regarded such men as martyrs. (Their approach, as one might expect, sometimes verges on hagiography.) The German Weimar-era antimilitarist Martha Steinitz, for instance, wrote a short play about Tarakin. Her play was a little romanticized with some fictional details, but accurate as to essentials. It was published in an English translation and performed several times by amateur companies in Britain.

18 Edgerton, ed., *Memoirs of Peasant Tolstoyans*, 181.

19 From two letters from Iakov Dragunovskii to Anna and Vladimir Chertkov, dated in December 1920 (ibid., 209–11). Dragunovskii gives the names of the ten COs who were shot.

20 See Dragunovskii's 'Memoirs,' printed in ibid., 199–209.

21 I am doubtful if such archival materials, even when fully accessible, will contain sufficient statistical data to justify serious quantification as to total numbers of COs at any given date or the regional spread of conscientious objection. That sensitive and percipient observer of the state of civil liberties in the Soviet Union during the 1920s, Roger Baldwin (*Liberty*, 263, 264), reports from 1927: 'No record is kept as to the numbers claiming exemption each year ... About fifty to sixty cases a year come up now in Moscow province, the only place where the facts are easily obtainable.' No reliable figures were then available either as to the number of COs on alternative service or of those few unconditionally exempted or of those whose applications for CO status had been rejected. For jailed COs, though, Baldwin cites a guess: 'the number in prisons all over the Union at any one time in recent years,' he writes, 'is estimated by the Tolstoyans at about two hundred and fifty to three hundred.' Of course, more precise figures are likely to exist for the two years when OSROG dominated the exemption process (January 1919 to December 1920). But we have to wait – alas, probably for a long time – until the Chertkov Papers in their entirety at last become open to scholars, before knowing if the data there can lead to meaningful quantification for this period at least. Until then our situation continues to resemble Baldwin's around seven decades ago. We are still largely guessing!

22 Vladimir F. Martsinkovskii, *Zapiski veruiushchego: Iz istorii religioznogo dvizheniia v Sovetskoy Rosii (1917–1923)* (Prague, printed privately, 1929), 86–93, 205–7, 272–8. German translation by W.L. Jack, *Gott-Erleben in Ssowjet-Russland: Erinnerungen aus der Freiheit und dem Gefängnis* (Wernigerode am Harz, 1927), 83–93, 197–9, 261–7. Study of the gospels had already made Martsinkovskii (1884–1972) an absolute pacifist during his student years before the war; and poor health saved him from imprisonment as a CO during the Great War. After the war the People's Court was to exempt him from service in the Red Army – on condition he continued his voluntary work with street children. Martsinkovskii's memoirs include some fascinating vignettes of COs, several of whom he met during time he spent subsequently in a Soviet jail: a charming Seventh-day Adventist boy from the country, a semi-literate and naïve Evangelical Christian peasant who delighted his fellow prisoners with his singing, an ex-army officer and former Tolstoyan communitarian who now felt any religious affiliation a hindrance to the freedom of the spirit, and finally an Orthodox student whom the People's Court, presided over in this case by a workman, eventually exempted unconditionally – to Martsinkovskii's amazement, since the courts often rejected out of hand the few Orthodox applicants for CO status appearing before them. The young man seemingly made a specially good impression because he was able to cite abundantly from the antiwar utterances of church authorities in the Orthodox tradition, for example, the Syrian saint Ephraem Syrus (c. 306–73) (Wilhelm Kahle, *Evangelische Christen in Russland und der Sovetunion: Ivan Stepanovič Prochanov [1869–1935] und der Weg der Evangeliumchristen und Baptisten* [Wuppertal and Kassel, 1978], 391 n. 19, 393 n. 24).

Compare with the above the experiences of two Baptist COs living in the Urals. On being incorporated into the Red Army during the summer of 1920, they declared their desire to receive exemption as COs on the basis of Lenin's decree. For a time they disappeared entirely from view. But then someone ran into them in a train carrying troops. Eventually, after various vicissitudes, the two men were set free by a People's Court to which their friends had managed to transfer their case. See Waldemar Gutsche, *Religion und Evangelium in Sovjetrussland zwischen zwei Weltkriegen (1917–1944)* (Kassel, 1959), 27, 28.

23 From 'Another Summer: 3.Iwana,' *The Dolphin* (1973).

24 Toews, 'The Mennonite *Selbstschutz*,' 30.

25 Baldwin, *Liberty*, 256: 'The authorities in White territories did not spare such men; many were shot, though no estimate of their number has been made.' But inevitably Baldwin's information in this regard cannot have

been so reliable as it was in the case of COs on territories controlled during the Civil War by the Red Army. The lives of more COs may have been 'spared' than Baldwin implies.

26 Dragunovskii, in Edgerton, ed., *Memoirs of Peasant Tolstoyans*, 208.

27 Rempel, ed., *Waffen*, 30–2. Another Mennonite conscripted into Kolchak's army was Peter Jakob Konrad, who had earlier served first as a draftee in the Mennonite Forestry Service and then as a volunteer medical orderly with the Russian forces during the Great War. With Kolchak, Konrad acted as an unarmed *Sanitäter*, along with his younger brother and his brother-in-law. As Kolchak's army headed for defeat, Konrad deserted – a wise move, though not without its dangers. See Anne Konrad, *And in Their Silent Beauty Speak: A Mennonite Family in Russia and Canada 1790–1990* ([Toronto], 2004), 147, 152, 153. The author is Konrad's daughter: she includes in her book many interesting details about the life of 'Russian' Mennonites before, during, and after the Revolution that help to illuminate the community's stance towards their traditional tenet of nonresistance during this period.

28 I have been greatly assisted in threading my way through a subject, indeed of great importance, but one in which I am, alas, an ignoramus, by Peter H. Solomon, Jr's, well-documented and stimulating article 'Soviet Penal Policy, 1917–1934: A Reinterpretation,' *Slavic Review*, vol. 39, no. 2 (June 1980), 195–217.

29 Solomon (ibid., 196, 200–3), while arguing with regard to Soviet penal policy in favour 'not [of] a straight line, but a sharp break ... before and after the summer of 1929,' is careful to point out the existence of labour camps known as 'concentration camps,' run by the Cheka during the Civil War for political prisoners. They came to include the notorious penal settlements on the Solovetski Islands in the frozen North. But the prevailing pattern in the Soviet prison system of that era was set by the 'progressive' penologists and not the secret police.

30 That is, repeated sentencing for what in fact was the same offence. In 1927, M.L. Salikin, for instance, was tried for a fourth time as a CO; I have found, however, no evidence indicating exactly how frequent was this sort of thing.

31 Baldwin, *Liberty*, 264, 265.

32 Solomon, 'Soviet Penal Policy,' 199.

33 In line with general prison policy, jailed COs also received short-term leaves of absence. Baldwin (*Liberty*, 267) gives a striking example of this 'leniency' from 1927. After his lecture at the Tolstoyan Moscow Vegetarian Society, he relates, 'two men came up to me ... and introduced themselves as objectors serving prison sentences. When I enquired how they happened

to be at the meeting, they replied that the warden had let them out to hear the lecture [its 'safely remote subject' was 'Militarism in the United States'] on their promise to be back for work Monday! They took the time from their two weeks vacation from prison allowed to them as to all well-behaved prisoners.' See appendix to essay 20 above.

34 Brock, ed., *Testimonies of Conscience Sent from the Soviet Union to the War Resisters' International, 1923–1929* (Toronto, 1997), 6, 7.

35 Solomon, 'Soviet Penal Policy,' 204. This program, however, was less effective in the provinces.

36 Despite the fact that, beginning in 1923 and continuing in subsequent years, successive government decrees withdrew recognition of certain major pacifist groups as qualifying their members to claim CO status, the *War Resister* of February 1927 printed a surprising judicial decision from October of the preceding year. Then the Moscow County Court Civil Division, hearing the appeal of an imprisoned objector belonging to the Evangelical Christian Church, ruled that, although members of that body did not fall any longer into a category recognized by the law as qualifying for CO status, the man should 'be exempted from military service on account of his religious convictions, and no alternative work be imposed on him.' The court based its decision first on the man's undoubted sincerity, proved by his willingness to suffer a jail term considerably longer than the period of army training which he had refused to attend, and secondly on 'fanaticism,' which made him unsuitable for service in the Red Army. 'To penalize him a second time,' the court declared, 'would be ... contradictory to the principles of the Soviet Government, which desires neither to revenge nor to punish, but to reform its criminal citizens.' This decision, however, seems to have been unique. See Brock, ed., *Testimonies*, 23, 24. The appellant, twenty-six-year-old Vasilii Chepikov, a Belarusian peasant, before he became an Evangelical Christian had performed his three-year conscript service in the Red Army. In 1925, now a pacifist, he was jailed for a *year* for refusing a summons to attend territorial training for a *month*. Next year, after release from jail, he had again been called up for a month's training.

37 Ibid., 37; also 8, 9.

38 Baldwin, *Liberty*, 266, 267. Baldwin correctly described such activities as 'very restrained.' They consisted in this case of privately circulating among sympathizers a letter asking for support of potential COs. The sentences of exile were based on a law punishing the use of 'the religious sentiments of the masses to excite resistance to the laws.' Chertkov, as chairman of the Society, took full responsibility for the actions of its staff and told the authorities it was he, and not they, who should be prosecuted. The secret

police, however, were unwilling to arrest the venerable old man, editor-in-chief of the official edition of Tolstoy's collected works and known at home and abroad as the Master's spiritual heir. 'A distinguished old idealist,' he was probably 'politically harmless. But' – Baldwin explains what he presumes was the OGPU's reasoning – 'organized work from an office might develop opposition; and the exile of secretaries breaks it up.'

39 The most notorious of such cases was that of Stanley Murphy and Louis Taylor, who went on a prolonged hunger strike in the penitentiary at Springfield (MO). The consent of three doctors was needed for certification. While the two prison doctors signed the certificate, the outside doctor, whose agreement was required by law, refused to sign. Murphy and Taylor, of course, did not yet become free men, but they remained in a civil prison and were not transferred to a mental institution, as they would have been in case of consensus on the part of the three examining physicians.

40 Martsinkovskii, *Zapiski*, 92, 93 (German translation, 92, 93); Kahle, *Evangelische Christen*, 408, n. 49. From supplementary materials Martsinkovskii included in an English version of his memoirs, *With Christ in Soviet Russia: A Russian Christian's Personal Experiences of the Power of the Gospel in Freedom and in Prison in Connection with the Religious Movements in U.S.S.R.*, translated by Hoyt E. Porter (Prague, printed privately, 1933), 325, we learn that later Asiev suffered even more severely for his religious convictions, first in the Solovetski Islands and then in Siberian exile, though I think not specifically now as a CO. Martsinkovskii is extremely vague as to the date of Asiev's incarceration in a mental institution; it is possible it occurred before the revolution! The report on the Tolstoyan is in Brock, ed., *Testimonies*, 36. It calls him simply Mazurin. He may be Boris Mazurin, a leading communitarian and author of one of the most compelling narratives printed in Edgerton's volume of memoirs of peasant Tolstoyans in the Soviet Union, referred to above. I am puzzled, though, by the fact that there Boris Mazurin nowhere mentions being imprisoned as a CO (though this was not at all unlikely), let alone incarcerated in a lunatic asylum. There may have been, of course, two Tolstoyans with the same surname, though such a coincidence seems to me unlikely.

41 If only I had at my disposal even a brief account of his CO soldier experiences by a Seventh-day Adventist! Or something perhaps from D.S. Vnukov, who did not belong to any religious group but was unwilling to carry a weapon. Called up in 1927, he had 'agreed to be a photographer in the army' (Brock, ed., *Testimonies*, 29).

42 Penner, *Mennoniten*, 104.

43 Ibid., 8. This story illustrates once again the fact that provincial officials

often ignored with impunity the Kremlin's regulations concerning CO exemption.

44 Ibid., 17, 18.

45 Penner (ibid., 44) lists a number of jobs to which the army assigned his Mennonite fellow soldiers, who obviously possessed varying levels of education. Occupations connected with the farm predominated among them, though also on the list were the following: blacksmith, carpenter, driver, laundryman, librarian, housepainter, shoemaker, stableboy, stenographer, wainwright. 'And all of us,' he comments, 'were quite content with the duties we were ordered to do.'

46 Namely, repositioning cannon. 'That,' said the officer-in-charge, 'is in no way a military exercise.' Penner and four other Mennonite lads carried out the task, for which some of their comrades criticized them. In the critics' view, they had failed to uphold the Mennonite peace witness (ibid., 43, 44).

47 Ibid., 112.

48 The bad impression left on Penner by these ten hours weekly of political instruction (pages 64–7) is confirmed in the recollections of another Mennonite soldier CO, Dietrich Klassen from the Old Colony (Chortitza), who served in the Red Army as a hospital attendant from September 1922 to May 1924 in five stints, first of twenty months and then four one-month stints. See Rempel, ed., *Waffen*, 33. Klassen in his free time was expected to read the communist and atheist propaganda in abundant supply in the hospital library. He failed to do so, and this gained him a bad reputation with the politruks attached to the staff.

49 Penner, *Mennoniten*, 92–4. Penner refers to the general as 'Fritz Friedrich,' obviously a pseudonym. Mystery surrounds his background, but he appears to have been an ethnic German, either on loan (so to speak) from Weimar Germany or an ex-Tsarist officer taken over by the new regime.

50 Ibid., 96, 97.

51 See, for example, the report 'In a Russian Civil Battalion,' printed in the *War Resister*, no. 24 (Autumn 1929), and reprinted in Brock, ed., *Testimonies*, 35, 36. 'During the Spring of 1928 over 1,000 Russian sectarians, who had been exempted from military service, were summoned by order of the Commissariat of the Interior to join the "Civil Battalion," to work for about four-and-a-half months in the forests of the Ural district. Conditions of life varied.' In some cases the men obtained 'decent food and shelter' and reasonable conditions of work. Others fared badly, 'having to walk many miles to fetch food. Their work was in a marsh where they toiled up to their knees in water, tormented by mosquitoes.' The battalion officers harped constantly on the theme of an imminent war between the Soviet Union and the capital-

ist states and 'the consequent duty of every man to defend the Fatherland.' Ninety-one of the men yielded to these arguments, sometimes skilfully presented, and decided to renounce their CO status and join the army. According to Kahle, *Evangelische Christen*, 411, n. 56, of the more than 1,000 men in the battalion, approximately 600 were Mennonites, 185 Baptists, 185 Evangelical Christians, and the remainder drawn from various smaller pacifist sects. Kahle also mentions (page 409) that in 1929, 62 sectarian COs in one of the labour battalions (presumably located in Ukraine) sent a telegram to the government of the Ukrainian Soviet Republic declaring their readiness to bear arms in defence of 'the achievements of the October Revolution' in case of an attack by the imperialist powers. As Kahle points out, resistance to pressures to sign such a document was not easy, at least for Baptist or Evangelical COs, who no longer enjoyed the support of their church in their stand as COs.

52 Rempel, ed., *Waffen*, 44, 45, 56, 63, 69, 76–8. In Rempel's collection, I found the reminiscences of A.W. Janzen particularly helpful.

53 Ibid., 69, 70.

54 The key text here was of course Romans 13:1–7. Penner, who had been drafted in 1924, explains clearly the Mennonite attitude in a section of his book he entitles: 'My personal position with regard to service required by the state [Staatsdienst]' (*Mennoniten*, 9, 10). All such calls from the government (*Obrigkeit*) for service must be obeyed without reservation and with a glad heart, unless indeed the duty required was morally wrong as in the case of training in weaponry for the purpose of killing other human beings.

55 Rempel, ed., *Waffen*, 85, 86. See also pages 47, 76, 106. At the end of the 1920s, though, several Mennonite ministers were jailed because they aided CO applicants in their efforts to gain exemption from military service.

56 Mennonite COs felt particularly close to the choristers: 'pleasant and good fellows'; 'We honour their memory' (Rempel, ed., *Waffen*, 105).

57 Ibid., 102–5; Klippenstein, 'Mennonites and Military Service,' 13: '1932 through 1935 has been designated the "worst years" of service, when the government was concerned not so much with offering alternative-service opportunities as with making those who refused to perform combatant service pay the bitter price of their "disloyalty."'

58 Rempel, ed., *Waffen*, 137–44. Hans Rempel, an eyewitness of the events he and his co-authors describe, states decisively (p. 146) that 1934 was the last year in which a CO option was possible for draftees satisfying the authorities of their qualifications for this status. He writes: '1935 nahmen die Volksgerichte keine Anträge auf Befreiung vom Wehrdienst mehr an.' If

most of the 1934 contingent also served a three-year term, that would make 1937 the last year in which conscientious objection formally existed in the Soviet Union. However, Klippenstein ('Mennonite Pacifism and State Service in Russia') accepts 1935 as the most probable terminal date for accepting applications. 'Little or no evidence,' he writes, 'has been found to indicate that Soviet courts continued to accept CO applications after 1935.' As I have shown, we shall probably have to push this date back by a year: that would coincide, too, with Rempel's memory.

59 Rempel, ed., *Waffen*, 146.

60 Klibanov, *Religioznoe sektantstvo*, 208.

61 Community life on the Tolstoyan model came to an end during the late 1930s. Since the beginning of that decade, agricultural colonists, numbering 'about one thousand,' had been concentrated in western Siberia.

62 Kahle, *Evangelische Christen*, 408.

63 The *Trudarmiia* persisted into the early 1950s. Some readers may have wondered why no mention has been made so far of Jehovah's Witnesses (JWs), who formed such a lively component of the Second World War community of conscientious objectors, especially in English-speaking countries. In fact – fortunately from the viewpoint of the authorities – there were few, if any, JWs in the Soviet Union before 1945, though after that date they steadily rose in numbers and consistently resisted the Soviet draft, as they did in other conscriptionist countries of the world. The incorporation into the Soviet Union, in 1939–41 and then from 1945 on, of Poland's former eastern borderlands (*kresy*), where JWs were already quite numerous, had as an unforeseen result the opening of the whole USSR to the JWs for missionizing effort. JWs were no longer aliens who could hopefully be kept out, but citizens of the Soviet Union. (There were, of course, other contributing factors to their post-1945 expansion, eventually from one end to the other of the Union.)

64 The point I want to make here is that the insistence of the church on refusal of combatant conscript service as a condition of continued membership illustrates its loyalty to the tradition of *Wehrlosigkeit*, shaken a little earlier by the *Selbstschutz* episode. Whether such rigidity ultimately strengthened the church's peace witness is another question. I doubt if it did. In the case of the Quakers, I certainly think the abandonment of disownment for serving as a combatant in the armed forces or as a militiaman did not lead to a weakening of the Quaker peace testimony, as that stalwart eighteenth-century Quaker pacifist Anthony Benezet realized; he failed, though, to convince his Friends of this. In fact, the subsequent decline of the peace testimony, where it has occurred, appears to be due to other factors.

65 Quoted in Klippenstein, 'Mennonite Pacifism and State Service in Russia,' 332.
66 Ibid. See also Rempel, ed., *Waffen*, 147.
67 Heinrich and Gerhard Woelk, *A Wilderness Journey: Glimpses of the Mennonite Brethren Church in Russia, 1925–1980*, translated from the German by Victor Doerksen (Fresno CA, 1982), 164, 165. Not until 1956 were Mennonites of draft age again liable for service in the army. My comments on the post-war era, therefore, apply to the period after 1956.
68 See, for example, A.B. Pchelintsev, *Pravo no streliat': Alternativnaia grazhdanskaia sluzhba* (Moscow, 1997).

22 Conscientious Objectors in Interwar Poland

Interwar Poland, like most other countries in continental Europe, imposed conscription on its able-bodied young men, who were required to serve in the armed forces for a period of two years before being placed on army reserve. Conscientious objection to military service remained there a peculiarity of a small number of religious sects; for in Poland, unlike the Netherlands, no objectors appeared with a stance based on anarcho-syndicalist or humanist grounds. In 1924 the Polish Ministry of War issued a circular exempting birthright members of certain pacifist sects from combatant service.[1] Eventually such persons were assigned noncombatant duties in the army. Recognition of this kind, however, covered only a small percentage of the men claiming to be conscientious objectors (COs). Those objectors refusing to enter the army, or not qualifying for exemption under the narrow terms of the circular, were tried by court martial and sentenced to long – and repeated – terms of imprisonment.[2] Though numerically the problem was small, still the principle of freedom of conscience was at stake.[3]

We know next to nothing about the fate of Poland's COs until in 1927 a section of the War Resisters' International (WRI) was set up in Warsaw with the task, above all, of defending the interests of those refusing to bear arms on grounds of conscience and of bringing their plight to international notice so as to pressure the Polish government into alleviating the harsh treatment they received at its hands.[4] Membership of the section, which remained small throughout the period, was predominantly middle-class, ethnic Poles working alongside persons from one or another of the country's national minorities. Practising Catholics, Orthodox, or Lutherans were noticeably absent, though several persons of Jewish extraction, like Amelia Kurlandzka or Rita Krauze, were among the section's most active members. Most of them religious liberals, humanists, or freethinkers, the Warsaw war resisters contrasted with the military objectors whose cause they espoused. The latter were drawn exclusively from primitivist sects of various shadings or from eschatological bodies like the Jehovah's Witnesses. With some objectors and WRI members practising vegetarianism, belief in the power of nonviolence and in the ultimate achievement of world brotherhood united them all in a fellowship that contrasted strongly with the rising tide of ethnic hatred and state violence already beginning to engulf central and eastern Europe.

The men who resisted military service came almost without exception from a different social stratum from the men and women forming WRI's Warsaw section. Peasants and artisans, they possessed little formal education. While some of them were barely literate, others had succeeded by their own efforts in acquiring a considerable stock of knowledge. Most of them had pondered the meaning of life; and they were prepared to accept prolonged hardship for themselves and their families in order to remain loyal to a code of ethics they believed was required by their religious faith.

A more unexpected aspect of conscientious objection in interwar Poland lies in the fact that an overwhelming majority of the objectors were drawn from the country's Belarusian minority inhabiting the north-eastern territories of the Polish state, even though Belarusians formed only about 6 per cent of the total population.[5] This situation emerges clearly in the reports received by the WRI from its Polish section and published in its journal.[6] There we discover, too, that the trials of most objectors took place in Military District Courts either at Wilno (Vilnius) or at Brześć (Brest),[7] that is, in military tribunals of the Belarusian area.

The comparatively rare instances when ethnic Poles, Germans, or Ukrainians refused to bear arms for conscience sake usually concerned Jehovah's Witnesses, a body with an international outreach whose members were expected to become conscientious objectors if drafted. But we do hear, too, of isolated Baptists and Adventists from these ethnic backgrounds taking the same stand. Of course, neither the Roman Catholicism of the Poles, nor mainstream German Protestantism, nor the Uniate Church of Poland's Ukrainians in the southeast provided a fertile soil for nurturing religious pacifism. Indeed, Polish patriotism, German nationalism, and the Ukrainianism inherited from former

Austrian Galicia created a hostile environment for the kind of war resistance that included refusal of military service.

The situation in the Belarusian area was different. This territory had formed an integral part of the Russian Empire, the most important area of the Empire incorporated by the peace settlement into the reborn Polish state.[8] Before 1914 the widespread sectarian movement in the Russian Empire had already taken root among the Belarusians, though possibly not quite with the same intensity as it had done among the Russians and Ukrainians under Tsarist rule. This development accounts for the presence among Poland's Belarusian minority of small sectarian groups (found also on the other side of the Polish-Russian frontier), whose principles forbade them to bear arms and kill their fellow men.

Among these groups were the Malevantsy, followers of the millenarian prophet Kondratii Malevannyi (d. 1913).[9] Tolstoy, whose pacifist writings were easily accessible to Belarusians because of the close kinship between their speech and the language of the Master, had found adherents, too, among the Belarusian peasantry.[10] Andrei Polishchuk was a typical objector from this milieu. A vegetarian and a teetotaler, he spent many years in a Polish prison – sometimes in chains – until international protest secured his release in 1931. From jail he had written defiantly: 'I can never be a slave or a beast. Never shall I serve [what I consider to be] base aims. I want to be a free man and work for a better future for mankind.'[11] Illiteracy, indeed, was no barrier to the spread of Tolstoyism; in the villages, a literate Belarusian peasant could read out loud Tolstoy's popular booklets, many of them simple tales expounding his philosophy of nonviolence in easy language, and find understanding among his listeners.

At the conclusion of the recent war, moreover, Russia's Baptists and the closely allied Evangelical Christians, then both rapidly expanding bodies, had abandoned their previous 'defencism' and officially adopted a pacifist position, with support for their young conscripts who were now refusing to bear arms. Thus, although these churches were soon forced by the Soviet government to reverse this trend and uphold armed defence of the workers' state, in the immediate post-war period many Baptists and Evangelical Christians, on being drafted into the Soviet Army, had claimed conscientious objector status, permitted by the decree of 4 January 1919.[12] The government indeed gradually restricted the originally very generous provisions of this enactment; but that did not prevent the continuance of conscientious objection in the Soviet Union, even if on a decreasing scale, until official recognition was withdrawn in the mid-1930s. After the Baptist (and Evangelical Christian) leadership had succumbed to Communist pressure on this issue, a dissident group continued to exist, though it had to endure severe persecution by the authorities. Baptists and Evangelical Christians living under Polish rule were well acquainted with these developments taking place just across the border. And it was from this awareness that we may attribute the comparatively high incidence of conscientious objection among Belarusian members of these two sects.

In West Belarus, the area incorporated into the new Polish state, most Belarusians belonged to the Orthodox Church, as did their conationals across the frontier; but a sizeable minority were Catholics. In addition, there were a number of religious sectarians belonging to a variety of – usually small – denominations. (Some of these, we have seen, espoused pacifism and nonviolence.) The two majority churches regarded the sectarians, on the whole, with suspicion and sometimes with open hostility, while the latter reciprocated such sentiments by adopting a negative stance towards both Orthodoxy and Catholicism.

This essay will concentrate on exploring some of the implications of the fact that the majority of interwar Poland's COs were Belarusians and not ethnic Poles or members of the country's other nationalities.

Neglected under Tsarist rule, the districts of Poland inhabited by Belarusians remained economically and socially backward throughout the interwar years; they constituted, in fact, the poorest area in a state that was suffering as a whole from severe economic problems. The overwhelming majority of Belarusians were peasants, many of them illiterate. Polish culture predominated everywhere, an inheritance from the period before the partitions of the late eighteenth century when Belarus had belonged to the old Polish-Lithuanian Commonwealth. With industry only in its infancy and the inhabitants of the small urban centres largely Jewish, political ascendancy rested jointly with the numerically small class of Polish – or Polonized – estate-owners, who were almost exclusively of noble (*szlachta*) origin, and the local Polish bureaucracy, which took its orders from the central government in Warsaw.

Belarusian national consciousness remained underdeveloped.[13] Whereas literary awakening dated back to the 1820s, Belarusian political nationalism had emerged only during the recent war. Thereafter, it continued to be weak.[14] Nevertheless, a strong sense of social apartness divided the Belarusian-speaking peasant masses from the small

Polish upper class and from Polish officialdom in the area. This consciousness led to the growth of political radicalism in the countryside, where rural poverty was widespread during the interwar years and sympathy for communism, though inchoate, was fostered by contacts maintained with Soviet fellow countrymen living just across the frontier. The latter enjoyed at least the right to develop their own language freely, even if in East Belarus civil liberties disappeared altogether and a reign of terror ensued under Stalin that has had few parallels in its severity. Yet as political and cultural repression on the part of the Polish authorities increased, the small Belarusian intelligentsia, hitherto not unfavourably disposed on the whole towards Poland, began to gravitate towards a pro-Soviet position.[15] In March 1927, the Polish government suppressed Hramada, by far the largest Belarusian political party, on the grounds of its being a crypto-Communist organization (an accusation that was indeed largely correct).

Nationalist opposition on the part of Belarusian political activists went underground, but it did not disappear. Moreover, rural discontent now merged with the still vague nationalistic aspirations felt by the peasantry to create a deepening sense of antagonism towards the Polish state, and in particular towards the civil administration responsible for carrying out the Polish government's policy of political repression as well as towards the Polish army, which conscripted for a long period of service the young men of the Belarusian village. These two state institutions, understandably, became for the Belarusian peasantry the most visible symbols of an alien rule, which seemed increasingly hard to bear.

The Belarusian peasant antimilitarists, who preferred to spend long years in jail rather than shoulder a rifle and fight for the Polish state, strove of course for the inauguration of the Kingdom of God and not for the establishment of an independent Republic of Belarus. They would have refused to fight if the national flag had been Belarusian. Yet the fact that the military authority they confronted was Polish, and therefore both socially and culturally alien, cannot have escaped them; that observation, in turn, could scarcely have failed to strengthen their consciousness of a separate Belarusian identity. Shortly before the outbreak of the Second World War, the WRI published in its organ a brief article based on information supplied by its section in Poland and entitled 'A White Russian Peasant's Stand for Peace.' The illusive connection between peasant antimilitarism and national consciousness is reflected in the text of the article:

> The Polish Government is collecting money for a National Defense Fund, and although officially the contributions are to be voluntary they are in part levied. Particularly cruel methods are used against the peasants, and officers and teachers in the Polish compulsory Elementary Schools, which are militaristic, are playing a sinister part.
>
> Jacob Wolczek [Iakub Volchek] lives in a village near Mir. He is an intelligent, but poor, White Russian [i.e., Belarusian] peasant. He is a member of the Village Council, and was asked to become a member of the Commission to raise money for the National Defense Fund. He refused continued invitations, although they were accompanied by threats.
>
> When people came to collect money from him he said, 'If the money were for disarmament I would like to give half my property, but for armaments I will not give a penny.' Because of his attitude he has been subjected to much petty persecution, and recently he has been fined 30 zloty by the District Authorities for his refusal. He remains firm in his refusal to have nothing to do with the fund.[16]

Though the sectaries did not participate in the still-weak political agitation of the Belarusian nationalists, in this period often closely allied – and sometimes actually identical – with the Communists, they remained close in spirit to the aspirations of their politically oriented brethren. Thus, while refusal to bear arms by interwar Belarusian village lads arose from their sect's Bible-centred nonresistance, and was a religious act, their war resistance was tinged, even if only lightly, with a cultural nationalist colouring. For, by refusing to serve in the Polish army, they were giving expression, in however veiled a form, to their deep attachment to a Belarusian national identity.

The WRI section in Warsaw did its best to bring all these cases to the attention of pacifists abroad who would, it was hoped, exert pressure on the Polish government to ameliorate the often harsh treatment meted out to objectors, whether of Belarusian or of other ethnic origin. Who, we may ask, acted as link between the urban humanist pacifists in the capital and the Belarusian peasant war resisters? Here, indeed, two cultural worlds met; contact might not be always easy. Since sources for interwar Polish pacifism are extremely exiguous, it is difficult to give an answer to the question just posed. But a brief obituary appearing in 1938 in the WRI's organ, published in England, points to its subject, Iosif Vigdorchyk (Józef Wigdorczyk), as the one who provided the liaison; he also seems to have supplied leadership to the hard-pressed peasant war resisters of interwar Poland, whether Belarusians or from another nationality.[17]

The obituary is not sparing in its praises, going so far as to describe Vigdorchyk as 'a great man.' The most striking trait of his character is said to have been 'indomitability.' 'In spite of an infirmity that entailed constant suffering, he became the friend and protector of countless war resisters who endured long years of imprisonment ... He visited them in prison, faced authorities with demands for their release, toured over Poland and became the centre of a great movement.' In addition, 'Josef's work was not limited to Poland'; he translated – 'and neatly duplicated' – WRI literature into Russian, thus becoming 'our instrument for much of our contact with the Russian people.'

Vigdorchyk, 'Brother Josef as we called him,' died in the town of Białystok in north-eastern Poland on 4 March 1938. Though the obituary just cited describes him as 'of Russian origin,' it seems almost certain that ethnically he was in fact a Belarusian. Białystok, his place of residence, was situated in a Belarusian area; his name is not infrequently found among Belarusians. That an educated Belarusian should know the Russian language as well as Vigdorchyk obviously did was not surprising, since he must have received his education in a Russian school. Moreover, the *War Resister*, in its reports on Poland, sometimes confuses 'Russian' with 'White Russian,' that is, Belarusian. It was not easy at that date for the English to get these subtle ethnic distinctions straight. But even were Vigdorchyk of Great Russian origin (which I think is very unlikely), surely he may be regarded as a Belarusian by adoption as a result both of his habitat and of his leadership role among Belarusian war resisters?

But, we may also ask, has Vigdorchyk not left some further trace of his existence in the surviving record? Is a thirteen-line obituary in a rather inaccessible journal the only notice we have of this man, who after all played a significant part in a vigorous, if small, movement of war resistance and gained the respect and admiration of his adherents, even to the point of adulation?[18] Unfortunately my quest for Vigdorchyk, unlike A.J.A. Symons's famous quest for Baron Corvo, has proved entirely fruitless, despite the assistance of kind friends in Poland.[19]

To begin with the public record office in Warsaw covering the more recent history of Poland, known as the Archiwum Akt Nowych. This does indeed hold a number of files dealing with the province of Białystok during the interwar years (*Zespół urząd wojewódzki białostocki*). While these files include materials relating to the interwar Communist movement in that area, there is nothing there on Vigdorchyk – or, indeed, on any pacifist activity in the province. The local Belarusian and Polish press seems also to have remained silent on the occasion of our 'great man's' death, so far at any rate as one may judge by copies that have survived the wartime destruction of newspaper depositories. Of course, somewhere in present-day Poland, Belarus, or even Lithuania a document or the file of some interwar newspaper or journal may be resting quietly on the shelves with just the information about Vigdorchyk that we have been seeking in vain. But if so, I failed, alas, to discover any clues to the whereabouts of such materials. And without preliminary clues of some sort, any research effort must in this instance resemble the proverbial search for a needle in a haystack!

What, indeed, adds a note of irony is that, first as a relief worker in post-war Poland and then as a graduate student and postgraduate researcher in Polish history, I had been personally acquainted with Amelia Kurlandzka, who was described in Vigdorchyk's obituary as his close associate in aiding COs. After his death, she was his successor in the leadership of the small Polish war resistance movement, until the outbreak of hostilities put an end to it in the following year. A question from me would undoubtedly have sufficed to elicit comprehensive answers from Kurlandzka to all the questions I have been asking here. But at that date I was ignorant of Vigdorchyk's existence; anyhow, my interests were focused on matters remote from the life of the elusive Belarusian.[20]

All we are left with, then, apart form the scraps of information supplied in Vigdorchyk's obituary, is the photograph reproduced here, showing 'Father Josef' surrounded by some of his war-resisting followers, mostly – and perhaps all – of Belarusian nationality. We may see him there in his 'home circle,' as it were, and can feel, if only remotely, something of the charisma that he radiated among these simple and devout peasant sectaries. But even now a certain ambiguity remains. The *War Resister*'s reproduction of the photograph is of poor quality. Vigdorchyk is, I presume, the frail and rather sad-looking man seated in the middle of the picture, for this person is marked with an 'x.' But one cannot be quite sure of this, and thus Vigdorchyk's identity even on the photograph remains unclear. But perhaps that, too, is symbolic: the obscure, but charismatic, leader and his humble followers are blended here in one design – to overthrow the incubus of militarism

Iosif Vigdorchyk and other war resisters in interwar Poland; Vigdorchyk is presumably the person marked with a white 'x.' (Courtesy the War Resisters' International)

in a land whose people had suffered from repeated wars through the centuries.

In conclusion, we may inquire what was the subsequent fate of these antimilitarist peasant sectarians in Belarus, whose young men, because of their pacifist beliefs, had stubbornly resisted the Polish military machine. How did they now react to the tragic events that successively overwhelmed their land: first Soviet occupation, then German invasion, and then reincorporation into the Soviet Union, a state which had suppressed all manifestations of pacifism along with most other aspects of religious life?

One of them, Daniel Skvornik, we know, was shot by the Germans. 'He lived in Kochovo, a small village near Skidel. The partisans had damaged the railway track not very far from the village. The German punitive expedition came to Kochovo and shot all inhabitants – men, women and children. Then the village was burned.'[21] For the rest, there is only silence.

NOTES

1 *War Resister* (Enfield, Middlesex, UK), no. 15 (February 1927), 7.

2 For further details, see my article 'The Small-Sect Antimilitarists of Interwar East Central Europe,' *Reconciliation Quarterly* (Autumn 1995), 6-16, where, alas, the printers made complete havoc of my page 12!

3 Exact figures are not available, but often there seem to have been as many as fifty objectors in prison at any one time, in addition to an unspecified number serving in the army in a noncombatant capacity.

4 *War Resister*, no. 17 (August 1927), 6. This journal, published at irregular intervals by the WRI, remains the most rewarding source for the history of conscientious objection in interwar Poland. Shortly before the outbreak of war, the Polish section's secretary, Amelia Kurlandzka, deposited its archives for safe-keeping in the Warsaw Public Library. They were destroyed by the Nazis, along with most of that library's collections, after the suppression of the Warsaw Insurrection of 1944. Probably materials on the subject have survived in government, including military, archives. But only a painstaking and lengthy investigation could unearth them, especially since some of these archives are now located in Belarus, Lithuania, and Ukraine.

5 In 1931, the official figure was 6.1 per cent, that is, 1,954,000 persons out of a total population of 31,916,000. See Jerzy Tomaszewski, *Ojczyzna nie tylko*

Polaków: Mniejszości narodowe w Polsce w latach 1918–1939 (Warsaw, 1985), 77. Assessments of the percentage differ, however, largely as a result of differing definitions of who counted as a Belarusian. Still, the official figures, though possibly an underestimation, are not likely to be too far wrong.

6 See, for example, the *War Resister*, no. 19 (March 1928), 8; no. 31 (Summer 1932), 16. Devi Prasad and Tony Smythe, eds, *Conscientious Objection – a World Survey: Compulsory Military Service and Resistance to It* (London, 1968), 109, refer to conscientious objection occurring in interwar Poland 'mostly amongst [White] Russian Tolstoyans living in the Eastern provinces.' In this statement the editors were drawing on reports published in the *War Resister*. So far as I know, the subject has not been dealt with in Belarusian. In the work of the Polish anti-Semite Mieczysław Skrudlik, *Agentury obce* (Warsaw, 1929), 11, 13, we learn that ordinarily almost half the conscripts belonging to the largely Belarusian Evangelical Christian sect requested assignment to the army medical corps because they objected to bearing arms. I must thank Professor Wojciech Modzelewski (University of Warsaw) for bringing my attention to this obscure booklet.

7 I do not know if the archives of these courts have survived the turbulent period that ensued after 1939. But from successive issues of the *War Resister*, their central role in judicial procedure against conscientious objectors is clear. The WRI Archives, deposited in the Institute of Social History (Amsterdam), contain very few manuscripts relating to interwar Poland. But materials there, dated 16 May 1932, refer specifically to the Military District Court No. III at Wilno and the Military District Court No. IX at Brześć as the locales for trials of conscientious objectors of Belarusian 'nationality' in the early 1930s.

8 Apart, that is, from the so-called Congress Kingdom of Poland, which enjoyed at least nominal separate status to the end. Because of the dominant position of Roman Catholicism and Polish culture, Russian sectarianism did not penetrate into this area.

9 In 1925, a delegation of three English Quakers visited their settlement at Raczkany near the Polish-Russian border. See *Friends in Europe: Handbook of the Society of Friends (Quakers) in Europe* (London, 1946), 51: 'These people were isolated from groups of their fellow-believers near Kiev ... they had, however, been visited and encouraged from time to time by a Polish Friend.' The latter was Wilhelm Tysz, who told me, when I was working in the Anglo-American Quaker Mission in Poland after the Second World War, that he had written a detailed survey of community life among the Malevantsy, but his report appears to be no longer extant. Tysz lived for a time as a teacher in their community.

10 There seems to have been a concentration of like-minded peace people at Skidal' near Grodno (Hrodna). I do not know if any contacts existed between the isolated Tolstoyans of Polish Belarus and the vigorous Tolstoyan pacifist movement in the Soviet Union, led by Vladimir Chertkov (see essay 20), but it is entirely possible that they did. A definitive answer may lie in the still uncatalogued – and therefore inaccessible – part of the Chertkov Papers (fond 435) in the Russian State Library (Moscow).

11 *War Resister*, no. 26 (Spring 1930), 6.

12 See Paul D. Steeves, 'The Russian Baptist Union, 1917–1935: Evangelical Awakening in Russia' (Ph.D. diss., University of Kansas, 1976), 557–92; also Z.K. Kalinicheva, *Sotsial' naia sushchnost' baptizma 1917–1929 gg.* (Leningrad, 1972), 59–60, a tendentious account. Professor Heather Coleman has completed a monograph (awaiting publication) on the Baptist Union in the early Soviet period. It contains a section on the Union's pacifism.

13 'The local people ... often failed to differentiate themselves from the Russians. Many had never heard the term "Belarusian"' (Piotr Wróbel, *Kształtowanie się białoruskiej świadomości narodowej a Polska* [Warsaw, 1990], 74, 75).

14 See Nicholas P. Vakar, *Belorussia: The Making of a Nation – a Case Study* (Cambridge, MA, 1956), chap. 9; Jan Zaprudnik, *Belarus: At a Crossroads in History* (Boulder, CO, and Oxford, UK, 1993), chap. 3. I would also like to thank Dr John Stanley for his comments concerning the history of Belarusian nationalism. I should add Dr Stanley disagrees with my major thesis here!

15 Wróbel, *Kształowanie*, 73, 74.

16 *War Resister*, no. 42 (Summer 1937), 7.

17 Ibid., no. 44 (Summer 1938), 2, 3. The obituary was unsigned; it was probably based on information sent to WRI headquarters by Amelia Kurlandzka. For Vigdorchyk, see my 'In Search of a "Lost" Belarusan Pacifist Leader,' in Peter Brock and Thomas P. Socknat, eds, *Challenge to Mars: Essays on Pacifism from 1918 to 1945* (Toronto, 1999), 60-6. Parts of this have been included in the present essay.

18 An anonymous article in the *War Resister*, no. 33 (n.d.[1933]), 13-17, entitled 'Until the End,' may contain references to Vigdorchyk, though it does not mention him by name. The article includes an account of a journey made by a middle-aged pacifist to see two imprisoned COs, one a Belarusian peasant lad and the other a working-class boy of Lithuanian nationality, both of whom were then on hunger strike in the hospital of a military jail in Wilno (Vilnius). 'I was one with them in thought,' the anonymous prison visitor stated; 'to me the two sentenced men were almost like sons.' Describing himself 'as a friend of the nearest friend of Tolstoi,' the visitor went on to explain that, living 'at a long distance,' he could make only 'very rare' visits

to the two jailed COs. If we accept that in those days Białystok might have seemed a long way from Wilno, especially if the traveller were in a poor state of health, the person in question could well have been Vigdorchyk himself. I suspect indeed that the latter was by religious affiliation a Tolstoyan. And 'the nearest friend of Tolstoi,' mentioned here as being a personal friend of the prison visitor, can only be Vladimir Chertkov, who led the antimilitarist movement in the Soviet Union from 1918 until his death in 1936. As the Chertkov Papers in the Russian State Library in Moscow (fond 435) become accessible to scholars, we may find materials there on Vigdorchyk, provided of course that my tentative identification of Vigdorchyk as the anonymous prison visitor is correct.

19 I would like to thank Professor Krzysztof Dunin-Wąsowicz, Dr Antoni Mironowicz, and Tadeusz A. Olszański for their investigations on my behalf in Warsaw and Białystok. They were not able, however, to uncover in archives and libraries there anything that would throw further light on Vigdorchyk either as man or as pacifist activist.

20 If, indeed, he really was a Belarusian ...

21 *War Resister*, no. 51 (Summer 1946), 33, 34, 36; from a report by Kurlandzka, one of the two known survivors of the WRI's Warsaw section. I am not sure if Skvornik had himself been a conscientious objector.

23 Six Weeks at Hawkspur Green: A Pacifist Episode during the Battle of Britain

Early in the 1980s the British Broadcasting Corporation (BBC) asked freelance writer Noel Currer-Briggs to help prepare a program on conscientious objectors (COs) in Second-World-War Britain. It was, in fact, never used, but it led Currer-Briggs, by now in his early sixties, to consider a further project: to write an account of an incident in his own career – 'a remarkable episode' – when in the summer of 1940 at the height of the Battle of Britain a small group of Oxford and Cambridge undergraduates, all of them pacifists and liable at any moment to confront conscription into the armed forces, had formed a Universities Ambulance Unit (UAU) and had started training in medical work.

After the lapse of forty years, Currer-Briggs found his memories of the six weeks he spent at Hawkspur Green, where the unit's training camp was located near the village of Little Bardfield in Essex, had grown hazy. Over the next few years, however, he successfully contacted a number of former participants in the camp. Some had died, while others he was unable to trace. Camp records did not exist – or had vanished without a trace. Eventually, on the basis of information gathered from participants, he pieced together a brief account of the camp. His narrative, though, never appeared in print.[1]

In 1939 pacifists formed a small minority among the undergraduates of England's two ancient, and especially prestigious, universities. They were, however, a vocal minority with their own pacifist societies, which attracted politically and socially aware members of the student body, as well as some of its best minds. The UAU had originated in Oxford, though its chronicler, Currer-Briggs, was at Cambridge along with several other unit members. At Oxford several prominent faculty publicly espoused pacifism, including church historian Cecil John

Cadoux at Mansfield College and the eccentric but brilliant philosopher Donald MacKinnon at Keble College. At Cambridge the Anglican Canon Charles Raven and the scientist and Peace Pledge Union (PPU) activist Alexander Wood at Emmanuel College defended pacifism in print and on the platform. If the UAU can be said to have had a place of origin, it was Balliol College, a thirteenth-century Oxford foundation then presided over by the dynamic – and left-wing – political philosopher A.D. Lindsay. In 1939 around 20 of its 150 undergraduates were pacifists. So let us begin the story of Hawkspur Camp there, with the commencement in October 1939 of the first wartime academic year.

Among college members who were to play an active role at Hawkspur was George Grant (1918–88), later to become Canada's best-known academic philosopher and exponent of progressive conservatism.[2] He had come to Oxford as a Rhodes Scholar to study ('read' in Oxfordese) law after successfully completing a B.A. in history at Queen's University in Ontario. At Canada's surrogate Eton, Upper Canada College, where his father was headmaster, young Grant, after reading Beverley Nichols's *Cry Havoc*,[3] had along with two of his schoolmates become a pacifist and sought – and obtained – exemption from the school's otherwise compulsory cadet corps.

For 'Choppy' Grant, as his father affectionately was called, his experiences as a soldier in the Great War had made him sympathetic to pacifism and ready to challenge the patriots on the school's board of governors on this issue.[4] George's pacifism at this time was not specifically Christian: 'As you know I am not a churchgoer,' he wrote to his mother from Oxford early in 1940.[5] But its Christian component grew steadily, and throughout his career Grant remained preoccupied with the religious aspect of life. One of his closest friends at Balliol, Peter Clarke, was a convinced Christian pacifist who went to prison for his beliefs: his stand continued to make a deep impact on Grant even after his own pacifism began to waver.[6]

Grant the 'colonial,' gauche and remaining rather uncertain of himself in the Balliol Junior Common Room, does not appear to have become acquainted there with two other particularly colourful Balliol undergraduates who were to be his colleagues at Hawkspur: Hallam Tennyson and Roddy (Roderic) Fenwick Owen. Tennyson was the great-grandson of the Victorian poet laureate and, on the female side, was a descendant of the seventh earl of Elgin, who had been responsible for removing the famous marbles from Athens to the British Museum; Roddy Owen was his slightly older cousin. Close friends at the real Eton College, Owen had converted Hallam to pacifism, and they had sold the PPU's paper, *Peace News*, together in Eton High Street, wearing the Eton boys' traditional top hats. Their introduction to pacifism reflected the same kind of reading as the Canadian Grant's – and that of so many other young people of that generation in English-speaking countries who came, if only temporarily, to espouse pacifism. It was the literature of disenchantment with war: primarily Beverley Nichols, A.A. Milne, Bertrand Russell, with the addition, of course, of the lively British *Peace News*. This was a humanist, humanitarian, ethical creed – no epithet fits it exactly. It could have religious, Christian undertones – or it might not.

These two boys were offspring of Britain's elite. At that date, even in Britain's upper-class 'public' schools and despite the ubiquitous cadet corps (otherwise known as the Officers' Training Corps [OTC]), the masters were often strongly antiwar and influenced the boys to become pacifists, a lesson sometimes – though by no means always – reinforced at home. Tennyson's mother indeed definitely disapproved of her son's association with his cousin Owen. She liked to entertain royalty at Farringford, the Tennyson family home on the Isle of Wight, where a butler in white gloves and two liveried footmen saw to the family's needs. There was no place there for pacifism. 'Roddy's influence,' she told her son, 'is pernicious ... Roddy [is] so pitifully misguided.' But the boys' close friendship – and their pacifism – continued, of course, in the freer atmosphere of the Balliol Junior Common Room. Tennyson writes in his autobiography:

> Roddy and I now entered on a period of preternaturally close friendship. We developed an elaborate cult based on a quick reading of the newly published Penguin volume of Freud. Our shrine, set up in his rooms, consisted of a retable with a dove on top representing the 'super-ego' and a teddy-bear in the middle representing the 'ego.' I have forgotten (significantly?) the 'id.' Through meditation we put ourselves in a state of semi-stupour and then indulged in the automatic writing of effusions ... which were threaded into an imitation gospel. Members of the sect were secretly selected by Roddy and me, though none of them were informed of the privilege.

A German refugee psychoanalyst, who gave Tennyson free sessions of psychoanalysis in exchange for a painting owned by Hallam that he admired, had 'insisted that Roddy and I were lovers and refused to listen to my denials.'[7] If Grant, though, was a member of this juvenile hocus-pocus, it must have been an unwitting one: that earnest young Canadian surely would not have been amused. But at Hawkspur he did at last come under Tennyson's charisma.

The Hawkspur campers were by no means drawn only from Balliol pacifists. Indeed, the man whom all recognized as the 'founder of the UAU,' Miles Vaughan Williams, was at Wadham College reading classics but already drawn to medicine, a field in which he eventually would make a name for himself. It was Vaughan Williams who, in the spring of 1940, as the 'phony' war turned into a shooting war, first realized a need to provide some service alternative for pacifist undergraduates like himself now facing call-up. They wished to help alleviate suffering – of soldiers as well as civilians – but were not willing to become soldiers themselves, even noncombatant ones. They were not service-absolutists, still less anarchists. They wished to help their country in its hour of need, but not as combatants. Grant at Balliol, for instance, had been perfectly willing to take part in an auxiliary fire brigade. 'Looking at these glorious buildings,' he told his mother, 'I have no scruples whatever about doing something to defend them, although at the same time it may indirectly help a war we doesn't like [*sic*]. It is as if someone attacked Chartres. Well, what the hell, you just couldn't sit still.'[8]

Quakers of the same ilk could join the Friends Ambulance Unit (FAU); it already had seen active service in Finland during the Winter War against the Soviet Union. Christian pacifists, even though not Quakers, possessed support societies to uphold them when they appeared before the tribunals that would decide their fate as COs. Vaughan Williams, full of energy and enterprise, now sought to provide for the unchurched pacifists at Oxford (and later through Currer-Briggs at Cambridge as well). Before the school year was over, he had organized first-aid classes for any interested members of the university's Pacifist Society with a local Quaker doctor as the instructor, and he invited applicants to join a Universities Ambulance Unit. Members, if accepted, would have to provide at least their own keep – or, rather, parents or guardians would have to be ready to provide this, for few undergraduates were yet breadwinners or were in possession of a private income.

In April and May 1940 first Norway and Denmark and then Holland and Belgium had been overrun by the German armed forces. As the Oxford school year neared its end, Grant had written home to his 'Dear

Mum,' 'England is no longer fighting for liberty but for her life. The whole atmosphere here ... has been tense ... nothing had touched this place really before but now it has come ... England [is] preparing for total warfare, this place is folding fast.' The dons were leaving to undertake various war jobs. 'Oxford, *you must realize,* is just ceasing to exist. It is a luxury commodity which England cannot afford if she is to win the war.' Yet, he cannot refrain from adding, the spring has been the most beautiful within living memory. 'Life is pleasant, pleasant, pleasant, physically beyond words.'[9]

Oxford undergraduates continued to punt on the river Cherwell (at Cambridge it was on the Cam). During that perfect summer, they socialized at cocktail parties and, as always, enjoyed endless talk. Some members of the press affected to be shocked by what they chose to regard as callous indifference to a world on fire: fiddling while Rome burned. In fact these young men knew that, if fit, they would soon be in the armed forces. They merely were filling in time as painlessly as possible before their call-up notices came. This in a way was a doomed generation, though some survived the conflict.

For a handful at Oxford the next step would be Hawkspur Camp. Early in June, Grant, for instance, had unburdened his troubled mind to his mother. Of one thing he was certain: he could not remain at Oxford, even though as a Canadian he was not so far liable to British conscription. 'My alternatives,' he told her, 'are to stay here [in England] and join an ambulance or else to go home and get a job. It is a hard decision ...' He felt, though, that his reluctance to become a combatant had been strengthened by his experiences since coming to Britain.[10] For Grant, training in first aid and subsequent ambulance work presented the most promising solution of his dilemma: how to combine personal pacifism with patriotic duty and his admiration of 'physical bravery' and the preservation of freedom. Grant's Balliol friend, Clarke, had given him Vaughan Williams's address, and early in June the Canadian went over to see the latter at Wadham College. Vaughan Williams accepted him at once for the forthcoming training camp, and Grant felt a sense of relief, though that would not last too long. At any rate, 'glad because [he] did not want to return to Canada at such a striking moment,' he soon went off to Hawkspur with high hopes. Probably most campers shared his feelings, at the beginning at any rate. In retrospect, David Morris, then a twenty-year-old pacifist undergraduate at Brasenose College, has expressed a more skeptical approach: 'I refused to admit that the force of the storm was too strong to beat against.' It was this feeling, he said, that took him, with twenty or so others, to a village in the county of Essex to start ambulance training.

What they found on arrival was not encouraging, but they were young and enthusiastic and strong enough to overcome preliminary obstacles. Morris writes:

> Hawkspur Camp had at one time been the scene of an experiment in the reform of boys who had gone astray. When we arrived the Camp was in a pretty bad way. There was a sort of Swiss chalet ... and down the slope of the hill were four more wooden huts, brown and bare, surrounded by long grass and nettles, heaps of rusty tins, cement and planks. The huts were full of dirt and bird-droppings, they smelt warm and dusty like the bird house at the Zoo. The last people using them seemed to have been tramps, and the walls were decorated with obscene drawings. Inside the Swiss chalet ... dark brown stuffing from a broken mattress covered half the room, the unswept ashes of the winter's fires spilled over the grates on to the hearth, dust lay everywhere. However we cleaned the place up, and when the doctor arrived got down to some training.[11]

Vaughan Williams had recruited this doctor from his pacifist network, and Dr Douglas Dunn seems to have done a good job even if several of the campers, despite academic brilliance, proved strangely allergic to the art of winding bandages and other nursing routines.

Dunn, a Scotsman then working in Newcastle-upon-Tyne, was himself a committed pacifist. He seems, though, to have regarded many of the campers as frivolous; perhaps he doubted the strength of their commitment to pacifism. Tennyson describes him rather unkindly as 'a raw bony man, very much aware of being a red-brick bull in a shop of Oxbridge porcelain ... It was soon obvious that he disliked most of us and that this dislike was heartily reciprocated.'[12] Nevertheless, training proceeded according to plan. It was fairly rigorous, especially after the undisciplined lifestyle of an Oxbridge undergraduate. The day began at 7:30 a.m. and included physical training and a route march, with supper at 7:30 p.m. and lights out by 11:00 p.m. Sundays, of course, were free of duties apart from camp maintenance.

'Our ages,' writes Currer-Briggs, 'ranged from 19 to 23. Life at Hawkspur was full of uncertainties ... no one knew how long our course was to last, or whether, at the end of it, we could continue as a unit or whether we would have to find work individually wherever our services might be needed.' The UAU proved something of an anomaly, at least in the eyes of the authorities, who could not make out whether it was a military unit or a civilian organization. 'There was no call for our services either in London or on the battlefield' – until the Blitz started in September. By then the UAU had ceased to function.[13]

At Hawkspur, although the going was tough during the day, there was time in the evenings and during the weekend to relax and to get to know colleagues. Introductions to three of the Balliol contingent – Grant, Tennyson, and Owen – as well as the camp 'leader,' Miles Vaughan Williams, have been made. Let us now meet some more campers, our choice necessarily being restricted to the information Currer-Briggs was able to gather, chiefly as the result of his questionnaire in the early 1980s. Otherwise we have only names – and, at that, a rostrum of names that may possibly be incomplete.

One of those who responded – in lively fashion – to Currer-Briggs's questionnaire was Robin Du Boulay (also a Balliol man), by that date one of Britain's most distinguished medieval historians.[14] Never either a diary or a letter keeper, Du Boulay retained 'some sharply-etched remembrances of Hawkspur [Camp], though,' he added, 'doubtless much has been blanked out.' With British (false?) modesty, he recalled himself 'as an immature, intolerant, scared, and objectionable youth who was treated with great forbearance' by his CO tribunal. He goes on to say,

> The UAU was possibly the most interesting and brilliant collection of men I have lived with for any length of time. It did more for my 'intellectual' (not emotional) education than any other episode. I used to go around [at the camp] with philosophers of a Christian-socialist kind whom I liked more than they liked me ... Ian Crombie [who] became a philosophy don at Wadham ... taught me to drive, out of sheer good nature, through the Essex lanes in his 1928 Hilman. It had to be cranked into starting and one day the handle slipped and pierced the exposed radiator. That was the first time I had heard an educated man say 'Fuck.' Needless to say I was awed ... His friend [at the camp], and mine, was Denys Munby, also later a don.[15]

Most of his fellow campers seem to have liked plump Hubert Fox ('dear Hubert'). The only Roman Catholic at Hawkspur, he described himself as 'an extreme sacramentalist' (with emphasis on the adjective). A humorist 'with a brilliant mind,' Fox was also 'good and kind': perhaps he derived his benevolence from his Quaker ancestors, while a

Spanish mother may have predisposed him to the reception of Catholicism, even though her family was staunchly anti-Franco. He was also a Mahler enthusiast and in their leisure regaled his fellow campers with that composer's Ninth Symphony. Played on a gramophone that he had brought with him to camp, it had thirty-two sides. 'It needed great devotion to listen to it from start to finish, but Hubert,' writes Currer-Briggs, 'succeeded in converting more than one of us' – not only to Mahler but also to Roman Catholicism.[16]

The unit held occasional business meetings. It also, in its leisure hours, organized play-readings and charades. Grant, fresh from his conservative Upper Canada background, recalls his surprise at one of these camp entertainments. He writes:

> One evening Ian Crombie put on a charade of Chamberlain meeting Mussolini on a balcony. It was intended to ridicule Chamberlain. I could hardly believe it, because I assumed that Chamberlain had been trying to maintain peace in Europe ... It seemed to me strange for a group of pacifists to be ridiculing him. But this was a minor ambiguous note in the midst of my enchantment with the niceness of the English.[17]

There were also evenings spent in a neighbouring pub. Currer-Briggs recalls playing duets with Brian Nunn (another Cambridge man) on a decrepit instrument in the lounge bar of the Fighting Cocks at Little Sampford. The villagers evidently did not quite know what to think of these young toffs who had taken the place of the young delinquents at the camp. Currer-Briggs characterized their general attitude towards the campers as 'suspicion tinged with hostility.' Some locals believed that they were nudists ('because during that hot summer most of us went about scantily clad'). That the campers were all 'conchies' or potential conchies does not appear to have been known. At least there were no serious incidents, though the campers do not seem to have succeeded in becoming part of the local community. There was not even time to get to know any of the local girls: Hawkspur remained an exclusively male society. Perhaps time might have changed the situation, but that was not to be.

Vaughan Williams had managed to obtain sufficient funds to cover the camp's electricity and fuel bills, while campers – or their parents – covered the cost of food. 'Some parents helped in kind.' Oliver (Nol) Wrightson's mother, for instance, contributed 'hampers of eggs and vegetables,' sent down from the family residence in County Durham.[18]

Wrightson – from Balliol too – was the younger son of Colonel Sir Thomas Garmondsway Wrightson, the second baronet of that name. Currer-Briggs aptly comments that 'most, if not all of us had been brought up in houses staffed with servants and cooks': now, though they had to cook for themselves, 'we managed to eat tolerably well.'[19]

On 13 June the Germans occupied Paris, and on 22 June Marshal Pétain concluded an armistice with Germany. Hitler now planned to invade Britain, but to achieve this he needed control of the air in the battle zone to offset Britain's naval predominance. The Luftwaffe prepared for combat. Thus, during June and July 1940 German air attacks extended from the Channel coastal area inland. Industrial plants and airfields were at first the main targets. The Battle of Britain had begun.

This was the background against which the Hawkspur Camp was set. Like the Oxbridge punters they had left behind in academe, the campers went about their business seemingly unconcerned, but actually never unaware of the tumultuous events in which they, like the rest of the country, inevitably were involved. In his letters home, the Canadian expatriate Grant, alone among the campers, provides an on-the-spot insight into the mindset of this most unusual group of pacifists at a crisis moment of history.

In the first letter he wrote to his mother after arriving in the camp, Grant gives his impressions of his fellow campers and of the novel environment in which his life now turned.[20] He assured her,

> All goes well here, busy, busy, busy – and yet nothing has happened – no invasion, nothing; but, by the time this letter gets to you, perhaps it will be different. This unit is in a strange way. It was meant to go to France, so that now it is rather at a loose end ... Last night we heard quite a few of the moaning, droning German planes, but no bombs dropped near enough to wake us up. Around here the air is just never silent, there are planes coming and going.

He was, on the whole, delighted with his new workmates. For instance, 'Hallam Tennyson [is] awfully nice but ineffectual.'[21] Of the others, whom Grant assessed as 'of varying degrees of niceness and efficiency, of strength and weakness,' he picked out Hubert Fox for comment:

> Half Spanish and of gigantic physical proportions, he lumbers round, clumsy, but effective, a superb European brain – different from the ordi-

> nary English kind. But to see this gigantic figure stumbling along on a route march with blisters on his feet, a frown on his face and dissertating (in hushed whispers) on André [Gide] is really a good sight. Most of his [mother's] family were destroyed by Franco.[22]

Grant's letters reflect intense if only occasional homesickness, which was of course peculiar to himself as the sole expatriate at the camp, but also reflect continuous if intermittent anxiety, a nagging uncertainty about what the future might hold.[23] This was a feeling probably shared by all his campmates. Currer-Briggs, for instance, confesses, 'Hawkspur rather added to my uncertainties [as a pacifist] than resolved them.'[24] Grant had bought a ticket home but now cancelled it. If the invasion came, he wanted to be here in Britain: as a pacifist and a Commonwealth patriot, he felt this was where duty lay. On the other hand, if invasion did not come and the UAU failed to find an outlet for its services, was it not his obligation to return to Canada and face the music as a CO, just as his fellow campers had to face their CO tribunals in Britain? He might, he knew, find himself in jail, as would happen to his closest friend at Balliol, Clarke. 'Perhaps jail, perhaps not. *Je ne sais pas.*' But of one thing he assured his mother: 'If I came home I would object, and what arrangements they have for that I just don't know.' He hoped his going to prison would not hurt either her or his brother-in-law, Geoffrey Andrew, who was a civil servant. 'I would try and do it somewhere else than Toronto.' Certainly it would finish any career as a lawyer in his native city. 'But that is as is – and must be ...'[25] 'Whatever happens or whatever people do say or feel just doesn't matter ... I am tired of doing the right thing to be liked. I am going to do what I feel – to hell with the career and the like ... It came across me how weak, weak, weak I'd been because of obeisance before social compromise.'[26]

Most of the day Grant and the other campers had plenty to occupy their minds and to keep them from anxious thoughts, including route marches that eventually covered twenty-five miles. ('This march today killed me,' Grant confessed to his mother on 2 August.) There were first-aid and nursing exams for which to prepare – no one wanted to fail – as well as additional camp duties. Grant surprisingly found himself in charge of the camp kitchen: His first soufflé proved a success and put to rest his doubts as to his competence as a cook. 'Life is never normal' was probably the reaction of most campers as the days hurried by.

By early September, training had come to an end. All campers now had become certified medics, even tubby Fox and the brilliant classicist

Oliver Coburn, whose 'involvement with a two-inch bandage,' Du Boulay reports, 'was the most unnerving sight of that kind I ever saw until my son, Tom, had to be extricated from the ribbon of my typewriter.'[27] Vaughan Williams and Dr Dunn, suspecting that divisions among campers might soon surface and cause irreparable harm, appear to have combined to put an end to the camp's formal existence.[28] Campers gradually dispersed.

Some, though, including Grant, stayed on for a little while doing forestry work, for which they earned eight shillings a day. That was more than enough to cover food; their accommodation, of course, was free. They worked 'like Trojans,' Grant told his mother. 'As a Canadian people feel I should be good [at it], so one must wield an axe till one's back aches.' He complained of feeling so tired at night that he had to go very early to bed in order to 'face tomorrow fresh.'[29] A few had left camp completely disillusioned by what seemed like a failed pacifist utopia. They abandoned their CO stance and hastened to join army, navy, or air force. The majority, however, still hoped that their ambulance unit eventually would become a reality. It was calculated that around £500 (a substantial sum in those days) would be needed to equip an ambulance. Tennyson and Owen were among those who stayed on in the neighbourhood and got temporary jobs, agreeing to pool their income to achieve the target of £500. The two friends also worked as household staff for a divorced white Russian countess, who claimed on very dubious evidence that her mother had been a friend of Tennyson's mother. As Tennyson tells the story, 'It was soon obvious that my main use was not to scramble reconstituted dried egg but my skill as a bridge player. Roddy's house cleaning became centred in the mistress's bedroom where there was a double bed with a lace canopy hungry for a second occupant.'[30]

The situation changed with the commencement of the London Blitz on 7 September. Hitherto, Vaughan Williams's efforts to find collective employment for the unit had failed:

> We offered our services as a mobile First-Aid-Squad, complete with a trained doctor and a small sum of money towards the cost of an ambulance. We had paid for our training and we were willing to work without wages. We did ask for our food and some place to sleep in. Opinion at that time was becoming a little less friendly towards conscientious objectors ... [Still, we] took it for granted ... that it would be easy to get work. So our leader wrote to about fifteen of the biggest town councils — only

Bristol and Newcastle considered the offer and they eventually turned it down.

Once the Blitz had started, the situation indeed altered radically. 'The prejudice against the employment of "conchies" had abruptly and mysteriously disappeared.'[31] Most unit members located themselves in the working-class district of Bermondsey in southeast London, where they worked in air-raid shelters and in rest centres and soup kitchens for the bombed-out homeless or in boys' clubs. Grant was among unit members who now sought – and found – in Bermondsey the kind of work that satisfied his desire for service while at the same time being under civilian auspices.

Just before leaving his forestry job, Grant had what he described to his mum as 'a tremendous experience.' Bombing, he told his mother, now had started in earnest, though so far not much damage had been done in Essex. 'The only thing they touched was the most local of local railways, which doesn't matter.' But then, out walking with several other ex campers, he suddenly had seen two planes crashing down in a nearby field. 'So we rushed, I wondering what I would do if I met a German.' Arriving at the spot, they found a 'big, white thing [that] didn't move.' It revealed a body. 'The German was dead – broken – the flaxen hair blowing all over his quiet face but his body smashed.' The pilot of the other plane was British, his body 'all burned up.' Then 'eight Germans came down in parachutes all round'; they surrendered at once. 'One man had been at Cambridge for eight months.'[32]

In London, Grant, who had gone to work among the bombed-out in a working-class district of the blitzed metropolis, soon abandoned hope in the UAU ever becoming a reality. 'Our ambulance has folded up,' he told a Canadian acquaintance; 'we were trained for France,' and France now had fallen to the invaders.[33] He was ready to return home at last. In 1941 five other ex-campers who, along with Grant, had migrated to Bermondsey, including Currer-Briggs, Owen, Tennyson, and Vaughan Williams, were accepted by a private organization attached vaguely to Northern Command. The British Volunteer Ambulance Corps (BVAC) operated on the northeast coast of England, where invasion was expected at any moment. The five conchies drove ambulances while contributing to the BVAC the savings accumulated in the aftermath of Hawkspur. 'This was an incredibly dotty enterprise,' writes Tennyson, 'staffed by a mixture of First World War veterans and bohemians from Chelsea.'[34] The conchies did not last long in this rather uncongenial milieu.

In the upshot at least six ex-Hawkspur campers joined the FAU.[35] At first ex-campers, the majority of whom were non-churchmen tending towards agnosticism, had viewed the prospect of joining the FAU, loosely associated as it was with a religious denomination to which none of them belonged, with a certain reserve. They were not sure if the FAU would accept any of them into membership.

Several expressed even stronger doubts about the propriety of pacifists joining the civil defence organization set up by the government throughout the country: Air Raid Precautions (ARP), they argued, directly assisted the war effort. 'The government makes out that ARP will give the people protection so that they'll accept the idea of war more docilely.' Nonviolent resistance on the Gandhian model was the only truly effective form of defence. Others, however, considered that the immediate objective of saving civilian lives, implicit in ARP, was not incompatible with the philosophy of pacifism. 'This led to arguments,' Currer-Briggs recalls, 'especially when those who had been members of the Peace Pledge Union proclaimed that it was the task of activists such as ourselves [to] find jobs wherever we could and influence our colleagues towards pacifism.'[36]

Many ex-campers had indeed been attracted to the idea of a UAU because they felt it answered their desire to fulfil their civic duty while at the same time giving expression to their abhorrence of war. For some, the necessity of resisting Hitlerism ultimately overrode their pacifist belief. The case of Grant was slightly different. In the late summer 1941, yielding to mounting pressure of family and friends, he decided to join the Merchant Marine. Hovering for months on the edge of a nervous breakdown, he described this decision in a letter to his mum as 'one of the stupidest, most useless, basest actions I have done. But people expect it so there one goes.' For some time he hesitated between the Royal Navy and the Merchant Marine. Finally he opted for the latter, but his medical examination uncovered tuberculosis, and he was rejected as a merchant seaman. The Blitz having temporarily abated, he left for Canada early in 1942.[37]

Not long before leaving London, Grant had received a visit from one of his Oxford and Hawkspur friends, Wrightson. 'Oliver came to town for a week's leave,' Grant informed his mother. 'He is a Balliol and Eton boy (whose father is an armament king ...). Oliver should have been a guard's officer but instead is a tough little private having refused a commission ... He knew he couldn't accomplish anything as an officer; so he is a private. It is hard for him, naturally, to be bossed and bullied by his inferiors, but [he] takes it without a word.'[38] Other ex-campers now abandoning pacifism and their CO stance included Du Boulay, Morris, and Owen, each of whom resigned from the FAU to join the armed forces, as well as the UAU's future chronicler, Currer-Briggs, who became an officer in the Intelligence Corps.[39] Rotund and much-loved Fox tried to join the Royal Air Force but was rejected – not surprisingly – on health grounds. He died not long afterward as the result of a bicycle accident.

Seemingly only one Hawkspur camper lost his life in action. He died in battle without having renounced his noncombatant status. Perhaps Anthony (Tony) Bass, in his death, best exemplified the UAU idea as Vaughan Williams, the unit's founder, had envisaged it and as most campers had seen it in those first heady days at Hawkspur: 'the scene of our earnest endeavours,' as Currer-Briggs, the camp's chronicler, put it.

At Hawkspur, Bass seems to have kept a low profile. The sometimes censorious Grant, however, thought him 'really the nicest' man in the camp. While not giving his name, Grant mentions him in a letter to his mum as being, along with Fox and Tennyson, particularly nice people. 'A small Jew from Oxford,' he goes on a little condescendingly, he 'looks as if he should be selling papers in the Bronx but [he has] just got a first in Greats, yet again that kindness [seen in Hubert Fox] that is neither softness or sentimentality.'[40] In retrospect, Du Boulay described Bass as a 'good man: a Jewish sceptic who later joined the paratroops as an RAMC [Royal Army Medical Corps] orderly.'[41] Sources available give no indication of how Bass fared during the years after he left Hawkspur. As a Jew – and a religious sceptic – he probably felt reluctant to apply for membership in the Quaker FAU. At some date he must have joined the RAMC; there he would not have been required to bear arms though otherwise subject to military discipline and training. Certainly this was a compromise in comparison to the UAU idea, for the UAU had envisaged working as a unit alongside but not as part of the army. (It was presumed, of course, that the military would accept them in this role.) Independence, indeed, was at the core of the UAU's idea – as it was of the Quaker FAU's. Without it, the UAU indeed lost its point. With the UAU dead and buried by 1941, however, Bass may have seen the RAMC as the closest way of serving his country as a civically minded pacifist in the Hawkspur spirit. He would not cease to be a conscientious objector to war at the same time he was helping – non-violently – the struggle against Hitlerism. As a Jew, he must have been aware of the enormity of that regime.

At any rate, Bass surfaces again in 1944 through the post-war memoirs of another CO, James Bramwell (Byrom), who had not been connected with Hawkspur. A professional writer before being conscripted, Bramwell, like Bass and other COs, had volunteered to serve as unarmed paramedics in a parachute unit, which would commence to operate after D-Day arrived on 4 June and the invasion of Normandy began (see essay 24 below). The two men trained together in an army barracks for the coming ordeal. Like Grant, the somewhat cynical Bramwell was captivated by Bass's unassuming character. 'He was a tall, short-sighted young man,' Bramwell writes, 'who loved humanity as did few conchies I came across. His steel-rimmed spectacles winked like beacons over the level of our collective military mediocrity.' It was, we may add, a wonder that, 'with his deficient sense of balance which often caused him to topple over backwards with his chair in the middle of a conversation,' he had survived both Hawkspur route marches and army medical examinations. Bramwell comments on Bass's sense of humour as well as on his 'penetrating intelligence.' 'His incredible clumsiness had made him the butt of the non-commissioned officers during his first weeks in the Field Ambulance, but at last he was accepted, a popular institution.' His fellow soldiers not merely tolerated his oddities and mannerisms but came to value his integrity and wisdom.

A few months later, someone remarked to Bramwell 'quite casually, "Have you heard about old Tony? Pity, wasn't it?" ... The phrase was not eloquent. Yet I thought it expressed a sound reaction to the death of close friends in battle.' Bramwell had attempted to stem his grief by employing the kind of 'formula the Colonel would have to use when writing his letter of condolence: ... killed picking up a wounded man under fire, doing his duty as a man and a conchie.' However, he remained acutely aware 'that a tiny splinter of metal had apparently triumphed over [a] lovable [and] gifted humanitarian.'[42] Perhaps, as Bramwell had felt intuitively, this triumph was only apparent. Perhaps clumsy Bass's death stands as a symbol of the generous idealism that had prompted the creation of the UAU – a service model of pacifism, churchless and religiously non-exclusionist, a stance that did not conflict with love of country or abhorrence of tyranny.

Looking back after nearly four and a half decades, the UAU's chronicler remarked, 'Most of us have come a long way since our rebellious youth.'[43] He ran through the names of Hawkspur campers he had been able to retrieve and came up with the following: two judges, one professor in the humanities in a British university and one in a Canadian university, a distinguished nuclear physicist who became the vice-chancellor of a British university, and three fellows of Oxford colleges including a 'world-famous' medical scientist. Others 'have become writers and/or broadcasters, and all have achieved success in their respective careers.'[44]

Despite the exceptional intellectual calibre of the Hawkspur campers, one cannot help wondering if their unit would have survived for very long. Circumstances, we have seen, prevented this from ever coming to the test. Few, indeed, were involved; its duration was brief. Moreover, its elitist educational and social composition would, today certainly, arouse strong reservations as to its fitness as an exemplar of pacifist service. It proved an abortive effort, leaving behind only a faint echo amid the din of mighty events. Even at the time, Vaughan Williams evidently had suspected the unit was not likely to function as he had planned, and others shared his view. What indeed became significant in the memories of those who had taken part in the camp was a vanished fellowship, their lost innocence, and their youthful rebellion. As Nol (now Judge) Wrightson put it, 'In varying degrees, and for different reasons, we were all young rebels – against the war.'[45] Perhaps those who subsequently abandoned their pacifism and joined the forces were the ones who felt the loss of innocence most keenly.

With the arrogance of youth (so, at least, they saw it in old age), they had imagined that they knew all the answers. They denounced war as the product of wrong-headed governments and stupid statesmen who already had decimated their fathers' generation in the holocaust of the war to end all wars. 'As young intellectuals,' writes the unit's chronicler, they had believed they understood the situation more clearly than their elders. Therefore, was it not their duty 'to stand aside from the idiocies at present being perpetrated by the leaders of Europe?'[46] At the same time, they realized that in a country coming under siege they could not in fact stand aside. Indeed, perhaps they had really never wished to stand aside, for they shared the basic ideals for which their countrymen were prepared to fight.

They were far from being saints; few of them belonged to any religious body, and intellectual scepticism offset their youthful enthusiasm and boundless energy and *joie de vivre*. It was indeed the rebel impulse that had brought them to Hawkspur. They were, however, 'gentle rebels' searching for a way to combine their abhorrence of war with the defence of humanist values. It was this search that afterwards led them in opposite directions. Miles Vaughan Williams, for instance, went back to Oxford to become a hospital porter at the Radcliffe Infirmary; Hallam Tennyson and Oliver Coburn joined the FAU; David Morris left the FAU's China Convoy for the armed forces;[47] Robin Du Boulay and Roddy Owen also left the FAU, eventually to become gunners engaged in armed combat; and Tony Bass ('so exuberantly, and yet sensibly alive') died on the battlefield a lonely noncombatant.[48]

NOTES

1 Noel Currer-Briggs, 'The Universities Ambulance Unit, 1939–40,' 18 pages. Apart from the introductory paragraph, I have used only pages 10–18 here. I must thank Professor William Christian (University of Guelph) for making a copy of Currer-Briggs's hitherto unpublished article accessible to me and also for sending me most generously copies of correspondence dated 1982–4 between Currer-Briggs and former participants in the Hawkspur Camp (referred to below as Chr.-x) as well as an incomplete list of participants compiled by Currer-Briggs. I think the plural form Universities Ambulance Unit, used by Currer-Briggs, is correct, though the singular form sometimes is found in the sources. (In a letter to Christian dated 31 May 1990, Currer-Briggs wrote, 'As the article was never published, I am perfectly agreeable for you to make what use of it you wish.')

2 Grant's most celebrated work was *Lament for a Nation: The Defeat of Canadian Nationalism* (Toronto, 1965). This slim volume made Grant a national icon for many of his younger intellectual contemporaries.

3 Beverley Nichols, *Cry Havoc!* (London, 1933).

4 William Christian, *George Grant: A Biography* (Toronto, 1993), 27–30, 59. The other two cadet corps COs were the future historian Kenneth McNaught and Michael (Sholome) Gelber. McNaught, in his *Conscience and History: A Memoir* (Toronto, 1999), writes, 'The passage of time has strengthened my admiration of [Choppy Grant's] decision. He demonstrated that a conservative confidence in the basic precepts of Canadian society need not be illiberal. Indeed ... such confidence is a requisite for genuine tolerance of dissent' (12). Of the three, only Grant maintained his pacifism after the outbreak of war: the other two reluctantly accepted it as their obligation to participate as combatants in the fight against Nazi Germany. Grant's letters

home, which were preserved by his mother, the dominating Maude Grant, form the only surviving primary source for life at Hawkspur Camp and its antecedents. The other evidence derives from the recollections of participants set down over four decades later.

5 Undated letter to Maude Parkin (Mrs W.L.) Grant, in George P. Grant Papers, National Archives of Canada (Ottawa), MG 30 D59, vol. 38 (referred to below as NAC and the volume number). I would like to thank Dr George Bolotenko at the National Archives for his assistance in my research there.

6 Christian, *George Grant*, 59, 60. Grant described Clarke to his mother as 'probably the only young person I know who is a saint.'

7 Hallam Tennyson, *The Haunted Mind* (London, 1984), 39, 40, 43–5, 56, 57, 59. This lively autobiography deals extensively with wartime pacifism in Britain and post-Gandhian nonviolence in India, but its major theme perhaps is the author's bisexuality and how he coped with it. Tennyson's publications include a study of the Gandhian Vinoba Bhave's 'Land-Gifts' mission entitled *Saint on the March* (1955).

8 Letter dated 9 November [1939], NAC, vol. 38.

9 Letter dated 19 May [1940], NAC, vol. 38. Italics in the original.

10 Letter dated 4 June [1940], NAC, vol. 39. This letter is printed in full in George Grant, *Selected Letters*, ed. William Christian (Toronto, 1996), 56, 57.

11 David Morris, *China Changed My Mind* (Boston, 1949), 18, 19. The book was published first in London by Cassell in 1948. The camp, temporarily inactive due to wartime conditions, belonged to Q Camps Association, an organization with pacifist connections that worked on the rehabilitation of delinquent boys. The association's secretary allowed the UAU to hold its training camp there without paying rent. Until the war, the school itself had been run by a Quaker, David Wills. See W. David Wills, *The Hawkspur Experiment: An Informal Account of the Training of Wayward Adolescence* (London, 1941).

12 Tennyson, *Haunted Mind*, 66. The author calls Dunn 'Andrew,' not wishing, I suppose, to identify him correctly in view of the hostile picture he presents of Dunn's personality and of the role he played in the camp.

13 Currer-Briggs, 'Universities Ambulance Unit,' 23.

14 Letter from Robin Du Boulay, dated 24 August, 1983, Chr.-x.

15 Crombie's two-volume *Examination of Plato's Doctrines* (1962–3) is generally regarded as a classic exposition of the subject. Munby became a Fellow of Nuffield College, Oxford, and wrote extensively on the relationship between theology and politics. He died prematurely – murdered while on holiday in Turkey in 1976.

16 Currer-Briggs, 'Universities Ambulance Unit,' 14, 15. Tennyson, in his autobiography, describes Fox more acerbically: 'Hubert was a rotund figure with tiny feet and spindly legs who was known as "the pansy hippo." He was a Roman Catholic convert ... with a ... delight in vestments and the minor idiocies of the Church' (66). Tennyson, though, does concede that Fox was 'the camp wit' and quotes with approval one of his risqué sallies directed in this case against Dr Dunn.

17 Quoted in Currer-Briggs, 15; text also in Grant, *Selected Letters*, 61, 62. If Du Boulay's memory has not led him astray, there was one Hawkspur camper whom Grant did not consider 'nice.' He writes, 'A Canadian Calvinist. ... George Grant ... absolutely loathed my guts and used to mock my Anglo-Catholic leanings.' Perhaps Du Boulay was being oversensitive. After all, as he tells us, Hubert Fox the Roman Catholic 'sacramentalist' used to call him 'Poppy' on the grounds he 'talked poppycock,' and in this case he did not take offence.

18 Currer-Briggs, 16, 17; Christian, *George Grant*, 66.

19 Oliver Wrightson told Currer-Briggs (letter dated 2 March 1982, Chr.-x) that he had published privately the letters he wrote to his mother from blitzed Bermondsey from October to December 1940. I do not know if 'this self-congratulatory diversion' (Wrightson's description) also contained letters from Hawkspur Camp, since I have been unable to locate a copy of a work evidently destined exclusively for friends and family, but it seems unlikely that it did. As Grant's biographer adds, these would-be ambulance men could not exist 'on Plato and poetry' alone; they did need food. Thus provisions from Lady Wrightson were very welcome.

20 Letter to Maude Grant, n.d. [June 1940]; printed in Grant, *Selected Letters*, 58, 59.

21 Ibid., 59. In a letter written circa 1984 (and reprinted by Christian in his edition of Grant's *Selected Letters*, 61), Grant told Currer-Briggs, 'My chief impression of the camp was what delightful and cultivated human beings they were.' He was 'enchanted,' indeed 'intoxicated,' by the culture these young men displayed, and their knowledge of subjects he had never heard discussed before coming to Oxford. Theirs was a world that in Canada he had known only from books; he had taken it 'for granted' then that such things were not truly serious. 'I was, of course, meeting directly contemporaries from a society which had some history from before the age of progress, who took the worlds of religion and art and morality seriously.' He selected Tennyson for special mention in this connection. Placed next to him on one of the unit route marches, Grant found that his conversation 'just enraptured me.' I am puzzled, though, by Grant's assertion that he

had never met Tennyson before. Was this indeed possible considering they both belonged to the same Oxford college and had entered the university the same year? Perhaps, after nearly half a century, Grant's memory led him astray on this point? But certainly, despite their shared pacifism, they cannot have been at all close during the year they shared at Balliol. Tennyson, for his part, does not mention Grant in his autobiography. When he wrote, he was of course unaware of the Canadian's admiration of his culture and wit – mixed with a feeling that the Englishman was delightfully crazy.

22 Ibid., 59. In a letter to his mother, hitherto unpublished in its entirety (dated 28 July [1940], NAC, vol. 39), Grant refers – anonymously – to Fox as 'an enormous fat man, who was in the [Spanish] civil war on the Loyalist side.' He was 'beyond words kind' (his kindness seems to have impressed everyone). 'This enormous body [was] carried by legs much too thin and with a lion's head.' Tennyson he describes here as 'mad and ineffectual but so pleasant, the kind of Etonian who is a success. I find so few of them.' Portions of this letter have been quoted by Christian, *George Grant*, 66.

23 See especially the letter to his mother (dated 1 July [1940], NAC, vol. 39), which begins, 'Today I have one of those ghastly attacks of homesickness that rarely come, but when they do one can think of nothing else.'

24 Currer-Briggs, 'Universities Ambulance Unit,' 16.

25 Letter to his mother, dated 2 August [1940], NAC, vol. 39; see also his letter dated 1 July [1940], NAC, vol. 39.

26 Letter, n.d. [early September 1940], NAC, vol. 39.

27 Du Boulay to Currer-Briggs, 24 August 1983, Chr.-x.

28 See Tennyson, *Haunted Mind*, 67. His account of events, though, may be slightly romancé. To a friend he described the incident as a 'happening.' He found it 'traumatic' and believed it resulted in 'the unit breaking up' (which may indeed be correct). Tennyson wrote a broadcast play about the incident but failed to persuade the British Broadcasting Company (BBC) to produce it. See letter from Roger Lockyear to Noel Currer-Briggs, dated 15 September 1983, Chr.-x. I should note here that I have failed to find in any of the sources available to me the exact dates of the opening or closing of the training camp. There is general agreement, though, that it lasted approximately six weeks – somewhere from late June to around mid-August or even a little later.

29 Letter, n.d. [early September 1940], NAC, vol. 39.

30 Tennyson, *Haunted Mind*, 67, 68. The author states that the countess's first name was Peryl and that she was 'a close friend' of Noel Coward. I have been unable to trace anyone of this name either in Coward's volumes of

autobiography or in his diaries, but considering the amatory propensities Tennyson attributes to the countess, he may be using a fictitious name here.

31 Morris, *China Changed My Mind*, 19–21.

32 Letter to Maude Grant, 31 August [1940], printed in Grant's *Selected Letters*, 63, 64; also letter, n.d. [early September 1940], NAC, vol. 39.

33 Grant to Professor R.A. Trotter, 18 September 1940, printed in his *Selected Letters*, 65. Already on 11 September he had confided to his mother his belief that 'the ambulance thing has come to an end.' See NAC, vol. 39.

34 Tennyson, *Haunted Mind*, 68, 69.

35 Oliver Coburn, Robin Du Boulay, David E. Morris, Paul T. Matthews, Roderic Fenwick Owen, and Hallam Tennyson.

36 Currer-Briggs, 'Universities Ambulance Unit,' 17. Unfortunately the author does not identify these PPU activists. My impression is that they formed a small minority of the Hawkspur Camp membership.

37 Christian, *George Grant*, 82. Christian, in *Selected Letters*, 87, comments: 'Under remorseless pressure ... to do his duty to king and country, Grant buckled and decided to join up. His options, as he saw them, were the Royal Navy or the Merchant Marine. Either, in his view, represented a betrayal of his pacifist principles. He opted for the Merchant Marine because he thought that he was most likely to serve there with the kind of people he had come to know and love in Bermondsey.' These words give Grant's intellectual position more accurately than does Christian's statement in his biography that Grant ceased to be an absolute pacifist immediately 'following his decision to join the British merchant marine late in 1941' (245). That only came over the next few years after his return to Canada. As a potential conscientious objector, even while engaged in often dangerous civil defence work during the Blitz, Grant had come to feel like almost a pariah in the eyes of his relatives, who included Vincent Massey, Canada's high commissioner in London. The crumbling of his will to resist the pressure to join up was indeed understandable. To his death, he remained strongly antiwar.

38 Letter to Maude Grant, n.d. [late 1941], printed in Grant's *Selected Letters*, 86. Later in the war, however, Wrightson became a lieutenant in the elitist Coldstream Guards. 'On 5 November [1944] Lt. [Oliver] Wrightson laid mines in a wood which was known to be visited by the enemy. A German patrol was duly caught in the trap, leaving one man wounded on the minefield who died towards daybreak.' Six days later he was himself wounded. See Michael Howard and John Sparrow, *The Coldstream Guards, 1920–1946* (London, 1951), 347, 519. When the war was over, Wrightson finished law and eventually was appointed a circuit judge.

39 The final chapter of Morris's book, *China Changed My Mind,* is titled 'The End of a Pacifist': it concludes with a terse paragraph stating, 'A few days [after arriving in Calcutta] I reported to the Recruiting Office in Chowringhee.' See also Lyn Smith, *Pacifists in Action: The Experience of the Friends Ambulance Unit in the Second World War* (York UK, 1998), 374, 415, 416, for some interesting comments by Morris (by that date an expert on family law) on the dilemmas faced by pacifists in wartime. He told Smith, 'I think one had always wanted to be fighting for one's country because one thought if ever there was a war which one ought to fight it was this one, so that one felt really that one was on the wrong side.' Owen became an official RAF historian, publishing a history of the Desert Air Force in 1948, and later wrote a life of Air Marshal A.W. Tedder. Tedder surely must be the only high ranking military officer whose semi-official biographer was an ex-conchie! On the book dust jacket, Owen, however, mentions having been a pacifist during the early part of the war. Owen also published novels and travel books with intriguing titles like *Roddy Owen's Africa* (1967) as well as several biographies, including the life of the exotic Mavis – alias Mabel – de Vere Cole, titled *Beautiful and Beloved* (1974).

40 Letter to Maude Grant, 28 July [1940], NAC, vol. 39, cited in part in Christian, *George Grant*, 66. The prestigious Oxford degree in classics was known colloquially as Greats.

41 Du Boulay to Currer-Briggs, 24 August 1983, Chr.-x.

42 James Byrom, *The Unfinished Man* (London, 1957), 147, 148, 202–5. James Byrom is a pseudonym for James Guy Bramwell.

43 Currer-Briggs to Paul T. Matthews, 19 February 1984, Chr.-x.

44 Estimates differ as to the exact number of participants in the Hawkspur Camp. Currer-Briggs speaks here of 'all,' but I do not think he retrieved all the names of the campers. Apart from the visiting instructor, Dr Douglas Dunn, I calculate that there were twenty-two campers. Fifteen of these men I have mentioned in my text, and, from Currer-Briggs's list (Chr.-x) and the signatures on a letter some of the campers sent to the *New Statesman and Nation* (N.S., 20, no. 494, 10 August 1940, 138), I have been able to add seven more names: Teddy Dewsbury, Mervyn Ellis-Williams, T.D. Green, F.E. Norris, Kenneth F. Urwin, Alan R. Waltham, and John West. Grant, we may note, told his mother that he was 'cooking for 22 persons' (Grant, *Selected Letters*, 58). In his autobiography, however, Tennyson introduces a camper whose name appears in no other source. 'We were a motley crew,' he writes, 'which included Desmond Stewart (later known as a Christian scholar and Arab expert) who, at that stage in his life, was an out-and-out Nazi. While most of us watched the Battle of Britain going on overhead

with bemused patriotism, Stewart vociferously encouraged the messerschmidts, jumping up and down in frantic excitement when they seemed to have scored a hit' (66). While most of the campers, including Tennyson, belonged to the socialist left, the presence of one Nazi sympathizer in the pacifist camp cannot be excluded (*ipso facto*). Still, why does not anyone else mention this unusual colleague, who we see made no attempt to hide his Fascist viewpoint? There is one further difficulty. According to the entry in *Who Was Who*, VIII (1891–1990), Desmond Stirling Stewart, an expert on the Arab world and early Christianity, was born on 20 April 1924. That would make him a schoolboy of sixteen (he was at Haileybury College) in 1940 – a circumstance that alone would have made him conspicuous at Hawkspur. In fact, he did not become an undergraduate until 1942 at Trinity College in Oxford. The next year, now aged nineteen, he was called up for military service. A conscientious objector, he served with the FAU from May to October 1943 and then resigned to take up paid hospital work. (His career as a CO finds no place in his entry in *Who Was Who*.) Even if Tennyson's memory recalled the wrong name for this rambunctious young fellow, in a pacifist fellowship he still would have remained conspicuous for such heterodox views. I must confess to remaining nonplussed! My thanks nevertheless to Joanna Clark of the Library of the Religious Society of Friends in Britain for supplying me with information about Stewart's brief connection with the FAU.

45 Wrightson to Currer-Briggs, 2 March 1982, Chr.-x.

46 Currer-Briggs, 'Universities Ambulance Unit,' 16. See also his letter to Du Boulay, 1 September 1983, Chr.-x.

47 Even after decisively rejecting pacifism, Morris could still state it as his belief 'that war was wrong and absolutely contrary to the life and teaching of Jesus Christ.' See his *China Changed My Mind*, 15; Byrom, *Unfinished Man*, 148, for Bass.

48 See essay 24 below.

24 British Conscientious Objectors as Medical Paratroopers in the Second World War

Lieutenant-General Sir Napier Crookenden, in his history of British and American airborne forces in the Normandy D-Day assault, praises the high standard of the medical personnel 'doctors, surgeons and medical orderlies attached to the Royal Army Medical Corps (RAMC)' who accompanied the paratroopers. Of the medical orderlies he writes: 'Many of these men were conscientious objectors ... who refused to bear arms but were quite willing to jump or glide into action as medical orderlies. Their levels of education, skill and courage were exceptional and every man ... could feel confident he would be looked after, if wounded, as well as was humanly possible.' General Crookenden singles out for special mention the officer commanding the 224th Parachute Field Ambulance in the 3rd Brigade of the British 6th Airborne Division: Lieutenant-Colonel Alistair Young, D.S.O. He was, writes Crookenden, 'a most able regular army doctor ... who but for his early death in 1971 would have reached high rank.'[1] Shortly after the conclusion of the conflict, Colonel Young, describing the work of the British army's parachute field ambulances, had commented on the conscientious objectors, who made up around one-third of the two parachute field ambulances taking part in the D-Day landings: 'These men were excellent in battle.'[2] My essay seeks to elucidate what at first sounds like an oxymoron: conscientious objection to combatant service and excellence in battle. The story of the British conscientious objectors who served as medical paratroopers in key campaigns of the Second World War has received little attention in the vast – and growing – literature on that conflict. Apart from two autobiographical accounts and two privately printed narratives, writers from the peace movement have almost entirely ignored the subject; yet it raises many moral issues that are central to pacifism and conscientious objection to military service. These issues will be discussed below.

According to the National Service (Armed Forces) Act of 1939,[3] the tribunals set up to deal with applications for exemption on grounds of conscience had been empowered to exempt those applicants they deemed sincere either unconditionally or on condition they undertook some form of civilian alternative service – or they could decide such men would be liable 'to be called up for [military] service but ... be employed only in non-combatant duties.' In April 1940 a Non-Combatant Corps (NCC) was formed to accommodate conscientious objectors in the armed forces. The NCC was divided into fourteen companies, and 6,766 men served in the Corps until its disbandment in November 1946.[4]

The duties of the NCC consisted mainly of 'the messy, laborious jobs of the Army' like construction of barracks and army hospitals as well as making roads and filling-in trenches. Other occupations included smokescreen duty, help in harvesting and ditching, as well as various administrative duties. On one occasion an NCC company put on a Christmas pantomime 'to entertain the troops': the Corps included a number of talented artists, writers, and actors, and men with university degrees, alongside the less sophisticated majority drawn from fundamentalist sects. The newsletters produced by the wartime NCC companies maintained a generally high intellectual and artistic level.[5] Sometimes NCC men were ordered to perform tasks like building machine-gun nests that clearly had a combatant purpose, though this occurred far less frequently than in the First World War. While some NCC men complied, others did indeed refuse to undertake such projects. Sustained by the Central Board for Conscientious Objectors (CBCO), 'refuseniks' of this kind were in the end not penalized for their stand. 'The Board,' writes Denis Hayes, 'was able to persuade the War Office to remind the Army Commanders concerned to give careful consideration to the duties required of men covered by the statutory guarantee of non-combatancy.' According to Hayes, 'the refusal to refuse [in such circumstances] can be explained only by extreme reluctance to risk court-martial,' though undoubtedly 'many in the ranks of the N.C.C. were religious fundamentalists whose whole outlook dictated strict obedience to authority.' Indeed, a majority of the men in the Corps belonged to sects like the Plymouth Brethren, whose objection to fighting was based primarily on the biblical injunction not to kill, interpreted in a narrowly personal way. ('In No. 12 N.C.C. Company,' for instance, 'men of twenty-eight different religious sects were recorded.') The consciences of the Brethren and their like were satisfied so long as they were not required actually to carry weapons, which had indeed been ruled out by the Army Council when the NCC was established in 1940. At best, labour was monotonous, and certainly unsatisfactory to those men who were anxious to alleviate suffering of soldier and civilian alike even if this involved personal danger. At any rate at first, some men found very trying the frequent hectoring and bullying of the Pioneers, who acted as the NCC's non-commissioned officers. Occasionally there were even cases of manhandling on the part of the latter: such treatment was often aimed at 'persuading' a corpsman to transfer to a combatant unit. Rapport was better with many of the regular officers assigned to command the NCC companies. As the chronicler of the wartime Pioneer Corps' activities observes: 'In the main these companies were easy enough to run, given tact and patience.'[6]

True, but Major Rhodes-Wood tells only part of the story. In fact, a strong bond of sympathy arose in many companies between the commanding officers and the corpsmen – despite basic differences of view on the question of war. The officers, and even some of the NCOs, were impressed by the 'team spirit' the corpsmen displayed and by their readiness to work hard at the job; and they came to respect their sincerity, even if they could not always comprehend their viewpoint. In the case of some companies, after the war was over an old-boys' linkage arose. For a number of years, annual reunion dinners were held by company associations; both former officers and the conchie ORs (i.e., 'other ranks') attended. When Captain F.A. Peach, second-in-command of No. 3 Company, died in 1955, a floral tribute at the funeral service was inscribed: 'With remembrance of a beloved skipper, from his troops, No. 3 N.C.C. Association.' The ORs of this company liked to refer affectionately to their commanding officer, Major Gilbert W. Clark, M.C., as the 'old man.'[7]

Early in the war the tribunals had been lavish in their assignments to the RAMC. But, in fact, to do so exceeded their powers, and most noncombatants ended up in the NCC.[8] With the onset of the Blitz on British cities, members of the NCC were allowed to volunteer for the job of bomb disposal; and 465 of them did this, being temporarily attached to the Royal Engineers for this purpose. 'The idea of danger seemed to act as a tonic to these men accustomed as they were to being kept away from hostilities.' They welcomed especially the opportunity of engaging in directly life-saving activity.[9]

The humanist-socialist objector Victor Newcomb expressed the feelings of this section of the NCC men when he wrote: after induction 'I [had] expected I might be able to undertake some purely humanitarian work alongside the armed forces,' for example, in the RAMC. But he soon became disillusioned, finding 'the shabbiness of the routines [he] was expected to follow' in the NCC 'pointless [and] depressing.' He came to regard the wearing of 'the distinctive letters NCC' on his forage cap as 'a stigma.'[10] For those who had volunteered for bomb disposal units, things now changed for the better. As Newcomb relates, 'we ... displayed the red flash of the bomb disposal units which identified us much more clearly with that than with the Non-Combatant Corps.'[11] At last, the stigma ceased to worry: several NCC men were awarded medals for their rescue work during the Blitz.[12] The slur of cowardice, whether generated by their own self-doubts or by a hostile general public, had been removed.

But by the beginning of 1943 there was a lull in the German bombardment of Britain: the bomb disposal units severely curtailed their activities, so that the NCC members were faced with the immediate prospect of returning to the dismal monotony from which they had so fortunately been able to escape. At this juncture, however, an unexpected offer came from the War Office: the army declared itself ready to accept volunteers from all sections of the NCC to begin training as airborne medical aidmen in the forthcoming invasion of the continent. On condition that they passed through the various stages of the vigorous training successfully, they would then be transferred from the NCC to the RAMC: in essence, a reversal of the policy observed hitherto. The military planners had indeed run up against a serious obstacle. Because of the nature of airborne operations, airborne personnel could only be recruited from volunteers: an unwilling parachutist could only prove a liability when the test came! And the army, to its alarm, had been unable to recruit sufficient volunteers from the RAMC so that the airborne combatants would be provided with enough medical corpsmen to care for the wounded.

The man the War Office sent to recruit those Non-Combatant Corpsmen recently with the bomb-disposal units was the flamboyant Colonel McEwan, 'a swaggering divisional medical officer,' according to Victor Newcomb. General Crookenden tells us that McEwan was known affectionately as 'old technicolour' because of the number of medals he liked to wear on his chest. 'With him to Normandy went a black tin box in which were ribbons of all the medals he might conceivably win there.'[13] 'This recruitment,' says Newcomb, 'was launched in great style, with great persuasion and with a wonderful image of the good work that conscientious objectors could do on the battlefield once the army had been dropped on Europe.'[14]

The next stage lasted a little over a year. First the volunteers from the NCC were located as a unit near Chesterfield in the English Midlands and subjected to a course of rigorous physical training, including exhausting route marches, the purpose of which was to eliminate those who might crack up in action. The army wished to train only those physically and psychologically able to parachute out of aeroplanes and to land successfully in enemy territory, whether combatants or non-combatants, that is, conscientious objectors. Newcomb described the process as one of 'hardening up.'[15] Next came training in working a parachute, including mock landings on the dropping zone. This occurred at Ringway aerodrome near Manchester; by now the conscientious objectors were training jointly with combatant medics, though of course they were not required to carry a weapon.[16] Finally assignment to one or another field ambulance took place, and at last they all received some first-aid training. The new location was now Bulford Barracks, in the vast army complex situated on Salisbury Plain. To quote Newcomb again: at this point 'we got to know officers and NCOs who were going to go into action with us.' Summing up the end result of the various forms of training he had been through, Newcomb says: 'I was nothing more really than a stretcher bearer with a reasonable knowledge of First-aid and treatment of wounds.'[17] Still, that was to prove enough to make each medical unit an effective reinforcement in combat.

During the weeks immediately prior to 6 June 1944, airborne troops were kept isolated from the rest of the community in a location in the Cotswolds. The atmosphere was one of expectation mixed with apprehension. A few weeks before D-Day, COs in training had been offered a revolver if they wanted to carry one. But Cedric McCarthy could remember only one CO in his unit who accepted this offer. The unofficial chroniclers of 224 Parachute Field Ambulance, both of them conscientious objectors, write of this period of anxious waiting:

> The weather was lovely and the freedom of the brown ploughed fields and stretches of summery grass invited us beyond the stone walls and barbed wire which shut us in ... [But] for us the operation had already begun. Almost without realizing it we had entered the tunnel which was to concentrate and intensify our lives until we emerged from it some-

> where in France. A detached observer might have missed this atmosphere of concentration. To see us supine in the sun, listening to gramophone records, playing cards in our tents or kicking footballs about among the guy-ropes, he might have thought our existence typical of troops in camp: or, knowing better, he might have thought our apparent indifference studied. Certainly we did our best to enjoy those last few days, for few of us had ever felt so conscious of being alive. But at the same time we were aware of another emotion, a sense of our collective importance. We knew that we were to be the spearhead of an invasion for which the world was waiting with bated breath.[18]

At last the order came to embark on the plane that was to carry them across the channel and behind the enemy lines. This is how one medical paratrooper, Roland Gant, who was also a conscientious objector, begins his story: 'Here sit I, Private Soldier number so-and-so, member of a medical section of twenty men [known as a "stick"] attached to a Parachute Battalion of the 6th Airborne Division.' Among the items of his equipment were 'a parachute, not to mention the sixty-pound kitbag to which my right leg was lashed ... Peering out of other masses of equipment I recognized the sweating faces of my friends,' including fellow 'conchies' as well as regular combatants like the captain and his batman and a Scots corporal.

The captain was the first to jump when the moment for this arrived. 'I began shuffling towards the door,' writes Gant, 'and suddenly there was nobody in front of me – nothing but the rectangle of night crisscrossed by red tracers [and] the six-foot-something Canadian Air Force dispatcher, who bawled "Good luck, kid" in my ear and helped me out of the door with a mighty shove between the shoulder blades.'[19] Gant made a successful landing. One of his fellow conscientious objectors, Phil Sargent ('about the nicest person I ever knew,' wrote another friend of his),[20] did not. He landed in a tree and was shot down by the Germans, thus becoming one of the few weaponless soldiers who would die on the Normandy battlefield (three of them on D-Day).[21]

Excitement mixed with fear possessed most paratroopers, whether combatants or weaponless. One of Gant's fellow conscientious objectors, the devoutly Anglican C. Hardinge Pritchard, describes how, the night before D-Day, 'lying in bed I found myself in a cold sweat.' He picked up his New Testament and read the Gospel of Mark 4:35–41. 'Why are ye so fearful? How is it that ye have no faith?' And Jesus' words restored his calm. Pritchard was number 13 in his 'stick' for the jump.[22] 'All jumps have a nightmarish quality.'[23] But it was probably the last positions in the 'stick' that needed just that extra pinch of courage; and there were cases of men refusing the leap, including one conscientious objector later in the war, 'who just could not jump through that door.'[24] According to Colonel Young, such refusals 'are very "infectious"'[25]: the army had, therefore, made it a court-martial offence. True, the 'static parachutes' then used for 'operational drops' almost always opened as soon as the parachutist left the plane: 'if it didn't, [as] on very ... odd occasions was the case, then you were very much out of luck.' However, states Newcomb, who had taken a course in parachute packing, only 'one in a thousand failed to open.'[26] Not all his comrades, of course, knew this; anyhow, a one-in-a-thousand chance was not in every circumstance a comforting thought!

After descending to the ground, members of the two medical units accompanied the troops as they slowly advanced into Normandy in the wake of the retreating Germans: the Germans unexpectedly put up a stubborn resistance, repeatedly counter-attacking and thus delaying the Allies' advance. But after three months, Operation 'Overlord' was at last over, its purposes achieved;[27] and the medical paratroop units returned to base at Bulford on Salisbury Plain on 6 September. From the medical point of view – number of casualties treated and surgical operations performed – the first fortnight had been the most satisfactory. The figures for that period, write Bramwell and Mowat, 'illustrate the value of a field Ambulance working in the front line.' In subsequent weeks, boredom and frustration ensued, and some medics began to doubt whether the units' existence was justified.[28] Though employment in, or near, the front line occurred again briefly, that intense satisfaction in their work was not again achieved.

'Ninety per cent of the Field Ambulance[s] who were dropped in Normandy on D-Day had never been in action before.' (This percentage referred not only to the conscientious objector contingent but to all personnel.) To adjust could not have been easy. 'In one place,' writes one of the 'conchies,' 'I found buttocks which appeared as though they had been cut off with a knife, in another a three-fingered hand unattached to anything else, curled in the dust with a horrible, almost surrealist fixity of purpose.' After they had landed, carnage had taken place among the combatant soldiers, who formed the airborne invaders. 'Many of the bodies were unrecognizable'; attempts at identification usually proved a waste of time.[29] But it was in circumstances like these that the medical paratroopers felt their job was worthwhile.

After recuperating in England, 224 Parachute Field Ambulance returned on Christmas eve to the continent: it took part in the Rhine Crossing and then continued on to the Baltic (late March to early May 1945).[30] Credit for the fact that the unit kept intact must go to its commanding officer, Colonel Young. He was also chiefly responsible for seeing that the work of the unit was recorded in detail, which did not happen in the case of the other three Parachute Field Ambulances active at this time (all of them including conscientious objectors as medical aidmen).[31]

The colonel entrusted the task of compiling this record to a small group of especially talented conscientious objectors attached to his unit. These writers and craftsmen set to work on the project during the final months of 1944. Young 'devoured each chapter [of the first volume] as we typed it,' one of them writes, 'spoiling our seamless paragraphs with new titbits of reminiscence, yet continually urging us to finish it.' Some of their comrades were indeed jealous of this 'inner circle,' as they liked to call Bramwell and Mowat, the authors, John Petts, the Welsh wood engraver and book designer, and John Ryder, 'a gifted amateur painter,' who 'made coloured maps of the battlefields.' During the advance to the Rhine, Ryder 'had spent his spare evenings ... cutting blocks by the light of a hurricane lamp.'[32] Printing of the second volume was completed in Palestine, where the unit found itself in May 1946 not long before it was finally disbanded.

Colonel Young succeeded in establishing an excellent relationship with the conscientious objectors who served under his command. And they responded positively to this approach, working 'happily' and 'efficiently' for as long as they were in his unit. The writer James Bramwell, more mature than were most of the other 'conchie' medical parachutists, enjoyed a relationship with Young that in other circumstances might perhaps have been described as friendship.[33]

The colonel claimed to have difficulty in understanding the mindset of the conscientious objector. 'Don't you bloody conchies ever think of anything else but your bloody consciences?' he expostulated once with Bramwell. Summarizing the colonel's attitude, the latter wrote: 'He was ... sympathetic to conscientious objectors without cherishing any illusions about them. What was more important he was a judge of character, with an interest in the welfare of individual men amounting almost to a vocation. And when, on the eve of the [D-Day] invasion, we acquired a [commander] of whom everybody approved we became a paradox of war-time society: a contented Unit.' Young, indeed, had very soon decided 'that conchies made better medics if their principles were left alone.'[34] Wartime experience taught him, too, that, in selecting personnel, individualism was an essential character trait of what he chose to call the 'parachute type.'[35] And this trait certainly seems to have predominated in those conscientious objectors who finally made it into his unit. Nonconformists, 'always in a state of argument against the military system of thoughtless repression,' abounded among the 'conchies' in 224 Parachute Field Ambulance (and presumably among the other medical parachute units), men like Johnny Ryder, whom the staff sergeant tried in vain to keep his hair cut, his sleeves done up, and his tunic buttoned up 'at the neck.'[36] Just as these highly individualistic types nevertheless 'greatly respected' the man who commanded them throughout three campaigns, he for his part recognized their sincerity and acknowledged the validity of their scruples in warfare. Though no pacifist, to some degree he succeeded in empathizing with his 'conchies.' When one of them, shortly after D-Day, was reported missing (he eventually surfaced as a POW in Stalag IV B), Colonel Young wrote to his parents, hitherto embarrassed by having a son who was a 'conchie': 'He was known by all ranks for his modesty and for the courage with which he bore his Christian convictions. Such men are rare.'[37]

Several different estimates have been given for the number of conscientious objectors who became medical paratroopers and, at intervals, took part in battle from D-Day on. According to Newcomb's recollections, there had been 'in the region of 150 or so' volunteers, forming 'in the end something like two-thirds of the strength of the Parachute Field Ambulance[s].'[38] The most accurate figure seems to be that given by Hayes: it was based on the records of the Central Board for Conscientious Objectors. According to him, 162 members of the NCC volunteered and were accepted 'for parachute duties' between June 1943 and August 1945.[39]

A complicating factor is that almost all the sources available on non-combatant medical paratroopers deal with only one unit, the 224 Parachute Field Ambulance commanded by Colonel Young, who, we have seen, was to sponsor the compilation and publication of his unit's history. Even if lists there of unit members do not appear to be quite complete, it seems clear that around fifty conscientious objectors served at one time or another in his unit.[40] The endeavours and dilemmas of the over one hundred objectors who served in other Parachute Field Ambulance units are unfortunately difficult now to follow:[41] they have faded from memory like so much of the past.

Conscientious objectors and combatant medics shared alike the achievements and frustrations their paratrooper work brought – first while still in training, and then in battle and in rest after combat. What, however, distinguished noncombatant from combatant soldier in these circumstances was, above all, the dilemmas which faced the first category and which the second category did not have to contend with. The remainder of my essay will be devoted to the problems that arose from this situation.

In the first place, their presence as an integral part of the fighting forces compelled men who had renounced violence to continually reconsider their position. One of them pointed to the humanitarian nature of their work, including 'more enemy casualties treated than allied,' as 'compensation, perhaps, for the grotesque compromise we'd made in serving in the army.'[42] Newcomb, who had at first contemplated going to prison rather than accept the appeals tribunal's decision in mid-1940 that he undertake noncombatant military service, came to feel after having 'rethought [his] position' that at that stage of the war his 'place was ... alongside my contemporaries' in the forces, if that were possible without renunciation of his pacifism. Nevertheless, the matter continued to bother him. Asked if he had not felt it was ironic – 'bearing in mind your pacifist stance' – that he should eventually go into battle, he replied:

> I'm not sure that irony is the right word. I can see the contradiction within it, and I could easily reflect upon the transition from being somebody who had originally persuaded himself that he wasn't going to take part in any single act which was directly connected with the war into somebody who was involved in what [was] a spearhead operation.

Pressed as to whether he did not consider working as a medical paratrooper was not 'rather a dangerous compromise with war activity,' Newcomb, however, denied that it had brought him any sense of 'discomfort.' As he explained:

> It took me, I think, some time to accept that once the war had begun in earnest, which it really did in 1940, ... the rules of the game were different ... [Since] I and my fellow [pacifists] had failed to persuade the population of the United Kingdom that passive resistance, a different national stance, was the appropriate one ... I began to think more and more strongly that it

was impossible for anybody to divorce themselves from the situation around them.

The war could no longer be stopped, but, as an individual, he could still help to reduce casualties to a minimum.[43]

In 224 Parachute Field Ambulance the conscientious objectors enjoyed a male bonding that they had carried over from their sojourn in the stigmatized NCC. The decision to train as medical paratroopers seems often to have been a joint one, made by close friends among NCC personnel attached to the bomb disposal squads. This situation presumably existed in other Parachute Field Ambulance units where objectors made up a considerable proportion of the personnel. Such solidarity, we may note, contrasts with the situation in which noncombatant medics sometimes found themselves in the U.S. armed forces of the Second World War: for example, the lonely objector attached to a Medical Corps unit in the Pacific theatre of operations, who refused to accept a weapon even though the rest of the unit carried arms.[44] Among British medical paratroopers, however, presence of a 'conchie' network came to coexist harmoniously with a wider camaraderie within the unit as a whole, shared in by all ranks. Stanley Rickman, a conscientious objector parachuted into Normandy on D-Day, wrote: 'Our fellow paratroopers regarded us [COs] as abnormal but we were accepted as comrades.'[45]

This camaraderie, though, presented a second dilemma. How far should it go? How far might the 'conchies' identify themselves with the combatant soldiers without compromising their pacifism? 'To treat and clear casualties sustained by' these soldiers[46] was – at any rate, in the eyes of the British army – the primary function of a Parachute Field Ambulance. From D-Day on, the 'conchies' would proudly wear the badge and maroon beret of the 'Red Devils,' the daredevil parachute brigade, some of the toughest fighters in the British army, who formed the 6th Airborne Division,[47] all of them volunteers – including the 'conchie' medics (the 'Red [Cross] Devils' as their chroniclers dubbed them). Some of the 'conchies' might indeed find it difficult to eliminate a certain swagger in their gait that they had taken over, unconsciously, from their combatant colleagues. Bramwell in his autobiography refers to the latter as 'the noble battalion.' 'In some ways,' he writes, 'I identified myself with the Battalion. Their courage and morale were extraordinary ... Conchie though I was, I admired them enormously. And it would be dishonest to conceal my gratitude for the cunning and marksmanship upon which my own life depended.' While deploring the unnecessary killings practised by a small minority of the Red Devils, Bramwell believed that his fellow 'conchies' 'now felt ... as the fighting grew hotter – that the part we were playing was of importance in sustaining the courage of the troops ... We were sustained in our turn by the knowledge that we were appreciated, a satisfaction quite apart from the deeper one of being able to save lives [including those of the enemy] when everyone else had the duty of destroying them.'[48]

Though Bramwell attributed the medics' care of wounded enemy soldiers 'as our own' to the hope that the Germans would do the same in the case of British captives as much as to humanitarian sentiment,[49] I think he was being unjust here, at least in so far as his fellow 'conchies' were concerned. On the basis of experience in the battle zone, his friend, the artist John Petts, disagreed and emphasized the compassion that the latter displayed towards the wounded irrespective of nationality, even in cases where a mercy killing of one of the wounded by means of a fatal dose of morphine was involved. 'Mind you,' Petts went on, 'I can think of ... particular cases of regular soldiers [in the RAMC] who displayed this lovely quality, so it's not entirely the possession of pacifists ... by any means.' But it proved an inspiration to him to see how his pacifist colleagues 'were serving their fellows' in that spirit.[50] Tony Bass, killed in action on 18 August 1944, appears as an exemplar of what Petts calls poetically 'the lovely quality of compassion.' An alumnus of Oxford as well as Hawkspur Green, this 'tall, short-sighted young man ... loved humanity as did few conchies I came across,' writes Bramwell, who also notes 'his incredible clumsiness,' surprising indeed in one who had succeeded in making a parachute landing in enemy territory. 'We doted on his awkward, coltish gambols when he suddenly felt pleased with life,' including the NCOs who had at first made him their butt. At the advanced dressing station – barn, dairy, farm outhouse – which his unit had set up at Le Mesnil behind the lines, Bass, because he knew German well, was entrusted with the task of dealing with wounded German POWs. '"*Lassen wir Tony fragen* [Let's ask Tony]," one used to hear' in the makeshift wards.[51]

A third problem distinctive to the 'conchie' contingent in the parachute Field Ambulances was that of promotion, though perhaps this bothered their well-wishers among the units' officers more than the men themselves. In 1941 the Army Council ruled against the promotion of conscientious objectors who had been assigned to noncombatant duties in the army. For the duration of the war, therefore, they would remain privates; the non-commissioned ranks were closed to them. The reason given for this decision was 'that a N.C.O. may be required to lead any British troops at hand to resist enemy airborne troops. A non-combatant N.C.O. could not carry out these duties.'[52] The matter was reopened in July 1943 after the War Office, 'because of the acute shortage of R.A.M.C. volunteers,' had agreed to accept volunteers from the NCC to train with the RAMC as medical paratroopers. It was now suggested informally that 'these men ... should be considered for non-commissioned rank. But this may still cut across general policy.'[53] The War Office, however, remained adamant in refusing its consent to a change of policy. Only if a man agreed to give up his noncombatant status, which had been guaranteed by his tribunal, could promotion to non-commissioned rank be considered. Otherwise, it argued, with a legally valid tribunal decision to support them, 'they ... might well refuse to give any orders requiring men to fire on and kill the enemy.'[54] And there the matter rested for the time being.

The promotion issue surfaced again in March 1945. There can be no doubt that the *spiritus movens* now was Colonel Young. The parachute operation on the Rhine was to open on 24 March. The previous day a junior official at the War Office wrote to his superior:

> I [have] received a very strong recommendation that we should modify the terms of A.C.I 1676 of 1941, to permit of the promotion of conscientious objectors in medical units. The actual cases which gave rise to this proposal were those of six medical orderlies in 6 Airborne Div. Each of these are genuine conscientious objectors and each is a volunteer for parachute duty, fully trained in their duties. They have all of them given proof of leadership in the performance of their own medical duties and great gallantry.

The writer of this memo, while his reaction to the recommendation was basically positive, was 'of the opinion that promotion of conscientious objectors should be very far from a routine matter.' The man must have 'proved his leadership in battle'; he should belong to a corps which consisted of 'protected personnel under the Geneva Convention'; and his commanding officer would have had first 'to take into account such views as men might have who were not conscientious objectors, and might be placed under [his] orders.' If all these conditions were satisfied, however, the memo writer could see no reason why such promotions should not be approved.[55] The Executive Committee of the Army Council considered the matter at its next meeting on 18 May 1945. As might perhaps have been expected, the committee decided to make no change in the existing policy. It conceded that a situation was unlikely to arise in which a conscientious objector, promoted to NCO rank, might in an emergency refuse 'to lead men in combat.' ('Indeed, being untrained in the use of weapons, [he] might be quite incompetent to do so, however courageous.') Nevertheless, 'these circumstances might be more common in the infiltration tactics of the Japanese war than they were in the war in Europe.'[56] By mid-August 1945, the conflict was over on all fronts; and the army's intention of sending CO medical paratroopers to the Far East was never carried out. The War Office had stubbornly upheld its ban on the promotion of conscientious objectors in the army.

The United States, we may note, both in the Second World War and in the Vietnam War, adopted a more reasonable policy with regard to promoting those of its noncombatant soldiers who took part in battle, as many of them did. In addition, three of these men – two posthumously – received the country's highest military award, the Medal of Honor (albeit the citations do not mention the fact of their being conscientious objectors). The British army was, however, much more sparing in allotting high awards to such men: only Private P.M. Lenton received a Military Medal for his rescue of wounded paratroopers, together with much needed stretchers left on the dropping zone, during the advance 'over the Rhine' at the end of March 1945. 'You'll never get there and back alive,' his section NCO had warned him. But Lenton insisted on trying, and his endeavours proved successful.[57] However, the recommendation of Colonel Young, indefatigable in support of his 'conchies,' to award both Privates J.G. Bramwell and W.H. Lewis Military Medals was rejected, while his recommendation of Private J.H.S. Mowat for mention in despatches was watered down into a mere 'C in C's Certificate for Good Service.'[58]

Lastly, the question of whether or not to accept a weapon as a last resort to ward off attack on wounded being cared for surfaced periodically: it remained a problem with which every conscientious objector had to grapple in his career as a medical paratrooper. 'When a C.O.,' writes Hayes, 'was sent to serve in the Army for non-combatant duties only, a special slip was to be attached to his documents indicating that by order of a statutory Tribunal he was to be employed on non-combatant duties only.'[59] There is no evidence of any man being forced to carry a weapon, as was customary in the case of RAMC paratroopers who were not conscientious objectors, 'so that they can use them for the protection of themselves and of casualties under their charge and so that they can take charge and dispose of the arms of casualties passing through their unit.'[60] But from the outset, some psychological pressure existed. Ernest Baxter, a member of the fundamentalist Church of Christ, reported: 'As training proceeded, the military authorities endeavoured to persuade the men to carry revolvers.' At this stage, at any rate, they all refused to do so.[61]

Participation in battle, though, created a new situation not easy to envisage beforehand. In his unit, Newcomb recalls, the 'conchies' were again – this time more politely – 'offered the opportunity of carrying a revolver' before going into action. Almost all – 'ninety-nine percent' – refused this offer. He thought, though, that the offer was indeed well meant on the part of the officers, who believed it might be a comfort to them in 'last resort situations.' 'Those people who were in the RAMC and not conscientious objectors couldn't understand why we didn't want to carry a revolver just in case.'[62]

As the war in Europe wound down and airborne forces prepared for possible action in east Asia against the Japanese, some pacifist medical paratroopers began to wonder where exactly the limits of their nonviolence lay in the case of an enemy who were believed unwilling to observe the rules of war followed even by Nazi Germany. The question, as it now appeared to be, was: since 'the Japanese give no quarter and [would] shoot all your patients ... are you going to defend your patients or not?' Because of Japan's surrender, the question remained a theoretical one, but not before it had troubled some consciences. Take the case of John Petts, 'one of the gladdest moments of [whose] life as a conchie' came near the end of the war when he took the captured Germans' weapons and smashed them. Nevertheless, after 'being briefed about service facing the Japanese,' he had decided to take a short course in arms training 'so that I knew how to load, and unload also, sten guns and hand guns and rifles ... Target practice and the handling and understanding and servicing of weapons, I considered that possibly useful knowledge and I pre-empted any decision about doing it ... I thought, "Well, knowledge can never be harmful."'[63]

Around this time Bramwell also took weapon training. His motivation was less pragmatic, more principled, than Petts's had been. As he explained, 'being a medic now meant more to me than being a pacifist.' If the two impulses ever came into conflict, he was ready to abandon pacifism, and he asked Colonel Young to allow him 'unofficially' to use a Sten gun, but only in an emergency.[64] Yet, so strong did he feel his ties with the other 'conchies' in the unit, he was unwilling to give up his conscientious objector status. ('In other words, you want to have your cake and eat it?' the colonel had interposed. 'Exactly, sir.') It was painful for men like Bramwell and Petts to break ranks over this issue with colleagues with whom they had shared the vicissitudes of battle and the ideals which had upheld them all in their weaponlessness. For the latter, pondering the matter 'in twos and threes' during the day 'and in bed at night,' remained firm 'that pacifism was a Cause and one that could not be fought with lethal weapons.'[65] They would not compromise.

Hayes has called Second-World-War Britain's 'conchie' paratroopers the 'Right Wing of the pacifist movement.'[66] In one way, this description is apt. It would scarcely have been possible to push 'conscientious cooperation' with the military further than they did in their Parachute Field Ambulances. As military historians have acknowledged,[67] without their courageous and dedicated and always physically exhausting endeavours, the airborne forces in 1944–5, during the most important campaigns on the Western front, would have functioned much less efficiently than these were able to do with their assistance. On the other hand, even in the combatant zone, these noncombatant medics remained loyal to their pacifist convictions: indeed, their presence on the battlefield reflected, above all, their desire to save life. That it also helped to legitimize conscientious objection in the eyes of many who would otherwise have been unsympathetic, was merely incidental. A handful had vacillated on the question of handling a weapon in exceptional circumstances, but even then they sought somehow to reconcile their stance with their conscientious objector status. It seems that in only one case did an objector transfer to full combatant duties.[68] This contrasts strikingly, for instance, with the independent Friends Ambulance Unit (FAU), where the transfer rate of its personnel was much higher. Yet few would wish to use a term like 'right-wing' with reference to the FAU.

Apart from the dilemmas they experienced in maintaining a pacifist stance in a battle situation, the conchies in the Parachute Field Ambulances made, we have seen, a perceptible impact on Britain's war strategy, even though the numbers involved were small, especially when considered within the framework of the masses then mobilized for war throughout the globe. True, other armies did without such assistance in their airborne operations. But if Britain had had to do so, its planning would surely have had to be different. Yet military historians have been even more reticent here than peace historians, their exiguous references to these men sometimes slurring over the fact that they are dealing with conscientious objectors.

This essay attempts to fill the historiographical gap.

NOTES

1 Napier Crookenden, *Dropzone Normandy: The Story of the American and British Airborne Assault on D Day 1944* (Shepperton UK, 1976), 56.
2 A.D. Young, 'The Parachute Field Ambulance,' *Journal of the Royal Army Medical Corps*, vol. 89, no. 5 (November 1947), 241.
3 2 & 3 Geo. 6, c. 81.
4 Denis Hayes, *Challenge of Conscience: The Story of the Conscientious Objectors of 1939–1949* (London, 1949), 123, 387.
5 For instance, the magazine of No. 9 Company, of which the British Library holds the first issue for spring 1941 (P.P. 4039. dbr.), includes articles on Ernst Toller, Thomas Mann's *Death in Venice*, William Walton's viola concerto, Charlie Chaplin's *Great Dictator*, and 'Fundamentals of Chess,' and a translation from the Russian by a corpsman, A. Harkness, of a poem by Lermantov, 'written while exiled for killing a man in a duel.' These newsletters concentrated on cultural topics after *Bless 'Em All: The Chronicle of No. 1. Company N.C.C.* was stopped early in 1941 when Conservatives in the House of Commons had protested against what they regarded as the antipatritic tone of an article there on Armistice Day.
6 Major E.H. Rhodes-Wood, *A War History of the Royal Pioneer Corps 1939–1945* (Aldershot, 1960), 75.
7 In his retirement Major Clark, with his wife, ran a home for 'mentally retarded people': he obviously empathized with the evangelical Christian outlook that predominated among the members of the post-war No. 3 N.C.C. Association. See Central Board for Conscientious Objectors (CBCO) Archives, Library of the Religious Society of Friends (London), TEMP MSS 914, Box COR 5/16-4. File 4 contains an incomplete file of the *News-Sheet* of No. 3 Company N.C.C. Association. In 1955 the *News-Sheet* announced the publication in a limited edition of 150 copies of a history of No. 3 Company N.C.C. 'First come, first served': priced at the modest sun of 12s. 6d, the *News-Sheet* expected it might soon go out-of-print, presumably through purchase by former No. 3 Company corpsmen. It seems that no

copy of this book is available in any library, though one may eventually surface.

8 One of those who did so was Keith Vaughan (1912–1977), an outstanding English painter of his generation and famous for his drawings of young male nudes. In his *Journals 1939–1977* (London, 1989), 14, 15, he describes his tribunal hearing – at Reading on 12 August 1940 – as follows: 'It all happened so quickly ... The president took a copy of my statement ... and asked me very politely whether I would consent to serve in the RAMC. I said yes.' Those who knew Vaughan have described him as a gentle person with great 'sweetness of character,' but at the same time a loner ready to challenge the values prevalent in society if he believed these to be wrong. Like the medical paratrooper-to-be, Johnny Ryder, also an artist of distinction, Vaughan responded negatively to the regimentation that service in the ranks of the army inevitably entailed. He wrote in his *Journals*: 'Driven and chivvied all day by NCOs we have no idea of the beginning or end of a job or what its purpose is' (ibid., 27, 28).

9 Hayes, *Challenge*, 120–8. See also Rachel Barker, *Conscience, Government and War: Conscientious Objection in Great Britain 1939–45* (London, 1982), 24–6, 78–85, 233; Felicity Goodall, *A Question of Conscience: Conscientious Objection in the Two World Wars* (Stroud UK, 1997), chaps. 13 ('Non-Combatant Corps') and 14 ('Bomb Disposal'); and Ernest Spring, *'Conchie': The Wartime Experiences of a Conscientious Objector* (London, 1975), 12–42; and *C.B.C.O. Bulletin*: 'Conchies in Battledress: The Non-Combatant Corps Does Its Job,' no. 26 (April 1942), 10–12; 'Trouble in the N.C.C.: Refusal to Fire-watch Shell-cases – C.O. Acquitted,' no. 32 (Oct. 1942), 3, 4; 'Non-Combatant Duties,' no. 35 (Jan. 1943), 2; 'N.C.C. Duties Allegation,' no. 39 (May 1943), 2; 'N.C.C. Charges Withdrawn,' no. 43 (Sept. 1943), 4; 'Non-Combatant Corps,' no. 44 (Oct. 1943), 8; 'What of the Non-Combatants?' no. 62 (April 1945), 111, 112. Hugh Mowat (letter dated 28 June 2004) wrote of his time in a bomb disposal unit: 'I suppose we [NCC volunteers] were all pleased to take this opportunity of work that would benefit the *community at large*, not just the war effort ... No parades, no spit-&-polish – as unmilitary as possible. The conchies included a cobbler, a student, a local-government clerk, an optician, & a deep-sea fisherman. It was thoroughly congenial ...' And, I may add, of course it had its spice of danger. In his novel *The English Patient* (1992), Michael Ondaatje, in the person of the young Sikh sapper, Kirpal Singh (Kip), presents a graphic picture of the hazards and rewards encountered in bomb disposal whether in Britain or in Italy.

10 Independently, Keith Vaughan came virtually to the same conclusion, noting 'the daily humiliation of going about with NCC flashes on their shoul-

ders' (*Journals*, 28). F.R. Coad, a corpsman from No. 12 Company, in some doggerel, which he entitled 'The Saga of 9700 – Pte Atkins T (with moral),' gave humorous expression to this widely spread feeling among members of the Non-Combatant Corps:

Young Tommy Atkins could not bear
Upon his battle-blouse to wear
Embroidered so, so tidily
the fateful letters – 'N.C.C.'

Till one day Tommy, homeward bound,
A red cap at the Underground
Stopped with a smile so very sweet:
'Let's see your pass!' Alas, so neat
Upon the pass is 'N.C.C.'
While Tommy's cap-badge boasts 'R.E.'

No eloquence could e'er persuade him
That R.E. badge it wasn't his'n –
But to the 'jug' he fast conveyed him –
Poor Tommy spent his leave in prison,
For pinching passes – what a shame
To all who bear clan Atkins' name.

Now Tommy's grown so very bold,
And wears his badge as good as gold.

Tommy Atkins = British private soldier; R.E. = Royal Engineers. From *Brains Trussed: No. 12. Company N.C.C. 1941–1944*, 20 (British Library: P.P. 4039. ega.).

11 Victor Noel Newcomb, typescript of taped interview, Department of Sound Records, Imperial War Museum (London), Accession No. 009400/15 A, (hereafter IWM 009400/15 A), 30, 31, 43, 44. See also Spring, *'Conchie,'* 42: 'We in BD were rather proud of the red and yellow bomb flash worn on the sleeve of the tunic. It lent a certain distinction, and there was satisfaction in knowing that the "Conchies" in BD were applying a spot of glistening to the reputation of the Corps.'

12 Hayes, *Challenge*, 128.

13 Crookenden, *Dropzone*, 56.

14 Newcomb, IWM 009400/15 A, 45. In fact, many of the NCC men who

became medical paratroopers attached to the RAMC now won the kind of assignment they had sought when they had applied for CO status and been put into the NCC instead. As Cedric McCarthy, who – unlike Mowat and Newcomb – was eventually assigned to 225 Parachute Field Ambulance, reports in a letter to me dated 25 August 2004: 'We were very pleased that we had been let into a medical unit, something some of us had asked for at our Tribunals, and perhaps a little smug that we had volunteered where regular combatants had not.' He himself, on registering as a CO, had 'expressed a wish to go into the navy' as a medical orderly. But his request was, of course, ignored, and he was called up for service in the NCC.

15 Ibid., 46, 47. Mowat (letter dated 26 June 2004) comments on this stage of the odyssey: 'The physical training instructors, excellent men, were baffled by having barrack-rooms full of conchies undifferentiated by any rank. So for 3 giddy weeks I (for example) was elected as the one to pin 2 stripes on my sleeve, becoming an acting, unpaid, unofficial Corporal for that period. It was a good period – challenging but not too challenging – & the food was good.' Cedric McCarthy reports that, at one stage, he too was made briefly an 'acting and unpaid' lance-corporal in charge of his unit by the commanding officer. 'This would suggest ... that there was no prejudice against COs,' he concludes.

16 Mowat (letter dated 26 June 2004) comments on this period: 'Another good experience! Did it really last only 8 days? The RAF instructors were super – cheerful, encouraging, but not too hearty. And we had confidence in the equipment; we were taken to see how the 'chutes were packed – by WAAF girls each working at a long bench with, just in front of their heads, "A MAN'S LIFE DEPENDS ON HOW YOU PACK THIS CHUTE." We quickly discovered how comfortable the harness was during the descent; & after the Rhine Crossing, in conversation with wounded German paratroopers, I discovered how *their* equipment led to many sprained & broken limbs on landing ... The training ... involved 8 drops – 2 from a scanty little platform suspended from a barrage balloon. I remember only one who failed the course ... We felt deeply for him. After the last training drop, parachuting was no longer optional. After all, we *had* volunteered – & our special status was thereafter acknowledged by an extra two shillings (20p) a day, in our weekly pay packet!'

17 Newcomb, IWM 009400/15 A, 50, 52. Knowledge of first-aid, writes Mowat (letter dated 26 June 2004), 'was imparted by our own officers – all doctors – & by knowledgable NCOs. I also took a course in blood transfusion, with a view to post-operative caring. Those selected for the two surgical teams had just 8 days in an army hospital – most of them conchies without any previous knowledge at all. And in the event, they performed prodigies,

being at times solely responsible for the anaesthesia, which meant injecting pentothal into the vein of a man whose state of traumatic shock had caused the veins to collapse. Such skill & self-mastery, in the face of life-or-death responsibility!' So far none of them ('except I suppose for the surgical teams?') had had 'any contact with a real casualty': such knowledge as a trainee possessed 'was still sketchy.' Robert Elmore, a CO who served from 1943 to 1947, for most of the time with 225 Parachute Field Ambulance under the command of Lt. Col. Bruce Harvey (attached to the 5th Parachute Brigade), writes in a letter dated 28 October 2004: 'I was a member of a surgical team which undertook emergency surgery in a field setting and assisted the surgeon with surgery.' 'A good number of the COs,' he adds, unlike most other RAMC personnel, acquired 'considerable knowledge and experience' and achieved the highest grade as nursing orderlies. Concerning 'those COs who served with the Medical Officers in the several parachute battalions,' Elmore writes: 'As medics they would accompany patrols exploring enemy territory and making raids. All COs, although they were medics, were part of fighting units and saw a good deal of action.' This was a risky occupation and 'their casualties were high.'

18 James Guy Bramwell and John Hugh Speke Mowat, eds, *Red [Cross] Devils: A Parachute Field Ambulance in Normandy ... Written by Members of 224 Parachute Field Ambulance and Published by the Unit* (N.p.p., 1945), 2. 'Published by kind permission of Major-General E.L. Bols, D.S.O. Divisional Commander, 6th Airborne Division.' Note that the word in square brackets in the title was represented on the title page by a symbol printed in red: this is usually overlooked by authors citing this work; for example, Neil Barber, *The Day the Devils Dropped In ...* (Barnsley UK, 2002), 11.

19 Roland Gant, *How like a Wilderness* (London, 1946), 7–10.

20 F.R. Davies, *Some Blessed Hope: Memoirs of a Next-to-Nobody* (Lewes UK, 1996), 42. For Davies' time in the NCC, see pages 37–48. A birthright Quaker, Davies became a combatant soldier before the war was over.

21 See 'Airborne Forces Roll of Honour, 1944,' in David Reynolds, *Paras: An Illustrated History of Britain's Airborne Forces* (Stroud UK, 1998), 230, 231.

22 C. Hardinge Pritchard, *In My Grave I Am Not* (London, 1998), 4–7. Cedric McCarthy recalls: 'People were nervous about being number 13 in a stick. My friend, the CO John Shirley, for the flight to Normandy changed places with someone, and in the event John jumping 13 survived while the person he changed with was killed very soon after landing.'

23 Bramwell and Mowat, eds, *Red [Cross] Devils*, 4.

24 John Petts, typescript of taped interview, Department of Sound Records, IWM, Accession No. 009732/16 A (hereafter IWM 009732/16 A).

25 Young, 'Parachute Field Ambulance,' 242.

26 Newcomb, IWM 009400/15 A, 49, 50. Cedric McCarthy reports: 'As parachutists we were always aware that the Americans had a spare emergency 'chute on their chest. We were jealous about this but also superior about it.'

27 For a competent summary of the contribution of the RAMC in the operation, see John S.G. Blair, *In Arduis Fidelis: Centenary History of the Royal Army Medical Corps* ([Aberdour, Scotland], 2001), 298–305, 312 n. 11; also F.A.E. Crew, *The Army Medical Services: Campaigns*, vol. 4 (*North-West Europe*) (London: Her Majesty's Stationery Office, 1962), 128–31, 283, 284.

28 Bramwell and Mowat, eds, *Red [Cross] Devils*, 41, 59–74. See also *224 Parachute Field Ambulance: Record of the Unit's Part in the War in Europe 6 June, 1944, to 8 May, 1945* (N.p.p., n.d.).

29 Gant, *How like a Wilderness*, 19, 20. See also Bramwell and Mowat, eds, *Red [Cross] Devils*, 4.

30 Bramwell and Mowat, eds, *Over the Rhine: A Parachute Field Ambulance in Germany ...* (Sarafand, Palestine, 1946). 'Privately printed [by the Canopy Press] at the Field Ambulance for its members only.'

31 See Young, 'Parachute Field Ambulance,' 235, 241. Because of this, the odyssey of 224 Parachute Field Ambulance has inevitably overshadowed, in the record as it exists today, the achievements of the other Parachute Field Ambulances in which COs served.

32 James Byrom (pseudonym for Bramwell), *The Unfinished Man* (London, 1957), 205–7. In this autobiography (which covers his time in the NCC on pages 121–36), Bramwell has hidden Colonel Young under the alias of Harding. See also Petts, IWM 009732/16 A, 53. In his obituary in the *Times* (25 January 2001), 25, John Ryder is described as the self-taught 'designer who grappled with *Ulysses*, made handsome books for Bodley Head, and encouraged a generation of enthusiasts to print for pleasure.' I must thank Hugh Mowat for drawing my attention to this item.

33 Bramwell's co-author, Hugh Mowat, in his letter dated 26 June 2004, described Bramwell as 'a very good mixer, at ease in any company. His command of detail in "Red Cross Devils" is masterly ... I was, & felt, a very subordinate assistant.'

34 Byrom (Bramwell), *Unfinished Man*, 143, 144, 196, 233.

35 Young, 'Parachute Field Ambulance,' 236.

36 Gant, *How like a Wilderness*, 8; Byrom (Bramwell), *Unfinished Man*, 134.

37 Pritchard, *In My Grave*, ix.

38 Newcomb, IWM 009400/15 A, 47.

39 Hayes, *Challenge*, 387.

40 Hugh Mowat and Ben Taylor, both former noncombatant members of 224

Parachute Field Ambulance, very kindly marked for me on otherwise undifferentiated lists the names of those members of the unit who were, like themselves, conscientious objectors. Since the few surviving medical paratroopers are now octogenarians or nonagenarians, the possibility of utilizing their memories is unfortunately limited.

41 See the Imperial War Museum's not especially revealing taped interview with the pharmacist 'conchie' Bernard Lionel Horne, who served with 225 Parachute Field Ambulance from D-Day to 1946 (IWM Accession No. 12908/3).

42 Letter from Hugh Mowat, 26 March 2003.

43 Newcomb, IWM 009400/15 A, 27–30, 65, 109, 110.

44 Mulford Q. Sibley and Philip E. Jacob, *Conscription of Conscience: The American State and the Conscientious Objector, 1940–1947* (Ithaca NY, 1952), 97.

45 Quoted in Goodall, *A Question*, 133. Elmore (letter dated 20 October 2004) writes: 'at no time did I encounter abuse or adverse comments for being a CO from fellow soldiers. Before I became a medical paratrooper it was a different story.'

46 Bramwell and Mowat, *Red [Cross] Devils*, 1.

47 G.G. Norton, *The Red Devils: From Bruneval to the Falklands*, 2nd edn (London and New York, 1984), chap. 6.

48 Byrom (Bramwell), *Unfinished Man*, 178, 182, 183.

49 Ibid., 184.

50 Petts, IWM 009732/16 A, 60–2.

51 Byrom (Bramwell), *Unfinished Man*, 147; Bramwell and Mowat, *Red [Cross] Devils*, 40. For Bass, see essay 23 above.

52 Army Council Instruction 1676 of 1941; quoted in War Office (WO) 32/9432, National Archives (Kew), formerly Public Record Office (PRO), London. See also Barker, *Conscience*, 133 n. 19.

53 Assistant director of medical services, 6 Airborne Division, to the undersecretary of state, War Office, 28 July 1944, WO 32/9432, National Archives. See also C.H. Pritchard, 'Promotion for Non-Combatants,' *C.B.C.O. Bulletin*, no. 78 (Sept. 1946), 265.

54 War Office, 10, 13, and 17 August 1943, ibid., National Archives.

55 War Office memo, 23 March 1945, ibid.

56 'Extract from the minutes of the 214th meeting of the Executive Committee of the Army Council held on Friday, 18th May, 1945,' ibid.

57 Lieutenant-Colonel Howard N. Cole, *On Wings of Healing: The Story of Airborne Medical Services, 1940–1960* (Edinburgh and London, 1963), 163.

58 '224 (Parachute) Field Ambulance R.A.M.C.: Account of Operations ... by Lieut.-Colonel A.D. Young,' Appendix 6, in 'War Diary of 224 Parachute

Field Ambulance,' WO 177/831, National Archives. Cf. list of 'honours and awards' in *224 Parachute Field Ambulance: Record*.

59 Hayes, *Challenge*, 12.

60 Memo dated 28 July 1943, WO 32/9432, National Archives.

61 'Captured by Nazis in Normandy: Ernest Spencer Interviews a Paratroop C.O.,' *C.B.C.O. Bulletin*, no. 54 (August 1944), 33.

62 Newcomb, IWM 009400/15 A, 54.

63 Petts, IWM 009732/16 A, 63, 64.

64 Byrom (Bramwell), *Unfinished Man*, 232: 'Would I look on and see my patients [killed], saving my conscience if not my life at their expense?' was how Bramwell formulated this agonizing dilemma.

65 Ibid., 197, 231–3.

66 Hayes, *Challenge*, 129.

67 For example, Barber, *The Day*, 11.

68 L./Sgt. C. Buckmaster.

25 Jehovah's Witnesses as Conscientious Objectors in Nazi Germany

Early in 1940 Judge Richardson, chairman of the local tribunal for conscientious objectors (COs) situated at Newcastle in northern England, remarked concerning some Jehovah's Witnesses (JWs) who had appeared before the tribunal over which he presided: 'I have the greatest contempt for your sort. You might pray and preach, but what good do you do?'[1] Such remarks were not unknown elsewhere in the case of officials dealing with COs either in Britain or North America. When Judge Richardson spoke, in wartime Nazi Germany JWs refusing to bear arms for Hitler's Reich were already being executed, and the death penalty continued to be imposed until the end of the war on most German JWs who resisted the draft. However, we should perhaps not be too severe on Judge Richardson and the authors of similar 'abusive' comments since, for at least half a century after the close of hostilities, German JWs, despite their staunch – while nonviolent – resistance to Hitler's regime, which the Nazi authorities branded as 'subversive,' still remained at the end of the century 'neglected' victims of Nazism, 'forgotten' by all but a few and 'virtually unknown to a wider public' whether inside or outside Germany.[2]

Background

Of American origin, the Bible Students (*die Ernsten Bibelforscher*), as the JWs called themselves at the outset, made their first converts in Germany around the year 1900. The sect grew slowly until, at the time Hitler came to power in 1933, they numbered around 25,000 with some 10,000 more sympathizers.[3] The JWs do not call themselves pacifists. Most of them accept self-defence. But until the coming of Christ at the battle of Armageddon (*Harmageddon*), JWs feel obliged to take up a position of neutrality with regard to all international conflicts. Even in the final apocalyptic conflict, they expect to be merely passive spectators while the destruction of the wicked will be carried out by God's avenging angels. Meanwhile, they must refrain from service in the armed forces of earthly powers as well as from participation in elections and all affairs of state. Their citizenship is in Jehovah's kingdom; 'they will "render unto Caesar." But [they] cannot take dual citizenship.'[4] 'The main task to which every Jehovah's Witness is regularly directed is that of evangelism,' which takes many forms, above all 'house-to-house visits' and 'door-to-door preaching.'[5] For this reason, JW draftees have often claimed exemption from military service on the grounds of being ministers of religion of equal status to the exempted clergy of other denominations.

In First-World-War Germany, as we have seen in a previous essay (no. 18), drafted JWs, along with other COs, were often confined as psychiatric patients in mental hospitals. This procedure occurred only very rarely during the Second World War. Already before war had broken out, leading German psychiatrists, like Professor Johannes Lange at the University of Breslau, had expressed the view that JWs and other religious COs, however mistaken and sometimes acting out of cowardice, were nevertheless indubitably sane. As Lange wrote: 'There seems to us to be no possibility of treating refusal of military service [Dienstverweigerung] on grounds of religion differently from any other form of refusal of military service.'[6] That opinion set the stage for the treatment of JW – and other – objectors once war had broken out.

The Framework of Military Conscription

Within a few months of the Nazis' coming to power, the JWs' organization was banned throughout the Reich. The confrontation with the state had already begun. In 1935 conscription was reintroduced: that added one more area of conflict. As Michael Barenbaum has put it: JWs 'would not enlist in the army, undertake air raid drills, stop meeting or proselytizing. They would not utter the words "Heil Hitler."' In addition, they opposed their teenager sons serving in the Hitler youth corps (Reicharbeitsdienst), which acted as a preparation for full military service later on.

According to the conscription law every able-bodied 'German man' between the ages of eighteen and forty-five was now liable for military service. No provision whatsoever was made for conscientious objection. Refusal to serve in the armed forces was punished by a prison term. In April 1937, for instance, Johannes Rauthe, a JW living in Leignitz, was sentenced by a military court to six months. He was sent to the army prison in Torgau, where he found a few of his coreligionists already incarcerated. At the end of his sentence, however, he was not freed but handed over to the Gestapo, who then attempted to 'persuade' him to change his mind and agree to become a combatant soldier. Failing in this, they despatched him in November to the concentration camp in Buchenwald. Ironically, this step saved his life since, so long as he remained a camp prisoner, he would not be called up and have to face the death penalty for persistent refusal to serve. Next year, Ernest Wilhelm Zehender, a thirty-two-year-old construction worker who had converted to the JWs from the Lutheran church at the beginning of the decade, was not so fortunate. Sentenced in mid-1938 to two years by a military court in Mannheim, he finished his sentence in a Germany now at war.[7] His subsequent fate is discussed below.

For the outbreak of war led to a sharpening of penalties for all draft resisters.[8] Those found guilty of 'undermining the country's military strength [Zersetzung der Wehrkraft]' were now liable to the death penalty; and a refusal to bear arms was considered an offence that came under that heading. True, a milder sentence remained a possibility, but such an option was only rarely applied in the case of JWs or other COs. With regard to the former, at any rate, capital punishment became the norm.[9] The majority of cases of draft refusal were tried before the State War Tribunal (Reichskriegsgericht), presided over from 12 September 1939 by Admiral Max Bastian until his retirement in November 1944. Bastian and several other members of this tribunal, which sat at first in Berlin-Charlottenburg and then (from the autumn of 1943) in Torgau, were old-fashioned conservatives rather than full-blown Nazis, and, after the war was over, the admiral admitted to having experienced qualms of conscience at sentencing men to death for following their religious convictions. Despite his 'uneasiness' at the time, he continued however to approve the sentencing of JWs to death.[10] At first the usual method of execution was by hanging, but this changed later to guillotining, though decapitation of that kind had been used earlier, too.

During the first four months of the war, at least forty JWs were executed for refusing induction into the army. The executions were not made public, presumably in the belief that such news would make a bad impression. As early as 17 November 1939 army command had issued an order: 'Information about the carrying out of the death sentence [on JW draft resisters] should not be displayed publicly, and notices of the same should not appear in the press.'

At the end of November the Führer himself confirmed the decision to impose the death penalty in such cases. In view of German soldiers' sacrifice of life and limb in the recent campaign against Poland, no mercy could be shown to such people. 'If they persisted in their resistance to army service, then the death penalty must be carried out.' Once Hitler had spoken, policy was set for dealing with COs, whether Witnesses or others, and it remained unchanged for the rest of the war.[11]

JWs receiving their call-up notices towards the end of August 1939, that is, prior to the outbreak of hostilities, were already marked down, as it were, for execution. For instance, Paul Frick, the forty-year-old father of four children, was summoned to the colours on 26 August, when he declared himself unwilling to be a soldier. He was sentenced to death on 23 October and executed shortly afterwards in the prison at Berlin-Plötzensee. Others shared the same fate.[12]

Some Statistics

Exact figures do not exist either regarding the total number of JWs who became COs, or the number of those who were executed as a result of their draft resistance. Wartime destruction of military and other archives have left gaps in the record that can only be filled by guesswork (hopefully intelligent guesswork). The JWs, on the basis of largely oral information and particularly the memories of relatives and friends of those 'martyred' by the Nazis, have made their own calculations. But they readily admit that the figures they have reached are likely to be an underestimation. Still, a roughly accurate answer is possible to the general question of how many JWs were executed as COs, though inevitably some confusion continues.

In her article on the JWs in the *Holocaust Encyclopedia,* Sybil Milton writes: 'The Witnesses' refusal to serve in the German military ... led [after 1938] to more than 250 death sentences and executions for subversion of the armed forces ... in Germany and incorporated Austria.'[13] The German scholar Hans Hesse gives a round figure of 250 JWs executed for refusing military service.[14] The sociologist Karsten Bredemeier, in his study of conscientious objection in Hitler's Germany, cites only the figures given in 1974 by the Wachturm Bibel- und Traktat-Gesellschaft (the German branch of the Watch Tower Bible and Tract Society): 253 JWs sentenced to death by the Reichskriegsgericht with 203 of these sentences actually carried out. And he warns his readers that these figures are almost certainly too low. Moreover, he does not attempt to estimate how many of those who suffered the death penalty did so on account of their refusal of military service.[15] Detlef Garbe, in his fine monograph on the JWs in Nazi Germany, also accepts the German Watch Tower Bible and Tract Society's figures as the most accurate we are likely to obtain, while adding that the offence of most of the men thus sentenced was 'their refusal to perform military service.' In Garbe's opinion, the surviving court records indicate that the figure for actual executions, given by the Watch Tower Society, needs to be increased by 'between a quarter and a third.' In addition, the Society later added another 48 executions of JWs belonging to the Witnesses' Austrian branch.[16] Thus, I think we shall not be far wrong if we say that the number of German and Austrian JWs, who were executed under the Nazis for refusing military service came to a little over 300.

Experiences of JWs as COs: Selected Cases

While incarcerated in Sachsenhausen concentration camp, Pastor Martin Niemöller observed how daily a JW was singled out at the morning roll-call and ordered to change his unwillingness, expressed hitherto, to perform *inter alia* military service. If the man persisted in refusing to sign a declaration to this effect, he was either hanged on the spot – to intimidate the other prisoners – or executed by shooting.[17] The few ready to sign such a document were released – to face in due course the inevitable call-up notice.

The most striking example of this brutal procedure, orchestrated by the Gestapo, took place on 15 September 1939. The victim, August Dickmann, was a twenty-nine-year-old JW who had been in the camp for nearly two years. In a moment of weakness, he had signed the declaration but later cancelled his signature. When, after the outbreak of war, his wife sent him his call-up notice, he reiterated his determination not to serve if released from the camp. The camp commandant, Baranowsky, then ordered Dickmann's execution to take place early in the morning in front of all the camp prisoners. The firing squad consisted of SS men. Before the event, Baranowsky had declared over the loudspeakers: 'The prisoner ... refuses military service, claiming he is a "citizen of God's kingdom." He has said: He who sheds human blood will have his blood shed. He has placed himself outside of society and in accordance with instructions from SS leader Himmler he is to be executed.' Calling Dickmann 'a swine,' Baranowsky gave the order to shoot. Among those forced to watch the execution was August's brother, Heinrich, also a Witness. Designed to intimidate, the execution failed to induce any of the camp JWs to sign the declaration: in fact, impressed by August Dickmann's resolute stance, two retracted the signatures they had already given. As for Heinrich, he later reported concerning the interview he now had with two 'high-ranking' Gestapo officers from Berlin:

> 'Did you see how your brother was shot?' My answer was: 'I did.' 'What did you learn from this?' 'I am and I shall remain one of Jehovah's witnesses.' 'Then you will be the next one to be shot.' I was able to answer several Bible questions, until finally an agent shouted: 'I don't want to know what is written, I want to know what you think.' And while he tried to show me the necessity of defending the fatherland, he kept throwing in sentences like: 'You will be the next one to be shot ... the next head to roll ... the next one to fall.' Until the other agent said: 'It is useless. Here, finish up the records.'

Not only did August Dickmann's courage make a deep impression on the other camp inmates, whether or not they were JWs; but the notorious Rudolf Höss, later the commandant at Auschwitz, who was present at the event in his capacity as adjutant and protective custody camp leader, noted in his memoirs that even those who carried out such executions (*Exekutionskommando*) were profoundly moved by the behaviour of the victims as were all those German officers and men present on these occasions.[18]

JWs in the camps who were lucky enough to escape execution for refusing to declare their readiness to serve in the army were punished in various ways. They might be assigned to labour in a penal division of the camp like the *Steinbruch-Kommando*,[19] or to so-called 'sport,' namely, 'exercises that taxed their abilities to the limit.' They could be refused medical attention for a prolonged period or subjected to dietary restrictions that adversely affected their health.[20] But these were hardships, severe indeed but something that could be borne, especially as it became increasingly clear that, by remaining in camp, a man might possibly survive. After all, God would protect those who remained firm in their faith. All such considerations helped these people to resist ill treatment and the threats of their captors as well as the well-meant advice of their non-Witness fellow prisoners to sign, as a gesture of appeasement that really signified little, and the efforts sometimes made by family and friends to induce them to abandon resistance and put their signature on the required declaration. Group pressure that might lead to expulsion from their religious community, as well as fear that apostacy of this kind would lose them the promised heaven in the afterlife, all added force to the men's decision to persist in their refusal.

A survivor later described his feelings while facing this dilemma: 'I was convinced that, if I signed, then all my happiness [mein ganzes Glück] would disappear.'[21] These JWs, as Garbe aptly puts it, had to face 'enormous mental pressure' exerted to make them give up their conscientious objection to service in the armed forces. The few who succumbed to this pressure were sentenced 'only' to two to three years, with the sentence postponed until the end of the war. Meanwhile, they were posted to a front-line penal battalion of the Wehrmacht, where, however, casualties were inevitably very high!

Did those JWs who agreed to serve either before or after incarceration in a concentration camp manage to reach some *modus vivendi* with their consciences? A way to do so, practised before by COs in other circumstances, was to resolve under no circumstances to use the weapons, which they had consented to carry, for the purpose of killing another human being. For instance, a father of four from Hamburg, who survived the war, declared afterwards: 'Throughout the whole war I never once killed a man.' A few lucky ones on joining their regiment, where they had at once declared they were Witnesses and therefore unwilling to use the arms with which they were issued for purposes of killing, discovered that they were under the command of an exceptionally understanding officer. One JW in this situation was told by his commanding officer: rest assured, you won't have to do this.[22]

We must now move on to the fate of the JWs who, after the outbreak of war, were drafted into the army from their various civilian occupations. With few exceptions these men were tried by a military tribunal, sentenced to death, and within a matter of weeks either hanged of guillotined. Verdicts of some trials (*Feldurteile*) have been preserved. One is that of the thirty-one-year-old Private Franz Steiner, Reserve Infantry

Battalion I/482, from Styria (Austria). When called up in April 1940, he sent a letter to the Draft Registration Office in Vienna, 'stating that as a true Christian ... he could not and would not bear arms. God prohibited killing. He had pledged to do God's will as written in the Holy Bible.' (The state had forbidden him to marry his partner, also a JW, 'since this woman is nearly blind.') Throughout a series of interrogations and during his trial before the Reichskriegsgericht in Berlin, Steiner had persisted in his decision not to serve. In the court's view, 'the fact that he has acted on religious convictions is not material to his guilt under criminal law. There is no evidence of temporary insanity or diminished mental capacity.' The court refused to consider a milder penalty than that of death: a possible option, as we have seen. 'It is true that the defendant has not acted out of cowardice or similar motives.' But 'his stubbornness and inflexibility' and 'implacable opposition to military service' set a dangerous example: without the imposition of capital punishment, others might be led to avoid military service, 'the honourable duty of a German.'[23] The death sentence was then carried out.

Families of the victims often kept – treasured – the farewell letters written shortly before the execution took place, and in some cases such letters have been published. The farmer Otto Friedrich Dups, for instance, was condemned to death by the Reichskriegsgericht for 'undermining military morale,' i.e., refusing induction into the army, and hanged in Berlin-Plötzensee prison on 22 December 1939. On the morning of his execution he wrote home: 'You, my dear ones, know what a Christian must do.'[24] Less concise but equally moving were the last words of Franz Mattischek, addressed from the same prison to his mother:

> I have only a few more hours to live ... Don't be sad, though. I put my trust in God and in Christ: that will bear me up until the end ... By the time you read my letter, I shall have gained my reward. I have in these final hours of mine felt very close to the Creator ... True, in the last few months I have gone through a lot. But now that I have found God's mercy, all is well. In all the troubles I have experienced I have learnt how to obey God ...
>
> It is now 9 p.m. on Friday evening, and I sit here in my cell awaiting my end. I leave everything in the hands of the Almighty ... I have so much to say to you. I believe, though, the time is not far distant when we shall all be together in 'peace and joy,' and when no one can take away our happi-

> ness. I feel so sorry for you, dear mother. I love you truly and I yearn for you. And this has caused me some difficult hours, though [I believe] the future will reunite us. Keep your Franz in your thoughts, and I will, until my last moment, pray for you ... My warmest greetings to Dad and Willi and Hubert.[25]

While confined on Death Row (*in 'Todeszellen'*), JWs continued to be subjected to various pressures aimed at getting them, even at that late moment, to change their mind and agree to serve as a combatant soldier. For instance, they might be told that their stance would lead to their families being penalized, too, including, of course, the removal of children from the care of their mother. If possible, a confrontation with wife and children would be so arranged as to lead the condemned man to 'soften.' In other instances, non-Witness relatives and friends would be brought in to plead with the man to cease his resistance. However, quite often the final result was the exact opposite of what the authorities had intended. As Admiral Bastian testified: 'Not seldom did it happen that the relatives of the condemned man begged him to remain firm under all circumstances, not to give in but to suffer death rather than yield.'[26]

A perhaps well meaning prison chaplain might add his voice in the attempt to persuade the man to give up his principles – and serve his country and at the same time save his life, at least for the time being. Garbe cites the case, from August 1942, of Dr Werner Jentsch, a Protestant theologian who was then *Standortpfarrer* at the Brandenburg-Görden prison. On 20 August he visited a nineteen-year-old Witness named Bernhard Grimm in his cell on Death Row. It was the night before the boy's execution. This is how Dr Jentsch later described his visit:

> According to the regulations of the State War Tribunal, the condemned man could, if need be even on the eve of his execution, write out a declaration expressing his agreement to serve in the army and swear the military oath. In this way he could save his life. And our conversation, in effect, was the last chance to get [Grimm] to sign. The discussion was a serious one: we went over together text after text of the Holy Scripture. In the end, he wanted once again to consider the whole matter by himself. I left him alone with his Lord. And when I returned early next morning, he was quite clear [ganz reif und klar] that he was not going to sign such a declaration. Nothing now remained for me to do except to respect his

> decision taken face to face with Jesus and to prepare him for his last journey.[27]

Together with Grimm there was another antimilitarist on the prison's Death Row. He was a Roman Catholic priest, Father Franz Reinisch. The Jehovah's Witness and the Catholic priest were executed on the same day. On this occasion, at any rate, adherents of two fiercely antagonistic faiths were united in death suffered in the name of peace.[28]

JW Women and Children as War Resisters

Resistance to war among Nazi Germany's JWs was not confined to men of draft age. Women as well as children in their early teens also bore witness to the sect's pacifist stance and suffered accordingly.

A confrontation with the SS over war production occurred in the concentration camp for women at Ravensbrück as early as the summer of 1940. JW inmates in the tailor shops, when ordered to make uniforms for the Waffen-SS, without exception refused to do so. When they likewise refused to make 'bags' after they had realized that such bags were designed to hold ammunition, they were punished by incarceration in what in American prisons would be described as 'the hole,' where they were subjected to severe dietary restrictions. Released from segregation in the punitive cell area, the women continued their resistance to successive attempts by the sadistic SS camp commandant, Koegel, to engage them in war work. 'They refused to unload hay for army horses, to wrap packages of bandages, and to build air-raid shelters.' All was to no avail: this was probably what Koegel expected when he issued the orders, the refusal of which would entitle him to further punish the women. A Catholic inmate, Nanda Habermann, has related what now happened:

> The commandant, extremely irritated, ordered ten strokes of the whip for each Bible Student. Everyone had to report for punishment. Even today, I still see the procession of mostly elderly, lovable mothers ... They were driven like a crowd of animals, each prisoner had to stand in line to be strapped to the whipping block, and then it started, one after the other ... But they prayed, quietly and humbly. ... When they left the camp jail, they tried to maintain their composure as far as possible. Many crawled, their elderly and battered bodies doubled-up and bent with pain. Many of

> these women were sixty and older ... some of these elderly mothers did not survive this beating.

Two years later, in the autumn of 1942, another crisis situation arose when first one group of JW inmates refused to work on breeding angora rabbits after learning that the wool would be used to line the jackets of air-force pilots, and then another group refused to tend garden plots after realizing that the vegetables grown there would be sent to the kitchens of an army hospital. The reaction of the camp commandant was swift. 'As punishment, about 90 women had to stand in the jail courtyard for three days and three nights; afterwards they were all flogged 25 times and forced to endure 40 days arrest in unlighted jail cells.' The ringleaders of the resistance were transferred to Auschwitz. 'Moreover, some of the women were executed by the SS in Ravensbrück.'[29]

In the camps, disagreement arose among female JWs, as it did among their male counterparts, with respect to precisely what types of labour should be considered war work and therefore refused on grounds of conscience. There could be no doubt about making weapons of various kinds and munitions. But what about the grey zone where it might not be entirely clear that the product was intended *primarily* for warlike purposes? In the concentration camp at Neuengamme, for instance, JW women worked at breeding rabbits, seemingly without qualms of conscience on this score.[30] Apart, however, from the occasional difference of opinion, the JW camp community of both genders remained firm in refusing to cooperate in war production, whatever the consequences might be.

The firmness of JW women in supporting their sect's antimilitarist position was naturally an important factor in leading the young folk to adopt the same view of the war and military service. Witness families were usually closely knit, and each family well integrated into church life as a whole, even after the JWs had become formally an illegal organization. The Nazi authorities, therefore, were psychologically correct in thinking that the removal of the Witnesses' children above the age of six from the care of their parents and placing them in a state-run institution would be an effective means of blocking the growth of the sect. And the JWs feared and resented this measure more perhaps than any other that the Nazis directed against them. Yet, as we shall see, it only partially succeeded in achieving its intended goal.

Let me quote Sybil Milton again:

> The children [of JWs], ostracized ... in school ... by classmates and teachers ... [for] noncompliance with the norms of Nazi education, were often declared juvenile delinquents and incarcerated in correctional institutions because of their unwillingness to enroll in the Hitler Youth. Parental custody was removed, in accordance with Paragraph 1666 of the German civil law code, on the pretext that Witness parents endangered their children's welfare by 'alienating them from German ways in the spirit of National Socialism.' By 1938 Witness children had been removed from more than 860 families to correctional institutions, reform schools, and Nazi homes.[31]

We do not know how many young JWs were 're-educated' in this way. However, the recent researches of Martin Guse into the fate of JW teenagers sent to the concentration camp for juveniles at Moringen (near Göttingen), which are based chiefly on extant camp records and interviews with survivors from the camp, have revealed the ineffectiveness in this case of the efforts of the Nazi rulers and, incidentally, 'the direct and indirect complicity of German welfare authorities' in this nefarious policy.[32] The majority of those incarcerated at Moringen were young thieves; a few might be described as juvenile political prisoners. The exact number of JWs is impossible to establish: former inmates told Guse that they formed 'a relatively large group' from the camp's opening in August 1940 until its closure in April 1945.

The young JW contingent were confronted with two issues that led them to clash with the camp authorities. First came the regimented daily routine, which included military drills and numerous head counts (not to speak of the inadequate food and long hours of labour). Resistance was savagely punished, 'above all [by] deprivation of food, standing at attention for many hours, and whippings.' Secondly, assignment to work in a neighbouring armaments factory (MUNA) presented an even more dangerous challenge. A former political prisoner assigned to work at MUNA recalled:

> The youngsters confined in Moringen because of their religious outlook ... refused to work in the armaments plants, which in any other camp would have resulted in death sentences. Even when they had been brutally beaten, their convictions did not change. I once witnessed a newly arrived prisoner stating the following at the entrance to MUNA ... 'This plant produces grenades. Grenades kill people, and human beings were not made to kill each other but to live in peace!' Of course this was reported and punished.

Another political prisoner told a similar story about a young Witness named Erich Meyer, who 'had just turned 18 and could [therefore] be drafted':

> Newly assigned to MUNA [Meyer] stood at the entrance to the shaft and said: 'I won't touch that! I don't touch guns, no weapons. I don't touch ammunition. I'm not allowed to.' The SS men then made fun of him and said: 'Now get to work!' But he replied: 'No. I'm not going to touch that!' The SS replied: 'So that you can go to heaven. You'll be going there without delay.' Then they filled his pockets with grenades, put them in his shirt – But he removed them all ... They then beat him till he was motionless. We thought he was dead, but he was tough ... Later he was again assigned to MUNA, and was allowed to sweep the work area; they never tried to force ammunition into his hands again.

The SS guards sometimes incited the other juvenile delinquents to beat up a refractory JW. They told the former that a JW who refused work did so because he was work-shy: that, they said, meant more work for the other prisoners. The latter 'didn't understand what it meant to be a Bible Student ... [so] they beat [the JW] to a pulp,' one of his interviewees told Guse.

When one of the imprisoned Witnesses reached the age of eighteen, he could be drafted into the army unless he escaped that fate by continued confinement. As in the case of adults, he could, however, gain an immediate release by signing a declaration of readiness to serve in the armed forces. Guse uncovered in Moringen camp archives two cases of JWs being called up and, after refusing induction, executed. One of them was that of Erich Meyer (see above). Guse writes of that obstinate antimilitarist: 'Incarcerated in Moringen, ... from the end of 1942 until the summer of 1943, ... and assigned prisoner number 839, ... he was sentenced to death for refusing military service and the SS transported him to the Berlin-Charlottenburg police prison where he was executed at the beginning of 1945.' Evidently his trial had taken place in the Moringen camp: a different procedure from that practised with respect to those JWs drafted from their civilian occupations. The second case discovered by Guse was that of eighteen-year-old Jonathan Stark from Ulm, whose Moringen prisoner number was 1140. Stark, who had trained in an art school to become a lithographer, maintained his antimilitarist witness as stubbornly as Meyer was to do. Before being sent to Moringen, Stark, only seventeen at that time, had resisted conscription into the Labour Service (Reichsarbeitsdienst), refusing the required oath to 'Führer and State.' In a letter smuggled out to his family, he reported of his subsequent treatment by the Gestapo: 'During my interrogation ... another official arrived ... a fat, unpleasant person, who screamed that I was a disloyal scoundrel and it would be best if I were shot without delay.' In fact, Stark after reaching draft age, was eventually hanged – on 1 November 1944 after being transferred from Moringen to Sachsenhausen, where he was lodged in Block 14 while awaiting execution.[33]

Another case of a JW juvenile war resister that ended more happily was that of the Austrian, Franz Wohlfart, who was incarcerated in Germany from 14 March 1940 to 24 March 1945. When at the age of nineteen he had been required to register he had refused. Arrested,

> I told them that I could never give my oath to Hitler. They threw me into solitary confinement for thirty-three days on bread and water. Then they brought me before a doctor ... who was visiting the camp as Hitler's personal representative. He said to me, 'I must admit that you Witnesses are giving us a lot of trouble.' He ordered me then to dress in the semi-military uniform I was given. I said no. Almandinger [presumably a guard] harangued me and said I was an Aryan who had been misled by criminals. He threatened me with death, but I said, 'Just three months ago my father was beheaded for his faith. Do you think I am afraid to die the same way?' He replied that the Nazis were going to rule the world and what a pity it would be if I did not share it with my fellow Aryans ... I told him I would rather die than break the laws of Jehovah by aiding a war effort, particularly the Nazi war effort, which was absolute aggression.[34]

Wohlfart was then tried for his offence in a special juvenile court and sentenced to five years' hard labour. Thus he survived the war.

Incarceration in a penal institution of the type represented by Moringen was clearly intended to break the resistance of boys like Meyer and Stark through the camp's military regime and by severing the children's ties with their parents, whom the Nazis rightly perceived as the prime source of the boys' stance. This motive is illustrated by a court ruling from Ruda in Upper Silesia, incorporated into the Reich at the outset of the war. The Witness parents of Bernhard and Heinrich D., though ethnically German, had refused to enrol on the *Volksliste* (which led eventually to the father's deportation to Auschwitz) and had prevented their sons from joining the Hitler Youth. In August 1944 the court, therefore, ordered that the two boys, now aged respectively nineteen and seventeen and already in protective custody, as 'the parents ... reject national and racial goals [and] their [sect's] teaching is subversive and dangerous to the state,' should be sent to Moringen. 'It seems that only strict and severe measures might be successful' in rescuing them from 'an advanced form of pathological religious fanaticism.' Both boys, according to the juvenile correctional institution at Grottkau, where they had been confined provisionally, regarded the war as 'the work of Lucifer.' 'God did not allow them to participate in any form of warfare, not even as medics.' And they joyfully welcomed the idea of suffering – dying – for their beliefs.

What happened to Bernhard and Heinrich after that is not altogether clear. Before leaving for Moringen, they had categorically rejected the Gestapo's attempt to make them sign the *Volksliste*. Guse discovered that they were fairly soon removed from Moringen and eventually lodged in the notorious concentration camp at Buchenwald ('the reason for this cannot be found in the surviving records').[35] We do not know, either, whether the two brothers, whose surname we do not know, persisted in their refusal to bear arms – which seems fairly certain from their previous stubborn adherence to the Witnesses' teachings – and were executed or whether – which seems very unlikely – they survived the war.

In conclusion, we may note that, at any rate towards the end of the war with Germany's rising casualties and growing shortage of manpower, the death penalty might be imposed if a pre-draft-age youth refused work in the Labour Service. This happened, for instance, in the case of seventeen-year-old Walter Appel in October 1944. Walter's father, Rolf Appel, a printer from Schleswig, had been executed in 1941 in the prison at Brandenburg-Görden as a Witness CO (*wegen Zersetzung der Wehrkraft*). A few months after his arrest his four children, then aged between nine and fifteen, were removed from the custody of their mother, who was also a JW, and placed in a state children's home. Re-education of this kind was evidently unsuccessful, at least in the case of Walter Appel, the eldest son. Called up for service in the Labour Corps, the boy refused and was executed in Köningsberg by the SS; as the record states, 'for refusal to perform either labour or military service [wegen Verweigerung des Arbeits- und Wehrdienst].'[36]

Conclusions

Students of the Nazi persecution of the Christian churches and various secular opposition groups, like John Conway, have noted the high proportion of victims among the JWs. 'In contrast to the compliance of the larger churches, the Jehovah's Witnesses maintained their doctrinal opposition to the point of fanaticism.' At the centre of their opposition, they put their resistance to the draft: an offence that in wartime, we know, was usually punished with death.[37] Even Himmler paid a backhanded tribute to the Witnesses when he suggested that they should be settled in areas to the East, which he expected the German forces would take over from the Russians: 'they were,' he wrote, 'sober, abstemious and hard-working people who kept their word; [and] they were excellent farmers' with the same otherworldly virtues possessed by the German Mennonites.[38] The JWs' pacifism, moreover, if it spread to the Slavic population (as Himmler in this case hoped it would), should keep them from seeking revenge against the expanded Reich. The same grudging admiration for the JWs was expressed by their SS tormenters in the concentration camps. When they were not torturing them, they were using them as 'trusties' around the camps. SS guards even allowed JWs to shave them every morning: they knew the Witnesses, besides being exceptionally honest and industrious, were also devoted to nonviolence even to the point of willingness to die for the principle of not hurting others. Thus, in some respects, JWs became privileged inmates: ironically, this resulted from their steadfast adherence to values that made them uncompromising opponents of the Nazi regime.

All writers on the JW experience in the Nazi concentration camps agree as to the vital role played by group solidarity in helping Witnesses to survive without seriously compromising their religious principles. It gave them the courage to face death when necessary. Those inmates who lacked such support were likely to succumb.[39] Garbe writes:

> Their unbreakable religious confidence, their strongly accentuated group solidarity and their mutual self-help gave the Jehovah Witnesses the inner strength to remain unconditionally true to their convictions even in the concentration camps. On this basis they succeeded, despite the harassment of the SS, in preserving intact throughout the whole time their will to hold out.[40]

Their draftees showed the same kind of spirit in holding out against pressures to become combatant soldiers. We have given examples of this above. The essential quality involved here was exemplified to perfection in the response made by Gustav Stange, a shoemaker, to the captain presiding at his court martial. When asked what would happen if everybody acted as he was doing, Stange replied: 'Then there would be no more war [Dann wäre der Krieg gleich zu Ende].'[41]

In perusing the available accounts of Witness COs, I have been struck by the fact that these men never allude to the future apocalyptic struggles, with the battle of Armageddon, that play so important a role today in Witness literature. Their thoughts are elsewhere. They speak of the wrongness of war and their unwillingness to kill other human beings. They brand the state that approves such behaviour as unchristian. They intend to have nothing to do with the war machine, including ambulance work in the army that aims only at patching up soldiers to fight again. They resembled Quakers or Tolstoyans in their emphasis on the Gospel law of love that will ultimately prevail over the existing hatred. 'Thou shalt not kill' and 'Resist not evil' are texts frequently on their lips. These were simple men, usually in their late teens or early twenties, and not theologians attempting to outline God's plan for humankind as expressed in the Book of Revelation.

Their witness was a truly heroic one. Observers, friends as well as foes, have pointed to the desire some JWs displayed for martyrdom either in the concentration camps or, as COs, on the hangman's rope or from the prison guillotine. But we should not forget that there were JWs of draft age who, while they strove to be true to their convictions, were neither heroes nor martyrs. Some JW draftees, for instance, went into hiding – and survived the war. Others agreed to serve but, as we have seen, resolved never to use a weapon to kill human beings. In Garbe's view, while 'Jehovah's Witnesses did not seek death, they preferred death to denying their faith.' And he illustrates this by an example. Rudi Auschner was condemned to death as a CO by the State Military Court in September 1944. Shortly before his execution, he wrote a farewell letter to his aunt. He had, he told her, done his best to prolong his case and postpone a death sentence. But in the end he had to submit to his fate. 'I must now end my letter with the hope that soon I shall see you and all my dear brothers again in God's kingdom.'[42]

The treatment of JW draftees in wartime Nazi Germany is unique in the history of conscientious objection.[43] The story is one of martyrdom, if sometimes reluctant, and nonviolent resistance. It deserves to be better known than it has been hitherto.[44]

NOTES

1 Rachel Barker, *Conscience, Government and War: Conscientious Objection in Great Britain 1939–45* (London, 1982), 41.

2 Hans Hesse, ed., *Persecution and Resistance of Jehovah's Witnesses during the Nazi Regime, 1933–1945* (Bremen, 2001), editor's preface (p. 12). The distinguished Holocaust scholar Michael Berenbaum (ibid., 11) calls attention to the post-war 'years of neglect' of the history of JWs in Nazi Germany spanning most of the second half of the twentieth century, while another distinguished Holocaust scholar, the late Sybil Milton, has written: 'In contrast to other victim groups, there are few published sources about the Witnesses' (ibid., 149), though the situation has recently begun to change. Surprisingly, Hesse's collection of essays is the first work in English to deal in detail with the subject. The German version, published in Bremen in 1998, is entitled *'Am mutigsten waren immer wieder der Zeugen Jehovas': Verfolgung und Widerstand der Zeugen Jehovas im Nationalsozialismus*. The standard work on the subject, however, has not been translated into English: Detlef Garbe, *Zwischen Widerstand und Martyrium: Die Zeugen Jehovahs im 'Dritten Reich'* (Studien zur Zeitgeschichte, vol. 42); hereafter Garbe, *Zwischen Widerstand*. With its six hundred closely packed and meticulously researched pages, I have found Garbe's monograph invaluable in preparing my essay, and I have used the fourth edition (Munich, 1999), which contains additional materials. For an overview of conscientious objection in Nazi Germany, see my essay in P. Brock and Thomas P. Socknat, eds, *Challenge to Mars: Essays on Pacifism from 1918 to 1945* (Toronto, 1999), 370–9. I regret that my treatment there of JW COs is very inadequate.

3 Hesse, ed., *Persecution*, 379, 380.

4 Christine King, 'Jehovah's Witnesses under Nazism,' chap. 18 in Berenbaum, ed., *A Mosaic of Victims: Non-Jews Persecuted and Murdered by the Nazis* (New York and London, 1990), 188. For an overall survey of JW history and doctrines, see M. James Penton, *Apocalypse Delayed: The Story of Jehovah's Witnesses*, 2nd edn (Toronto, 1997); also David L. Weddle's entry on 'Jehovah's Witnesses' in Hans J. Hillerbrand, ed., *The Encyclopedia of Protestantism* (New York and London, 2004), vol. 2, 977–82.

5 Penton, *Apocalypse*, 242–5.

6 Garbe, *Zwischen Widerstand*, 379. Garbe is quoting here from Lange's article

'Dienstverweigerung aus religiösen Grunden,' *Münchener Medizinische Wochenschrift*, vol. 84, no. 1 (1 January 1937), 16. Lange had noted that the major Christian denominations everywhere approved their members' participation as combatants when conscripted to fight for their country. This, they considered, was the duty of every citizen (p. 13). In support of his thesis, on the other hand, concerning the sanity of the average small-sect CO, Lange cited the two JWs he had recently examined in his own clinic. True, such men were fanatics, with a martyr-complex usually too; but they were not mentally ill (pp. 13–15). During the Second World War, COs, including the Witnesses, were normally considered to be 'strafrechtlich voll verantwortlich' and subject, therefore, to be tried and sentenced in a military court.

7 Garbe, *Zwischen Widerstand*, 361, 362. A few JW draftees during this period agreed to induction into the army but then refused the loyalty oath to Hitler. This, of course, was also an offence bringing a prison sentence.

8 'Mit kriegsbeginn veränderte sich die Situation für die wehrdienstverweigernden Zeugen Jehovas entscheidend' (ibid., 364).

9 'Gegen den hartnäckigen Überzeugungstäter wird wegen der propagandischen Wirkung seines Verhaltens im Normalfall nur die Todesstrafe angezeigt sein' (quoted from *Rechtsgrundsätze des Reichkriegsgerichts*, 5, in ibid., 365).

10 Ibid., 370.

11 Ibid., 367–9, 371. 'Mit diesem "Führerwort" war die allgemeine Richtung für die "Handhabung" der Verweigerfälle vorgegeben' (371).

12 Ibid., 365, 368.

13 S. Milton in Walter Laqueur, ed., *The Holocaust Encyclopedia* (New Haven and London, 2001), 350. Cf. her article in Hesse, ed., *Persecution*, 146, where she gives the figure of 'ca. 250' as the number of death *sentences* passed at trials of Witness COs, leaving unanswered the question of how many of these sentences were actually carried out.

14 Hesse, ed., *Persecution*, 12. See also 283. Cf. note 16 below.

15 Karsten Bredemeier, *Kriegsdienstverweigerung im Dritten Reich: Ausgewählte Beispiele* (Baden-Baden, 1991), 85, 86.

16 Garbe, *Zwischen Widerstand*, 500. See also 350 n. 118, 375. See also Garbe's essay in Hesse, ed., *Persecution*, 251. In addition to the Reich's JWs, who refused to serve in the German army, there were about 30 other COs, most of whom were executed. Of these men, about a dozen were Catholics, half that number Adventists, with one lonely Baptist. The best-known of the non-Witness COs is undoubtedly the Catholic Franz Jägerstätter, due largely to the moving biography by Gordon C. Zahn, *In Solitary Witness: The Life and Death of Franz Jägerstätter* (New York, 1964).

17 Bredemeier, *Kriegsdienstverweigerung*, 85.

18 Garbe, *Zwischen Widerstand*, 420–5; Antje Zeiger, 'Jehovah's Witnesses in Sachsenhausen Concentration Camp,' in Hesse, ed., *Persecution*, 80, 81; *Yearbook of Jehovah's Witnesses* (1974), 166–9.

19 Kirsten John-Stücke, 'Jehovah's Witnesses in Wawelsburg Concentration Camp,' in Hesse, ed., *Persecution*, 66: in this camp 'the Witnesses had continually to carry rocks at the double up a steep slope; the SS brutally beat and abused them.'

20 Garbe, *Zwischen Widerstand*, 426; Zeiger 'Jehovah's Witnesses,' 80.

21 Garbe, *Zwischen Widerstand*, 427, 428.

22 Ibid., 388, 390, 391, 398.

23 Milton, ed., Document 8, in Hesse, ed., *Persecution*, 161–4. The original German text is printed here and also in Albrecht Hartmann and Heidi Hartmann, *Kriegsdienstverweigerung im Dritten Reich* (Frankfurt am Rhein, 1986), 79–82; hereafter Hartmanns. In civilian life, Steiner was a farm labourer; he had completed only primary school.

24 Hubert Roser, 'The Religious Association of Jehovah's Witnesses in Baden and Würtemberg, 1933–1945,' in Hesse, ed., *Persecution*, 206, 207.

25 Hartmanns, 63, 64. The letter was lent to the Hartmanns by Franz Mattischek's brother, Hubert. See also Garbe, *Zwischen Widerstand*, 388–90; Guy Canonici, *Les témoins de Jéhovah face à Hitler* (Paris, 1998), 110–12; Hartmanns, 68–70.

26 Garbe, *Zwischen Widerstand*, 388, 389.

27 Ibid., 387. Garbe correctly points out the ambiguous character of these pastoral attempts to undermine the victim's resolution. I have not read of any instances when they were successful.

28 Ibid., Reinisch was not a pacifist, but he believed Nazi Germany was waging a war of aggression. His refusal to take the military oath led to his being sentenced to death.

29 Ursula Krause-Schmitt, 'Persecution and Resistance of Female Jehovah's Witnesses,' in Hesse, ed., *Persecution*, 200; and John-Stücke, 'Jehovah's Witnesses,' in ibid., 70 n. 25,

30 John-Stücke, 'Jehovah's Witnesses,' 70 n. 25. However, among male JWs incarcerated in Buchenwald a similar question led to a schism. Some of the Witnesses there had been assigned to a workshop making ski-boards (*Skibrettern*). The majority, backed by the sectarian camp leader (*der Wortführer der Bibelforschergemeinde*), Willi Töllner, a man of strong character – indeed a charismatic figure – exercising great influence over his coreligionists, decided that skis must in this case be considered a weapon of war since they would be used by the troops. A minority of JW inmates dissented. Ski-

boards, they said, would not kill anybody, whereas hand-grenades, for instance, would. Those inmates who took this position were disfellowshipped by the majority. See Garbe, *Zwischen Widerstand*, 430.

31 Milton in *Holocaust Encyclopedia*, 348, 349. Milton has also printed (Document 7, in Hesse, ed., *Persecution*, 160, 161) the decision of the Karlsruhe District Court, dated 15 April 1937, 're: Removal of parental custody for the minor male son, Willi Josef Seitz.' Both parents were JWs. According to the court decision, 'the youth had refused to participate in national school ceremonies, to salute the flag, to use the German greeting, and to sing national songs. The boy informed the school director that he would not be a soldier.' The father, an unemployed stoker, told the court that his son's behaviour was entirely the result of the boy's independent thinking. The court, however, disagreed: 'the son's beliefs are the result of parental influence.' It, therefore, ordered that the boy be placed in the reformatory at Schloss Flehingen. Unfortunately I have not been able to discover what happened to Willi Josef after that.

32 Martin Guse '"The Little One ... He Had to Suffer a Lot": Jehovah's Witnesses in the Moringen Concentration Camp,' in Hesse, ed., *Persecution*, 110.

33 Ibid., 96–100, 104–9.

34 Jerry Bergman, 'The Jehovah's Witnesses' Experience in the Nazi Concentration Camps: A History of Their Conflicts with the Nazi State,' *Journal of Church and State*, vol. 38, no. 1 (Winter 1996), 95, quoting from Allen Spraggett, 'The Faith Hitler Couldn't Break,' *Toronto Daily Star* (17 June 1966), 1.

35 Guse, 'Little One,' 102–4.

36 Garbe, *Zwischen Widerstand*, 208, 209, 364 n. 179.

37 J.S. Conway, *The Nazi Persecution of the Churches, 1933–45* (Toronto, 1968), 196–8.

38 Ibid., 198, 199.

39 Socialists and communists in the camps possessed a similar solidarity.

40 Garbe, *Zwischen Widerstand*, 436. Bergman, 'Jehovah's Witnesses' Experience,' 94–101, refers to the JWs' sense of 'community under hardship' as 'a major key to their camp survival.'

41 Garbe, *Zwischen Widerstand*, 386. Quoted from a report by the Stuttgart Stadtpfarrer, Rudolf Dauer.

42 Ibid., 523. Recently, Michael W. Casey (Pepperdine University) kindly drew my attention to several Seventh-day Adventist Reform Movement COs executed in Nazi Germany under conditions similar to those endured by JW COs. On the eve of his execution on 29 March 1940, Gustav Psyrembel from Lower Silesia had written to his wife: 'The Lord be thanked and praised!

He has ... given me His joy and love in rich measure. He will not leave me in the last hour.' He felt happy in his cell, for it was 'a privilege to suffer and die for His sake ... I would not give up this faith for all the world.' The only shadow saddening him was the letter addressed by a minister of the pre-war main Seventh-day Adventist body to the war tribunal which tried his case: if other Adventists are ready to bear arms in defence of their country, 'why can't you do the same?' the officers now asked Psyrembel. At 6:00 p.m. on 3 February 1943 the Austrian 'Reformer' Anton Brugger, was executed as a CO in the prison at Brandenburg-Goert. On the morning he was put to death, he wrote to his fiancée, his 'cherished treasure,' asking her to comfort his grieving mother. 'I trust I have not lived in vain ... I love you dearly to the end. Farewell, darling, *auf Wiedersehn*. Your Anton.' For these cases, see A. Balbach, *The History of the Seventh Day Adventist Reform Movement* (Roanoke VA, 1999), 202–8, 214, 215.

43 The 'sufferings' of German Witness COs re-emerged after the war in communist East Germany (DDR), beginning with the reintroduction there of military conscription in 1962 and ending with the fall of communism in 1990. See Hans-Hermann Dirksen, *'Keine Gnade den Feinden unserer Republik': Die Verfolgung der Zeugen Jehovahs in der SBZ/DDR 1945–1990* (Berlin, 2001), 749–87, 871, 874–8. For a summary paragraph in English on JWs and 'Military Service,' see Dirksen's essay, 'Jehovah's Witnesses in the German Democratic Republic,' in Hesse, ed., *Persecution*, 223. Note 4 in essay 16 above documents a few brief remarks in the text concerning the noncombatant army service for COs (*Baueinheiten*), which existed in the DDR from 1964 to 1990, though it was boycotted by JWs. Three writers have contributed more than any others to the history of these units: Bernd Eisenfeld, Stephan Eschler, and Uwe Koch.

Worth noting, too, is the contemporary savage treatment in Greece of COs belonging to the Witnesses. 'It was common for a Jehovah's Witness to stay 10–15 years in a military jail. Throughout the Civil War (1946–9) some of them were given the death penalty and shot (Ioannis Tsoukaris in February 1949 and Georgios Orfanidis on 2 March 1949).' The last Greek JW CO to receive a death sentence was Hristos Kazanis in 1966, 'but under ... international pressure, his penalty was reduced to 4 years in prison.' Only in 1997 did the Greek government give – limited – recognition to conscientious objection. See Yannis Chryssoverghis, 'The History of CO Struggle in Greece,' *The Broken Rifle: Newsletter of War Resister: International*, no. 66 (May 2005), 3.

44 It was only after completing this essay that I learnt about M. James Penton's book, *Jehovah's Witnesses and the Third Reich: Sectarian Politics under Persecu-*

tion (Toronto, 2004). Its appearance is one more proof that the story of the Jehovah's Witnesses in Nazi Germany is becoming better known in English-speaking countries. Penton's approach, I should add, is more critical of the Witnesses' official stance vis-à-vis the Nazi regime than Garbe's is. A meticulous scholar (and an ex-JW), Penton argues convincingly *inter alia* that, during the summer months of 1933, the JWs in Germany attempted to gain Hitler's favour by thinly veiled anti-Semitism and that, thereafter, the then president of the Watch Tower Society in Brooklyn, Judge J.F. Rutherford, imperilled the German branch of the organization by switching policy and ordering reckless opposition to the Nazi regime. More controversial is Penton's belief that 'the Witnesses ... were in part responsible for their sufferings' in Nazi Germany as elsewhere (p. 236) and that 'it is difficult to give ... very much credence' to the view that, in Germany at least, JWs until recently have been 'forgotten victims' of Nazi oppression (p. 95). The book, however, deals only peripherally with the JWs as conscientious objectors to military service. Its main thrust is directed against the sect's treatment of the history of the JWs in Nazi Germany, his book's subject; understandably the author's major concern is to refute JW 'hagiolatry' (p. 240) and the sect's scholarly 'apologists.'

Index

Note: The letter *n* in a page citation refers to a note (e.g., 99n2 refers to page 99, note 2). Non-English characters are alphabetized as if in English (e.g., Ø is treated as O).